The Diagnosis
of Stupor and Coma

Contemporary Neurology Series available:

Fred Plum, M.D., and Fletcher H. McDowell, M.D., *Editors-in-Chief*

The Diagnosis

of Stupor and Coma

FRED PLUM, M.D.

Anne Parrish Titzell Professor of Neurology
Cornell University Medical College
Neurologist-in-Chief, The New York Hospital

JEROME B. POSNER, M.D.

Professor of Neurology
Cornell University Medical College
Chairman, Department of Neurology
Memorial Sloan-Kettering Cancer Center

EDITION 3

 F. A. Davis Company, Philadelphia

Library of Congress Cataloging in Publication Data

Plum, Fred.
  The diagnosis of stupor and coma.

  (Contemporary neurology series; 19)
  Bibliography: p.
  Includes index.
  1. Coma. 2. Stupor. I. Posner, Jerome B.,
joint author. II. Title. III. Series.
[DNLM: 1. Brain diseases—Diagnosis. 2. Brain
injury, Acute—Diagnosis. 3. Coma—Diagnosis.
W1 C0769N v. 19/WB182 P734d]
RB150.C6P55 1980   616'.047   80-10300
ISBN 0-8036-6992-5

CASES

OF

APOPLEXY AND LETHARGY:

WITH

Observations

UPON

THE COMATOSE DISEASES.

By J. CHEYNE, M.D.

FELLOW OF THE ROYAL COLLEGE OF PHYSICIANS, EDINBURGH;
LICENTIATE OF THE KING AND QUEEN'S COLLEGE OF
PHYSICIANS IN IRELAND; ONE OF THE PHYSICIANS
TO THE MEATH HOSPITAL, AND COUNTY
OF DUBLIN INFIRMARY, &c.

LONDON:

PRINTED FOR THOMAS UNDERWOOD, MEDICAL BOOKSELLER
40, WEST SMITHFIELD; ADAM BLACK, EDINBURGH;
WALTER DUNCAN, GLASGOW; AND
GILBERT AND HODGES, DUBLIN.

1812.

I HAVE every wish to avoid unnecessary distinctions in medicine, and to see simplicity in the nosological arrangement; yet, at the expense of restoring another genus to the table of diseases, I conceived it right again to draw the line between apoplexy and lethargy. I found great confusion arising from the attempt which had been made to identify these two affections of the brain; and those who best understand the nature of apoplexy, will be the most ready to admit, that it is a disease which requires an undivided attention. If in describing the morbid appearances which are connected with apoplexy, I shall be thought tedious, I beg to remind the reader, that, independent of the practical tendency of such a detail, the anatomy of apoplexy is connected with a forensic question of great importance. Being aware of many defects in the following pages, I beg leave to say, that, until lately, I have not had the benefit of leisure to make the proper use of my opportunities of observation; and that in a work compiled under the disadvantages of the fatigue and hurry of professional employment of the most laborious kind, neither deep research into the writings of medical authors, nor the most orderly disposition of materials, can reasonably be expected.

Preface to the Third Edition

During the eight years since the second edition of *The Diagnosis of Stupor and Coma* the development of computerized transaxial tomography has transformed the process of diagnosis in clinical neurology. Where CT units are available, technology has replaced clinical deduction in the capacity to identify and localize many intracranial mass or destructive lesions. But the art of diagnosis is to comprehend the whole picture: where the lesion is, what it comprises, and, above all, what it is doing to the patient. CT scanning cannot answer the sometimes difficult question of whether a visualized lesion is of sufficient size and location to explain the associated symptoms, nor does it provide an answer to the metabolic or diffuse disturbances that cause or worsen severe disability of the brain. These steps require the thought of an informed doctor. Accordingly, we have kept our original goal for *Stupor and Coma:* to provide a clinically slanted volume that will help the reader understand and diagnose severe brain dysfunction both as it exists and as it evolves in the seriously ill. The book remains a treatise on pathophysiology because radiologic, electrophysiologic, and chemical technology by themselves are insufficient substitutes for the physician's educated mind in the management of patients.

Advances in knowledge or at least in our understanding of our subject have led to substantial changes in this edition. Chapter 1 has been largely rewritten and extensive additions and revisions have been made in Chapters 2 through 5. Chapter 6, on prognosis, has been substantially lengthened to reflect the results of recent studies on outcome from head trauma and medical coma. Finally, since outcome from coma often depends to a very great extent on how the general physician treats the patient during the first hours after onset and even before the diagnosis is reached, we have added a chapter outlining principles of early management. Many illustrations have been either redrawn or added, thanks to the skill of the medical illustrator, Hugh Thomas.

Many people generously have given time and thought to the material included in this revision and we thank them. Especially helpful have been Drs. J. P. Blass, J. J. Caronna, W. E. Crill, T. E. Duffy, M. P. Earnest, M. S. Gazzaniga, G. E. Gibson, W. M. Landau, D. E. Levy, R. Y. Moore, J. R. Nelson, C. A. Pagni, P. F. Prior, W. Pulsinelli, C. B. Saper, P. Safar, B. Sigsbee, J. V. Snyder, and D. S. Zee. We are indebted to Dr. A. I. Arieff and the Williams & Wilkins Company for permission to reprint Figure 36 and to Dr. R. G. Ojemann and the American Medical Association for permission to reprint Figure 32. Professor B. K. Siesjö graciously gave us permission to adapt Figure 34 from one of his earlier drawings. The manuscript would never have reached publication without the great help of Reba M. Deane, Carol D'Anella,

Adele Ahronheim, and Garie Posner. It is a special pleasure to acknowledge the attention and care that Christine H. Young, Robert H. Craven, and the staff of the F. A. Davis Company have given to every aspect of this and the other 18 volumes of the *Contemporary Neurology Series*.

Fred Plum, M.D.
Jerome B. Posner, M.D.

Preface to the First Edition

Stupor and coma are such common clinical states that it is unusual for a busy hospital emergency room to pass a day without facing a diagnostic problem involving one or the other. Despite this ubiquity of the problem, however, no current volume has directed itself at the clinical approach to diagnosis of states of impaired consciousness, and Cheyne's monograph of 150 years ago, from which we have appropriated the charming frontispiece, is now medically somewhat out of date. It has been our good fortune to be associated with hospitals and colleagues serving wide segments of the community and receiving many diagnostic problems from other physicians. The demands of patients for care forced us to develop for ourselves a systematic approach in diagnosing coma, and the lively interest among our associates in the whys and hows of unconsciousness prompted us to explain our approach and summarize some of the lessons learned. This book is the result.

The clinical material came from the King County Hospital and University of Washington Hospital, Seattle, between 1953 and 1963, and from the Cornell University services at The New York Hospital and Bellevue Hospital since 1963. We are indebted to many medical and nursing associates at these institutions for their help and personal contributions. Certain colleagues deserve particular mention and thanks. Drs. August G. Swanson, Harold W. Brown, Gian E. Chatrian, Henry Leffman, Richard M. Torack, Raymond F. Hain, and Ellsworth C. Alvord contributed many of the ideas and some of the studies included here. Misses Helen Goodell and Carol Manning provided particular assistance in manuscript preparation and we give them thanks. Before he died in 1961, Dr. Donald E. McNealy was a valued and stimulating co-worker who left many of his ideas and the stamp of his enthusiasm and energy on these pages.

FRED PLUM, M.D.
JEROME B. POSNER, M.D.

Contents

CHAPTER 1

The Pathologic Physiology
of Signs and Symptoms of Coma

ALTERED STATES OF CONSCIOUSNESS

And men should know that from nothing else but from the brain came joys, delights, laughter and jests, and sorrows, griefs, despondency and lamentations. And by this, in an especial manner, we acquire wisdom and knowledge, and see and hear and know what are foul, and what are fair, what sweet and what unsavory ... —The Hippocratic writings

Since the days of the Greeks, men have known that normal conscious behavior depends on intact brain function and that disorders of consciousness are a sign of cerebral insufficiency. However, the range of awake and intelligent behavior is so rich and variable that clinical abnormalities are difficult to recognize unless there are substantial deviations from the norm. Impaired, reduced, or absent conscious behavior implies the presence of severe brain dysfunction and demands urgent attention from the physician if potential recovery is to be expected. The brain can tolerate only a limited amount of physical or metabolic injury without suffering irreparable harm. Stupor and coma mean advanced brain failure, just as, for example, uremia means renal failure, and the longer such brain failure lasts the narrower becomes the margin between recovery and the development of permanent neurologic invalidism.

A wide spectrum of specific conditions can injure the brain so as to result in coma or progressive defects of consciousness. Table 1 lists some of the common and/or perplexing causes of unconsciousness that the physician is likely to encounter in the emergency room of a general hospital. The purpose of this monograph is to describe a systematic approach to the diagnosis of the patient who is comatose, based on anatomic and physiologic principles. Accordingly, this book divides the causes of unconsciousness into four major categories that can be differentiated by the principles, tests and examinations described in Chapters 1 and 8 and are discussed as specific disease entities in Chapters 2 through 5. Before considering the anatomic and physiologic principles which underlie the examination of the comatose patient, some of the terms used in this monograph as well as in the extensive literature on consciousness and coma will be defined.

Definitions

Consciousness

Consciousness is the state of awareness of the self and the environment and coma is its opposite, i.e., the total absence of awareness of self and environment even when the subject is externally stimulated. Between the extreme states of consciousness and coma stand a variety of altered states of consciousness, defined in detail

Table 1. Cause of Stupor or Coma in 500 Patients Initially Diagnosed as "Coma of Unknown Etiology"*

I. Supratentorial Lesions   101
  A. Rhinencephalic and subcortical destructive lesions   2
    1. thalamic infarcts   2
  B. Supratentorial mass lesions   99
    1. hemorrhage   76
      a. intracerebral   44
        (1) hypertensive   36
        (2) vascular anomaly   5
        (3) other   3
      b. epidural   4
      c. subdural   26
      d. pituitary apoplexy   2
    2. infarction   9
      a. arterial occlusions   7
        (1) thrombotic   5
        (2) embolic   2
      b. venous occlusions   2
    3. tumors   7
      a. primary   2
      b. metastatic   5
    4. abscess   6
      a. intracerebral   5
      b. subdural   1
    5. closed head injury   1
II. Subtentorial Lesions   65
  A. Compressive lesions   12
    1. cerebellar hemorrhage   5
    2. posterior fossa subdural or extradural hemorrhage   1
    3. cerebellar infarct   2
    4. cerebellar tumor   3
    5. cerebellar abscess   1
    6. basilar aneurysm   0
  B. Destructive or ischemic lesions   53
    1. pontine hemorrhage   11
    2. brainstem infarct   40
    3. basilar migraine   1
    4. brainstem demyelination   1
III. Diffuse and/or Metabolic Brain Dysfunction   326
  A. Diffuse intrinsic disorders of brain   38
    1. "encephalitis" or encephalomyelitis   14
    2. subarachnoid hemorrhage   13
    3. nutritional   1
    4. hepatic encephalopathy   17
    5. uremia and dialysis   8
    6. pulmonary disease   3
    7. endocrine disorders (including diabetes)   12
    8. remote effects of cancer   0
    9. drug poisons   149
    10. ionic and acid-base disorders   12
    11. temperature regulation   9
    12. mixed or nonspecific metabolic coma   1
IV. Psychiatric "Coma"   8
  A. Conversion reactions   4
  B. Depression   2
  C. Catatonic stupor   2

*Represents only patients in whom the initial diagnosis was uncertain and a final diagnosis was established. Thus, obvious diagnoses such as known poisonings and closed head injuries, and never-established diagnoses such as mixed metabolic encephalopathies are under-represented.

2

below, to which have been applied a bewildering number of terms such as "vegetative state," "akinetic mutism," "coma vigil," and "apallic syndrome." The limits of consciousness are hard to define satisfactorily and quantitatively and we can only infer the self-awareness of others by their appearance and by their acts. For example, a paralyzed and mute patient suffering from polyneuritis may be fully awake and alert, i.e., fully conscious, but completely unable to communicate his consciousness to others.[38] Furthermore, psychologic factors can influence behavior as much as physiologic ones and usually require different medical management. Coma produced by drug overdosage and psychogenic unresponsiveness produced by emotional stress may appear clinically similar to the inexperienced observer, but it is essential that the physician distinguish between them.

Two physiologic components govern conscious behavior, namely, content and arousal. Brain diseases of different types and distributions affect each component differently. The *content* of consciousness represents the sum of cognitive and affective mental functions. Any lesion that interferes with full cognitive function diminishes the content of consciousness and renders the patient less than fully conscious. For example, an aphasic individual may appear awake and alert, but his inability to comprehend or manipulate language (as opposed to speech) decreases his full awareness of himself and his environment. *Arousal* is the other aspect of consciousness and at least behaviorally is closely linked to the appearance of wakefulness. An individual who has taken an overdose of sedative drugs may become aroused by noxious stimulation so as to carry out near-normal cognitive functions, but be unable to maintain contact with his environment unless sufficiently stimulated. He too is less than fully conscious. It should be evident that cognition is not possible without at least some degree of arousal. Later sections of this book will make it clear that mere arousal does not guarantee cognition.

Sleep is not fully conscious behavior, and whatever significance dreams may have, they resemble delirium too closely for us to conclude that they have any value in that adaptation to the external milieu that constitutes full biological consciousness.

Patients who have a sleep-like appearance and remain behaviorally unresponsive to all external stimuli qualify as being unconscious by everyone's definition. However, continuous sleep-like coma almost never lasts more than 2 to 4 weeks, no matter what the brain injury. After that point in time, or even before, many seriously brain-injured patients develop a chronically unresponsive state in which they look awake but give little or no evidence of possessing either sentient recognition of the environment or any other cognitive mental content. Terminologic differences surround descriptions of these chronic states of wakeful responsiveness, variously called vegetative states, akinetic mutism, coma vigil, or the apallic syndrome. Some workers regard them as forms of coma; others consider them as examples of profound dementia and restrict the term "coma" to sleep-like states in which the eyes remain closed. This book takes the latter view, but only agreement on definitions will settle the matter. By clarifying and agreeing upon definitions, clinicians, physiologists, and psychologists can reach a common discussion ground where they can add their special expertise to unraveling the brain's unknowns.

States of Acutely Altered Consciousness

Restricted impairments of psychologic functions, such as aphasia or memory loss, reduce the total content of consciousness, but these localizable cerebral defects are not generally regarded as altered states of consciousness. By contrast, acute, diffuse psychologic losses, i.e., the confusional states and deliria, almost always combine a generalized reduction or alteration in the content of consciousness with at least some reduction in total arousal; these conditions comprise the incipient states of altered or "clouded" consciousness. In stupor and sleep-like coma, the defect in arousal predominates, making it impossible to estimate the potential mental content. With chronic states in which the content of consciousness is profoundly reduced but the capacity for arousal is retained or returns, it is best to avoid global, imprecise terms such as coma and to describe the mental content and the capacity for wakefulness separately. *When pathologic processes strike the brain acutely or develop rapidly, the loss of cerebral function is proportionately large in relation to the size of the lesion. Sleep-like stupor and coma tend to reflect acute or subacute brain diseases; dementia more often characterizes insidiously developing or chronic processes, particularly those that spare the brainstem. Even with acute lesions of the brain, however, the normal cerebral reserves are so extensive and pluripotential that altered or reduced consciousness can always be taken to reflect either diffuse or bilateral impairment of cerebral functions or failure of the brainstem ascending reticular activating system or both.*

CLOUDING OF CONSCIOUSNESS is a term applied to states of reduced wakefulness or awareness that in their minimal form may include hyperexcitability and irritability alternating with drowsiness. The major defect is one of attention. [163] The patient is easily distracted and sometimes startled by stimuli; he sometimes misjudges sensory perceptions, particularly visual ones. Although not necessarily disoriented, he thinks neither quickly nor clearly. More advanced clouding produces an acute or subacute *confusional state* in which stimuli are more consistently misinterpreted. Confused patients are bewildered and often have difficulty following commands. They have at least a minor disorientation for time and sometimes for place or person. (Except in rare instances of acute delirium, disorientation for self is confined to psychologic disturbances.) Memory is faulty in confusional states and such subjects have difficulty in repeating numbers backward (the normal number is at least four or five) and in repeating the details or even the meaning of stories. Drowsiness often is prominent and daytime drowsiness may alternate with nighttime agitation.

Few investigators have examined in any detail the physiological or metabolic functions of patients with clouded consciousness, but what studies do exist indicate the existence of generalized brain dysfunction. In lethargic confused patients with liver disease, for example, Posner and Plum [225] found that cerebral oxygen consumption had fallen 20 percent below the normal level. Shimojyo, Scheinberg, and Reinmuth [258] noted a similar reduction in cerebral metabolism in confused subjects with Wernicke's disease.

DELIRIUM is a floridly abnormal mental state characterized by disorientation, fear, irritability, misperception of sensory stimuli, and, often, visual hallucinations. The behavior of such patients commonly places them completely out of contact with the environment; often one finds it difficult to determine whether they even retain self-recognition. Lucid periods can alternate with delirious episodes and such patients are commonly terrified of the potential implications of their own mental failure. Delirium commonly produces complex, systematized, and protracted delusions of a dream-like nature during which the subject is completely out of contact with the environment and psychologically unreachable by the examiner. The patients are commonly loud, talkative, offensive, suspicious, and agitated. Full-blown delirious states always come on rapidly and rarely last more than 4 to 7 days. Fragments of misperceptions and

4

hallucinations can last as long as several weeks, however, especially among some alcoholics or patients with cerebral involvement from collagen vascular disease.

Delirium is prominent with toxic and metabolic disorders of the nervous system, such as acute poisoning with atropine or its congeners, the alcohol-barbiturate withdrawal syndrome, acute porphyria, uremia, acute hepatic failure, encephalitis, and the collagen vascular diseases. Certain forms of status epilepticus involving the limbic system produce a syndrome indistinguishable from delirious states. Severe head injury often leads to delirium during recovery from unconsciousness. At one time delirium frequently accompanied acute febrile systemic infections such as pneumonia. The state is much less common now that antibiotics have blunted the severity of the infectious illnesses.

Delirium accompanies diffuse metabolic and multifocal cerebral illnesses and its presence implies a generalized impairment of brain functions or at least a bilateral involvement of limbic structures. Cerebral metabolic studies on delirious patients are lacking, but Romano and Engel[237] reported that the EEG was always slowed in delirium, although others disagree.[226] Because for all practical purposes the terms "clouding of consciousness" and "delirium" define equivalent alterations of arousal that commonly emerge as preludes or sequels to stupor or coma, this book usually employs the term delirium to refer to either condition.

OBTUNDATION literally means mental blunting or torpidity. In the medical setting, one generally applies the term to patients with a mild to moderate reduction in alertness, accompanied by a lessened interest in the environment. Such patients have slower psychological responses to stimulation and an increase in number of hours of sleep, often with drowsiness between.

STUPOR is a condition of deep sleep or behaviorally similar unresponsiveness from which the subject can be aroused only by vigorous and repeated stimuli. As soon as the stimulus ceases, stuporous subjects lapse back into the unresponsive state. Most stuporous patients have diffuse organic cerebral dysfunction, although deep physiologic sleep can sometimes produce a degree of stupor indistinguishable from that caused by organic brain disease. Catatonic schizophrenia or a severe depressive reaction can lead to a state of stupor that behaviorally closely resembles the unresponsiveness associated with structural diseases of the brain and may require great skill to differentiate (see Chapter 5).

COMA is a state of unarousable psychologic unresponsiveness in which the subjects lie with eyes closed. Subjects in coma show no psychologically understandable response to external stimulus or inner need.[178] They neither utter understandable words nor accurately localize noxious stimuli with discrete defensive movements. It is possible that the psychological aspects of coma have gradations in depth, but these can hardly be estimated once patients no longer respond to the environment. Some authors equate the presence or absence of various motor responses with depth of coma, which tends to confuse the issue. The neural structures regulating consciousness have an anatomical distribution that differs from those that regulate motor function. As a result, diseases causing coma can differ widely in the degree to which they impair motor mechanisms.

States of Subacute or Chronic Alterations in Consciousness

DEMENTIA defines an enduring or permanent decline in mental processes owing to an organic process and not accompanied by a reduction in arousal. Conventionally, the term implies a diffuse or disseminated reduction in cognitive functions rather than the impairment of a single psychologic activity such as language. The reader will recognize this definition as an arbitrary restriction. Usually, the term dementia is applied to the effects of primary disorders of the cerebral hemispheres, such as degenerative conditions, traumatic injuries, and neoplasms. Occasionally, dementia can be at least partially reversible, such as when it accompanies thyroid or vitamin B_{12} deficiency or results from a reversible communicating hydrocephalus; more often, however, the term applies to chronic conditions carrying limited hopes for improvement. Further discussion of the scope and implication of dementia as well as its structural associations and causes can be found in the monographs edited by Wells[300] and Katzman, Terry, and Bick.[135] As subsequent sections of the present book will show, a major reason for reaching early diagnosis and effective treatment of states causing stupor or coma is the attempt to prevent irreversible brain damage with subsequent dementia.

HYPERSOMNIA refers to excessive drowsiness. Particularly in the European literature, states of sleep-like coma are sometimes designated hypersomnia, but the physiologic relationship to sleep has not been established and the usage is potentially confusing. The term hypersomnia is best restricted to subacute or chronically developing states characterized by excessive but normal-appearing sleep from which the subject readily, even if briefly, awakens when stimulated.

VEGETATIVE STATE is the term proposed by Jennett and Plum[123] to describe the subacute or chronic condition that sometimes emerges after severe brain injury and comprises a return of wakefulness accompanied by an apparent total lack of cognitive function. An operational definition is that the eyes open spontaneously in response to verbal stimuli. Sleep-wake cycles exist. The patients spontaneously maintain normal levels of blood pressure and respiratory control. They show no discrete localizing motor responses and neither offer comprehensible words nor obey any verbal commands.[160] *Persistent or chronic vegetative state* refers to this condition in its permanent form and designates subjects who survive for prolonged periods (sometimes years) following a severe brain injury without ever recovering any outward manifestations of higher mental activity. In most instances the vegetative state follows upon a period of sleep-like coma. As discussed later in this chapter, nearly all patients in coma begin to awaken within 2 to 4 weeks no matter how severe the brain damage. Once sleeping and waking cycles return it becomes contradictory to describe such subjects as still in coma, even though their behavior may never again demonstrate evidence of a conscious intelligence. Since several different types of neuropathologic abnormalities involving the cerebral cortex or brainstem can underly such behavioral states, the descriptive word *vegetative* seems preferable to applying to a clinical syndrome anatomic terms, such as "neocortical death" or "apallic state," that presume greater knowledge of the associated morphological lesion than often turns out to be present. Likewise, although many such patients are akinetic and mute, others with apparently similar degrees of brain damage may be restless, noisy, and hypermobile. The term *vegetative state* focuses on the contrast between the severe mental loss and the subject's preserved autonomic or vegetative functions. Physicians and laymen both immediately understand its connotations and it has greater dignity than many of the terms sometimes applied vulgarly to the hopelessly brain damaged.

Several other terms have been invoked to describe the condition of patients in the vegetative state, including coma vigil, the apallic syndrome, cerebral death,[150] neocortical death, and total dementia. Although sometimes connoting minor differences in clinical appearance, these descriptions apply to a state in which sleeping and waking behavior have returned to a subject who lacks all evidence of cognition.

6

The neuropathologic basis of the chronic vegetative state is well described by Brierley,[25] Ingvar,[112] Dougherty,[68] and their colleagues. The patients involved all were initially in coma from anoxic-ischemic brain insults. Most of them awakened, in that they opened their eyes and regained waking and sleeping cycles, but they never again showed recognizable signs of cognitive function. Brainstem functions remained intact as expressed by pupillary activity, oculocephalic responses, chewing, swallowing, breathing, and the control of circulation. Owing to extraordinary attention, the described patients survived their acute illnesses for periods lasting from 2 weeks to as long as 8 and in one instance 17 years. Cerebral blood flow was reduced in six such patients studied by Ingvar, dropping to 10 to 20 percent of the normal level in the longstanding cases. Apparent metabolic rates of the forebrain were similarly reduced. EEGs in several instances were essentially isoelectric, but in others regained various patterns of rhythm and amplitude, not consistent from one case to the next.

Neuropathologic studies on the brains of the above-mentioned patients in a chronic vegetative state invariably showed damage to forebrain structures. Injury to the cerebral cortex varied widely between the extremes, occasionally appearing hardly sufficient to explain the patients' premortem mindless behavior.[68] Most often present was cortical laminar necrosis, especially involving occipital and hippocampal areas, but sometimes so extensive as to approach total decortication. Scattered areas of infarction marked the hemispheres in many cases, with neuronal loss and gliosis involving basal ganglia in a majority. Ammon's horn of the hippocampus was necrotic in nearly all described instances. In late cases much of the cortical neuropil was essentially replaced by gliosis, the hemispheres were shrunken and collapsed, and the white matter vacuolated. Striking among all these cases was a relative sparing of brainstem structures where pathologic involvement ranged from scattered areas of microinfarction in a few instances to complete morphologic sparing in others. Cerebellar structures were almost always damaged, Purkinje cell loss being the most frequent feature.

The difference in the behavioral state (early sleep-waking, absence or near-absence of all cognitive activity, maintenance of intact brainstem function) of these vegetative patients with predominantly or exclusively telencephalic damage stands in sharp contrast to the chronic hypersomnia, occasional verbal responses, and frequent pupillary abnormalities that one observes in patients with posterior hypothalamic-midbrain injury (see patient 2-15, p. 143).

AKINETIC MUTISM describes a condition of silent, alert-appearing immobility that characterizes certain subacute or chronic states of altered consciousness in which sleep-wake cycles have returned, but externally obtainable evidence for mental activity remains almost entirely absent and spontaneous motor activity is lacking.

Many different structural pathologic lesions will sooner or later after their onset produce variations on the state of akinetic mutism. The subject, although usually lying with eyes closed, retains cycles of self-sustained arousal, giving the appearance of vigilance but vocalizing little or not at all. He is doubly incontinent and makes only the most rudimentary skeletal muscle movements even in response to noxious or disagreeable stimuli.[32] The crucial factors that attract the examiner's attention are (1) the seeming wakefulness without recognizable content and (2) the relative paucity of signs that would ordinarily imply severe damage to descending motor pathways despite the unmoving state. Cairns's original description was of a girl with a craniopharyngiomatous cyst that compressed the walls of the third ventricle.[33] More or less similar behavior has been described in association with many different lesions. These have included large bilateral frontal lobe lesions, particularly those that interfere with the anterior cerebral arteries so as to produce infarcts of the cingulate gyri and limbic system;[7] bilateral diffuse destruction of the cerebral cortical mantle, as following cardiac asystole or profound hypoglycemia; bilateral hemispheric demyelination, as sometimes follows carbon monoxide poisoning or head injury; hydrocephalus;[180] large bilateral lesions of the corpus striatum,[78] globus pallidus,[64] or dorsomedial or ventrolateral thalamus;[152] paramedian lesions of the reticular formation of the midbrain and posterior diencephalon;[265] and cerebellar hemorrhage with brainstem compression.[66]

Inspection of the protocols of the above reports and others in the medical literature discloses two problems of interpretation. In many instances the inferred anatomic lesions were unverified by postmortem examination or were only part of more widespread pathologic alterations. Furthermore, among the several pathologic states only some of them truly were accompanied by the distinctive appearance of motionless, mindless wakefulness that Cairns sagely recognized. Fewer still of the patients developed this as a presenting or early manifestation of illness. Thus, following severe head injury and other bilateral severe diffuse insults to the cerebrum, sleep-like coma tends to last for up to several weeks, and when the subject finally does reach a state of intermittent wakefulness devoid of mental content, the clinical state tends to be regarded as either a variation of coma or a profound dementia. Also, most patients with large acute paramedian destructive lesions of the posterior diencephalon and midbrain have a clinical picture better termed hypersomnia than akinetic mutism, at least if one is to follow Cairns's lead in the matter. Jouvet concluded from experimental work in the cat that bilateral destruction of nigrostriatal projections or descending extrapyramidal pathways in the diencephalon produced a state of coma-like motor immobility or catatonia.[131] Pathologic descriptions of human postmortem material following akinetic mutism have been insufficiently exact to determine whether damage to such pathways may operate in man, but the structures incriminated in Jouvet's experimental work lie in the ventral diencephalon where many of the lesions associated with akinetic mutism are described in man.

The best clinical and pathologic evidence indicates that the classic appearance of akinetic mutism can arise early in the course of three types of lesions, all of which interfere with reticular-cortical or limbic-cortical integration but largely spare corticospinal pathways. These include: large, bilateral, basal-medial, frontal lobe lesions involving the orbital cortex, septal area, and cingulate gyri; small (and probably incomplete) lesions interrupting the paramedian reticular formation of the posterior diencephalon and adjacent midbrain; and, less often, subacute communicating hydrocephalus of an advanced degree. Even with the frontal lesions it is still an open question as to how much of the unresponsive akinesia can be attributed directly to frontal lobe damage and how much must be assigned to secondary compression or circulatory changes in the adjacent hypothalamus. As mentioned earlier, patients with frontal mutism are more wakeful (vigilant) than those with diencephalic-mesencephalic lesions and some even demonstrate episodically agitated behavior[78] (p. 24).

APALLIC SYNDROME is Kretschmer's term[58,153] to describe the behavior that accompanies the diffuse bilateral degeneration of the cerebral cortex that sometimes follows anoxic head injury or encephalitis. Ingvar has urged the use of the term "apallic syndrome" for patients suffering from absent neocortical function but with relatively intact brainstem function.[112] He describes eight patients who had suffered severe cerebral anoxia and remained permanently in a state that indicated absence of all cerebral hemisphere function. Behaviorally, patients such as Ingvar describes are vegetative, as noted above. Anatomically, one can hardly assure oneself of the extent of the cerebral damage during the patient's life,[68] and the term apallic state has found little usage in English-speaking countries.

8

LOCKED-IN SYNDROME describes a state in which selective supranuclear motor deefferentation produces paralysis of all four extremities and the lower cranial nerves without interfering with consciousness. The voluntary motor paralysis prevents the subject from communicating by word or body movement. Usually, but not always,[317] the anatomy of the responsible lesion in the brainstem is such that locked-in patients are left with the capacity to use vertical eye movements and blinking to communicate their awareness of internal and external stimuli. Although occasional case histories describing patients with such abnormalities date back to the 19th century, the first edition of this monograph (1966) emphasized the psychological implications of the state and gave it a distinctive name. Since then, several clinical pathologic studies of the locked-in syndrome have appeared, indicating that it is not uncommon, especially among patients with cerebral vascular disease.

Although clinically it somewhat resembles akinetic mutism because of the motor paralysis, and it is therefore sometimes confused with it, the pathogenesis of the locked-in state and the accompanying suffering of the affected patients are entirely different. When "locked-in," or deefferented, the patient gives signs of being appropriately aware of himself and the environment, whereas in akinetic mutism little or no awareness appears to exist. Deefferentation can occur to some degree with purely peripheral neurologic lesions such as polyneuritis, poliomyelitis, or myasthenia gravis. However, because of the nature of their illness, such patients are immediately recognized to be conscious, so that hospital attendants are sensitive to their emotional needs. A more harrowing circumstance occurs when an acute destructive lesion strikes the efferent motor tracts in the brainstem but spares the reticular formation. Most such patients, like Patient 3-2, on page 159, have had large ventral infarcts of the pontine base.[104,141,199] One can sometimes encounter a similar clinical picture in patients with ventral midbrain infarction,[133] pontine tumor,[44] pontine hemorrhage, central pontine myelinolysis, or head injury.

To the unwary, the combination of acute tetraplegia owing to brainstem corticospinal tract involvement, plus aphonia owing to interruption of corticobulbar fibers to the lower cranial nerves can easily give the false impression of coma or mindless akinetic mutism. Since the supranuclear ocular motor pathways travel caudally in the brainstem via Dejerine's bundle, which lies dorsal to the main destructive lesion and remains unscathed, such patients can usually reveal their awareness by initiating appropriate eye movements or by blinking. Because the lesion in the basis pontis often destroys the efferent abducens nerve fibers, however, vertical eye movements may be all that remain. Patients chronically in this state have been taught to signal by Morse code with their eyes and have been able to communicate complex ideas.[79] Sleep may be abnormal. Clinical pathologic studies of locked-in patients with paramedian destruction of the pontine tegmentum suggest that such lesions result in a striking reduction in both activated and nonactivated sleep patterns.[174]

BRAIN DEATH is a state in which all functions of the brain, including cortical, subcortical, and brainstem functions, are permanently lost. The definition of brain death and its distinction from irreversible coma are considered in Chapter 6.

Clinical Guides to Diagnosis

Determining the cause of coma or, at times, even whether an unresponsive patient suffers primarily from a physical or psychiatric illness can be challengingly difficult. Unfortunately for those who seek simple solutions, no single laboratory test or screening procedure will sift out the critical initial diagnostic categories nearly so effectively as does a prompt and careful clinical appraisal. Faced with an

9

acutely ill patient with severe neurologic or behavioral symptoms suggesting impaired consciousness, the physician must accurately answer the following questions: Is the disturbance functional or organic? If organic, is it focal or diffuse? Is the patient getting better, holding his own, or getting worse? What is the specific pathologic process causing coma? Does medical or surgical treatment carry the greater likelihood of being effective? The rest of this book attempts to answer some of these questions. How to differentiate between functional and organic causes of unresponsiveness is discussed in Chapter 5. Later sections of the present chapter will indicate that although focal lesions of the cerebral hemispheres produce aphasia, apraxia, agnosia, or unilateral motor or sensory defects, they do not produce stupor or coma unless they engender secondary changes in remote intracranial structures so as to induce diffuse bilateral dysfunction in the cerebral hemispheres. It will be emphasized that in the brainstem small focal lesions must lie in critical sites in order to produce coma directly. *Therefore, delirium, stupor, or coma complicating cerebral hemispheric disease implies the presence of brain dysfunction that is either diffuse or multifocal. The physician must constantly remind himself that the course of signs and symptoms in patients with impaired consciousness is a crucial indicator of the progression of disease, the effectiveness of treatment, and the potential outcome of the illness.*

In keeping with the above precepts, two general types of pathologic processes can impair consciousness. One consists of conditions that widely and directly depress the function of the cerebral hemispheres (and, usually, some brainstem structures at the same time). The other comprises abnormalities that depress or destroy the brainstem activating mechanisms that lie in or near to the central core of the gray matter of the diencephalon, midbrain, and rostral pons. These principles imply that diseases producing stupor or coma either must affect the brain widely or encroach directly upon its deep central structures or have both such effects. Such diseases fall into three categories: (1) supratentorial mass lesions, the effects of which secondarily encroach upon deep diencephalic structures so as to compress or damage physiologic systems interacting with both hemispheres; (2) subtentorial mass or destructive lesions, which directly damage the systems that lie in the central core of the upper brainstem and normally activate both cerebral hemispheres; and (3) metabolic disorders that widely depress or interrupt the function of brain structures lying in both the supratentorial and subtentorial cavities. Table 1 lists some of the specific causes of unconsciousness for these three categories and also includes psychogenic states that may at first resemble coma but are physiologically distinguishable from it. Subsequent chapters will explain and justify this classification.

Once having decided that a patient is in stupor or coma, the next question is anatomic, i.e., where does the lesion lie? A corollary question is: In what direction is the process evolving? The answers to these two place the disease in one of the above three categories and greatly reduce the number of inferences required to solve the final question: What is the specific pathologic process and what can be done about it and its effects on the brain? *The physician must always remember, that even before he attempts to answer these questions, the brain must be protected immediately against more serious or irreversible damage.* Even preceding his detailed examination, he must guarantee the airway (the oxygen supply), the circulation (the oxygen-transport system), and the substrate requirements for the brain's metabolism.

The diagnosis of coma can be accomplished logically and accurately by moving from general causes to more restricted categories, and finally to specific causes that can be verified objectively and promptly by laboratory methods. Chapter 8 develops this approach in greater detail. A full and accurate history often gives the preliminary answer and telephone calls to a patient's family, associates, and local physicians can obviate the need for extensive, time-consuming, and expensive screening laboratory tests. Police and ambulance drivers may provide similarly valuable data.

In many cases of stupor or coma a reliable history cannot be obtained and the cause remains obscure, necessitating heavy reliance on the physical and laboratory examinations. A complete neurologic examination must be made, but changes in some functions give more information than others. We have found that the pattern of changes in five physiologic variables gives particularly valuable information about the level of the brain involved, the nature of the involvement, and the direction the disease process is taking. These variables are (1) the state of consciousness, (2) the pattern of breathing, (3) the size and reactivity of the pupils, (4) the eye movements and the oculovestibular responses, and (5) the skeletal muscle motor responses.

The following sections discuss these functions and relate the pathologic physiology of their abnormalities to the various states of unconsciousness. First, however, one must examine what is known about the fundamental mechanisms that govern consciousness and coma themselves.

Physiology and Pathology of Consciousness and Coma

A human being's state of consciousness reflects both his level of arousal and the sum of the cognitive functions of his brain (the content of consciousness). Furthermore, sleep-like abnormalities of consciousness almost always imply an acute or subacute onset of brain dysfunction rather than a chronic process. *Arousal* in mammalian species depends on the integrity of physiologic mechanisms that take their origin from the reticular formation and other structures that lie in the upper brainstem extending from the level of the middle pons forward into the hypothalamus. *Conscious behavior* depends upon the presence in the cerebral hemispheres of relatively intact functional areas that interact extensively with each other as well as with the deeper activating systems of the upper brainstem, hypothalamus, and thalamus. Studies in lower animals complement observations made in man in illuminating the location in the brain of the structures that mediate an aroused consciousness. Animal studies also have been especially useful in defining the extraordinarily rich manner in which brainstem-cortical and cortical-cortical systems interact to produce higher level, integrative behavior. As for cognitive functions, observations indicate that the property of conscious self-awareness is far richer in human beings than in animals, with evidence that this richness at least partially relates itself to the intact language functions of the dominant cerebral hemisphere. The following paragraphs of this section discuss in greater detail the mechanisms that underlie arousal and cognition. The bibliography contains several additional sources that thoughtfully discuss various aspects of the neurobiology of consciousness.[71,72,96,119,144,156,224]

Studies in Animals

Although Carpenter's textbook of physiology in 1853 alluded to the importance of the diencephalon in consciousness,[37] physiologists gave short shrift to the concept

11

until Berger's discovery in 1928 that sleep is associated with a slower and more synchronous electroencephalograph (EEG) than is wakefulness.[14] The symmetrically increased synchrony of the sleep EEG could only be explained as the physiologic expression of a subcortical pacemaker diffusely affecting the cortex but lying outside of it. Bremer in 1937 provided further evidence of the importance of the brainstem to the hemispheres when he compared in the cat the effects of transection of the brainstem at the pontine-midbrain level and at the medullary-spinal junction.[23] Neither of the surgical preparations produced appreciable damage to the rostral diencephalon or the hemispheres, and the animals' systemic functions were physiologically well maintained. The cats with the midbrain transection appeared to be continuously behaviorally asleep and had unarousable synchronous sleep-like waves in their EEGs. By contrast, animals with a cervical-medullary transection had the facial appearance of wakefulness, and their EEGs contained desynchronized patterns, resembling normal arousal. Bremer emphasized that the animals with cervical-medullary transections retained auditory and trigeminal sensory inputs and concluded that wakefulness required stimulation of the cerebral hemispheres by incoming sensory impulses. He neglected to comment as to why the still-intact visual and olfactory pathways of animals with midbrain transections failed to provide the necessary sensory stimulation. Nevertheless, he concluded that coma resulted passively when specific sensory stimulation of the forebrain was silenced or interrupted.

Bremer was largely correct in his inferences, but did not realize at the time that the brainstem might also contain ascending, nonspecific mechanisms that influenced arousal. The presence of such a system first became clear when Morison and Dempsey in 1942 demonstrated a diffuse thalamocortical recruiting system that was independent of any specific primary sensory system.[187] A few years later, Moruzzi and Magoun discovered additional regions in the reticular formation located in the rostral brainstem that, when stimulated, produced a generalized nonspecific activation of the cerebral cortex.[189] These they termed the *ascending reticular activating system (ARAS)*.[172,188] Moruzzi and Magoun identified their ARAS as lying within the center of the brainstem, extending from the midbrain into the hypothalamus and thalamus, and demonstrated that structures lying within this region either directly or indirectly transmitted diffuse physiologic effects to the cerebral cortex that profoundly influenced arousal and the EEG. When the ARAS of a sleeping animal was stimulated directly with an electrode placed in its substance, diffuse EEG desynchronization and behavioral arousal promptly resulted. When the ARAS was destroyed, a slow synchronized EEG and coma ensued; neither of these abnormalities could be reversed by strong sensory stimulation even if the main somatic sensory pathways from the periphery via the thalamus to the cortex were preserved. In contrast, destruction of the primary thalamocortical sensory relays did not produce coma as long as the ARAS and its connections with the rostral forebrain were preserved. Several early studies seemed to agree with the inference that the ARAS was central to consciousness, including the finding that anesthetic drugs apparently selectively depressed the brainstem core. Accordingly, the view gradually became prevalent that consciousness was due to the distinctive arousal effects induced by the ARAS stimulating the cerebral hemispheres and that most unconscious states resulted from selective depression or destruction of the reticular formation. More advanced electrophysiologic, neuroanatomic, and pharmacologic studies of recent years have required some revisions of these early interpretations. Nevertheless, the fundamental concept of nonspecific physiologic arousal mechanisms arising in the upper brainstem has stood well the test of time and further experiment.

Anatomy and Physiology of the Brainstem Activating Systems

THE RETICULAR FORMATION. Anatomically, the reticular formation constitutes the central core of the brainstem, extending from caudal medulla to rostral midbrain. Although its borders often are not clearly defined, the human reticular formation does contain a number of distinct nuclei as well as others that are less well-defined.[206] Neurons of the reticular formation vary considerably in size, but many fall into the category of medium-sized cells with an "isodendritic" array of dendrites that radiate from the cell body in a plane perpendicular to the long axis of the brainstem. The organization of the reticular formation is most distinctive in the medulla and caudal pons. Here the lateral two thirds of the reticular substance is composed of small and medium-sized neurons and forms the region of termination of afferents into the reticular formation. The medial one third contains a population of very large neurons (the "gigantocellular" region), which produce many of the long ascending and descending reticular formation projections.[26] Many short and long axons provide rich interconnections within the reticular formation, endowing it with the properties of both slow and rapid conduction. Long axons from the ARAS ascend mainly through the central tegmental fasciculus.[193] Although to be expected from the observed physiologic property of slowly initiated, long-sustained arousal, no short axonal Golgi type II cells have been found in the reticular formation at any level.[247] Individual reticular neurons extend their dendritic fields over large areas, providing a continuum of overlapping fibers and a free intermingling of dendrites with ascending and descending myelinated and unmyelinated bundles. The entire architecture creates optimal anatomic opportunities for stimulation by collaterals coming from many different specific afferent fiber pathways as well as from adjacent brainstem nuclear masses.[229]

The reticular activating system receives collaterals from and is stimulated by every major somatic and special sensory pathway. Spinothalamic collaterals to the medullary and pontine tegmentum are especially numerous and may provide a morphologic pathway for mediating the particularly arousing qualities of noxious stimuli. The trigeminal sensory input is particularly important in this regard. The cerebral cortex not only is stimulated by the ARAS but reciprocally innervates the reticular formation to stimulate and modulate its activity, providing one of the major feedback mechanisms by which the forebrain regulates incoming information.[190] Such mechanisms help to explain why incoming messages of equal physical intensity but different psychologic "meaning" possess profoundly different capacities to arouse.

Because of the many reticular components that contribute to it, the ascending reticular activating system is perhaps better regarded as a physiologic entity than a precise anatomic one. Certain well-marked bundles such as the lateral reticulothalamic tract conduct in a cephalad direction.[239] In addition, clusters of cells projecting rostrally can be found at several levels of the brainstem, but anatomists disagree as to how much such systems comprise a part of the reticular formation. Anatomic and physiologic details of all projections of brainstem nuclei to the cerebral cortex are not yet fully understood. At present, however, one can identify at least three principal ascending pathways from the reticular formation. One projects to the thalamic reticular nucleus and then to the cortex via a projection to specific thalamic nuclei.[227,307] The second ascends through the hypothalamus to influence basal forebrain structures including the limbic system.[193] The third is comprised of axons of serotonin neurons of the midbrain raphe[186] and norepinephrine neurons of the locus ceruleus,[128,159] both of which provide a diffuse, widespread innervation of the neocortex.

Physiologic studies indicate that stimulation of the *thalamic reticular nucleus* predominantly inhibits the cerebral cortex, as reflected by the appearance of recruiting responses and related synchronous cortical activities.[307] Purpura demonstrated several years ago that the thalamic recruiting responses take their origin in this nuclear structure.[227] Since anatomic studies by the Scheibels[248] show that the thalamic reticular nucleus projects only into the thalamus, its diffuse physiologic effects on the cerebral cortex must be mediated by way of the specific thalamic nuclei. Stimulation of the mesencephalic reticular region reduces or abolishes the otherwise tonic inhibitory influence of the thalamic reticular nucleus as does stimulation of the caudally directed frontal-thalamic pathway that travels back towards the thalamus by way of the thalamofrontal cortical system. By increasing or decreasing thalamic inhibitory mechanisms on the cerebral cortex, the ARAS thus provides a gating mechanism that limits or enhances the influence on the cortex of both specific ascending stimuli and the caudally directed cortical stimulation that flows constantly back to the thalamic nuclei during the waking state.[55]

The *limbic system relay* of ascending influences to the cerebral cortex is also of major importance in conscious behavior. From the hypothalamus, many fiber projections reach the amygdala and septal area.[55,245,246] From these sites, relays reach other components of the limbic system, including the hippocampus, the medial dorsal nucleus of the thalamus, and the amygdala.[192,281] Especially important is the major projection carried to the neocortex of the prefrontal lobes via the medial-dorsal thalamus.[154,158] Nauta speculates that this reticular-hypothalamic-neocortical reciprocal relationship modulates not only the organism's level of arousal but his external responses to instinctual vegetative and emotional drives.[192] The fact that every area of sensory cortex projects back via multiple relays into the limbic system underscores the key integrating influences of reticular projections to this region.[129,281] The possible relationship of limbic forebrain dysfunction to the clinical state of akinetic mutism is discussed on page 7.

DIRECT AFFERENT SYSTEMS. Recent neuroanatomic studies, especially ones employing autoradiographic techniques, have demonstrated several direct afferent pathways in the center of the brainstem. These circuits cannot properly be considered reticular in origin, yet they lie within the regions of ablation-stimulation originally considered to encompass the ARAS by Moruzzi and Magoun.[189] Their functions remain only partly elucidated, but they project to the upper brainstem and limbic system and conceivably may contribute to arousal and integrative cognitive mechanisms. The origins of these direct projections include the neurons of several pontine nuclei, especially the locus ceruleus, raphe nuclei, and parabrachialis. The pathways project mainly through the dorsal tegmental bundle, dorsal hypothalamus and the central tegmental tract-median forebrain bundle. They terminate mainly in the cingulate, orbital frontal, and medial temporal lobe cortex, all areas that also relate to the medial dorsal nucleus of the thalamus.[18,53,128,162,243,282]

In animals, major damage to the central tegmental region anywhere in the upper third of the pons, the midbrain, or the dorsal hypothalamus is sufficient to interrupt or greatly reduce the rostrally projecting mechanisms that normally maintain

14

consciousness.[189] The caudal extent of the structures critical to cortical arousal probably extends not much lower than the level of the trigeminal nerve entry. In animals, the central region of the lower pons and medulla confers important influences on certain stages of sleep and on the EEG, but does not seem to be directly required for the maintenance of sustained arousal. Batini and associates[8] describe the appearance of alertness in cats with brainstem transections at midpons (midpontine pretrigeminal preparation), and Jouvet[131] reports a similarly alert appearance in his "retropontine" preparations, which have their brainstems transected at the level of the trapezoid body, just rostral to the pontine-medullary junction.

The Cerebral Cortex and Conscious Behavior

As already emphasized, patterns of self-aware consciousness and conscious behavior in man depend on the integrity of an aroused cerebral cortex. Experimental studies of the last 20 years have produced major advances in understanding the normal physiology of this structure in mammals. One of the most important discoveries has been the recognition that all parts of the cortex possess a basically columnar functional organization of their neuronal populations with the columns being oriented roughly perpendicular to the surface.[110,190,305] Not only are the cells of single columns linked orthogonally to the cortex, but throughout the neocortex an organization exists wherein several adjacent columns appear to be linked in functional units by local circuit neurons.[228] The result is a modular organization of neocortical structures receiving afferents from several areas. These transmitting areas include the specifically related nuclei of the dorsal thalamus, other cortical areas of the same and opposite hemisphere, the more diffusely projecting areas in the basal forebrain, the nonspecific thalamic nuclei, and even the above-described widely projecting pontine nuclei.[190] Massive reciprocal relationships interconnect cortical areas with their specific thalamic nuclei, as well as other areas of the neocortex, the basal ganglia and cerebellum, homotypic cortical areas across the corpus callosum, and many other neural systems. The result provides a far richer connectivity for any given area and subarea of the neocortex than was recognized to exist even a few years ago. Selective fractionation of these cortical-cortical connections by still unknown mechanisms must underlie much of the astonishing complexity and variability of individual animal and human behavior.

The discoveries of the columnar-modular organization of cortical function and the exuberant extent of associated neocortical connectivity may begin to resolve some of the long-standing questions that scientists have raised as to whether qualitative or quantitative influences of the cerebral cortex exert the greater effect on conscious behavior. Regional specificity of cerebral cortical function has been well established since the 19th century for motor, visual, auditory, and language function. Psychologic and psychophysiologic studies of the past 25 years have increasingly demonstrated that the ultimate integrations of many additional sensory and cognitive functions are regionally and sometimes precisely localized in the cerebral hemispheres and, sometimes, even in separate hemispheres. As discussed in a later section, even the property of self-aware consciousness may be disproportionately linked to the language-producing areas of the dominant hemisphere.

Set against the incontrovertible evidence that the cerebrum preferentially "localizes" many and perhaps most of the specific cognitive functions that it subserves, stands the equally strong record that, wherever located, cerebral lesions of increasing

15

size increasingly dampen the general alertness and mental faculties of the patient. Chapman and Wolff for example, collected considerable evidence that demonstrated that large cerebral lesions or injuries damaged cognitive functions roughly in proportion to the amount of tissue lost and almost irrespective of what part of the hemispheres sustained the structural injury.[42] Other studies[40] also have shown that with increasingly large cerebral lesions, patients become less and less alert until, finally, if the cortex is totally or near-totally obliterated, behavioral evidence for the cognitive content of consciousness disappears, even in the absence of brain-stem lesions.[68,112,222]

Connections between cortical regions provide a mechanism to explain why lesions in one part of the brain can alter the functions of other, undamaged cerebral modules. Fully active function in any given cerebral area depends on that particular region receiving continuous afferent stimulation from specific thalamic relays and the known nonspecific thalamocortical pathways; it also depends on interactions with a myriad of cortical-cortical connections whose activity fluctuates according to internal and external stimuli and whose precise origins are sometimes only dimly understood. Removal of a large cerebral area thus causes nonspecific effects somewhat comparable to the well-established effects of removal or depression of deeply lying arousal mechanisms. At least acutely, such gross cerebral damage results in physiologic changes that extend well beyond the loss of the specific functions regulated by the injured region.

One can cite many clinical examples to illustrate that damage to one cerebral area produces physiologic and, therefore, metabolic depression in cerebral regions remote from the injury. Large brain tumors, even when they produce no substantial increase in intracranial pressure or discernible shift of the intracranial contents, can reduce the blood flow and metabolic rate of other regions of the cerebral hemispheres.[75] Acute ischemic injury (stroke) to one hemisphere in man commonly is followed by reduced blood flow, depressed physiologic activity, and a lowered metabolic rate in the other hemisphere.[179,266] In experimental animals, experimental stroke confined to the region of one middle cerebral artery similarly induces prompt impairments in the physiology and metabolism of the mirror area of the opposite hemisphere, to which it is linked by the massive fiber pathways of the corpus callosum.[149]

Neuropharmacologic Mechanisms in Consciousness

Studies of recent years have identified in the central nervous system an almost bewildering number of chemical agents that fulfill some or most of the criteria for being neurotransmitters. Several of these biochemical substances undoubtedly act on pathways that influence waking or nonwaking behavior, but knowledge of this action for most of the compounds remains too fragmentary to discuss here. Several considerations explain this limitation. Anatomic studies of the cellular origins of putative neurotransmitters and the distribution of their central pathways far outdistance in number and definitiveness experimental work that clarifies their specific functional effects. Little is known about how one pharmacologic subsystem may interact with others, yet such connections compound and complicate the apparent effect of stimulating a "specific" system. Finally, apparently similar pharmacologic systems can sometimes mediate dissimilar effects in different species, so that animal experimental results must be applied cautiously to human physiology.

16

Given the above precautions in interpreting the evidence, it appears that central acetylcholine and monoamine systems deserve the greatest attention as potential mediators of mechanisms governing arousal, cognition, stupor, and coma.

Investigators have implicated cholinergic mechanisms in arousal since the 1950s.[62,131] Cholinergic drugs, such as physostigmine, that cross the blood brain barrier produce behavioral arousal and EEG activation in many forms of human and animal coma. Cholinoceptive neurons, however, exist at many levels of the cerebral cortex, diencephalon, and brain stem, so that some of these pharmacologic results could reflect direct cerebral stimulation rather than activation of an ascending activating system. However, histochemical studies of acetylcholine esterase provide somewhat stronger evidence for the existence of a cholinergic arousal mechanism originating in the brainstem or basal nuclei. According to Shute and Lewis, cholinergic fibers ascend from the mesencephalic reticular formation in the dorsal tegmental pathway that supplies the tectum, pretectal area, geniculate bodies, and thalamus.[259] The system receives afferents from, among other areas, the locus ceruleus. They found that a ventral tegmental cholinergic pathway arises from the pars compacta of the substantia nigra and adjacent substantia innominata and perhaps provides cholinergic connections between the reticular formation and neocortical areas. Initially, this latter conclusion was uncertain, because histochemical staining for acetylcholinesterase sometimes marks noncholinoceptive cell membranes, implying specific connections where none exist. Recently, however, Johnston and associates have reported that in the rat neuron-specific lesions in the area of the basal nucleus of Meynert result in a 50 to 60 percent reduction in cholinergic markers in the frontal and dorsolateral parietal cortex.[127] At least with unilateral lesions, the animals demonstrated no grossly evident behavioral changes.

Only limited evidence exists about the relative distribution and functional importance of nicotinic versus muscarinic cholinergic systems in the brain. According to Kawamura and Domino, the cortical arousal induced by nicotine in intact animals is blocked by lesions of the mesencephalic reticular formation.[136] The finding implies that reticular cholinergic synapses operate via nicotinic receptor pathways. Furthermore, centrally acting cholinergic agonists interrupt cortical recruitment, just as does physiologic stimulation of the brain stem reticular formation.[67]

Central monoamine systems, especially serotonin (5-hydroxytryptamine) and noradrenaline, comprise substantial components of the brainstem reticular formation. Both of these neuropharmacologic systems are highly collateralized, give off widely distributed projections, and innervate large portions of the forebrain. These anatomic properties seem especially well suited to providing nonspecific modulating or regulating influences on receptor fields and have led several investigators to seek evidence for their participation in generating behavioral responses, including arousal and sleep.[185,186]

Jouvet has advanced the most elaborate theory for the participation of monoamine systems in arousal, sleep, and coma.[131] Based to a considerable extent on his own experimental observations, he postulates that slow wave sleep is initiated by the release of serotonin from the central synapses of neurons taking their origin in the rostral part of the brainstem raphe system. This nuclear complex extends along the midline from the midbrain anteriorly to the mid pons posteriorly. He regards tonic behavioral or cortical arousal, on the other hand, as depending upon the projections of noradrenaline containing neurons arising from the anterior portion of the locus ceruleus. In Jouvet's view, dopamine containing neuron systems that

17

project from substantia nigra to other extrapyramidal nuclei may activate aroused motor behavior. If so, interruption of the dopamine system could result in coma-like motor inactivity.

To what degree Jouvet's imaginative synthesis and extension of experimental findings apply to human states of arousal and pathologic unconsiousness remains to be demonstrated. Chemical ablation studies of serotonergic neurons employing 5,6 di-hydroxytryptamine in animals indicate neither loss of slow wave sleep nor detectable long-term effects on arousal or alertness. Similarly, efforts up until now to produce pharmacologic or physical blocking of the locus ceruleus in animals have had little evident effects on arousal. These seemingly contradictory findings are difficult to reconcile with the view that monoamines play a central role in regulating waking and sleeping.

Considerable evidence supports the view that gamma amino butyric acid (GABA) is a naturally occurring centrally acting inhibitory transmitter, widely distributed in the brain.[115] It has been demonstrated that GABA is released from the cortex during periods of cortical inhibition and that cortical release of the neurotransmitter falls during periods of wakefulness induced by stimulation of the brainstem reticular formation. Beyond that fragment of evidence, no convincing data presently indicate that selective activation or blocking of a GABA system causes coma or arousal.

Relationship of Sleep to Coma

Coma and slow wave sleep share many behavioral and EEG characteristics. Both abolish conscious interaction with the environment and the behavioral appearance of the subject often is similar in the two states, the exception being in patients with prominent metabolic abnormalities or motor system damage. The EEG can be slow (1–5 Hz) in both sleep and coma, and many lesions or illnesses that cause coma in their late states produce excessive drowsiness in their less severe or earlier periods. Our medical forebears regarded sleep and coma as one, and until even a few years ago there was a widespread tendency among physiologists to regard both sleep and coma as caused by a damping or failure of the normal tonic flow of impulses from the reticular activating system to the cerebral hemispheres. This unitary concept, however, was hard to reconcile with the early findings by Mangold and coworkers [173] that human cerebral oxygen uptake remains at or above the normal level during sleep, while it declines below the awake normal level in most studied examples of coma.[70] It also was hard to reconcile the older view with the fact that EEG and behavioral manifestations that consistently accompany each other during sleep often part company during pathologic unconsciousness. For example, some patients in coma from pontine lesions have EEGs with normal rather than slow frequencies,[301] and drugs such as atropine can slow the EEG without blocking behavioral arousal.[264]

The premise that sleep and coma are physiologically identical was gradually superseded by evidence from several laboratories, especially those of Moruzzi[188] and Jouvet.[131] Such studies established that sleep is an active physiologic process with several distinct EEG and behavioral stages, which depend for their full expression on specific individual brainstem nuclear areas extending rostrally to caudally from the posterior diencephalon to the upper medulla. At present no one equates physiologic sleep with pathologic clouding of consciousness, and the unsolved problem lies more in determining where the two overlap and why they so often seem to blend into one another in patients with cerebral dysfunction.

Some examples of coma, particularly metabolic coma, resemble deep sleep during

18

their early stages. In deep sleep, as in pathologic coma, the subject can be almost unarousable with vigorous stimuli. The muscle tone is flaccid, the EEG is slow, and the volume of respiration, the degree of body temperature, and the level of the blood pressure all fall below levels found during wakefulness. Furthermore, almost all patients in coma wake up to some degree with the passage of time, the only exceptions being certain subjects with destructive lesions of the posterior dorsal hypothalamus and adjacent midbrain who may remain indefinitely in a more or less continuous sleep-like state. Depending on the cause of coma and the accompanying structural damage in the brain, the reawakening from sleep-like coma may come in hours, days, or even a few weeks, after onset. Its rate of reappearance seems to depend on the integrity of upper brainstem and hypothalamic function and not on any necessary preservation of forebrain structures. A characteristic feature of patients in the chronic vegetative state is that they demonstrate sleep-wake cycles. When awakening does occur, the behavior and, often, the EEG of such patients sooner or later show the several stages of sleep characteristic of normals. Whether or not the duration of such sleep-wake cycles returns completely to normal is unknown.

The above considerations imply two things about the sleep-like quality of most comas. One is that waking and sleeping reflect primitive vegetative functions whose activity requires little more than the preservation of relevant brainstem mechanisms to express themselves in total body behavior. The other is that the sleep-like quality of coma reflects a state of temporary inhibition of arousal mechanisms, a form of reticular "shock" perhaps analogous to the inhibition of motor activity that occurs in the distal spinal segments when an acute high spinal injury produces spinal shock.

Evidence from neonates with malformations of the brain may not necessarily be applicable to patients suffering injuries to fully developed nervous systems, but anencephalic infants with brains intact only as far rostral as the midbrain level are reported to display normal behavioral sleep-wake cycles as well as primitive changes in emotional expression.[92,93] The findings reinforce the conclusion that in man all the necessary mechanisms for sleeping-waking behavior reside in the brainstem and are acutely inhibited rather than destroyed in most examples of coma.

Studies of Altered Consciousness in Man

Most animal experimental studies on mechanisms of consciousness consist of correlating anatomic and electrophysiologic data with the behavioral appearances of the organism under study. Such an approach produces unavoidable limitations. Different species do not always react similarly to similar lesions, and one cannot tell whether animals other than man possess the capacity of self-awareness that ultimately defines our consciousness. In animals, lesions that block arousal usually have been produced abruptly; the neurologic effects differed when similar destructive changes were induced more slowly to resemble what often happens with human pathologic processes.[1] Even in animals it turns out that acute lesions often produce behavioral and EEG effects that change substantially if the animal is nursed successfully to long survival. Demonstrating this, Batsel in dogs[9] and Villablanca in cats[296] observed that mesencephalic transections of the brainstem were followed at first by coma and EEG slowing, but later by substantial neurologic recovery with the isolated forebrain and diencephalon developing EEG patterns characteristic of alternating sleep and wakefulness. Such cycling activity of the isolated forebrain suggests that a functional reorganization occurs. Presumably, stimuli from visual

19

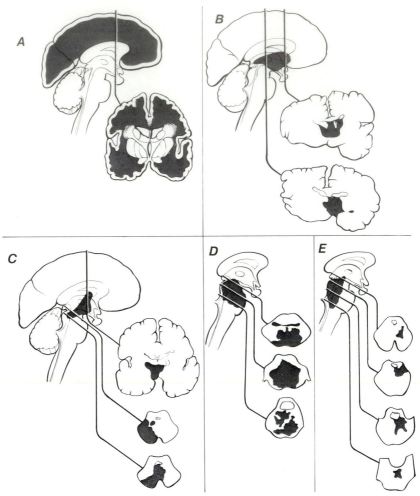

Figure 1. Brain lesions causing coma.

A, Diffuse demyelination of the hemispheral subcortex following anoxia (see Patient 1-1).

B, Lymphoma of diencephalon. The findings are presented in full in Patient 2-14, p. 143.

C, Diencephalic-midbrain infarct. A 66-year-old man was found unconscious in the street. For 6 months after his admission to the hospital he remained comatose, with eyes closed, and no spontaneous movement, but he grimaced and withdrew when stimulated noxiously. During the subsequent 2 months he opened his right eye in response to loud noises and once mumbled his first name. However, he never responded appropriately to command. He died 8 months after admission. There was severe arteriosclerosis of his cerebral arteries and a cystic infarct as diagrammed involving the gray matter surrounding the posterior third ventricle and the aqueduct as well as the left cerebral peduncle.

D, High pontine infarct. A 56-year-old man with diabetes and hypertension was admitted to the hospital complaining of generalized weakness and vomiting. The day after admission he suddenly became unconscious and behaviorally unresponsive to noxious stimuli. He hyperventilated and developed skew deviation of his eyes. He died 26 days later without regaining consciousness. His basilar artery was thrombosed in its midportion. A large infarct involved the tegmentum of both the upper pons and lower midbrain.

E, Brainstem hemorrhage. A 49-year-old man with severe hypertension suddenly developed an occipital headache and right-sided weakness. Several hours later he lapsed into coma with decerebrate posturing in response to noxious stimuli. He remained in coma for 2 months and then gradually recovered consciousness, but was left with severe dysarthria and dysphagia as well as bilateral weakness of the extremities. When he died 7 months after the original episode, residual damage from several small hemorrhages was scattered throughout the tegmentum of the lower midbrain, pons, and upper medulla.

and olfactory inputs form thalamocortical and cortical-cortical connections, and those as well as a reactivated hypothalamo-limbic-frontal loop interact to restore at least some normal cortical function. In this regard, even acute animal experiments have sometimes produced a dissociation between electroencephalographic activation and behavioral arousal. According to Feldman and Waller, hypothalamic destruction sparing the midbrain reticular formation is followed by sustained somnolence, even though stimulation of the midbrain or a peripheral afferent pathway can still evoke a low-voltage desynchronized EEG record.[82] These inconsistencies and the difference between the neurologic effects of anatomically comparable lesions in lower animals and man make well-documented clinical and pathologic observations crucial to an understanding of the pathogenesis of impaired consciousness.

As will be seen, to produce stupor or coma in man a disorder must damage or depress the function of extensive areas of both cerebral hemispheres, or similarly impair the function of structures lying in the paramedian diencephalon and upper brainstem, or involve both the hemispheres and brainstem together. Figure 1 illustrates examples of such lesions causing coma, while Figure 2 illustrates examples of less extensive damage with which patients retained the aroused state throughout.

HISTORICAL BACKGROUND. The record of well-studied patients having anatomic lesions that illuminate the basis for human consciousness and coma goes back more than a century. Gayet in 1875 described a patient who was apathetic and limp when aroused and lapsed into a coma-like sleep when not actively stimulated.[95] The illness

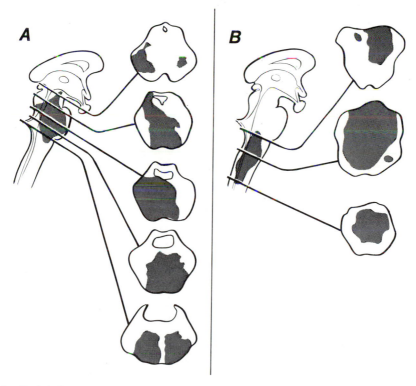

Figure 2. Brain lesions not causing sustained coma. **A,** Brainstem infarct. The clinical details are given as Patient 3–2, p. 159. **B,** Medullary hemorrhage. Patient 1–2, p. 29.

21

lasted 5 months and at autopsy the brain contained inflammation, softening, and sclerosis of the central gray matter surrounding the third ventricle, aqueduct, and fourth ventricle. Mauthner in 1890 reviewed Gayet's data, cited the association between somnolence and the presence of hemorrhagic necrosis in the same regions in patients with Wernicke's superior polioencephalitis, and correlated similarly distributed periaqueductal lesions with the somnolence of encephalitis. Mauthner concluded that midbrain lesions blocked wakefulness by blocking neural impulses between the periphery and the cerebral cortex: "I . . . view the nature of sleep as an interruption of the centripetal and centrifugal conductor. . . . The location of sleep is in the central hollow gray."[176]

Mauthner's view was singular for the times and his contemporaries regarded sleep and coma as being caused by cerebral anemia, or depression of conduction in the corona radiata of the cerebral hemispheres. Hughlings Jackson placed consciousness in the frontal lobes and clinicians, at least, were disinclined to challenge him.[116] In the 1920s, however, the finding of prominent midbrain damage in patients dying from encephalitis lethargica led von Economo to refocus attention on the importance of brainstem lesions as a cause of coma.[297] Similarly located abnormalities in patients in coma from brain tumors,[6,91] brain infarcts,[22] and cerebral trauma[120] all demonstrated that relatively restricted lesions interrupted or markedly reduced consciousness if they involved the paramedian gray matter anywhere between the posterior hypothalamus and the tegmentum of the lower pons.

Studies in recent years that have added new and useful details to these earlier findings are discussed in the following paragraphs. However, it should be noted that with many of the observations on humans as well as on animals the follow-up data are insufficient to tell whether lesions that acutely block consciousness would necessarily forever prevent its emergence were the patient to survive.

CEREBRAL HEMISPHERES. Most studies of humans indicate that to produce either coma or, chronically, the vegetative state, the larger part of both cerebral hemispheres must be damaged or rendered functionless. Several observers, however, have questioned whether the left hemisphere bears a stronger relationship to consciousness than the right. During the past 40 years, studies from several laboratories, especially those of Milner,[182] Teuber,[286] Hecaen,[105] Sperry,[272] and Gazzaniga,[96] have gradually replaced the older concept that language represents the only anatomically localized psychologic function in the human cerebral hemispheres. Observations on patients with hemispheric brain lesions as well as extensive and ingenious psychologic evaluations of subjects with surgical section of the anterior two thirds of the corpus callosum have disclosed striking lateralization of cortical areas dealing with the recognition of form, the spatial perception of nonverbal as opposed to verbal memory, and a variety of other visual and other cognitive functions. An important part of these findings suggests that in man a special relationship exists between language and self-awareness.[156]

Both clinical and experimental reports have suggested that the left hemisphere influences consciousness to a degree more than can be accounted for by the relative amount of tissue involved. Since the evidence is conflicting, it is repeated in some detail.

Serafitinides, Hoare, and Driver first reported in 1965 that amobarbital sodium more often produced a transient loss of consciousness when injected into the carotid artery of the dominant (usually left) speech-containing hemisphere than the nondominant.[252] The transient unresponsiveness occurred even when only homolateral EEG slowing occurred; the inference was that consciousness, like speech, sometimes depended on the dominant hemisphere. Rosadini and Rossi were unable to confirm these findings, perhaps because they required as a criterion that any observed loss of consciousness last longer than one minute.[238] Two additional groups, however, report that apparent loss of consciousness is more frequent among patients with ischemic stroke involving the language dominant hemisphere than among those with nondominant infarcts. Schwartz noted that 38 of 46 patients with ischemic lesions in the dominant hemisphere suffered an initial loss of consciousness, while this occurred in only 3 of 54 patients with a similar lesion in the nondominant hemisphere.[250] This was a postmortem study and many of the clinical data were fragmentary and retrospectively collected; the results are so different from general experience that one should perhaps view them cautiously. Nevertheless, Albert and associates prospectively studied 47 such patients, examining the same question, with somewhat similar results.[3] Fifty-seven percent of patients with left hemisphere lesions reportedly had an initial impairment of consciousness (eight somnolent, three stuporous, two in coma) in contrast to 25 percent with right sided damage (none were in coma). Detailed analysis of the case material revealed no evidence that the size of the ischemic injury was any larger in the patients with left hemisphere than right hemisphere strokes.

Behaviorally, one can estimate another person's self-aware consciousness only by his response to the examiner's verbal commands or gestures. Therefore, conclusions about the localization of self-aware consciousness in the language-dominant hemisphere are immediately relevant to the context of this monograph only insofar as they relate to the apparently high incidence of stupor or coma in association with acute left hemisphere lesions. From the evidence available one must conclude that self-aware consciousness and language function impose a physiologically greater activity upon the dominant than the nondominant hemisphere. Sudden loss of such function results behaviorally in loss of more than half of the functioning cerebral hemispheres, and stupor can often be the result.

To epitomize, then: Except, possibly, for the special case of sudden, large aphasia-producing lesions of the dominant hemisphere, unilateral dysfunction of the cerebral hemispheres does not by itself cause stupor or coma. Furthermore, unless they produce secondary effects that extend beyond their original confines, even large dominant hemisphere lesions produce only briefly lasting coma if they produce any at all. Large unilateral lesions in either hemisphere blunt alertness acutely in rough proportion to their size and remote effects (see Chapter 2), but it requires bilateral and extensive damage or dysfunction of the cerebral hemispheres or diencephalon before stupor or unarousable coma ensue. The following case study is an example (Fig. 1A).

Patient 1–1. A 59-year-old man was found unconscious in a room filled with illuminating gas. A companion already had died. On admission the man was unresponsive. His blood pressure was 120/80 mm. Hg, pulse 120, and respirations 18 and regular. His rectal temperature was 102°F. His stretch reflexes were hypoactive, and plantar responses were absent. Coarse rhonchi were heard throughout both lung fields.

He was treated with nasal oxygen and began to awaken in 30 hours. On the second hospital day he was alert and oriented. On the fourth day he was afebrile, his chest was clear, and he was ambulated. The neurologic examination was normal, and a psychologic evaluation by a psychiatrist revealed a clear sensorium with "no evidence of organic brain damage." He was discharged to his relatives' care 9 days after the anoxic event.

At home, he remained well for 2 days but then became quiet, speaking only when spoken to. The following day he merely shuffled about and responded in monosyllables. The next day (13 days after the anoxia) he became incontinent and unable to walk, swallow, or chew. He neither spoke to nor recognized his family. He was admitted to a private sanatorium and diagnosed as having a depression. Deterioration continued, and 28 days after the initial anoxia he was readmitted to the hospital. His blood pressure was 170/100 mm. Hg, pulse 100, respirations 24, and temperature 101°F. There were coarse rales at both lung bases. He perspired profusely and constantly. He did not respond to pain but would open his eyes momentarily to loud sounds. His extremities were flexed and rigid, his deep tendon reflexes were hyperactive, and his plantar responses extensor. Laboratory studies, including examination of the spinal fluid, were normal. He died 3 days later.

An autopsy examination showed diffuse bronchopneumonia. The brain was grossly normal. There was no cerebral swelling. Coronal sections appeared normal with no evidence of pallidal necrosis. Histologically, neurons in the motor cortex, hippocampus, cerebellum, and occipital lobes appeared generally well preserved, although a few sections showed minimal cytodegenerative changes and reduction of neurons (Fig. 3). There was occasional perivascular lymphocytic infiltration. Pathologic changes were not present in blood vessels, nor was there any interstitial edema. The striking alteration was diffuse demyelination involving all lobes of the cerebral hemispheres (Fig. 4) and sparing only the arcuate fibers (the immediately subcortical portion of the cerebral white matter). Axis cylinders were also reduced in number but were better preserved than was the myelin. Oligodendroglia were preserved in demyelinated areas. Reactive astrocytes were considerably increased. The brain stem and cerebellum were histologically intact.[222] (The condition of delayed postanoxic cerebral demyelination observed in this patient is discussed at greater length in Chapter 4.)

Unresponsive behavior also has been described in children in whom adreno-leuko-dystrophy has produced diffuse demyelination of the hemispheres but spared the brainstem. Additional examples of loss of consciousness and cognition with extensive bilateral damage to the cerebral hemispheres but preservation of largely intact brainstems are discussed in the section on the chronic vegetative state, page 6.

Following severe head injury one also finds evidence that damage confined to the cerebral hemispheres can produce at least a transient sleep-like coma replaced after several weeks or even months by a state of wakefulness devoid of cognitive content. Stritch reported a series of patients in whom the cerebral hemispheres were extensively and bilaterally demyelinated following head injury, yet the brainstem was spared from any extensive pathologic change.[278] Stritch describes her patients as severely demented, although only after several weeks had any of them opened their eyes. At least two of the patients never recovered more than the most rudimentary nonreflex responsiveness to the environment, and none recovered anything approaching the full faculties of consciousness. Crompton, Teare, and Bowen[57] and Jellinger and Seitelberger[122] report that in their extensive studies on posttraumatic encephalopathy, coma was always associated with lesions at the base of the third ventricle and in the brainstem, while injuries confined to the hemispheres resulted only in a profound or progressive dementia. Since they include no clinical details, one cannot deduce whether by coma they refer exclusively to states in which sleeping and waking fail to return. In their reports, however, patients with entirely hemispheric lesions are described as spending days or weeks in coma, implying either that they had nonmorphologic injury to brainstem arousal centers or that these centers were physiologically inhibited acutely following hemispheric injury. In either case, much evidence from patients with many different kinds of neurologic injury indicates that severe bilateral damage to the cerebral hemispheres alone is sufficient to produce at least temporary coma and is capable of permanently erasing the cognitive content of man's consciousness.

FRONTAL LIMBIC SYSTEM LESIONS, COMA, AND AKINETIC MUTISM. Many authors have reported changes in cognitive consciousness in association with deep, medially placed lesions of the frontal lobes. These reports deserve special attention because at first they may appear to contradict the principle that only lesions that produce diffuse and bilateral dysfunction of the cerebral hemispheres produce stupor or coma.[30,78,90,121,142,198]

The clinical disorder in this group of patients holds fairly true to form. When the associated disease has come on abruptly, as with vascular occlusions of the anterior

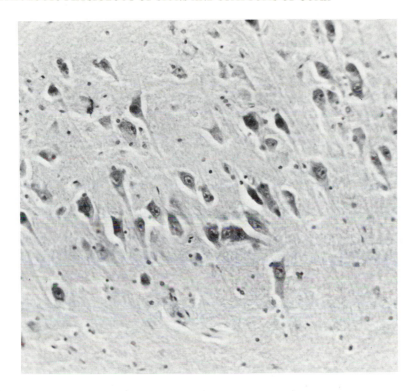

Figure 3. Normal appearance of cortical neurons of hippocampal gyrus ($\times$ 100) in Patient 1–1.

cerebral arteries or hemorrhages from anterior communicating aneurysms into the frontal lobes, the patients commonly lapse initially into coma, usually to awaken in a few days with the clinical picture of attentive-appearing akinetic mutism. Wakeful periods are prolonged, and the eyes often appear to be interestedly heeding much that surrounds them, but the subject rarely, if ever, speaks. Despite their appearance of cognitive readiness and sustained wakefulness, such patients neither respond to commands nor move, an appearance that inspired the picturesque French term, *coma vigil*.

The pathologic changes that accompany this state of attentive-appearing mute akinesia are fairly consistent from patient to patient and are usually fairly widespread, although a number of reports have appeared under titles that suggest an anatomically more restricted lesion. Mostly, however, the anatomic changes have included major bilateral damage to the cingulate gyri, the septal area, varying portions of the frontal poles, and, often, portions of the thalamus or hypothalamus. Details of the neuropathologic protocols almost always indicate either associated lesions, acute compressive abnormalities elsewhere in the cerebral hemispheres,[30,90] or the presence of preexisting cerebral lesions that could enhance the physiologic ill-effects of the frontal damage. Where reported, EEGs have almost always shown diffuse bilateral abnormalities over the hemispheric convexities.

The above considerations imply that the akinetic mutism of frontal lobe origin reflects widespread physiologic dysfunction of the cerebral hemispheres, which may be morphologically most severe in the frontal lobes, but functionally, almost cer-

25

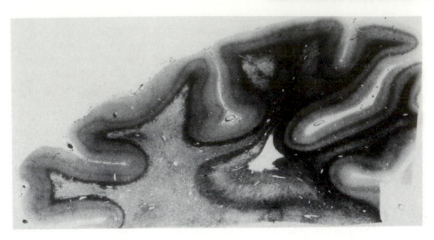

Figure 4. Myelin sheath stain of occipital cortex from Patient 1-1 showing extensive subcortical demyelination, essentially sparing only the subcortical arcuate fibers (the dark staining bands immediately beneath the cortex).

tainly involves other parts of the cerebrum as well. Surgical cingulectomy, for example, produces in man neither coma, nor akinesia, nor mutism.[290] It appears most likely that large, deep, midline frontal lesions in man interrupt the major reciprocal pathways that normally interconnect the frontal lobe with the thalamus, the amygdala, and the midbrain.[128,162,192] Such interruptions not only affect frontal lobe function directly, but secondarily influence large parts of the remaining neocortex that normally receive cortical-cortical connections and limbic modulation transmitted via the frontal lobe circuits. The interruption of such limbic influences can be expected to have profound effects on cognitive thought and behavior, just as interruption of the mesencephalic ascending reticular influence has profound effects on arousal and somatic activity.

THALAMUS. Pure anatomic lesions of the thalamus that neither accompany a generalized disease nor involve adjacent structures are unusual, and selective bilateral thalamic injury is rare. Unilateral thalamic destruction is not recorded as being associated with behavioral unresponsiveness nor have we encountered such an association. Bilateral lesions restricted to the thalamus can alter conscious behavior, however. Such injuries are nearly always the consequence of vascular occlusion of perforating arteries that arise either from the apex of the basilar artery or from the short segments of the posterior cerebral arteries that extend from where it originates at the bifurcation of the basilar artery to where it is joined by the posterior communicating arteries (see Fig. 27 in Chapter 2). This segment is called the mesencephalic artery or, more graphically, the *basilar communicating artery*. Percheron has detailed the potential vascular variations in this critical area, pointing out that minor congenital anomalies can result in a thalamic perforating artery that arises unilaterally but supplies both sides of the thalamus.[218,219]

Occlusion either of the basilar artery at its apex or of the origin of an anomalous perforating vessel from the basilar communicating artery can produce bilateral medial thalamic ischemia. More anteriorly placed bilateral lesions presumably are due to occlusion of the anterior thalamo-subthalamic artery. Such occlusions may produce infarcts anatomically confined to the thalamus, but the early symptoms in the involved patients suggest that functional changes extend caudally into the mesencephalon. Patients with anterior thalamo-subthalamic artery occlusions generally have had an abrupt onset of unresponsiveness, characteristically accompanied by small reactive or unequal pupils along with intact horizontal caloric responses but, often, impaired vertical eye movements.[181] Coma subsides in 10 days or so but is followed by several days or weeks of hypersomnia and then by a permanent condition of apathetic, semimute hypokinesia coupled with a profound amnesic dementia. Castaigne and associates describe such a clinical disorder in two elderly women in whom postmortem studies demonstrated softening confined to the thalamus.[39,40] The described abnormalities were located especially in the distribution of the intralaminar nuclei, the parafascicular region, and the centromedian nuclei area of the thalamus extending towards, but not destroying, the red nucleus. (The dorsal tegmental bundle conveying ascending pontine tegmental fibers courses through this same region.) No lesions were found in the midbrain. Similar clinical and anatomic findings were present in a patient earlier described by Schuster.[249]

Segarra believes that more posteriorly placed thalamic lesions are caused by infarcts resulting from occlusion of the posterior thalamo-subthalamic paramedian artery.[251] These produce a somewhat different syndrome from the above. Patients with such lesions are described as resembling the above description except for remaining much longer in sleep-like coma, being almost permanently akinetic and mute, and having a high incidence of oculomotor abnormalities reflecting their midbrain damage. Certainly, the anatomic lesions in the paramedian region of the midbrain in Segarra's cases would make one predict that they would remain permanently deprived of their main arousal mechanisms. Bilateral ptosis due to oculomotor paralysis sometimes makes it difficult to determine whether or not such patients are awake and it is more difficult, therefore, to comment on the mechanism of their reported hypersomnia.[317]

HYPOTHALAMUS. In experimental animals, stimulation of the periventricular gray matter of the posterior hypothalamus produces arousal while anterior hypothalamic stimulation, at least in some species, induces the behavioral and physiologic appearances of sleep.[107] Bilateral paramedian destructive lesions of the posterior hypothalamus in man cause in direct proportion to their size a progressively more severe clouding of consciousness, drowsiness, and eventually totally unresponsive coma. An example of such a condition is diagrammed in Figure 1B and described in detail on page 143 (Patient 2-14). Since either ischemic or compressive lesions in this paramedian hypothalamic area rarely spare the adjacent midbrain reticular formation, it is difficult to assign symptoms solely to injury of one or the other structure. Patients with hypothalamic hypersomnia, however, characteristically demonstrate the behavioral manifestations of normal sleepiness; they yawn, stretch, and sigh, and these features generally are lacking in patients with coma from midbrain lesions. The extensive literature describing hypersomnia with hypothalamic inflammation in epidemic encephalitis,[297] as well as that on neoplasms in this area,[91] suggests that intrinsic posterior hypothalamic injury or destruction characteristically induces prolonged sleep-like coma.

MIDBRAIN AND PONS. Abundant recent material corroborates the early clinical-pathologic conclusions by Gayet, Mauthner, and von Economo about the relation of the central area of these brainstem structures to wakefulness. Indeed, some of the described lesions destroying the paramedian reticulum and producing well-documented coma in man are as precise and restricted as those created by Lindsley in the early animal studies that experimentally established the physiologic importance

27

of the midbrain reticular formation in producing arousal.[161] Brain, for example, described a comatose state in a patient with a precisely defined paramedian infarct of the midbrain.[22] The loss of consciousness of the man whose pathologic lesion is illustrated in Figure 1C gives another example of clinical pathologic correlation nearly as precise as one finds in animals with experimentally placed lesions.

Evidence gained from clinical-pathologic analyses firmly establishes that the midbrain and pontine area critical to consciousness in man lies in the paramedian tegmental zone immediately ventral to the ventricular system and extends continuously from the posterior hypothalamic area rostrally to approximately the lower third of the pontine tegmentum caudally. Just how much of this critical region must be damaged to interrupt cerebral activation is difficult to establish because only a small number of clinically well-studied patients have had small and restricted brain lesions, and few analyses differentiate between the immediate and long-term effects of such damage. To draw physiologic conclusions one generally must rely on the examination of patients who have had acute infarctions from vascular occlusions, since the tissue alterations caused by hemorrhages or neoplasms generally change too much between the time of onset and autopsy to allow reliable inferences.

Small lesions involving the critical paramedian zone and producing coma have been reported by only a relatively few workers.[22, 113, 202, 251] All recorded examples, however, have involved both sides of the midline and most of the dorsal-ventral axis of the tegmentum. Chase, Moretti, and Prensky reviewed the findings in 20 patients, 8 of their own, with autopsy-confirmed tegmental lesions of the pons and lower midbrain.[43] None of the 9 whose brain contained bilateral lesions remained alert, and 8 were deeply obtunded. By contrast, only 3 of the 11 patients with unilateral tegmental destruction were obtunded, and 2 of those were febrile or hypoxic. Lesions confined to the periaqueductal gray matter in man[103, 256] do not impair conscious behavior, an observation consistent with experimental findings.[265] According to von Glees and Bailey, bilateral surgical severance of the medial lemnisci and spinothalamic tracts at midbrain level in man did not interrupt consciousness.[298]

It is difficult to estimate precisely how far caudally the tegmental area that is critical to consciousness extends because most lesions that damage the lower pontine area also damage the lower cranial nerve pathways and both corticospinal tracts, cutting off the patient's ability to communicate (see page 6). The EEG is of little differentiating value in such instances since in the presence of lesions of the pontine tegmentum its pattern can resemble wakefulness despite the behavioral unresponsiveness of the patient.[301] Patients with bilateral infarcts of the midpontine paramedian tegmentum are not arousable, at least acutely. We made a special effort to evoke appropriate behavioral responsiveness in two closely studied patients with such lesions, and no glimmer of consistent reaction in ocular or any other movement, could be elicited by any but noxious stimuli. We have not discovered well-studied examples of chronically surviving patients with lesions confined to the lower pontine tegmentum, although Figure 5 shows a lesion that extended into this region in a patient who retained conscious responses until a few hours before death.

MEDULLA OBLONGATA. All evidence indicates that in man paramedian medullary destruction does not interfere with conscious responses. Earlier workers, including Cairns[32] and Jefferson,[121] thought that medullary injuries did cause coma, but they drew their conclusions from observing patients with expanding lesions of a type that notoriously exerts widespread effects. Reichardt's experience has been cited to prove that medullary damage provokes coma.[233] The example is equivocal, however. Reichardt described a woman who suffered an apparent medullary puncture during a cisternal tap. She cried out and became unresponsive, but promptly recovered after the needle was withdrawn. She complained bitterly of unilateral paresthesias of the body, and her pulse rate slowed to 55 per minute. The blood pressure was not taken, but it would seem that the attack could as easily have been one of vasovagal syncope as one resulting from interruption of specific physiologic pathways subserving consciousness.

Our own material indicates that, in man, medullary structures exert little direct effect on neural functions regulating consciousness. The following patient preserved quick and accurate responses to commands as well as the behavioral appearance of consciousness almost until death, despite extensive destruction of the central medulla extending rostrally into the lower third of the pons. The findings at autopsy are diagrammed in Figure 2B and pictured in Figure 5.

Patient 1-2. A 62-year-old woman was examined through the courtesy of Dr. Walter Camp. Twenty-five years earlier she had developed weakness and severely impaired position and vibration sense of the right arm and leg. Two years before we saw her she developed paralysis of the right vocal cord and wasting of the right side of the tongue, followed by insidiously progressing disability with an unsteady gait and more weakness of the right limbs. Four days before coming to the hospital, she became much weaker on the right side, and two days later she lost the ability to swallow.

When she entered the hospital, she was alert and in full possession of her faculties. She had no difficulty breathing and her blood pressure was 162/110 mm. Hg. She had upbeat nystagmus on upward gaze.

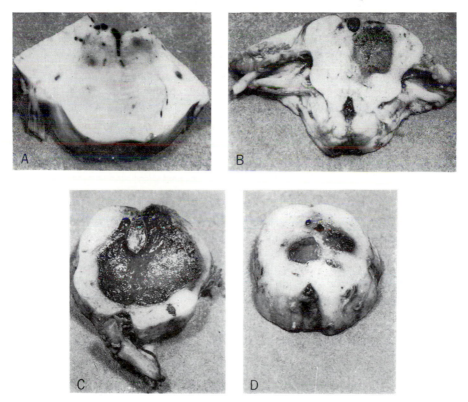

Figure 5. Section from lower pons (**A**) to upper cervical spinal cord (**D**), Patient 1-2.

29

and decreased appreciation of pinprick on the left side of the face. The right sides of the pharynx, palate, and tongue were paralyzed. The right arm and leg were weak and atrophic, consistent with disuse. Stretch reflexes below the neck were bilaterally brisk and the right plantar response was extensor. Position and vibratory sensations were reduced on the right side of the body and the appreciation of pinprick was reduced on the left.

The next day she was still alert and responsive, but she developed difficulty in coughing and speaking and finally she ceased breathing. An endotracheal tube was placed and connected to a ventilator. Later, on that third hospital day, she was still brightly alert and quickly and accurately answered questions by nodding or shaking her head. The opening pressure of cerebrospinal fluid (CSF) at lumbar puncture was 180 mm. of water, and the xanthochromic fluid contained 8500 RBC and 14 WBC per cu. mm.

She lived for 23 more days. During that time she developed complete somatic motor paralysis below the face. Several hypotensive crises were treated promptly with infusions of pressor agents, but no pressor drugs were needed during the last 2 weeks of life. Intermittently during those final days, she had brief periods of unresponsiveness, but then awakened and signaled quickly and appropriately to questions demanding a yes or no answer and opened or closed her eyes and moved them laterally when commanded to do so. There was no other voluntary movement. Four days before she died, she developed ocular bobbing when commanded to look laterally, but although she consistently responded to commands by moving her eyes, it was difficult to know whether or not her responses were appropriate. During the ensuing 3 days, evidence of wakefulness decreased. She died of gastrointestinal hemorrhage 26 days after entering the hospital.

The brain at autopsy contained a moderate amount of dark, old blood overlying the right lateral medulla adjacent to the fourth ventricle. A raspberry-appearing arteriovenous malformation, 1.4 cm. in greatest diameter, protruded from the right lateral medulla, beginning with its lower border 2.5 cm. caudal to the obex. On section the vascular malformation was seen to originate in the central medulla and to extend rostrally to approximately 2 mm. above the obex. From this point a large hemorrhage extended forward to destroy the central medulla all the way to the pontine junction (Fig. 5). Microscopic study demonstrated that, at its most cranial end, the hemorrhage destroyed the caudal part of the right vestibular nuclei and most of the adjacent lower pontine tegmentum on the right. Caudal to this, the hemorrhage widened and destroyed the entire dorsal center of the medulla from approximately the plane of the nucleus of the glossopharyngeal nerve down to just below the plane of the nucleus ambiguus. From this latter point caudally the hemorrhage was more restricted to the reticular formation of the medulla. The margins of this lesion contained an organizing clot with phagocytosis and reticulum formation indicating a process at least 2 weeks old. The center of the hemorrhage contained a degenerating clot estimated to be at least 72 hours old; at several places along the lateral margin of the lesion were small fresh hemorrhages estimated to have occurred within a few hours of death. It was considered unlikely that the lesion had changed substantially in size or extent of destruction in the few days before death.

CIRCULATION

A series of central nervous pathways and structures that extend from the spinal cord forward all the way to the forebrain influence the cardiac rhythm and systemic blood pressure.[151] Under normal resting circumstances, the integrity of the ponto-medullary reticular formation and its descending pathways is essential for maintaining a normal peripheral vasomotor resistance and, therefore, blood pressure. Prepontine cardiovascular areas mediate their influences via descending autonomic pathways that originate from various regions of the limbic forebrain, the hypothalamus, and the midbrain reticulum. In normal man these regions provide rapid adjustments to actual or anticipated behavioral needs, thereby "setting" appropriate cardiovascular responses in advance of physiologic requirements. With disease or dysfunction of the brain, however, damage to central cardiovascular regulating areas can produce a variety of abnormalities, including temporary hypertension, as well as prominent disturbances in heart rate, rhythm, and electrical activity. These considerations sometimes make cardiovascular changes important in neurologic diagnosis.

To review briefly the autonomic anatomy:[34] At the spinal cord level, sympathetic preganglionic fibers arise from perikarya in the intermediolateral columns of the first five thoracic segments, whence they emerge to innervate the three cervical and upper four or five thoracic sympathetic ganglia. From these ganglia, especially the three cervical and first thoracic, postganglionic fibers proceed to the region of the heart and intertwine themselves in the cardiac plexus, eventually to reach the myocardium and its blood vessels. Sympathetic stimulation produces predominantly cardiac acceleration and arterial vasodilation. Parasympathetic fibers arise in man from the nucleus ambiguus complex of the vagus nerve in the medulla oblongata. From that point they project caudally in the descending vagus nerves to join the cardiac plexus and innervate the intracardiac ganglia of the atria, and thence the heart. Vagal action produces cardiac slowing by suppression of excitability of the sinoatrial (SA) node; when intense or in the presence of hypoxia, such parasympathetic stimulation can produce asystole or even sustained cardiac arrest.

At the medullary level of the brainstem, afferent fibers from the vagus as well as from the baroreceptors and chemoreceptors of the carotid sinus project largely into the nucleus solitarius complex. The presence of tachycardia, hypertension and susceptibility to arrhythmia in patients with severe peripheral neuropathy generally can be attributed to involvement of these afferent nerves by the neuropathic process. Major sympathomimetic vasomotor influences arise from neuronal areas located in the reticular formation of the pontomedullary region that extends over an area from the lower end of the pons down to approximately the level of the medullary obex. Within this region, a median zone subserves largely vasodepressor influences, while stimulation of a somewhat less well-defined, more dorsal and lateral region induces systemic vasoconstriction and cardiac acceleration. Some evidence indicates that the lateral vasomotor area projects heavily toward the medial reticular region and that the latter may relay the ultimate vasomotor outflow to the spinal cord.[234] Micro-regions within both the medial and lateral pontomedullary areas possess substantial functional discrimination. The main projection from both areas travels caudally via the lateral spinal funiculus to the intermediolateral columns of the spinal cord with excitatory fibers lying somewhat more dorsal than vasodepressor fibers.

Stimulation in animals of the orbital-frontal cortex of the cerebral hemispheres evokes bradycardia owing to increased vagal activity as well as inhibition of sympathetic constrictor tone and of adrenal catecholamine secretion. When frontal lobotomy was being practiced more widely several years ago, stimulation in this same region on patients was found to induce hypertension.[41] Limbic stimulation around the edges of the temporal lobe cortex, in the area of the cingulum and even in the amygdaloid nucleus, induces in animals mostly vasodepressor responses. In man, however, Penfield and Rasmussen found this area of cortex relatively unsusceptible to producing cardiovascular responses to stimulation.[216]

Descending autonomic pathways from the forebrain converge in the hypothalamus where interneurons integrate these impulses with other afferent messages received from the diencephalon and brainstem and, in turn, discharge their descending fibers to the lower brainstem and spinal cord.

Research over the years has demonstrated that the classic Kocher-Cushing response of a rise in blood pressure and slowing of the pulse in association with increased intracranial pressure results mainly from compression or ischemia of a restricted pressor area lying just beneath the floor of the fourth ventricle.[235] Because intracranial lesions commonly compartmentalize their abnormal pressure effects (see page 94), the classic Cushing changes prove not to be of much use in the diagnosis of stupor and coma, except perhaps in children, where the presence of a more expansile skull frequently allows shifts of tissue and fluid in the intracranial cavity to transmit their effects directly to the medulla. Blood pressure control, however, can be crucial in the management of hypertensive encephalopathy, subarachnoid hemorrhage, potential shock, and many other aspects of the course of patients in coma. These aspects of management rather than diagnosis make the monitoring of blood pressure an important consideration in patients in coma.

In contrast to the relatively low diagnostic importance of blood pressure changes in patients with stupor or coma, recognition of certain EKG abnormalities can point toward the primary neurologic origin of certain unconscious states and sometimes even can hint at specific disease causes. Table 2 lists the more common neurogenic abnormalities of heart rhythm and EKG configuration.

Neurologists now recognize that many and perhaps most patients with severe subarachnoid hemorrhage (SAH) have abnormal EKG tracings. Arrhythmias are common. Reversible, ventricular tachycardia has been recorded, and neurogenic cardiac arrhythmia has been incriminated as the probable mechanism of sudden death in patients with acute intracranial bleeding. The combination of intense para-sympathetic-sympathetic stimulation with an increased level of circulating catechol-amines has been held responsible for these changes. Based on findings in experimental animals, Estanbul and associates suggest that arrhythmias accompanying acute bleeding in SAH reflect massive autonomic discharges resulting from sudden increases in intracranial pressure, while more delayed changes in the EKG and cardiac rhythm are the result of increasing circulating and tissue catecholamine concentrations.[77]

Cardiac arrhythmias also show a high association with acute stroke and in generating stroke-like symptoms. A recent study by Dimant and Grob indicated that 90 percent of 100 patients with acute stroke (78 infarction, 22 hemorrhage) had abnormal EKGs.[65] Of these, 14 demonstrated conduction defects, 21 auricular fibrillation, and 13 premature ventricular beats. Only 5 percent of the patients had EKG changes compatible with recent myocardial infarction, and it must be assumed that many of the rhythm changes were neurogenic in origin. The question of cardiac arrhythmias as a cause of syncope or transient stroke-like symptoms is discussed in Chapter 4.

RESPIRATION

Breathing is a sensorimotor act integrated by nervous influences that arise from nearly every level of the brain and upper spinal cord. In higher mammals and especially man, respiration subserves two major functions, one of metabolism the other of behavior.[220] Metabolic respiratory control is directed principally at maintaining normal oxygenation and acid-base balance; it is principally regulated by the classically known respiratory "centers" that lie in the reticulum of the lower brainstem between the mid pons and the cervical-medullary junction. The detailed anatomy and physiology of these brainstem respiratory areas is well described in recent reviews.[13] The behavioral control, which in man has its most obvious expression in speech, but extends to nonverbal and emotional communication as well, takes its origins from prepontine structures lying mainly at forebrain level. The two controlling systems integrate with each other largely in the lower brainstem, but to some degree also at the level of the spinal cord, and each system projects

Table 2.   Major EKG Changes With Acute Intracranial Disease*

Large upright T waves with long QT interval
Q waves with ST depression
Supraventricular tachycardia; flutter-fibrillation
Sinus bradycardia, arrest; nodal rhythms
A-V block or dissociation
PVCs; ventricular flutter-fibrillation

* Many of these changes are brief.

by a distinct descending pathway to the spinal respiratory motoneurons. The presence of these dual control mechanisms, arising at several different levels of the neuraxis and affecting breathing in separate ways, means that diseases causing stupor or coma commonly induce respiratory abnormalities that can reflect either the pathologic anatomy or the pathologic chemistry of the illness (see review by Plum and Leigh[221]). These considerations make the recognition of respiratory changes useful in diagnosis.

This section considers the neuroanatomic basis of respiratory abnormalities that accompany coma (Table 3, Fig. 6). Chapter 4 discusses respiratory responses to metabolic disturbances. A word of caution is appropriate. Metabolic and neurogenic influences on breathing often overlap and interact so that one must interpret respiratory changes cautiously. This precaution particularly applies to patients in whom pulmonary congestion and hypoxia accompany altered respiratory patterns.

Localizing Value of Breathing Abnormalities in Coma

Posthyperventilation Apnea (PHVA)

Normally, if the arterial carbon dioxide tension is lowered by a brief period of hyperventilation, most awake subjects continue to breathe regularly with a reduced tidal volume until the blood carbon dioxide tension returns to normal. By contrast, subjects with bilateral metabolic or structural forebrain disease commonly demonstrate posthyperventilation apnea, i.e., their respirations stop after deep breathing has lowered the arterial carbon dioxide content below its usual resting level. Rhythmic breathing returns when endogenous CO_2 production raises the arterial value back to normal.

The demonstration of posthyperventilation apnea requires that the patient voluntarily take several deep breaths, so that, strictly speaking, the test is useful in differential diagnosis of obtunded or confused patients but not of truly comatose ones. One instructs the patient to take five deep in-and-out breaths. No other instructions are given and no inferences should be provided about breath-holding or even that the respiratory rhythm is being watched. If the lungs function well, the manuever usually lowers the arterial carbon dioxide tension by 8 to 14 mm. Hg. At the end of the deep breathing, wakeful patients without brain damage experience little or no apnea (less than 10 seconds is the rule), but in abnormal subjects the period of apnea lasts 12 to 30 seconds or more. The neural stimulus that normally activates rhythmic breathing when CO_2 is reduced is believed to arise from the forebrain, since it disappears with sleep, obtundation, or bilateral hemispheric dysfunction.

33

Table 3. Neuropathologic Correlates of Breathing Abnormalities

Forebrain Damage
    Epileptic respiratory inhibition [194,215]
    Apraxia for deep breathing or breath-holding [220]
    "Pseudobulbar" laughing or crying
    Posthyperventilation apnea
    Cheyne-Stokes respiration
Hypothalamic-Midbrain Damage
    Central reflex hyperpnea (neurogenic pulmonary edema)
Basis Pontis Damage
    Pseudobulbar paralysis of voluntary control
Lower Pontine Tegmentum Damage or Dysfunction
    Apneustic breathing
    Cluster breathing
    Short-cycle anoxic-hypercapnic periodic respiration
    Ataxic breathing (Biot)
Medullary Dysfunction
    Ataxic breathing
    Slow regular breathing
    Loss of automatic breathing with preserved voluntary control
    Gasping

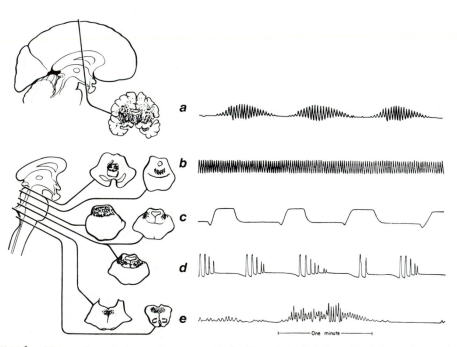

Figure 6. Abnormal respiratory patterns associated with pathologic lesions (shaded areas) at various levels of the brain. Tracings by chest-abdomen pneumograph, inspiration reads up. **a,** Cheyne-Stokes respiration. **b,** Central neurogenic hyperventilation. **c,** Apneusis. **d,** Cluster breathing. **e,** Ataxic breathing.

Cheyne-Stokes Respiration (CSR)

This is a pattern of periodic breathing in which phases of hyperpnea regularly alternate with apnea. The breathing waxes from breath to breath in a smooth crescendo and then, once a peak is reached, wanes in an equally smooth decrescendo. The hyperpneic phase usually lasts longer than the apneic phase.

CSR is a neurogenic alteration in respiratory control that usually results from intracranial causes, although hypoxemia, a prolonged circulation time, and congested lungs enhance its appearance. Brief episodes of CSR sometimes occur during sleep in normal persons, apparently without pathologic significance. Sustained or prolonged periodic breathing, however, usually implies the development of a serious neurologic or circulatory abnormality or both. CSR is almost certainly neurologic in origin if the periodicity is "obligate" (i.e., the patient cannot voluntarily breathe during the apneic phase or hold his breath during the hyperpneic phase). Metabolic brain dysfunction also can cause CSR, presumably by impairing the neurologic mechanisms described below.

The pathogenesis of CSR is the outcome of a combination of an abnormally increased ventilatory response to CO_2 stimulation causing hyperpnea, and an abnormally decreased forebrain ventilatory stimulus permitting posthyperventilation apnea.[312] Patients with bilateral hemispheric lesions overbreathe when stimulated by carbon dioxide, a phenomenon reminiscent of other facilitated neurologic responses to stimulation. As a result of the overbreathing, the blood's carbon dioxide content drops below the level where it stimulates the respiratory centers and, in the presence of brain dysfunction, breathing stops. During apnea, CO_2 reaccumulates until it exceeds the respiratory threshold, and the cycle repeats itself to oscillate indefinitely, particularly if the circulation time is prolonged. Arterial blood gases reflect mild overall hyperpnea with moderately lowered CO_2 values and with oxygen tensions usually slightly below normal.

The presence of CSR implies bilateral dysfunction of neurologic structures usually lying deep in the cerebral hemispheres or diencephalon, rarely placed as low as the upper pons. In reports of patients where CSR was associated with structural lesions of the brain, the site of damage found at autopsy has ranged widely. Descriptions of affected subjects with fairly chronic neurologic defects disclosed mainly cortical and subcortical infarctions of the cerebral hemispheres. Recently published analyses of more acutely ill subjects with head injury have emphasized that CSR can accompany bilateral damage of descending pathways anywhere from forebrain down to the upper pons.[201] Most of the latter examples have included bilateral injury to corticospinal or corticobulbar pathways, but more widespread injury almost always accompanies such traumatic lesions, making it difficult to construct specific anatomic-clinical correlations. CSR is frequent in patients with bilateral cerebral infarction, with hypertensive encephalopathy, and with metabolic diseases, such as uremia or profound heart failure producing cerebral hypoxia. In addition, the emergence of CSR in patients with supratentorial mass lesions sometimes provides a valuable sign of incipient transtentorial herniation (Chapter 2).

A number of other vegetative functions, including alterations in arousal, pupillary size, and cardiac rhythm, sometimes fluctuate in concert with the breathing variations in CSR. It seems likely that most of these are secondary and due to the nonspecific stimulating influences of fluctuating $PaCO_2$ tension. The cardiac arrhythmias sometimes noted with CSR are probably due to hypoxia and mediated via vagus nerve stimulation.

Occasionally, periodic breathing that somewhat resembles CSR but with a shorter cycle develops in association with severe increases in intracranial pressure that approach the systemic blood pressure or with expanding lesions of the posterior fossa, such as cerebellar hemorrhage. Such breathing patterns usually reflect intermittent ischemia of the brainstem. The respiratory thresholds to blood gas stimulation are often elevated, the breathing phase is foreshortened, the patient appears to be underventilated, and the respiratory periodicity tends to be less regular than when CSR accompanies hemispheric lesions. The hypoventilatory periodic breathing of low brainstem injury often changes into cluster breathing or gasping (see below), patterns which more clearly incriminate the presence of pontomedullary failure.

Hyperventilation with Brainstem Injury

Sustained, rapid, and fairly deep hyperpnea often occurs in patients with dysfunction involving the rostral brainstem tegmentum. At autopsy examination in such individuals, destructive lesions have been found between the low midbrain and the middle third of the pons, destroying the paramedian reticular formation just ventral to the aqueduct and fourth ventricle. Such observations have suggested that perhaps central nervous system damage or disease can result directly in a sustained primary hyperventilation of the blood gases. The available evidence, however, indicates that central neurogenic or primary hyperventilation (CNH) in man is rare and except for hypothalamic panting has not been reproduced in experimental animals.

A diagnosis of CNH requires that with the subject breathing room air, the blood gases show an elevated PaO_2, a lowered $PaCO_2$, and, at least acutely, a commensurately elevated arterial pH. (In the absence of cyanide poisoning such findings effectively rule out chemoreceptor stimulation of the respiratory system, and a high arterial blood oxygen tension provides strong evidence against pulmonary congestion with its associated respiratory reflex stimulation.) In the spinal fluid the pH should also be above normal and cells should be absent to rule out abnormal central stimuli to respiration by hemorrhage, infection, or neoplastic meningitis. The respiratory changes must persist during sleep to eliminate psychogenic hyperventilation and one must exclude the presence of stimulating drugs such as salicylates. Cases fulfilling all these criteria have rarely been observed and never described with postmortem examination of the brain.

Plum and Swanson initially regarded a group of tachypneic hypocapnic patients with destructive lesions of the central tegmentum of the rostral pons and adjacent midbrain as having neurogenic hyperventilation.[223] All the subjects, however, had below normal PaO_2 values and, when studied at autopsy, had congested lungs. Similarly, Lange and Laszlo's hyperventilating patient with a midbrain tumor lacked analysis of PaO_2 and the pH was not measured in either blood or CSF.[155] A child with a pontine tumor whom we studied showed intense hyperventilation awake and asleep and had a low pH in the CSF owing to a high lactic acid content. Presumably, lactic acid diffused from the brainstem tumor cells into adjacent respiratory centers to stimulate breathing.[221]

From a purely clinical point of view we have observed during many years of study only three patients who fulfilled all the criteria mentioned above for diagnosing primary hyperventilation. Two were in the early stages of hepatic coma, a condition well established to cause hyperpnea. The other was an elderly woman thought on the basis of somewhat imprecise clinical signs to be suffering from a restricted brainstem ischemic attack. The patients with hepatic encephalopathy later died and the brains showed no morphologic abnormalities other than the typical astrocytic alterations of that disease. The other patient recovered uneventfully.

If true neurogenic hyperventilation is so rare, what explains the tachypneic hypocapnia commonly observed in unconscious persons? The best evidence suggests that most if not all examples of such hyperpnea are secondary to the stimulation by pulmonary congestion of afferent peripheral reflexes arising in the lung and chest wall. Patients with such hyperpnea have a below-normal level of $PaCO_2$ but while breathing room air also have in the arterial blood a subnormal oxygen tension for the degree of hyperpnea, a finding that implies substantial pulmonary shunting. Hypoxic chemoreceptor stimulation does not explain the hyperpnea since oxygen therapy sufficient to raise the PaO_2 to normal levels does not immediately suppress the overbreathing. The precise neural pathway whereby pulmonary congestion mediates tachypneic hyperpnea is not always known. Experimentally, in animals, excitation of nonmyelinated vagal afferent fibers by lung congestion or inflammation[291] produces a pattern of rapid breathing associated with hypocapnia; usually, the congestion also produces a below-normal PaO_2, but correcting the hypoxemia fails to alter the hyperventilation. Similar reflexes are presumably involved in man.

Several pathogenetic mechanisms can account for pulmonary abnormalities in patients with brain damage. In many and perhaps most instances, pulmonary lesions result from the combination of aspiration, passive dependent congestion and infection that affects many sick patients. One finds tachypneic hypocapnia in many severely ill patients, whether or not they have neurologic abnormalities, and the degree of hypocapnia correlates closely with a poor outcome.[177] Leigh and Shaw found that in unconscious patients the presence and intensity of regular rapid breathing correlated more closely with pulmonary complications and a bad outcome than it did with the site of the neurologic lesions.[157]

In addition to these nonspecific pulmonary complications, patients with hypothalamic or brainstem injury may suffer from the effects of more directly related pulmonary disease. Many observers have recorded in man that pulmonary edema and congestion can occur almost instantaneously following head injury.[262] Experimentally in animals, either raising the intracranial pressure or delivering blunt trauma to the cranium induces similar changes. In at least some such animals the sequence of events consists of a neurologically mediated rise in systemic blood pressure that is sufficiently severe to lead to heart failure and pulmonary edema.[11] Lesions that produce bilateral destruction of the anterior hypothalamus or nucleus tractus solitarius (NTS) or that compress the floor of the fourth ventricle all will induce the hypertensive response, although by different mechanisms.[235] The anterior hypothalamic lesions lead to peripheral vasoconstriction by neurogenically initiating the release of adrenal medullary catecholamines, while the nucleus tractus solitarius lesions and medullary compression act by directly stimulating efferent sympathetic vasoconstrictor pathways.

It is possible that other, yet unknown neural pathways also can induce the pulmonary congestion that so frequently accompanies upper brainstem injury. Only clinical circumstances suggest such additional mechanisms, but in some subjects pulmonary edema appears so rapidly following injuries of the brain that it seems hardly possible to attribute the effect to the secondary consequences of peripheral hypertension. Indeed, in a few patients careful examinations immediately after injury have failed to demonstrate any rise in blood pressure despite the rapid development of wet lungs.[69]

Apneustic Breathing and Its Variants

Apneusis is a prolonged inspiratory cramp—a pause at full inspiration. Fully developed apneustic breathing is rare in man but does occur. A more common abnormality consists of brief end-inspiratory pauses lasting 2 to 3 seconds, often alternating with end-expiratory pauses as well as with other irregularities of the respiratory rhythm. Apneustic breathing is a localizing sign of great value that reflects damage to the respiratory control mechanisms located at the mid- or caudal-pontine level, approximately at and below the location of the nucleus parabrachialis, which lies adjacent to the trigeminal motor nucleus. The brainstem lesions reported in patients with apneustic breathing usually have been extensive, consisting of a nearly complete dorsal transection, with a predilection for the dorsolateral tegmental areas. More prolonged apneusis has developed when these dorsolateral lesions extended caudally to involve the dorsolateral pontine nuclei.

Clinically, apneustic breathing most often accompanies pontine infarction caused by basilar artery occlusion. Occasionally, one observes apneustic breathing with hypoglycemia, anoxia, or severe meningitis. Apneusis occurs rarely in patients with progressive brainstem dysfunction secondary to transtentorial herniation, possibly because the major injury in these cases affects medial rather than lateral brainstem structures.

Ataxic Breathing

The respiratory centers that ultimately regulate the to-and-fro of breathing are located in the reticular formation of the dorsomedial part of the medulla and extend down to or just below the obex. Lesions in this area in man cause respiratory ataxia. Ataxic breathing has a completely irregular pattern in which both deep and shallow breaths occur randomly. Irregular pauses appear haphazardly, and there is no predicting the future respiratory rhythm from the pattern of past breaths. The respiratory rate tends to be slow and may progressively decelerate to apnea. Ataxia is the respiratory abnormality that Biot described in severe meningitis. Its irregularity differentiates it from the regular waxing and waning of Cheyne-Stokes respiration.

Physiologically, ataxic breathing represents primary functional disruption of the medullary neuronal populations that normally generate the respiratory rhythm. The irregular pattern usually is accompanied by hyposensitivity of the respiratory center to endogenous chemical stimuli, as well as by an undue susceptibility to depressant drugs. As a result, mild sedation or natural sleep sometimes induces apnea in affected subjects.

Many different pathologic processes in the posterior fossa can impair the respiratory rhythm. It is typical of medullary compression that respiration fails long before circulation. Rapidly expanding lesions such as cerebellar hemorrhage, pontine hemorrhage, or cerebellar tonsillar herniation are prone to produce acute respiratory arrest, and direct medullary destruction from trauma or hemorrhage will do the same (Fig. 5). Lesions that expand more slowly affect respiration less often unless they directly compress or destroy the central part of the caudal medulla. With ischemia from cerebral vascular disease, medullary respiratory involvement is rare, since it ordinarily requires an unusual abnormality such as bilateral involvement of the vertebral arteries to produce infarction of the central medulla. Chronic demyelinating illnesses seldom cause ataxic breathing, but acute parainfectious demyelination is prone to involve the medulla and leads directly to respiratory failure. Similar involvement is frequent in poliomyelitis. Complete respiratory assistance should be readied for patients who show ataxic breathing.

Other Abnormal Patterns of Breathing with Medullary Lesions

When the lesion is high in the medulla, or low in the pons, clusters of breaths may follow each other in disorderly sequence with irregular pauses between. These merge with various patterns of gasping respiration in which deep "all-or-none" breaths occur, usually at a slow rate. One of our patients with an intramedullary glioma breathed with slow ratchet-like, jerky inspirations followed by expiration, then pauses lasting 6 to 10 seconds. Overdoses of opiate and sedative drugs can depress the medulla so gradually that breathing fails almost imperceptibly with the tidal volume insidiously decreasing and the rate slowing until the system stops altogether.

Failure of Automatic Breathing While Asleep

The partial anatomic separation of metabolic (automatic) and behavioral (voluntary) influences on breathing occasionally results in a striking abnormality characterized by normal or near-normal respiration during wakefulness or attention, but severe hypoventilation or even potentially fatal apnea with the advent of sleep or inattention. The abnormality occurs most often in association either with subacute medullary disease or after inadvertent surgical section of the respiratory reticulospinal projection during the course of ventrolateral upper cervical cord section designed to interrupt afferent spinothalamic projections. Such processes damage the automatic rhythmic respiratory generator and its spinal projections but spare the corticospinal pathways that carry influences from higher centers directly to the spinal respiratory motor neuron pools. A similar pattern of hypoventilation accentuated by sleep also can develop during the course of nonspecific disorders of the brainstem, termed "idiopathic primary alveolar hypoventilation," as well as in a small number of patients with chronic muscular or neuromuscular diseases. Sometimes called "Ondine's curse" after the mythological water nymph whose human suitor was cursed to lose automatic functions while asleep,[253] the abnormality represents a potential cause of asphyxial coma in susceptible subjects. It should be borne in mind, however, that upper airway obstructive disorders are a more frequent cause of sleep apnea than the neurologic dysfunctions described here.

Yawning, Vomiting, and Hiccup

All three of these stereotyped complex acts involve the respiratory musculature, yet only the first has a primary respiratory function. Their importance to neurologic diagnosis is that each is integrated by neural mechanisms in the lower brainstem, a site where disease or dysfunction can produce the reflex by direct stimulation, bypassing the normal afferent pathway.

Yawning is physiologically the least well studied of the three. Closely related to generalized body stretching, yawning must certainly help maintain chest, lung, and respiratory muscle compliance, but whether this is its primary function is unknown. The sparse available literature on yawning practically confines itself to descriptions of its behavioral associations and often whimsical speculations about its possible biologic advantages. It is likely that the medulla oblongata contains an integrating area for yawning similar to that for hiccup and vomiting. Gamper stated that his well-studied anencephalic human neonate, who possessed no brain higher than the midbrain, yawned and stretched in normal fashion.[92,93] Yawning commonly accompanies posterior fossa expanding lesions, but these also raise the intracranial pressure, thereby detracting from their localizing value. Many such patients are not drowsy, however. Both Penfield and Jasper[215] and Wilson[304] describe forced and repeated yawning in association with structural lesions located around the medial temporal lobe and the third ventricle; the material is hard to interpret, however, because of uncertain remote effects from the lesion and scanty clinical details in the published reports.

Vomiting is primarily a gastrointestinal reflex with a strong efferent component involving the respiratory muscles. The act is integrated by an area in the lateral reticular formation of the medulla oblongata in the region of the tractus solitarius.[19] Nausea and gastrointestinal atony characteristically accompany vomiting evoked by visceral stimulation. By contrast, direct involvement of the central vomiting mechanism by neurologic lesions sometimes short-circuits the afferent arc to produce vomiting without preceding nausea; unheralded by warning nausea, vomitus may escape as a "projectile" with the full force of the suddenly contracted thoracoabdominal muscles behind it. Most intracranial lesions that produce vomiting, however, also produce nausea.

In proportion to the total incidence of vomiting, central neurologic lesions only seldom take the blame, but for this reason they are often overlooked while other body systems are fruitlessly explored. Central neurologic lesions that produce vomiting are, respectively, those that involve the vestibular nuclei or their immediate projections, particularly when they cause diplopia as well; those that directly impinge on the floor of the fourth ventricle, such as the medulloblastoma or ependymoma; and, less often, those that produce brainstem compression secondary to increased intracranial pressure. Since this last group includes many posterior fossa neoplasms, general and local medullary compression is often hard to differentiate.

Hiccup, like vomiting, appears to be mainly a gastrointestinal reflex involving the respiratory musculature.[197] Sustained hiccupping is peculiarly an abnormality of males. In the Mayo Clinic series of 220 cases, for example, there were only 39 women, 36 of whom ostensibly had "psychogenic" hiccup.[271]

Most hiccups are stimulated by thoracoabdominal disease or by the ingestion of drugs. Neurologic causes include parenchymal abnormalities of the medulla oblongata such as infections, syringomyelia, neoplasm, and infarction, as well as lesions that surround or compress the medulla such as neoplasms, hematomas, or bleeding into the fourth ventricle.

Although central mechanisms in hiccup are less well worked out experimentally than those involved in vomiting, the peripheral physiology has been well studied. According to Newsom Davis the reflex is accentuated by a low arterial carbon dioxide tension and inhibited by hypercarbia or breath-holding.[197] The act consists of spasmodic bursts of inspiratory muscle activity followed within 35 milliseconds or so by abrupt glottic closure so that the ventilatory effect is negligible. If a tracheotomy bypasses the glottis, however, the vigorous inspiratory spasm produces a tidal volume large enough to hyperventilate the patient, thereby accentuating the hiccups. As an example, one such patient at the New York Hospital with a low brainstem infarct and tracheotomy maintained his total ventilation for several days by hiccup alone.

PUPILS

The pupillary reactions, constriction and dilatation, are controlled by the sympathetic and parasympathetic nervous system (Fig. 7). The sympathetic pathways begin in the hypothalamus and traverse the entire brainstem, predominantly ipsilaterally, to reach the intermediolateral cell column of the thoracic spinal cord. The afferent parasympathetic pathways begin in the retinal ganglion cells and follow the optic nerve and tract to reach the pretectum. The efferent pathways follow the oculomotor nerve to the orbit. Because the brainstem areas controlling consciousness are anatomically adjacent to those controlling the pupils, pupillary changes are a valuable guide to the presence and location of brainstem diseases causing coma. *In addition, because pupillary pathways are relatively resistant to metabolic insult, the presence or absence of the light reflex is the single most important physical sign potentially distinguishing structural from metabolic coma.*

Functional Anatomy

Sympathetic stimulation contracts the pupillodilator muscle, and the pupil widens (mydriasis). Parasympathetic stimulation contracts the pupilloconstrictor

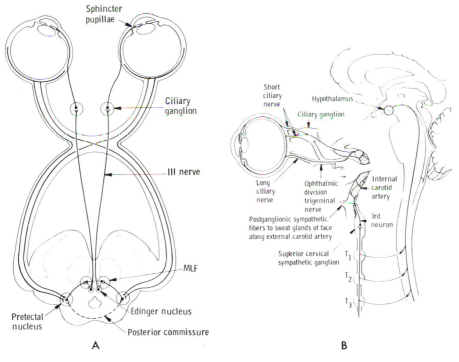

Figure 7. **A,** The parasympathetic pupilloconstrictor pathway. **B,** The sympathetic pupillodilator pathway.

41

fibers, and the pupil narrows (miosis). Inhibition of either of these two systems has the opposite effect, but inhibitory fibers play a lesser role in pupillary control in man.[164] Both anatomic innervations are tonically active, and the resting pupil represents a balance, with a moderate preponderance of one innervation over the other, depending on incident light and other factors. A constantly changing dominance between sympathetic and parasympathetic tone controlled by both external and internal environmental factors keeps the pupil in the awake person in constant motion through a small range (hippus). Tonic neural input to the pupil is considerable, since when either the sympathetic or parasympathetic supply is completely blocked, the remaining unopposed systems evoke a near maximal pupillary response of miosis (1.5–2 mm.) with sympathetic paralysis or mydriasis (8–9 mm.) with parasympathetic paralysis. Partial denervation leads to correspondingly smaller changes in pupillary size and a decrease in normal hippus.[270]

Sympathetic Fibers

The neural regulation of the pupil by the sympathetic nervous system has been the subject of recent reviews.[165] Experimental evidence suggests that pupillary regulation begins in the cerebral cortex. Jampel produced pupillary dilatation, greater on the contralateral side, by stimulating the middle frontal gyrus of the macaque monkey.[118] Stimulation of other areas of the frontal lobe produced dilatation of either the ipsilateral or contralateral pupil. By contrast, stimulation of the occipital lobe produced pupillary dilatation greater in the ipsilateral eye. These pupillary changes were usually associated with contralateral deviation of the eyes (see below, Ocular Movements). Stimulation of the superior temporal gyrus produced ipsilateral miosis without associated eye movement. Evidence also exists in man for a cortical influence on pupillary size. Rasmussen and Penfield produced contralateral pupillary dilatation by stimulation of the frontal cortex.[231] Pant and associates reported six patients in whom unilateral dilatation of the pupil either accompanied generalized convulsions or occurred during the postictal state.[210] In some of these patients, the pupillary dilatation was ipsilateral and in others contralateral to the presumed site of the cerebral discharge.

Zee, Griffin, and Price describe a patient with adversive seizures accompanied by unilateral pupillary dilatation.[308] Neuropathologic examination showed a contusion involving the middle frontal gyrus contralateral to the pupil that dilated during the seizure. The authors suggested that the anatomic pathway known to project from the frontal cortex to the ipsilateral pretectum and mesencephalic tegmentum could mediate the pupillary reflex pathway. These several studies indicate, then, that pathways producing unilateral (both contralateral and ipsilateral) pupillary dilatation and constriction originate in the cerebral cortex, but the routes they follow to deeper structures are not known.

The exact site of origin of the descending pupillodilator pathway from the hypothalamus also is not known, but at least four hypothalamic nuclei (paraventricular, lateral, posterior, and zona incerta) send fibers directly to the spinal cord.[244] Stimulating the ventrolateral hypothalamus in animals produces pupillary dilatation.[107,134] Destruction or functional depression of this area results in pupilloconstriction. In man, focal lesions in either the lateral hypothalamus or the overlying thalamus produce ipsilateral pupillary constriction,[36,39] suggesting that the sympathetic pathway for pupillodilation resides in this area. Loewy and associates identified three pathways concerned with pupillodilation in the brainstem of the cat.[166]

42

The first, a descending pathway originating in the hypothalamus, lies dorsolateral to the medial lemniscus close to the spinothalamic tract at collicular and pontine levels. At more caudal levels, the pathway moves to a position dorsolateral to the pyramidal tract, and then in the cervical spinal cord it shifts to a superficial position in the lateral funiculus near the insertion of the denticulate ligament. This pathway carries the sympathetic pupillodilator fibers that emerge from the thoracic spinal cord. Two pathways that inhibit pupilloconstrictor fibers and thus lead to pupillary dilatation have also been identified. One pathway begins in the paramedian reticular area of the medulla and ascends to inhibit the Edinger-Westphal nucleus. The second pathway, which may originate in the spinothalamic tract, is anatomically associated with the lateral descending pupillodilator pathway. Loewy and associates believe this last ascending pathway to be associated with nociceptive reflex pupillary dilatation[166] (see below, Ciliospinal Reflex). In man, however, inhibitory pathways appear to play little role in pupillary dilatation.[164]

The pathway for fibers stimulating pupillodilatation is less well worked out in humans than in experimental animals. It appears to be predominantly ipsilateral, descending from the hypothalamus through the caudal diencephalon, midbrain, and pons. Lesions in the upper brainstem immediately rostral and dorsal to the red nucleus and at the subthalamic nucleus produce ipsilateral pupillary constriction. In the medulla the pathway lies dorsolaterally, since lesions in this area produce a homolateral Horner's syndrome (Wallenberg's syndrome). In the cervical spinal cord the descending sympathetic pupillodilator fibers descend superficially to synapse with neurons in the intermediolateral cell column of the upper three thoracic segments. Preganglionic fibers leave the cord, pass through the inferior and middle cervical ganglia, and synapse in the superior cervical ganglion. This ganglion lies near the respective ganglia of the glossopharyngeal and vagus nerves, between the internal carotid artery and the internal jugular vein, just below the base of the skull. Postganglionic sympathetic fibers travel with the internal carotid artery into the skull. Pupillodilator fibers first follow the ophthalmic branch of the trigeminal nerve and finally its branch, the nasociliary nerve, to reach the pupillodilator muscle. Other sympathetic fibers follow the ophthalmic artery to reach the lacrimal gland and orbital blood vessels.

Parasympathetic Innervation

The parasympathetic innervation of the pupil travels a more direct route than the sympathetic. Whether or not the parasympathetic supply has a cerebral representation is not known. Stimulation of either the occipital or frontal lobes in animals evokes pupillary constriction, as does stimulation of the pretectal region (that part of the thalamic gray matter lying immediately rostral to the midbrain tegmentum). Comparable observations are unavailable in man. It has been generally assumed that the major source of the parasympathetic preganglionic supply to the pupil is the Edinger-Westphal nucleus lying in the midbrain between the oculomotor nuclei and sending fibers that accompany the oculomotor nerve. However, little direct evidence supports this assumption.[165] In the cat, retrograde cell labeling after injection of horseradish peroxidase into the ciliary ganglion labels cells dorsolateral and ventral to the Edinger-Westphal nuclei and only a few cells within the nucleus itself; in the monkey, however, it is the Edinger-Westphal neurons that are primarily labeled. Maximal pupillary constriction is elicited by electrical stimulation of regions ventral to the Edinger-Westphal nucleus.[260]

Afferent Arc of the Pupillary Light Reflex

Figure 7 diagrams the neural pathway for the pupillary light reflex. The afferent stimulus is relayed from certain retinal ganglion cells via fibers that travel in the optic nerves and accompany homotopic fibers from the retinal visual receptors through crossed and uncrossed chiasmatic pathways into the optic tracts. From the optic tracts, pathways bypass the lateral geniculate body, turning medially to terminate bilaterally in the nucleus of the optic tract and the olivary pretectal nucleus. The posterior and anterior pretectal regions may also receive retinal afferents. From these nuclei, fibers project first to the contralateral nucleus of the posterior commissure and then to the region of the Edinger-Westphal nucleus.[167]

Ciliospinal Reflex

The ciliospinal reflex consists of bilateral 1 to 2 mm. pupillary dilatation evoked by noxious cutaneous stimulation. It is most easily elicited by a pinch to the face, neck, or upper trunk. The reflex is more prominent during sleep or coma than during wakefulness and clinically tests the integrity of sympathetic pathways in lightly comatose patients. However, because the synapse between afferent pain pathways and efferent pupillodilator pathways lies in the spinal cord, the reflex is not particularly useful in evaluating brainstem function.[232]

Localizing Value of Pupillary Abnormalities in Coma

The incidence of pupillary abnormalities in comatose patients is high and justifies giving careful attention to pupillary size and shape. The light reflex should be examined with a bright light, and if the pupils are small, a magnifying glass should be used to disclose any reflex constriction not apparent to the naked eye. Some important pupillary abnormalities in comatose patients are illustrated in Figure 8.

CEREBRAL EFFECTS on the pupil are not helpful in diagnosis.

HYPOTHALAMIC DAMAGE, especially in the posterior and ventrolateral portions, produces ipsilateral pupillary constriction, usually associated with ptosis and anhidrosis (Horner's syndrome). The associated anhidrosis involves the entire ipsilateral half of the body and not just the face, neck, and arm as in cervical sympathetic lesions. The importance of recognizing hypothalamic dysfunction in coma is that downward displacement of the hypothalamus with a unilateral Horner's syndrome is often the first clear sign of incipient transtentorial herniation (Chapter 2). Crill reported five cases of supratentorial hemorrhage associated with ipsilateral Horner's syndrome.[56] In none was there carotid occlusion (see below). Of the four patients who died and underwent autopsy, two had cerebral hemorrhages directly involving the thalamus and hypothalamus, and one had a subdural hematoma with transtentorial herniation and a secondary hemorrhage involving the upper midbrain and diencephalon. The fourth had hemorrhage into a cortical metastatic tumor with no direct hypothalamic destruction. Supporting the view that unilateral diencephalic lesions can produce Horner's syndrome is the observation of Carmel in 15 patients that stereotactic thalamic surgery produced ipsilateral sympathetic defects including ptosis, miosis, and hemianhidrosis.[36] Keane[315] reports that 14 out of 100 patients referred with Horner's syndrome had hemispheral lesions (hemorrhage, tumor, infarct).

44

Horner's syndrome sometimes accompanies occlusion of the internal carotid artery and often has been attributed to involvement of nerves in the perivascular sheath in such instances. However, asymptomatic carotid artery occlusion almost never causes Horner's syndrome, so we suspect that hypothalamic damage rather than a peripheral sympathetic lesion is probably the explanation for most examples of the Horner's syndrome reported in association with carotid artery occlusion.[126] In keeping with this suggestion is the fact that several of the patients with Horner's syndrome attributed to carotid artery disease in clinical reports did not have an actual occlusion of the artery but only stenosis or, rarely, even a normal vessel.[204] However, all had ipsilateral cerebral symptoms. One of our patients with a carotid occlusion and ipsilateral Horner's syndrome was anhidrotic on the entire ipsilateral side, a finding that points to a central lesion.

The pupils shrink in sleep and also become symmetrically small when the diencephalon is bilaterally involved during rostral-caudal deterioration secondary to supratentorial mass lesions. In both instances, the reaction to light is preserved.

MIDBRAIN DAMAGE produces clear-cut pupillary signs.[118] Dorsal tectal or pretectal lesions interrupt the pupillary light reflex (Fig. 8), but may spare the response to accommodation. The result is midposition or slightly widened (5 to 6 mm. in diameter), round, and regular pupils that are light-fixed, but spontaneously fluctuate in size and may show hippus and retain their ciliospinal reflex. Recognition of these tectal effects on the pupil is important since small lesions in the midbrain tegmental area often involve the periaqueductal gray matter and interrupt consciousness. In such instances, the accompanying pupillary changes localize the anatomic lesion. Nuclear midbrain lesions nearly always interrupt both the sympathetic and parasympathetic pathways to the eye (Fig. 8). The resulting pupils are midposition (4 to 5 mm. in diameter), fixed to light, usually slightly irregular, and often unequal. Midposition fixed pupils are most commonly caused by midbrain damage from transtentorial herniation, but also occur when neoplasms, granulomas, hemorrhages, or infarcts involve the midbrain. Lesions involving the third nerves between their nuclei and point of emergence from the brainstem produce external oculomotor paralysis accompanied by wide pupillary dilation. Such parenchymal third nerve paralyses are frequently bilateral, in contrast to peripheral third nerve palsies, which are usually unilateral.

PONTINE LESIONS in the tegmentum interrupt descending sympathetic pathways and produce bilaterally small pupils. If no drugs have been taken or instilled in the eye, pinpoint pupils generally mean pontine hemorrhage and are believed by Walsh and Hoyt[299] to result from parasympathetic irritation in combination with sympathetic interruption. The pupillary light reflex with pontine hemorrhage is usually present if examined with a magnifying glass,[85] although the degree of constriction is sometimes so intense that the casually observed light reflex is absent for several hours after onset of the primary brain injury.

LATERAL MEDULLARY AND VENTROLATERAL CERVICAL SPINAL CORD LESIONS cause a homolateral mild Horner's syndrome with slight ptosis and pupillary constriction, never obliterating the light reflex.

PERIPHERAL LESIONS involving either the third nerves or the sympathetic pathways can affect the pupils of comatose patients. The pupillary fibers in the third nerve are particularly susceptible when uncal herniation compresses the nerve against the posterior cerebral artery or tentorial edge.[143,280] In these instances, pupillary dilatation often precedes extraocular motor abnormalities. More distally along the nerve, the oculomotor and pupillomotor fibers are equally susceptible to damage,

45

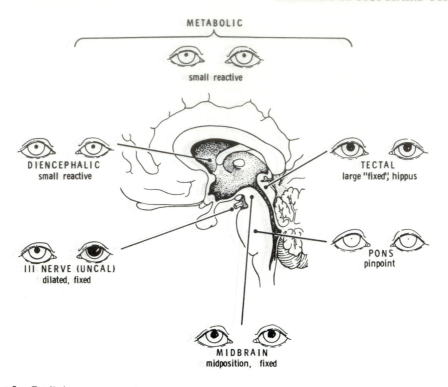

Figure 8. Pupils in comatose patients.

although occasionally the pupil is spared. More rarely, lesions compressing the third nerve near its origin can produce oculomotor palsy without pupillary dilatation. The reason for this selective involvement is unknown.

Pharmacologic and Metabolic Effects on the Pupil

The following drugs and disorders have effects that may confuse the interpretation of pupillary changes in coma.

Atropine and scopolamine, when ingested in large amounts, produce fully dilated and fixed pupils, often accompanied by delirium or stupor. Further, anticholinergic drugs such as atropine frequently are given during resuscitation from cardiac arrest and may produce mydriatic pupils that respond poorly or not at all to light. A distinction can be made between an anoxic and pharmacologic dilated pupil by the use of 1 percent pilocarpine instilled into the eye. If the dilatation of the pupil is due to parasympathetic denervation, prompt miosis occurs since this cholinergic substance acts directly on the smooth muscle constricting the pupil. The smooth muscle receptors, however, are blocked by atropine, and if pupillary dilatation is due to pharmacologic mydriatic agents, miotic responses to pilocarpine will be diminished or absent.[288]

Glutethimide (Doriden) characteristically produces midposition or moderately dilated (4 to 8 mm.) pupils that are unequal and frequently fixed to light for several hours following ingestion of enough of the drug to produce profound coma. Fixed pupils in glutethimide poisoning do not necessarily signify a poor prognosis as they do under most other circumstances. Brown and Hammill reported a patient with a

46

unilaterally dilated fixed pupil (10 mm.) after glutethimide overdose.[28] The contralateral pupil was 5 mm. and reacted sluggishly. Both became normal when the woman recovered consciousness.

Opiates, particularly heroin and morphine, produce pinpoint pupils resembling those seen with pontine hemorrhage. The light reflex may be difficult to elicit but can be demonstrated with a bright light.

Anoxia or *ischemia*, if severe, may lead to bilaterally wide and fixed pupils. The clinical paradigm is that observed after cardiac arrest, in which, if resuscitative measures are successful, the pupils rapidly become small and reactive. Pupillary dilatation is not an invariable accompaniment of anoxia, however, and the pupils can sometimes remain small or midposition throughout an episode of profound hypoxia leading to death.[130] Experimentally, acute anoxia produces pupillary constriction until asystole occurs or the cardiac output is reduced more than 70 percent,[17] at which point the pupils dilate only to return to the midposition 3 to 20 minutes after death. Pupillary dilatation follows circulatory arrest even in pupils with sympathetic or parasympathetic denervation. If the pupil has lost both sympathetic and parasympathetic supply, maximum dilatation follows restoration of circulation,[132] suggesting that circulating humors as well as neural impulses play a role in anoxic pupillary dilatation. Clinically, anoxic pupillary dilatation lasting more than a few minutes implies very severe and usually irreversible brain damage, although successful resuscitation has been reported after the pupils ostensibly were fixed and dilated for hours.[47]

Hypothermia[289] and, rarely, *severe barbiturate intoxication* can fix the pupils. Patients with barbiturate intoxication sufficiently severe to fix the pupils are usually apneic as well as hypotensive.

Pant and associates reported transient anisocoria in 12 patients during or following seizures.[210] The larger pupil usually reacted sluggishly to light.

Small pupils accompany many *metabolic encephalopathies*. The difference between pharmacogenic and destructive lesions causing sympathetic hypofunction cannot be determined by examining the eyes alone. The most important point is that, with the exceptions noted above, the pupillary light reflex is preserved until the near-terminal stages of most metabolic brain diseases producing coma. Since destructive lesions of the midbrain abolish the light reflex, it follows that patients who show other signs of severe midbrain depression, yet retain the pupillary light reflex, have a metabolic disturbance.

OCULAR MOVEMENTS

The pathways that mediate the oculomotor reflexes lie adjacent to brainstem areas necessary for consciousness, making it clinically useful to search for both gross and subtle oculomotor abnormalities when evaluating patients in stupor or coma. An important clinical tenet is that *asymmetrical oculomotor dysfunction more often accompanies structural than metabolic causes of unconsciousness.*

Anatomy

Figures 9, 10, and 11 schematically represent our concept of the major neural pathways for ocular motility. Although there is dispute about the exact anatomic course of these pathways, the general outlines are sufficiently reproducible to help in localizing clinical lesions, even if some morphologic details remain controversial or unknown.[60] Lynch and associates[170] provide a good review of physiologic evidence

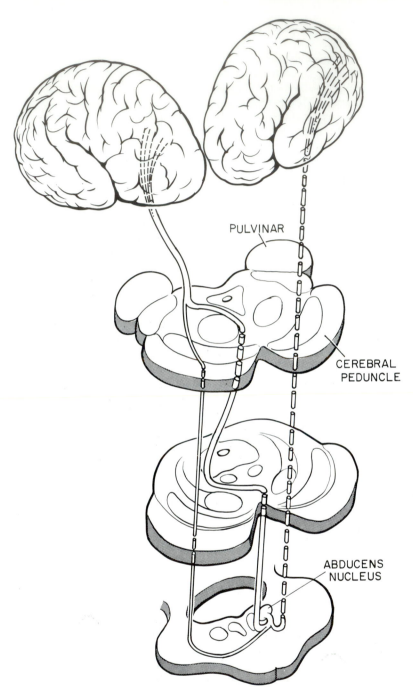

Figure 9. The supranuclear pathways subserving lateral conjugate gaze. The pathways from the "frontal eye fields" are shown descending in two bundles through the midbrain, crossing to the contralateral side in the midbrain and upper pons to synapse in the contralateral midpons close to or within the abducens nucleus. The pathway from the parietooccipital eye fields, which probably has both ipsilateral and contralateral components, is shown descending ipsilaterally to synapse in or near the abducens nucleus in the pons. The anatomic and physiologic evidence supporting the presence and course of these pathways is referenced in the text.

48

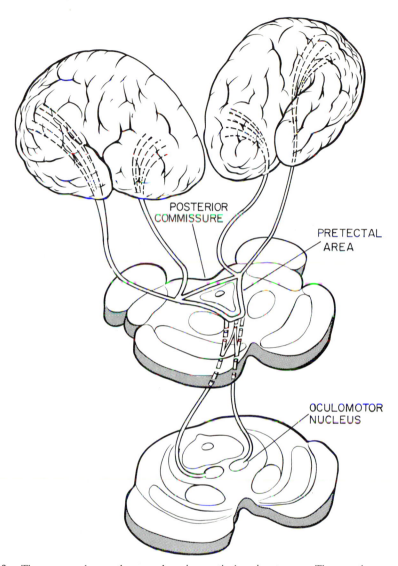

Figure 10. The supranuclear pathways subserving vertical conjugate gaze. These pathways are shown originating from the "frontal and occipital eye fields" of both hemispheres and descending through the ipsilateral hemisphere to the pretectal area of the upper midbrain. Some of the fibers cross in the posterior commissure, and others cross in the midbrain tegmentum ventral to the sylvian aqueduct. The fibers then descend, probably through the midbrain tegmentum, to reach both contralateral and ipsilateral oculomotor nuclei. The anatomy of these pathways is less well worked out than that of the pathways subserving lateral conjugate gaze.

for cerebral control of eye movements, and other reviews describe brainstem mechanisms for controlling eye movements.[49,230,236]

Supranuclear Centers and Pathways

The "frontal gaze center" (Brodman's area 8) subserves rapid voluntary or saccadic eye movements. Saccadic eye movements are rapid (up to 700°/sec.), ballistic,

49

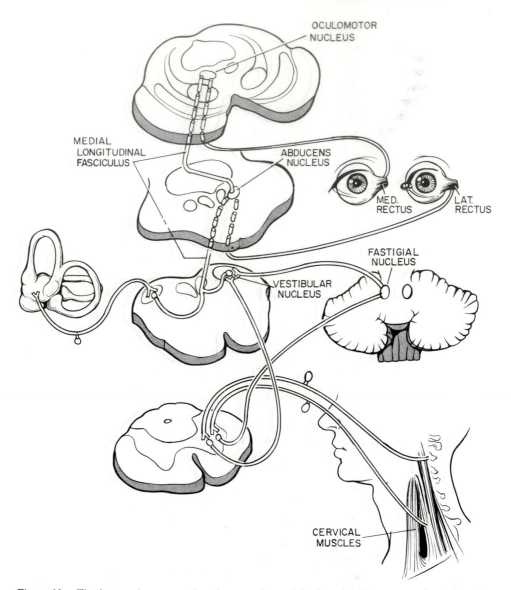

Figure 11. The internuclear connections between the nuclei subserving eye movement and how they are influenced by proprioceptive, cerebellar, and labyrinthine fibers. At the lower right, proprioceptive fibers from posterior cervical muscles and ligaments are shown entering the spinal cord to reach the vestibular nuclei, either directly or via a relay through the fastigial nucleus of the cerebellum. In the left middle of the drawing, vestibular fibers from the labyrinth are shown reaching the ipsilateral and contralateral vestibular nuclei of the medulla. In the middle right of the drawing, fibers from the cerebellum are shown leaving the fastigial nucleus to reach ipsilateral and contralateral vestibular nuclei. Fibers from the vestibular nuclei then ascend in the medial longitudinal bundle to reach the abducens nucleus. Fibers from the abducens area cross in the midpons and ascend in the medial longitudinal fasciculus to reach the contralateral oculomotor nuclei. As shown in the drawing, the left abducens nucleus, which moves the left eye laterally, is linked to the right oculomotor nucleus, which moves the right eye medially via the medial longitudinal fasciculus, which also links incoming fibers from cervical muscles, cerebellum, and labyrinth, allowing these structures to influence conjugate movement of the eyes by oculovestibular and oculocephalic reflexes.

50

conjugate eye movements used to change fixation voluntarily. The quick phase of nystagmus is also a saccadic eye movement. In response to a new visual target, saccades occur after a latency of 200 milliseconds. The frontal region is probably the site of origin of voluntary eye movements. Even though electrophysiologic studies of the frontal area in waking animals have yielded controversial results, stimulation of one frontal gaze center does move the eyes conjugately to the opposite side, and after ablation of the frontal regions in monkeys or acute damage in man, the eyes are held conjugately toward the side of the lesion (implying unopposed stimulation from the undamaged side). Combined stimulation of both frontal lobes together produces vertical eye movements. A bilateral loss of frontal lobe function impairs voluntary eye movements as well as the fast phase of optokinetic and vestibular nystagmus.

Posterior cerebral hemispheric structures subserve slow tracking or pursuit eye movements. ("Slow eye movements" are smooth conjugate deviations of the eyes that occur when an individual tracks a moving target, during head turning when the eyes are fixed on a point, or during the slow phase of nystagmus.) Slow eye movements begin after a latency of 125 milliseconds. Voluntary pursuit movements cannot track beyond 50°/sec. Vestibuloocular reflex pursuit movements can track up to 400°/sec. Loss of parietal lobe function impairs smooth following responses toward the diseased hemisphere.[59] For this reason, some believe that oculomotor pathways from the parietal-occipital area descend ipsilaterally, radiating forward parallel to the optic radiation and then entering the midbrain.[94] In Figure 9 the posterior hemisphere gaze center is pictured as projecting an ipsilateral course.

The anatomy of descending corticobulbar oculomotor pathways is imprecisely known. Fibers from the cerebral frontal cortex probably reach the brainstem by descending through the genu of the internal capsule and then by dividing into two bundles. The major pathway descends caudally and medially along the ventral surface of the thalamus through the zona incerta and fields of Forel into the ipsilateral reticular formation of the rostral midbrain.[29] The fibers then decussate in the lower midbrain and upper pons and descend in the contralateral pontine paramedian reticular formation to the segmental level of the abducens nucleus. This area, classically called the paraabducens nucleus, represents a gaze center for conjugate gaze. Recent evidence suggests that the premotor staging center for fine horizontal conjugate eye movements appears to be within the abducens nucleus itself.[98] The second bundle, Dejerine's aberrant pyramidal system, passes through the cerebral peduncle at the base of the pons and turns dorsally to enter the pontine tegmentum. Since in man ventral lesions of the cerebral peduncle and at the base of the pons do not cause disturbances of oculomotor function, the clinical significance for eye movements of this latter system is not clear.

The pathway followed by fibers from the posterior hemisphere gaze center to the oculomotor nuclei is even less well-defined than those from frontal gaze centers, although it too must descend in the tegmentum of the midbrain and pons to reach predominantly the ipsilateral paramedian pontine reticular formation. The cerebellum also contributes to smooth visual tracking since hemicerebellectomy causes an ipsilateral deficit in pursuit movements.

Available evidence indicates that fibers controlling vertical gaze pass through the cerebral hemispheres with those subserving lateral gaze (Fig. 10). Those from the frontal eye fields probably reach the oculomotor and trochlear nuclei via Brucher's pathway, described above. Those from the posterior hemisphere eye fields apparently reach the oculomotor nuclei bilaterally, traveling through the regions of the pretectal and posterior commissural nuclei.

The final common pathways for vertical eye movements, the oculomotor and trochlear nuclei, are influenced by caudal fibers ascending through the medial longitudinal fasciculus and by rostral fibers descending from the cortex to reach the nuclei and the fasciculus by way of the midbrain tectum and tegmentum. In the clinical situation the descending fibers appear to be the most important ones since it is usually lesions in the midbrain rather than the pons that selectively impair vertical eye movements.

The supranuclear pathways for vertical eye movement are only partially understood. In experimental animals, both voluntary and reflex upward gaze can be abolished by selective lesions of the posterior commissure,[212] and this is the pathway that probably is damaged by structural lesions involving the region of the superior colliculus. The earlier view that fibers subserving vertical gaze traveled through the superior colliculi is probably incorrect since removal of this structure alone does not affect ocular motility.[211] There is some physiologic evidence for a system of supranuclear vertical gaze fibers descending to the pons before reaching the oculomotor nuclei. Bender and Shanzer produced loss of vertical gaze in both upward and downward directions by placing bilateral lesions in the pontine reticular formation.[12] The clinical significance of this observation is somewhat doubtful since patients with pontine lesions sufficient to produce total absence of conjugate lateral gaze characteristically retain vertical gaze movements (Patient 3-2, p. 159). Hoyt and Daroff report transient loss of vertical gaze with retention of normal eyelid and pupillary function after surgical procedures in the posterior fossa.[109] They assume that midbrain structures were not damaged and that the vertical gaze palsy resulted from bilateral edema of the pontine tegmentum.

Christoff has reported the clinical and pathologic findings in 27 patients with paralysis of vertical gaze.[46] Upward gaze paralysis occurred mainly with bilateral lesions involving the area of the pretectum, posterior commissure, and dorsal midbrain tegmentum. Unilateral lesions caused paralysis of upward gaze only if the posterior commissure was involved. When the lesions were bilateral and in the tegmentum of the rostral and midpons, many patients had paralysis of downward as well as upward gaze. Paralysis of downward gaze also resulted from bilateral involvement of the prerubral region of the diencephalon and midbrain and this finding has been confirmed experimentally in monkeys.[316] Isolated paralysis of downward gaze is less common than paralysis of upward gaze. Anatomic studies suggest that such paralysis results from bilateral lesions of the rostral mesencephalic reticular formation in the region of the so-called rostral interstitial nucleus of the medial longitudinal fasciculus.[31,102,117] Mills and Swanson have reported a patient with paralysis of voluntary vertical saccades but intact pursuit vertical eye movements, resulting from bilateral infarcts involving the medial thalamic regions.[181] The localization was supported by CT scanning, and they concluded that the pathogenesis of the lesion had been acute infarction in a territory supplied by the thalamo-sub-thalamic paramedian arteries.

Internuclear, Vestibular, and Proprioceptive Pathways (Fig. 11)

The medial longitudinal fasciculus (MLF) connects the oculomotor trochlear and abducens nuclei. This pathway lies immediately ventral to the periaqueductal gray matter and decussates in the pons just rostral to the abducens nerve.[50] Interruption

52

of one MLF prevents abduction of the ipsilateral medial rectus when conjugate lateral gaze is attempted voluntarily or when one tries to evoke it by optokinetic,[268] vestibular, or oculocephalic stimulation. Bilateral MLF lesions cause bilateral paresis of adduction as well as impaired vertical vestibuloocular and pursuit responses. However, vertical saccades are unaffected by MLF lesions.[146] Fibers from the semicircular canals and the fastigial nucleus of the cerebellum synapse in the vestibular nuclei and traverse the medial longitudinal fasciculus to supply the ocular nuclei, thereby linking the semicircular canals and the cerebellum with the eye muscles.[27,284] This gives the cerebellum a role in modulating the vestibuloocular response.[309]

Cerebellar influences particularly from the flocculus[318-320] assure the accuracy of saccades and the quick-phase of nystagmus without affecting their velocity characteristics.[310,313] The cerebellum also contributes to the genesis of pursuit eye movements and the ability to hold eccentric positions of gaze. At least in the monkey, total cerebellectomy abolishes smooth pursuit and causes gaze-paretic nystagmus. Lesions restricted to the cerebellum result in disorders of saccadic eye movements (e.g., ocular dysmetria, ocular flutter, or opsoclonus).[48,73]

Neck influences also can affect eye movements. Fibers subserving proprioception from vertebral joints, ligaments, and possibly neck muscles[16] enter the spinal cord through the dorsal roots of C2, C3, and C4. They ascend both by direct pathways and through spinocerebellar and spinal reticular tracts to reach the vestibular nuclei.[89] From there the pathways project to the medial longitudinal fasciculus. Fibers of the medial longitudinal fasciculus probably subserve both the slow and fast phases of vestibular nystagmus.[146] Additional fibers subserving the fast phase may also ascend in the pontine tegmentum via a polysynaptic pathway.[283]

Examination of Ocular Motility

One examines extraocular movements in awake, cooperative patients by comparing both voluntary and reflex eye movements. In patients in stupor or coma, reflex eye and eyelid movements must suffice. The paragraphs that follow give our methods for examining ocular motility, including the oculocephalic and oculovestibular responses. The next section gives the physiologic explanation for these responses.

One begins by noting the position of the eyes and eyelids at rest and observes the patient for spontaneous eye movements. A small flashlight or bright ophthalmoscope, when held 50 cm. or so from the face and shined in the eyes, reflects from the same point on each pupil if the eyes lie on conjugate axes.

Eyelid and Corneal Reflexes

Observe the position of the eyelids. In most patients with stupor or coma, as in sleep, the eyes are closed by tonic contraction of the orbicularis oculi muscles. (The situation changes in chronic coma when sleep-wake cycles return.) Lift the lids and release them, noting their tone. In unconscious patients the eyelids close gradually after they are released, a movement that cannot be duplicated voluntarily by a hysterical patient.[86] Absence of tone or failure to close either lid suggests facial nerve dysfunction on that side. Strong resistance to eye opening or rapid closure upon release, or both, can be voluntary, as in psychogenic unresponsiveness, or a result of reflex blepharospasm, which occurs in both structural and metabolic brain disease. Caplan reviewed 25 patients with ptosis occurring as a result of acute infarction of the brain.[35] Either unilateral or bilateral ptosis could occur from hemispheric lesions, with the ptosis usually being present or more marked on the side of the hemiparesis. In the brainstem, unilateral ptosis usually occurred as part of Horner's syndrome. Unilateral ptosis without pupillary changes occurred with medial pontine infarction, and bilateral ptosis resulted from rostral brainstem infarction and could either accompany or be independent of changes in oculomotor or pupillary function. Some patients in coma show tonically retracted eyelids, most often associated with pontine infarction. Keane reported three such patients who exhibited tonic, uninhibited lid elevation in the unconscious state.[138] Despite being unconscious, the eyes were held widely open and never blinked or spontaneously closed. If closed by the examiner, they would immediately spring open. In the two patients examined at autopsy, the pathologist found large pontine infarctions.

Observe if blinking is present either at rest or in response to a bright light, a threat, or a loud sound. The presence of spontaneous blinking implies that the pontine reticular formation is intact, and if blinks can be provoked by light or sound, the relevant special sensory afferent pathways must also be intact. Blinking in response to a bright light may be present when there is no response to threat and probably does not imply an intact visual cortex since the reflex can be elicited in decorticate animals[212] and in man when visual evoked responses are absent and the EEG isoelectric.[314] Absence of blinking on one side is usually a sign of facial nerve dysfunction. Bilateral absence of blinking suggests either structural or metabolic dysfunction of the reticular formation.

Test the corneal response. In unconscious patients, a stronger stimulus must often be used to elicit this reflex than in alert patients. Observe both the eyelid and the eye. A positive bilateral response of eyelid closure and upward deviation of the eye (Bell's phenomenon) indicates normal function of the brainstem tegmental pathways from the midbrain (third nerve nucleus) to the low pons (seventh nerve nucleus). With structural brainstem lesions above the midpons (trigeminal nucleus) Bell's phenomenon disappears, but the jaw may deviate to the opposite side (corneal pterygoid reflex). When Bell's phenomenon is present but eyelid closure absent, the facial nerves or nuclei are damaged.

Oculocephalic Reflex (Proprioceptive Head-Turning Reflex, Doll's Head Eye Phenomenon) (Fig. 12)

One holds the patient's eyelids open and briskly rotates the head from one side to the other, at least briefly holding at the endpoints. Both lateral directions should be tested. A positive response is contraversive conjugate eye deviation (e.g., if the head is rotated to the right, the eyes deviate to the left). Next, the neck is briskly flexed and then extended. A positive response is deviation of the eyes upward when the neck is flexed and downward when the neck is extended. The eyelids may open reflexly when the neck is flexed (doll's head phenomenon),[86] allowing one to test levator palpebrae function as well. Within several seconds after the head is moved the eyes return to the resting position, even if the new head position is maintained. Oculocephalic maneuvers should not be attempted if the physician suspects that the patient has sustained trauma sufficient to cause a cervical fracture or dislocation.

Oculovestibular Reflex (Caloric Stimulation) (Fig. 12)

After the auditory canal is examined to be certain that the tympanic membrane is intact and any impacted cerumen is removed, the head is elevated 30 degrees

54

CONDITION: OCULAR REFLEXES IN UNCONSCIOUS PATIENTS

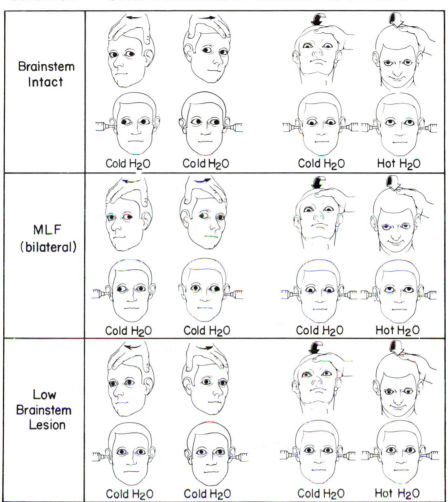

Figure 12. Ocular reflexes in unconscious patients. The upper section illustrates the oculocephalic (above) and oculovestibular (below) reflexes in an unconscious patient whose brainstem ocular pathways (see Fig. 11) are intact. Horizontal eye movements are illustrated on the left and vertical eye movements on the right: lateral conjugate eye movements (upper left) to head turning are full and opposite in direction to the movement of the face. A stronger stimulus to lateral deviation is achieved by douching cold water against the tympanic membrane(s). There is tonic conjugate deviation of both eyes toward the stimulus; the eyes usually remain tonically deviated for 1 or more minutes before slowly returning to the midline. Because the patient is unconscious, there is no nystagmus. Extension of the neck in a patient with an intact brainstem produces conjugate deviation of the eyes in the downward direction, and flexion of the neck produces deviation of the eyes upward. Bilateral cold water against the tympanic membrane likewise produces conjugate downward deviation of the eyes, whereas hot water (no warmer than 44°C) causes conjugate upward deviation of the eyes.

In the middle portion of the drawing, the effects of bilateral medial longitudinal fasciculus lesions on oculocephalic and oculovestibular reflexes are shown. The left portion of the drawing illustrates that oculocephalic and oculovestibular stimulation deviates the appropriate eye laterally and brings the eye, which would normally deviate medially, only to the midline, since the medial longitudinal fasciculus, with its connections between the abducens and oculomotor nuclei, is interrupted. Vertical eye movements often remain intact. The lower portion of the drawing illustrates the effects of a low brainstem lesion. On the left, neither oculovestibular nor oculocephalic movements cause lateral deviation of the eyes because the pathways are interrupted between the vestibular nucleus and the abducens area. Likewise, in the right portion of the drawing, neither oculovestibular nor oculocephalic stimulation causes vertical deviation of the eyes. On rare occasions, particularly with low lateral brainstem lesions, oculocephalic responses may be intact even when oculovestibular reflexes are abolished (see Patient 1–3).

above the horizontal so that the lateral semicircular canal is vertical and stimulation can evoke a maximal response. A small catheter is placed in the external canal near the tympanic membrane and up to 120 cc. of ice water is slowly introduced from a syringe into the canal of unresponsive patients. Cool water (30°C) or small amounts of ice water (<1 cc.)[195] are effective and less noxious for awake patients. In a normal awake patient the response to ice water caloric testing is nystagmus with the slow component toward the irrigated ear and the fast component away from the irrigated ear. Normal nystagmus is regular, rhythmic, and lasts 2 to 3 minutes. One observes little excursion of the eye from the midline. As consciousness is lost acutely from metabolic or supratentorial brain disease, the fast component progressively disappears and the slow component carries the eyes tonically toward the irrigated ear. In obtunded or lightly comatose patients there may be a slow drift toward the irrigated ear with a quick return to the midline. Even in unresponsive patients, occasional irregular beats of nystagmus are encountered, but the eyes usually deviate fully and conjugately toward the irrigated ear for as long as 2 to 3 minutes before returning to their original position. One should allow 5 minutes for the oculovestibular system to stabilize before performing the caloric test in the opposite ear. When structural brainstem lesions produce coma and involve the oculovestibular system as well, abnormal caloric responses may sometimes be observed, e.g., caloric irrigation may produce downward deviation of the ipsilateral eye with a few rotatory nystagmoid jerks (see Patient 1–3). Severe brainstem injury or deep metabolic depression of brainstem function obliterates the caloric response.

Maccario and associates reported paradoxical caloric responses in patients with altered states of consciousness resulting from metabolic encephalopathy.[171] In these patients, nystagmus was present and enhanced by eye opening rather than reduced or abolished, as occurs in normal individuals. The physiologic meaning of this finding is unclear.

With chronic brain injuries producing coma, the oculovestibular responses are less predictable than those just outlined. Mentally unresponsive patients surviving for several weeks after severe supratentorial injuries, for example, may demonstrate unsustained conjugate ocular movements down and away from the caloric irrigation as well as a number of other less well-characterized responses. The pathologic physiology of these responses is not clear.

The above caloric stimuli test lateral eye movements. To test vertical eye movements, one can irrigate both auditory canals simultaneously with ice water. In a comatose patient with intact brainstem function, the eyes deviate downward. To produce upward gaze, either irrigate both canals simultaneously with warm water (44°C) or position the head in the supine position, 30 degrees above the horizontal and use ice water.

Physiology of Oculocephalic and Oculovestibular Reflexes

Despite its empirical value in diagnosis, the physiologic basis of the oculocephalic reflex is debated. Neither visual fixation nor occipital connections are involved in the reflex since it persists after blindness,[108] in coma or darkness,[311] and after occipital lobectomy.[211] Awake patients whose eyes are open do not have doll's head eye responses unless they either voluntarily fix vision or suffer from bilaterally interrupted frontopontine pathways.[5] With the latter lesion, full doll's head responses are present but are said by Bielschowsky[15] to reflect a different reflex, requiring visual fixation. The stimulus for the oculocephalic reflex involves either the vestibular system or the proprioceptive afferents from the neck, or possibly both. Ford

56

and Walsh favor a vestibular basis for the reflex.[88] They point out that in healthy subjects neck reflexes elicit only 2 to 3 degrees of ocular movements and that the doll's head response can be elicited with the neck fixed if the patient is moved through space or tilted on a table. However, Barnes and Forbat have found large deviations of the eyes in oculocephalic testing in some normal subjects.[311] Thus, many observers believe that the doll's head phenomenon is simply the slow phase of the vestibuloocular reflex occurring in the absence of a quick phase. However, evidence for a contribution from proprioceptor impulses originating in neck muscles is compelling, since the oculocephalic reflexes can be elicited in patients with vestibular systems unresponsive to caloric stimulation.[108] Patient 1–3 illustrates this phenomenon.

Patient 1–3. A 51-year-old man was admitted in deep coma. Eight years earlier he had suffered a subarachnoid hemorrhage treated by ligation of the left internal carotid artery and followed by right hemiplegia and aphasia.

His body temperature was 32.6°C (92°F), his blood pressure was 110/70 mm. Hg, and his pulse was 64 beats per minute and regular. The respiratory pattern was apneustic. His pupils were 2 mm. in diameter and constricted briskly at a bright light stimulus. The right eye was in the straight-ahead position at rest, and the left eye showed intermittent, spontaneous, rotatory jerking movements from the straight-ahead position to an inferomedial position. Cold caloric testing intensified the movements of the left eye, but neither eye deviated appropriately. Vigorous head turning elicited a full range of lateral and vertical movements. Noxious stimuli to the right side of the body elicited flexion of the legs and decerebrate posturing of the right arm. The EEG showed 3 to 4 cps background with lower voltage over the left hemisphere. He died several days later.

Autopsy disclosed a recent occlusion of the basilar artery from its midpoint to a level 2 to 3 cm. rostrally. There was an old left internal carotid thrombosis with an old cavitary left hemispheral infarct. There was a large recent infarct almost transecting the pons at the level of the trigeminal motor nucleus. Below and above this level, the infarction was primarily in the lateral tegmentum, and medial tegmental structures were relatively spared.

The fundamental physiology of the caloric response has been extensively studied by Szentágothai,[283,284] Cohen and associates,[51,52] and others.[87] It is generally accepted that in caloric tests, convection currents in the endolymph activate receptors in the semicircular canals. Cold stimuli produce downward currents away from the ampulla of the horizontal canal when the head is 30 degrees above horizontal, and warm stimuli produce upward currents[83] toward the ampulla. The vestibular nerve is tonically active at rest; stimulation with electrical impulses increases activity, as does warm water. Cold water gives the opposite response, decreasing the frequency of discharge below the resting level.[97] When individual semicircular canals are selectively activated by pressure or electricity, stimulation of the horizontal canal concurrently excites the contralateral lateral rectus and the ipsilateral medial rectus muscles (an opposite effect is produced by ice water caloric tests). Stimulation of the posterior canal excites the ipsilateral superior oblique and the contralateral inferior rectus muscle. Stimulation of the superior canal excites the ipsilateral superior rectus muscle and the contralateral inferior oblique muscle. The excitatory stimuli to the extraocular muscles travel over three neuron arcs via the medial longitudinal fasciculus. Neural influences inhibiting reciprocal muscles during caloric stimulation appear to travel not in the medial longitudinal fasciculus but perhaps through the reticular formation.[284]

Abnormal Eye Movements in Coma

Resting Eye Position and Spontaneous Eye Movements

ROVING EYE MOVEMENTS. The eyes of comatose patients with intact oculomotor function in the brainstem often rove spontaneously with slow, random deviations much like the slow eye movements of light sleep in normal persons. The movements may vary from conjugate to dysconjugate in the same patient, the dysconjugate aspect having no known additional pathologic significance. The movements are usually horizontal, but vertical eye movements also occur. Roving eye movements cannot be mimicked voluntarily,[86] and their presence rules out psychogenic unresponsiveness. Most patients with roving eye movements also have active oculocephalic reflexes (see below). If brainstem function becomes depressed, roving eye movements disappear, much as slow eye movements disappear in deep sleep. Roving eye movements are slower than the always conjugate rapid eye movements (REM) of the dreaming phase of sleep.[63]

Periodic alternating or "Ping-Pong" gaze is a term used to describe repetitive, rhythmic, and conjugate horizontal ocular deviations occurring spontaneously in stuporous or comatose patients. The eyes move conjugately to the extremes of lateral gaze, pause for 2 to 3 seconds, and then move conjugately in the other direction. The episodic movement of the eyes may occur every few seconds for hours or days.[323] Various pathologic lesions have been associated with periodic alternating gaze, including vermian hemorrhage and bilateral cerebral infarcts. Structural involvement of the brainstem does not appear necessary to produce the syndrome, which is probably a variant of roving eye movements.

Nystagmus. Spontaneous nystagmus is uncommon in coma since the quick or compensatory phase depends upon interaction between the oculovestibular system and the cerebral cortex and disappears as cortical influences are reduced. One does encounter, however, the following patterns of spontaneous eye movements resembling nystagmus, which may be of localizing value in comatose states:

Retractory Nystagmus. This was first described by Koeber.[148] The movements consist of irregular jerks of the eyes backward into the orbit, sometimes occurring spontaneously but usually precipitated by attempted upward gaze. The phenomenon usually accompanies mesencephalic tegmental lesions.[74] Daroff and Hoyt reviewed the electromyographic findings in this disorder, which showed simultaneous contraction of all six ocular muscles.[59] They suggested that the mesencephalic lesion produces dysfunction of cortical mesencephalic inhibitory fibers, and thus all six muscles contract when any one is stimulated.

Convergence Nystagmus.[321] This consists of spontaneous, slow, drifting, ocular divergence followed by a quick convergent jerk. The abnormality also reflects a mesencephalic lesion and may be interspersed with retractory nystagmus.

Ocular Bobbing. This is Fisher's term[84] for attacks of intermittent, usually conjugate, brisk, downward eye movement followed by return to the primary position "in a kind of bobbing action." The movement most often accompanies severe destructive caudal pontine lesions (see Patient 1–2) and is not altered by caloric tests. Ocular bobbing also can occasionally accompany pontine dysfunction resulting from more remote lesions. Ocular bobbing has been reported in a patient with brainstem compression from cerebellar hematoma,[20] in a conscious patient with pontine lesion, [196] with obstructive hydrocephalus, and in patients with metabolic encephalopathy.[21] One of our patients had ocular bobbing associated with early transtentorial herniation from a frontal lobe hematoma.

Nystagmoid Jerking of a Single Eye. Such jerking in a lateral, vertical, or rotational direction accompanies severe midpontine to lower pontine damage. Patient 1–3 illustrates this phenomenon. Like other patients with this disorder, this man had severe abnormalities of his resting ocular position. Occasionally, slow, irregular, rotatory movements of the eyes occur in patients with pontine lesions;

these are bilateral and sometimes reciprocal so that one eye moves down and extorts as the other moves up and intorts.

Not to be confused with these reciprocal eye movements is "seesaw" nystagmus,[168] a rapid, pendular, disjunctive movement of the eyes in which, as one eye rises and intorts, the other falls and extorts. The nystagmus is most marked on visual fixation, decreases with relaxation of visual attention, and rarely occurs in comatose patients. Patients with seesaw nystagmus most often have lesions in the region of the anterior third ventricle or the rostral mesencephalon and not of the lower brainstem. Such nystagmus is usually associated with severe visual field defects (bitemporal hemianopia) and loss of visual acuity. On the other hand, Keane has recently reported an exceptional patient who exhibited spontaneous intermittent seesaw nystagmus while in coma resulting from a head injury.[139] Also present was ocular bobbing. At autopsy the brain was found to contain scattered small cerebral and cerebellar cortical contusions as well as hemorrhagic lesions of the periaqueductal gray matter at the pontomesencephalic junction. The lower pons and medulla were severely damaged with lacerations. A seesaw-like rotatory nystagmus has been described in other patients with clinical evidence of lesions in the medulla or pons.[175] Some evidence indicates that lesions of the interstitial nucleus of Cajal may be important in the generation of seesaw nystagmus.[242]

EYE POSITION AT REST. Patients with intact extraocular muscle pathways have eyes directed straight ahead[49] or slightly divergent during both consciousness and unconsciousness. Deviation of either eye more than a few degrees of arc from the physiologic position of rest signifies abnormal extraocular function, although the abnormality may represent the emergence of latent strabismus rather than a new oculomotor lesion.

ABNORMALITIES OF LATERAL GAZE. Most lateral conjugate gaze disorders occurring in unconscious patients result from destructive lesions since neither compressive nor metabolic disorders usually affect the supranuclear oculomotor pathways asymmetrically. Conditions causing coma are likely to produce one of three types of abnormal conjugate lateral gaze, two originating with disorders of the hemisphere and the third with dysfunction in the brainstem. The first is a temporary loss of contraversion when a hemispheral lesion disrupts supranuclear cerebral pathways. Contralateral gaze being suddenly deprived of descending neural influences, the eyes deviate fully and conjugately to the still innervated side (the side of the lesion). The cerebral lesion usually also causes associated contralateral hemiparesis so that the eyes "look" at the normal arm and leg. There is usually no nystagmus.

The second hemispheral abnormality is an irritative or epileptic phenomenon that conjugately deviates the eyes away from a cerebral lesion. This contraversion of the eyes often accompanies cerebral hemorrhage and lasts only a matter of minutes or hours, to be replaced by the more common supranuclear paralysis of conjugate gaze. Less frequently, contraversion of the eyes provides a clue that coma is associated with status epilepticus. Under these circumstances, the ocular contraversion has a jerking, nystagmoid, clonic quality with a frequency similar to that of focal motor seizures in the extremities.

The third conjugate gaze abnormality comes from the brainstem. Lesions in the pons involving supranuclear oculomotor fibers below their decussation (e.g., in the region of the abducens nucleus) produce conjugate ocular deviation, in which the eyes usually cannot be brought past the midline toward the lesion and spontaneously deviate away from the lesion. The deviation usually is less than with hemispheral lesions. If the responsible lesion affects the corticospinal pathways as well, the hemiparesis is contralateral to the lesion so that the eyes "look" at the paralyzed side.

Fisher reports three patients with supratentorial hemorrhage whose eyes deviated to the "wrong" side.[85] In each instance the hemorrhage was located in the medial thalamus with rupture into the third ventricle. All three patients had signs of upper brainstem disease as well (i.e., unreactive pupils in all three, downward deviation of the eyes in one, and absence of full oculocephalic responses in two), suggesting that the eye deviation was produced by midbrain impairment just below the decussation of the corticobulbar pathways. We have made similar clinical observations, but our material lacks pathologic confirmation. Daroff and Hoyt describe ipsilateral conjugate paresis with preserved reflex eye movements in patients with acute deep medial cerebellar hemispheral lesions.[59] We have not observed such a patient.

To epitomize: Sustained, involuntary, conjugate ocular deviation toward a normal arm and leg suggests a hemispheral lesion, and toward a paralyzed arm and leg, a pontine brainstem lesion. Localization of conjugate gaze disorders is aided by caloric and oculocephalic testing as discussed below.

A resting dysconjugate lateral position of the eyes results when nuclear or infranuclear oculomotor pathways are damaged. Lesions involving the oculomotor nucleus or nerve cause the involved eye to deviate outward. If the oculomotor lesion is in the brainstem, the pupil is dilated to at least some degree, and light fixed. If the oculomotor lesion is in the peripheral fibers, the pupil is usually, but not always, dilated (see page 109). With unilateral abducens paralysis, the involved eye deviates inward; with bilateral abducens paralysis, the eyes converge.

Latent strabismus can be accentuated or made manifest by acute neurologic illness, even when oculomotor function is not directly involved. Brainstem lesions causing strabismus produce defects in a neurologic distribution as described above, whereas congenital strabismus involves single muscles. Conversely, in deeply comatose patients preexisting dysconjugate gaze defects disappear, since when innervation is removed from all ocular muscles the eyes assume the physiologic position of rest.

ABNORMALITIES OF VERTICAL GAZE. Many otherwise healthy elderly patients have a limited capacity for upward gaze; with that exception, abnormalities of upward gaze imply a brainstem lesion. The most common abnormality is paralysis of upward gaze, which usually results from a lesion compressing or destroying the pretectal and posterior commissural areas at the midbrain-diencephalic junction. Bilateral lesions of the medial longitudinal fasciculus also may produce defects in upward gaze, particularly if the lesion extends ventrally into the adjacent reticular formation. In patients in light coma, upward gaze can be tested by holding the lid open and stimulating the cornea. This normally results in lid closure and upward ocular deviation (Bell's phenomenon). In patients in deeper coma, oculocephalic or caloric stimulation is usually required. Resting deviation of the eyes below the horizontal meridian always denotes brainstem dysfunction, which most often results from compression upon the midbrain tectum. However, extensive brainstem destruction or metabolic depression, as in hepatic coma, can also cause conjugate downward deviation.[140] Simon has recently reported that forced downward deviation of the eyes following oculovestibular testing occurs commonly in patients comatose from sedative or hypnotic drug overdose.[263]

Resting vertical dysconjugate gaze implies a lesion of internuclear or, rarely, supranuclear pathways. Bielschowsky reports this phenomenon following interruption of supranuclear fibers with a midbrain lesion involving the tectum but sparing the oculomotor nuclei.[15] Presumably, the supranuclear fibers are involved unilaterally after they separate to innervate their respective oculomotor nuclei.

In skew deviation the eyes diverge, one "looking" down, the other up. Patients able to cooperate and who possess this ocular abnormality may show mild vertical nystagmus in either eye and occasionally have slow seesaw movements of both eyes. The specific fibers involved in skew deviation have not been identified, but the causative lesions are characteristically localized either in or around the brachium pontis or dorsolateral medulla on the side of the inferiorly rotated eye[269] or in the medial longitudinal fasciculus on the side of the elevated eye.[267] Since skew deviation is diagnostic of brainstem lesions, it is imperative to be certain that one is not misinterpreting preexisting vertical strabismus.

Abnormalities of Oculocephalic (Doll's Head) and Oculovestibular (Caloric) Reflexes (Fig. 12)

With certain important exceptions, discussed below, the oculomotor responses to caloric stimulation and passive head turning relate to each other as if the two stimuli differed only in degree, the first being stronger than the second. These reflexes, therefore, are discussed together.

In normal awake subjects or those with psychogenic unresponsiveness, oculocephalic responses are inconsistent and caloric stimulation produces nystagmus. Awake patients with bifrontal[292] or diffuse hemispheral and basal ganglia disease[275] have active doll's head oculomotor responses, possibly, as Bielschowsky pointed out, because frontal eye field pathways are damaged and no longer inhibit visual fixation. In such patients caloric stimulation may produce tonic deviation rather than nystagmus.

In light supratentorial coma caused by supratentorial lesions cortical influences are lost. The oculocephalic reflexes can be demonstrated consistently, and caloric stimuli produce tonic lateral deviation rather than nystagmus. Several vigorous turns of the head may be necessary to elicit the oculocephalic response, particularly if the subject has roving eye movements. With greater cortical depression, but still leaving the brainstem intact, both doll's head and caloric responses become very brisk, and the oculocephalic responses can be elicited by a single turn of the head.

Oculocephalic and particularly oculovestibular reflexes are usually powerful enough to overcome the conjugate lateral eye deviation that results from unilateral lesions of the frontal or occipital eye fields. However, in the first few hours after a massive hemispheral lesion, it may require both vigorous passive head turning and caloric stimulation in combination to overcome the ocular deviation toward the damaged hemisphere.

Patients with metabolic cerebral depression generally retain reflex eye movements even when certain other signs of brainstem depression such as decerebrate rigidity and central hyperventilation have already appeared. With more severe depression of brainstem function, as with deep sedative poisoning, the reflexes become sluggish and finally disappear, caloric responses outlasting oculocephalic reflexes.

Lesions that destroy or compress the brainstem produce oculocephalic and caloric reflex abnormalities that depend on the location of the lesion. Pretectal or midbrain tegmental compression destroys reflex upward gaze. Compression or destruction of the oculomotor nerves or nuclei obliterates all homolateral oculocephalic and caloric responses except as mediated by the external rectus muscle.

One must interpret absent oculovestibular responses in a comatose patient with caution. Although the presence of normal oculovestibular reflexes implies intact brainstem function, the absence of such reflexes in a comatose patient need not imply that brainstem function is absent nor that the oculovestibular reflex absence is due to the same cause that produced the coma. Table 4 lists a variety of agents that block oculovestibular responses in comatose patients but that may not be related to the cause of coma or even may have been used to treat it. Preexisting vestibular disease, which may have altered or destroyed semicircular canal functioning without having produced major symptoms, may also block oculovestibular responses in comatose patients. Simmons reported 43 of 2500 consecutive electronystagmograph-monitored caloric-induced nystagmus examinations gave no response to 5 cc. of ice water in either ear.[261] Among the causes of the absence of the bilateral loss of caloric response were drugs in 5 patients, inflammatory or infectious diseases in 12, and congenital abnormalities of vestibular function in 9. In some patients a cause could not be established. Thus, the physician should interpret the bilateral loss of caloric responses in a comatose patient with great caution, always considering the possibility that preexisting vestibular disease or concurrent administration of vestibulotoxic agents has caused a peripheral failure of vestibular function and is not directly related to the cause of coma.

Midbrain or pontine lesions involving the medial longitudinal fasciculus (MLF) produce internuclear ophthalmoplegia. In comatose patients, the effects of MLF lesions can be detected by passive head turning or caloric irrigation. The eye ipsilateral to the lesion fails to adduct when the other eye abducts. Strictly speaking, the presence of intact convergence (this function not requiring MLF pathways) is required to distinguish between internuclear ophthalmoplegia and an isolated medial rectus palsy. However, isolated medial rectus weakness is so rare that reflex failure of one or both eyes to adduct is by itself almost diagnostic of internuclear ophthalmoplegia. The clinical usefulness of this identification is that unilateral or bilateral internuclear ophthalmoplegia occurs frequently in patients with structural brainstem lesions. Internuclear ophthalmoplegia is less common with metabolic brain disease. Nathanson failed to demonstrate internuclear ophthalmoplegia by caloric tests in any of 250 subjects after giving amobarbital intravenously.[191] Our experience is that internuclear ophthalmoplegia may often be encountered transiently at some stage during barbiturate intoxication, but seldom lasts long enough to confuse the diagnosis. We have also noted the phenomenon in other forms of metabolic coma (e.g., hepatic encephalopathy), especially when small quantities of ice water were used. In these instances, the stronger stimulus of a larger irrigation may produce

Table 4. Agents or Conditions that Potentially Block Vestibuloocular Responses in Comatose Patients

1. Ototoxic drugs
   antibiotics (e.g., gentamicin[61])
2. Vestibulosuppressant drugs[295]
   a. barbiturates and other sedative drugs
   b. phenytoin[207]
   c. tricyclic antidepressants[183]
3. Neuromuscular blockers
   succinylcholine[294]
4. Preexisting vestibular disease[261]

adduction of the contralateral medial rectus, a finding not encountered with structural disease of the MLF.

Acute or subacute lateral pontine lesions in the area of the abducens nuclei produce conjugate gaze paralysis, which cannot be modified by either passive head turning or caloric stimulation. It is believed that vestibular and proprioceptive impulses enter the neural pathways controlling extraocular movements at this locus and are involved in the lesion. In bilateral lateral brainstem lesions involving the vestibular nuclei, caloric responses are absent, but oculocephalic reflexes may be retained because the pathways remain that connect the oculomotor system with proprioceptive afferent impulses from the neck (Patient 1–3). This or circumstances in which both labyrinths are destroyed (e.g., streptomycin toxicity) are the only conditions in which absence of caloric responses accompanies preserved oculocephalic responses.

Summary of Abnormal Oculomotor Signs

In awake alert patients the eyes are directed straight ahead at rest and there are no involuntary movements. The full range of oculocephalic eye movements cannot normally be elicited passively since saccadic eye movements keep the eyes near the midline and caloric stimulation yields nystagmus rather than sustained deviation.

Unconscious patients suffering from diffuse or bilateral hemispheral dysfunction without direct destruction or compression of the neural pathways influencing ocular movements have eyes directed straight ahead or slightly divergent with no involuntary movements except slow roving eye movements. Oculocephalic responses are brisk, and caloric stimulation causes sustained eye deviation.

Unconscious patients with acute damage to a frontal eye field have eyes deviated to the side of the lesion, occasionally with some nystagmus to that side. Oculocephalic and caloric responses are usually present, although they may be difficult to elicit in the early hours after injury.

In most metabolic coma (poisoning with barbiturate-hypnotics and phenytoin being the exception), responses to oculocephalic and caloric stimulation at first are brisk, then become more difficult to demonstrate as coma deepens. In very deep metabolic coma, the eyes are immobile.

The eyes of comatose patients with midbrain lesions are immobile and directed straight ahead. The eyes of patients with small lesions involving the medial longitudinal fasciculus look straight ahead, but the globe on the side of the lesion fails to adduct to oculocephalic or caloric stimulation. More laterally placed unilateral pontine lesions cause the eyes to deviate conjugately away from the lesion with absence of oculocephalic and caloric responses in the paralyzed field. Skew deviation results from dorsolaterally placed pontine lesions or from lesions of the medial longitudinal fasciculus.

Eyes that are directed straight ahead have no localizing value in the unconscious patient. Eyes that are conjugately deviated in the horizontal meridian mean either an ipsilateral hemispheral lesion (usually frontal) or a contralateral pontine lesion. If the eyes are fully deviated but can be brought beyond the midline toward the other side by either passive head turning or caloric stimulation, the lesion is almost certainly hemispheral. If the eyes are partially deviated and repeated efforts fail to bring them beyond the midline toward the other side, the lesion is almost certainly pontine. If the eyes are conjugately deviated downward, a lesion is either compressing or metabolically depressing the mesencephalon; downward deviation rarely occurs with direct destruction of the mesencephalon. If the eyes can be raised above the horizontal meridian by oculocephalic or caloric response, the lesion is probably metabolic; if not, it is probably compressive.

Except for mild ocular divergence, dysconjugate ocular deviation in coma means a structural brainstem lesion if preexisting strabismus can be ruled out. Dysconjugate eye movements may be evoked by caloric or oculocephalic responses. If one or both eyes selectively fail to adduct, the lesion is in the medial longitudinal fasciculus (if pupillary responses indicate that there is no oculomotor palsy). Failure of abduction with intact contralateral adduction indicates a lesion of the abducens nerve below its nucleus. Oculocephalic and caloric stimulations only rarely produce dysconjugate vertical movements, but if they do, the lesion is intrinsic to the brainstem.

MOTOR FUNCTION

The examination of motor function in comatose patients provides valuable localizing information and in appropriate cases can serve as a guide to the course of the illness. Abnormal motor responses can result from dysfunction of structures that lie at several different levels of the brain, and the pattern of the motor behavior often provides a reliable clue to the area of maximal dysfunction. However, one must be cautious about directly equating the pattern of the motor responses with the depth of coma. The nuclear masses and pathways that specifically regulate skeletal muscle movement lie in areas largely separate from those that mediate conscious arousal or mental activity. As a result, neurologic diseases of equal severity but different anatomic distribution can produce very dissimilar motor abnormalities. These differences become especially useful in appraising some of the metabolic disorders discussed in Chapter 4.

Motor abnormalities in most patients in coma include the typical and well-known patterns of monoplegia, hemiplegia, and abnormal reflexes that reflect more or less selective involvement of the cerebral motor neurons and their descending corticospinal pathways. Other less frequently emphasized motor changes involve a variety of synergistic activities that are "released" when other motor areas, usually lying more rostrally, are damaged or undergo a loss of function.

Signs of Impaired Forebrain Function

Any of several abnormal patterns of motor behavior or motor responses to stimulation emerge in patients who, by radiographic or later postmortem examination, show a large-sized loss or impairment of forebrain gray matter. Most of the abnormalities have little precise localizing value and all of them tend to be more useful in appraising the neurologic basis of dementia than in the specific diagnosis of stupor or coma. Paulson reviews the nature and significance of the presence of or changes in, respectively, gait and posture, pelvicrural flexion postures, oculomotor avoidance and blepharospastic responses, motor perseveration and avoidance, reflex sucking and snouting responses, the palmomental and nuchocephalic reflexes, and other related abnormalities.[213] He, as have others, points out that the normal infant spontaneously possesses most of these reflexes and behavior patterns; such an analysis perhaps helps one to understand the reemergence of these signs as the forebrain deteriorates with age or disease.

Reflex grasping of the hand or foot usually arises in association with disease of the opposite frontal lobe and has somewhat more localizing value than the signs of diffuse dysfunction mentioned above. Even when the grasp response is strongly unilateral, however, it is almost always accompanied by an evidence of bilateral cerebral dysfunction. One seldom elicits manual grasping, for example, in patients with small frontal lobe neoplasms or infarcts, and its presence usually provides a reliable indication not only of contralateral frontal lobe disease, but also of increased intracranial pressure, abnormal intracranial displacements, or diffuse vascular or metabolic changes.[254]

The precise pathologic physiology of the grasp reflex is unknown, although its association with destructive lesions of the contralateral frontal lobe is well established. Clinical-pathologic publications on the subject almost always depict the presence of widespread abnormalities in the frontal lobes, the basal ganglia, and even the diencephalic reticular formation.[2] Reflex tonic grasping seems to be an exaggerated and distorted flexion reflex containing two components, one mediated as a short latency, primitive, cutaneous spinal reflex analogous to the normal finger flexor or flexor plantar response,[214] and the second (a sign of frontal lobe damage) combining the abnormally emergent spinal reflex with motor perseveration.[225] Thus, a very brisk, brief palmar flexor without sustained grasping is readily elicited by finger or palmar extension in patients with decerebrate rigidity.

Paratonia or gegenhalten (motor negativism)[147] is a plastic-like increase in muscle resistance to passive movements of the extremities, head, or trunk. The resistance is felt as constant or nearly so throughout the movement arc and of similar intensity regardless of the initial position of the body part. The phenomenon is differentiated from parkinsonian rigidity in that it almost disappears if the part is moved very slowly, is made worse by rapid passive movement, and is unaccompanied by any sense of cogwheel resistance. In awake patients, gegenhalten is generally greatly enhanced by brusque urgings to " relax," often giving to the resistance a quality suggesting that the patient actively opposes every effort to move his parts. The degree of resistance varies widely from a just perceptible molasses-like "stickiness" to an intense rigidity that can involve the entire body. The associated stretch reflexes are unaltered, but one often can elicit a weak palmar grasp reflex and a tonic plantar or extensor plantar response on the same side as the more prominent paratonia. The physiologic basis of paratonic rigidity is unknown, although it blends into the more familiar extrapyramidal rigidity of certain forms of parkinsonism. Normal infants between the second and eighth week of life show both paratonia and bilateral grasp reflexes.

In adults, the presence of paratonic rigidity usually reflects diffuse forebrain dysfunction such as occurs with metabolic encephalopathy, diffuse cerebral atrophy, or hypertensive vascular disease. Paratonia is usually bilateral and symmetrical, but occasionally can be more marked on one side of the body, and in such instances the phenomenon often reflects a mass lesion residing in or compressing the deeper portions of the opposite cerebral hemisphere.

Abnormal Postural Responses and Their Significance (Fig. 13)

Motor function in patients with reduced consciousness is commonly appraised by applying a noxious stimulus to various parts of the body and observing the response. Depending upon the patient's depth of stupor or coma, clinicians resort to a variety of stimuli to elicit these responses, e.g., supraorbital pressure, pinching of various parts of the extremity or trunk, or compressing the sternum. For patients difficult to

65

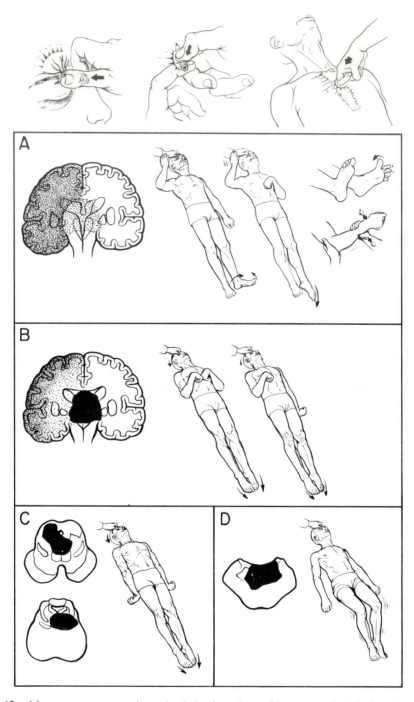

Figure 13. Motor responses to noxious stimulation in patients with acute cerebral dysfunction. Noxious stimuli can be delivered with minimal trauma to the supraorbital ridge, the nail bed, or the sternum as illustrated at top. Levels of associated brain dysfunction are roughly indicated at left. The text provides details.

arouse, we have found that placing a pencil or pen across the fingernail bed and applying increasingly firm pressure produces a consistently noxious stimulus with a minimum of tissue trauma. Such stimuli generally evoke one of three patterns of movement: appropriate, inappropriate, or no response. Normal responses include pushing the stimulus away, a quick and nonstereotyped withdrawal of the limb, or movement of the body and limb away from the stimulus. A facial grimace or a groan often accompanies the movement. Such responses imply the presence of functioning sensory pathways as well as partially intact descending motor pathways from cerebral cortex to effector. Provided that one applies stimuli to both sides of the body so as to rule out sensory lesions, unilateral absence of response implies impairment of corticospinal tract functions somewhere along their length. Bilateral absence of motor responses accompanied by facial grimacing or groaning suggests the presence of either bilateral corticospinal tract impairment or peripheral motor weakness.

Abnormal motor responses include several stereotyped postures of the trunk and extremities. Most appear only in response to noxious stimuli or are greatly exaggerated by such stimuli. Seemingly spontaneous postural spasms most often represent the presence of excess endogenous stimulation, such as come from the meningitis caused by subarachnoid bleeding or infection, from peripheral bodily injuries, or from internal irritants, such as a distended bladder. The pattern of these abnormal responses varies according to the site and severity of the brain involvement and includes flexor spasms, extensor spasms, or flaccidity.[322] The predominant response in the upper and lower extremities can differ according to the rostral caudal site of the major central nervous system damage and whether the stimulus is delivered to the arm or leg. Also, the two sides of the body can show different patterns of abnormality reflecting the distribution of injury to the brain. Even within the same patient, upper extremity flexor responses can give way to extensor postures and vice versa in the presence of changing systemic complications such as fever, infection, or pain-producing injury.

Clinical tradition has transferred the terms *decorticate rigidity* and *decerebrate rigidity* from experimental physiology to certain of the patterns of motor abnormality in man. The terms have a certain shorthand advantage in conveying the appearance of particular abnormal postures. One should recall, however, that even in experimental animals the terms decorticate or decerebrate tend to describe motor abnormalities that can be produced by lesions of several different kinds and locations in the brain and that the motor changes in individual animals can fluctuate in their intensity, form, and duration. In man these anatomic and physiologic associations are even less precise. Accordingly, it is desirable in analyzing abnormal motor responses to describe them noncommittally as abnormal flexor, abnormal extensor, or absent (flaccid) and designate the specific limbs involved. This permits more accurate following of the patient and prevents making undeservedly specific inferences about the anatomic distribution of the lesion. Furthermore, evidence indicates that observers agree with each other significantly better about the presence of the relatively simple designations of "normal-avoidance responses," "abnormal flexor," or "abnormal extensor" than they do about the presence or absence of the complexities of decorticate rigidity or decerebrate rigidity.[285]

Neither experimental physiologic studies nor human postmortem material provides a precise anatomic basis for the origins of the several abnormal postural responses described in the following paragraphs. On the other hand, much evidence indicates that the responses correlate with the presence of functional or structural impairment of certain cortical and subcortical *regions* of the brain and to some degree with the severity of impairment as well. Within that framework, the responses contribute information about both the rostral-caudal level and the side of the brain that is maximally damaged. To anticipate: Abnormal flexor responses in the arms with or without extensor responses in the leg appear to reflect more rostral and less severe supratentorial impairment. Extensor responses in arm and leg correlate best with the presence of deeper or more severe but still mainly supratentorial dysfunction. Extensor responses in the arms combined with flexion in the legs are associated with pontine brainstem dysfunction. Diffuse muscle flaccidity, with little or no response to stimulation, correlates most strongly with damage to the brainstem lying within or distal to the lower pontomedullary region.

ABNORMAL FLEXOR RESPONSE IN THE ARM WITH EXTENSION OF THE LEG. In fully developed form, this is the pattern often referred to as decorticate rigidity. The response is often incomplete, however. Physiologically, flexor muscle hypertonus predominates in the upper extremity with predominantly extensor hypertonus in the lower. The fully developed response consists of a relatively slow (as opposed to quick withdrawal) flexion of the arm, wrist, and fingers with adduction in the upper extremity and extension, internal rotation, and vigorous plantar flexion of the lower extremity. Less vigorous degrees of response can be confined to the stimulated member and consist, for example, of no more than stereotyped flexion of the arm. Such fragmentary patterns have the same localizing significance as the fully developed postural change, but often reflect either a less irritating or smaller central lesion. Physiologically, in experimental animals, destructive lesions including cerebral decortication and classic decerebration can produce the abnormal arm-flexor leg-extensor posture.[80] In general, animals with more superficially placed cerebral decortication or those surviving more chronically after decerebration are disposed more towards the arm-flexor response, while those with more extensive decerebration or with acute irritative lesions tend to show the classic Sherringtonian extensor response.

In man the large size of fatal lesions usually precludes using autopsy material to make accurate localization of the brain abnormalities that underly the pathogenesis of the arm flexor-leg extensor responses or that differentiate them from those that cause the arm extensor response. On empirical grounds, clinicians have long recognized that abnormal arm flexion carries a less serious prognosis than does arm extension, and recent statistical studies of head injury confirm the impression. Jennett and Teasdale reported that in patients comatose from head injury, flexor responses in the upper extremity were associated with a 37 percent recovery rate, whereas the presence of arm extensor responses indicated only a 10 percent recovery.[124] Bricolo and associates gave similar percentages.[24] The fact that 90 percent of patients with "decorticate rigidity" in Bricolo's series were free of any neuroophthalmologic signs of brainstem dysfunction emphasizes the hemispheric origin of the motor abnormality. Greenberg and coworkers analyzed somatosensory evoked responses (p. 72) in patients with either "decorticate" or "decerebrate" rigidity: in both groups the resulting electrophysiologic evidence pointed mainly to dysfunction of the cerebral hemispheres rather than of the brainstem.[99,100]

ABNORMAL EXTENSOR RESPONSE IN ARM AND LEG. This is the pattern termed decerebrate rigidity. When fully developed in man it consists of opisthotonos with the teeth clenched; the arms stiffly extended, adducted, and hyperpronated; and the legs stiffly extended with the feet plantar flexed. Tonic neck reflexes usually can be elicited. The full decerebrate response commonly requires the application of an external noxious stimulus. With acute lesions of the brain, however, waves of shivering and hyperpnea may accompany seemingly spontaneous recurrent decerebrate spasms.

Such a pattern is particularly likely when subarachnoid bleeding, massive cerebral and intraventricular hemorrhages, or compression upon the brainstem provide endogenous noxious stimulation. In less severely ill patients suffering from the appropriate neurologic lesions, external noxious stimulation sometimes elicits fragments of the decerebrate response consisting of brief hyperextension of the body or an arm, pronation of the hand, or clenching of the jaws with head retraction. Clinical disease sometimes blurs the dividing line between arm flexor and arm extensor responses, particularly in the presence of deep hemispheric lesions that are beginning to exert pressure effects on the upper brainstem. In such instances, the motor responses can shift back and forth from one combination to the other, presumably reflecting the physiologic effects of changes in the amount of compression or irritation delivered to the tissue. With acute expanding intracranial lesions, one sometimes observes decerebrate responses on one side of the body (usually contralateral to the hemispheric lesion), while the other less functionally impaired side demonstrates either an appropriate response or shows arm flexion.

Physiologically in animals and man, the decerebrate state consists of an excessive excitation of synergistic extension movements, often accompanied by simultaneous contraction of flexor antagonists.[24,81] Decerebrate rigidity in experimental animals classically results from midbrain transections that pass between the colliculi and spare the more caudally placed vestibular nuclei and the adjacent pontine reticular formation.[257] As noted above, lesions found in patients at autopsy almost never provide an anatomic correlation as precise as surgical section in animals. Thus, at autopsy examination of subjects who have had fully developed decerebrate responses, one can find bilateral diencephalic and hemispheric damage, upper brainstem injury, or, even in hepatic coma for example, no structural lesions of the brain at all. Most frequently there is evidence of bilateral and fairly deep diencephalic injury, often but not always in association with rostral central brainstem injury. Such anatomic findings are consistent with clinical studies in patients with head injury that indicate that between 50 and 75 percent of patients showing motor decerebrate responses have associated neuroophthalmologic signs of brainstem dysfunction. As mentioned above, however, evoked response analyses in such subjects most often indicate dysfunction of the cerebral hemispheres rather than the brainstem.

The clinician usually encounters decerebrate rigidity under one of four circumstances: (1) accompanying massive and bilateral forebrain lesions such as occur with acute head trauma and cerebral hemorrhage; (2) during the course of rostral-caudal deterioration as diencephalic dysfunction evolves into the stage of midbrain dysfunction (Chapter 2); (3) with destructive or expanding posterior fossa extraaxial or cerebellar lesions that compress or partially damage the midbrain and rostral pons; or (4) with severe metabolic disorders such as hepatic coma, hypoglycemia, anoxia, or drug intoxication that relatively selectively depress the function of the deep diencephalon and forebrain. Less often, decerebrate rigidity is observed with certain subacute and severe bilateral, diffuse hemispheric abnormalities, such as postanoxic cerebral demyelination and the metabolic disease of white matter called adrenoleukodystrophy.

ABNORMAL EXTENSOR RESPONSE IN ARMS WITH FLACCID OR WEAK FLEXOR RESPONSE IN LEGS. The 1972 edition of this monograph described this abnormal response as occurring in patients with damage to the brainstem tegmentum at approximately the level of the vestibular nuclei. Since then we have confirmed the observation on several additional patients shown at postmortem examination to have primary hemorrhages, infarcts, or other forms of structural damage involving the pontine tegmentum. Other workers have confirmed this association.[24,293] Thus, the localizing value of the response appears to be well established. The motor pattern has no exact counterpart in experimental physiology, but presumably represents the beginning transition from the abnormal synergistic extensor response evoked by damage to the mid to upper brainstem and the predominantly flexor response that characterizes the reaction to stimulation of the isolated spinal cord.

FLACCIDITY. Flaccid or absent motor responses can reflect either peripheral denervation or depression of central motor mechanisms in the medullopontine reticular formation. Skeletal muscle flaccidity marks the initial motor phase of acute functional spinal cord transection ("spinal shock"). Both clinical and experimental evidence indicate that transections producing such flaccidity can lie as high as the junction between the lower and middle third of the pons.

MAJOR DIAGNOSTIC LABORATORY PROCEDURES

Electroencephalogram (EEG)

The EEG helps to differentiate coma from psychogenic unresponsiveness (e.g., hysteria and catatonia) (see Chapter 5) and sometimes helps distinguish among the various causes of coma. It is, however, considerably less useful than the CT scan in distinguishing structural from metabolic lesions. Detailed descriptions of the physiology of normal and abnormal EEGs can be found elsewhere. A few clinical statements may clarify the role of the EEG in the differential diagnosis of the apparently unconscious patient: an entirely normal EEG, i.e., a background activity of bilateral and symmetrical 8 to 13 Hz. (alpha activity) present with the patient at rest but inhibited by eye opening, indicates that the subject is awake and reasonably alert. However, there are important exceptions to this general rule.[111] Occasionally, patients who are unconscious because of brainstem infarcts maintain normal alpha activity (*alpha coma*). The alpha activity in comatose patients is usually more regular and less variable than in awake patients. It is usually not affected by light, noise, eye opening, or other stimuli, as is the alpha activity of the awake patient. So-called alpha pattern coma has also been reported after cardiopulmonary arrest and respiratory arrest.[101,301] Wilkus and associates reported on a patient unconscious from a pontine infarct whose alpha activity drove to photic stimulation.[303]

It is often not possible to distinguish alpha pattern coma from the awake state by the EEG alone. The patient with psychologic unresponsiveness usually has alpha activity that is very responsive to passive eye opening, to loud noises, and to noxious stimuli. In the patient with alpha pattern coma, on the other hand, the alpha activity is usually regular and affected little or not at all by these stimuli. When combined with other findings, including oculovestibular responses to caloric testing, one usually has little difficulty in making the differentiation. More difficult to distinguish is alpha pattern activity accompanying the locked-in state (see page 159). Here the clinical examination, including oculovestibular responses, may not be helpful, but the EEG of the patient with the locked-in state usually shows more reactive alpha activity than that of the comatose patient, although the two may overlap.[38,101]

As normal subjects become drowsy, alpha activity disappears and is replaced by slower waves in the theta (3–7 Hz.) or delta (1–3 Hz.) range. Bilateral delta activity implies that the patient is either deeply asleep or unconscious. Supratentorial lesions generally cause focal EEG abnormalities because they either directly involve the cortex or interrupt thalamic cortical projections. The first change is the appearance of unilateral or focal slow activity, usually of high voltage, which occurs in the vast majority of supratentorial hemorrhages, infarcts, tumors, and abscesses. By the time the patient becomes deeply comatose, however, the slow activity becomes bilateral, and one may not be able to identify the site of major damage. With transtentorial herniation, EEG activity may be of higher voltage on the side opposite the major damage.[169] Infratentorial lesions usually produce bilateral slow activity; the exception of alpha coma is noted above.

Metabolic brain disease usually produces diffuse and symmetrical slowing of the EEG, with the severity of the encephalopathy and the degree of slowing generally paralleling one another. Even the mildest delirium is usually accompanied by a reduction in alpha frequency, but this may be difficult to ascertain unless previous records are available from the patient. For example, the background activity of a patient suffering from metabolic encephalopathy may slow from its normal 12/second to 8 or 9/second. If one had known that the patient's normal alpha activity was 12/second, the slowing would be recognized as a substantial alteration from that normal, even though the 8 to 9/second activity is within normal limits for the entire population. In some patients with agitated delirium, particularly in the delirium of drug or alcohol withdrawal, low to moderate voltage fast activity (13–30 Hz.) predominates, replacing normal alpha activity. Pro and Wells, in a comprehensive review of the literature on the EEG and delirium, were unable to find "a single example in which a patient has been followed with EEG's from a normal state into delirium or vice versa in whom EEG changes were not discernible over time."[226] Moreover, the EEG in metabolic encephalopathy is often as much or more sensitive than the clinical examination. Changes in the EEG may precede discernible changes in cognitive function,[241] and EEG abnormalities often persist after the mental status examination returns to normal.

A recent study has evaluated EEGs in 95 patients with "acute confusional states."[203] In 52 patients, the EEG was grossly abnormal, and in 31 mildly so. Twelve patients, including three believed to be suffering from psychiatric disease, had normal EEGs. The other 9 normal EEGs occurred in 4 of 48 patients with intracranial disorders causing the confusional state, and 5 of 42 patients with extracranial disorders (presumably metabolic brain disease). No follow-up studies are reported. Focal abnormalities, such as asymmetry of delta activity and localized paroxysmal features, were prominent in about half of the patients with intracranial disease, but rare in those suffering from extracranial disease. On the other hand, bifrontal delta activity in triphasic waves was encountered both in patients with structural brain disease and in those with metabolic brain disease.

A characteristic EEG abnormality in metabolic coma, particularly that due to liver disease, is the so-called triphasic or paroxysmal wave. These are bilaterally synchronous 2 to 4 Hz. waves occurring in bursts, predominantly in the frontal area and then spreading laterally and posteriorly as cerebral depression deepens. These waves were originally thought to be pathognomonic of hepatic encephalopathy, but have been reported in metabolic brain diseases of other causes, including uremia.[200]

The EEG is often helpful in identifying status epilepticus from partial complex seizures (see Chapter 4) as a cause of stupor or coma.[76] Patients who are unresponsive because they are suffering from continuous seizure discharges frequently show on the EEG either focal or diffuse spike activity or spike and wave activity. Because the treatment of this form of metabolic coma with anticonvulsants is different from that of other forms, the EEG is a vital diagnostic test.

In summary, with the possible exception of anoxic ischemic encephalopathy (alpha coma), a normal EEG in an unresponsive patient rules out metabolic brain disease as the cause. Slowing of the EEG may be the earliest sign of metabolic brain disease, preceding even changes in a careful mental status examination. Moreover, EEG recovery may lag behind clinical recovery and very slow, coma-like records may persist for days or weeks after a patient awakens from metabolic coma.

The EEG in patients suffering from psychologic disorders is usually normal. Pro and Wells indicate that in acutely agitated schizophrenic patients the EEG may be of the low voltage fast variety,[226] and others have reported slowing of the EEG in some patients with catatonic schizophrenia. However, in a patient with psychogenic unresponsiveness, the EEG is almost always normal and easily differentiated from the tracings of all patients with physiologic unconsciousness, including those with alpha coma.

Evoked Responses

Signal averaging allows one to record from the scalp short latency evoked responses generated from the somatic (SER), visual (VER), and auditory (AER) systems using conventional EEG oscillographs.[45,100,125] Furthermore, in the case of SER and AER, one not only records the direct cortical projection of the system (near-field potential), but short latency, secondary potentials that are generated by neural structures at several different levels of the brainstem. These latter are also called far-field potentials.[125] In the case of SER, the first short latency far-field response is believed to emanate from the spinal cord, while experimental and clinical data indicate that later components take their origins from several levels of the brainstem, cerebellum, and thalamus.[114,276,302] In the case of auditory far-field potentials, Starr and Hamilton concluded that of the seven components observed in the initial 10 msec. following click signals, loss of all responses after wave I implies interruption of the auditory pathway at the junction of the VIII nerve with the brainstem.[274] Waves II and III, on the other hand, reflect brainstem activity at the level of the cochlear nucleus and trapezoid body, while waves IV and V according to Starr reflect activity of the lateral lemniscus and inferior colliculus.

Potentially, the above findings imply that the judicious analysis of evoked responses may aid in making an anatomic diagnosis in patients in coma. Furthermore, because the location of structural lesions has an important influence on potential recovery, evoked response studies may provide an aid to prognosis.

Only limited applications have so far been used to test these implications. Starr's group found that far-field responses beyond wave I were absent in patients with brain death. They also concluded from clinical testing that in drug poisoned patients the normal response remained even with deep coma.[273]

Greenberg and associates carried out an extensive appraisal of near-field and far-field responses in patients with head injury.[99,100] Using a multimodality system, Greenberg found that evoked response measurements provided a powerful tool for functional measurements and for estimating prognosis. Abnormal multimodality evoked responses, recorded acutely, "consistently defined dysfunction of the visual, auditory and motor systems in comatose patients and were considerably more effective than the clinical neurological exam" in predicting residual neurologic deficits. Furthermore, the presence of severely abnormal far-field potentials recorded soon after head injury predicted that functional recovery would not be seen even after 3 months or more. The authors did not provide data as to the earliest post-injury time that accurate predictive analyses could be obtained, their earliest mean testing times having been day three. Nor did they indicate whether a brief and simple system could be devised that would offer practical use in a large population of comatose patients.

These experimental studies represent a promising beginning. Critical studies plotting the significance for neurologic recovery of abnormal responses recorded within the first minutes or hours following global or regional cerebral ischemia have not been reported in detail. What must be determined is whether evoked response methods will discriminate any better than clinical signs between patients destined to recover spontaneously and those with a poor natural prognosis. An ideal application of evoked response studies would be to test their effectiveness in situations where analysis of clinical indicants leaves the outcome in doubt; such applications have not yet been described.

CT Scanning

Computerized tomographic (CT) scanning of the brain is a relatively new radiologic technique that allows the direct visualization of intracranial structures.[205] With the newest scanners, the physician can distinguish gray matter from white matter and can identify the shape and location of the cerebral ventricles and sulci. After the intravenous injection of iodinated contrast material, one can identify major vascular structures of the brain as well as areas of blood-brain barrier breakdown. A CT scan of the brain is taken by passing an x-ray beam through the skull around a 360° axis. The density of the tissue at each point along the beam is reconstructed by the computer, and a section of brain is displayed on an oscilloscope. The depth of brain sections can be varied from 4 to 15 mm., and the resolution in the plane of section is usually about 5 mm. A single section can be taken in about 2 seconds with the newest CT scanners. The sections are usually taken in the horizontal plane but can be taken in the coronal plane as well. Computer reconstructions can be made in any other plane. CT scanning is an ideal way to view the anatomy of the brain and to identify either abnormal structures (larger than 5 mm. in diameter) or shifts of normal structures.[208,277]

The scanners hold promise of being able to quantify the various compartments of the brain, including gray matter, white matter, CSF, edema content,[4,240,287] and blood volume.[217] CT scanning has revolutionized the differential diagnosis of comatose patients. It is particularly useful for identifying mass lesions in the brain in either the supra- or infratentorial compartments. Acute hemorrhages, because their density is greater than that of any normal intracranial structures, are especially easy to identify. More chronic hemorrhagic lesions such as subdural hematomas may become isodense with brain after 2 to 3 weeks, but even when the lesion itself is not apparent, the shift of the ventricular system and the obliteration of cortical sulci it produces usually make the diagnosis relatively simple.[145] Cerebral tumors may be isodense with or less dense than brain, but because most of them disrupt the blood-brain barrier, they enhance their image when iodinated contrast material is given.

Virtually all patients suspected of harboring a supratentorial mass or an infratentorial mass or destructive lesion (see Chapters 2 and 3) should have an emergency CT scan whenever such a study is available. Many of the lesions seen on CT scan are surgically remediable if treated sufficiently early, but irreversible if there is excessive delay in instituting treatment. CT scans do not identify the lesions in metabolic encephalopathy or in psychogenic coma; in these instances the EEG is often more helpful.

The major problem with CT scanning in comatose patients is that many patients are restless and movement artifacts can obscure abnormal findings. A new generation of CT machines that scan each section in 2 seconds reduces this problem but does not eliminate all difficulty with movement artifacts. Often, restless patients must be sedated in order to assure an interpretable scan. Diazepam (3-10 mg. I.V.) is usually an effective sedative, but it produces prolonged sedation that may obscure changing neurologic signs. Narcotic drugs have the advantage that their effects can be reversed by naloxone. However, most narcotics, including morphine, act rather slowly and cause sedation and respiratory distress for several hours. Naloxone given at the completion of the scan may reverse the effects of morphine only temporarily, and the patient may later develop respiratory depression when the effect of the naloxone has worn off. Some workers prefer a rapidly acting narcotic drug such as fentanyl (0.05-0.1 mg. I.V.). The onset of sedation is almost immediate. Respiratory depression appears several minutes later, often after the scan is completed. The drug's effects can be fully and permanently reversed by intravenous injection of the opiate antagonist naloxone (0.4 mg. I.V.). Whatever sedation is used, the patient's respiratory state must be carefully monitored and provision made for artificial ventilation.

When an emergency CT scan is to be performed, the physician must be present throughout the scan for two reasons: first, he may have to administer sedative drugs to quiet an obtunded patient whose spontaneous movements preclude an accurate scan, and second, the physician should always accompany a stuporous or comatose patient with rapidly developing neurologic signs because sudden changes in the neurologic state, including respiratory failure, can occur rapidly and require emergency treatment.

The CT scan is a powerful diagnostic tool, and its interpretation often appears deceptively simple. Because the computer prints out a picture of the brain in sections rather than the vague shadows seen on arteriography or radionuclide brain scanning, the novice is often fooled into believing that he can interpret the pictures as easily as the expert. In many instances, particularly with large lesions such as intracerebral hemorrhage, this is true. However, subtle changes on CT scanning such as isodense subdural hematomas and transtentorial herniation require great skill and experience for correct interpretation. Expert neuroradiologic assistance should be sought in making a final interpretation of the CT scan.

REFERENCES

1. ADAMETZ, J.H.: *Rate of recovery of functioning in cats with rostral reticular lesions. An experimental study.* J. Neurosurg. 16:85-98, 1959.

2. ADIE, W.J., AND CRITCHLEY, M.: *Forced grasping and groping.* Brain 50:142-170, 1927.

3. ALBERT, M.L., SILVERBERG, R., RECHES, A., ET AL.: *Cerebral dominance for consciousness.* Arch. Neurol. 33:453-454, 1976.

4. ALLEN, J.C., THALER, H.T., DECK, M.D.F., ET AL.: *Leukoencephalopathy following high-dose intravenous methotrexate chemotherapy: quantitative assessment of white matter attenuation using computed tomography.* Neuroradiology 16:44-47, 1978.

5. ALTROCCHI, P.H., AND MENKES, J.H.: *Congenital ocular motor apraxia.* Brain 83:579-588, 1960.

6. BAILEY, P.: *Concerning the localization of consciousness.* Trans. Am. Neurol. Assoc. 80:1-12, 1955.

7. BARRIS, R.W., AND SCHUMAN, H.R.: *Bilateral anterior cingulate gyrus lesions. Syndrome of the anterior cingulate gyri.* Neurology 3:44-52, 1953.

8. BATINI, C., MORUZZI, G., PALESTINI, M., ET AL.: *Effects of complete pontine transections on the sleep-wakefulness rhythm: the midpontine pretrigeminal preparation.* Arch. Ital. Biol. 97:1-2, 1959.

9. BATSEL, H.L.: *Electroencephalographic synchronization and desynchronization in the chronic "cerveau isole" of the dog.* Electroencephalogr. Clin. Neurophysiol. 12:421-430, 1960.

10. BAUMGARTEN, H.G., BJORKLUND, A., HOLSTEIN, A.F., ET AL.: *Chemical degeneration of indolamine axons in rat brain by 5,6-dihydroxytryptamine.* Z. Zellforschl. 129:256-271, 1972.

11. BEAN, J.W., AND BECKMAN, D.L.: *Centrogenic pulmonary pathology in mechanical head injury.* J. Appl. Physiol. 27:807-812, 1969.

12. BENDER, M.B., AND SHANZER, S.:"Oculomotor pathways defined by electric stimulation and lesions in the brainstem of monkey." In Bender, M.B. (ed.): *The Oculomotor System.* Harper and Row, New York, 1964.

13. BERGER, A.J., MITCHELL, R.A., AND SEVERINGHAUS, J.W.: *Regulation of respiration.* N. Engl. J. Med. 297:92-97, 138-143, 194-201, 1977.

14. BERGER, H.: *Ueber das Elektroenkephalogramm des Menschen.* Arch. Psychiat. Nervenkr. 87: 527-570, 1929.

15. BIELSCHOWSKY, A.: *Lectures on motor anomalies of the eyes. X. Supranuclear paralyses.* Am. J. Ophthalmol. 22:603-613, 1939.

16. BIEMOND, A., AND DEJONG, J.M.B.V.: *On cervical nystagmus and related disorders.* Brain 92:437-458, 1969.

17. BINNION, P.F., AND MCFARLAND, R.J.: *The relationship between cardiac massage and pupil size in cardiac arrest in dogs.* Cardiovasc. Res. 3:915-917, 1967.

18. BOBILLIER, P., SEGUINS, J., PETITJEAN, F., ET AL.: *The raphe nuclei of the brain stem. A topographical atlas of their efferent projections as revealed by autoradiography.* Brain Res. 113:449-486, 1976.

19. BORISON, H.L., AND WANG, S.C.: *Physiology and pharmacology of vomiting.* Pharmacol. Rev. 5:193-230, 1953.

20. BOSCH, E.P., KENNEDY, S.S., AND ASCHENBRENER, C.A.: *Ocular bobbing: the myth of its localizing value.* Neurology 25:949-953, 1975.

21. BRAEMS, M., DEHAENE, I.: *Ocular bobbing: clinical significance.* Clin. Neurol. Neurosurg. 78:99-106, 1975.

22. BRAIN, R.: *The physiological basis of consciousness.* Brain 81:426-455, 1958.

23. BREMER, F.: *Cerebral hypnogenic centers.* Ann. Neurol. 2:1-6, 1977.

24. BRICOLO, A., TURAZZI, S., ALEXANDRE, A., ET AL.: *Decerebrate rigidity in acute head injury.* J. Neurosurg. 47:680-698, 1977.

25. BRIERLEY, J.B., ADAMS, J.H., GRAHAM, D.I., ET AL.: *Neocortical death after cardiac arrest.* Lancet 2:560-565, 1971.

26. BRODAL, A.: *The Reticular Formation of the Brain Stem. Anatomical Aspects and Functional Correlations.* Oliver and Boyd, Edinburgh, London, 1957.

27. BRODAL, A., POMPEIANO, O., AND WALBERG, F.: *The Vestibular Nuclei and Their Connections, Anatomy and Functional Correlations.* Charles C Thomas, Springfield, Ill., 1962.

28. BROWN, D.G., AND HAMMILL, J.F.: *Glutethimide poisoning: unilateral pupillary abnormalities.* N. Engl. J. Med. 285:806, 1971.

29. BRUCHER, J.M.: *The frontal eye field of the monkey.* Int. J. Neurol. 5:262-281, 1966.

30. BUGE, A., ESCOUROLLE, G., RANCUREL, G., ET AL.: *Akinetic mutism and bicingular softening.* Rev. Neurol. 131:121-137, 1975.

31. BÜTTNER-ENNEVER, J.A., AND BÜTTNER, V.: *A cell group associated with vertical eye movements in the rostral mesencephalic reticular formation of the monkey.* Brain Res. 151:31-47, 1978.

32. CAIRNS, H.: *Disturbances of consciousness with lesions of the brain stem and diencephalon.* Brain 75:109-146, 1952.

33. CAIRNS, H., OLDFIELD, R.C., PENNYBACKER, J.B., ET AL.: *Akinetic mutism with an epidermoid cyst of the 3rd ventricle.* Brain 64:273-290, 1941.

34. CALARESU, F.R., FAIERS, A.A., AND MOGENSON, G.J.: *Central neural regulation of heart and blood vessels in mammals.* Prog. Neurobiol. 5:1-35, 1975.

35. CAPLAN, L.R.: *Ptosis.* J. Neurol. Neurosurg. Psychiatry 37:1-7, 1974.

36. CARMEL, P.W.: *Sympathetic deficits following thalamotomy.* Arch. Neurol. 18:378-387, 1968.

37. CARPENTER, W.B.: *Principles of Human Physiology.* Blanchard and Lea, Philadelphia, 1853.

38. CARROLL, W.M., AND MASTAGLIA, F.L.: *"Locked-in coma" in postinfective polyneuropathy.* Arch. Neurol. 36:46–47, 1979.

39. CASTAIGNE, P., BUGE, A., CAMBIER, J. ET AL.: *Demence thalamique d'origine vasculaire par ramollissement bilateral limite au territoire du pedicule retro-mamillaire.* Rev. Neurol. 114:89–107, 1966.

40. CASTAIGNE, P., AND ESCOURELLE, R.: *Etude topographic des lesions anatomiques dans les hypersomnies.* Rev. Neurol. 116:547–584, 1967.

41. CHAPMAN, W.P., LIVINGSTON, R.B., LIVINGSTON, K.E., ET AL.: "Possible cortical areas involved in arterial hypertension." In Wolff, H.G., Wolf, S.G., and Hare, C.C. (eds.): *Life Stress and Bodily Disease.* Res. Publ. Assoc. Res. Nerv. Ment. Dis. 29:775–798, 1950.

42. CHAPMAN, L.F., AND WOLFF, H.G.: *The cerebral hemispheres and the highest integrative functions of man.* Arch. Neurol. 1:357–424, 1959.

43. CHASE, T.N., MORETTI, L., AND PRENSKY, A.L.: *Clinical and electroencephalographic manifestations of vascular lesions of the pons.* Neurology 18:357–368, 1968.

44. CHERINGTON, M., STEARS, J., AND HODGES, J.: *Locked-in syndrome caused by a tumor.* Neurology 26:180–182, 1976.

45. CHIAPPA, K.H., GLADSTONE, K.J., AND YOUNG, R.R.: *Brainstem auditory evoked responses. Studies of wave form variations in 50 normal human subjects.* Arch. Neurol. 36:81–87, 1979.

46. CHRISTOFF, N.: *A clinicopathologic study of vertical eye movements.* Arch. Neurol. 31:1–8, 1974.

47. CLEVELAND, J.C.: *Complete recovery after cardiac arrest for three hours.* N. Engl. J. Med. 284:334–335, 1971.

48. COGAN, D.G.: *Ocular dysmetria: flutter-like oscillations of the eyes, and opsoclonus.* Arch. Ophthalmol. 51:318–335, 1954.

49. COGAN, D.G.: *Neurology of the Ocular Muscles,* ed. 2. Charles C Thomas, Springfield, Ill., 1956.

50. COGAN, D.G., KUBIK, C.S., AND SMITH, W.L.: *Unilateral internuclear ophthalmoplegia: report of eight clinical cases with one post-mortem study.* Arch. Ophthalmol. 44:783–796, 1950.

51. COHEN, B.: *Eye, head and body movements from semicircular canal nerve stimulation.* Neurology 15:270, 1965.

52. COHEN, B., SUZUKI, J.I., SHANZER, S., ET AL.: "Semicircular canal control of eye movements." In Bender, M.B. (ed.): *The Oculomotor System.* Harper and Row, New York, 1964.

53. CONRAD, L.C.A., LEONARD, C.M., AND PFAFF, D.W.: *Connections of the median and dorsal raphe nuclei in the rat: an autoradiographic and degeneration study.* J. Comp. Neurol. 156:179–206, 1974.

54. CONRAD, L.C.A., AND PFAFF, D.W.: *Efferents from medial basal forebrain and hypothalamus in the rat. II. An autoradiographic study of the anterior hypothalamus.* J. Comp. Neurol. 169:221–262, 1976.

55. CREUTZFELDT, O.: "Physiological conditions of consciousness." In den Hartog Jager, W.A., Bruyn, G.W., and Heijstee, A.P.J. (eds.): Proc. 11th World Congress of Neurology. Excerpta Medica, Amsterdam, 1978, pp. 194–208.

56. CRILL, W.E.: *Horner's syndrome secondary to deep cerebral lesions.* Neurology 16:325, 1966.

57. CROMPTON, M.R., TEARE, R.D., AND BOWEN, D.A.L.: *Prolonged coma after head injury.* Lancet 2:938–940, 1966.

58. DALLE ORE, G., GERSTENBRAND, F., LUCKING, C.H., ET AL. (eds.): *The Apallic Syndrome.* Springer-Verlag, New York, 1977.

59. DAROFF, R.B., AND HOYT, W.F.: "Supranuclear disorders of ocular control systems in man: clinical, anatomical and physiological correlations." In Bach-y-Rita, P., Collins, C.C., and Hyde, J.E. (eds.): *The Control of Eye Movements.* Academic Press, New York, 1971, p. 175.

60. DAROFF, R.B., AND TROOST, B.T.: "Supranuclear disorders of eye movements." In Glaser, J.S. (ed.): *Neuro-ophthalmology.* Harper & Row, New York, 1978, Chapter 10.

61. DAYLA, V.S., CHAIT, G.E., AND FENTON, S.S.A.: *Gentamicin vestibulotoxicity. Long term disability.* Ann. Otol. Rhinol. Laryngol. 88:36–39, 1979.

62. DEFEUDIS, F.V.: "Cholinergic roles in consciousness." In DeFeudis, F.V. (ed.): *Central Cholinergic Systems and Behaviour.* Academic Press, London, 1974, pp. 7–32.

63. DEMENT, W., AND KLEITMAN, N.: *Cyclic variations in EEG during sleep and their relation to eye movements, body motility and dreaming.* Electroencephalogr. Clin. Neurophysiol. 9:673–690, 1957.

64. DENNY-BROWN, D.E.: *The Basal Ganglia and Their Relation to Disorders of Movement.* Oxford University Press, London, 1962.

65. DIMANT, J., AND GROB, D.: *Electrocardiographic changes and myocardial damage in patients with acute cerebrovascular accidents.* Stroke 8:448–455, 1977.

66. DINSDALE, H.B.: *Spontaneous hemorrhage in the posterior fossa.* Arch. Neurol. 10:200–217, 1964.

67. DOMINO, E.F., DREN, A.T., AND YAMAMOTO, K.I.: *Pharmacologic evidence for cholinergic mechanisms in neocortical and limbic activating systems.* Prog. Brain Res. 27:337–364, 1967.

68. DOUGHERTY, J.H., JR., RAWLINSON, D., LEVY, D.E., ET AL.: *Hypoxic-ischemic brain injury and the vegetative state. Clinical and neuro-pathologic correlation.* Neurology 29:591, 1979.

69. DUCKER, T.B.: *Increased intracranial pressure and pulmonary edema. Part I: Clinical study of 11 patients.* J. Neurosurg. 28:112–117, 1968.

70. DUFFY, T.E., AND PLUM, F.: "Seizures, coma and major metabolic encephalopathies and comatose states." In Siegal, G.J., Albers, R.W., Katzman, R., et al. (eds.): Basic Neurochemistry, ed. 3. Little, Brown and Company, Boston, 1980.

71. ECCLES, J.C. (ed.): *Brain and Conscious Experience.* Springer Publishing Co., Inc., New York, 1966.

72. EDELMAN, G.M., AND MOUNTCASTLE, V.B.: *The Mindful Brain.* MIT Press, Cambridge, Massachusetts, 1978.

73. ELLENBERGER, M.A.J.C., AND NETSKY, M.G.: *Anatomic basis and diagnostic value of opsoclonus.* Arch. Ophthalmol. 83:307–310, 1970.

74. ELSCHNIG, A.: *Nystagmus retractorius: ein cerebralis Herdsymptom.* Med. Klin. 9:8–11, 1913.

75. ENDO, H., LARSEN, B., AND LASSEN, N.A.: *Regional cerebral blood flow alterations remote from the site of intracranial tumors.* J. Neurosurg. 46:270–281, 1977.

76. ENGEL, J. JR., LUDWIG, B.I., AND FETELL, M.: *Prolonged partial complex status epilepticus: EEG and behavioral observations.* Neurology 28:863–369, 1978.

77. ESTANBUL, B.V., LOYO, M.V., MATEOS, J.H., ET AL.: *Cardiac arrhythmias in experimental subarachnoid hemorrhage.* Stroke 8:440–447, 1977.

78. FARIS, A.A.: *Limbic system infarction. A report of two cases.* Neurology 19:91–96, 1969.

79. FELDMAN, M.H.: *Physiological observations in a chronic case of locked-in syndrome.* Neurology 21:459–478, 1971.

80. FELDMAN, M.H.: *The decerebrate state in the primate. 1. Studies in monkeys.* Arch. Neurol. 25:501–516, 1971.

81. FELDMAN, M.H., AND SAHRMANN, S.: *The decerebrate state in the primate. 2. Studies in man.* Arch. Neurol. 25:517–525, 1971.

82. FELDMAN, S.M., AND WALLER, H.J.: *Dissociation of electrocortical activation and behavioral arousal.* Nature 196:1320–1322, 1962.

83. FISCHER, J.J.: *The Labyrinth-Physiology and Functional Tests.* Grune and Stratton, New York, 1956.

84. FISHER, C.M.: *Ocular bobbing.* Arch. Neurol. 11:543–546, 1964.

85. FISHER, C.M.: *Some neuro-ophthalmological observations.* J. Neurol. Neurosurg. Psychiatry 30:383–392, 1967.

86. FISHER, C.M.: *The neurological examination of the comatose patient.* Acta Neurol. Scand. 45 (Suppl. 36):1–56, 1969.

87. FLUUR, E.: *Influences of semicircular ducts on extraocular muscles.* Acta Otolaryngol. Suppl. 149, 1959.

88. FORD, F.R., AND WALSH, F.B.: *Tonic deviations of the eyes produced by movements of the head.* Arch. Ophthalmol. 23:1274–1284, 1940.

89. FREDRICKSON, J.M., SCHWARZ, D., AND KORNHUBER, H.H.: *Convergence and interaction of vestibular and deep somatic afferents upon neurons in the vestibular nuclei of the cat.* Acta Otolaryngol. 61:168–188, 1966.

90. FREEMON, F.R.: *Akinetic mutism and bilateral anterior cerebral artery occlusion.* J. Neurol. Neurosurg. Psychiatry 34:693–697, 1971.

91. FULTON, J.F., AND BAILEY, P.: *Tumors in the region of the third ventricle: their diagnosis and relation to pathological sleep.* J. Nerv. Ment. Dis. 69:1–25, 145–164, 261–277, 1929.

92. GAMPER, E.: *Bau und leistungen eines menschlichen mittelhirnwesens (arhinencephalie mit encephalocele)*. Z. Ges. Neurol. Psychiat. 102:154–235, 1926.

93. GAMPER, E.: *Bau und leistungen eines menschlichen mittelhirnwesens (arhinencephalie mit encephalocele) zugleich ein beitrag zur teratologie und fasersytematik*. Z. Ges. Neurol. Psychiat. 104: 49–120, 1926.

94. GAREY, I.J., JONES, E.G., AND POWELL, T.P.S.: *Interrelationships of striate and extra-striate cortex with the primary relay sites of the visual pathway*. J. Neurol. Neurosurg. Psychiatry 31:135–157, 1968.

95. GAYET, M.: *Affection encephalique (encephalite diffuse probable)*. Arch. Physiol. Norm. Path. 2^e ser 2:341–351, 1875.

96. GAZZANIGA, M.S., AND LeDOUX, J.E.,: *The Integrated Mind*. Plenum Press, New York, 1978.

97. GERNANDT, B.E.: *Response of mammalian vestibular neurons to horizontal rotation and caloric stimulation*. J. Neurophysiol. 12:173–184, 1949.

98. GRAYBIEL, A.M.: *Direct and indirect preoculomotor pathways of the brainstem: an autoradiographic study of the pontine reticular formation of the cat*. J. Comp. Neurol. 175:37–78, 1977.

99. GREENBERG, R.P., BECKER, D.P., MILLER, J.D., ET AL.: *Evaluation of brain function in severe human head trauma with multimodality evoked potentials. Part II: Localization of brain dysfunction and correlation with posttraumatic neurological conditions*. J. Neurosurg. 47:163–177, 1977.

100. GREENBERG, R.P., MAYER, D.J., BECKER, D.P., ET AL.: *Evaluation of brain function in severe human head trauma with multi-modality evoked potentials. Part I: Evoked brain-injury potentials, methods and analysis*. J. Neurosurg. 47:150–162, 1977.

101. GRINDAL, A.B., SUTER, C., AND MARTINEZ, A.J.: *Alpha-pattern coma: 24 cases with 9 survivors*. Ann. Neurol. 1:371–377, 1977.

102. HALMAGYI, G.M., EVANS, W.A., AND HALLINAN, J.M.: *Failure of downward gaze*. Arch. Neurol. 35:22–26, 1978.

103. HATCHER, M.A., JR., AND KLINTWORTH, G.K.: *The sylvian aqueduct syndrome. A clinicopathologic study*. Arch. Neurol. 15:215–222, 1966.

104. HAWKES, C.H.: *"Locked-in" syndrome: report of seven cases*. Br. Med. J. 4:379–382, 1974.

105. HECAEN, H., AND ALBERT, M.L.: *Human Neuropsychology*. John Wiley, New York, 1978.

106. HESS, R. JR., KOELLA, W.P., AND AKERT, K.: *Cortical and subcortical recordings in natural and artificially induced sleep in cats*. Electroencephalogr. Clin. Neurophysiol. 5:75–90, 1953.

107. HESS, W.R.: *The Functional Organization of the Diencephalon*. Grune & Stratton, New York, 1957.

108. HOLMES, G.: *The cerebral integration of the ocular movements*. Br. Med. J. 2:107–112, 1938.

109. HOYT, W.F., AND DAROFF, R.B.: *"Supranuclear disorders of ocular control systems in man."* In Bach-y-Rita, P., Collins, C., and Hyde, J.E. (eds.): *The Control of Eye Movements*. Academic Press, New York, 1971.

110. HUBEL, D.H., AND WIESEL, T.N.: *Sequence regularity and geometry of orientation columns in the monkey striate cortex*. J. Comp. Neurol. 158:267–294, 1974.

111. HUGHES, J.R.: *"Limitations of the EEG in coma and brain death."* In Korein, S. (ed.): *Brain Death: Interrelated Medical and Social Issues*. Ann. N.Y. Acad. Sci. 315:121–136, 1978.

112. INGVAR, D.H., BRUN, A., JOHANSSON, L., ET AL.: *"Survival after severe cerebral anoxia with destruction of the cerebral cortex; the apallic syndrome."* In Korein, J. (ed.): *Brain Death: Interrelated Medical and Social Issues*. Ann. N.Y. Acad. Sci. 315:184–214, 1978.

113. INGVAR, D.H., AND SOURANDER, P.: *Destruction of the reticular core of the brain stem. A pathoanatomical follow-up of a case of coma of three years' duration*. Arch. Neurol. 23:1–8, 1970.

114. IRAGUI-MADOZ, V.J., AND WIEDERHOLT, W.C.: *Far-field somatosensory evoked potentials in the cat*. Electroencephalogr. Clin. Neurophysiol. 43:646–657, 1977.

115. IVERSON, L.L.: *"The uptake, storage, release, and metabolism of GABA in inhibitory nerves."* In Snyder, S.H. (ed.): *Perspectives in Neuropharmacology*. Oxford University Press, New York, 1972, pp. 75–111.

116. JACKSON, J.H., *Selected writings of John Hughlings Jackson*, J. Taylor (ed.). Basic Books, New York 1958, vol. 2.

78

117. JACOBS, L., ANDERSON, P.J., BENDER, M.B.: *The lesions producing paralysis of downward but not upward gaze.* Arch. Neurol. 28:319-323, 1973.

118. JAMPEL, R.S.: *Convergence, divergence, pupillary reactions and accommodations of the eye from faradic stimulation of the macaque brain.* J. Comp. Neurol. 115:371-399, 1960.

119. JASPER, H.H., PROCTOR, L.D., KNIGHTON, R.S., ET AL. (eds.): *Reticular Formation of the Brain.* Little, Brown and Co., Boston, 1958.

120. JEFFERSON, G.: *The nature of concussion.* Br. Med. J. 1:1-15, 1944.

121. JEFFERSON, G.: "The reticular formation and clinical neurology." In Jasper, H.H., et al. (eds.): *Reticular Formation of the Brain.* Little, Brown and Co., Boston, 1958, Chapter 36, pp. 729-738.

122. JELLINGER, K., AND SEITELBERGER, F.: *Protracted post-traumatic encephalopathy. Pathology, pathogenesis and clinical implications.* J. Neurol. Sci. 10:51-94, 1970.

123. JENNETT, W.B., AND PLUM, F.: *The persistent vegetative state: a syndrome in search of a name.* Lancet 1:734-737, 1972.

124. JENNETT, W.B., AND TEASDALE, G.,: Aspects of coma after severe head injury. Lancet 1:878-881, 1977.

125. JEWETT, D.L., ROMANO, M.N., AND WILLISTON, J.S.: *Human auditory evoked potentials; possible brain stem components detected on the scalp.* Science 167:1517-1518, 1970.

126. JOHNSON, H.C., AND WALKER, A.E.: *The angiographic diagnosis of spontaneous thrombosis of the internal and common carotid arteries.* J. Neurosurg. 8:631-659, 1951.

127. JOHNSTON, M.V., McKINNEY, M., COYLE, J.T.: *Evidence for a cholinergic projection to new cortex from neurons in basal forebrain.* Proc. Natl. Acad. Sci. 76:5392-5396, 1979.

128. JONES, B.E., AND MOORE, R.V.: Ascending projections of the locus coeruleus in the rat. II. Autoradiographic study. Brain Res. 127:23-53, 1977.

129. JONES, E.G., AND POWELL, T.P.S.: *An anatomical study of converging sensory pathways within the cerebral cortex of the monkey.* Brain 93:793-820, 1970.

130. JORDANOV, J., AND RUBEN, H.: *Reliability of pupillary changes as a clinical sign of hypoxia.* Lancet 2:915-917, 1967.

131. JOUVET, M.: *The role of monoamines and acetylcholine containing neurons in the regulation of the sleep-wake cycle.* Rev. Physiol. (Ergeb. Physiol.) 64:166-307, 1972.

132. KAPP, J., AND PAULSON, G.: *Pupillary changes induced by circulatory arrest.* Neurology 16:225-229, 1966.

133. KARP, J.S., AND HURTIG, H.I.: *"Locked-in" state with bilateral midbrain infarcts.* Arch. Neurol. 30:176-178, 1974.

134. KARPLUS, J.P., AND KREIDL, A.: *Gehrin und sympathicus. I. Zwischenhirnbasis und halssympathicus.* Pfluegers Arch. Ges. Phsyiol. 129:138-144, 1909.

135. KATZMAN, R., TERRY, R.D., AND BICK, K.L. (eds.): *Alzheimer's Disease: Senile Dementia and Related Disorders.* Raven, New York, 1978.

136. KAWAMURA, H., AND DOMINO, E.F.: *Differential actions of m and n cholinergic agonists on the brainstem activating system.* Int. J. Neuropharmacol. 8:105-117, 1969.

137. KEANE, J.R.: *Contralateral gaze deviation with supratentorial hemorrhage. Three pathologically verified cases.* Arch. Neurol. 32:119-122, 1975.

138. KEANE, J.R.: *Spastic eyelids. Failure of levator inhibition in unconscious states.* Arch. Neurol. 32:695-698, 1975.

139. KEANE, J.R.: *Intermittent see-saw eye movements. Report of a patient in coma after hyperextension head injury.* Arch. Neurol. 34:173-174, 1978.

140. KEANE, J.R., RAWLINSON, D.G., LU, A.T.: *Sustained downward deviation. Two cases without structural pretectal lesions.* Neurology 26:594-595, 1976.

141. KEMPER, T.L., AND ROMANUL, F.C.A.: *State resembling akinetic mutism in basilar artery occlusion.* Neurology 17:74-80, 1967.

142. KENNARD, M.: *The cingulate gyrus in relation to consciousness.* J. Nerv. Ment. Dis. 121:34-39, 1955.

143. KERR, F.W.L., AND HOLLOWELL, O.W.: *Location of pupillomotor and accommodation fibres in the oculomotor nerve: experimental observations on paralytic mydriasis.* J. Neurol. Neurosurg. Psychiat. 27:473-481, 1964.

144. KETY, S.S., EVARTS, E.V., AND WILLIAMS, H.L. (eds.): *Sleep and Altered States of Consciousness.* Res. Publ. Assoc. Nerv. Ment. Dis. Proc. vol. 45, 1967.

145. KIM, K.S., HEMMATI, M., WEINBERG, P.E.: *Computed tomography in isodense subdural hematoma.* Radiology 128:71–74, 1978.

146. KING, W.M., LISBERGER, S.G., AND FUCHS, A.F.: *Response of fibers in medial longitudinal fasciculus (MLF) of alert monkeys during horizontal and vertical conjugate eye movements evoked by vestibular or visual stimuli.* J. Neurophysiol. 39:1135–1149, 1976.

147. KLEIST, K.: *Gegenhalten (motorischer negativismus) zwangreifen und thalamus opticus.* Monatsschr. Psychiat. Neurol. 65:317–396, 1927.

148. KOEBER, H.: *Trois observations de mouvements de rétraction de sulbe (Nystagmus retractorius).* Clinique Ophthal. p. 147. Abs. Jahresb. Ophthal. 34:683, 1903.

149. KOGURE, K., BUSTO, R., SCHEINBERG, P., ET AL.: *Energy metabolites and water content in rat brain during the early stage of development of cerebral infarction.* Brain 97:103–114, 1974.

150. KOREIN, J.: "Terminology, definitions and usage." In Korein, J. (ed.): *Brain Death: Interrelated Medical and Social Issues.* Ann. N.Y. Acad. Sci. 315:6–10, 1978.

151. KORNER, P.I.: *Integrative neural cardiovascular control.* Physiol. Rev. 51:312–367, 1971.

152. KRAYENBUHL, H., WYSS, O.A.M., AND YASARGIL, M.G.: *Bilateral thalamotomy and pallidotomy as treatment for bilateral parkinsonism.* J. Neurosurg. 18:429–444, 1961.

153. KRETSCHMER, E.: *Das apallische syndrom.* Z. Ges. Neurol. Psychiat. 169:576–579, 1940.

154. KRETTEK, J.E., AND PRICE, J.L.: *The cortical projections of the mediodorsal nucleus and adjacent thalamic nuclei in the rat.* J. Comp. Neurol. 171:157–192, 1977.

155. LANGE, L.S., AND LASZLO, G.: *Cerebral tumor presenting with hyperventilation.* J. Neurol. Neurosurg. Psychiatry 28:317–319, 1965.

156. LE DOUX, J.E., WILSON, D.H., AND GAZZANIGA, M.S.: *A divided mind: observations on the conscious properties of the separated hemispheres.* Ann. Neurol. 2:417–421, 1977.

157. LEIGH, R.J., AND SHAW, D.A.: *Rapid regular breathing in unconscious patients.* Arch. Neurol. 33:356–361, 1976.

158. LEONARD, C.M.: *The connections of the dorsomedial nuclei.* Brain Behav. Evol. 6:524–541, 1972.

159. LEVITT, P., AND MOORE, R.Y.: *Noradrenaline neuron innervation of the neocortex in the rat.* Brain Res. 139:219–232, 1978.

160. LEVY, D.E., KNILL-JONES, R.P., AND PLUM, F.: *The vegetative state and its prognosis following nontraumatic coma.* Ann. N.Y. Acad. Sci. 315:293–306, 1978.

161. LINDSLEY, D.B.: "Attention, consciousness, sleep and wakefulness." In Field, J., Magoun, H.W., and Hall, V.E. (eds.): *Handbook of Physiology.* Sect. I, Neurophysiology. American Physiological Society, Washington, D.C., 1960, vol. 3, Chapter 64.

162. LINDVALL, O., AND BJORKLUND, A.: *The organization of the ascending catecholamine neuron systems in the rat brain.* Acta Physiol. Scand. 412:1–48, 1974.

163. LIPOWSKI, Z.J.: *Organic brain syndromes: a reformulation.* Compr. Psychiatry 19:309–322, 1978.

164. LOEWENFELD, I.E.: "Mechanisms of reflex dilatation of the pupil. Historical review and experimental analysis." In von Bahr, G., ten Doesschate, J., Fischer-von Bunau, H., et al. (eds.): *Documenta Ophthalmologica, Advances in Ophthalmology,* vol. XII. Uitgeverij Dr. W. Junk, S-Gravenhage, 1958.

165. LOEWY, A.D.: "Neural regulation of the pupil." In Brooks, C.M., Koizumi, K., and Sato, A. (eds.): *Integrative Functions of the Autonomic Nervous System.* University of Tokyo Press, Tokyo, 1979.

166. LOEWY, A.D., ARAUJO, J.C., AND KERR, F.W.L.: *Pupillodilator pathways in the brain stem of the cat: anatomical and electrophysiological identification of a central autonomic pathway.* Brain Res. 60:65–91, 1973.

167. LOEWY, A.D., SAPER, C.B., AND YAMODIS, N.D.: *Re-evaluation of the efferent projections of the Edinger-Westphal nucleus in the cat.* Brain Res. 141:153–159, 1978.

168. LOURIE, H.: *Seesaw nystagmus.* Arch. Neurol. 9:531–533, 1963.

169. LUNDERWOLD, A.: "The EEG in patients with coma due to localized brain lesions." In Harner, R., and Naquet, R. (eds.): *Handbook of Electroencephalography and Clinical Neurophysiology,* vol. 12. Elsevier, Amsterdam, 1975, pp. 37–46.

80

170. LYNCH, J.C., MOUNTCASTLE, V.B., TALBOT, W.H., ET AL.: *Parietal lobe mechanism for directed visual attention.* J. Neurophysiol. 40:362–389, 1977.

171. MACCARIO, M., BACKMAN, J.R., AND KOREIN, J.: *Paradoxical caloric responses in altered states of consciousness. Clinical and EEG correlations in toxic metabolic encephalopathies.* Neurology 22:781–788, 1972.

172. MAGOUN, H.W.: *The Waking Brain,* ed. 2. Charles C Thomas, Springfield, Ill., 1963.

173. MANGOLD, R., SOKOLOFF, L., CONNER, E., ET AL.: *Effects of sleep and lack of sleep on cerebral circulation and metabolism of normal young men.* J. Clin. Invest. 34:1092–1100, 1955.

174. MARKAND, O.N., AND DYKEN, M.L.: *Sleep abnormalities in patients with brain stem lesions.* Neurology 26:769–776, 1976.

175. MASTAGLIA, F.L.: *See-saw nystagmus: an unusual sign of brain-stem infarction.* J. Neurol. Sci. 22:439–443, 1974.

176. MAUTHNER, L.: *Zur Pathologie und Physiologie des Schlafes nebst Bemerkungen ueber die "Nona,"* Wien. Klin. Wochenschr. 40:961, 1001, 1049, 1092, 1144, 1185; 1890.

177. MAZZARA, J.T., AYRES, S.M., AND GRACE, W.J.: *Extreme hypocapnia in the critically ill patient.* Am. J. Med. 56:450–456, 1974.

178. Medical Research Council, Brain Injuries Committee: *A glossary of psychological terms commonly used in cases of head injury.* Medical Research Council War Memorandum #4 HMSO, London, 1941.

179. MELAMED, E., LAVY, S., PORTNOY, Z., ET AL.: *Correlation between regional cerebral blood flow and EEG frequency in the contralateral hemisphere in acute cerebral infarction.* J. Neurol. Sci. 26:21–27, 1975.

180. MESSERT, B., HENKE, T.K., AND LANGHEIM, W.: *Syndrome of akinetic mutism associated with obstructive hydrocephalus.* Neurology 16:635–649, 1966.

181. MILLS, R.P., AND SWANSON, P.D.: *Vertical oculomotor apraxia and memory loss.* Ann. Neurol. 4:149–153, 1978.

182. MILNER, B.: "Hemispheric specialization: scope and limits." In Schmitt, F.O., and Worden, F.G. (eds.): *The Neurosciences Third Study Program.* MIT Press, Cambridge, Mass., 1974, pp. 75–89.

183. MLADINICH, E.K., AND CARLOW, T.J.: *Total gaze paresis in amitriptyline overdose.* Neurology 27:695, 1977.

184. MOORE, R.Y., AND BLOOM, F.E.: *Central catecholamine systems: anatomy and physiology of the dopamine systems.* Ann. Rev. Neurosci. 1:129–169, 1978.

185. MOORE, R.Y., AND BLOOM, F.E.: *Central catecholamine neuron systems: anatomy and physiology of the norepinephrine and epinephrine systems.* Ann. Rev. Neurosci. 2:113–168, 1979.

186. MOORE, R.Y., HALARIS, A.E., AND JONES, B.E.: *Serotonin neurons of the midbrain raphe: ascending projections.* J. Comp. Neurol. 180:417–438, 1978.

187. MORISON, R.S., AND DEMPSEY, E.W.: *A study of thalamo-cortical relations.* Am. J. Physiol. 135:281–292, 1942.

188. MORUZZI, G.: *The sleep-waking cycle.* Rev. Physiol. (Ergeb. Physiol.) 64:1–165, 1972.

189. MORUZZI, G., AND MAGOUN, H.W.: *Brain stem reticular formation and activation of the EEG.* Electroencephalogr. Clin. Neurophysiol. 1:455–473, 1949.

190. MOUNTCASTLE, V.B.: "An organizing principle for cerebral function: the unit module and the distributed system." In Edelman, G.M., and Mountcastle, V.B. (eds.): *The Mindful Brain.* MIT Press, Cambridge, Massachusetts, 1978.

191. NATHANSON, M.: "Caloric responses in barbiturate coma." In Bender, M.B. (ed.): *The Oculomotor System.* Harper & Row, N.Y., 1964, pp. 484–487.

192. NAUTA, W.J.H.: *The problem of the frontal lobe: a reinterpretation.* J. Psychiatr. Res. 8:167–187, 1971.

193. NAUTA, W.J.H., AND KUYPERS, H.G.J.M.: "Some ascending pathways in the brainstem reticular formation." In Jasper, H.H., et al. (eds.): *Reticular Formation of the Brain.* Little, Brown and Company, Boston, 1958, Chapter 1, pp. 3–30.

194. NELSON, D.A., AND RAY, C.D.: *Respiratory arrest from seizure discharges in limbic system.* Arch. Neurol. 19:199–207, 1968.

195. NELSON, J.R.: *The minimal ice water caloric test.* Neurology 19:577-585, 1969.

196. NEWMAN, N., GAY, A.J., HEILBRUN, M.P.: *Dysconjugate ocular bobbing. Its relation to midbrain, pontine and medullary function in a surviving patient.* Neurology 21:633-637, 1971.

197. NEWSOM DAVIS, J.: *An experimental study of hiccup.* Brain 93:861-872, 1970.

198. NIELSEN, J.M., AND JACOBS, L.L.: *Bilateral lesions of the anterior cingulate gyri.* Bull. Los Angeles Neurol. Soc. 16:231-234, 1951.

199. NORDGREN, R.E., MARKESBERY, W.R., FUKUDA, K., ET AL.: *Seven cases of cerebral medullary disconnexion: the "locked-in syndrome."* Neurology 21:1140-1148, 1971.

200. NORIEGA-SANCHEZ, A., MARTINEZ-MALDONADO, M., AND HAIFFE, R.M.: *Clinical and electroencephalographic changes in progressive uremic encephalopathy.* Neurology 28:667-669, 1978.

201. NORTH, J.B., AND JENNETT, S.: *Abnormal breathing patterns associated with acute brain damage.* Arch. Neurol. 31:338-344, 1974.

202. OBRADOR, S., SUAREZ-REINOSO, F., CARBONELL, J., ET AL.: *Comatose state maintained during eight years following a vascular ponto-mesencephalic lesion.* Electroencephalogr. Clin. Neurophysiol. 38:21-26, 1975.

203. OBRECHT, R., OKHOMINA, F.O.A., AND SCOTT, D.F.: *Value of EEG in acute confusional states.* J. Neurol. Neurosurg. Psychiatry 42:75-77, 1979.

204. O'DOHERTY, D.S., AND GREEN, J.B.: *Diagnostic value of Horner's syndrome in thrombosis of the carotid artery.* Neurology 8:842-845, 1958.

205. OLDENDORF, W.H.: *The quest for an image of brain: a brief historical and technical review of brain imaging techniques.* Neurology 28:517-533, 1978.

206. OLSZEWSKI, J., AND BAXTER, D.: *Cytoarchitecture of the Human Brain Stem.* J. B. Lippincott Co., Philadelphia, 1954.

207. ORTH, D.N., ALMEIDA, H., WALSH, F.B., ET AL.: *Ophthalmoplegia resulting from diphenylhydantoin and primidone intoxication. Report of four cases.* J.A.M.A. 201:225-227, 1967.

208. OSBORN, A.G.: *Diagnosis of descending transtentorial herniation by cranial computed tomography.* Radiology 123:93-96, 1977.

209. OSBORN, A.G., HEASTON, D.K., AND WING, S.G.: *Diagnosis of ascending transtentorial herniation by cranial computed tomography.* A.J.R. 130:755-760, 1978.

210. PANT, S.S., BENTON, J.W., AND DODGE, P.R.: *Unilateral pupillary dilatation during and immediately following seizures.* Neurology 16:837-840, 1966.

211. PASIK, P., AND PASIK, T.: "Oculomotor functions in monkeys with lesions of the cerebrum and superior colliculi." In Bender, M.B. (ed.): *The Oculomotor System.* Harper & Row, New York, 1964, Chapter 3, pp. 40-80.

212. PASIK, P., PASIK, T., AND BENDER, M.B.: *The prectectal syndrome in monkeys. I. Disturbances of gaze and body posture. II. Spontaneous and induced nystagmus, and "lightning" eye movements.* Brain 92:521-534, 871-884, 1969.

213. PAULSON, G.W.: "The neurological examination in dementia." In Wells, C.E. (ed.): *Dementia,* ed. 2. F. A. Davis Co., Philadelphia, 1977, Chapter 8, pp. 169-188.

214. PEDERSEN, E.: *Studies on the central pathway of the flexion reflex in man and animal, and changes in the reflex threshold and the circulation after spinal transection.* Acta Psychiatr. Neurol. Scand. Suppl. 88, 1954.

215. PENFIELD, W., AND JASPER, H.: *Epilepsy and the Functional Anatomy of the Human Brain.* Little, Brown and Co., Boston, 1954.

216. PENFIELD, W., AND RASMUSSEN, T.: *The Cerebral Cortex of Man.* Macmillan, New York, 1950.

217. PENN, R.D., WALSER, R., AND ACKERMAN, L.: *Cerebral blood volume in man. Computer analysis of a computerized brain scan.* J.A.M.A. 234:1154-1155, 1975.

218. PERCHERON, G.: *The anatomy of the arterial supply of the human thalamus and its use for the interpretation of thalamic vascular pathology.* Z. Neurol. 205:1-13, 1973.

219. PERCHERON, G.: *Les artères du thalamus humain. II. Artères et territoires thalamique paramédians de l'artère basilaire communicante.* Rev. Neurol. 132:309-324, 1976.

220. PLUM, F.: "Neurological integration of behavioural and metabolic control of breathing." In Porter, R. (ed.): *Ciba Foundation Symposium on Breathing: Hering-Breuer Centenary Symposium.* Churchill, London, 1970, pp. 159-181.

221. PLUM, F., AND LEIGH, R.J.: "Abnormalities of central respiratory mechanisms." In Lenfant, C., and Hornbein, T. (eds.): *Lung Biology in Health and Disease*, vol. 12, *Respiratory and Clinical Applications*. Marcel Dekker, New York. In press.

222. PLUM, F., POSNER, J.B., AND HAIN, R.F.: *Delayed neurological deterioration after anoxia.* Arch. Intern. Med. 110:18–25, 1962.

223. PLUM, F., AND SWANSON, A.G.: *Central neurogenic hyperventilation in man.* Arch. Neurol. Psychiatry 81:535–549, 1959.

224. POPPER, K.R., AND ECCLES, J.C.: *The Self and Its Brain.* Springer International, New York, 1977.

225. POSNER, J.B., AND PLUM, F.: *The toxic effects of carbon dioxide and acetazolamide in hepatic encephalopathy.* J. Clin. Invest. 39:1246–1258, 1960.

226. PRO, J.D., AND WELLS, C.E.: *The use of the electroencephalogram in the diagnosis of delirium.* Dis. Nerv. Syst. 38:804–808, 1977.

227. PURPURA, D.P.: "Operations and processes in thalamic and synaptically related neural subsystems." In Schmitt, F.O., (ed.): *The Neuroscience: Second Study Program.* Rockefeller University Press, New York, 1970, pp. 458–470.

228. RAKIC, P.: *Local Circuit Neurons.* MIT Press, Cambridge, Mass., 1977.

229. RAMON-MOLINER, E., AND NAUTA, W.J.H.: *The isodendritic core of the brainstem.* J. Comp. Neurol. 126:311–336, 1966.

230. RAPHAN, T., AND COHEN, B.: *Brainstem mechanisms for rapid and slow eye movements.* Ann. Rev. Physiol. 40:527–552, 1978.

231. RASMUSSEN, T., AND PENFIELD, W.: *Movement of head and eyes from stimulation of human frontal cortex.* Res. Publ. Assoc. Res. Nerv. Ment. Dis. 36:346–361, 1948.

232. REEVES, A.G., AND POSNER, J.B.: *The ciliospinal response in man.* Neurology 19:1145–1152, 1969.

233. REICHARDT, M.: *Hirnstamm und Psychiatrie.* Monatsschr. Psychiat. Neurol. 68:470–506, 1928. (Translation in J. Nerv. Ment. Dis. 70:390–396, 1929.)

234. REIS, D.J., AND DOBA, N.: *The central nervous system and neurogenic hypertension.* Prog. Cardiovasc. Dis. 17:51–71, 1974.

235. REIS, D.J., NATHAN, M.A., AND DOBA, N.: *Two specific brainstem systems which regulate the blood pressure.* Clin. Exp. Pharmacol. Physiol. Suppl. 2:179–183, 1975.

236. ROBINSON, D.A.: "Oculomotor control signals." In Lennerstrand, G., and Bach-y-Rita, P. (eds.): *Basic Mechanisms of Ocular Motility and their Clinical Implications.* Pergamon Press, New York, 1975, pp. 337–374.

237. ROMANO, J., AND ENGEL, G.L.: *Delirium: I. Electroencephalographic data.* Arch. Neurol. Psychiatry 51:356–377, 1944.

238. ROSADINI, G., AND ROSSI, G.F.: *On the suggested cerebral dominance for consciousness.* Brain 90:101–112, 1967.

239. ROSSI, G.F., AND ZANCHETTI, A.: *The brain stem reticular formation.* Arch. Ital. Biol. 95:199–235, 1957.

240. ROTTENBERG, D.A., PENTLOW, K.S., DECK, M.D.F., ET AL.: *Determination of ventricular volume following metrizamide CT ventriculography.* Neuroradiology 16:136–139, 1978.

241. SACHDEC, N.S., CARTER, C.C., SWANK, R.L., ET AL.: *Relationship between post-cardiotomy delirium, clinical neurological changes, and EEG abnormalities.* J. Thorac. Cardiovasc. Surg. 54:557, 1967.

242. SANO, K., SEKINO, H., TSUKAMATO, Y., ET AL.: *Stimulation and destruction of the region of the interstitial nucleus in cases of torticollis and see-saw nystagmus.* Confin. Neurol. 34:331–338, 1972.

243. SAPER, C.B., AND LOEWY, A.D.: *Efferent projections of the parabrachial nucleus.* Neurosci. Abstr. 4:24, 1978.

244. SAPER, C.B., LOEWY, A.D., SWANSON, L.W., ET AL.: *Direct hypothalamoautonomic connections.* Brain Res. 117:305–312, 1976.

245. SAPER, C.B., SWANSON, L.W., AND COWAN, W.M.: *The efferent connections of the ventromedial nucleus of the hypothalamus of the rat.* J. Comp. Neurol. 169:409–442, 1976.

246. SAPER, C.B., SWANSON, L.W., AND COWAN, W.M.: *The efferent connections of the anterior hypothalamic area of the rat, cat and monkey.* J. Comp. Neurol. 182:575–599, 1978.

247. SCHEIBEL, M.E., AND SCHEIBEL, A.B.: "Structural substrates for integrative patterns in the brainstem reticular core." In Jasper, H.H., et al. (eds.): *Reticular Formation of the Brain.* Little, Brown and Company, Boston, 1958, Chapter 2, pp. 31–55.

248. SCHEIBEL, M.E., AND SCHEIBEL, A.B.: *The organization of the nucleus reticularis thalami: a Golgi study.* Brain Res. 1:43–62, 1966.

249. SCHUSTER, P.: *Beitrage zur pathologie des thalamus opticus.* Arch. Psychiatr. Nervenkr. 105: 358–432, 550–662; 1936.

250. SCHWARTZ, B.: *Hemispheric dominance and consciousness.* Acta Neurol. Scand. 43:513–525, 1967.

251. SEGARRA, J.M.: *Cerebral vascular disease and behavior. I. The syndrome of the mesencephalic artery (basilar artery bifurcation).* Arch. Neurol. 22:408–418, 1970.

252. SERAFETINIDES, E.A., HOARE, R.D. AND DRIVER, M.V.: *Intracarotid sodium amylobarbitone and cerebral dominance for speech and consciousness.* Brain 88:107–130, 1965.

253. SEVERINGHAUS, J.W., AND MITCHELL, R.A.: *Ondine's curse—failure of respiratory center automaticity while asleep.* Clin. Res. 10:122, 1962.

254. SEYFFARTH, H., AND DENNY-BROWN, D.: *The grasp reflex and the instinctive grasp reaction.* Brain 71:109–183, 1948.

255. SHAHANI, B., BURROWS, P., AND WHITTY, C.W.M.: *The grasp reflex and perseveration.* Brain 93:181–192, 1970.

256. SHELDEN, W.D., PARKER, H.L., AND KERNOHAN, J.W.: *Occlusion of the aqueduct of Sylvius.* Arch. Neurol. Psychiatry 23:1183–1202, 1930.

257. SHERRINGTON, C.S.: *Cataleptoid reflexes in the monkey.* Proc. R. Soc. Lond. 60:411–414, 1897.

258. SHIMOJYO, S., SCHEINBERG, P., AND REINMUTH, O.: *Cerebral blood flow and metabolism in the Wernicke-Korsakoff syndrome.* J. Clin. Invest. 46:849–854, 1967.

259. SHUTE, C.C.D., AND LEWIS, P.R.: *The ascending cholinergic reticular system: neocortical, olfactory and subcortical projections.* Brain 90:497–520, 1967.

260. SILLITO, A.M., AND ZBROZYNA, A.W.: *The localization of pupilloconstrictor function within the mid-brain of the cat.* J. Physiol. 211:461–477, 1970.

261. SIMMONS, F.B.: *Patients with bilateral loss of caloric response.* Ann. Otol. Rhinol. Laryngol. 82: 1–4, 1973.

262. SIMMONS, R.L., MARTIN, A.M., HEISTERKAMP, C.A., ET AL.: *Respiratory insufficiency in combat casualties.* Ann. Surg. 170:39–62, 1969.

263. SIMON, R.P.: *Forced downward ocular deviation. Occurrence during oculovestibular testing in sedative drug-induced coma.* Arch. Neurol. 35:456–458, 1978.

264. SKINNER, J.E.: *Electrocortical desynchronization during functional blockade of the mesencephalic reticular formation.* Brain Res. 22:254–258, 1970.

265. SKULTETY, F.M.: *Clinical and experimental aspects of akinetic mutism. Report of a case.* Arch. Neurol. 19:1–14, 1968.

266. SLATER, R., REIVICH, M., GOLDBERG, H., ET AL.: *Diaschisis with cerebral infarction.* Stroke 8:684–690, 1977.

267. SMITH, J.L., AND COGAN, D.: *Internuclear ophthalmoplegia: a review of fifty-eight cases.* Arch. Ophthalmol. 61:687–694, 1959.

268. SMITH, J.L., AND DAVID, N.J.: *Internuclear ophthalmoplegia. Two new clinical signs.* Neurology 14:307–309, 1964.

269. SMITH, J.L., DAVID, N.J., AND KLINTWORTH, G.: *Skew deviation.* Neurology 14:96–105, 1964.

270. SMITH, S.E., SMITH, S.A., BROWN, P.M., ET AL.: *Pupillary signs in diabetic autonomic neuropathy.* Br. Med. J. 2:924–927, 1978.

271. SOUADJIAN, J.V., AND CAIN, J.C.: *Intractable hiccup. Etiologic factors in 220 cases.* Postgrad. Med. 43:72–77, 1938.

272. SPERRY, R.W.: "Lateral specialization in the surgically separated hemispheres." In Schmitt, F.O., and Worden, F.G. (eds.): *The Neurosciences Third Study Program.* MIT Press, Cambridge, Mass. 1974, pp. 5–19.

273. STARR, A.: *Auditory brain stem responses in brain death.* Brain 99:543–554, 1976.

274. STARR, A., AND HAMILTON, A.E.: *Correlation between confirmed sites of neurological lesions and abnormalities of far-field auditory brain stem responses.* Electroencephalogr. Clin. Neurophysiol. 41:595–608, 1976.

275. STEELE, J.C., RICHARDSON, J.C., AND OLSZEWSKI, J.: *Progressive supranuclear palsy.* Arch. Neurol. 10:333–359, 1964.

276. STOCKARD, J.J., AND ROSSITER, V.S.: *Clinical and pathologic correlates of brain stem auditory response abnormalities.* Neurology 27:316–325, 1977.

277. STOVRING, J.: *Descending tentorial herniation: findings on computed tomography.* Neuroradiology 14:101–105, 1977.

278. STRITCH, S.J.: *Diffuse degeneration of cerebral white matter in severe dementia following head injury.* J. Neurol. Neurosurg. Psychiatry 19:163–185, 1956.

279. SULLIVAN, K.N., MANFREDI, F., AND BEHNKE, R.H.: *Hippus in Cheyne-Strokes respiration. Observations in three patients with rhythmic respiratory and pupillary changes.* Arch. Int. Med. 122:116–121, 1968.

280. SUNDERLAND, S., AND BRADLEY, K.C.: *Disturbances of oculomotor function accompanying extradural haemorrhage.* J. Neurol. Neurosurg. Psychiatry 16:35–46, 1953.

281. SWANSON, L.W., AND COWAN, W.M.: "Autoradiographic studies of the development and connections of the septal area in the rat." In DeFrance, J.F. (ed.): *The Septal Nuclei.* Plenum Press, New York, 1976, pp. 37–63.

282. SWANSON, L.W., AND HARTMAN, B.K.: *The central adrenergic system. An immunofluorescence study of the location of cell bodies and their efferent connections in the rat utilizing dopamine-β hydroxylase as a marker.* J. Comp. Neurol. 163:467–506, 1975.

283. SZENTÁGOTHAI, J.: *The elementary vestibulo-ocular reflex arc.* J. Neurophysiol. 13:395–407, 1950.

284. SZENTÁGOTHAI, J.: "Pathways and synaptic articulation patterns connecting vestibular receptors and oculomotor nuclei." In Bender, M.B. (ed.): *The Oculomotor System.* Harper & Row, New York, 1964, Chapter 8.

285. TEASDALE, G., KNILL-JONES, R., AND VAN DER SANDE, J.: *Observer variability in assessing impaired consciousness and coma.* J. Neurol. Neurosurg. Psychiatry 41:603–610, 1978.

286. TEUBER, H.L.: *Unity and diversity of frontal lobe functions.* Acta Neurobiol. Exp. Neurobiol. 32:615–656, 1972.

287. THALER, H.T., FERBER, P.W., AND ROTTENBERG, D.A.: *A statistical method for determining the proportions of gray matter, white matter, and CSF using computed tomography.* Neuroradiology 16:133–135, 1978.

288. THOMPSON, H.S., NEWSOME, D.A., AND LOEWENFELD, I.E.: *The fixed dilated pupil. Sudden iridoplegia or mydriatic drops? A simple diagnostic test.* Arch. Ophthalmol. 86:21–27, 1971.

289. TOLMAN, K.G., AND COHEN, A.: *Accidental hypothermia.* Can. Med. Assoc. J. 103:1357–1361, 1970.

290. TOW, P.M., AND WHITTY, C.W.M.: *Personality changes after operations on the cingulate gyrus in man.* J. Neurol. Neurosurg. Psychiatry 16:186–193, 1953.

291. TRENCHARD, D., GARDNER, D., AND GUZ, A.: *Role of pulmonary vagal afferent nerve fibres in the development of rapid shallow breathing in lung inflammation.* Clin. Sci. 42:251–263, 1972.

292. TROOST, B.T., WEBER, R.B., AND DAROFF, R.B.: *Hemispheric control of eye movements. I. Quantitative analysis of refixation saccades in a hemispherectomy patient.* Arch. Neurol. 27:441–448, 1972.

293. TURAZZI, S., AND BRICOLO, A.: *Acute pontine syndromes following head injury.* Lancet 2:62–64, 1977.

294. TYSON, R.N.: *Simulation of cerebral death by succinylcholine sensitivity.* Arch. Neurol. 30:409–411, 1974.

295. VESTERHAUGE, S., AND PEITERSEN, E.: "Effects of some drugs on the caloric induced nystagmus." In Stahle, J. (ed.): *Advances in Oto-Rhino-Laryngology,* vol. 25. S. Karger, Basel, 1979, pp. 173–177.

296. VILLABLANCA, J.: *Electroencephalogram in the permanently isolated forebrain of the cat.* Science 133:44–46, 1962.

297. von Economo, C.: *Encephalitis Lethargica: Its Sequelae and Treatment.* Newman, K.O. (trans.) Oxford University Press, London, 1931.

298. von Glees, P., and Bailey, R.A.: *Schichtung und fasergrosse des tractus spino-thalamicus des menschen.* Monatsschr. Psychiat. Neurol. 122:129–141, 1951.

299. Walsh, F.B., and Hoyt, W.F.: *Clinical Neuro-ophthalmology,* vol. 1, ed. 3. Williams and Wilkins Co., Baltimore, 1969.

300. Wells, C.E. (ed.): *Dementia,* ed. 2. F. A. Davis Co., Philadelphia, 1977.

301. Westmoreland, B.F., Klass, D.W., Sharborough, F.W., et al.: *Alpha coma. Electroencephalographic, clinical, pathologic and etiologic correlations.* Arch. Neurol. 32:713–718, 1975.

302. Wiederholt, W.C., and Iragui-Madoz, V.J.: *Far field somatosensory potentials in the rat.* Electroencephalogr. Clin. Neurophysiol. 42:456–465, 1977.

303. Wilkus, R.J., Harvey, F., Ojemann, L.M., et al.: *Electroencephalogram and sensory evoked potentials. Findings in an unresponsive patient with pontine infarct.* Arch. Neurol. 24:538–544, 1971.

304. Wilson, S.A.K.: *Epileptic variants.* J. Neurol. Psychopath. 8:223–240, 1928.

305. Woolsey, T.A., and Vanderloos, H.: *The structural organization of layer IV in the somatosensory region (S_1) of mouse cerebral cortex: the description of a cortical field composed of discrete cytoarchitectonic units.* Brain Res. 17:205–242, 1970.

306. Yin, T.C.T., and Mountcastle, V.B.: *Visual input to the visuomotor mechanisms of the monkey's parietal lobe.* Science 197:1381–1383, 1977.

307. Yingling, C.D., and Skinner, J.E.: *Regulation of unit activity in nucleus reticularis thalami by the mesencephalic reticular formation and the frontal granular cortex.* Electroencephalogr. Clin. Neurophysiol. 39:635–642, 1975.

308. Zee, D.S., Griffin, J., and Price, D.L.: *Unilateral pupillary dilatation during adversive seizures.* Arch. Neurol. 30:403–405, 1974.

309. Zee, D.S., Yee, R.D., Cogan, D.G., et al.: *Ocular motor abnormalities in hereditary cerebellar ataxia.* Brain 99:207–234, 1976.

310. Avanzini, G., Girotti, F., Crenna, P., et al.: *Alterations of ocular motility in cerebellar pathology. An electrooculographic study.* Arch. Neurol. 36:274–280, 1979.

311. Barnes, G.R., and Forbat, L.N.: *Cervical and vestibular afferent control of oculomotor response in man.* Acta Otolaryngol. 88:79–87, 1979.

312. Cherniack, N.S., von Euler, C., Homma, I. et al.: *Experimentally induced Cheyne-Strokes breathing.* Respir. Physiol. 37:185–200, 1979.

313. Estanol, B., Romero, R., and Corvera, J.: *Effects of cerebellectomy on eye movements in man.* Arch. Neurol. 36:281–284, 1979.

314. Keane, J.R.: *Blinking to sudden illumination. A brain stem reflex present in neocortical death.* Arch. Neurol. 36:52–53, 1979.

315. Keane, J.R.: *Oculosympathetic paresis. Analysis of 100 hospitalized patients.* Arch. Neurol. 36:13–15, 1979.

316. Kompf, D., Pasik, T., Pasik, P., et al.: *Downward gaze in monkeys: stimulation and lesion studies.* Brain 102:527–558, 1979.

317. Meienberg, O., Mumenthaler, M., and Karbowski, K.: *Quadriparesis and nuclear oculomotor palsy with total bilateral ptosis mimicking coma. A mesencephalic "locked-in syndrome"?* Arch. Neurol. 36:708–710, 1979.

318. Noda, H., and Suzuki, D.A.: *The role of the flocculus of the monkey in saccadic eye movements.* J. Physiol. 294:317–334, 1979.

319. Noda, H., and Suzuki, D.A.: *The role of the flocculus of the monkey in fixation and smooth pursuit eye movements.* J. Physiol. 294:335–348, 1979.

320. Noda, H., and Suzuki, D.A.: *Processing of eye movement signals in the flocculus of the monkey.* J. Physiol. 294:349–364, 1979.

321. Ochs, A.L., Stark, L., Hoyt, W.F., et al.: *Opposed adducting saccades in convergence-retraction nystagmus: a patient with Sylvian aqueduct syndrome.* Brain 102:497–508, 1979.

322. Schepelmann, F.: *Human motor activity in decerebrate states and their sequelae.* Acta Neurochirurgica 46:185–217, 1979.

323. Stewart, J.D., Kirkham, T.H., and Mathieson, G.: *Periodic alternating gaze.* Neurology 29:222–224, 1979.

CHAPTER 2

Supratentorial Lesions Causing Coma

Three types of supratentorial processes have been reported to cause loss of consciousness. (1) Lesions producing diffuse bilateral impairment of either the cortical mantle or its underlying white matter without abnormalities in the brainstem. Some of these can follow traumatic head injuries, as discussed in this chapter, but more often such diffuse lesions have a metabolic origin and are discussed in Chapter 4. (2) Bilateral subcortical destructive lesions ostensibly selectively involving rhinencephalic structures. As discussed below, these lesions probably extend to involve structures beyond the rhinencephalon as well, making it doubtful that abnormalities confined to the rhinencephalon cause coma. (3) Localized hemispheric mass and destructive lesions. *Hemispheric mass lesions* cause stupor or coma when they either encroach directly upon deep diencephalic structures or secondarily compress those structures in the process of transtentorial herniation. *Hemispheric destructive lesions* that cause stupor or coma usually are of an acute or subacute nature and bilaterally involve either the entire cerebrum (e.g., Patient 2–1) or the thalamic or hypothalamic activating systems. Most such destructive lesions are ischemic, although a few invasive tumors can produce coma by deep bilateral diencephalic involvement. As noted in Chapter 1 (p. 22), some workers also report examples of coma with acute left hemisphere lesions damaging language centers, but proof that this is due to unilateral hemispheric damage has not been verified by autopsy.

RHINENCEPHALIC AND SUBCORTICAL DESTRUCTIVE LESIONS

Several workers have described patients in whom coma was associated with lesions of the corpora striata,[23] the cingulate gyri,[88] or the territorial distribution of the anterior cerebral arteries.[22] However, other patients with similar lesions have not been unconscious,[79] and a review of the available protocols of the unconscious patients suggests that in some of them metabolic or circulatory complications caused the coma, while in many of the others the pathologic changes were distributed more widely than was at first suspected or emphasized. An example of the latter is a patient in whom coma was attributed to bilateral infarction of the cingulate gyrus.[88] She had a cerebral hemorrhage above the cingulum and, while there certainly was cingulate gyrus damage, the accompanying illustration of a sagittal brain section shows downward displacement of the diencephalon consistent with tentorial coning. Another example is a patient in whom coma was ascribed to occlusion of the anterior cerebral artery proximal to the origin of Heubner's recurrent artery,[19] but the autopsy description indicated pathologic changes considerably beyond the usual territorial distribution of this vessel. Thus, it appears unlikely that restricted rhinencephalic or subcortical hemispheral destructive lesions cause coma, although acute, large, bilateral frontal-medial destruction does appear capable of producing such apathy (abulia) that the patient neither speaks nor moves spontaneously and appears similar to a patient with akinetic mutism.

EFFECTS OF SUPRATENTORIAL MASS LESIONS

Clinicopathologic correlations repeatedly have demonstrated that large, one-sided cortical and subcortical lesions of the cerebral hemispheres dampen total behavior and produce dull apathy, particularly when they involve the thalamoparietal sensory radiations. By and large, however, disease processes causing unilateral destruction confined to a single cerebral hemisphere, basal ganglia, or lateral thalamus do not cause coma unless their effects extend beyond these anatomical boundaries. The way that supratentorial mass lesions do produce coma is by enlarging sufficiently so that they displace adjacent and remote brain tissue. This displacement occurs across the midline to compress the other hemisphere (not usually symptomatic) or more importantly, moves in a caudal direction so as to compress and damage the deep diencephalic and midbrain structures that normally activate or arouse the cerebrum. Occasionally a supratentorial mass directly invades these deep structures; more often the mass evokes local and remote intracranial tissue reactions that secondarily displace the brain down toward the tentorial incisura, compressing the diencephalon, interfering with its blood supply, and, eventually, distorting the midbrain. To understand these processes requires a close knowledge of the anatomy and physiology of the intracranial compartments.

Anatomy of the Intracranial Compartments

The dural and meningeal supporting structures have a negligible volume. The remaining intracranial contents are divided approximately as follows: brain (of which 77 percent is water) 87 percent, blood 4 percent, and cerebrospinal fluid 9 percent. Since the intracranial volume is essentially constant, a new mass must develop and enlarge at the expense of an existing component.

Several factors limit the brain's ability to adjust to a space-occupying mass. The skull is inelastic and allows for only minimal expansion through the foramen magnum and the smaller foramina that transmit blood vessels and nerves. Furthermore, supporting septa that divide the intracranial cavity into fossae normally protect the brain against excessive movement, but limit the amount of compensatory shift and displacement that can develop in response to abnormal conditions.

The tentorium cerebelli divides the cranial vault into anterior and posterior fossae (Fig. 14). This inflexible fibrous dural lamina extends posteriorly from the petrous ridges and anterior clinoid processes, sloping downward and outward from its medial edge to attach laterally to the occipital bone along the line of the lateral sinus. Posteriorly, the tentorium slopes down to attach to the internal occipital protuberance. Extending posteriorly into the center of the tentorium from the posterior clinoid processes is a large semioval opening, the incisura or tentorial notch, whose diameters are usually between 50 and 70 mm. in the frontooccipital axis and 25 and 40 mm. on the interparietal axis. [31,50,124]

The temporal lobes rest on the tentorial incisura, and their medial surfaces slightly overhang it so that ordinarily 3 to 4 mm. of the medial-anterior part of the temporal uncus bulges into the notch. A small crescent of the hippocampal gyrus also overhangs the edge and becomes more narrow posteriorly. At postmortem

88

examinations, the uncus normally contains a visible, shallow, 1- to 2-mm. groove marking its tentorial edge. In pathologic herniations this groove deepens and extends back over the hippocampal gyrus as well (Fig. 15).

Changes in the relationships between the tentorial incisura and the neurovascular structures that surround it explain most of the complications and many of the symptoms of supratentorial mass lesions producing coma. The midbrain occupies the anterior portion of the tentorial notch (Fig. 14). The important anatomic relationships of the midbrain are those to the arteries, the third nerves, and the cisterns, whose size varies considerably among different individuals. The cerebellum is closely apposed to the dorsum of the midbrain and fills the posterior part of the notch. Ventral to the brainstem lies the basilar artery, which splits into the two diverging posterior cerebral arteries just below the tentorial incisura. Each posterior cerebral artery crosses the oculomotor nerve that emerges caudal to it. The artery then circles around the homolateral cerebral peduncle and the adjacent lateral midbrain and reaches the ventral surface of the hippocampal gyrus of the temporal lobe, where it crosses the tentorial edge and proceeds toward the occipital lobe. Another important vascular structure in this region is the anterior choroidal artery, which branches directly from the internal carotid artery and runs in a narrow space between the dentate gyrus of the temporal lobe and the free lateral margin of the tentorium, over which it is sometimes displaced by masses pressing the temporal lobe downward.

The oculomotor nerves emerge from the medial-basal surface of each cerebral peduncle just caudal to the tentorium. They proceed across the basal cistern (or tentorial gap, as Sunderland[124] calls it), first passing between the superior cerebellar (below the nerve) and posterior cerebral (above the nerve) arteries. These nerves then lie adjacent to each temporal lobe uncus at the point where this structure overhangs the lateral incisural edge. Each nerve passes over the homolateral petroclinoid ligament just lateral to the posterior clinoid process, and enters the cavernous sinus. The trochlear nerve is clinically unimportant, being protected on the under surface of the tentorium. The abducens nerve is infratentorial and becomes impaired by supratentorial lesions only when progressive herniation displaces the entire brainstem downward, stretching the nerve.

The foramen magnum is another potential site for intracranial herniation. Here the medulla, the cerebellum, and the vertebral arteries are juxtaposed, and their normal relationships to one another often vary. Usually a small portion of the cerebellar tonsils protrudes into the aperture, and the inferior surface of the cerebellum is grooved against the foramen's posterior lip. Variations in the normal degree of grooving make it difficult to interpret cerebellar impaction or tonsillar herniation at the autopsy table unless changes are extensive.

Pathology and Pathologic Physiology

Recognition of the Importance of Tentorial Herniation

Many early investigators attempted to explain the mechanisms whereby supratentorial lesions produce stupor, coma, and other signs of widespread neurologic dysfunction. In the nineteenth century, Macewen,[71] Gowers,[40] Oppenheim,[92] and Déjerine[24] all cited coma with supratentorial lesions as a manifestation of widespread or rapid involvement of the cortical mantle. This view was largely supplanted during the first part of this century by Cushing's belief that the major

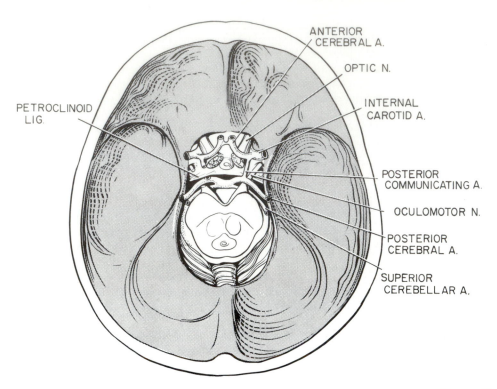

ANTERIOR
CEREBRAL A.

OPTIC N.

INTERNAL
CAROTID A.

PETROCLINOID
LIG.

POSTERIOR
COMMUNICATING A.

OCULOMOTOR N.

POSTERIOR
CEREBRAL A.

SUPERIOR
CEREBELLAR A.

Figure 14. The floor of the anterior and middle fossae, illustrating the tentorial notch and how the third nerve passes between the posterior cerebral and superior cerebellar arteries and over the petroclinoid ligaments.

remote or indirect symptoms of cerebral compression were due to capillary anemia of the medulla oblongata.[20] Cushing, however, based many of his conclusions upon acute animal experiments in which he produced rapidly enlarging supratentorial masses.[21] Such acute expanding masses produce tissue shifts that tend to bypass intermediate brain segments and result in medullary dysfunction early in their course.[51,129] As models their effects resemble acute clinical conditions such as those produced by sudden intracerebral hemorrhage, but they are less useful in explaining the more common symptoms of patients harboring gradually enlarging supratentorial masses. Experimentally, when a mass lesion expands over minutes or hours, the Cushing reflex occurs at a critical volume of added intracranial mass and is independent of the rate at which that mass formed.[143] Most clinically occurring masses enlarge more slowly than do such experimentally produced lesions, however, and such patients almost always develop symptoms reflecting more rostral brainstem dysfunction before showing evidence of medullary failure.[74]

Understanding how supratentorial mass lesions cause coma and other signs of serious brainstem dysfunction in man has come as much from studies of postmortem pathology as from experimental physiology. Adolph Meyer,[78] in 1920, first called attention to temporal lobe herniation into the tentorial gap in cases of brain tumor. He wrote a sparse accompanying text and perhaps for that reason his contemporaries paid little attention to the tentorial notch. During the next decade, several observers reemphasized the earlier point made by Hutchinson[48] and Mace-

90

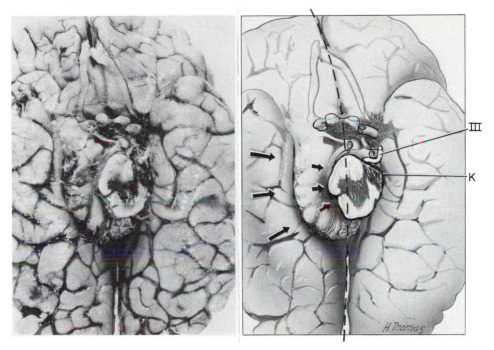

Figure 15. The under-surface of the forebrain in transtentorial herniation. Compare the positioning of the III nerve and the adjacent posterior cerebral artery, as well as the shape of the midbrain, with Figure 14. Large arrows point to the edge where the hippocampus herniated through the tentorium. Small arrows and the dotted line indicate the lateral shift of the mesencephalon, which produces a hemorrhagic Kernohan's notch at K.

wen[71] that the pupil may dilate on the same side as a cerebral mass because of pressure of the temporal lobe on the third nerve.

In 1929, Kernohan and Woltman[59] demonstrated grooving and histological change in the cerebral peduncle as it was compressed against the edge of the tentorium opposite to a supratentorial mass, thus explaining why some patients with brain tumor show paresis homolateral to the cerebral lesion (see Fig. 16). Thenceforth, attention turned increasingly to how changes at the tentorial region explained the remote and catastrophic effects of certain supratentorial masses. Spatz and Stroescu[121] in 1934 published detailed illustrations of the intracranial cisterns and how they were altered by various hernias, and 2 years later Vincent, David, and Thiebaut[134] related the development of anxiety, stiff neck, vasomotor troubles, and cardiac arrhythmias in patients with brain tumor to transtentorial herniation. Van Gehuchten[133] drew attention to the hemorrhages in the midbrain and the pons that sometimes accompany tentorial pressure cones. Both he and Vincent stressed that death might follow lumbar puncture in patients with tentorial herniation. This was the period during which much of the physiology of the hypothalamus in respiratory, circulatory, and thermal regulation was delineated. As a result, when Jefferson[50] in 1938 reviewed the problems of tentorial pressure cone, he cited four general signs that indicated its presence: (1) "vegetative storm"; (2) stiff neck; (3) bilateral motor signs (often decerebrate rigidity); and (4) a dilated pupil. Jefferson attributed death in these patients to subthalamic vegetative damage and pointed out that signs

91

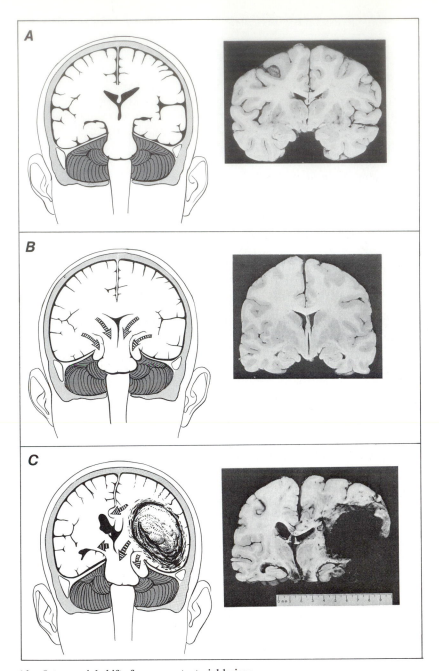

Figure 16. Intracranial shifts from supratentorial lesions.

  A, The relationships of the various supratentorial and intratentorial compartments as seen in a coronal section.

  B, Central transtentorial herniation. The photograph is taken from a patient with carcinoma of the lung and multiple cerebral metastases (none are apparent in this section) who died after developing signs and symptoms of the central syndrome of rostral-caudal deterioration (see text). The brain is swollen: the diencephalon is compressed and elongated, and the mammillary bodies lie far caudal to those in the normal brain. Neither the cingulate gyrus nor the uncus is herniated.

  C, Uncal and transtentorial herniation. The photograph is taken from a patient who developed a massive hemorrhagic infarct and who died after developing the syndrome of uncal herniation (see text). The cingulate gyrus is herniated under the falx; there is hemorrhagic infarction of the opposite cerebral peduncle, and marked swelling and grooving of the uncus on the side of the lesion. Central downward displacement is also present but is less marked than in the figure above.

of medullary failure are uncommon and, if present at all, are late manifestations of decompensating supratentorial masses.

Since Jefferson's paper it has generally been accepted that the dividing line between survival and death with supratentorial masses is whether or not irreversible tentorial herniation can be prevented. For this reason, a clear understanding of the mechanisms leading to this process and their accompanying symptoms becomes a major step in diagnosis and planning effective treatment.

Mechanical Factors Enhancing the Effects of Intracranial Masses

The pathologic tissue reactions surrounding all intracranial masses are qualitatively similar, whether the masses are neoplasms, infections, infarcts, hemorrhages, or foreign bodies. They include glial proliferation, dilatation and multiplication of blood vessels, invasion by histiocytic and inflammatory cells, and at least some edema of the adjacent brain. The histologic type of the lesion itself and the rate of its development modify these reactions: acute lesions such as bacterial abscesses, parenchymal hemorrhages, or metastatic tumors for reasons unknown evoke more edema and a brisker vascular and inflammatory response than do slow-growing lesions such as intracranial neoplasms that lie outside the brain. Sooner or later, however, nearly all masses enlarge so much, either through their own growth or by the edema added to their periphery, that the surrounding brain can no longer accommodate them. The expanding cerebral structures shift across the midline or downward toward the base of the brain; the sheer bulk of the shifting tissues compresses new regions, and these, in turn, begin to swell and shift. Eventually, the brain, thus progressively increased in volume, has no choice but to squeeze into the only available supratentorial exit, the tentorial notch.

Vascular Factors Influencing the Effects of Intracranial Lesions

Alteration or abolition of physiologic responses of the cerebral vascular bed contributes to the pathologic effects of intracranial injuries and masses. Cerebral arteries contain a muscular but not an elastic coat, and the vessel walls are generally thinner than systemic arteries. A rich adrenergic and cholinergic plexus sheathes the arteries at the base of the brain but thins out progressively as the vessels branch to supply the cortical mantle and the hemispheric parenchyma.[94,101] Cholinergic fibers appear to be limited to vessels at the base and those traversing the pial surface, but adrenergic fibers penetrate the cerebral parenchyma, in many areas accompanying the arterial bed all the way to the level of the capillaries and even the venules. Other peptide neurotransmitter systems also can be identified in the proximity of the vascular bed, but their function presently remains unexamined.

Present evidence indicates that the resistance and cross-sectional diameter of the cerebral arterial and arteriolar bed are governed predominantly by a combination of the metabolic demands of the local tissues and the intrinsic capacity of vascular smooth muscle to resume its resting length when rapidly stretched. Whether local neurogenic fibers in some way mediate the metabolic stimulus is unknown but seems improbable. More likely is that neurogenic effects exert mild tonic influences on the vascular contractility and provide rapid compensatory vasoconstriction or dilatation to sudden rises or falls in the systemic arterial pressure; perhaps neural influences also modify cerebral capillary permeability.[102]

Two major physiologic properties characterize the cerebral vascular bed. First, it is *autoregulated*, i.e., it intrinsically constricts or dilates when the systemic arterial pressure is raised or lowered so as to assure a constant blood supply as long as the tissue itself remains metabolically constant. Second, it is *chemically regulated*, i.e., its smooth muscle contracts or relaxes in response to appropriate changes in carbon dioxide and oxygen tensions in the blood and to these and possibly other metabolites in local tissue. Except during the prodromes of migraine, the normal intracranial vessels do not spontaneously go into spasm. Intracranial disease can disrupt both of these physiologic properties of blood vessels, with autoregulation being the more sensitive to injury. Indeed, loss of autoregulation represents the most important vascular abnormality enhancing the pathologic effects of still-reversible mass lesions. With loss of autoregulation, the arterial bed passively dilates or constricts as the arterial blood pressure rises or falls, but the result almost always is to congest the vascular compartment. The additional loss of chemical regulation is a more severe physiologic injury, probably confined to areas of profound ischemia or necrosis. *Vasospasm* mainly follows more or less direct vascular injuries caused by direct trauma, blood extravasation, or perivascular inflammation and is usually a diffuse response (see Chapter 4).

The normal cerebral autoregulation is at least briefly but diffusely suspended after traumatic concussion, after generalized seizures,[100] and following brief generalized ischemia or anoxia.[66] Local areas of traumatic injury,[110] infarcts,[96] and neoplasms[95] are commonly surrounded by pressure-passive hyperemic zones that retain their endogenous ability to constrict if one lowers the arterial blood CO_2 tension, but passively increase or decrease their diameter (and therefore their blood volume and flow) if the systemic arterial pressure rises or falls. Even well-localized infarcts or neoplasms can cause a widespread loss of autoregulation that sometimes includes the entirety of the same or even both hemispheres. Such wide margins of vasodilatation can considerably extend the pathologic boundaries of the primary lesion since the increased bulk of blood creates an additional mass and the arteriolar vasodilatation leads to edema by increasing the local capillary hydrostatic pressure. These changes in turn lead to local increases in tissue pressure that augment shifts of intracranial structures.[103] Marked increases in local tissue pressure may exceed capillary pressure, producing a focal decrease in cerebral blood flow with its attendant ischemia. Neither the mechanisms that normally govern cerebral autoregulation nor those that destroy it are precisely known, but an abnormal, passive cerebral vascular response to pressure is a significant factor contributing to "decompensation" in progressive supratentorial mass lesions.

Changes in Intracranial Pressure as a Cause of Symptoms

The intracranial pressure at any given moment reflects the net effect of static and dynamic forces affecting the intracranial contents.[82,105] The skull and spinal canal and their contents constitute a semirigid compartment partially vented to the atmosphere via the cardiovascular system. Largely because of the craniospinal vascular bed, pressure-volume relationships inside the skull are nonlinearly related. As the pressure rises, intracranial compliance (i.e., the capacity of the pressure to adapt to increases in volume) decreases, so that relatively small increases of volume are potentially more dangerous in the presence of increased intracranial pressure than when the initial pressure is normal.

So long as the steady-state relationships between cerebrospinal fluid (CSF) formation and absorption remain constant, the static intracranial pressure reflects primarily the sum of the dural venous sinus pressure plus the product of CSF formation and the resistance to CSF absorption.[73] Sustained, static elevations of intracranial pressure require either an increase in the dural sinus pressure, an increase in CSF or intracellular fluid production, or an increase in resistance to CSF absorption. So long as these values are normal, mass lesions in and of themselves do not alter intracranial pressure.[132] (Extracellular fluid production and CSF absorption mechanisms are influenced in complex ways by mass lesions, partial obstructions in CSF outflow pathways, and meningeal inflammation.)

Dynamic, rapid changes in intracranial pressure result from rapid changes in brain volume or blood volume, or from sudden changes in the relation between CSF production and absorption, as occurs, for example, when the CSF circulation is suddenly obstructed or when CSF is removed by lumbar or ventricular puncture.

An increase in intracranial pressure per se produces few or no troublesome symptoms beyond at times headache and little in the way of neurologic signs except for papilledema, until the pressure rises high enough to impair the normal flow of cerebral circulation. In the normal brain, the perfusion pressure (mean arterial pressure minus mean intracranial pressure) must drop below 40 mm. Hg before cerebral blood flow is impaired because normal cerebral autoregulation produces compensatory vasodilatation. In the damaged brain, the point at which a decreasing perfusion pressure seriously interferes with circulation to all or a portion of the brain cannot easily be determined. The exact figure may vary from area to area within the central nervous system. Either a rise in systemic arterial pressure or a drop in intracranial pressure increases perfusion pressure; conversely, a fall in systemic arterial pressure or an increase in intracranial pressure diminishes perfusion pressure. The relatively benign effects of moderately high intracranial pressure are seen in many circumstances. No serious cerebral symptoms accompany increased intracranial pressure caused by obstruction of venous outflow, such as occurs with blockage of the superior vena cava, of the jugular veins in the neck, or even of the anterior part of the sagittal sinus. Similarly, when Browder and Meyers[11] and Schumacher and Wolff[109] raised the intracranial pressure in man by injecting saline into the lumbar subarachnoid space, the subjects developed no adverse symptoms, not even headache, until the subarachnoid pressure approached the diastolic blood pressure (800 to 1000 mm. CSF). If normal cerebral blood flow is maintained, the electrical activity of the cerebral cortex remains normal even when intracranial pressure is raised above 50 mm. Hg.[128]

The above examples demonstrate the benign nature of intracranial hypertension caused either by obstructing the large draining sinuses or by directly increasing the spinal fluid pressure, but what of raising the pressure by increasing the size of the intracranial substance, the brain itself? Here again, the evidence is that if the brain substance expands relatively slowly and does not shift so as to obstruct the flow of arterial blood or spinal fluid, the ensuing increase in intracranial pressure has a relatively benign effect on the central nervous system.* In the condition known as pseudotumor cerebri, brain bulk is increased and the intracranial pressure is raised, but the intracranial structures maintain their normal anatomic relationships to one another as nothing obstructs the flow of CSF within either the ventricles or the subarachnoid space. The remarkable thing under these cir-

---

*Very rapid, diffuse increases in brain volume, such as occur with Reye's syndrome (p. 268), acute meningitis in children, acute herpes simplex encephalitis (p. 264), or the vasomotor paralysis that follows head injury, may behave differently, presumably because the larger and more extensively myelinated cerebral hemispheres swell earlier and more rapidly than the brainstem, producing transtentorial herniation.

cumstances is that despite intracranial pressures that often rise as high as 400 to 600 mm. CSF and sometimes even closely approach the systemic arterial pressure,[81] most of these patients look and feel well and remain free of confusion, obtundation, and coma. It is important to recognize that these high intracranial pressures are asymptomatic in relatively normal brains because autoregulation of cerebral blood vessels maintains a relatively normal blood flow. In the damaged brain, where autoregulation is impaired, much lesser changes in intracranial pressure may cause cerebral ischemia.

Acute dynamic changes in intracranial pressure represent more clinically serious processes than the static, diffuse pressure changes described above. Such dynamic changes can be due either to paroxysmal pressure rises or to more sustained pressures that create gradients between different intracranial compartments.

The frequent presence of paroxysmal symptoms suggesting transient vascular insufficiency in patients with increased intracranial pressure was first emphasized by Ethelberg and Jensen in 1952.[30] Lundberg in 1960 noted that intraventricular recordings from patients with expanding brain lesions showed a variety of fluctuating abnormal pressure patterns.[69] Particularly important were large variations in pressure that occurred at intervals as often as 15 to 30 minutes apart, sometimes maintaining sustained *plateau waves* for considerable periods with pressures approaching the mean systemic blood pressure. Although some of the pressure fluctuations precipitated no apparent neurologic worsening, others were associated with alarming, although often temporary, neurologic deterioration.

The pathogenesis of plateau waves, which typically occur only during the advanced stages of intracranial hypertension associated with enlarging parenchymal lesions, relates to episodic arterial dilatation,[69] which dynamically and promptly raises the pressure in an intracranial compartment that already suffers from a reduced compliance. The vasodilation in these circumstances can have either a physiologic basis (the waves commonly occur during sleep, with its attendant CO_2 retention, or upon arousal when arterial dilation accompanies increased cerebral metabolism) or a pathologic source in vasoparalysis. Plateau waves may also be precipitated by sudden postural change[72] or by changes in intrathoracic pressure, such as those produced by tracheal suctioning with its associated bronchospasm and coughing.

The crucial factor in the symptoms produced by intracranial pressure relates to the development of abnormal intracranial compartmentation. Pathologic intracranial compartmentation occurs when mass lesions or brain hernias begin to obstruct the tentorial incisura or foramen magnum. The result is that pressures generated by CSF and arterial pulsations are no longer transmitted freely along the intracranial and intraspinal tissues and fluid spaces, so that gradients develop between one compartment and another; as a consequence, pressure recordings from one compartment no longer reflect accurately the pressure in another[27,56] and compliance falls sharply in the now smaller individual compartments. Consequently, small volume changes lead to large pressure changes. The inevitable result is to accentuate and accelerate the process of compartmental herniation.

Intracranial Shift in the Pathogenesis of Coma

There are three major patterns of supratentorial brain shift, and they can be identified by their end stages: cingulate herniation, central transtentorial herniation, and uncal herniation (Fig. 16).

96

CINGULATE HERNIATION. This occurs when the expanding hemisphere shifts laterally across the intracranial cavity, forcing the cingulate gyrus under the falx cerebri and compressing and displacing the internal cerebral vein. The main danger of cingulate herniation is that it compresses blood vessels, particularly the ipsilateral anterior cerebral artery,[120] and tissues, causing cerebral ischemia, congestion, and edema which, in turn, enhance the expanding process.

CENTRAL OR TRANSTENTORIAL HERNIATION (Fig. 17). Central or transtentorial herniation of the diencephalon is the end result of downward displacement of the hemispheres and the basal nuclei, compressing and eventually displacing the diencephalon and the adjoining midbrain rostrocaudally through the tentorial notch.[108] Shift of this kind occurs mainly in response to parenchymal lesions of the frontal, parietal, and occipital lobes and to extracerebral lesions lying more toward the intracranial vertex or the frontal-occipital poles. With unilateral expanding lesions, shift across the midline and herniation of the cingulate gyrus under the falx commonly precede downward shift and central transtentorial herniation.

The changes at the tentorium in central transtentorial herniation consist of an actual caudal displacement of the diencephalon, sometimes to such a distance that it partially avulses the pituitary stalk[52] and buckles the diencephalon against the midbrain[47] (Fig. 17B). Cross-section examinations of such cases show the diencephalon to be edematous and enlarged, often containing hemorrhages in the pretectal region and sometimes also in the thalamus adjacent to the thalamostriate veins, which normally drain into the internal cerebral vein. These severe paramedian changes need not necessarily be accompanied by prominent morphological evidence of uncal or hippocampal herniation into the incisura. Severe secondary brainstem changes develop caudal to the incisura and are discussed in the next section.

UNCAL HERNIATION. *When the abscess is seated in the temporosphenoidal or frontal lobe, the pupil on the same side as the abscess may become ... mydriatic, accompanied by a degree of stability. ... Sections of the frozen head show well the relationships of the third nerve to the temporal lobe and how destruction of this lobe may exercise pressure on the third nerve.* These words of Macewen,[71] written more than 80 years ago, emphasize that the earliest warnings of uncal herniation signify dysfunction in structures that lie outside the brain parenchyma, in contrast to central herniation, where the first signs are of diencephalic dysfunction. Uncal herniation characteristically occurs when expanding lesions arising in the temporal fossa or temporal lobe shift the inner, basal edge of the uncus and hippocampal gyrus toward the midline so that they bulge over the incisural edge of the tentorium. The resultant crowding at the notch flattens the adjacent midbrain, pushing it against the opposite incisural edge (Figs. 15 and 16). At the same time, the third nerve and the posterior cerebral artery on the side of the expanding temporal lobe are often caught between the overhanging swollen uncus and the free edge of the tentorium or some other resistant structure such as the petroclinoid ligament.

The particular danger of supratentorial displacements and herniations is that they initiate vascular and obstructive complications that aggravate the original expanding lesion and convert a potentially reversible into an irreversible pathologic process. Herniation under the falx compresses the anterior cerebral artery and accentuates already existing ischemia and edema of the herniating hemisphere. Displacement across the midline posteriorly compresses the great cerebral vein and raises the hydrostatic pressure of the entire deep cerebral territory it drains. Either central or uncal herniation into the tentorial notch compresses the posterior

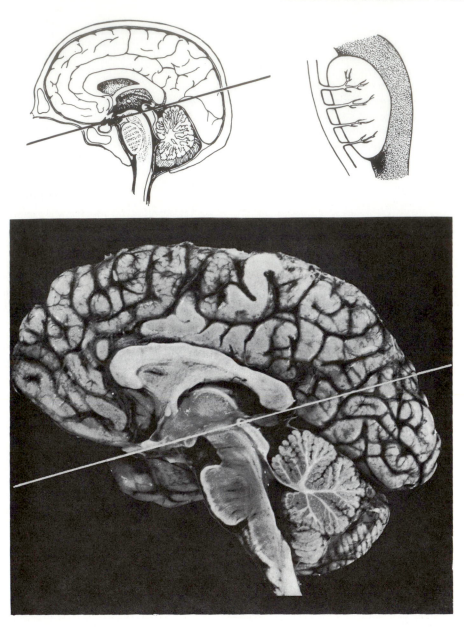

Figure 17. Downward displacement of the brainstem with transtentorial herniation. The drawings in the upper part of each figure illustrate the relationship of the brainstem to the supratentorial compartment (left) and to the penetrating branches of the basilar artery (right). In drawing **B** there is downward displacement of the diencephalon and stretching of the penetrating branches of the basilar artery. The photograph in **A** is that of a sagittal section of a normal brain. The line drawn between the inferior margin of the splenium of the corpus callosum and the optic chiasm passes just above the quadrigeminal plate and either

98

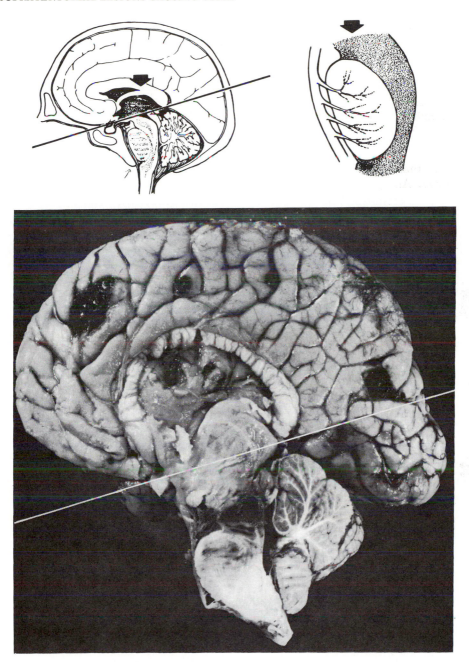

through or just above the mammillary body. The photograph in **B** is from a patient with multiple metastatic brain tumors (melanoma) who died following a clinical course suggesting central transtentorial herniation (see text). The multiple tumors are apparent in the supratentorial compartment. The line drawn from landmarks similar to those in **A** now passes well above both the quadrigeminal plate, which is foreshortened as well as displaced posteriorly, and the mammillary bodies. A midbrain hemorrhage is apparent in this section as well.

cerebral artery to produce occipital infarction and swelling. Equally important to any of these processes is that both uncal and transtentorial herniation can compress the aqueduct and subarachnoid spaces so as to interfere with spinal fluid circulation.[112] The blockage has two consequences. One is that spinal fluid can no longer escape from the ventricular system to accommodate an enlargement in the brain, so that the pressure in the supratentorial cavity rises above that in the posterior fossa. As a result, lumbar CSF pressure may be normal despite grossly elevated supratentorial pressure (see p. 96). The other is that when the ventricular system is obstructed, no pulse of escaping CSF can compensate for the expansion of the supratentorial volume that accompanies each systolic beat.[139] As a result, the brain is pounded between the pulsating arterial bed and the unyielding cerebral extracellular and ventricular fluid. This pounding may be a factor impacting the posterior diencephalon into and through the tentorial incisura, which is the eventual common denominator of both the central and the uncal patterns of herniation. The increased intracranial pressure in the supratentorial compartment that accompanies many of these cases directly leads to pressure necrosis in the parahippocampal gyrus.[2]

Herniation into or across the tentorium also produces brainstem ischemia and hemorrhages that characteristically involve the central core of the brainstem from the diencephalon to the lower pons; such lesions are particularly prominent when the supratentorial lesion enlarges rapidly. The exact pathogenesis of these secondary brainstem vascular abnormalities is debated, and both a venous and arterial origin were originally suggested. Their arterial origin now seems well established, however. Transtentorial herniation displaces the midbrain and pons downward, stretching the medial perforating branches of the basilar artery, because the artery itself is tethered to the circle of Willis and cannot shift downward. Pathologically, the first brainstem change is that of paramedian ischemia,[140] and when Johnson and Yates[52] injected the intracranial arteries in such cases postmortem, contrast media leaked out of the necrotic arteries along the brainstem, just as blood would have done had their perfusion continued during life. Indeed, Klintworth[61] produced midbrain hemorrhages experimentally by following a procedure of first markedly increasing the supratentorial pressure, then releasing the pressure and producing hypertension sufficient to reperfuse the ischemic arteries.[61] Friede and Roessmann serially sectioned the brainstem in patients with midbrain hemorrhages and found 101 of arterial to 1 of venous origin.[34]

Clinical evidence as outlined in the next section suggests that the ischemic process rather deliberately advances down the brainstem once transtentorial herniation occurs. Pathologic confirmation of this kind of steady advancement is almost always impossible to reconstruct from postmortem material, which usually discloses only the terminal stage of severe central brainstem destruction down to lower pontine levels.

To epitomize: Pathologic changes in most brains with supratentorial mass lesions consist of vasomotor paralysis, congestion, and edema that spread from the lesion, at first radially and then rostral-caudally in a progressively contiguous manner. Even when tentorial herniation and downward displacement finally damage the brainstem, the pathologic changes tend to move in an orderly rostral-caudal plane almost as if an inexorably advancing wave were producing serial functional transections.

Two infrequent exceptions break the rule that untreated supratentorial mass lesions paralyze the brain in a progressively contiguous rostral-caudal direction.

One occurs in patients with acute cerebral hemorrhage, the other follows ill-timed lumbar punctures in patients with incipient transtentorial herniation. In both instances, clinical signs can jump from reflecting hemispheral or diencephalic dysfunction to indicating sudden medullary failure. Special pathologic circumstances explain both of these exceptions to the usual rostral-caudal progression. Most cerebral hemorrhages produce rapid medullary failure only after bleeding extends into the ventricular system. Presumably the sudden outpouring of blood produces a fluid pressure wave that compresses the region around the fourth ventricle almost as much as the parenchyma of the immediately surrounding brain. Experimentally, this effect can be reproduced in animals: An intraventricular injection of saline produces medullary failure much more rapidly than comparable amounts of saline injected into the cerebral parenchyma.[129] Similar considerations explain the lumbar puncture effect, except that here the stopper has been removed from below rather than the compression applied from above. Anatomic lesions in patients with supratentorial lesions dying from sudden medullary failure following lumbar puncture usually are not distinctive except that all such patients show either incipient or fully developed tentorial herniation and most have compression of the aqueduct as well. Apparently, withdrawal of spinal fluid from the reservoir of the posterior fossa must suddenly reduce its supporting pressure so that the intracranial contents are abruptly pushed downward, compressing the medulla into the foramen magnum. As already mentioned, this sudden sequence of events is difficult to reconstruct at autopsy.

DIAGNOSIS OF COMA FROM SUPRATENTORIAL MASS LESIONS

The previous section described how intracranial pathologic changes radiate progressively downward and away from supratentorial mass lesions. Abnormal clinical signs develop the same way, so that patients with progressing, unreversed supratentorial lesions develop a sequence of respiratory, ocular, and motor signs that indicate the gradual, orderly failure of first diencephalic, and then midbrain, pontine, and medullary functions, in that order. Indeed, this orderly progression is almost invariable unless a hemorrhage or abscess ruptures into the ventricles or an ill-advised lumbar puncture rapidly changes the intracranial dynamics so that medullary compression occurs. The classical Kocher-Cushing signs of a rising blood pressure and slow pulse rate do not occur with most supratentorial masses. These "classical" signs of increased intracranial pressure are more common with posterior fossa lesions, and on the rare occasions when they do accompany supratentorial lesions, they usually imply that an epidural hemorrhage or a massive cerebral hemorrhage has *suddenly* increased the supratentorial and intraventricular pressure and transmitted its effects directly to the posterior fossa.

Decompensating focal cerebral lesions produce either of two distinct clinical pictures. One, the *uncal syndrome*, is the classical picture of uncal herniation and includes the early signs of compression of the third nerve and lateral midbrain. The uncal syndrome is particularly likely to develop in neurosurgical emergencies, especially with rapidly expanding traumatic supratentorial hematomas and overwhelmingly severe head injuries associated with generalized intracranial vasomotor paralysis. In these instances, the pathologic sequence resembles that produced by inflating balloons in the heads of experimental animals. The other, the *central syndrome*, is sometimes less immediately recognized but occurs more frequently among subacute or chronically ill patients, where diagnosis is a greater problem, and reflects bilateral progressive parenchymal impairment of the diencephalon.[74] The syndromes conform to the differences in pathology between uncal and central tentorial herniation. Clinically, they are recognizably distinct early in their course, but both merge into a similar picture once pathologic changes extend to involve the midbrain level or below.

Whether patients with intracranial disease develop a central syndrome or an uncal syndrome depends partly on the site of the lesion and partly on unknown influences. Table 5 includes 67 well-documented cases of supratentorial lesions producing transtentorial herniation. All the patients were studied for the evolution of signs and symptoms leading to coma. The diagnoses were confirmed by autopsy in 42 cases, by surgery in 15, and by radiographic procedures or a combination of these in the remainder. Radiographic evidence alone was accepted only in patients having entirely consistent clinical findings and a neurologic disability that was fully reversed by treatment; this minimized the possibility that undiagnosed primary brainstem lesions caused the symptoms. As can be seen from the table, medially placed supratentorial lesions of relatively slow development more often produced signs of the central syndrome, while temporal lobe and lateral extracerebral masses most often caused the uncal syndrome. In only a small proportion of cases, how-

Table 5. The Nature and Location of Supratentorial Lesions Producing Rostral-Caudal Deterioration in 67 Verified Cases*

	No. of Cases	Type of Syndrome		
		Central	Uncal	Combined
Infarction				
Massive middle cerebral a. distribution	8	8		
Parietooccipital	1	1		
Parietotemporal	3	3		
Hemorrhage				
Basal ganglia	6	4	1	1
Frontotemporal	3	2	1	
Frontoparietal	2	2		
Frontal	3	3		
Parietal	1	1		
Temporal	5	1	3	1
Neoplasm				
Frontal	3	3		
Parietal	5	4		1
Thalamic	3	3		
Abscess				
Temporal	2		2	
Thalamoparietal	1	1		
Trauma (acute epidural 3, acute subdural 4, chronic subdural hematoma 14)				
Hemisphere	12	7	3	2
Frontal	4	3	1	
Biparietal	2	2		
Temporal	3		2	1

*These patients do not in all instances correspond with those in Category 1 of Table 1 because coma was not a problem in diagnosis in many of these patients and, conversely, several patients in Table 1 were not observed fully for evidence of rostral-caudal deterioration.

ever, were these anatomic correlations sufficiently consistent to predict confidently the site of the lesion or its histology from the pattern of herniation alone.

The Central Syndrome of Rostral-Caudal Deterioration

Diencephalic Stage—Clinical Signs

Figures 18 and 19 illustrate the clinical signs that accompany the early and late diencephalic stages of the central syndrome. The first evidence that a supratentorial mass is beginning to impair the diencephalon is usually a change in alertness or behavior. Initially, subjects with such lesions find it difficult to concentrate and tend to lose the orderly details of recent events. Some patients become agitated; others sink slowly into torpid drowsiness. Admittedly, it sometimes is difficult to distinguish between the apathy accompanying purely unilateral hemispheric abnormalities such as aphasia or severe hemisensory defects and a more global reduction in consciousness caused by direct encroachment on subcortical neural structures. Under such circumstances the respiratory, ocular, and motor signs described below can provide evidence for or against the presence of bilateral dysfunction in these other neurologically controlled systems. If the supratentorial lesion continues to enlarge and displace tissues toward the deep midline of the cerebrum, stupor and then coma

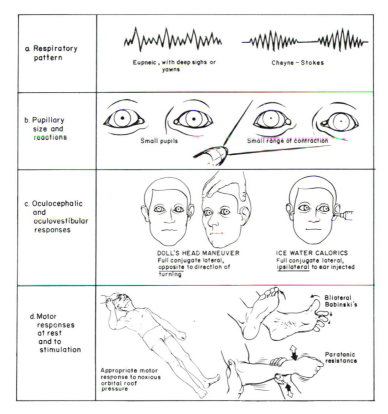

Figure 18. Signs of cerebral transtentorial herniation, early diencephalic stage.

103

occur. Once this stage is reached, the state of consciousness per se becomes less useful as a localizing sign and has little value as an immediate index to whether patients are improving or worsening. When consciousness is lost, paying careful attention to respiratory, ocular, and motor signs not only helps in diagnosing supratentorial causes of coma, but also in determining whether the direction of the disease process is for the better or worse.

Respiration in the early diencephalic stage of the central syndrome is commonly interrupted by deep sighs, yawns, and occasional pauses. Many patients have periodic breathing of the Cheyne-Stokes type, particularly as they sink into deeper somnolence. The pupils are small (1 to 3 mm.) and, if examined superficially, may appear to have lost their reaction to light. Close scrutiny with a bright light brings out reactions that are brisk, but with a small range of contraction. Whether these small pupils reflect the effects of functional decortication or hypothalamic sympathetic dysfunction is unknown; either mechanism could explain them.

Examination of eye movements reveals one of two abnormalities in the early diencephalic stage of the central syndrome. Some patients show conjugate or slightly divergent roving eye movements that either resist a consistent response to the doll's head maneuver or are only weakly interrupted by it. Roving conjugate eye movements always mean that the brainstem is intact and probably indicate a relatively slight degree of diencephalic impairment. More frequently, the eyes are conjugate

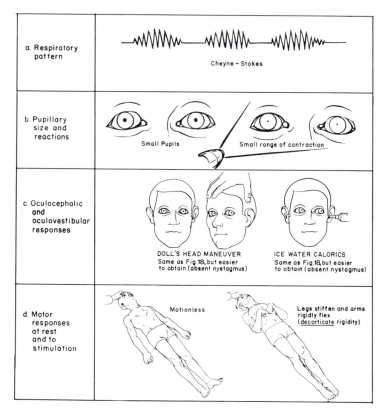

Figure 19. Signs of central transtentorial herniation, late diencephalic stage.

104

and quiet at rest but respond briskly to passive side-to-side head rotation. Caloric tests with cold water evoke a full and conjugate slow tonic movement to the side irrigated with impairment or absence of the fast component of the response. (Temporarily, patients with large acute primary lesions of a frontal lobe may not demonstrate reflex lateral eye movement to the contralateral side with the doll's head maneuver and on rare occasions even the caloric response on the hemiplegic side may disappear for a few hours. Tests of vertical reflex eye movements also furnish valuable information in this early stage. Lesions producing downward pressure through the posterior part of the tentorial incisura compress the region of the superior colliculi and the adjacent diencephalic pretectum and impair upward conjugate deviation of the eyes. This can be demonstrated in stuporous patients by briskly flexing the head and observing that the eyes fail to roll upward.

In the motor system, early diencephalic involvement is signaled by the development of bilateral signs of corticospinal and extrapyramidal dysfunction. Commonly with hemispheral lesions, there is a preexisting hemiparesis or hemiplegia contralateral to the original focal brain lesion. As the diencephalic stage of the central syndrome evolves, the contralateral hemiplegia may worsen, but in addition the extremities *homolateral* to the brain lesion commonly develop paratonic resistance, or gegenhalten, but continue to respond appropriately to noxious stimuli. The generalized muscular hypertonus often extends to the neck, which initially resists both flexion and lateral motion. (A truly stiff neck or head retraction without lateral limitation of movement results from stretching pain-sensitive meninges at the base of the brain and is more consistent with meningitis or cerebellar tonsillar herniation than with tentorial herniation.) Along with the development of paratonic rigidity homolateral to the hemispheral lesion, both plantar responses commonly become extensor, although the response ipsilateral to the hemispheric lesion generally remains less vigorous in its expression. Later, as diencephalic impairment progresses, paratonic resistance to passive stretch increases and grasp reflexes commonly emerge, particularly when the initiating lesion lies in the contralateral prefrontal area. Finally, "decorticate" responses appear—nearly always at first contralateral to the primary expanding lesion and in response to a noxious stimulus such as supraorbital pressure or firm compression of the pectoralis muscle. In some patients with a hemispheral lesion whose deterioration indicates rostral-caudal progression, the initially hemiplegic side responds to noxious stimulation with extensor posturing, while the opposite extremity, homolateral to the primary lesion, responds with the decorticate posture. The physiologic explanation for this difference is unknown.

PATHOGENESIS AND SIGNIFICANCE OF THE DIENCEPHALIC STAGE. Many of the above-mentioned signs could result from either diffuse bilateral hemispheral dysfunction or impaired function of the diencephalon-upper brainstem. Obtundation and progressively increasing stupor are more compatible with bilateral diencephalic or brainstem dysfunction than with unilateral hemispheric dysfunction, but a hard and fast distinction is not always possible because hemispheral shift across the midline is a possible cause of bilateral functional changes. The few patients coming to autopsy at this early stage usually have had at least some edema in both hemispheres. Almost all patients at this stage also have functional abnormalities of their cerebral circulation with reduction in cerebral blood flow in areas remote from the primary lesion.[75] How much these changes contribute to their symptoms is unknown. Some investigators, as reviewed by Heiskanen,[43] have suggested that increased intracranial pressure in these patients compresses the intracranial blood vessels, which, in turn, decreases the cerebral blood flow. Since intracranial pressures exceeding arteriolar-capillary pressure would be required, it seems unlikely that this happens very often, although sudden rises of increased pressure sufficient to impede the circulation have also been suggested by Ethelberg and Jensen[30] and Lundberg[69] to cause visual obscurations and other transient worsenings in patients with brain tumor. The mechanism merits direct investigation as a potential cause of symptoms. Often, however, slowed cerebral circulation as measured by angiography or other techniques is observed in these patients only after intracranial bleeding or meningitis, and in these instances, at least, a direct effect of the disease on the blood vessels can be held responsible for much of the arterial narrowing.

It is our view that the clinical course of patients having signs of the early central syndrome is most compatible with early diencephalic dysfunction. Most commonly the intracranial pressure is not high enough to compress the vascular bed, and radiographic studies of many patients with central signs show downward displacement of the anterior choroidal artery or other structures, indicating diencephalic displacement. If patients with diencephalic signs of the central syndrome continue to worsen, they tend rapidly to develop manifestations of midbrain damage, suggesting that the pathologic process has simply extended to the next more caudal level.

The clinical importance of the diencephalic stage of stupor or coma caused by supratentorial mass lesions is that it warns that a potentially reversible lesion is about to become irreversible by progressively encroaching on the brain at the level of the tentorium or below. If the enlarging supratentorial process can be alleviated or removed before the aforementioned signs of diencephalic dysfunction give way to signs of midbrain damage, chances are good for complete neurologic recovery. Once signs of lower diencephalic and, particularly, midbrain dysfunction appear, it becomes increasingly likely that they will reflect infarction rather than reversible ischemia and compression, and although a few patients may still be treatable, the outlook for neurologic recovery is poor.

Midbrain-Upper Pons Stage

If treatment is delayed or ineffective and patients progress beyond the diencephalic stage of the central syndrome, the clinical signs give way to those of midbrain failure (Fig. 20). A few patients develop diabetes insipidus, reflecting severe downward traction on the pituitary stalk and the hypothalamic median eminence.[52] Abnormally wide fluctuations of body temperature are common and hyperthermia often surrenders to hypothermia. Cheyne-Stokes respiration gradually changes to sustained tachypnea. The initially small pupils dilate moderately to fix irregularly at midposition (3 to 5 mm.), but do not dilate widely except terminally, when generalized anoxia may cause a systemic release of epinephrine. Ciliospinal reflexes may disappear and the oculovestibular responses become progressively more difficult to elicit, requiring either repeated side-to-side head movement or a combination of lateral head movement and cold caloric irrigation. When elicited, the eye movements often are dysconjugate with the medially moving eye failing to move as far as the laterally moving eye (internuclear ophthalmoplegia). Meanwhile, motor dysfunction progresses from decorticate to bilateral extensor rigidity in response to noxious stimulation. Extensor rigidity sometimes occurs spontaneously and sporadically, particularly in the presence of irritative intracranial processes such as

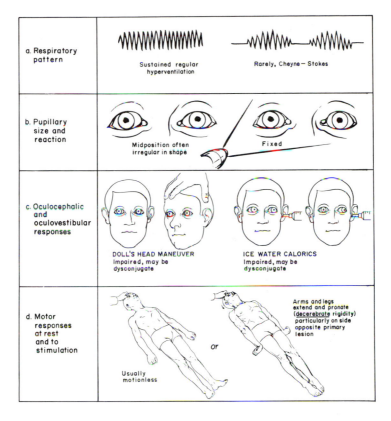

Figure 20. Signs of transtentorial herniation, midbrain-upper pons stage.

hemorrhages or infections; more commonly, patients rest quietly until stimuli are applied.

Midbrain damage after tentorial herniation is due to secondary ischemia, which rapidly produces necrosis, particularly in paramedian structures. In our adult patients, no subject with a supratentorial lesion has recovered full neurologic function once midbrain signs were fully developed, and most have either died, remained in coma for months, or have been severely disabled when transferred for custodial care. Zervas and Hedley-White[142] and Brendler and Selverstone[9] report a happier outcome in some patients, with full recovery following vigorous treatment of the "decerebrate" state, but even their series implies a high incidence of neurologic residua. The prognosis for recovery is often considerably better in children.

Lower Pontine—Upper Medullary Stage

Gradually, ischemia marches down the brainstem (Fig. 21). Hyperventilation quiets down and a more or less regular breathing pattern resembling eupnea supervenes, but often with a more rapid rate (20 to 40 per minute) and shallow depth. Unless the patient has been severely anoxic or has been given drugs that affect the autonomic nervous system, the pupils maintain midposition and do not respond

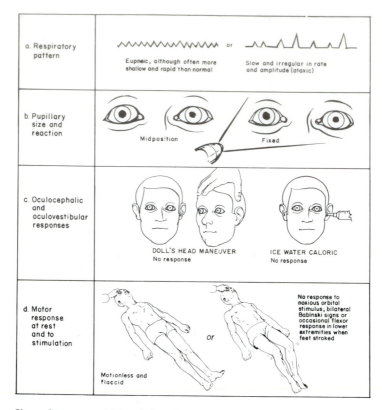

a. Respiratory pattern	Eupneic, although often more shallow and rapid than normal	or	Slow and irregular in rate and amplitude (ataxic)
b. Pupillary size and reaction	Midposition		Fixed
c. Oculocephalic and oculovestibular responses	DOLL'S HEAD MANEUVER No response		ICE WATER CALORIC No response
d. Motor response at rest and to stimulation	Motionless and flaccid	or	No response to noxious orbital stimulus; bilateral Babinski signs or occasional flexor response in lower extremities when feet stroked

Figure 21. Signs of transtentorial herniation, lower pons-upper medulla stage.

to light. Oculovestibular responses are unobtainable, and the subject becomes flaccid, retaining bilateral extensor plantar responses and, occasionally, flexor responses in the lower extremities to noxious stimulation.

Medullary Stage

The medullary stage is terminal. Respiration slows, often becomes irregular in rate and depth, and frequently is interrupted by deep sighs or gasps. Occasionally, brief episodes of hyperpnea alternate with relatively long periods of apnea. The pulse is variably slow or fast and the blood pressure drops. Finally, after a few gasps, breathing stops and during the ensuing hypoxia the pupils often dilate widely. With artificial respiration the blood pressure can be maintained for several hours, but death is inevitable.

The following case illustrates the full development of the central syndrome owing to an acute cerebral hemorrhage:

Patient 2-1. A 74-year-old retired lawyer had mild hypertension for several years but was otherwise in excellent health. On the day of admission he suddenly developed pain behind the right ear along with weakness of the left side of his body and dysarthria. He was brought immediately to the hospital where he was observed to be afebrile, to have a pulse rate of 88 per minute, regular breathing at a rate of 16 per minute, and blood pressure 200/112 mm. Hg. He was awake, oriented, and followed commands.

108

He was dysarthric and complained of a steady, moderately severe pain above and behind the right ear. His head and eyes deviated moderately to the right, and there was a left homonymous hemianopsia.

He was able voluntarily to deviate his eyes just past the midline to the left. With the doll's head maneuver, however, the eyes conjugately deviated all the way to the left. The pupils were unequal, the right being 2 mm. and the left 3 mm.; both reacted to light. The inequality was interpreted as a right partial Horner's syndrome caused by incipient diencephalic compression. Sensation was reduced in the left side of the face and cornea. There was a moderately severe, flaccid left hemiparesis interrupted intermittently by clonic movements of the left leg and tonic flexor movements of the left arm. Stretch reflexes on the left side were reduced, but the plantar response was extensor. Laboratory work was unremarkable. At lumbar puncture, the opening pressure of the CSF was 200 mm. with brisk arterial pulsations and clear fluid containing 1143 red cells per cu. mm. The protein content was 57 mg./dl. The clinical diagnosis of cerebral hemorrhage was made.

By an hour after admission, the patient was having periodic decorticate postural spasms on the left side. The right plantar response had become extensor. He gradually lost consciousness and by 4 hours after admission was unresponsive except to noxious stimuli, which produced at first extensor responses on the left but decorticate responses on the right, and finally bilateral extensor posturings slightly more pronounced on the left than on the right. By this time the right pupil had dilated and fixed in an oval shape, being vertically 7 mm. and horizontally 3 mm. Minimal oculomotor responses could be elicited to cold caloric stimulation, and the patient was hyperventilating. The blood pressure had risen to 235/150 mm. Hg.

Treatment with intravenous urea was started and during the next hour the patient's condition stabilized except that the right pupil became round and regained a minimal reaction to light. The blood pressure dropped to 160/60 mm. Hg. The patient began to vomit, and his temperature rose to 39.6°C. He began to sweat profusely. By 6 hours after admission, decerebrate responses became less intense; the pupils were fixed, slightly irregular at 3 to 4 mm. diameter, and unequal; oculocephalic responses were absent; respiration was quiet and shallow. By 8 hours after admission, respiration was ataxic; the pupils remained slightly unequal with absence of oculovestibular responses; the patient was diffusely flaccid but had bilateral extensor plantar responses and mild flexor responses in the legs to noxious stimulation of the soles of the feet. He died half an hour later.

At postmortem examination there was hypertrophy of the heart and a massive right-sided cerebral hemorrhage arising in the region of the posterior aspect of the basal ganglia and creating both uncal and transtentorial herniations. The posterior diencephalon was displaced an estimated 8 mm. caudally through the tentorial incisura. Secondary hemorrhages and hemorrhagic infarction extended down the brainstem to the lower third of the pons.

The Syndrome of Uncal Herniation and Lateral Brainstem Compression

Early Third Nerve Stage

As discussed on page 97, expanding lesions in the lateral middle fossa or temporal lobe commonly push the medial edge of the uncus and hippocampal gyrus toward the midline and over the free lateral edge of the tentorium. Because the diencephalon may not be the first structure encroached upon, impaired consciousness is not consistently an early sign of impending uncal herniation, and the state of alertness in different subjects may vary from near-wakefulness through stupor to coma. The earliest consistent sign is the unilaterally dilating pupil (Fig. 22).

Moderate anisocoria with a sluggish light reaction of the dilated pupil can sometimes last for several hours before other signs appear. During early uncal herniation, this may be the only abnormality, respiration remaining eupneic, extraocular movements and oculovestibular responses being unimpaired, and motor abnormalities, if any, reflecting no more than could be expected in someone with a supratentorial lesion. But the alarming feature of uncal herniation is that once any signs of herniation or brainstem compression appear, deterioration may proceed rapidly, with patients slipping from full consciousness to deep coma in a few hours.

109

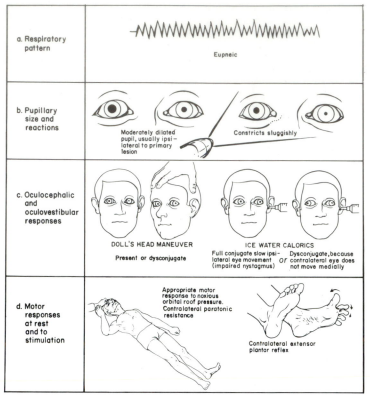

Figure 22. Signs of uncal herniation, early third nerve stage.

Late Third Nerve Stage

A striking feature of the clinical syndrome of uncal herniation is that, once the patient progresses beyond the stage where his signs are entirely explained by a restricted cerebral lesion, there is a tendency for midbrain dysfunction to occur almost immediately (Fig. 23). This quick progression with a tendency to bypass the rostral diencephalon is associated with rapid encroachment upon the brainstem by the herniating hippocampal gyrus and implies great clinical danger since delays in effective treatment invite irreversible damage. Once the pupil fully dilates, external oculomotor ophthalmoplegia soon follows. Concomitantly, patients usually become deeply stuporous, then comatose. The oculovestibular responses at first reveal oculomotor impairment, then rapidly become sluggish and disappear as ischemia spreads to the midbrain. As the opposite cerebral peduncle becomes compressed against the contralateral tentorial edge (producing Kernohan's notch),[59] hemiplegia commonly develops *ipsilateral* to the expanding supratentorial lesion. Soon afterward, bilateral motor signs evolve and noxious stimuli elicit bilateral extensor plantar responses succeeded by extensor posturing of the limbs. Decorticate posturing is unusual. Treatment must remove the initiating lesion or alleviate the brain swelling at this point or the patient will not recover. The example described in Patient 2–9 illustrates the rapid development of uncal herniation in a young woman with a cerebral hemorrhage and its equally prompt reversal by treatment.

110

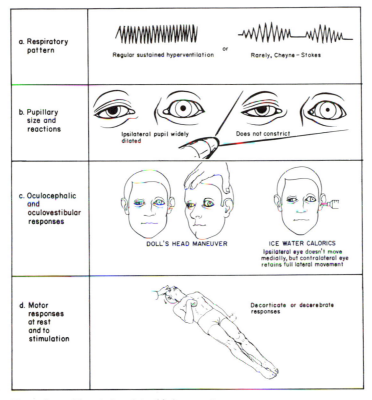

a. Respiratory pattern	Regular sustained hyperventilation	or Rarely, Cheyne – Stokes
b. Pupillary size and reactions	Ipsilateral pupil widely dilated	Does not constrict
c. Oculocephalic and oculovestibular responses	DOLL'S HEAD MANEUVER	ICE WATER CALORICS Ipsilateral eye doesn't move medially, but contralateral eye retains full lateral movement
d. Motor responses at rest and to stimulation		Decorticate or decerebrate responses

Figure 23. Signs of uncal herniation, late third nerve stage.

Midbrain-Upper Pons Stage

If treatment is delayed or is unsuccessful in reversing uncal herniation, signs of midbrain damage appear and progress caudally. The pupil opposite the one originally dilated may show either of two reactions: it may dilate widely and fix or it may enlarge to fix in midposition. Sooner or later both pupils assume the midposition (5 to 6 mm.) and remain fixed. Most patients at this stage show the combination of sustained hyperpnea, impairment or absence of oculovestibular responses, and bilateral decerebrate rigidity. From this point onwards, progression of the uncal syndrome is clinically indistinguishable from that of the central syndrome.

Pathogenesis of the Uncal Syndrome

Macewen's description quoted on page 97 can hardly be improved upon. As the temporal lobe slides medially over the edge of the tentorium, the uncus herniates over the free edge, pushes the posterior cerebral artery down, and in turn compresses the third nerve. The midbrain is squeezed directly, and the cerebral peduncle presses against the opposite tentorial edge. The temporal lobe tissue herniating into the notch traps the posterior cerebral artery against the free edge of the tentorium: Ischemia of the occipital lobe, obstruction of the aqueduct, and expansion of the original lesion all combine to produce an increase in the supratentorial contents.

111

Transtentorial impaction and secondary brainstem ischemia follow. Once this occurs, few survive.

The following account illustrates the development of the uncal syndrome in a young man with cerebral hemorrhage.

Patient 2-2. A previously well 16-year-old boy suddenly complained of frontal headache, collapsed, and was admitted to hospital.

His blood pressure was 158/64 mm. Hg, his pulse 44 per minute, and his breathing eupneic at 18 per minute. The general examination was normal. He was obtunded but with encouragement could be aroused to complain of headache. He retched frequently. The pupils were equal (4 mm.) and reacted to light and cervical pinch. The eyes roved spontaneously with a full lateral range. The corneal reflexes were present. There was a flaccid left hemiplegia and hemihypalgesia with complete areflexia, including no plantar response. His neck was slightly stiff. The right retina contained small flame-shaped hemorrhages.

The CSF pressure was 280 mm., and the fluid was bloody with a hematocrit of 14 percent. Shortly after lumbar puncture, the right pupil dilated to 6 mm. but remained sluggishly reactive; the left pupil was 4 mm. and reactive. The right eye failed to move completely medially on doll's head maneuvers (internuclear ophthalmoplegia). He became more difficult to arouse. Five hours after admission, the right pupil dilated widely (8 mm.) and became fixed. Right medial rectus function was absent. He developed sustained regular hyperventilation at a rate of 26 per minute. He was unresponsive, and the left arm and leg showed fragmentary extensor responses following supraorbital pressure. Hypertonic urea solution was given intravenously. During the next 15 to 30 minutes he became agitated and pulled out his oral airway and intravenous infusion. The pupils became equal to 4 mm. and were equally reactive. Respiration lessened in depth and rate but continued to be slightly labored. The eye movements were again roving and complete. The blood pressure was 120/60 mm. Hg (intramuscular reserpine had been given), and the pulse rate was 60 per minute. Ten hours after admission he was restless, had intense nuchal rigidity, and his pupils were 2 to 3 mm. and reactive. One hour later he suddenly became deeply comatose with widely dilated and fixed pupils and flaccid areflexia. The blood pressure had increased to 210 mm. Hg systolic, and the pulse had risen to 140 per minute. Respiration ceased for 5 minutes, then resumed with occasional irregular gasps. The blood pressure disappeared 1 hour later.

At autopsy, the lungs weighed 870 gm. and were congested. The heart weighed 310 gm. and was normal. The formalin-fixed brain revealed a 1×3 mm. aneurysm at the bifurcation of the right internal carotid artery. Coronal section of the hemispheres showed a large hematoma in the right frontal lobe, which had ruptured into a lateral ventricle and filled the entire ventricular system with blood. There was a right uncal hernia, and the right third nerve was compressed by the posterior cerebral artery. The right calcarine cortex was infarcted. There were no gross brainstem hemorrhages.

Combined Central and Uncal Herniation

The differences between the pathologic anatomy of diencephalic compression with central herniation and lateral temporal lobe shift with uncal herniation are usually sufficiently distinct that patients show either the central or the uncal syndromes in relatively pure form. But occasionally the same patient will display the combined features of both clinical pictures with an equally serious progression of neurologic dysfunction. Such patients show moderate pupillary dilatation or even early signs of peripheral third nerve weakness combined with early stupor and periodic breathing. The whole picture evolves more in the slow, deliberate rostral-caudal fashion of the central syndrome than in the rapid jump from early third nerve signs to midbrain damage and coma, as so commonly happens in the uncal syndrome.

Combined Supratentorial and Subtentorial Damage

Head injury, diffuse intracranial bleeding (as with blood dyscrasias), encephalitis, and meningitis often damage both brainstem and supratentorial functions simultaneously. Initially, the appearance of signs different from the expected rostral-caudal pattern helps to estimate the extent and locus of the immediate brainstem injury. Later, if the supratentorial lesion swells and induces secondary brainstem compression, signs of rostral-caudal deterioration may be limited to changes in only one or more functions (respiratory, oculomotor, skeletal muscle) because others are already impaired. Nevertheless, a change in only a single function can help to indicate increasing secondary brainstem compression requiring active therapy. The following patient illustrates this principle: A change in respiratory abnormalities led to the diagnosis of an expanding supratentorial lesion needing surgical relief.

Patient 2–3. A 15-year-old boy was struck by an automobile and brought to hospital within 30 minutes in deep coma. His blood pressure was 168/60 mm. Hg. He had a pulse rate of 60 per minute, Cheyne-Stokes breathing, widely dilated and fixed pupils, absence of oculocephalic reflexes, and decerebrate posturing. A lumbar puncture yielded moderately bloody spinal fluid with a pressure of 330 mm. A sagittal fracture line across the coronal suture was seen in the skull x-ray film. During the next 2 hours, sustained hyperventilation replaced periodic breathing and the patient became flaccid. Both of these signs suggested deterioration in the rostral-caudal direction: Burr holes were placed in the skull and subdural and epidural hematomas containing an estimated 90 cc. were encountered over the left hemisphere and drained. Postoperatively, the pupils shrank to approximately 3 mm., left greater than right, and the oculovestibular responses returned. Breathing quieted and he moved his left arm spontaneously. The patient gradually regained consciousness, but with the passage of time was left with mild residual aphasia and a right hemiparesis.

False Localizing Signs with Supratentorial Lesions

When obstructive hydrocephalus or supratentorial masses develop slowly, they sometimes distort and displace the intracranial tissues a great deal before they dampen the function of the brainstem core enough to produce stupor or coma. The results can be to produce dysfunction in cranial nerve and brainstem structures that lie remote from the primary lesion, and the resulting abnormal clinical signs can trap an unwary observer into incorrect localizing diagnoses.[37] The most frequent deception, as Collier[17] long ago pointed out, is for a supratentorial tumor or obstruction to induce signs suggesting primary trouble in the posterior fossa. A striking example of this from our own service was a girl of 16 years with an unsuspected chronic aqueductal stenosis. Because of symptoms that included trigeminal neuralgia, nystagmus, and intermittent deafness, she was at first thought to have disseminated sclerosis and treated inappropriately for 2 years before her hydrocephalus was discovered and all her posterior fossa symptoms were cured by the placement of a lateral ventricular shunt.

Although most signs of remote dysfunction involve the cranial nerves, a few can take a parenchymal origin. A cerebellar-like ataxia can emerge if a frontal lobe tumor interrupts or compresses cerebellofrontal projection pathways, and the same mimicry can confuse the clinical picture if a parietal lobe lesion blunts or destroys proprioception. Nystagmus sometimes accompanies supratentorial mass lesions, presumably as the result of severe downward displacement of the vestibular region of the brainstem. Evidence of just how misleading such changes can be comes from the neurosurgical writings of 50 years ago: Accurate diagnostic radiology was lacking, and despite the clinical skills of the day, inappropriate posterior fossa exploration was by no means rare in patients with entirely supratentorial tumors.

Dysfunction of each and every cranial nerve sometimes results as the indirect effect of increased intracranial pressure or downward displacement of the brainstem. Description of the details of these impairments and their individual pathogenesis are beyond our scope, but the changes can include anosmia; papilledema; congruent and incongruent visual field defects; unilateral (tentorial herniation) or bilateral pupillary change; unilateral or bilateral ophthalmoplegias involving the sixth, fourth, and third nerves; ocular bobbing; trigeminal sensory loss (rarely accompanied by tic douloureux); facial monoplegia or diplegia; bilateral deafness; and even bilateral weakness in swallowing, speaking, or use of the tongue.[86] Except for papilledema, unilateral or bilateral abducens paralysis is both the most frequent and the earliest of these remote changes to appear.

The pathogenesis of remote intracranial abnormalities includes, in varying degree, compression of the involved nerves against their cranial outflow foramina (much as toothpaste is squeezed from a tube), stasis-ischemia and edema of the nerves, and traction of the involved nerves downward with compression against various angular protuberances of the dura and skull as the brainstem is pushed further caudally by the supratentorial mass.[47] In some instances the lower cranial nerve defects involving facial, speaking, and swallowing movements are undoubtedly part of a pseudobulbar palsy induced by hydrocephalic impairment of supratentorial corticobulbar motor pathways; other examples of these lower cranial nerve weaknesses appear to be part of a generalized akinesia that accompanies extensive frontal lobe dysfunction. But whether due to direct traction, to compression of corticobulbar pathways, or to supranuclear akinesia, the weakness usually quickly resolves if the surgeon can relieve the abnormal supratentorial pressure and the resulting displacement of the brainstem.

The false localizing signs of intracranial lesions are potentially puzzling diagnostically and clinically important because they reflect hydrocephalus, brainstem distortion, or (as with oculomotor paralysis) transtentorial herniation. They should, however, seldom confuse or interfere with the orderly diagnosis of coma. For one thing, the abnormalities are most frequent in the still-conscious patient whose central brainstem function has accommodated to mechanical displacement, and with the exception of oculomotor or abducens nerve paralysis, their development rarely parallels any acute decline in consciousness. For another, when diencephalic and central brainstem dysfunction finally do reach a stage to cause stupor or coma, more prominent and characteristic changes in respiration, pupillary, oculovestibular, and motor function still evolve in their characteristic progression, only partly obscured by these independent cranial nerve weaknesses.

Lumbar Puncture in Patients with Mass Lesions

The question is often asked, "Under what circumstances is a lumbar puncture indicated in patients suspected of suffering from an intracranial mass lesion?" Lumbar puncture is often useful in the differential diagnosis of such lesions: Bloody spinal fluid is present in all but a few patients with supratentorial hemorrhages; xanthochromia without red cells is a frequent finding in patients with subdural hematoma; malignant cells are occasionally identified in the spinal fluid of patients with primary or metastatic supratentorial tumors if the tumors have reached the subarachnoid or ventricular surface.[145] At times acute bacterial meningitis may mimic supratentorial mass lesions, and a lumbar puncture becomes essential in establishing both the diagnosis and the etiologic agent. However, lumbar puncture also can be dangerous in patients with supratentorial mass lesions. There are often large pressure gradients between the supratentorial compartment and the lumbar compartment,[56] and lowering the lumbar pressure by removing CSF may increase the gradient, promoting both transtentorial and foramen magnum herniation. How frequently a lumbar puncture produces or hastens the clinical signs of transtentorial herniation is unclear because it is difficult to be certain in an individual patient whether the patient would have spontaneously developed transtentorial herniation had the diagnostic procedure not been undertaken. The literature presents conflicting opinions. Lubic and Marotta[68] analyzed 401 lumbar punctures in patients with brain tumors, of whom 127 had increased intracranial pressure. Only one patient became worse following the procedure. Of their 127 patients with increased intracranial pressure, only 33 had papilledema, and in another 40 the funduscopic findings were equivocal. Korein, Cravioto, and Leicach[63] reported the findings in 129 patients with either papilledema or increased intracranial pressure on lumbar puncture. Fifteen patients (or 11.9 percent) developed possible complications of the lumbar puncture (any change for the worse in 48 hours). The authors, however, estimate the actual complication rate at 1.2 percent. Another series[114] reports 38 patients with papilledema secondary to brain tumors, of which 10 were subtentorial and the remainder supratentorial masses. The authors noted no complications but noted that seven of their patients had normal lumbar pressure despite the obvious evidence of increased intracranial pressure. A much more disturbing series was reported by Duffy[27] involving 30 patients referred to a neurosurgical service in 1 year because of complications of lumbar puncture. Twenty-nine of the patients had had headache and 22 had had focal neurologic signs before the puncture. Thirteen patients lost consciousness immediately following the lumbar puncture, and another 15 showed decreases in their state of consciousness within 12 hours following lumbar puncture. Three patients stopped breathing, and seven developed unequal pupils during or immediately after the procedure; 12 died within 10 days of the lumbar puncture. Of the 30 patients, only 10 had papilledema, and in half of the patients the lumbar puncture pressure was normal.

Our own experience has been that lumbar punctures, even when meticulously performed, can be dangerous in patients with increased intracranial pressure, as the case below illustrates:

Patient 2–4. A 43-year-old woman was admitted complaining of "terrible headache with nausea and vomiting for 3 days." She had been employed at the hospital for 5 years and during that time had visited the outpatient department over 30 times for evaluation and treatment of headache. The headaches, which had troubled her for 25 years, were usually right-sided and throbbing, occasionally preceded by blurred vision. They had been treated with ergotamine tartrate, aspirin and other analgesic drugs (including narcotics), and tranquilizing and antidepressant drugs. She was depressed and had often visited the psychiatrist. Two months before her admission she complained that she had fallen and bumped her right parietal area and had developed daily headaches. Her physical and neurologic examinations at that time were normal, as were skull x-ray studies; the pineal gland was not calcified. Ten days before her hospital admission she returned to the outpatient department complaining of 5 days of bilateral frontal and occipital headache unlike her usual headache and unrelieved by aspirin. The headache did not respond to ergotamine tartrate or to an interview with the psychiatrist, and she was admitted to the hospital.

On examination she was depressed, crying, apparently exhausted, and complaining of severe head pain. Her physical and neurologic examinations were reportedly normal, as were routine blood and urine examinations. At 9:30 the evening of admission a lumbar puncture was performed with an opening pressure of 125 mm. of CSF. The fluid was crystal clear; there was one mononuclear cell and no red cells were seen; the protein concentration was 10 mg./dl. and the glucose concentration 60 mg. During the night she was given 100 mg. pentobarbital, 10 mg. prochlorperazine, 30 mg. pentazocine, and 50 mg. meperidine. At 6:00 A.M. the nurse found her unarousable. Neurologic examination at that time revealed her to be unresponsive to all verbal stimuli, but she withdrew appropriately from noxious stimuli. There was equivocal blurring of the right optic disc; the right pupil was 3 mm. and the left pupil was 1.5 mm.; both reacted sluggishly. Doll's eye reactions were sluggish, but the ice water caloric test produced tonic movement toward the appropriate side. Her neck was supple; deep tendon reflexes were symmetrical, and plantar responses were extensor bilaterally. Despite the anisocoria, it was the impression of her physicians that she was suffering from depressant drug poisoning; however, 4 hours later she was unresponsive to noxious stimuli and the oculocephalic and oculovestibular responses had disappeared; her pupils were 6 mm. and unreactive, and stretch reflexes were absent. Respirations ceased and an endotracheal tube was placed and she was put on artifical respiration. Lumbar puncture was repeated and again the opening pressure of the clear fluid was 125 mm. of CSF. Bilateral trephination yielded 150 to 200 cc. of subdural blood that was removed from over the right cerebral hemisphere. No subdural blood was found on the left side. She did not recover spontaneous respirations and died 4 days later. At autopsy there was evidence of the evacuated subdural hematoma as well as cerebral swelling with uncal and transtentorial herniation.

Experiences such as this indicate that lumbar puncture can induce intracranial herniation even in patients who are relatively stable. A meticulous neurologic examination should be performed before lumbar puncture is undertaken in any patient. When there is evidence of a mass lesion increasing the intracranial pressure, we believe that lumbar punctures should be performed as the *primary* diagnostic procedure only if there is a suspicion of infection. In all other instances, when an intracranial mass lesion is suspected, a CT scan if available should be performed before lumbar puncture is undertaken. A CT scan will reliably identify cerebral and cerebellar hemorrhages and will usually identify subarachnoid hemorrhage from aneurysms. Weisberg[137] reported 50 patients with subarachnoid hemorrhage from ruptured aneurysms; CT scan demonstrated evidence of bleeding in 28 patients, and others report similar findings.[44] In patients with normal CT scans, lumbar puncture can usually be undertaken without significant risk or herniation. If CT scanning is not available and an intracranial mass lesion is suspected, arteriography or even trephination should be performed before lumbar puncture is undertaken.

Most complications of lumbar puncture occur within 12 hours after the procedure. Therefore, elective lumbar punctures should be performed during the daytime, permitting careful observations of the patient during his waking hours.

SPECIFIC SUPRATENTORIAL LESIONS AS CAUSES OF COMA

The preceding pages have described how the normal relationships among intracranial structures "decompensate" in response to supratentorial space-occupying lesions and have delineated the general clinical syndromes that result. Because of the physiologic implications of coma, it follows that when any supratentorial process impairs consciousness, the physician must either find a way promptly to halt the progression or take the risk of seeing his patient suffer irreversible brain damage or death. Beyond this generality, different supratentorial lesions have individual characteristics that govern their rate of development, modify their treatment, and sometimes hint at their specific diagnosis. The following sections of this chapter group these lesions according to their geographic distribution within the supratentorial space and discuss their symptoms. It has not been possible to discuss in detail every space-occupying lesion, and the examples selected have been those that most frequently present problems in the diagnosis and management of coma.

Extracerebral Lesions

General Characteristics

Neoplasms, infections, and hematomas are included in this category. Except with acute head injuries, these extracerebral lesions seldom produce a problem in the diagnosis of stupor or coma except when they and their surrounding tissue reaction change the intracranial dynamics so as to impair consciousness without producing prominent focal neurologic signs. Under such circumstances, the signs and symptoms of diffuse brain dysfunction often can be more prominent than those of focal brain disease. In the early stages, such a course of events is sometimes misdiagnosed as having a psychogenic or metabolic origin.

Neoplasms

The major intracranial extracerebral neoplasms rarely produce problems in the diagnosis of coma. Most meningiomas, neuromas, pituitary adenomas, and lymphomas tend to evoke prominent focal localizing signs in the form of headaches, seizures, motor and sensory abnormalities, cranial nerve defects, or endocrine changes *before* they impair alertness or awareness. Lymphomas and metastatic carcinomas can sometimes grow in the subdural space over the cerebral convexity to produce a clinical syndrome similar to that of chronic subdural hematomas, discussed below. However, only in the rare instance of hemorrhage into a tumor (e.g., pituitary apoplexy) is coma a presenting complaint with most extracerebral neoplasms. Rarely, large meningiomas underlying the frontal lobes grow so insidiously and displace the brain so gradually that quiet apathy bordering on akinetic mutism overcomes the patient before he presents for medical care. But even in such patients, brain tumors seldom escape clinical suspicions, and conventional objective tests confirm the diagnosis.

Closed Head Trauma

When acute head injury causes unconsciousness, the fact of the trauma seldom escapes attention, so that diagnostic problems related to impaired consciousness usually center on secondary questions, particularly on whether the patient might have an intracranial hemorrhage requiring neurosurgical treatment. Jennett and Teasdale discuss the full spectrum of head injuries and their treatment in the forthcoming *Volume 20* of this series, *Management of Head Injuries*. Blunt cranial trauma produces both extracerebral and intracerebral lesions and damage to the brainstem as well. However, almost all the directly treatable acute and subacute conditions are extracerebral and supratentorial, so that it is convenient to present the whole problem in this section insofar as it relates to supratentorial structures.

MECHANISM OF UNCONSCIOUSNESS FOLLOWING CLOSED HEAD INJURY. This is not precisely known. Our knowledge is deficient not because of any lack of good experimental or clinical-pathologic studies, of which many exist,[25,91,127] but because several mechanisms undoubtedly operate, producing more potential abnormalities than one can analyze accurately with available methods. These considerations make it presently impossible to say whether the changes that cause concussion and those that are responsible for prolonged post-traumatic coma differ from one another in kind or only in degree.

Acute unconsciousness following head injury represents one of the major causes of the comatose state. Physiologically, the loss of consciousness implies at the least that the subject has suffered widespread dysfunction of cerebral hemispheres or brainstem or both. Immediately following injury it may be difficult to distinguish on clinical grounds between subjects destined to awaken promptly and those who will remain in prolonged coma. Generally speaking, however, signs of pupillary dysfunction, oculomotor abnormalities, or abnormal posturings point towards a more severe injury with sustained loss of consciousness to be expected.

Brief unconsciousness from which the subject recovers in minutes to hours with no detectable residua other than transient post-traumatic amnesia and, perhaps, some more slowly subsiding nonspecific symptoms of giddiness and headache is universally termed *concussion*. The diagnosis can be made only in retrospect, since it describes a transient state. Symonds[127] would make this only quantitatively different from more long-lasting unresponsive states, while others suspect that the pathologic vascular-necrotic and nerve fiber damage[122] that one finds in the brains of patients dying after protracted coma have no anatomic counterpart in commonplace, brief concussion. One problem is that most reports of large series of patients with head injury are singularly free of the detailed clinical observations on breathing, oculomotor function, and motor responsiveness that one requires to evaluate whether the brainstem was functioning normally or abnormally.

Several pathogenic mechanisms act as potential causes of acute coma in closed head injuries.[1] Both physiologic and pathologic studies emphasize that shearing forces disrupt axons in the white matter of the hemispheres[1,25,91,123] and brainstem. In rapidly fatal cases it appears that such forces may also damage blood vessels, producing diffuse potential hemorrhages throughout the brain. Large areas of cerebral ischemia can be found at postmortem examination, presumably reflecting the combined effects of contusion, vasomotor paralysis, post-traumatic increases in intracranial pressure, and arterial hypotension, the last a result of systemic injuries. Soon after the trauma, intracerebral and extracerebral hemorrhages accumulate and enlarge, and these, plus vasoparalysis and tissue edema, raise the bulk and pressure of the supratentorial compartment and compress the diencephalon and hippocampal gyri into the tentorial notch.[2]

The nature of postmortem studies makes it difficult to determine precisely how much of the initial impact of the above processes affects the upper brainstem as opposed to the cerebral cortex. Nor can one be completely certain as to how changes thenceforth evolve. Several years ago, Foltz and Schmidt[33] reported that when they delivered a concussive blow to experimental animals, the physiologic activity of neuronal units in the brainstem reticular formation was temporarily suspended; regrettably, the observation has not been extended physiologically to include simultaneous recordings from other brain areas. Other studies conclude that the mesencephalon enjoys relative resistance to the morphologic lesions of head trauma, and that the axons and neurons of the hemispheres suffer proportionately greater damage.[2,3] Ommaya and Gennarelli[91] from physiologic and clinical analyses similarly conclude that more centripetally located structures suffer the greater functional and structural impairment from traumatic injuries, and that the diencephalic-mesencephalic core suffers last and least. Clinical observations support the conclusion that the brainstem receives relatively less damage in traumatic coma. Patients who recover to the vegetative state or remain with severe disability after head injury generally show relatively few signs of primary brainstem injury despite evidence of severe hemispheric disease. Even the occasional third nerve paralysis in such patients usually can be ascribed to either uncal compression of the nerve itself or to Duret hemorrhages in the brainstem, both being secondary to transtentorial herniation. There are exceptions, however, especially in very severe cases. Turazzi and Bricolo described acute pontine syndromes following head injury in 13 of 1000 patients admitted to their intensive care unit during a 3-year period.[131] Lindenberg and Freytag described 21 accident victims with traumatic hyperextension injuries of the head that led to hemorrhages at the junction of the medulla and pons and extending into the pontine tegmentum.[67] All these latter patients were dead on arrival at the hospital.

CONCUSSION. Patients with brief concussion are almost always arousable to semiappropriate responses by vigorous stimuli or possess conjugate or dysconjugate roving eye movements, responsive pupils that spontaneously fluctuate considerably in size, and a motor abnormality that at worst is confined to paratonia and extensor plantar responses. When neurologic abnormalities exceed these limits, the coma usually lasts a minimum of several hours and often much longer, and the patients suffer substantial post-traumatic amnesia and confusion coupled with a recovery period that stretches out over several days and often longer.

The adequate stimulus to produce concussion is either a rapid acceleration-deceleration injury[25] or a sudden blow that deforms the skull sharply. According to Gurdjian and associates,[42] the common denominator of both injuries is a sudden pressure rise in the region of neurons critical to consciousness. Cerebral ischemia, cerebral edema, depolarization of neurons from sudden acetylcholine release, and destruction of neurons and nerve fibers from shearing effects have all been invoked to explain how sudden deceleration or pressure changes interfere with neuronal function.[1,127] Although no gross neuropathologic changes consistently follow experimental concussion, individual neuronal disruption of many neurons together with scattered capillary damage can usually be found on microscopic examination, especially in the brainstem reticular formation.

Clinically, the coma of concussion is usually brief, with consciousness returning within minutes or at most a few hours after the blow. Respiration is usually eupneic and pupillary and ocular reflexes are retained, caloric tests often producing quick-phase nystagmus.[80] Decorticate or decerebrate rigidity may be present for a few brief moments, but usually patients are flaccid, although they do have bilateral extensor plantar responses. After consciousness is regained, confusion persists for variable periods but seldom for more than 24 hours. At least some amnesia is always present and includes the brief period of confusion after re-awakening (post-traumatic amnesia) as well as a shorter period before the concussion (retrograde amnesia).

The coma and post-traumatic confusion of concussion is nonspecific and resembles a number of other unconscious states, including the postictal state and some metabolic abnormalities. Unless there is direct physical evidence of head injury, the diagnosis can only be inferred from the situation in which the patient is found, so that a careful examination of the head should be made to uncover contusions or lacerations of the scalp. Diffuse or localized scalp edema without lacerations suggests multiple underlying fractures produced by a blunt instrument (e.g., "sandbagging"). An ecchymosis over the mastoid area (Battle's sign) results from a fracture through the temporal bone, and bilateral medial orbital ecchymoses ("raccoon eyes") suggest an anterior basal skull fracture. Both the nose and ears should be examined for blood or cerebrospinal fluid leakage. A clear, glucose-containing fluid in these cavities is CSF, which can only have seeped out via a basal skull fracture. Fracture lines over the vault also may be evident on skull x-rays films. Lumbar puncture is normal with uncomplicated concussion. Blood in the CSF suggests more severe brain damage (e.g., contusion or laceration), but in the absence of focal neurologic signs does not necessarily carry a worse prognosis.

ADVERSE FACTORS IN HEAD TRAUMA. Neurologic worsening often is delayed for hours or days after severe head injuries and this delayed response implies that a substantial degree of the morbidity and mortality may be preventable or treatable.

Some such patients may be initially conscious (the *lucid interval*), then deteriorate into coma. Others are never awake following the initial impact, but deteriorate neurologically within a matter of hours or days following the trauma. Many such patients suffer a progressive and seemingly irreversible degree of cerebral edema and vasomotor paralysis leading to increased intracranial pressure and various intracranial herniations. In others, preventable abnormalities may contribute to the deterioration. Rose and associates described 116 such deteriorating patients who eventually had autopsy examinations.[104] Avoidable abnormalities were identified in 74 percent of the patients and in 54 percent were regarded as contributing directly to death. The most common avoidable factor was delay in treating an intracranial hematoma. Other frequent abnormalities included poorly controlled epilepsy, meningitis, hypoxia, and hypotension. Increased intracranial pressure arises as a complication largely among patients with severe head injury, and its diagnosis and management generally require the advanced technical skills of neurologic specialists. Post-traumatic intracranial hemorrhages, however, are likely to arise in patients who initially may seem to have suffered relatively mild injuries and thus receive the care of the general physician. The same applies to post-traumatic stupor. Accordingly, the following paragraphs discuss the diagnosis of these conditions in some detail.

POST-TRAUMATIC INTRACRANIAL HEMORRHAGES. These include acute and delayed intracranial hematomas, extradural hemorrhages, and subdural hematomas.

Intracerebral hematomas occur in only about 2 percent of all serious head injuries, but are found in nearly half the fatal cases. Acutely, the effects of large hematomas can hardly be differentiated from the clinical consequences of other effects of severe brain trauma. Cerebral hematomas have more important clinical consequences when they produce subacute or delayed neurologic effects.[6,26,85]

Clinically, *delayed post-traumatic cerebral parenchymal hemorrhages* usually follow episodes of mild to moderately severe head trauma, sufficient perhaps to cause concussion. Following brief unconsciousness, a period relatively free of symptoms lasts for hours to weeks, after which time neurologic symptoms abruptly recur. Symptoms include drowsiness and progressive hemiparesis with or, often, without the typically apoplectic onset of a large cerebral hemorrhage. Headache and hemiplegia lead to coma and, in many instances, death. Surgical treatment generally carries the only hope, but has not met much success in patients already in coma.

Patient 2–5. A 14-year-old boy was thrown against a wall and stunned in a street fight. He broke his arm and had contusions of the scalp, but no other neurologic defect. At another hospital, skull x-rays were unremarkable, and the arm was set in a plaster cast. He was observed for 48 hours and discharged as neurologically well. Subsequently, he seemed lethargic to his parents, but otherwise unremarkable. Three weeks later the parents awakened to observe the first of four motor seizures starting in the boy's left arm and spreading to become generalized. When examined 2 hours later, he was unresponsive to verbal stimuli, had roving eye movements with small, unequal, sluggishly reactive pupils, and responded to noxious stimuli with either abnormal flexor or abnormal extensor postures. A CT scan (Fig. 24) showed a large parenchymal hemorrhage in the region of the left caudate nucleus and adjacent basal ganglia. The child rapidly developed midposition fixed pupils, absent oculocephalic reflexes, flaccid motor responses, and shallow breathing. He died 3 hours later. Autopsy examination by the medical examiner showed a large fresh left cerebral hemorrhage involving the region of the basal ganglia, internal capsule, and thalamus on the left without evidence of aneurysm, arteriovenous malformation, or subacute traumatic changes in the brain.

No one has provided a satisfactory explanation for the pathogenesis of delayed traumatic hematomas. Some may represent acute traumatic hemorrhages that enlarge to produce symptoms either because of surrounding edema and tissue reaction or because of new bleeding into the clot. Many, and perhaps most, however,

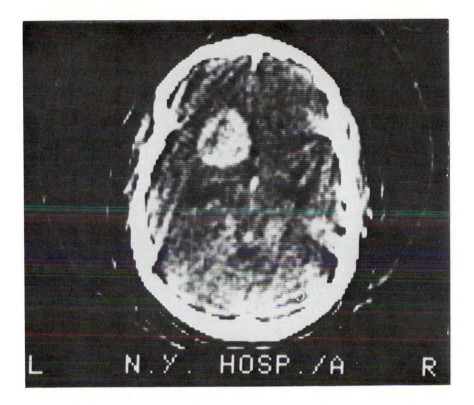

Figure 24. Delayed post-traumatic intracerebral hemorrhage in Patient 2-5.

arise *de novo* in the traumatized brain: successive CT scans have demonstrated delays up to 12 days after injury before the intracerebral hemorrhage appeared.[77] Most delayed traumatic intracerebral hemorrhages have been diagnosed within 4 weeks of the time of trauma, although examples are cited in which as many as 120 days or more separated the acute injury from the acute symptoms. The longer the interval the more difficult it is to relate the hemorrhage directly to the trauma except by the extraordinary association. Autopsy studies provide no strong clue as to mechanism. Young persons under age 40 years have been affected more than the elderly, but this may reflect only the epidemiology of head injury. Nevertheless, the youthful distribution provides evidence against intrinsic vascular disease causing the hemorrhages.

EXTRADURAL HEMORRHAGE. These lesions can arise frontally, laterally, or occipitally, with the lateral two presentations running the more rapid and usually more dangerous course. The bleeding can originate from veins, arteries, or both.

Frontal extradural hematomas most often arise in children and in the elderly, are relatively self-limited, and often run a slow course more like that of subdural hematoma. Occipital hematomas tend to compress posterior fossa structures and are discussed in Chapter 3. The most common extradural hemorrhages arise in the lateral temporal fossa as a result of laceration of the middle meningeal artery or vein by skull fracture. Such hemorrhages tend to enlarge rapidly until they self-seal the bleeding vessel, are surgically repaired, or cause the death of the subject.

121

Although an occasional hematoma arrests its own progress after 30 to 50 cc. of blood has accumulated and thereafter acts as a unilateral focal mass lesion, the more frequent course is for extradural hematomas to produce a rapidly progressing uncal syndrome within a few hours or days after injury.

Extradural hematomas push the brain laterally away from the skull and in so doing stretch and tear pain-sensitive meninges and blood vessels at the base of the middle fossa. They then compress the ipsilateral temporal lobe and adjacent hemispheric tissue, finally inducing uncal herniation and pressure on the third nerve, resulting in dilatation of the homolateral pupil *early* as brain swelling, shift, and herniation evolve.

As one might expect with such a sequence, the first symptom in conscious patients with extradural hematoma is headache, followed by clouding of consciousness or agitation and then by signs and symptoms of the uncal syndrome. Once clouding of consciousness develops, pupillary signs, hemiparesis, and deeper coma evolve within a few hours because, as the shifting uncus reaches far enough to compress the third nerve, it also encroaches upon the midbrain. Sunderland and Bradley[125] emphasized the sensitivity of pupillary signs as indicators in this condition and described their evolution and frequency: Only 2 of their 25 patients with epidural hemorrhage lacked pupillary abnormalities, and both of these had evidence of subacute or chronic lesions rather than acute ones. In the remaining patients the homolateral pupil first constricted, then gradually dilated to become widely fixed, and oculomotor palsy ensued. Each of these three distinct signs of dysfunction, i.e., pupillary dilatation, pupillary fixation, and oculomotor paralysis, passed from the homolateral to the contralateral eye before the next more severe ophthalmologic change occurred. Maximum pupillary dilatation and fixation were ominous, requiring urgent action since patients failed to survive if fixed bilateral mydriasis persisted longer than 30 minutes.

Motor signs occur only late in the course of extradural hematoma and usually are those of an acute uncal syndrome. In addition, the rapid development of the lesion and the irritative effect of the blood frequently produce focal or general convulsions.

The diagnosis of extradural hemorrhages can be puzzling, for many of them follow trivial blows to the head such as can arise in minor home accidents or sports. Another, smaller, group must be detected by signs of clinical worsening in patients who remain unconscious from the time of the initial head injury. Among Jamieson and Yelland's 167 patients with extradural hemorrhage[49] almost half had no initial loss of consciousness, and in Gallagher and Browder's equally large series,[36] two thirds had an initial injury too mild to command hospital attention. Only about 15 to 20 percent of patients undergo the "classical" sequence of an initial traumatic unconsciousness followed by a lucid interval and then a relapse into coma.

Headache is the most common symptom among conscious patients, but a subtle change in behavior, consisting of irritability, a lessening of mental alertness, or somnolence, is usually the first clear warning of impending trouble. Once stupor, pupillary or motor signs, or convulsions evolve, the chance of death increases rapidly, and less than half of the patients operated on in coma survive. Plain skull x-ray films will identify a fracture line in 80 percent but miss approximately 10 percent of fractures that turn up later at autopsy or operation. If the fracture line overlies the middle meningeal groove, it is essentially diagnostic.

Computerized tomography is the most informative laboratory tool in the diagnosis of nearly all cerebral hemorrhages, subdural hematomas providing the occasional exception. The specific attenuation differences caused by blood delineate accurately the hematoma from surrounding areas of brain injury and also indicate the presence of clinically unsuspected associated lesions. If CT scanning is unavailable, carotid arteriography is the diagnostic procedure of choice and usually outlines the lesion, showing separation of the cerebral vasculature from the inner table of the skull. However, with rapid clinical progression, particularly when altered consciousness or pupillary dilatation has already developed and there is a history of recent head trauma or a known temporal bone skull fracture, delay can be fatal. In such instances, diagnosis and treatment can be made simultaneously by proceeding immediately to trephination, which should be done quadrantically in the frontoparietal and temporoparietal regions of the skull.

SUBDURAL HEMATOMA. Acute and subacute hematomas are complications of acute, severe head injuries, and their effects usually are ancillary to the primary cause of coma, which is usually one of diffuse injury to the cerebral hemispheres and brainstem. These acute traumatic lesions seldom present problems of differential diagnosis and are not discussed in this book.

Chronic subdural hematoma is a more difficult diagnostic problem that is a fairly frequent cause of stupor or coma and often deceptive in its manifestations. Although the hematomas occur in all age groups, they are more frequent among the elderly, in chronic alcoholics, and in patients receiving anticoagulant drugs.

Chronic subdural hematomas are collections of weeks-to-months-old partially decomposed blood, blood pigments, and proteins in the subdural space. The lining of the hematoma is supplied with luxuriously proliferating small vessels, and fresh blood that leaks from the delicate channels undoubtedly is one factor that explains why chronic hematomas can suddenly cause symptoms after many months of clinical silence. Small clots containing 40 to 60 cc. probably cause no symptoms. Larger clots vary greatly in their size by the time they cause symptoms because of differences in how fast they accumulate as well as in the degree of brain displacement and compression that they produce. Since subdural hematomas do not directly invade the brain, it is not uncommon for them to produce signs of generalized supratentorial dysfunction in advance of or instead of paralysis, seizures, or other focal changes.

Recently, we reviewed the course of 73 patients with subdural hematomas treated at The New York Hospital (Table 6); 27 were in stupor or coma. Many of the patients were initially admitted to general medical or surgical services where it was notable that a supratentorial mass lesion was correctly diagnosed in less than half and not even considered in more than one third. The most serious and frequent error was to diagnose a subdural hematoma as cerebral infarction, although infection of the central nervous system was an incorrect diagnosis made almost as frequently.

Subdural hematomas cause coma because they compress the brain and displace it downward or laterally to produce central or uncal herniation. About 80 percent of all patients with subdural hematoma have headache and even if stuporous will recoil if the skull is percussed over the hematoma. Beyond this, the diagnosis is suggested by either of two clinical pictures. (A history of trauma cannot be relied upon). One is that of a straightforward expanding hemispheral mass lesion, and the physician needs only the history of headache combined with signs of progressive clouding of consciousness and hemispheric dysfunction to suspect the diagnosis and proceed with specific diagnostic studies. The other is more frequent and consists of headache, diffuse mental changes, obtundation, and signs signifying bilateral cerebral dysfunction (the presence of posthyperventilation apnea, sucking

Table 6. Clinical Features of 73 Patients with Subdural Hematoma

Unilateral hematoma	62
Bilateral hematomas	11
Mortality	14 (3 unoperated)
Number of patients in stupor or coma	27

Principal clinical diagnosis before hematoma discovered:	
Intracranial mass lesion or subdural hematoma	24
Cerebral vascular disease, but subdural hematoma possible	17
Cerebral infarction or arteriosclerosis	12
Cerebral atrophy	5
Encephalitis	8
Meningitis	3
Metabolic encephalopathy secondary to systemic illness	3
Psychosis	1

and snouting reflexes, diffuse paratonic resistance, minor stretch reflex differences), blending into the early symptoms of the central herniation syndrome. In their early stages, these imprecise symptoms may remotely suggest a subacute delirious reaction or even a primary dementia, but headache, drowsiness, asymmetry of signs, and a neurologic picture that characteristically changes or fluctuates under observation usually recommends the diagnosis. Neither psychiatric nor metabolic brain disease produces the typical rostral-caudal deterioration that sooner or later characterizes a progressive subdural hematoma.

The symptoms of subdural hematoma have a remarkable tendency to fluctuate from day to day and even from hour to hour, and the nature of these fluctuations is both alarming and suggestive of their possible cause. The more brief fluctuations undoubtedly are associated with plateau waves of increased intracranial pressure (see p. 96). The longer periods of intermittent neurologic dysfunction probably reflect the actual development of diencephalic compression. Many types of expanding supratentorial mass lesions produce fluctuations in their symptoms once they reach the stage where the intracranial structures can barely compensate for the mass and the associated downward shift it produces. When these masses are brain tumors, the fluctuations are usually associated with worsening or improvement of motor, sensory, or other focal signs. What is different (and deceptive) with subdural hematoma is that the downward shift and generalized supratentorial dysfunction often occur without substantial accompanying focal signs of a hemispheral mass lesion. Under these circumstances, as Patient 2-6 illustrates, the fluctuations are associated with changes in pupillary, ocular, and motor function that indicate the patient is moving in and out of the diencephalic stage of the central syndrome.

In making the diagnosis of chronic subdural hematoma, one cannot depend on distinctive pupillary abnormalities being present. Most patients in our own series had small, reactive pupils consistent with the early stages of the central syndrome. Cameron[13] has recently reported clinical findings in 114 patients with chronic subdural hematomas; only 6 (5 percent) had unilateral pupillary dilatation; 23 (20 percent) had papilledema; and 45 (40 percent) were hemiparetic, with the hemiparesis being ipsilateral to the hematoma in 18 and contralateral in 28. Fifteen patients (13 percent) were in coma at the time of admission to hospital. Treatment led to complete recovery in 89 percent of the patients, including 14 of the 15 in coma.

General laboratory aids help only moderately when subdural hematoma is suspected (Table 7). In The New York Hospital series, examination of the spinal fluid was undependable as the fluid was xanthochromic or under increased pressure in less than half of the patients. The EEG was frequently abnormal but often not focally so. Skull x-ray pictures contained evidence of a pineal shift in only 12 of 73 cases, although, when present, this was an obviously valuable sign of a mass lesion. Brain scanning after radionuclide injection detects an abnormal uptake in the region of the hematoma in about 80 percent of such cases, and in an even higher percentage when the lesion is over 2 weeks old and membranes have formed.

CT scanning, especially when performed with contrast-enhancing techniques and interpreted with experience and care, almost always detects a subdural hematoma. Even when the biologic degradation of the blood produces a fluid isodense with brain, and even when bilateral isodense subdural hematomas do not cause midline shifts, the absence of cortical sulci[60] and the presence of downward herniation[93] and contrast-enhancement of cortical vessels pushed from the inner table of the skull insure an accurate diagnosis if the scans are read attentively. The only circumstance in which an error is likely to be made is when the hematoma is against the vertex of the skull, arising from the sagittal sinus or low in the posterior fossa. Even here, coronal CT scans may be helpful in the former instance.

In doubtful cases, carotid angiography provides the advantage of outlining other intracranial structures as well as unusually placed hematomas tucked between or underneath the hemispheres. When clinical signs strongly suggest subdural hematoma, the exact diagnosis and treatment should not be delayed. As implied above, symptoms in these patients often reflect a delicate balance between compensation and decompensation of the neural and vascular structures grouped around the tentorial notch, and patients can rapidly develop serious and irreversible cerebral damage if not properly and promptly treated.

Patient 2–6. A 35-year-old woman had been well until the last trimester of her uncomplicated pregnancy in September, when she became lethargic. After the uncomplicated delivery of a premature child, she continued to be drowsy, and, despite the demands of the newborn, she slept for long periods during both the day and night. In early November, she had a brief tonic seizure. Her lethargy increased, and by mid-November she developed headaches, which were at first bioccipital and subsequently changed position to become dull and constant behind the left eye. Concurrently she developed intermittent nausea and vomiting. A neurologic examination was reportedly negative at that time. At the beginning of December she was found by her husband early one morning speaking incoherently. She was admitted to The New York Hospital later the same day, irrational, bewildered, and agitated. The somatic neurologic examination was unremarkable at that time. Her serum potassium was 2.5 mEq./L. (the patient had been receiving chlorothiazide) and her serum bicarbonate was 30 mEq./L. The lumbar puncture yielded faintly xanthochromic, clear fluid, with a pressure of 205 mm., no cells, and 56 mg./dl. of protein. An electroencephalogram showed bursts of high amplitude 2 cps waves in the frontal areas bilaterally, but predominating on the left side. Skull x-ray findings were negative.

Table 7. Diagnostic Features of 73 Patients with Subdural Hematoma

Skull X-Ray Examination		Spinal Fluid (51 patients)	
Negative	53	Protein under 50	24
Fracture	8	Protein over 50	25
Pineal shift	12	Less than 5 RBC	21
		More than 5 RBC	28
Electroencephalogram		More than 2 WBC	11
Focal abnormality	19	Xanthochromia	23
General abnormality	18	CSF pressure < 150	24
Normal	8	CSF pressure > 150	25
Unsatisfactory	1		

The electrolyte abnormalities were corrected parenterally, and later the same day the patient had recovered remarkably. She was alert, oriented, and cooperative and had no memory of her recent confusion. She continued to have left-sided headaches, however. Six hours later she became obtunded—indeed, almost stuporous—and she was disoriented when aroused. Her pupils were 2 mm. and reactive, and she had bilateral paratonic resistance to passive stretch in the extremities as well as mild right-sided weakness and an abnormal plantar response on the right. The fluctuation of signs in and out of stupor along with bilateral motor signs suggested incipient transtentorial herniation, and biparietal burr holes were placed by a neurosurgeon. These yielded a large chronic subdural hematoma on the left containing both fresh and decomposed blood. Within minutes after evacuation of the hematoma she became alert, oriented, and rational. A detailed neurologic examination performed 3 days later encountered no abnormalities. Subsequently it was learned that the patient probably suffered from recurrent alcoholism and falls, but this information was pointedly withheld by the family when she was first examined.

Comment: This is a typical history for subdural hematoma and illustrates how difficult it is to determine retrospectively when these lesions begin or first produce clinical symptoms. Whether her bouts of exacerbation represented additional head trauma with fresh bleeding cannot be known. When she came under our care, her fluctuating symptoms clearly reflected diffuse, intermittent, bilateral cerebral dysfunction, and these fluctuations plus the other clinical and EEG signs of diencephalic dysfunction suggested early transtentorial herniation. Her rapid recovery when the hematoma was evacuated was evidence that her clinical picture was due to shift and displacement of the brain rather than to structural compression of vessels and neurons, for the latter would hardly have responded so rapidly.

The following patient with subdural hematoma illustrates well the fluctuating nature of rostral-caudal signs of upper brainstem dysfunction in this disorder, as well as the close relation between delirium and coma in cerebral disorders.

Patient 2-7. A 34-year-old male clerk of exemplary habits had had bitemporal headaches for a month, and for 5 days had had an increase in headache accompanied by confusion, agitation, and somnolence. He had noted some weakness of his right side the day before admission, and his wife, a nurse, had noted that his left eye lagged behind the right when he looked to the right.

When he was admitted to The New York Hospital, his blood pressure, pulse, respiration, and body temperature were unremarkable. He was obtunded, restless when aroused, and oriented only to person. The pupils were dilated to 7 mm. bilaterally but reacted to light. Examination of extraocular movements showed loss of upward conjugate gaze. There was a mild right hemiparesis, the stretch reflexes were bilaterally hyperactive, and both plantar responses were extensor.

During the 2 hours after admission the patient became more agitated and developed more spasticity and intermittent decorticate spasms on the right. His pupils shrank symmetrically to 5 mm. but retained their light reaction. At lumbar puncture the CSF pressure was 240 mm., and the fluid was otherwise unremarkable. Following the puncture, the right facial weakness was briefly more pronounced, but within 2 hours he was alert, talking coherently, and the right-sided signs had almost disappeared. Diffuse headache persisted, however.

The improvement misled his examining physicians into believing that he might have a metabolic cerebral lesion, and it was decided to observe him and obtain more laboratory work. During the next 5 hours he again developed obtundation accompanied by increased spasticity on the right side and bilateral extensor plantar responses. The cycle reversed again, and by the next morning, 6 hours later, he was alert and responsive and a neurologic consultant found a loss of upward conjugate gaze as the only certain abnormality. The patient was scheduled for arteriography, but as preparation for the procedure was made he became progressively more somnolent. The right pupil shrank to 3 mm. and lost its light reaction. The left pupil remained at 5 mm. but with a minimal light and ciliospinal reaction. The right eye turned outward (third nerve palsy) and did not move during the doll's eye maneuver. Decorticate posturing developed first on the right, then on the left side of the body. The arteriogram demonstrated a large nonvascular area in the left parietotemporal subdural space. On the way to the operating room, the man became first extremely agitated, then quiet and unresponsive. The left pupil became fixed, and the left eye deviated laterally. Shortly thereafter, the patient's eyes deviated in a skewed manner: the right up and the left down. Respiration rose to 30 per minute, then quieted and became small in amplitude and slow (8 per minute) in frequency.

126

Burr holes were placed promptly, and 150 cc. of dark red blood were removed from the subdural space on the left. The underlying brain was slack and reexpanded only after lumbar subarachnoid saline injection. During operation, the respiratory rate gradually rose to 60 per minute. One hour later the pupils were 3 mm. and reacted to light, and the eyes were conjugately midposition with intact horizontal oculovestibular responses to head turning. Four hours after the surgical procedure the patient responded verbally to vigorous stimulation and moved all four extremities. Thereafter, he made an uneventful recovery and left the hospital on the twelfth day with no neurologic residuals other than a slight weakness on the lower right side of the face. No history of relevant head trauma could be recalled.

POST-TRAUMATIC STUPOR IN CHILDREN. This syndrome involves a lesion of neither the epidural nor the subdural space, but since its symptoms are often confused with these more serious conditions its description is included here.

Head injuries in children often initiate a clinical picture of post-traumatic stupor, which is briefly alarming but ultimately benign. The children are typically under 14 years of age and suffer a moderate or severe direct closed head injury such as occurs after falling from a tree, being hit on the head by a ball, or being struck in an accident. Usually there is brief unconsciousness after which children go through either of two early courses. Most recover immediately and are clinically well so that physicians rarely see them. A smaller number recover for 30 to 60 minutes but then relapse and undergo several hours of lethargy accompanied by fluctuating but consensual changes in the pupil size, muscular hypertonus shifting from one side of the body to the other, and unilateral or bilateral extensor plantar responses. Focal seizures[98] and cortical blindness[39] have been observed during such periods. The children often are nauseated and vomit, but as a rule awaken from their lethargic state within 2 to 6 hours after the injury and are alert with no apparent residua. Sometimes, however, that night the child declines into a stuporous sleep and is abnormally difficult to arouse, a state that superficially may suggest the presence of a cerebral contusion or even an intracranial hematoma. The arousability, the lack of focal signs, and the lack of progression belie these more serious diagnoses, and the children usually recover with no residua the following day.

The cause of childhood post-traumatic stupor is unknown (see the next section). The patients have normal x-ray findings and EEG records. Lumbar puncture usually is unremarkable except for occasional high pressures of 160 to 200 mm., a finding difficult to interpret in children. The illness is short-lived, and the benign features that distinguish it from serious head injury are that, after brief worsening, the children improve spontaneously and progressively, do not show evolving focal cerebral signs, and, despite sleeping deeply, can be awakened at least briefly if vigorously stimulated.

DELAYED NONHEMORRHAGIC ENCEPHALOPATHY FOLLOWING MILD HEAD TRAUMA. This disorder may differ only in degree and permanence from the delayed encephalopathy in children described above. Delayed post-traumatic cortical blindness, for example, occurs in younger adults as well as children,[39] although it is more common in the latter. Fortunately, delayed encephalopathy in adults is rare, for the course of the clearly documented cases observed in our own hospital and by others has been devastating. The reported patients have been young people below the age of 25 years, mainly adolescents. Following a relatively mild head injury sufficient to stun but not cause sustained unconsciousness, the patients lapse into coma or develop a severe focal neurologic deficit (cortical blindness, hemiplegia, aphasia) after an awake, relatively symptom-free, post-traumatic period lasting from 15 minutes to 2 or more hours. In no instance has the clinical examination at the time of delayed unconsciousness been sufficiently detailed to estimate how much brainstem function was lost. A 24-year-old woman examined by us several years ago at The New York Hospital had signs of a progressive left hemispheric dysfunction without brainstem dysfunction that began after a closed head injury and a 30-minute clear period following the trauma. The duration and evolution of her signs over a period of less than 2 hours resembled the course of ischemic cerebral infarction. Trephination and ventriculography were unremarkable and failed to reveal the expected epidural hematoma. Arteriography was not performed. She was left with a significant residual motor and language defect.

Autopsy findings have been reported on four such patients.[41,119,122] The brains of all four contained multifocal ischemic or necrotic lesions. In two the abnormalities were confined to the cortical diencephalic and brainstem gray matter, but the other two lacked such a clear geographical distribution. The ultimate pathogenesis of this lesion is unknown. Neither the appearance of any of the patients nor the pathologic changes at autopsy suggested that they suffered from an unsuspected period of hypotension or an asystole. The obviously ischemic lesions found at postmortem examination suggest a link to the functional cerebral vascular abnormalities that follow trauma (described on p. 118), but no direct evidence supports this speculation.

Subdural Empyema

Subdural empyema is a rare but important cause of stupor or coma, which can be cured if treated promptly by surgical drainage, but damages the brain irreversibly if neglected.[55] The condition is usually a complication of otorhinologic disease, particularly of acute sinusitis. Less commonly, the empyema follows acute meningitis or the rupture of an intracerebral abscess, complicates a penetrating wound of the skull, or follows upon a surgical procedure. Males are affected more than females, and a significant proportion of the patients give a history of either ear, nose, and throat surgery or head trauma shortly before they develop symptoms of the empyema. The infection reaches the subdural space either by extending directly through the skull (otitic infection) or along the penetrating veins, the latter route being most common with sinus infection. Rarely, hematogenous infection of a previously sterile subdural effusion has been reported. Pus sometimes accumulates in the subdural spaces between the hemispheres or at the base of the brain, but the most frequent distribution is a collection extending posteriorly from the frontal pole over the dorsolateral part of the hemisphere.[46] Streptococci are the most common causative organisms, the anaerobes being frequent.

Subdural empyema produces stupor or coma by two mechanisms. The principal mechanism results from an expanding supratentorial mass, which, together with the adjacent brain swelling that results from inflammation and venous congestion, produces rostral-caudal displacement and compression of the brain at its base. The other is that of an intracranial infection, which either spreads to involve the adjacent brain or whose toxic effects impair brain metabolism. At least in the early stages, the latter effect is usually less prominent because the arachnoid membrane is relatively impermeable to both toxins and infection. As the illness evolves, however, meningitis, underlying bacterial encephalitis, and especially cortical thrombophlebitis become more prominent and are accompanied by increasing focal signs of seizures, hemiplegia, or aphasia.[65]

The clinical picture of subdural empyema resembles in many ways the symptoms of subdural hematoma except that there is a greater tendency to produce stupor or coma in advance of focal hemispheral signs, the time course is greatly truncated, and the patient with empyema has fever and toxic signs. A small proportion of patients have cutaneous swelling over the infected sinus (Pott's puffy tumor). The diagnosis should be suspected in a patient with clouded consciousness who has the history or x-ray findings of rhinootitic infection, headache, skull tenderness, fever, and the early signs of transtentorial herniation, combined with focal signs of early frontal lobe dysfunction. These localizing features, which include hemiparesis, seizures and aphasia, provide the principal differentiating features from acute, uncomplicated meningitis. Typically, patients with subdural empyema have mild bilateral motor signs at this early stage. Meningismus is sometimes present, and the spinal fluid is under increased pressure. The spinal fluid contents are rarely normal, although their cell count is often low (we view more than 2 lymphocytes suspiciously and even a single neutrophil as abnormal) and the CSF protein may be only modestly elevated. Organisms can almost never be cultured from the CSF in the early stage of the illness. Skull x-ray films are helpful only if they disclose evidence of sinusitis or sinus or mastoid osteomyelitis.

When subdural empyema is suspected, cerebral angiography is probably the most valuable indirect technique to establish the diagnosis and also frequently reveals sites of clinically unsuspected pus.[46] The relative value of CT scanning has not been fully established in this uncommon condition. Kaufman and Leeds, however, report that in five cases, CT scans equalled the accuracy of cerebral angiography in identifying the size and extent of the empyema.[54] When patients are severely and acutely ill, it is sometimes desirable to proceed immediately to trephination, which not only provides a definitive diagnosis but permits drainage as well. Appropriately selected antimicrobial agents in large doses are indicated as soon as one suspects an intracranial infection.

The following young man had subdural empyema. It was of interest that burr holes were delayed several hours because asterixis, fever, and vomiting originally suggested metabolic disease. The importance of only a few cells in the CSF was not initially recognized.

Patient 2–8. A 28-year-old man had been healthy except for chronic sinusitis. Two weeks before his admission to the hospital, he developed a dull, right frontal headache that gradually became more severe. His physician gave him penicillin intramuscularly and for 12 hours after this he developed fever (39.6°C), nausea, and vomiting. He then improved for 3 days, after which increasing headache and a return of fever led to another penicillin injection, which again was followed by transient nausea and vomiting and then improvement. Five days before we saw him, his headaches became "excruciating" and he was admitted to another hospital. A diagnosis of sinusitis was made and penicillin was given, 1,200,000 units every 4 hours. During the ensuing 3 days he gradually became first obtunded and finally almost unresponsive.

When admitted to The New York Hospital, his rectal temperature was 37.5°C, his pulse 70 per minute, his respirations 40 per minute and regular, and his blood pressure 120/75 mm. Hg. He was stuporous and responded only to vigorous stimuli. Once aroused, he was disoriented to time, but followed commands slowly and appropriately. He complained of right hemicranial headache, and the right side of the skull was tender. The neck was not stiff. He had had an old injury of the left iris that reduced its light reaction, but both pupils were 2 mm. in diameter and reacted to light, the right briskly so. The retinal veins were full. Testing of extraocular movements showed limitation of both voluntary and reflex upward gaze. There was bilateral paratonic resistance to passive stretch in the extremities and very mild right-sided hemiparesis. Bilateral extensor plantar responses were elicited, more briskly on the left than on the right. A striking finding was the presence of asterixis involving particularly the left upper and lower extremity with occasional myoclonic twitches involving the same members.

A lumbar puncture released crystal-clear spinal fluid with a pressure of 120 mm. There were 32 red blood cells and 3 lymphocytes per cu. mm. The protein content was 47 mg./dl. The white blood count was 13,000 with 80 percent neutrophilic forms. Skull x-ray films showed evidence of bilateral frontal and maxillary sinusitis.

The asterixis was puzzling, and the sinusitis and fever not at first given sufficient weight. However, the progressive obtundation, small pupils, loss of upward gaze, and bilateral mild motor signs all suggested a poorly localized supratentorial mass, producing the diencephalic stage of the central syndrome. With the history of sinus infection and fever, abscess formation was considered. Bilateral parietal-occipital burr holes were placed, and copious amounts of pus were evacuated from the right subdural space. The next day a frontal sinus antrotomy was performed to drain that cavity as well. Postoperatively, the patient developed left-sided motor seizures and weakness. Transient left homonymous hemianopsia was noted at the same time, but he had not previously been sufficiently alert to enable vision to be tested. Cultures of the empyema yielded a microaerophilic streptococcus. Penicillin was continued for 2 weeks parenterally. Recovery was uneventful, and the patient has subsequently remained well and returned to work.

Comment: This patient developed the typical signs of the central syndrome of transtentorial herniation with rostral-caudal deterioration. The persistent headache and lack of clear localizing signs suggested a lesion in the subdural space, and the fever, rapid course, and history of sinusitis should have made us suspect empyema more promptly. The asterixis was a finding of great interest, particularly as it developed maximally in the extremities opposite to the abscess. We tentatively ascribed this to "toxic" effects of the infection, but the important thing was to learn that it did not rule out a mass lesion.[144]

Intracerebral Lesions

Neoplasms, hemorrhages, infarctions, and abscesses are included in this category. Most of these lesions are easier to localize and identify than are extracerebral lesions because they impinge upon or directly destroy the cerebral structures dealing with movement, sensation, speech, or the special senses. By the time they produce coma, therefore, most intracerebral masses have also produced specific localizing neurologic signs that warn of their presence and sometimes imply their histologic construction. There are two exceptions to the rule that intracerebral masses produce focal signs before generalized ones: Frontal lobe and intraventricular masses both arise in neurologically "silent" areas and even when they produce widespread anatomic effects they may result in few recognizable focal symptoms in advance of confusion, stupor, or coma.

Cerebral Vascular Disease

The most frequent type of cerebral vascular disease producing altered consciousness is cerebral hemorrhage, acting as an expanding mass to produce diencephalic compression and transtentorial herniation. Large cerebral hemispheric infarcts sometimes act to impair consciousness by a similar mechanism. Bilateral thalamic and hypothalamic infarction is a rare and difficult-to-diagnose form of supratentorial vascular lesion causing coma. The following paragraphs describe these several conditions in greater detail.

CEREBRAL HEMORRHAGE. About one fourth of all cerebral hemorrhages produce unconsciousness at their onset,[84] making them the most common cause of coma among supratentorial vascular lesions. Hemorrhage into the cerebral parenchyma is due to: (1) most commonly, rupture of an intracerebral blood vessel in the parenchyma, usually an artery, occasionally a vein; (2) leakage from or rupture of arterial aneurysms at the base of the brain; (3) leakage from or rupture of arterio-venous malformations or microangiomas; and (4) hemorrhage into a small and asymptomatic primary or metastatic brain tumor. In the case of aneurysms or of large arteriovenous malformations, the source of bleeding can usually be identified, but with hypertensive hemorrhages deep in the parenchyma, it is almost the rule for the pathologist not to find the actual bleeding vessel.

Spontaneous parenchymal cerebral hemorrhages producing coma arise deep in the hemisphere and measure 2 to 3 cm. in diameter by CT scan or at autopsy. They usually involve structures in and around the internal capsule, especially the putamen and thalamus. This anatomic distribution means that hemorrhages severe enough to cause coma produce hemiplegia or hemisensory defects as well. Although cerebral hemorrhage is almost the only supratentorial vascular lesion that produces coma within minutes of its onset, unconsciousness is rarely the very first sign of even these catastrophes. Thus, almost all patients with parenchymal cerebral hemorrhage have at least a brief period of headache, aphasia, hemisensory defect or hemiparesis before losing consciousness, and many suffer for several hours a gradual or stair-step progression of symptoms. Some of these worsenings result because swelling and inflammation of the brain progressively surround the fresh area of bleeding, but most instances probably reflect progressive bleeding.

The presentation of a large series of parenchymal hemorrhages diagnosed by CT scan at the Massachusetts General Hospital provides an excellent profile of this condition.[45,135] Forty-two hemorrhages involved the putamen or thalamus. Most of the patients were hypertensive, only five having diastolic blood pressures below 100 mm. Hg on admission. The development of altered consciousness correlated directly with the size of the hematoma. Hematomas 3 to 4 cm. in diameter invariably produced severe neurologic defects, while in several instances small bleeds were regarded clinically as embolic strokes prior to obtaining CT scan. The level of consciousness also correlated with outcome, so that 12 of the 13 patients in coma died, as did 5 of 12 who were obtunded or stuporous from thalamic hemorrhage.

Headache was a less prominent symptom in these patients than previous analyses have suggested and was recorded in only 42 percent.[84] The evolution of the disorder was abrupt in one third and smooth in two thirds, with hemiparesis, hemisensory defects, and abnormal eye signs being the most prominent physical changes. More than half the patients worsened in the hospital, several abruptly. Abnormal eye signs with putamenal hemorrhage included anisocoria, fixed dilated pupils, and lateral gaze preference towards the side of the lesion; all were associated with larger hematomas and a poorer prognosis. With thalamic hemorrhage ophthalmologic abnormalities typically included limitation of vertical gaze, downward or down and lateral positioning of the eyes, and small pupils with fixed or sluggish reactions to light. Occasionally ocular deviation was unexpectedly towards the side of the hemiplegia rather than away. Two patients with putamenal hemorrhage had lumbar cerebrospinal fluids essentially free of blood. Many patients, especially with thalamic hemorrhage, bled into the ventricular system.

The Harvard group indicated that no patient with cerebral hemorrhage admitted in coma survived.[84] Our own findings drawn from a prospective study of medical coma are slightly less gloomy: 6 of 47 patients admitted in coma with parenchymal cerebral hemorrhage survived.[8] However, only three regained an independent existence, emphasizing the serious neurologic implications of coma with cerebral hemorrhage.

Examples of cerebral hemorrhages producing the central and uncal syndromes, respectively, have been given in Patients 2–1 and 2–2. The following report illustrates how patients with cerebral hemorrhage sometimes rapidly develop signs of diencephalic dysfunction and how effective treatment can equally rapidly reverse these signs.

Patient 2–9. A 34-year-old woman developed a sudden right-sided headache that rapidly spread over the right hemicranium. She could not see clearly to the left, and her family noted that she was confused. Two days later she was brought to the hospital. At that time she had a blood pressure of 160/100 mm. Hg. She was lethargic, oriented, and coherent but had left homonymous hemianopsia and a left hemisensory defect for stereoperception. She denied her neurologic abnormalities in a manner typical of patients with parietal lobe damage.

Laboratory work was unremarkable, lumbar puncture being omitted because cerebral hemorrhage was suspected. A right internal carotid arteriogram showed evidence of a moderately large right posterior temporal lobe mass with the internal cerebral vein shifted 10 mm. to the left.

The day after admission her blood pressure slowly rose from 140/110 to 190/100 mm. Hg and her pulse rate fell from 72 to 54 per minute. After 60 to 90 minutes, she became unresponsive with periodic breathing, bilaterally dilated (8 mm.) and fixed pupils, flaccid extremities, and extensor plantar responses. She was given sodium mannitol, 50 gm. in 250 cc. of 5 percent dextrose in water, over the next hour. Corticosteroids were given intravenously, a tracheostomy was performed, and she was placed on artificial respiration. (Hyperosmotic agents shrink the brain, and lowering the arterial carbon dioxide content by artificial ventilation reduces the intracranial blood volume, also shrinking the intracranial contents.) After 60 minutes of treatment, the pupils constricted to 5 mm. and regained their light reflex. She began to move to her right side.

Over the next 3 days she gradually improved and awakened, although she remained obtunded when not stimulated. She was oriented but showed almost complete denial of her rather severe left homonymous hemianopsia, her left-sided hemisensory defect, and her mild left hemiparesis. The breathing pattern was normal, and the pupils were 4 mm., reacted to light, and were equal. She could gaze conjugately to both lateral extremes but could not follow an object with her eyes to the left of the midline. There was paralysis of voluntary and reflex upward gaze.

She continued to improve, but suddenly one evening she became apneic and flaccid with dilated fixed pupils and divergent eyes. She died after receiving artificial respiration and pressor agents for 2 days.

At postmortem examination, the brain was soft, reflecting the 2-day period of artificial survival. The inferior and posterior portions of the right temporal lobe were destroyed by a large, partly clotted and partly fresh hemorrhage, which had lacerated the base of the temporal lobe, pushing the homolateral uncus into the tentorial incisura and displacing the opposite third nerve downward and compressing it against the petroclinoid ligament. The entire upper brainstem was displaced caudally, but the brainstem was free of gross hemorrhage. The exact source of the hemorrhage could not be found.

Only 6 percent of patients with thalamic hemorrhage can be considered alert according to Walshe and associates.[135] Findings in the following patient from The New York Hospital with a thalamic hemorrhage suggest that the pathogenesis of both the stupor and the ophthalmologic abnormalities in such cases result from downwards compression of the midbrain-tectal region.

Patient 2–10. A 55-year-old man with known malignant melanoma developed a right thalamic hemorrhage with stupor, tetraparesis, deepening coma, and left decerebrate rigidity. The eyes deviated conjugately down and to the left, initially failing to move upwards on oculocephalic responses and eventually coming to rest substantially below the horizontal meridian. Lateral oculocephalic reflex movements were intact. A ventricular catheter was placed to drain the supratentorial ventricular system after a CT scan showed a right thalamic hemorrhage. The subject awakened shortly and the abnormal eye movements disappeared.

INTRAVENTRICULAR HEMORRHAGE. Intraventricular hemorrhage usually occurs from dissection of an intracerebral hemorrhage into the lateral ventricles. Much less often such hemorrhages result from bleeding from an intraventricular neoplasm. The effects of such hemorrhages vary with their size. Intraventricular hemorrhage occurred in 24 of 34 of our own patients who died from cerebral hemorrhage, and a retrospective analysis suggested that in many this catastrophe produced a characteristic group of symptoms. Ten patients presented with sudden profound coma after either very brief or no recognized initial symptoms. They died within minutes to hours and often demonstrated signs of pontine or medullary failure within a few minutes following onset. The 14 remaining patients had a double-phased illness: Their early symptoms clinically resembled those of any kind of progressive supratentorial mass lesion producing incipient rostral-caudal deterioration. Suddenly this orderly progression of signs was interrupted by deeper coma, convulsions, and the abrupt appearance of signs indicating low brainstem damage. We believe that these signs reflect sudden pressure transmitted through the ventricular system to the floor of the fourth ventricle at the moment of intraventricular rupture. Experimental data are consistent with this interpretation. Blood, per se, in the ventricular system has little or no ill effects on the brain. However, the sudden injection of fluid into a lateral cerebral ventricle adversely affects blood pressure, pulse rate, and respiration and can produce acute pressure gradients between the anterior and posterior fossae with rapid medullary failure.

The following patient's course was typical of intraventricular hemorrhage. The effects of sudden bleeding into the ventricular system were difficult to distinguish from primary pontine hemorrhage (p. 163).

Patient 2–11. A 79-year-old man had a history of long-standing hypertension with blood pressures in the range of 170–190/100–110 mm. Hg. On the night of admission he awakened his wife by noisy breathing. He was difficult to arouse and could only mumble. Weakness on the left side of the body from a previous hemiparesis was noted by the wife to have become a total hemiplegia. Within the hour he became entirely unresponsive to his wife's entreaties. Examination in the emergency room approximately 1 hour later showed ataxic irregular breathing, midposition fixed pupils, eyes conjugately fixed in the straight ahead position, and absent oculovestibular responses bilaterally. Noxious stimulation to the fingernail beds elicited bilateral extensor postural responses in all four extremities, more prominent on the left than the right and more vigorous in the arms than the legs. The patient was placed on a ventilator pending objective diagnosis. However, the story of abrupt hemiplegia progressing within an hour to coma accompanied by signs of upper and middle brainstem dysfunction led the resident to a clinical diagnosis of cerebral hemorrhage with intraventricular rupture and dissection down the aqueductal system into the fourth ventricle. A CT scan (Fig. 25) confirmed the clinical impression. The patient's heart stopped several days later with no intervening neurologic improvement.

Not all intraventricular hemorrhages produce neurologic devastation. One often observes extension of small cerebral hemorrhages into the lateral or third ventricle on CT scans with little associated evidence that serious symptoms have resulted. As illustrated in the following patient, the intraventricular blood in such subjects disappears rapidly, leaving no apparent residua.

Patient 2–12. A 16-year-old boy awakened in the early morning with occipital headache and a left hemiparesis. He vomited and fell to the floor in attempting to arise. Several hours later, he was noted to be oriented, but drowsy and had a dense left hemiplegia and hemisensory defect. Twenty-four hours later, the blood pressure was 120/80 and the general examination was unremarkable. The youngster complained of severe generalized headache, photophobia, and stiff neck. He was oriented but uncooperative. Papilledema was absent; the right pupil was 2 mm., the left was 3 mm., and both reacted to light and accommodation. Miosis was noted on the right. No conjugate gaze abnormality was observed, but there was a consistent skew deviation with the anteroposterior axis of the right eye raised approximately 3 mm. above that of the left and the change being consistent in all directions of gaze. This abnormality lasted approximately 24 hours. Supranuclear left facial weakness was observed as was a left hemiparesis with residual strength in the extremities graded 1 out of a potential 5. On the left side of the body, including the cornea and face, sensation was reduced to pain and temperature. Position sense was reduced in the left upper extremity but not in the left lower. CT scan showed a high density lesion, presumed to represent a hematoma in the right thalamus with extension of bleeding into the ventricular system (Fig. 26). Cerebral angiography outlined a small arteriovenous malformation lying in the region of the pulvinar of the right thalamus and overlaid by hematoma. The angioma subsequently disappeared following treatment by proton beam irradiation. Three years later the young man showed only a mild residual increase in stretch reflexes in the left extremities with slight reduction in all sensory modalities on the left side of the body and mild athetosis in the left upper and lower extremity.

CEREBRAL INFARCTION. Unconsciousness is seldom the initial sign of uncomplicated cerebral hemispheric infarction. Among 106 patients with hemispheric infarcts whom we studied,[99] the only instances of coma at the onset of illness were in patients with an associated systemic hypotension caused by myocardial infarction, cardiac arrhythmias, acute pulmonary infarction, or anesthetic accidents; all these conditions reduce the cardiac output and the cerebral blood flow.[28] Several patients with large infarcts, however, were initially dull, drowsy, and apathetic. This, combined with severe aphasia, sometimes led the family or the referring medical examiners to call them unconscious, but a detailed appraisal almost always indicated a less global reduction of faculties. Since few clinical details were provided, it is difficult to judge reports in the literature in which coma is reported to accompany acute hemispheric infarcts.[4,84] Most of the material was published before CT scanning became widely available for purposes of diagnosis. Accordingly, we suspect that in most instances either systemic hemodynamic abnormalities or undetected cerebral hemorrhages were responsible for the altered states of consciousness.

Although coma is rare with the onset of an uncomplicated hemispheric infarct, several conditions favor its development during the ensuing few days. Many patients with acute strokes develop pneumonitis, heart failure, or electrolyte disorders, and these complications can further impair brain metabolism and lead to stupor. In addition, a cerebral infarct becomes an expanding mass as vascular congestion, inflammation, and edema increase its bulk. This can be a life-threatening complication.

Shaw, Alvord, and Berry pointed out that patients dying within a week after acute cerebral hemispheric infarction of large size have considerable brain swelling with hemispheral shift across the midline and usually transtentorial herniation.[115] In their pathologic material, swelling reached a maximum within 2 to 4 days and then gradually became less as the interval from the onset of the stroke lengthened. Ng and Nimmannitya similarly emphasize the fatal significance of cerebral edema in hemispheric infarction.[87] In 47 of their 353 patients dying with acute hemispheric stroke, edema and transtentorial herniation were the predominant or major contributing causes of death.

Clinical criteria suggest that cerebral edema causes worsening of signs in about one out of every five cases of acute hemiplegic cerebral infarction. We studied 106 patients with large cerebral hemispheric infarctions specifically for this complication. Fourteen patients developed a gradual worsening into stupor and then deep coma with signs of progressive rostral-caudal deterioration typical of an expanding supratentorial mass. Eight of the fourteen died and were examined postmortem. The brain of each of the eight showed large cerebral infarctions in the territory of the middle cerebral artery accompanied by gross cerebral edema and secondary transtentorial herniation. An additional eight patients developed part of this progression, but the signs of dysfunction halted at the diencephalic level and were followed by slow recovery. Most of the patients who developed coma secondary to cerebral infarction had clinical signs of the central syndrome of rostral-caudal deterioration.

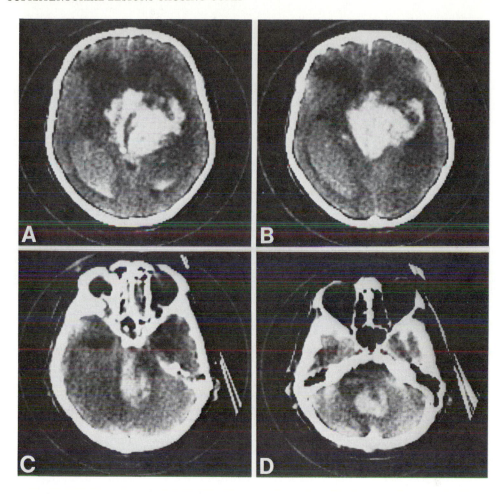

Figure 25. Rostral-caudal CT scans showing intracerebral hemorrhage with intraventricular rupture in Patient 2–11. The hemorrhage shows as the comparatively radiopaque density against background. **A,** Hemorrhage in right basal ganglia extending into lateral and third ventricle. **B,** Massive amounts of blood fill the third ventricle and adjacent parenchyma. **C,** Blood dissects into aqueduct of Sylvius and rostral fourth ventricle. **D,** Blood fills fourth ventricle.

Pupillary dilatation was recorded only twice in this series, although such a change is reported more frequently by others.[87]

CEREBRAL EMBOLISM. Acute cerebral embolism is sometimes regarded as a potential cause of coma, even when the region of ischemic infarction is limited to the cerebral hemispheres. Wells,[138] for example, states that 20 of 63 episodes of clinically diagnosed acute cerebral embolism were associated with coma, and his statistics indicate that at least some of these patients had hemispheric lesions.

Our experience, cited below, is that coma uncommonly accompanies the onset of embolism to the cerebral hemispheres. Fisher[32] implies the same conclusion since his diagnostic criteria for suspecting cerebral embolism include the preservation of consciousness in the presence of a severe neurologic deficit. Carter[14] also regards un-

135

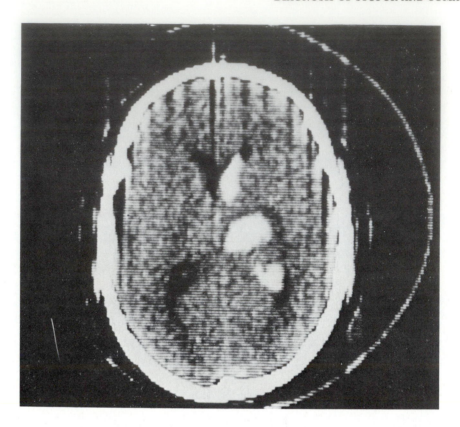

Figure 26. CT scan of right thalamic hemorrhage with extravasation into the right lateral ventricle in Patient 2-12. Two weeks later the CT scan showed a smaller herniation and no ventricular blood.

consciousness as uncommon, although it is difficult to assess exact incidence from his figures. CT scanning sometimes discloses parenchymal hematomas in patients clinically diagnosed as having emboli, perhaps explaining some of the diagnostic discrepancies.

We have examined 17 patients who, by autopsy or a combination of clinical history and examination plus an arteriogram, were diagnosed as having an embolus restricted to the internal carotid or proximal middle cerebral artery with large hemispheric infarcts. Two had convulsions with transient unconsciousness immediately, and four more progressed into coma within 8 to 24 hours after the onset of the acute lesion. All four of these died, and the three in whom autopsy was done were found to have extensive edema of the infarcted hemisphere with a tentorial pressure cone. Among the remaining 13 patients, 1 with a dominant hemisphere lesion was apparently in coma from the onset of his illness, and 9 others had signs of bilateral hemispheric dysfunction (usually consisting of paratonia and an extensor plantar response opposite to the major hemiplegia plus varying degrees of obtundation) but not coma when they were first examined. Most of these patients became drowsier during the next 48 to 72 hours, but the mechanism of the immediate bilateral functional impairment with an ostensibly unilateral vascular lesion is, physiologically, still something of a mystery. (The time course is too rapid for cerebral swelling.)

136

At least three explanations have been offered for the immediate development of bilateral neurologic signs with acute embolism producing massive infarction. One is that sudden hemispheral loss alone can cause coma. That, we think, is unlikely, as discussed on page 22. A second is that emboli may have gone to both sides of the brain in these acutely comatose patients, a postulate that is hard to evaluate. In experimental cerebral embolism, emboli are usually found in all parts of the cerebral circulation, even when great care is taken to inject them only into a single carotid artery.[76] In man, however, it is rare to find bilateral emboli at postmortem examination except when a source exists for multiple and repeated embolism such as mitral valvular disease or endocarditis. The third is that the effect on the contralateral hemisphere is physiologic, i.e., it is a sudden inhibition of remote neural or vascular tissue function owing to the injury, a process called by von Monakow "diaschisis."

Although there is little doubt that remote effects on neurologic metabolism can follow cerebral injury, this mechanistic basis is unknown. Some have postulated that diffuse vascular shock or vasospasm occurs when embolism strikes one part of a previously healthy cerebral circulation. No evidence supports this contention, and most workers liken the contralateral hemispheric depression to the sudden depression of the remaining intact, spinal cord that follows a rostral transection (spinal shock). Several studies in man[75,118] and animals[62,89] show that acute massive infarction arising in one cerebral hemisphere produces substantial abnormalities in the cerebral blood flow and neurologic function of the other. Kempinski[58] some years ago demonstrated that the electrophysiologic effect, at least, was mediated via the corpus callosum; whether a similar pathway underlies the vascular changes is not known. Changes in blood flow do not necessarily correlate well with either the clinical or EEG changes. However, the blood flow in the contralateral hemisphere does decline progressively during the first week after cerebral infarction,[118] with a time course somewhat similar to that by which post-acute edema develops in the infarcted hemisphere.

In summary, the likelihood is that most instances of stupor and coma after a hemispheral cerebral embolism imply a very large infarct that secondarily affects the opposite hemisphere or diencephalon. In a few cases the sequence can reflect the fact that the embolus has lodged opposite to a previously damaged hemisphere or that dissemination of embolic material has either caused bilateral hemispheric abnormalities or has directly struck the diencephalon or brainstem. With large emboli occluding the internal carotid or middle cerebral arteries and causing extensive unilateral injury, there is probably an acute physiologic inhibition of neural and vascular function, and for this there is presently no known treatment. Later, within the first hours or days after the embolus strikes, cerebral edema forms in and around the fresh infarct and produces a supratentorial mass lesion that induces or accentuates coma by producing rostral-caudal deterioration.

BILATERAL THALAMIC INFARCTION. An unusual syndrome characterized acutely by coma followed by permanent defects in arousal, motivation, and mental content accompanies bilateral infarctions that involve the medial portions of the thalamus and extend posteriorly towards and sometimes into the adjacent paramedian mesencephalic region. Cases of this type are relatively rare, and only a few satisfactory descriptions exist that include both clinical and anatomic details. Segarra,[113] Castaigne and associates,[15] and Mills and Swanson[83] review the anatomic, neurologic, and neuroophthalmologic aspects.

Selective or relatively selective bilateral thalamic infarction results from ischemia in the distribution of the anterior and/or posterior thalamo-subthalamic perforating arteries. These vessels arise from the short segment of the posterior cerebral artery that lies between its origin at the apex of the basilar artery and its junction with the posterior communicating artery (Fig. 27). The segment is termed the mesencephalic artery by developmental anatomists or, more descriptively, the basilar communicating artery by Percheron.

Percheron described in detail the variations by which the thalamo-subthalamic and mesencephalic paramedian perforating arteries take their origin from the basilar communicating trunk.[97] Figure 28 is reconstructed from his drawings and diagrams the principal patterns.

Infarction resulting from bilateral occlusion of the above perforating vessels all cause coma at onset with accompanying signs and recovery patterns that vary according to the rostral-caudal extent of the thalamic infarction and whether or not it extends into the midbrain.

Patients with bilateral involvement of the anterior-medial thalamic nuclear groups have the abrupt onset of coma, characteristically accompanied by signs that indicate sparing of the brainstem. The pupils are equal and small, the corneal responses intact, and oculovestibular reflexes are full. Most have signs of bilateral corticospinal tract dysfunction.[15,83] Within several days, a hypokinetic, drowsy, apathetic awakening follows, accompanied by a return of verbal responses and apparent recognition of the environment, but profound disturbances of memory and cognitive function. With infarction of the posteromedial thalamus, and especially if the distribution of the mesencephalic perforating arteries is involved, more prolonged coma gives way to a long-lasting or permanent semi-vegetative state characterized by excessive sleepiness, hypokinesia, and such limited verbal responses as to preclude appraisal of cognitive functions (akinetic mutism).

Neuroophthalmologic abnormalities are prominent in both the above syndromes. Bilateral paramedian thalamic infarction that spares the mesencephalon characteristically produces few or no eye signs during coma, but can interrupt supranuclear pathways controlling vertical gaze.[83] The result is detected when wakefulness reappears and consists of a loss of voluntary upward gaze and sometimes downward gaze as well. When the infarction extends into the pretectal area or involves the paramedian areas of the mesencephalon, eye signs reflect the degree to which pupillary reflexes and oculomotor nuclei are damaged. The changes include, in descending order of frequency, loss of voluntary upward gaze, unilateral or bilateral pupillary dilatation, and impairment of pupillary light reflexes and oculomotor functions, depending upon whether third nerve nuclei and outflow pathways are impaired.

Diagnosis of restricted thalamic infarction is difficult because the condition is unusual and confirmatory laboratory support of one's clinical impression can be entirely lacking in the acute stage. The acute infarcts are likely to be too small to produce interpretable attenuation abnormalities on CT scan. Unless the apex of the basilar artery is occluded or contains a large plaque, arteriography is not helpful because asymmetries in the size and pattern of the proximal posterior cerebral arteries are common and the thalamo-perforating arteries are too small to allow satisfactory visualization of their patterns or abnormalities. EEG findings in these patients have included only those of nonspecific slowing. The spinal fluid usually is unremarkable. Conditions to exclude in differential diagnosis include acute cerebral or subarachnoid hemorrhage, pontine hemorrhage, acute encephalitis, and, especially, acute metabolic forebrain depression, such as occurs with hypoxia, hypoglycemia, or hepatic coma.

CEREBRAL VENOUS AND VENOUS SINUS THROMBOSES. Occlusion of cerebral

138

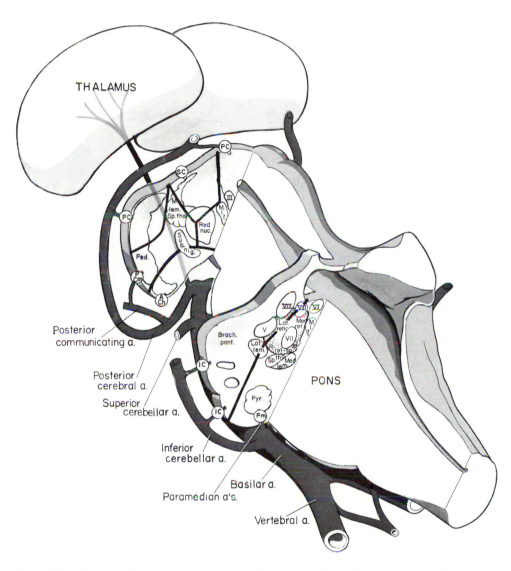

Figure 27. The arterial blood supply to the base of the brain and its relation to structures critical to consciousness. The basilar artery gives off paramedian branches throughout its length, which irrigate the deep midline nuclei and ascending pathways critical to maintaining arousal and cerebral integration. Lateral circumferential arteries (superior, and anterior inferior cerebellar arteries) supply more peripherally placed brainstem structures and much of the cerebellum. (The posterior inferior cerebellar artery is not shown.) The short segment of the posterior cerebral arteries that lies between the apex of the basilar and the junction of the posterior communicating artery gives rise to the thalamic perforating arteries and is called the mesencephalic or basilar communicating artery (see text and Fig. 28).

veins or cerebral venous sinuses arises in one of four settings: (1) It may result from extracranial bacterial infection that spreads to involve either the large venous sinuses at the base of the brain (e.g., cavernous sinus occlusion) or from bacterial meningitis leading to cortical thrombophlebitis. (2) Venous sinuses may be occluded by direct compression from epidural tumors. (3) Venous sinus occlusion may arise

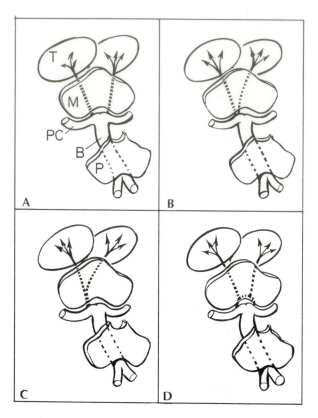

Figure 28. Diagrammatic representation of the variations in the origins of the thalamic-subthalamic perforating arteries that arise from the basilar communicating arteries, as described by Percheron.[97] Either arrangement **B** or **C** enhances the risk of bilateral arterial occlusion and bilateral thalamic infarction from a localized thrombus or embolus.

as a complication of a generalized hypercoagulable state. The principal stage-setters for the last-mentioned include pregnancy and the postpartum period, the ingestion of contraceptive pills, systemic cancer (particularly lymphoma),[116] inflammatory bowel disease,[117] collagen-vascular disease, or marked dehydration. (4) Krayenbuhl reported that 20 percent of venous sinus occlusions arose in the setting of good health.[64]

Local venous thrombosis or occlusion of the cavernous or lateral sinuses complicating facial or oral infections produces signs and symptoms that depend on the site of the occlusion, and the clinical picture is likely to be dominated by signs of local infection plus cerebral deficits (see earlier section, Subdural Empyema). Thrombosis of the superior sagittal sinus, which is more common, presents a more difficult diagnostic picture.[5,16,38] The onset may be sudden, with headache and focal or generalized seizures. In our experience, the occlusion usually runs a benign course, with symptoms clearing without residua. However, sagittal sinus occlusion may precipitate serious neurologic illness, particularly when the occlusion is in the posterior portion of the sinus and occurs suddenly. Then bifrontal or generalized headaches usually develop early, often associated with nausea and vomiting. Irritability, drowsiness, and delirium follow, proceeding to stupor or coma. Papilledema arises in about half the cases. Kalberg and Wolf[53] found lower extremity sensory loss more often than motor impairment, but lower extremity monoparesis, paraparesis, hemiparesis, and language deficits all may develop, depending on the exact site of the thrombosis and whether it occludes the venous drainage of the central fissure or more lateral hemispheric area. The history of Jacksonian, multi-focal or generalized convulsions corresponds at autopsy with those patients in whom the thrombosis is found at autopsy to extend into cortical veins.

Because the signs and symptoms are often diffuse and nonlocalizing, the diagnosis of sinus thrombosis is often not suspected clinically but encountered accidentally at arteriography or autopsy. Sagittal sinus occlusion should be suspected in patients with acute headache and focal or generalized convulsions, particularly those occurring during the puerperium or when women are receiving oral contraceptive drugs. About two thirds of the patients have an elevated CSF pressure. The spinal fluid may contain both red and white cells. Barnes has reported that flow study radio-nuclide scanning often establishes the diagnosis of sagittal sinus occlusion,[7] but our own experience has been that there are many false-negative nuclide scans. The con-trast-enhanced CT scan may establish the diagnosis by showing an "empty sagittal sinus" (empty delta sign).[12] The cerebral arteriogram establishes the diagnosis by demonstrating the occluded venous sinus or a near absence of veins draining into it (Fig. 29).

The exact incidence of sagittal sinus occlusion is difficult to determine; however, Towbin reported 17 cases in 182 consecutive autopsies from a chronic care facility.[130] Recent series by Gettelfinger and Kokmen[38] and by Averback[5] review the literature and suggest that the diagnosis is more common than heretofore suspected. The following patient's natural history is characteristic of severe sagittal sinus occlusion.

Patient 2–13. A 50-year-old woman was admitted to hospital on July 14, 1978, because of severe head-ache. She had been treated 4 years before for carcinoma of the breast and 3 years later had developed a malignant pleural effusion, which was being treated with chemotherapy. Metastatic lesions in her bone had been treated with local radiation therapy as well. Despite these problems, she felt well and did her usual housework. About 3 weeks before admission, she developed pain behind her left ear. The pain persisted until the morning of admission, when she awoke with a severe headache associated with vomiting, dizziness, and an unsteady gait. The dizziness improved when she lay down, but the headache was not relieved by analgesic agents. Her admission neurologic examination was normal and her general physical state had not changed from previous examinations. CT scan performed be-fore and after the injection of contrast material was normal. Lumbar puncture revealed an opening pressure of 200 mm. CSF, 98 red cells, 10 white cells, a protein of 42 mg./dl. and a glucose of 64 mg./dl. The tap was believed to be traumatic. Her symptoms persisted and she was intermittently confused and disoriented. She also developed slight weakness of the right arm and bilateral asterixis more marked on the right side than the left side. A second lumbar puncture revealed an opening pressure of 250 mm. of CSF, xanthochromic fluid with 1000 red cells and 3 white cells. A coagulogram including partial thromboplastin time, prothrombin time, thrombin time, and fibrinogen was within normal limits. Her confusion and the right-sided weakness increased. A carotid arteriogram performed on July 21 revealed occlusion of the superior sagittal sinus, irregularity of the wall of the inferior sagittal sinus, and suggestion of small venous occlusive disease in the posterior parietal region (Fig. 29). There was tortuosity of cortical veins bilaterally, especially those of smaller caliber, probably repre-senting collateral circulation. A CT scan was within normal limits. By the following day she appeared to be cortically blind and aphasic, with a marked right hemiparesis. There were bilateral extensor plantar responses. Despite treatment with steroids and mannitol, she developed the signs of transten-torial herniation and died on July 28, 1978.

At autopsy widespread metastatic carcinoma was restricted to extracranial sites. The brain was edematous and there was bilateral hemorrhagic infarction of the hemispheres. The superior sagittal sinus, inferior sagittal sinus, lateral sinuses, and the superior portion of both internal jugular veins were occluded by thrombus. The thrombus in the left lateral sinus appeared old and well organized. The thrombus in the remaining venous sinuses, although clearly antemortem, had been present for no more than a week.

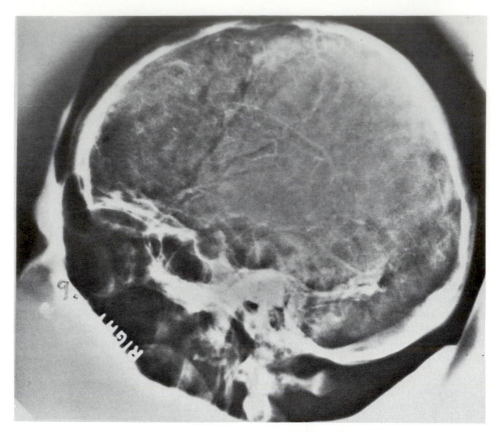

Figure 29. Venous phase of the cerebral arteriogram from Patient 2–13. The superior sagittal sinus is completely occluded; the inferior sagittal sinus is irregular, and small cortical veins are occluded, particularly in the posterior parietal region. The cortical veins are tortuous, especially those of smaller caliber, probably representing collateral circulation. The lateral sinuses or straight sinus do not fill.

Comment: This patient's story illustrates the clinical picture produced by slowly progressive occlusion of the venous outflow pathways of the brain. The clinical diagnosis was difficult because focal signs on admission were lacking and the CT scan did not reveal the characteristic changes of venous sinus occlusion. It was only later, with the extention of the thrombus from the lateral sinus into the sagittal sinus and the development of focal signs, that the clinical diagnosis became clear. At no time were the hematologists able to identify a hypercoagulable state by laboratory test, and there was no evidence of metastases, either grossly or microscopically, within the central nervous system.

Intracerebral Tumors

The early symptoms of brain tumor have become generally recognized in recent years, and during the same time the diagnostic accuracy of electroencephalography and neuroradiology has very greatly improved. As a result, supratentorial brain tumors are now usually diagnosed before they impair consciousness and are a relatively uncommon cause of coma of unknown origin. Nevertheless, these masses sometimes present vexingly difficult diagnostic problems, particularly when the patient's past history is unknown and the tumor's effects have impaired consciousness so much that a clear story cannot be obtained.

If supratentorial neoplasms produce coma, they do so by one or more of the following mechanisms: (1) They cause convulsions followed by a postictal state in all ways similar to that which follows other convulsive disorders (p. 280). (2) Bleeding occurs into the neoplasm superimposing the effects of a cerebral hemorrhage onto the natural history of the tumor. This is comparatively unusual. (3) A neoplasm enlarges progressively and evokes swelling and displacement of the brain to produce the central or uncal syndromes of tentorial herniation. The type of tumor usually influences only the rate at which the symptoms develop. (4) A tumor, located in the lateral or third ventricle, suddenly obstructs ventricular flow, which produces acute, ventricular hypertension and sudden downward compression or displacement of the brainstem. This may be the mechanism of the recurrent attacks of unconsciousness that mark the natural history of third ventricle cysts.[57] More often, however, the effect of supratentorial tumors is to produce plateau waves that increase intracranial pressure and displace cerebral structures.[69] (5) A neoplasm directly infiltrates or destroys the cerebral activating structures located in the thalamus and hypothalamus and thereby produces an encephalitis-like picture of progressively deepening obtundation.

Among the above causes of coma with supratentorial brain tumors, the first four involve mechanisms that have already been discussed. The final mechanism, that of a neoplasm directly invading the diencephalon, merits more comment. The early stages of these lesions are often marked primarily by changes in mentation, behavior, and consciousness, and they may produce very few accompanying long tract signs of abnormal motor or sensory function. At such times, physicians must give particular heed to evidence of excessive drowsiness, memory loss, impaired concentration, or changes in personal habits, as these early signs of dementia signify that a structural lesion rather than a purely emotional illness is causing the obtundation. An additional source of potential difficulty in diagnosis is that many diencephalic neoplasms lie adjacent to the meninges and may produce in the CSF an encephalitic-like or meningitic picture, complete with pleocytosis and, sometimes, a lowered sugar content as well. Similar EEG abnormalities accompany either infections or neoplasms involving this region, and, in such instances, radiologic contrast procedures are required to decide the cause of the progressive signs of diencephalic failure. The following report illustrates such a course.

Patient 2-14. A 44-year-old petroleum engineer noted gradual difficulty in concentration, accompanied by lethargy, approximately 3 months before he was first examined by a physician. These symptoms insidiously progressed so that he was sleeping for longer and longer periods at night and napping during the day as well. His wife found him increasingly inattentive, but he had no headache, no evidence of motor or sensory abnormalities, and no apparent symptoms of autonomic dysfunction. Finally, his drowsiness became so severe that he fell asleep driving his automobile and his wife insisted that he see a physician.

At another hospital he was noted to be lethargic but had few other neurologic abnormalities. A diagnosis of encephalitis was suspected and seemed to be supported by the spinal fluid findings of 138 lymphocytes per cu. mm. and 120 mg. of protein and 70 mg. of sugar per dl. Cultures of the CSF were sterile. Agglutination tests for viruses and rickettsia were inconclusive, and when the patient failed to improve he was referred to The New York Hospital 4 weeks later.

Upon admission he was only intermittently responsive and appeared to sleep most of the time. When

143

he did answer, he was disoriented for time and he perseverated. He was unable to perform even simple calculations and could not follow commands. Language function per se appeared preserved. Respiration was marked by intermittent deep sighs. The pupils were bilaterally tiny, 1 to 2 mm., but equal, and they retained their light reaction. Extraocular movements were intact, and it was possible during his intermittent periods of unresponsiveness to elicit full lateral and vertical oculovestibular responses. The motor examination showed an occasional myoclonic jerk, occurring in either arm and sometimes the trunk. One observer thought that the right lower face drooped, but there were no other focal neurologic signs. Laboratory work added nothing to what was already known except that an EEG was diffusely moderately slow, particularly in the right posterior temporal-occipital lead, and showed bursts of bilateral frontal 2 cps slow activity, typical of deep midline supratentorial lesions.

The coma, pinpoint pupils, intact oculovestibular responses, and typical EEG all indicated a hypothalamic lesion. Radiographic contrast procedures failed to fill the posterior part of the third ventricle and aqueduct of Sylvius, and an arteriogram indicated a mass in the right thalamus.

He gradually declined into uninterrupted coma. Periodic breathing and intermittent spasms of decerebrate rigidity followed. He finally developed brainstem failure and died 3 weeks after admission. The general autopsy was unremarkable. The brain showed moderately dilated lateral ventricles. There was a yellow-gray tumor involving both thalamic regions, more on the left than on the right (Fig. 1B). The neoplasm invaded the floor of the third ventricle and the paraventricular region of the diencephalon from the posterior commissure dorsally to the mammillary bodies ventrally. The third ventricle was compressed and shifted to the right, and the rostal portion of the aqueduct appeared to be closed by adjacent tumor. There was no tumor in or caudal to the midbrain, but central hemorrhages down the brainstem had occurred terminally. Histologically, the tumor was a reticulum cell sarcoma of the brain of the microglial type.

Comment: Primary lymphomas of the brain are notorious for invading the base of the diencephalon and producing an encephalitis-like illness of the type demonstrated by this patient. Many of these tumors run a slow and even relapsing course, and examples have been recorded where exacerbations and remissions lasted as long as 8 years or more.[107] The tumor can infiltrate widely into the brainstem and cerebral basal nuclei, and most cases are associated with pleocytosis and elevation of the protein content of the CSF. The tumor usually but not always produces sufficient mass effect to be detected by CT scan and other neuroradiologic contrast procedures.

PITUITARY APOPLEXY. Pituitary apoplexy is a term applied to sudden enlargement of a pituitary tumor caused either by infarction or hemorrhage. The syndrome usually occurs in a patient with a known pituitary tumor, often during a course of radiation therapy, but it may be the presenting complaint in a patient not previously known to harbor a pituitary tumor.[136] In the former instance, the clinical diagnosis is easy; in the latter it is often difficult. The exact incidence of pituitary apoplexy is not known. Weisberg reported 14 instances in 300 patients with pituitary tumors; in 5, pituitary apoplexy was the presenting complaint.[136]

The pathogenesis of pituitary apoplexy is not clearly established. Adams and his colleagues suggested that pituitary apoplexy occurred when a tumor, as a result of its rapid growth, outgrew its blood supply.[10] Rovit and Fein conclude that mechanical events, e.g., compression and distortion of the arterial supply to the pituitary tumor, might be more important than tumor growth.[106] Sussman and Porro reported a case of pituitary apoplexy in which the hemorrhagic necrosis probably resulted from cholesterol emboli to the pituitary tumor.[126]

Whatever the pathophysiologic changes that lead to spontaneous infarction or hemorrhage in pituitary tumors, the clinical picture is often dramatic. The first symptom is headache, usually sudden in onset and severe.[18,136] The headache is often retro- or peri-orbital and may be unilateral in the beginning, but it rapidly becomes generalized. Visual loss resulting from compression of the optic chiasm and diplopia resulting from compression of ocular nerves traversing the cavernous sinus just lateral to the pituitary fossa frequently accompany the headache. Obtundation and stupor are common, making it difficult to examine visual fields and acuity, and frank coma occasionally occurs. Focal neurologic signs including hemiparesis, hemiataxia, or lower cranial nerve dysfunction occur rarely, probably as a result of hemorrhage upward into the hypothalamus and backward into the midbrain. As mentioned above, diagnosis can be difficult. The typical patient is stuporous or comatose without focal signs except for extraocular palsies suggesting isolated but often bilateral third and/or sixth nerve dysfunction. The pupils are usually reactive, but if visual loss is sufficient, may be sluggish or fixed. The patients frequently have a stiff neck. Rarely are they hemiparetic or ataxic. Except for the ocular palsies, the clinical picture suggests metabolic more than structural coma, and often one's first impression is of acute subarachnoid hemorrhage (see Chapter 4).

The spinal fluid is always under increased pressure and may contain evidence of recent hemorrhage. However, an identical clinical picture may occur in the absence of blood in the spinal fluid. In these instances, the spinal fluid may either be acellular or contain large numbers of white cells with sufficient polymorphonuclear cells to lead to the erroneous diagnosis of acute bacterial meningitis. The pleocytosis probably results from irritation of the meninges by parameningeal necrotic tumor. If the diagnosis is suspected, a lateral skull film will often reveal an enlarged sella turcica making pituitary apoplexy likely. Occasionally, however, the sella turcica appears entirely normal on skull films, and then the diagnosis can be established by only CT scanning.[136] The CT scan characteristically reveals a dense mass reflecting hemorrhage in the sella or suprasellar area. There may also be enhancement after the injection of contrast material, indicating the presence of tumor into which the hemorrhage occurred.

The pathogenesis of altered consciousness in pituitary apoplexy is not clear. In some patients, direct compression of the diencephelon and brainstem by the mass leads to changes in consciousness, but these probably represent a minority. In others, the sudden increase in intracranial pressure combined with the blood or other noxious substances released into the suprasellar cistern may interfere with cerebral metabolism in a manner similar to what happens with subarachnoid hemorrhage or bacterial meningitis. It is doubtful that acute endocrine failure plays a major role.

The symptoms of pituitary apoplexy, including stupor or coma, sometimes resolve spontaneously with conservative treatment.[141] Often, however, surgical evacuation of the necrotic tissue is necessary, especially in deteriorating patients.

Patient 2–15. A 70-year-old woman had been well until the night prior to admission, when she complained of headache and a restless night. The following morning she had a generalized convulsion. She arrived at the hospital somnolent but arousable. While being examined she had a brief generalized convulsion. Examination in the postictal state revealed equal and reactive pupils, a supple neck, and no pathologic reflexes. While in the emergency room she had several more brief seizures. In the postictal state after 5 mg. of diazepam, she was stuporous but withdrew appropriately from pain. Respirations were regular at 18, neck supple, pupils equal and reactive, optic fundi normal, and cold water calorics induced tonic deviation of the eyes. Corneal reflexes were depressed but present. The deep tendon reflexes were diffusely decreased, muscle tone was flaccid, and plantar responses were flexor. A lumbar puncture revealed cloudy fluid with 150 red cells and 900 white cells (92 percent polymorphonuclear cells). A glucose was 113 mg./dl. and the protein 182 mg./dl. Gram stain was negative. Her temperature was 38.8° C, and a presumptive diagnosis of bacterial meningitis was made. She was started on antibiotics. She awoke rapidly. A CT scan performed the next morning revealed a dense mass in the suprasellar area (Fig. 30), which did not enhance after contrast injection. Lumbar puncture performed that morning had an opening pressure of 270, with 3000 white cells (88 percent polymorphonuclear cells) and 100 red cells. The glucose was 102

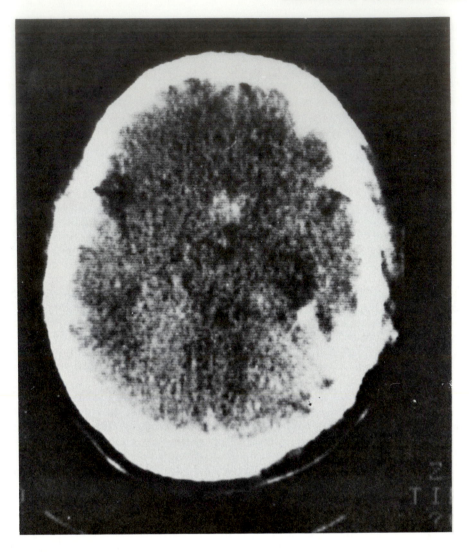

Figure 30. Noncontrast CT scan of Patient 2-15 with pituitary apoplexy. The hemorrhagic tumor is seen as a dense mass in the suprasellar area.

and the protein 60. She was given corticosteroids for a presumptive diagnosis of pituitary apoplexy and rapidly recovered full neurologic function. Skull tomograms performed 6 days after admission revealed a slight enlargement of the sella turcica with a calculated volume of 18 cu. mm. The enlargement was symmetrical, with a slight downward bowing of the floor. There appeared to be a faint cloud of calcification in the suprasellar region and fairly prominent hyperostosis in the tuberculum. CT scan 2 weeks after onset revealed evidence of an enhancing lesion reaching into the sella turcica with some suprasellar extension. Pituitary function tests examined during the recovery stage were within normal limits. She remained clinically well for at least the following 18 months.

REFERENCES

1. ADAMS, J.H.: "The neuropathology of head injuries." In Vinken, P.J., and Bruyn, G.W. (eds.): *Handbook of Clinical Neurology*, vol. 23, *Injuries of the Brain and Skull, Part I.* Amsterdam, North Holland, 1975. Chapter 3, pp. 35-65.

2. ADAMS, J.H., AND GRAHAM, D.: *The relationship between ventricular fluid pressure and the neuropathology of raised intracranial pressure.* Neuropathol. Appl. Neurobiol. 2:323-332, 1976.

3. ADAMS, J.H., MITCHELL, D.E., GRAHAM, D.I., ET AL.: *Diffuse brain damage of immediate impact type.* Brain 100:489-502, 1977.

4. ALBERT, M.L., SILVERBERG, R., RECHES, A., ET AL.: *Cerebral dominance for consciousness.* Arch. Neurol. 33:453-454, 1976.

5. AVERBACK, P.: *Primary cerebral venous thrombosis in young adults: the diverse manifestations of an unrecognized disease.* Ann. Neurol. 3:81-86, 1978.

6. BARATHAM, G., AND DENNYSON, W.G.: *Delayed traumatic intracerebral haemorrhage.* J. Neurol. Neurosurg. Psychiatry 35:698-706, 1972.

7. BARNES, B.D., AND WEINSTOCK, D.P.: *Dynamic radionuclide scanning in the diagnosis of thrombosis of the superior sagittal sinus.* Neurology 27:656-661, 1977.

8. BATES, D., CARONNA, J.J., CARTLIDGE, N.E.F., ET AL.: *A prospective study of nontraumatic coma: methods and results in 310 patients.* Ann. Neurol. 2:211-220, 1977.

9. BRENDLER, S.J., AND SELVERSTONE, B.: *Recovery from decerebration.* Brain 93:381-392, 1970.

10. BROUGHAM, M., HEUSNER, A.P., AND ADAMS, R.D.: *Acute degenerative changes in adenomas of the pituitary body, with special reference to pituitary apoplexy.* J. Neurosurg. 7:421-439, 1950.

11. BROWDER, J., AND MEYERS, R.: *Behavior of the systemic blood pressure, pulse rate and spinal fluid pressure associated with acute changes in intracranial pressure artificially produced.* Arch. Surg. 36:1-19, 1938.

12. BUONANNO, F.S., MOODY, D.M., BALL, M.R., ET AL.: *Computed cranial tomographic findings in cerebral sinovenous occlusion.* J. Comp. Assist. Tomography 2:281-290, 1978.

13. CAMERON, M.M.: *Chronic subdural haematoma: a review of 114 cases.* J. Neurol. Neurosurg. Psychiatry 41:834-839, 1978.

14. CARTER, A.B.: *Cerebral Infarction.* Pergamon Press, Oxford, 1964.

15. CASTAIGNE, P., BUGE, A., CAMBIER, J., ET AL.: *Demence thalamique d'origine vasculaire par ramollissement bilateral, limite au territoire du pedicule retro-mamillaire.* Rev. Neurol. 114:89-107, 1966.

16. CASTAIGNE, P., LAPLANE, D., AND BOUSSER, M.G.: *Superior sagittal sinus thrombosis* (letter to the editor). Ann. Neurol. 34:788-789, 1977.

17. COLLIER, J.: *The false localizing signs of intracranial tumors.* Brain 27:490-507, 1904.

18. CONOMY, J.P., FERGUSON, J.H., BRODKEY, J.S., ET AL.: *Spontaneous infarction in pituitary tumors: neurologic and therapeutic aspects.* Neurology 25:580-587, 1975.

19. CRITCHLEY, M.: *The anterior cerebral artery and its syndromes.* Brain 53:120-165, 1930.

20. CUSHING, H.: *Concerning a definite regulatory mechanism of the vasomotor centre which controls blood pressure during cerebral compression.* Bull. Hopkins Hosp. 12:290-292, 1901.

21. CUSHING, H.: *Some experimental and clinical observations concerning states of increased intracranial tension.* Am. J. Med. Sci. 124:375-400, 1902.

22. DANDY, W.E.: *Changes in our conceptions of localization of certain functions in the brain.* Am. J. Physiol. 93:643, 1930.

23. DANDY, W.E.: *The location of the conscious center in the brain—the corpus striatum.* Bull. J. Hopkins Hosp. 79:34-58, 1946.

24. DEJERINE, J.: *Sémiologie des Affections du Système Nerveux.* Masson et Cie, Paris, 1926.

25. DENNY-BROWN, D.E., AND RUSSELL, W.R.: *Experimental cerebral concussion.* Brain 64:91-164, 1941.

26. DEVET, A.C.: "Traumatic intracerebral haematoma." In Vinken, P.J., and Bruyn, G.W. (eds.): *Handbook of Clinical Neurology*, vol. 24, *Injuries of the Brain and Spine, Part II.* North Holland, Amsterdam, 1976, Chapter 19, pp. 351-368.

27. DUFFY, G.P.: *Lumbar puncture in the presence of raised intracranial pressure.* Brit. Med. J. 1:407-409, 1969.

28. EISENBERG, S., MADISON, L., AND SENSENBACH, W.: *Cerebral hemodynamic and metabolic studies in patients with congestive heart failure: II. Observations in confused subjects.* Circulation 21:704-709, 1960.

29. ENDO, H., LARSEN, B., AND LASSEN, N.A.: *Regional cerebral blood flow alterations remote from the site of intracranial tumors.* J. Neurosurg. 46:270-281, 1977.

30. ETHELBERG, S., AND JENSEN, V.A.: *Obscurations and further time related paroxysmal disorders in intracranial tumors.* Arch. Neurol. Psychiatry 68:130-149, 1952.

147

31. FINNEY, L.A., AND WALKER, A.E.: *Transtentorial Herniation.* Charles C Thomas, Springfield, Ill., 1962.

32. FISHER, C.M.: "Clinical syndromes in cerebral arterial occlusion." In Fields, W.S. (ed.): *Pathogenesis and Treatment of Cerebrovascular Disease.* Charles C Thomas, Springfield, Ill., 1961, pp. 151–181.

33. FOLTZ, E.L., AND SCHMIDT, R.P.: *The role of the reticular formation in the coma of head injury.* J. Neurosurg. 13:145–154, 1956.

34. FRIEDE, R.L., AND ROESSMANN, U.: *The pathogenesis of secondary midbrain hemorrhages.* Neurology 16:1210–1216, 1966.

35. GALBRAITH, S., AND TEASDALE, G.: *Computerised tomography and subdural hematomas.* Lancet 1:983–984, 1979.

36. GALLAGHER, J.P., AND BROWDER, J.: *Extradural hematoma. Experience with 167 patients.* J. Neurosurg. 29:1–12, 1968.

37. GASSEL, M.M.: *False localizing signs. A review of the concept and analysis of the occurrence in 250 cases of intracranial meningioma.* Arch. Neurol. 4:70–98, 1961.

38. GETTELFINGER, D.M., AND KOKMEN, E.: *Superior sagittal sinus thrombosis.* Arch. Neurol. 34:2–6, 1977.

39. GJERRIS, F., AND MELLEMGAARD, L.: *Transitory cortical blindness in head injury.* Acta Neurol. Scand. 45:623–631, 1969.

40. GOWERS, W.R.: *A Manual of Diseases of the Nervous System.* The Blakiston Co., Philadelphia, 1893.

41. GRAHAM, D.I., AND ADAMS, J.H.: *Ischemic brain damage in fatal heal injuries.* Clin. Develop. Med. 39/40:34–40, 1971.

42. GURDJIAN, E.S., ET AL.: *Studies on experimental concussion.* Neurology 4:674–681, 1954.

43. HEISKANEN, O.: *Cerebral circulatory arrest caused by acute increase of intracranial pressure.* Acta Neurol. Scand. (Suppl. 7) 40: 1964.

44. HEYWARD, R.D., AND O'REILLY, G.V.A.: *Intracerebral hemorrhage.* Lancet 1:1–14, 1976.

45. HIER, D.B., DAVIS, K.R., RICHARDSON, E.P., JR., ET AL.: *Hypertensive putaminal hemorrhage.* Ann. Neurol. 1:152–159, 1977.

46. HITCHCOCK, E., AND ANDREADIS, A.: *Subdural empyema: a review of 29 cases.* J. Neurol. Neurosurg. Psychiatry 27:422–434, 1964.

47. HOWELL, D.A.: *Longitudinal brain stem compression with buckling.* Arch. Neurol. 4:572–579, 1961.

48. HUTCHINSON, J.: *Four lectures on compression of the brain.* Clin. Lect. Reps. London Hosp. 4:10–55, 1867.

49. JAMIESON, K.G., AND YELLAND, J.D.N.: *Extradural hematoma. Report of 167 cases.* J. Neurosurg. 29:13–23, 1968.

50. JEFFERSON, G.: *The tentorial pressure cone.* Arch. Neurol. Psychiatry 40:857–876, 1938.

51. JENNETT, W.B., AND STERN, W.E.: *Tentorial herniation; the midbrain and the pupil. Experimental studies in brain compression.* J. Neurosurg. 17:598–609, 1960.

52. JOHNSON, R.T., AND YATES, P.O.: *Clinico-pathological aspects of pressure changes at the tentorium.* Acta Radiol. 46:242–249, 1956.

53. KALBAG, R.M., AND WOOLF, A.L.: *Cerebral Venous Thrombosis.* Oxford University Press, London, 1967.

54. KAUFMAN, D.M., AND LEEDS, N.E.: *Computed tomography (CT) in the diagnosis of intracranial abscesses.* Neurology 27:1069–1073, 1977.

55. KAUFMAN, D.M., MILLER, M.H., AND STEIGBIGEL, N.H.: *Subdural empyema: analysis of 17 recent cases and review of the literature.* Medicine 54:485–498, 1975.

56. KAUFMANN, G.E., AND CLARK, K.: *Continuous simultaneous monitoring of intraventricular and cervical subarachnoid cerebrospinal fluid pressure to indicate development of cerebral or tonsillar herniation.* J. Neurosurg. 33:145–150, 1970.

57. KELLY, R.: *Colloid cysts of the third ventricle.* Brain 74:23–65, 1951.

58. KEMPINSKY, W.H.: *Experimental study of distant effects of acute focal brain injury.* Arch. Neurol. Psychiatry 79:376–389, 1958.

59. KERNOHAN, J.W., AND WOLTMAN, H.W.: *Incisura of the crus due to contralateral brain tumor.* Arch. Neurol. Psychiatry 21:274–287, 1929.

60. KIM, K.S., HEMMATI, M., AND WEINBERG, P.E.: *Computed tomography in isodense subdural hematoma.* Radiology 128:71–74, 1978.

61. KLINTWORTH, K.G.: *Paratentorial grooving of human brains with particular reference to transtentorial herniation and the pathogenesis of secondary brainstem hemorrhages.* Am. J. Pathol. 53:391–399, 1968.

62. KOGURE, K., BUSTO, R., SCHEINBERG, P., ET AL.: *Energy metabolites and water content in rat brain during the early stage of development of cerebral infarction.* Brain 97:103–114, 1974.

63. KOREIN, J., CRAVIOTO, H., AND LEICACH, M.: *Reevaluation of lumbar puncture. A study of 129 patients with papilledema or intracranial hypertension.* Neurology 9:290–297, 1959.

64. KRAYENBUHL, H.A.: *Cerebral venous and sinus thrombosis.* Clin. Neurosurg. 14:1–23, 1967.

65. KUBIK, C.S., AND ADAMS, R.D.: *Subdural empyema.* Brain 66:18–42, 1943.

66. LANGFITT, T.W.: *Increased intracranial pressure.* Clin. Neurosurg. 16:436–471, 1969.

67. LINDENBERG, R., AND FREYTAG, E.: *Brainstem lesions characteristic of traumatic hyperextension of the head.* Arch. Pathol. 90:509–515, 1970.

68. LUBIC, L.G., AND MAROTTA, J.T.: *Brain tumor and lumbar puncture.* Arch. Neurol. Psychiatry 72:568–572, 1954.

69. LUNDBERG, N.: *Continuous recording and control of ventricular fluid pressure in neurological practice.* Acta Psychiatry Neurol. Scand. (Suppl. 149) 36:1–193, 1960.

70. MACEWEN, W.: *The pupil in its semeiological aspects.* Am. J. Med. Sci. 94:123–146, 1887.

71. MACEWEN, W.: *Pyrogenic Infective Diseases of the Brain and Spinal Cord.* J. Maclehose and Sons, Glasgow, 1893.

72. MAGNAES, B.: *Body position and cerebrospinal fluid pressure. Part 1: Clinical studies on the effect of rapid postural changes. Part 2: Clinical studies on orthostatic pressure and the hydrostatic indifferent point.* J. Neurosurg. 44:687–697, 698–705, 1976.

73. MARMAROU, A., SHULMAN, K., AND ROSENDE, R.M.: *A nonlinear analysis of the cerebrospinal fluid system and intracranial pressure dynamics.* J. Neurosurg. 48:332–344, 1978.

74. McNEALY, D.E., AND PLUM, F.: *Brainstem dysfunction with supratentorial mass lesions.* Arch. Neurol. 7:10–32, 1962.

75. MELAMED, E., LAVY, S., PORTNOY, Z., ET AL.: *Correlation between regional cerebral blood flow and EEG frequency in the contralateral hemisphere in acute cerebral infarction.* J. Neurol. Sci. 26:21–27, 1975.

76. MELDRUM, B.S., PAPY, J.J., AND VIGOUROUX, R.A.: *Intracarotid air embolism in the baboon.* Brain Res. 25:301–315, 1971.

77. MERINO-DE VILLASANTE, J., AND TAVERAS, J.M.: *Computerized tomography (CT) in acute head trauma.* Am. J. Roentgenol. 126:765–778, 1976.

78. MEYER, A.: *Herniation of the brain.* Arch. Neurol. Psychiatry 4:387–400, 1920.

79. MEYERS, R.: *Dandy's striatal theory of "The center of consciousness"; surgical evidence and logical analysis indicating its improbability.* Arch. Neurol. Psychiatry 65:659–671, 1951.

80. MIGRINO, S., AND FRUGONI, P.: *Significance of vestibulo-ocular reflex alterations in comatose patients after head injury.* Acta Neurochir. 16:321–322, 1967.

81. MILLER, J.D., STANEK, A., AND LANGFITT, T.W.: *Concepts of cerebral perfusion pressure and vascular compression during intracranial hypertension.* Prog. Brain Res. 35:411–432, 1972.

82. MILLER, J.D., AND SULLIVAN, H.G.: "Severe intracranial hypertension." In Trubuhovich, R.V. (ed.): *Management of Acute Intracranial Disasters. International Anesthesiolology Clinics,* vol. 17. Little, Brown and Company, Boston, 1979, pp. 19–75.

83. MILLS, R.P., AND SWANSON, P.D.: *Vertical oculomotor apraxia and memory loss.* Ann. Neurol. 4:149–153, 1978.

84. MOHR, J.P., CAPLAN, L.R., MELSKI, J.W., ET AL.: The Harvard Cooperative Stroke Registry: a prospective registry. Neurology 28:754–762, 1978.

85. MORIN, M.A., AND PITTS, F.W.: *Delayed apoplexy following head injury ("traumatische Spät-Apoplexie").* J. Neurosurg. 33:542–547, 1970.

86. NEEDHAM, C. W., BERTRAND, G., AND MYLES, S.T.: *Multiple cranial nerve signs from supratentorial tumors.* J. Neurosurg. 33:178–183, 1970.

87. NG, L.K.Y., AND NIMMANNITYA, J.: *Massive cerebral infarction with severe brain swelling.* Stroke 1:158–163, 1970.

88. NIELSEN, J.M., AND JACOBS, L.L.: *Bilateral lesions of the anterior cingulate gyri.* Bull. Los Angeles Neurol. Soc. 16:231–234, 1951.

89. O'BRIEN, M.D., WALTZ, A.G., AND JORDAN, M.M.: *Ischemic cerebral edema.* Arch. Neurol. 30:456–460, 1974.

90. OLESEN, J.: *Cerebral blood flow methods for measurement regulation, effects of drugs and changes in disease.* Acta Neurol. Scand. 50 (suppl. 57):1–134, 1974.

91. OMMAYA, A.K., AND GENNARELLI, T.A.: *Cerebral concussion and traumatic unconsciousness: correlation of experimental and clinical observations on blunt head injuries.* Brain 97:633–654, 1974.

92. OPPENHEIM, H.: *Diseases of the Nervous System,* ed. 2. E.E. Mayer (trans.). J. B. Lippincott Co., Philadelphia, 1900.

93. OSBORN, A.G.: *Diagnosis of descending transtentorial herniation by cranial computed tomography.* Radiology 123:93–96, 1977.

94. OWMAN, C., AND EDVINSSON, L. (EDS.): *Neurogenic Control of the Brain Circulation.* Pergamon Press, Oxford, 1977.

95. PALVOLGYI, R.: *Regional cerebral blood flow in patients with intracranial tumors.* J. Neurosurg. 31:149–163, 1969.

96. PAULSON, O.B., LASSEN, N.A., AND SKINHØJ, E.: *Regional cerebral blood flow in apoplexy without arterial occlusion.* Neurology 20:125–138, 1970.

97. PERCHERON, G.: Les artères du thalamus humain. II. Artères et territoires thalamique paramédians de l'artère basilaire communicante. Rev. Neurol. 132:309–324, 1976.

98. PICKLES, W.: *Acute focal edema of the brain in children in head injuries.* N. Engl. J. Med. 240:92–95, 1949.

99. PLUM, F.: *Brain swelling and edema in cerebral vascular disease.* Res. Publ. Assoc. Res. Nerv. Ment. Dis. 41:318–348, 1966.

100. PLUM, F., AND BRENNAN, R.W.: *Dissociation of autoregulation and chemical regulation in cerebral circulation following seizures.* Trans. Am. Neurol. Assoc. 95:27–30, 1970.

101. PURVES, M.J., (Chairman): *Cerebral Vascular Smooth Muscle and Its Control.* CIBA Foundation Symposium 56. Elsevier-Excerpta Medica, North Holland, Amsterdam, 1978.

102. RAICHLE, M.E., HARTMAN, B.K., EICHLING, J.O., ET AL.: *Central noradrenergic regulation of cerebral blood flow and vascular permeability.* Proc. Natl. Acad. Sci. USA 72:3726–3730, 1975.

103. REULEN, H.J., GRAHAM, R., SPATZ, M. ET AL.: *Role of pressure gradients and bulk flow in dynamics of vasogenic brain edema.* J. Neurosurg. 46:24–35, 1977.

104. ROSE, J., VALTONEN, S., AND JENNETT, B.: *Avoidable factors contributing to death after head injury.* Br. Med. J. 2:615–618, 1977.

105. ROTTENBERG, D.A., AND POSNER, J.B.: "Intracranial pressure control." In Cottrell, J.E., and Turndorf, H. (eds.): *Anesthesia and Neurosurgery.* C. V. Mosby Company, St. Louis, 1979.

106. ROVIT, R.L., AND FEIN, J.M.: *Pituitary apoplexy: a review and reappraisal.* J. Neurosurg. 37:280–288, 1972.

107. SCHAUMBERG, H.H., PLANK, C.R., AND ADAMS, R.D.: *The reticulum cell sarcoma-microglioma group of brain tumors.* Brain 95:199–212, 1972.

108. SCHEINKER, I.M.: *Transtentorial herniation of the brain stem; a characteristic clinicopathologic syndrome; pathogenesis of hemorrhages in the brain stem.* Arch. Neurol. Psychiatry 53:289–298, 1945.

109. SCHUMACHER, G.A., AND WOLFF, H.G.: *Experimental studies on headache.* Arch. Neurol. Psychiatry 45:199–214, 1941.

110. SCHUTTA, H.S., KASSELL, N.F., AND LANGFITT, T.W.: *Brain swelling produced by injury and aggravated by arterial hypertension. A light and electron microscopic study.* Brain 91:281–294, 1968.

111. SCHWARTZ, B.: *Hemispheric dominance and consciousness.* Acta Neurol. Scand. 43: 513–525, 1967.

112. SCHWARTZ, G.A., AND ROSNER, A.A.: *Displacement and herniation of the hippocampal gyrus through the incisura tentorii; a clinicopathological study.* Arch. Neurol. Psychiatry 46:297–321, 1941.

113. SEGARRA, J.M.: *Cerebral vascular disease and behavior. I. The syndrome of the mesencephalic artery (basilar artery bifurcation).* Arch. Neurol. 22:408–418, 1970.

114. SENCER, W.: *The lumbar puncture in the presence of papilledema.* J. Mt. Sinai Hosp. 23:808–815, 1956.

115. SHAW, C.M., ALVORD, E.C., JR., AND BERRY, R.G.: *Swelling of the brain following ischemic infarction with arterial occlusion.* Arch. Neurol. 1:161–177, 1959.

116. SIGSBEE, B., DECK, M.D.F., AND POSNER, J.B.: *Non-metastatic superior sagittal sinus thrombosis complicating systemic cancer.* Neurology 29:139–146, 1979.

117. SIGSBEE, B., AND ROTTENBERG, D.A.: *Sagittal sinus thrombosis as a complication of regional enteritis.* Ann. Neurol. 3:450–452, 1978.

118. SLATER, R., REIVICH, M., GOLDBERG, H., ET AL.: Diaschisis with cerebral infarction. Stroke 8:684–690, 1977.

119. SMALL, J.M., AND WOOLF, A.I.: *Fatal damage to the brain by epileptic convulsions after a trivial injury to the head.* J. Neurol. Neurosurg. Psychiatry 20:293–301, 1957.

120. SOHN, D., AND LEVINE, S.: *Frontal lobe infarcts caused by brain herniation. Compression of anterior cerebral artery branches.* Arch. Pathol. 84:509–512, 1967.

121. SPATZ, H., AND STROESCU, G.J.: *Zur Anatomie und Pathologie der äusseren Liquorräume des Gehirns. Die Zisternenverquellung beim Hirntumor.* Nervenarzt 7:481–496, 1934.

122. STRICH, S.J.: *Diffuse degeneration of cerebral white matter in severe dementia following head injury.* J. Neurol. Neurosurg. Psychiatry 19:163–185, 1956.

123. STRICH, S.J.: "The pathology of brain damage due to blunt head injuries." In Walker, A.E., Caveness, W.F., and Critchley, M. (eds.): *The Late Effects of Head Injury.* Charles C Thomas, Springfield, Ill., 1969.

124. SUNDERLAND, S.: *The tentorial notch and complications produced by herniations of the brain through that aperture.* Br. J. Surg. 45:422–438, 1958.

125. SUNDERLAND, S., AND BRADLEY, K. C.: *Disturbances of oculomotor function accompanying extradural haemorrhage.* J. Neurol. Neurosurg. Psychiatry 16:35–46, 1953.

126. SUSSMAN, E.B., AND PORRO, R.S.: *Pituitary apoplexy: the role of atheromatous emboli.* Stroke 5:318–323, 1974.

127. SYMONDS, C.P.: *Concussion and its sequelae.* Lancet 1:1–5, 1962.

128. TEASDALE, G., ROWAN, J.O., TURNER, J., ET AL.: "Cerebral perfusion failure and cortical electrical activity." In Ingvar, D.H., and Lassen, N.A. (eds.): *Cerebral Function, Metabolism and Circulation.* Acta Neurol. Scand. 56 (suppl. 64):430–431, 1977.

129. THOMPSON, R.K., AND MALINA, S.: *Dynamic axial brainstem distortion as a mechanism explaining the cardiorespiratory changes in increased intracranial pressure.* J. Neurosurg. 16:664–675, 1959.

130. TOWBIN, A.: *Syndrome of latent cerebral venous thrombosis: its frequency and relation to age in congestive heart failure.* Stroke 4:419–430, 1973.

131. TURAZZI, S., AND BRICOLO, A.: *Acute pontine syndromes following head injury.* Lancet 2:62–64, 1977.

132. VAN CREVEL, H.: *Papilloedema, CSF pressure, and CSF flow in cerebral tumours.* J. Neurol. Neurosurg. Psychiatry 42:493–500, 1979.

133. VAN GEHUCHTEN, P.: *Le Méchanisme de la Mort dans Certains Cas de Tumeur Cérébrales.* Rev. Neurol. (Paris) 65:702, 1936.

134. VINCENT, C., DAVID, M., AND THIEBAUT, F.: *Le Cône de Pression Temporal dans les Tumeurs des Hémisphères Cérébraux. Sa Symptomatologie; Sa Gravité; Les Traitments qu'il Convient de lui Opposer.* Rev. Neurol. 65:536–545, 1936.

135. WALSHE, T.M., DAVIS, K.R., AND FISHER, C.M.: *Thalamic hemorrhage: a computed tomographic-clinical correlation.* Neurology 27:217–222, 1977.

136. WEISBERG, L.A.: *Pituitary apoplexy.* Am. J. Med. 63:109–115, 1977.

137. WEISBERG, L.A.: *Computed tomography in aneurysmal subarachnoid hemorrhage.* Neurology 29:802–808, 1979.

138. WELLS, C.E.: *Cerebral embolism.* Arch. Neurol. Psychiatry 81:667–677, 1959.

139. WHITE, D.N., WILSON, K.C., CURRY, G.R., ET AL.: The limitation of pulsatile flow through the aqueduct of Sylvius as a cause of hydrocephalus. J. Neurol. Sci. 42:11–51, 1979.

140. WOLMAN, L.: *Ischaemic lesions in the brain-stem associated with raised supratentorial pressure.* Brain 76:364–377, 1953.

141. WRIGHT, R.L., OJEMANN, R.G., AND DREW, J.H.: *Hemorrhage into pituitary adenomata. Report of two cases with spontaneous recovery.* Arch. Neurol. 12:326–331, 1965.

142. ZERVAS, N.T., AND HEDLEY-WHITE, J.: *Successful treatment of cerebral herniation in five patients.* N. Engl. J. Med. 286:1075–1077, 1972.

143. ZIDAN, A.H., AND GIRVIN, J.P.: *Effect on the Cushing response of different rates of expansion of a supratentorial mass.* J. Neurosurg. 49:61–70, 1978.

144. DEGOS, J.D., VERROUST, J., BOUCHAREINE, A., ET AL.: *Asterixis in focal brain lesions.* Arch. Neurol. 36:705–707, 1979.

145. GLASS, J.P., MELAMED, M., CHERNICK, N.L., ET AL.: *Malignant cells in cerebrospinal fluid (CSF): the meaning of a positive CSF cytology.* Neurology 29:1369–1375, 1979.

151

CHAPTER 3

Subtentorial Lesions Causing Coma

PATHOLOGY AND PATHOLOGIC PHYSIOLOGY

Two kinds of posterior fossa lesions cause coma: those located within the brainstem that *destroy* the paramedian midbrain-pontine reticular formation and its associated pathways, and those located outside the brainstem that *compress* its reticulum.

Brainstem Destruction

Lesions within the brainstem can cause coma either by directly invading and destroying the brainstem central core or by impairing its blood supply to produce ischemia, necrosis, or hemorrhage. The most common pathologic process that causes such primary destruction of the brainstem is cerebral vascular disease, but demyelinating disorders, neoplasms, granulomas, and abscesses produce similar effects, which are individually discussed in the second half of this chapter. Head trauma also can damage the subtentorial brainstem core, but this usually presents no problem in diagnosis.

Brainstem Compression

Posterior fossa lesions lying adjacent to but outside the brainstem cause coma in three ways: (1) They exert direct pressure on the tegmentum of the pons and midbrain, leading to ischemia and swelling of the reticular activating formation. (2) They produce upward herniation of the superior vermis of the cerebellum through the tentorial notch, compressing the upper midbrain and the diencephalon. (3) They cause downward herniation of the cerebellar tonsils through the foramen magnum, compressing and displacing the medulla. A given lesion of the posterior fossa, depending on its size and location, can produce one, two, or all three of the shifts described above, and if the lesion is large enough, all three shifts are inevitable. Such a large lesion and the shifts of brainstem structures caused by it are illustrated in Figure 31.

Direct Compression

The anatomic and physiologic principles that underlie swelling, displacement and compression of the brain were discussed in Chapter 2. With posterior fossa lesions, just as with supratentorial lesions, the rate at which these changes develop has an important bearing on the severity of symptoms. However, the smaller size of the posterior fossa necessarily reduces its ability to tolerate expanding lesions

153

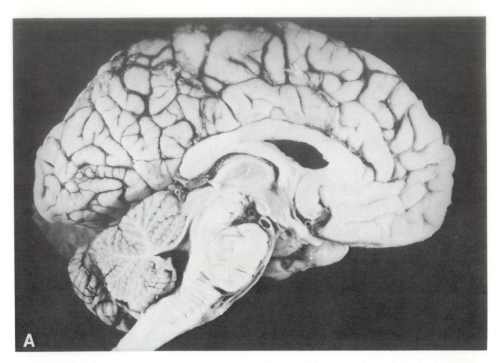

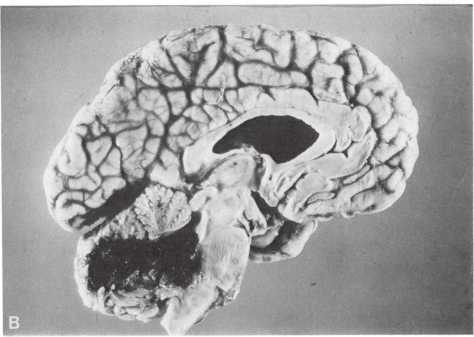

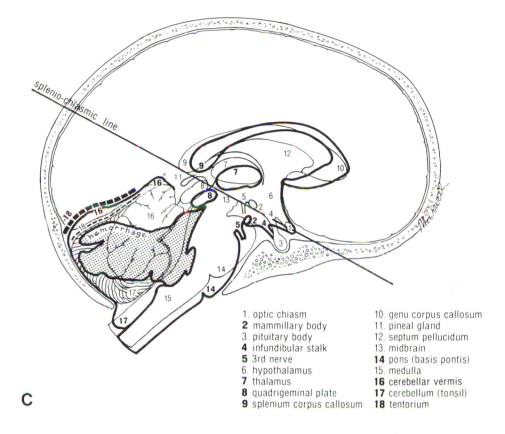

1. optic chiasm
2. mammillary body
3. pituitary body
4. infundibular stalk
5. 3rd nerve
6. hypothalamus
7. thalamus
8. quadrigeminal plate
9. splenium corpus callosum
10. genu corpus callosum
11. pineal gland
12. septum pellucidum
13. midbrain
14. pons (basis pontis)
15. medulla
16. cerebellar vermis
17. cerebellum (tonsil)
18. tentorium

C

Figure 31.   The anatomy of posterior fossa herniation.

Compare the normal brain in midsagittal section (**A**) with that of a patient who died of a cerebellar hemorrhage (**B**). Diagrams of the two brains are superimposed to emphasize the abnormal shifts in brainstem structures (**C**). The position of the normal brain is indicated by the fine lines and numbers and that of the *herniated* brain by the **bold** lines and numbers. The entire brainstem and corpus callosum of the herniated brain is indicated boldly. The structures that have not undergone significant shifts are indicated below the figure by the fine numbering. The bold numbers depict those structures which have been shifted by the hemorrhage. As **B** and **C** indicate, hemorrhage has replaced the middle and inferior vermis of the cerebellum and dissected into the fourth ventricle. The hemorrhage itself, plus the swelling of the adjacent cerebellum, has produced three major areas of shift:

1. Downward displacement of the cerebellar tonsils (#17) through the foramen magnum; this has displaced the caudal medulla forward.

2. Upward displacement of the cerebellum. This has resulted in rostral movement of the tentorium itself (#18) and in herniation of the anterior vermis through the tentorial opening (#16). Herniation of the anterior vermis has caused shifts of supratentorial structures, including the isthmus of the cingulate gyrus (indicated by the asterisk [*] above #16), the splenium of the corpus callosum (#9), and the quadrigeminal plate (#8). The result is a swelling of the entire diencephalon. This diencephalic swelling is less prominent than that produced by supratentorial mass lesions with downward herniation (see Figs. 17A and 17B). Nevertheless, shifts of supratentorial structures occur that are similar to but less severe than those accompanying supratentorial mass lesions. For example, the mamillary bodies are displaced 0.5 cm. downward from the splenio-chiasmic line. There is no shift of the optic chiasm or the anterior wall of the third ventricle.

3. Anterior displacement of the brainstem results partly from mass of the hemorrhage itself and partly from tonsillar herniation. The entire brainstem has been displaced anteriorly and compressed upon the clivus. Both the pons and the midbrain are swollen.

so that expanding lesions show an even greater tendency to alter the function of adjacent and remote normal tissues than they do in the supratentorial compartment. Accordingly, large or rapidly developing masses, such as cerebellar hemorrhages or infarcts, are frequently associated with coma, presumably because there is insufficient time for other posterior fossa structures, such as the brain itself, the CSF, and the blood vessels, to readjust their size and compensate for the lesion. By contrast, more slowly developing lesions sometimes reach an equal or greater size and produce substantial brainstem deformities without impairing consciousness. Sooner or later, however, compression of the brainstem directly damages neural tissue and distorts the blood vessels to produce ischemia. Whichever the initial step, necrosis of both neural and vascular elements is the ultimate effect, and the resulting coma is an ominous development.

Upward Transtentorial Herniation

When tissues in the posterior fossa selectively expand, the cerebellum and mesencephalon may herniate upward through the tentorial notch. This compresses the dorsal aspect of the mesencephalon as well as adjacent blood vessels and induces changes in the midbrain and surrounding structures drained by the central cerebral veins.[2] The posterior third ventricle is distorted, and the potential vascular obstructions can be appreciated. The spinal fluid flow can be blocked either by obstruction of the aqueduct, which prevents caudal exit of CSF from the lateral ventricles, or by obliteration of the pontine and ambient cisterns, which dams back the rostral flow of CSF from the posterior to the anterior fossa over the surface of the brain. Upward herniation also compresses and distorts the veins of Galen and Rosenthal, raising the supratentorial venous pressure, a process which partly counteracts and compensates for the upward herniation from below. Finally, the superior cerebellar arteries can be compressed against the tentorium from upward herniation, resulting in infarcts of the superior cerebellum.

Upward tentorial herniation occurs frequently with expanding lesions in the posterior fossa. Vastine and Kinney[52] reported that the pineal body was displaced upward in one third of their 15 patients with subtentorial gliomas and in 22 percent of their 28 patients with acoustic neurinomas. More "normally placed" pineal bodies in their patients with subtentorial tumors were nearer the upper than the lower margin of the normal range.

Several recent reports review the radiographic changes of upward herniation of the cerebellum through the tentorial notch. Wackenheim and associates describe the arteriographic changes of upward cerebellar herniation, emphasizing upward displacement of the superior vermian vein as a critical sign in establishing the diagnosis.[53] Eisenberg and Sarwar describe the ventriculographic features of a single patient who herniated following treatment of hydrocephalus with a low resistance shunt.[16] They emphasize the elevation and deformation of the posterior portion of the third ventricle, with obliteration of pineal and suprapineal recesses.

Osborn, Heaston, and Wing have described the CT findings in ascending transtentorial herniation.[40] They observe that early upward herniation causes compression and slight posterior flattening of the quadrigeminal plate cistern. With progressively more severe herniation, the cisterns become progressively more distorted and finally completely obscured by the herniated cerebellar vermis. Obstructive hydrocephalus occurred in most of the patients whom they examined.

156

Downward Herniation into the Foramen Magnum

The cerebellar tonsils may normally project as much as 2 cm. into the cervical canal,[23] and five out of six normal brains show grooving of the under surface of the cerebellum against the foramen magnum. In patients with foraminal impaction, the groove extends more deeply and ventrally to involve cerebellar tissue on either side of the medulla. If such patients survive long enough, the tonsils as well as the medulla and upper cervical spinal cord become infarcted. This is an extreme situation, however, and the usual problem for the pathologist is that foraminal herniation with medullary compression produces fatal respiratory and circulatory arrest so quickly that morphologic changes are equivocal. Physiologically the mechanism of coma in foraminal impaction is anoxia secondary to the respiratory and circulatory changes and not medullary compression per se.

CLINICAL SIGNS OF SUBTENTORIAL LESIONS

Destructive Lesions

Patients with destructive subtentorial lesions often lose consciousness immediately, and the ensuing coma is accompanied by distinctive patterns of respiratory, pupillary, oculovestibular, and motor signs that clearly indicate whether it is the tegmentum of the midbrain, the rostral pons, or the caudal pons that initially is most severely damaged. The brainstem reticulum lies so close to nuclei and pathways influencing the pupils, the eye movements, and other major functions that primary brainstem destructive lesions characteristically produce restricted and asymmetrical signs of focal neurologic disease that often can be precisely localized anatomically by the clinical findings, with all the signs pointing to a single lesion that produces less than a full physiologic brainstem transection. This restricted, discrete localization is unlike metabolic lesions causing coma, where the signs commonly indicate incomplete but symmetrical dysfunction that commonly affects several different levels. It also is unlike the secondary brainstem dysfunction that follows supratentorial herniation, in which *all* functions at any given brainstem level tend to be lost as the process descends from rostral to caudal along the neuraxis.

Certain combinations of signs stand out prominently in patients with subtentorial destructive lesions causing coma. At the *midbrain* level, centrally placed brainstem lesions interrupt the pathway for the pupillary light reflex and often damage the oculomotor nuclei as well. The resulting deep coma commonly is accompanied by pupils that are fixed at midposition or slightly wider, by a nuclear or infranuclear type of ophthalmoplegia, and by abnormal, long-tract motor signs. These last mentioned result from involvement of the cerebral peduncles and commonly are bilateral, although asymmetrical. Destructive lesions of the *rostral pons* commonly spare the oculomotor nuclei but interrupt the medial longitudinal fasciculus and the adjacent ocular sympathetic pathways. One observes tiny pupils, internuclear ophthalmoplegia, and in many instances, cranial nerve signs of trigeminal or facial weakness betraying pontine destruction.

Severe *lower pontine destruction* sometimes causes a functional transection with physiologic effects that may be difficult to differentiate from metabolic coma. The pupils of such patients are miotic but may react minimally to light since midbrain parasympathetic oculomotor fibers are spared. Reflex lateral eye movements are

157

absent since the pontine structures for lateral conjugate eye movements are destroyed. However, upward and downward ocular deviation occasionally is retained either spontaneously or in response to the oculocephalic maneuvers, and, if present, this dissociation between lateral and vertical movement clearly identifies pontine destruction. Ocular bobbing sometimes accompanies such acute destructive lesions and when present usually, but not always, indicates primary posterior fossa disease. The motor signs of severe pontine destruction are not the same in every patient and can include flaccid quadriplegia, less often extensor posturing, or, occasionally, extensor posturing responses in the arms with flexor responses or flaccidity in the legs. Respiration may show any of the patterns characteristic of low brainstem dysfunction described in Chapter 1, but cluster breathing, apneusis, gasping, and ataxic breathing are characteristic.

Compressive Lesions

With posterior fossa lesions the effects of direct brainstem compression can be difficult to separate clinically from the effects produced by upward or downward herniation of the brain out of the posterior fossa, since all three processes accompany almost every sizable lesion. Abnormal lateral conjugate gaze, ocular bobbing, and other oculomotor signs frequently occur because pontine ocular pathways are compressed. Vomiting and cranial nerve abnormalities accompany many of these compressive lesions.

It is not certain whether or not posterior fossa lesions causing *upward transtentorial herniation* produce a consistent syndrome.[61] As herniation occurs, it compresses the pretectal area, an effect that results in either conjugate downward deviation of the eyes or at least failure to elicit voluntary or reflex upward deviation of the eyes. Severe upward herniation also obstructs the vein of Galen, and this may be the mechanism of certain rare instances of proptosis with acute posterior fossa hemorrhage. Cuneo and associates have suggested that the sequence in brainstem compression begins with direct compression of the pons, leading to reactive but miotic pupils, asymmetric or absent caloric responses, and decerebrate motor movements.[10] In their experience, upward herniation of the cerebellum, compressing the midbrain, was heralded by a change from equal, reactive pupils to anisocoria, which gave way to midposition and fixed pupils.

The following patient illustrates the clinical picture of a combination of direct brainstem compression and upward transtentorial herniation owing to an expanding cerebellar abscess.

Patient 3-1. A 52-year-old alcoholic male became progressively obtunded in jail. By the time he reached the hospital, he was unable to give a history. His body temperature was 39.2° C, and he was diffusely rigid and hyperventilating at a rate of 34 per minute. At lumbar puncture the opening pressure of CSF was 230 mm. The CSF contained 4 mononuclear cells, and the protein content was later reported to be 242 mg./dl. Despite the ominous story, he was initially suspected of having delirium tremens and little was done. The next morning he was in coma and had abnormal extensor motor responses on the left side of his body and decorticate posturing on the right. He was mildly hyperpneic with a rate of 28 per minute. His pupils measured 1.5 mm. and were *unreactive* to a bright light. Vertical doll's eye movements were absent but the lateral responses were hyperactive. His extremities and neck were diffusely rigid and his plantar responses were extensor. Skull x-ray findings were unremarkable, and a right carotid arteriogram showed a sweeping anterior cerebral artery consistent with dilation of the lateral ventricles, as well as elevation of the basal vein consistent with upward transtentorial herniation. Air could not be introduced into the aqueduct or fourth ventricle by ventriculography, and air injected into the lumbar subarachnoid space stopped at the cervical region, a finding compatible with cerebellar tonsillar herniation. The posterior fossa was explored, and 10 cc. of pus was removed from the greatly swollen right cerebellar hemisphere. The patient recovered.

158

Comment: The combination of coma, hyperventilation, miotic fixed pupils (pontine compression), loss of upward gaze (pretectal compression), and brisk lateral oculocephalic responses was, in retrospect, diagnostic of a posterior fossa lesion with upward herniation. Before obtaining the ventriculogram, observers failed to heed these signs and believed that the patient had a metabolic or diencephalic lesion despite the hyperventilation, the nearly pinpoint, fixed pupils, and the dissociated oculovestibular responses, all of which spelled direct brainstem dysfunction.

Compression of the middle third of the pons, by either slowly enlarging masses in the floor of the fourth ventricle or midline cerebellar masses, also produces a recognizable clinical syndrome. As we have observed such patients, prior to surgical treatment or to their decompensation with secondary brainstem infarction, they have been drowsy rather than stuporous or in coma. Pupils were small, 1 to 2 mm. in diameter, and reacted minimally but briskly. Progressive external ophthalmoplegia developed, first on lateral gaze, then vertical. Nystagmus, when present, appeared to be predominantly of the gaze paretic type. Oculocephalic and oculovestibular responses were at first somewhat better preserved than voluntary movement, but the two disappeared almost in parallel. Respiration was normal or slow, but eventually slowed with intermittent deep sighs or ataxia. Signs of corticospinal tract dysfunction were initially mild. Mild appendicular ataxia was present. Gait and truncal ataxia generally were prominent in instances where they could be tested, but with the patient in the supine position, signs of cerebellar dysfunction often were minimal or uncertain.

Brainstem Lesions Sparing Consciousness

Brainstem lesions lying outside the pontine-midbrain reticular formation sometimes destroy a remarkable amount of brain without causing coma. Patient 1–2 described in Chapter 1, who was awake despite widespread destruction of the medulla, illustrates this principle, as does the following patient who retained consciousness and responded appropriately despite almost total destruction of the basis pontis.

Patient 3–2. A 44-year-old white man was healthy until he suddenly had a 15-minute episode of vertigo and nausea. A physical examination the following day was normal. Seven days later, the patient again experienced vertigo, nausea, and vomiting, followed by weakness of all extremities and inability to talk. On admission to a hospital, the diagnosis of basilar artery thrombosis was made. He was transferred to our observation 1 month later. His blood pressure was 140/80 mm. Hg. He was well developed and well nourished. He was awake but unable to move his limbs or talk. When instructed to respond to questions by moving his eyes up and down to indicate yes or no, he could do so appropriately. He apparently recognized large images although detailed testing of visual acuity was not possible. There was no lateral motion of the eyes either on command or on passive head turning. Cold caloric irrigation on the left evoked no response; on the right it evoked ipsilateral tonic deviation of the eyes. Nystagmus was not present in either direction. The corneal reflexes and facial sensation appeared to be present bilaterally. There was bilateral facial weakness. The brow had a normal contour but no voluntary motion. Hearing was intact bilaterally. There was no voluntary movement in structures innervated by cranial nerves IX to XII or in the extremities, which lay motionless and flaccid. Perception of noxious stimuli appeared to be preserved. The stretch reflexes were equally hyperactive bilaterally throughout the arms and legs, with bilateral extensor plantar responses.

The EEG contained symmetrical, well-formed parietal-occipital 8 per second alpha activity and was interpreted as being within normal limits. The course in hospital was unremarkable except for the development of some voluntary motion in the left ankle. The patient died 1 month later from pneumonia, having retained responsiveness to questions almost until death.

Autopsy revealed severe arteriosclerosis of the basilar artery with complete occlusion 1 cm. above its

159

origin from the vertebrals. The cerebral hemispheres were normal. There was a cystic infarct in the brainstem that destroyed most of the upper two thirds of the basis pontis and a small portion of the cerebral peduncles. The mesencephalic tegmentum was intact, and a small portion of the periventricular pontine tegmentum was also spared. At no point did the reticular formation appear to be completely interrupted in its course. The lower pons and medulla were not involved by the lesion.

Comment: Like M. Noirtier de Villefort in Dumas' *The Count of Monte Cristo*, this patient was awake but had lost all power to communicate except with his eyes —"a corpse with living eyes." Although both akinetic and mute, he did not suffer from the syndrome of akinetic mutism in which patients are unconscious and make no appropriate responses.[7,9] Great care must be exercised in distinguishing such locked-in patients with "a mind ... encumbered by a body over which it has lost the power of compelling obedience" from typical akinetic mutism in which self-aware consciousness is lost. The implications for humane patient care are profound.

SPECIFIC SUBTENTORIAL LESIONS CAUSING COMA

Basilar Artery Occlusion with Midbrain-Pontine Infarction

Occlusion of the basilar artery either by thrombosis or embolism is a relatively common cause of coma, and several patients with this disorder are admitted every year to large clinical services. The occlusions are usually the result of atherosclerotic or hypertensive disease, since rarer vascular diseases such as periarteritis and other collagen diseases tend to spare the basilar artery. Vascular syphilis sometimes produces basilar artery occlusion but is now rare. Emboli to the basilar artery are unusual with valvular heart disease but do occur with arteriosclerosis. Kubik and Adams[26] reported that 7 of their 18 patients with basilar occlusion had an embolism, but did not identify the origin.

Brainstem infarction with coma caused by vertebral artery occlusion can be caused by chiropractic manipulation of the neck. Several such patients have been reported with severe and permanent brainstem damage.[38] Cranial arteritis involving the vertebral arteries in the neck also can lead to secondary basilar artery ischemia with brainstem infarction and coma.[55]

Most patients in coma from brainstem infarction are over 50 years of age, but this is not an exclusive limit. One of our patients was only 34 years old. Characteristic transient symptoms and signs owing to brief ischemia of the brainstem often precede coma by days or weeks. These transient attacks typically change from episode to episode but always reflect subtentorial central nervous system dysfunction and include headaches (mainly occipital), diplopia, vertigo, dysarthria, dysphagia, bilateral or alternating motor or sensory symptoms, or drop attacks[5] (sudden spontaneous falls while standing or walking, without loss of consciousness and with complete recovery in seconds). The attacks usually last for as short a period as 10 seconds or as long as several minutes. Seldom are they more prolonged, although recurrent transient attacks of otherwise unexplained akinetic coma lasting 20 to 30 minutes occurred in one of our patients who later died from pontine infarction caused by total occlusion of the middle portion of the basilar artery. Except in patients who additionally have recurrent asystole or other severe cardiac arrhythmias, transient ischemic attacks caused by vertebrobasilar artery insufficiency nearly always occur in the erect or sitting position.

Segmental thrombi can occlude the midportion of the basilar artery, producing only limited and temporary symptoms of brainstem dysfunction. Such limited

160

occlusions are rare, however, and most patients with basilar artery occlusion are much more seriously ill—about half are in coma from the onset of their disease, and most of the rest are either confused, obtunded, or delirious. The degree of impairment of consciousness presumably depends on how much the collateral vascular supply protects the central brainstem and the reticular formation. The coma usually begins abruptly or within a few hours of other clinical signs and is accompanied by other signs reflecting infarction of the midbrain or pons. Most patients have respiratory abnormalities that include periodic breathing, or various types of irregular or ataxic respiration. The pupils are almost always abnormal and may be small (pontine), midposition (midbrain), or dilated (third nerve outflow in midbrain). Most patients have divergent or skewed optical axes reflecting direct nuclear and internuclear damage. Other cranial nerve functions are often impaired. Signs of motor long-tract abnormalities are characteristically bilateral and include defects in swallowing as well as hemiplegia or quadriplegia and extensor plantar responses.

The differential diagnosis of acute brainstem infarction can usually be made from clinical clues alone. With brainstem infarction, the fact that signs of midbrain or pontine damage accompany the *onset* of coma immediately places the site of the lesion as subtentorial. The illness is maximal at onset or evolves rapidly and in a series of steps, as would be expected with ischemic vascular disease. Supratentorial ischemic vascular lesions, by contrast, are not likely to cause coma that comes on with such an abrupt onset, and they never begin with pupillary abnormalities or other signs of direct brainstem injury. Pontine and cerebellar hemorrhages, since they also destroy or depress the brainstem, sometimes resemble brainstem infarction in their manifestations. However, most such hemorrhages have a distinctive picture (see below). Furthermore, they nearly always arise in hypertensive patients, often cause occipital headache (which is unusual with infarction), and are accompanied by a bloody spinal fluid under increased pressure. Metabolic depression of the brainstem only rarely is mimicked by brainstem infarction; in the few cases in which one has difficulty with this distinction, it is usually because the history of onset is unavailable and the infarct has involved the low pons. Such infarcts can produce defects in the sympathetic control of the pupil as well as interruption of oculovestibular reflexes. The differentiation between pontine infarction and a metabolic lesion is made easier by recalling that among metabolic causes for coma only glutethimide produces deep coma with fixed pupils and that metabolic lesions rarely produce a sustained dissociation between the lateral and vertical oculovestibular responses.

Patient 3-2 illustrated the symptoms of one type of basilar artery occlusion with sparing of much of the tegmentum. The following example illustrates the syndrome of acute infarction of the lower midbrain tegmentum owing to basilar artery occlusion.

Patient 3-3. A 79-year-old white woman was admitted in coma. She had been in good health, except for known hypertension, until 4 hours earlier when she suddenly vomited and became unconscious. Her blood pressure was 180/100 mm. Hg. She had sighing respirations, which shortly changed to a Cheyne-Stokes pattern. The pupils were 4 mm. in diameter and unreactive to light. The oculocephalic responses were absent, but cold caloric irrigation induced a bilateral, dysconjugate response with abduction of the eye only on the side being irrigated. She responded to noxious stimuli with extensor posturing and occasionally was wracked by spontaneous waves of extensor rigidity. On the way to the ward from the emergency room, she vomited bloody material. Her subsequent blood pressure was 120/80 mm. Hg, her pulse 80 per minute, and her respirations periodic at 11 per minute. The pineal gland was seen in the midline on a skull x-ray film. The CSF pressure on lumbar puncture was 140 mm.; the fluid was clear, without cells, and contained 35 mg./dl. of protein. Two days later, the patient continued in coma with extensor responses to noxious stimulation; the pupils remained fixed in midposition, and there was no ocular response to cold caloric irrigation. Respirations were eupneic. The next day she died. The brain was examined postmortem. The basilar artery was occluded in its midportion by a recent thrombus 1 cm. in length. There was extensive infarction of the upper portion of the basis pontis and of the medial pontine and midbrain tegmentum. The lower portion of the pons and the medulla were intact.

Comment: This woman suffered an acute brainstem infarction with unusually symmetrical neurologic signs. It was at first thought that she might have had a cerebral hemorrhage with sudden acute transtentorial herniation producing a picture of acute midbrain transection. However, such rapid progression to a midbrain level (within 4 hours) almost never occurs in cerebral hemorrhage, probably because overwhelmingly severe hemorrhages are fatal within minutes. Patients with large cerebral hemorrhages rarely vomit initially, and their spinal fluid is almost never completely free of red cells. Finally, the neurologic signs of midbrain damage in this patient remained nearly constant from onset, whereas transtentorial herniation would rapidly have produced further rostral-caudal deterioration.

Subtentorial Hemorrhage

Posterior Fossa Subdural and Extradural Hematomas

In the posterior fossa, space-occupying lesions in the subdural and extradural space produce similar clinical disorders. These are rare, but their recognition is important because proper treatment leads to a high incidence of full recovery. Underlying cerebellar hematomas accompany many of these lesions[8] but with no distinguishable differences in symptoms. A history of trauma can be obtained in about three fourths of the cases.

These hematomas usually originate from veins rather than arteries, which may explain why most of the patients have a subacute or chronic illness. Direct occipital injury with skull fracture frequently precedes bleeding into either space, but extradural hematomas generally originate from tears in the sinuses or torcular, while subdural collections have more often been described in association with cerebellar lacerations. With severe head injury, both supratentorial and subtentorial extracerebral bleeding can combine.[43]

The history and findings are characteristic. In acute cases, occipital injury produces acute unconsciousness or a dazed state followed in most instances by a lucid interval lasting hours or days during which occipital headache appears and becomes progressively more severe. If seen early, the patients characteristically show nystagmus, some ataxia, and, sometimes, papilledema. If ignored, these changes are followed within a few hours by vomiting, vertigo, ataxia, stiff neck, drowsiness, restlessness, and, finally, coma with bilateral corticospinal tract dysfunction plus signs of diffuse posterior fossa dysfunction and, eventually, respiratory failure. Skull x-ray examinations disclose an occipital fracture line in about three quarters of the patients, and vertebral arteriograms or ventriculograms are usually diagnostic. Delay is dangerous in acute cases with a strong clinical story since these illnesses when untreated can run their full course to severe brain damage or death in less than 12 to 15 hours.

Subacute or chronic hematomas tell a similar tale, but more slowly. Post-traumatic lucid intervals lasting as long as 4 months have been reported, followed by occipital

162

headache, stiff neck, papilledema, ataxia, and dysarthria, plus other signs of cerebellar dysfunction and, finally, impaired consciousness. Occipital fracture lines are usually present. The CSF is noncharacteristic and lumbar puncture risky so that most hematomas are ultimately diagnosed by contrast studies, surgical exploration, or postmortem examination. Surgical drainage, if initiated early, results in a cure.

Primary Pontine Hemorrhage

Hemorrhage into the pons arises from the paramedian arterioles, begins at the base of the tegmentum, and usually dissects in all directions in a relatively symmetrical fashion.[12] Rupture into the fourth ventricle occurs in most patients, but dissection into the medulla is rare. Because at one time the diagnosis was made almost exclusively by postmortem examination, pontine hemorrhages once were believed essentially always to cause coma. The development of CT scanning, which clearly outlines those lesions, has brought us to realize that about one third are confined to the basis pontis and produce an acute locked-in state, often with considerable recovery. Larger hemorrhages nearly always produce coma, but are a comparatively uncommon cause, accounting for only 2 percent of our cases of intracranial hemorrhage. Almost all primary pontine hemorrhages occur in hypertensive persons, few of whom, according to Dinsdale[12] have prior symptoms of cerebral vascular disease. Among our own patients, however, almost half had histories of previous hemiplegic strokes.

Coma caused by pontine hemorrhage begins abruptly, usually during the hours when patients are awake and active and usually without prodromata.[12,46] As far as we could tell from witnesses, few of our patients had symptoms such as sudden occipital headache, vomiting, speechlessness, and collapse before losing consciousness. Almost every patient has had respiratory abnormalities of the brainstem type: Cheyne-Stokes breathing, apneustic or gasping breathing, and progressive slowing of respiration or apnea occur. Steegman[46] reported that 30 percent of his patients developed progressive respiratory failure.

The pupils are nearly always abnormal and usually pinpoint. The light reaction is often lost immediately after the hemorrhage but ordinarily returns if the patient survives 24 hours or more. The ciliospinal response disappears. Large hemorrhages, extending to the midbrain, may cause asymmetrical or dilated pupils. About one third of the patients suffer from oculomotor abnormalities such as skewed or lateral ocular deviations or ocular bobbing, and the oculocephalic responses disappear. Motor signs vary according to the extent of the hemorrhage. Some subjects become diffusely rigid and tremble and suffer repeated waves of decerebrate rigidity. More frequently, however, the patients are quadriplegic and flaccid with flexor responses at hip, knee, and great toe to plantar stimulation, a reflex conbination characteristic of acute low brainstem damage when it accompanies acute coma. Nearly all patients with pontine hemorrhage who survive more than a few hours develop fever with body temperatures of 38.5 to 41°C.

The diagnosis of pontine hemorrhage is usually straightforward. Almost no other lesion, except an occasional cerebellar hemorrhage with secondary dissection into the brainstem, produces sudden coma with periodic or ataxic breathing, pinpoint pupils, absence of oculovestibular responses, quadriplegia, and bloody spinal fluid. Before lumbar puncture, a severe metabolic disease might be suspected, but in metabolic coma the pupils are rarely so small and, even if pinpoint, are not light fixed. Finally, the flexor spasms that accompany the flaccid quadriplegia of low brainstem injury do not occur in patients who have motor flaccidity from metabolic disease. CT scan, if available, is diagnostic and eliminates the need for diagnostic lumbar puncture. The patient reported below had a clinical picture typical of pontine hemorrhage.

Patient 3–4. A 75-year-old man had a "stroke" with a left hemiparesis from which he subsequently recovered. Seven months later he collapsed in coma. The blood pressure was 170/90 mm. Hg; the pulse was 84 per minute; respirations were Cheyne-Stokes in character and 16 per minute. The pupils were pinpoint but reacted equally to light. The ocular globes were still and oculovestibular responses were absent. The patient was flaccid with symmetrical stretch reflexes of normal amplitude and bilateral flexor withdrawal responses in the lower extremities to plantar stimulation. The spinal fluid was bloody with an opening pressure of 200 mm. and a protein content greater than 100 mg./dl. There was no shift of the well-calcified pineal gland in the x-ray films. The next morning he was still in deep coma, but now was diffusely flaccid except for flexor responses to noxious stimuli in the legs. He had slow, shallow, eupneic respiration, small, equally reactive pupils, and eyes in neutral position. Shortly thereafter, breathing became irregular and he died. A 3-cm. primary hemorrhage destroying the central pons and its tegmentum was found at autopsy.

Okudera and associates recently reviewed the clinical and radiographic features of 23 patients who died of primary pontine hemorrhages.[39] All patients had a rapid onset of coma. In many, coma occurred with no prodromata, while in others headache, vomiting, and vertigo preceded loss of consciousness, usually by no more than a few minutes. Miotic pupils were the rule, with midposition or mydriatic pupils encountered in about a quarter of the patients. Eighty percent of the patients became hyperthermic, with temperatures over 39°C. Cerebrospinal fluid was grossly bloody in all 18 of the patients who received lumbar puncture. Most patients died within a few days of admission. At autopsy, the hematomas were localized to the mid-pons. In 11 patients, the entire pons was involved; in the other 12, hemorrhage was limited primarily to the tegmentum. Rupture into the fourth ventricle had occurred in 20 patients, upward extension into the tegmentum of the midbrain in 15, and downward extension into the medulla in only 1 patient.

Cerebellar Hemorrhage

Cerebellar hemorrhages account for about 10 percent of parenchymal intracranial hemorrhages and frequently cause coma and death by compressing or infiltrating the brainstem. Increasing numbers of reports in recent years[4,30,33,41,44] indicate that if the diagnosis can be made promptly, many such patients can be treated successfully by evacuating the clot or removing an associated angioma. Approximately three quarters of patients with cerebellar hemorrhage have hypertension; most of the remaining have angiomas of the posterior fossa or are receiving anticoagulant drugs. Among our own 28 patients, 5 had posterior fossa arteriovenous vascular malformations, 1 had thrombocytopenic purpura, 3 were normotensive but receiving anticoagulants, and the remainder, who ranged between 39 and 83 years of age, had hypertensive vascular disease. Hemorrhages in hypertensive patients arise in the neighborhood of the dentate nuclei; those coming from angiomas tend to lie more superficially. Both types usually rupture into the subarachnoid space or fourth ventricle and appear to produce coma chiefly by compressing the brainstem.

Fisher's paper in 1965[17] did much to stimulate efforts at clinical diagnosis in this disorder and encouraged attempts at successful treatment. Subsequent reports from several large centers have increasingly emphasized that one must make prompt, early diagnosis to effect satisfactory treatment of cerebellar hemorrhage and that once patients become stuporous or comatose, surgical drainage represents a near-hopeless exercise. Figure 32 gives background factors of age and cause in 56 patients with cerebellar hematoma reported by Ott and associates.[41] The influence of age, hypertension, and anticoagulants is evident.

Brennan and Bergland[4] have summarized the experience with 12 patients treated in the pre-CT scan era at The New York Hospital, with findings generally similar to those of Ott and associates from the Massachusetts General Hospital.

The most common initial symptoms of cerebellar hemorrhage are headaches (most often occipital), nausea and vomiting, dizziness or vertiginous sensations, unsteadiness or an inability to walk, dysarthria, and, less often, drowsiness. Table 8 lists the most frequent early physical signs as recorded in the two large series.[4,41] Both studies emphasize that deterioration from alertness or drowsiness to stupor often comes within a few hours of admission and that even brief delays to carry out radiographic procedures can prove fatal. An additional sign of cerebellar hemorrhage sometimes consists of unilateral eyelid closure. Messert and associates observed this in two patients, apparently as a voluntary attempt to prevent diplopia.[34] Because the cerebellar hematoma caused mild ipsilateral facial weakness by compressing the brainstem, the closed eye was on the side contralateral to the cerebellar hemorrhage.

Our experience with acute cerebellar hemorrhage points to a gradation in severity that can be divided roughly into four relatively distinct clinical patterns. The least serious form occurs with small hemorrhages, usually less than 1.5 to 2 cm. in diameter by CT scan, and includes a self-limited acute disturbance of unilateral cerebellar dysfunction accompanied by headache.[21] Without CT scanning, this

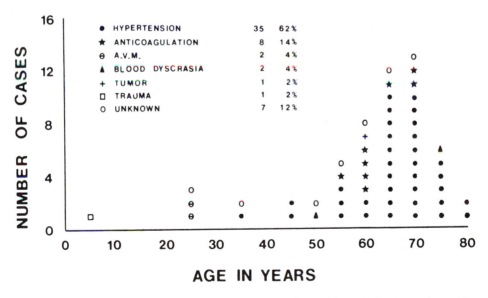

Figure 32. Etiologic factors and age distribution of 56 patients with cerebellar hemorrhage. (From Ott, K.H., Kase, C.S., Ojemann, R.G., and Mohr, J.P.: *Cerebellar hemorrhage: diagnosis and treatment.* Arch. Neurol. 31:160–167, 1974, with permission.)

165

disorder undoubtedly would go undiagnosed, but it blends in severity into a less benign disorder in which occipital headache is more prominent and signs of cerebellar or oculomotor dysfunction develop gradually or episodically over 1 to several days. There may be some associated drowsiness or dull behavior. Patients with this degree of impairment have been reported to recover spontaneously, particularly from hemorrhages measuring less than 3 cm. in diameter by CT scan.[30] However, the condition requires extremely close evaluation because, as noted, patients almost always do badly if one waits until coma develops to initiate surgical treatment. The most characteristic and therapeutically important syndrome of cerebellar hemorrhages describes individuals who develop acute or subacute occipital headache, vomiting, and progressive neurologic impairment including ipsilateral ataxia, nausea, vertigo, nystagmus, and gaze paresis toward the side of the hematoma and ipsilateral facial paresis together with weakness of paralysis of the legs. Confusion or obtundation can appear at varying points along the course of the illness and is a symptom of impending decompensation. In this group, surgical decompression and drainage can be life saving. Finally, about one fifth of patients with cerebellar hemorrhage suddenly lose consciousness and develop respiratory irregularity, pinpoint pupils, absent oculovestibular responses, and quadriplegia; the picture is clinically indistinguishable from primary pontine hemorrhage and almost always fatal.

Since in many instances the clinical evidence provides strong evidence for the diagnosis of cerebellar hemorrhage, both The New York Hospital and Massachusetts General Hospital studies concluded that unless facilities for rapid CT scanning are available, one should proceed immediately with surgical drainage in worsening patients with typical pictures. Rosenberg and Kaufman, however, record a less optimistic experience with clinical diagnosis: in their institution the clinical approach correctly identified only 13 of 23 cerebellar hemorrhages, while physicians incorrectly made the diagnosis on 10 patients who had other disorders.[44] Table 9 outlines the major points that differentiate clinically between cerebellar hemorrhage and other acute cerebral vascular lesions potentially causing stupor or coma.

Table 8. Frequent Clinical Signs of Cerebellar Hemorrhage in 12 Alert New York Hospital Patients[4] Compared with 38 Noncomatose Patients at Massachusetts General Hospital.[41]

Brennan		Ott
	Nuchal rigidity	14/35
8/9	Dysarthria	20/32
5/12	Respiration irregularity	6/28
	Abducens palsy	10/36
	Decreased corneal	10/33
	Facial palsy	22/36
	Gag reflex loss	6/30
5/12	Skew deviation	4/33
12/12	Miosis	11/37
6/12	Nystagmus	18/35
9/12	Gaze palsy	20/37
6/12	Ophthalmoplegia	
	Hemiparesis	4/35
7/8	Appendicular ataxia	17/26
5/6	Gait or truncal ataxia	11/17
10/12	Extensor plantar response	23/36

Table 9. Typical Clinical Profiles of Acute Cerebrovascular Lesions Affecting Consciousness

---

Acute massive cerebral infarction with or without hypotension.   Distribution: internal carotid-proximal middle cerebral artery or middle cerebral plus anterior cerebral arteries. Onset during wakefulness or sleep. Massive hemiplegia with aphasia, hemisensory defect. Obtundation from the start or within hours, progressing to stupor in 12 to 24 hours, coma usually in 36 to 96 hours. Convulsions rare. Pupils small and reactive, or constricted ipsilateral to lesion (Horner's), or moderately dilated ipsilateral to lesion (III nerve). Conjugate gaze paresis to side of motor weakness; contralateral oculovestibulars can be suppressed for 12 hours or so. Contralateral hemiplegia, usually with extensor plantar response and paratonia ipsilateral to lesion. Cheyne-Stokes breathing 10 to 20 percent. Signs of progressive rostral-caudal deterioration begin in 12 to 24 hours. Spinal fluid usually unremarkable or with mildly elevated pressure and cells.

Frontoparietal hemorrhage.   Hypertensive, onset during wakefulness. Sudden onset headache, followed by more or less rapidly evolving aphasia, hemiparesis to hemiplegia, conjugate ocular deviation away from hemiparesis. Convulsions at onset in approximately one fifth. Pupils small and reactive, or ipsilateral Horner's with excessive contralateral sweating, or stupor to coma and bilateral motor signs within hours of onset. Bloody spinal fluid.

Thalamic hemorrhage.   Hypertensive, onset during wakefulness. Clinical picture similar to frontoparietal hemorrhage but seizures rare, vomiting frequent, eyes characteristically deviated down and laterally to either side. Pupils small and reactive. Conscious state ranges from awake to coma. Bloody spinal fluid.

Pontine hemorrhage.   Hypertensive. Sudden onset of coma or speechlessness, pinpoint pupils, ophthalmoplegia with absent or impaired oculovestibular responses, quadriplegia, irregular breathing, hyperthermia. Bloody spinal fluid.

Cerebellar hemorrhage.   Hypertensive and awake at onset. Acute and rapid onset and worsening within hours of occipital headache, nausea and vomiting, dizziness or vertigo, unsteadiness, dysarthria, and drowsiness. Small and reactive pupils, nystagmus or horizontal gaze paralysis towards the side of the lesion. Midline and ipsilateral ataxia, ipsilateral peripheral facial palsy, and contralateral extensor plantar response. Occasionally, course may proceed for 1 to 2 weeks. Spinal fluid bloody.

Acute cerebellar infarction.   Mostly hypertensive, mostly males. Onset at any time. Vertigo, ataxia, nausea, dull headache, nystagmus, dysarthria, ipsilateral dysmetria; 24 to 96 hours later: drowsiness, miosis, ipsilateral gaze paresis and facial paresis, worsening ataxia, extensor plantar responses. Coma, quadriplegia, and death may follow if not decompressed. Spinal fluid sometimes microscopically bloody.

Acute subarachnoid hemorrhage.   Awake at onset, sometimes hypertensive. Sudden headache, often followed within minutes by transient unconsciousness. Pupils small or unilaterally dilated. Subhyaloid hemorrhages, hemiparesis or aphasia may or may not be present, hemisensory changes rare. Neck stiff within 24 hours. Bloody spinal fluid.

The following history describes a patient with a progressively evolving cerebellar hemorrhage.

Patient 3–5. A 64-year-old woman had a 15-year history of hypertension that was medically well controlled with blood pressures in the region of 160/95 mm. Hg. At 7:30 in the evening, while cooking dinner, she experienced a sudden onset of vertigo associated with nausea and vomiting. She sat down and did not have occasion to walk thereafter. She also developed a severe occipital headache, but this was far overshadowed by the vertigo in terms of subjective distress. A physician examined her at 9:00 P.M. and noted that her head and eyes were deviated to the right. When she arrived at The New York Hospital 1½ hours later she was lethargic, anxious to sleep, experiencing vertigo, and vomiting in a nonprojectile fashion. Her blood pressure was 230/130 mm. Hg. Her pupils were 3 mm. in diameter and reactive, but her head and eyes deviated to the right and she did not follow commands to move them

167

from that position. She had decreased rapid alternating movements in the left upper and lower extremities along with mild dysmetria and striking hypotonia in the left arm. A left extensor plantar response was noted. Ice water (50 cc.) irrigated against the left tympanum failed to bring the eyes beyond the midline. Forty-five minutes later the patient had become more lethargic and had developed bilateral extensor plantar responses. A lumbar puncture opening pressure was 345 mm. with the patient in the lateral recumbent position, and the fluid contained 3800 red cells in the third tube. The protein was 150 mg./dl. At midnight the patient had a posterior fossa exploration, and 3 to 4 cm fresh hematoma was evacuated from the left cerebellar hemisphere. The next day she was greatly improved, with normal extraocular movements and near-complete resolution of cerebellar and corticospinal tract dysfunction. She recovered gradually and by 2 months later had barely detectable cerebellar abnormalities on the left side. Postoperatively the blood pressure returned to the pre-illness level and was easily controlled medically.

Comment: The sudden onset of vertigo and occipital headache associated with conjugate ocular deviation away from the side of cerebellar signs strongly suggested a posterior fossa lesion. Had the hemorrhage, which was proved by lumbar puncture, been in the brainstem, consciousness would surely have been lost since the neurologic signs indicated a pontine defect and not a medullary one. The steady and rapid progression led her physicians to act promptly and directly, without wasting valuable time on x-ray contrast studies. In retrospect, even the lumbar puncture probably needlessly delayed things.

Acute Cerebellar Infarction

Recent years increasingly have brought the recognition that acute cerebellar infarction can produce a fatal subtentorial mass lesion with clinical manifestations somewhat resembling cerebellar hemorrhage. We have had less experience with this disorder than have other authors,[29,49,57] but it appears that occlusion of the vertebral or cerebellar arteries can produce variable clinical syndromes that depend partly on the site of the occlusion and partly on unknown factors presumably having to do with collateral vascular supply. Sypert and Alvord, in 52 cases of cerebellar infarction studied at autopsy, found no history of neurologic difficulties in 12, a history of a remote neurologic "stroke" in 12, and evidence of an immediately antemortem subacute illness with progression to coma and death in 28.[49] In all instances of the last subacute disorder, post-infarction swelling of the cerebellum had compressed the brainstem to cause death.

Most patients with acute cerebellar infarction causing an altered state of consciousness have had moderate degrees of hypertension, and the great majority have been men between the ages of 34 and 69 years. Most have had occlusions of the vertebral and/or inferior cerebellar arteries. Their illness somewhat resembled that of cerebellar hemorrhage, but with a slower tempo and important distinctions. The onset was characteristically marked by acute or subacute dizziness, vertigo, unsteadiness, and, less often, dull headache. Most of the patients examined within hours of onset showed ataxia of gait, nystagmus with gaze in either direction but predominantly towards the infarct, and dysmetria ipsilateral to the infarct. Dysarthria and difficulty swallowing were evident in some patients and presumably reflected associated lateral medullary infarction. In most instances, further progression was delayed for 24 to 96 hours after onset, at which time more alarming symptoms began, including drowsiness leading to stupor, miotic and poorly reactive pupils, conjugate gaze paralysis ipsilateral to the lesion, ipsilateral peripheral facial paralysis, more intense ipsilateral dysmetria, and extensor plantar responses. Once the symptoms appeared, unless surgical decompression was conducted promptly, the illness progressed rapidly to coma, quadriplegia, and death within 2 to 4 days.

Diagnosis in patients with enlarging cerebellar infarction depends upon clinical acumen and suspicion supplemented by well-chosen laboratory studies. As with cerebellar hemorrhage, a successful outcome depends upon prompt action if consciousness is threatened. In most instances, the CSF pressure is elevated and the fluid often is microscopically bloody (hemorrhagic infarction). The diagnosis is suspected on clinical grounds and a CT scan; the same test determines whether or not the mass is causing hydrocephalus. Only the evaluation of clinical signs can determine whether the swelling is resolving or the enlarging mass must be surgically treated (by ventricular shunt or extirpation of infarcted tissue).[18] Survival follows prompt surgery, but as with the following young woman, patients may have distressing neurologic residua.

Patient 3–6. A 32-year-old athletically inclined woman was in good health except for labile hypertension until 5 days prior to a New York Hospital admission, when she noted the onset of vertex headache. She attributed this to a fall the day before, which occurred while she was attempting a headstand. Her headache was dull and generalized, and made worse by any movement of the head. She was otherwise well and continued to work, but sought medical help because of persistent headache. Her neurologic examination was entirely normal, and a lumbar puncture was cell free and the fluid under normal pressure. CT scanning was not available. Over the next 3 days she remained at home complaining of increasingly more severe headache and some dizziness. She was admitted for further evaluation.

The general physical and neurologic examinations were normal except for slight restriction of neck flexion. On lumbar punctures performed during the first 2 days of hospitalization, there were 300 to 800 red blood cells, with protein concentrations of 42 and 111 mg. per 100 ml. Her headache continued without lateralizing features and required narcotic analgesics for relief. On the third hospital day the patient developed horizontal nystagmus and a slight conjugate gaze palsy, both to the left. The left pupil was 1 mm. smaller than the right and there was mild left ptosis. Rapid movements in the left upper extremity were dysmetric. There was mild flattening of the left lower face without weakness and some depression of gag reflex on the left. A left vertebral and a right brachial arteriogram revealed narrowing of the extracranial portions of the left vertebral artery together with signs of a mass in the left cerebellar hemisphere. The posterior inferior cerebellar arteries were angulated forward and depressed, and the superior cerebellar arteries were stretched upward. The right lateral ventricle was minimally enlarged. Twelve hours later she developed a left lateral rectus muscle palsy and the posterior fossa was explored. At operation, the lateral inferior portion of the left cerebellar hemisphere was soft and the left tonsil of the cerebellum was widened, discolored, and extended well below the margin of the foramen magnum. The abnormal tissue was resected and had the gross and microscopic consistency of a hemorrhagic infarction. She made a gradual recovery.

Brainstem Angiomas

Arteriovenous malformations and hemangiomas can occur at any level of the brainstem.[50] These lesions, when small, are sometimes asymptomatic until they bleed; the larger ones may induce progressive cranial nerve changes and motor loss, but in both instances coma occurs only with rupture, producing the characteristic picture of brainstem hemorrhage.[31] Those that directly communicate with a lateral sinus sometimes produce homolateral proptosis at the time of rupture.

Vertebrobasilar Artery Aneurysm

Increased attention is being focused on ruptured aneurysms of the vertebral and basilar arteries as causes of coma since some of them apparently can be treated surgically without paying too high a price in associated neurologic damage.[13,56] Unruptured aneurysms of the basilar and vertebral arteries sometimes grow to a size

169

of several centimeters and act like posterior fossa extramedullary tumors.[6,15,36] They do not cause coma unless they rupture.

When a vertebrobasilar aneurysm ruptures, the event is characteristically abrupt and frequently is marked by the complaint of suddenly weak legs, collapse, or coma. Most patients also have sudden occipital headache, but in contrast with anterior fossa aneurysms in which the story of coma, if present, is usually clear cut, it sometimes is difficult to be certain whether a patient with a ruptured posterior fossa aneurysm had briefly lost consciousness or merely collapsed because of paralysis of the lower extremities. Ruptured vertebrobasilar aneurysms are often reported as presenting few clinical signs that clearly localize the source of the subarachnoid bleeding to the posterior fossa. In Logue's 12 patients,[31] 4 had unilateral sixth nerve weakness (which can occur with any subarachnoid hemorrhage), 1 had bilateral sixth nerve weakness, and only 2 had other cranial abnormalities to signify a posterior fossa localization. Duvoisin and Yahr[15] say that only about half of their patients with ruptured posterior fossa aneurysms had signs that suggested the origin of their bleeding. Jamieson[24] reported 19 cases with even fewer localizing signs: 5 patients suffered third nerve weakness, and 2 had sixth nerve palsies.

Our own experience differs somewhat from the above. We have had eight patients with ruptured vertebrobasilar aneurysms found at arteriography or autopsy, and six had respiratory, pupillary, or oculomotor signs indicating a primary fossa lesion (Table 10). Despite these clinical hints, however, posterior fossa angiography ultimately must be resorted to in order to diagnose vertebrobasilar aneurysms and should be employed without hesitation whenever acute subarachnoid hemorrhage is accompanied by signs of primary brainstem dysfunction or is unexplained by the findings of carotid angiography.

Basilar Migraine

Altered states of consciousness are an uncommon but distinct aspect of what Bickerstaff[3] called basilar artery migraine, associated especially with prodromal symptoms that suggest vascular insufficiency involving the tributaries of the basilar artery. The alteration in consciousness can take any of four major forms: confusional states, brief syncope, stupor, and unarousable coma.[3,28,60] The precise cause of these prodromal symptoms is unknown, but the alterations in consciousness often last longer than the usual sensorimotor auras of complicated migraine. Blood flow studies concurrent with migraine prodromata have demonstrated both diffuse and focal cerebral vasoconstriction,[20] but this seems somehow an insufficient explanation for the strikingly focal symptoms in basilar migraine. Basilar migraine carries a strong family history of migraine, up to 80 percent in Bickerstaff's series. Bickerstaff found the disorder more often in adolescents and in girls, but Lapkin and Golden[27] found an even sex and age distribution in 30 children. One death with brainstem infarction has been reported,[19] but most attacks clear spontaneously, leaving no residua. Evidence for epilepsy is slight, although anticonvulsant drugs appear to help perhaps 40 percent of the patients.

Selby and Lance observed that among 500 consecutive patients with migraine, 6.8 percent had prodromal episodes of confusion, automatic behavior, or transient amnesia, while 4.6 percent actually fainted.[45] The confusional and stuporous attacks can last from minutes to as long as 24 hours or, rarely, more; they range in content from quiet disorientation through agitated delirium to unresponsiveness in which

170

Table 10. Localizing Signs in 6 Cases of Ruptured Vertebrobasilar Aneurysms

Occipital headache	5
Skew deviation of the eyes	3
Third nerve paralysis	2
Cerebellar signs	3
Acute paraplegia before loss of consciousness	2

the patient is barely arousable. Transient vertigo, ataxia, diplopia, hemianopsia, hemisensory changes, or hemiparesis changes may immediately precede the mental changes. During attacks, most observers have found few somatic neurologic abnormalities, although occasional patients are reported as having oculomotor palsies, pupillary dilatation, or an extensor plantar response. A few patients, at least briefly, have appeared to be in unarousable coma. No medicament has been predictably effective in reversing attacks. EEG changes have varied: some patients show no abnormalities, while others show symmetrical slowing, focal slowing, or photomyoclonic responses. In most instances, but not all, headache succeeds the disappearance of the confusional-stuporous episode. In cases in which the results of contrast studies have been reported, no abnormalities have been found. The natural history is for the attacks gradually to decline in frequency over succeeding years, but little evidence predicts when this will happen in the individual patient.

Nonvascular Brainstem Destructive Lesions

Abscesses, granulomas, and both primary and secondary neoplasms occasionally arise in the pontine and midbrain tegmentum and destroy or compress the reticular formation. Generally speaking, coma is a late or nonexistent development with these lesions, presumably because the primitive brainstem reticulum undergoes a considerable physiologic adjustment to partial destruction and distortion if given time. For example, slowly proliferating neoplasms such as pontine gliomas in children may enlarge the brainstem to twice the usual size, disrupt motor pathways almost completely, and paralyze extraocular function, all without altering consciousness until their terminal stages. Even when the content of consciousness is impaired with slowly expanding brainstem lesions, the result is more frequently the locked-in syndrome,[63] dementia, memory loss, and abnormal behavior than coma.[37,42]

The differential diagnosis of posterior fossa infiltrative or destructive lesions depends heavily on indirect evidence. Abscesses produce acute or subacute meningitis plus focal brainstem signs, which continue despite the adequate use of antibiotics. The diagnosis of brainstem abscess has rarely been suspected during life, but can be considered when fever, occipital-nuchal headache, cranial nerve signs, low-grade persistent meningitis, and stupor or coma develop in a patient with an extrameningeal source of infection.[54] In about one fourth of the cases reported in the literature the infection extended from the middle ear; the others stemmed from a more remote source.

The presence of brainstem granulomas or metastatic tumors is suggested by signs of a posterior fossa infiltrating lesion in patients with identifiable primary lesions elsewhere in the body. Usually the exact diagnosis must be made by x-ray contrast studies or posterior fossa surgical exploration.

171

Nonvascular Lesions Compressing the Brainstem

These are rare causes of coma. Cerebellar abscesses may cause coma if they suddenly rupture into the fourth ventricle and compress the brainstem, but most abscesses are clinically evident long before this. Cerebellar neoplasms may produce drowsiness and dementia if they cause obstructive hydrocephalus, but they rarely cause coma except as a terminal event when foraminal impaction produces respiratory arrest, neurogenic hypotension, and asphyxia. Extramedullary neoplasms in the posterior fossa may produce drowsiness, but they rarely cause coma as an early sign, even if they distort, compress, and displace the brainstem.

Demyelinating Lesions

Multiple Sclerosis

The plaques of multiple sclerosis frequently involve the brainstem, and in this region, where areas of gray and bundles of white matter lie closely juxtaposed, acute lesions frequently produce drowsiness or even stupor. Mental changes resulting from brainstem lesions may be an early feature of multiple sclerosis.[58,62] The diagnosis of multiple sclerosis presents no difficulty when a new exacerbation of a chronic problem produces acute signs of cranial nerve, internuclear, or vestibular dysfunction coupled with reduced alertness. However, when the first attack of demyelination involves the brainstem, multiple sclerosis cannot with any certainty be differentiated from other causes of focal encephalitis or demyelination of this region, except at autopsy or by finding serologic evidence of one of the specific viral encephalitides. CT scans will delineate plaques as small as 0.5 cm. in diameter and may be useful in diagnosing obscure cases.[22]

Central Pontine Myelinolysis

This is an uncommon disorder in which the myelin sheaths in the central basis pontis are destroyed in a single confluent and symmetrical lesion. Similar lesions can coexist in the cerebral hemispheres.[51,58] The lesions vary from a few millimeters in size to ones large enough to spare only a rim of peripheral myelin, and these latter also involve the ventral part of the tegmentum. Children as well as adults are affected. The cause is unknown, but hyponatremia is a frequent associated finding. Messert and associates have actually proposed that central pontine myelinolysis is an iatrogenic disease produced by excessive hydration leading to severe hyponatremia with its attendant cerebral edema.[35] Many of the patients who develop the disorders are alcoholics, and attempts to rehydrate them may cause hyponatremia because alcohol withdrawal has led to an increase in circulating antidiuretic hormone. Among patients reported in the literature with pontine myelinolysis proved at autopsy, 88 percent had a history of electrolyte disturbance and 78 percent a history of alcoholism.[35] Iatrogenic factors leading to hyponatremia, such as the use of intravenous fluids or diuretics, were present in 77 percent. Messert proposed that the central pons, because of its grid-like anatomy, is particularly susceptible to damage when edema occurs, the edema literally strangling the myelin sheaths and small blood vessels. According to this view, other areas of the brainstem and hemispheres are spared because they lack the tight grid-like structure of the basis pontis.

Small demyelinations cause no symptoms. The larger lesions characteristically produce ocular and pupillary paralyses, dysarthria or mutism, quadriparesis, and incontinence. About a quarter of the patients become drowsy, stuporous, or unresponsive as their illness progresses. In the literature reports of patients with the disease proved at autopsy, 65 percent had been "locked-in" at some time during their course.[35] The diagnosis of central pontine myelinolysis should be suspected in a chronic alcoholic or patient with severe nutritional deficit who develops cranial nerve weakness, quadriplegia, and reduced consciousness despite receiving thiamine and other vitamins. Confirmation of the larger lesions can be made by CT scanning. Auditory-evoked far field responses help to identify the locus of the pontine lesion, but not its nature.[47]

REFERENCES

1. ADAMS, R.D., VICTOR, M., AND MANCALL, E.L.: *Central pontine myelinolysis. A hitherto undescribed disease occurring in alcoholic and malnourished patients.* Arch. Neurol. Psychiatry 81: 154–172, 1959.

2. AZAMBUJA, N., LINDGREN, E., AND SJÖGREN, S.E.: *Tentorial herniations: I. Anatomy; II. Pneumography; III. Angiography.* Acta Radiol. 46:215–241, 1956.

3. BICKERSTAFF, E.R.: *Basilar artery migraine.* Lancet 1:15–17, 1961.

4. BRENNAN, R.W., AND BERGLAND, R.M.: *Acute cerebellar hemorrhage. Analysis of clinical findings and outcome in 12 cases.* Neurology 27:527–532, 1977.

5. BRUST, J.C.M., PLANK, C.R., HEALTON, E.B., ET AL.: *The pathology of drop attacks: a case report.* Neurology 29:786–790, 1979.

6. BULL, J.: *Massive aneurysms at the base of the brain.* Brain 92:535–570, 1969.

7. CAIRNS, H.: *Disturbances of consciousness with lesions of the brain stem and diencephalon.* Brain 75:109–146, 1952.

8. CIEMBRONIEWICS, J.E.: *Subdural hematoma of the posterior fossa.* J. Neurosurg. 22:465–473, 1965.

9. CRAVIOTO, H., SILBERMAN, J., AND FEIGIN, I.: *A clinical and pathologic study of akinetic mutism.* Neurology 10:10–21, 1960.

10. CUNEO, R.A., CARONNA, J.J., PITTS, L., ET AL.: *Syndrome of upward cerebellar herniation.* Arch. Neurol. 36:618–623, 1979.

11. DIMSDALE, H., AND LOGUE, V.: *Ruptured posterior fossa aneurysms and their surgical treatment.* J. Neurol. Neurosurg. Psychiatry 22:202–217, 1959.

12. DINSDALE, H.B.: *Spontaneous hemorrhage in the posterior fossa.* Arch. Neurol. 10:200–217, 1964.

13. DRAKE, C.G.: *Ligation of the vertebral (unilateral or bilateral) or basilar artery in the treatment of large intracranial aneurysms.* J. Neurosurg. 43:255–274, 1975.

14. DUNCAN, G.W., PARKER, S.W., AND FISHER, C.M.: *Acute cerebellar infarction in the PICA territory.* Arch. Neurol. 32:364–368, 1975.

15. DUVOISIN, R.C., AND YAHR, M.D.: *Posterior fossa aneurysms.* Neurology 15:231–241, 1965.

16. EISENBERG, H.M., AND SARWAR, M.: *Ventriculographic features of ascending transtentorial herniation.* Acta Neurochir. 42:255–228, 1978.

17. FISHER, C.M., PICARD, E.H., POLAK, A., ET AL.: *Acute hypertensive cerebellar hemorrhage: diagnosis and surgical treatment.* J. Nerv. Ment. Dis. 140:38–57, 1965.

18. GREENBERG, J., SKUBICK, D., AND SHENKIN, H.: *Acute hydrocephalus in cerebellar infarct and hemorrhage.* Neurology 29:409–413, 1979.

19. GUEST, I.A., AND WOLFF, A.L.: *Fatal infarction of brain in migraine.* Br. Med. J. 1:225–226, 1964.

20. HACHINSKI, V.C., OLESEN, J., NORRIS, J.W., ET AL.: *Cerebral hemodynamics in migraine.* Can. J. Neurol. Sci. 4:245–249, 1977.

21. HEIMAN, T.D., AND SATYA-MURTI, S.: *Benign cerebellar hemorrhages.* Ann. Neurol. 3:366–368, 1978.

22. HERSHEY, L.A., GADO, M.H., AND TROTTER, J.L.: *Computerized tomography in the diagnostic evaluation of multiple sclerosis.* Ann. Neurol. 5:32–39, 1979.

173

23. HOWELL, D.A.: *Upper brain-stem compression and foraminal impaction with intracranial space-occupying lesions and brain swelling.* Brain 82:525–550, 1959.

24. JAMIESON, K.G.: *Aneurysms of the vertebrobasilar system.* J. Neurosurg. 21:781–797, 1964.

25. KOSARY, I.Z., GOLDHAMMER, Y., AND LERNER, M.A.: *Acute extradural hematoma of the posterior fossa.* J. Neurosurg. 24:1007–1012, 1966.

26. KUBIK, C.S., AND ADAMS, R.D.: *Occlusion of the basilar artery—a clinical and pathological study.* Brain 69:73–121, 1946.

27. LAPKIN, M.L., AND GOLDEN, G.S.: *Basilar artery migraine.* Am. J. Dis. Child. 132:278–281, 1978.

28. LEE, C.H., AND LANCE, J.W.: *Migraine stupor.* Headache 17:32–38, 1977.

29. LEHRICH, J.R., WINKLER, G.F., AND OJEMANN, R.G.: *Cerebellar infarction with brain stem compression. Diagnosis and surgical treatment.* Arch. Neurol. 22:490–498, 1970.

30. LITTLE, J.R., TUBMAN, D.E., AND ETHIER, R.: *Cerebellar hemorrhage in adults.* J. Neurosurg. 48:575–579, 1978.

31. LOGUE, V.: "Posterior fossa aneurysms." In *Clinical Neurosurgery.* The Proceedings of the Congress of Neurological Surgeons. Williams and Wilkins Co., Baltimore, 1964, vol. 11, pp. 183–219.

32. LOGUE, V., AND MONCKTON, G.: *Posterior fossa angiomas.* Brain 77:252–273, 1954.

33. McKISSOCK, W., RICHARDSON, A., AND WALSH, L.: *Spontaneous cerebellar hemorrhage: a study of 34 consecutive cases treated surgically.* Brain 83:1–9, 1960.

34. MESSERT, B., LEPPIK, I.E., AND SATO, S.: *Diplopia and involuntary eye closure in spontaneous cerebellar hemorrhage.* Stroke 7:305–307, 1976.

35. MESSERT, B., ORISON, W.W., HAWKINS, M.J., ET AL.: *Central pontine myelinolysis.* Neurology 29:147–160, 1979.

36. MORLEY, T.P., AND BARR, H.W.K.: *Giant intracranial aneurysms: diagnosis, course and management.* Clin. Neurosurg. 16:73–94, 1969.

37. NETSKY, M.G., AND STROBOS, R.R.J.: *Neoplasms within the midbrain.* Arch. Neurol. Psychiatry 68:116–129, 1952.

38. NYBERG-HANSEN, R., LØKEN, A.C., AND TENSTAD, O.: *Brainstem lesion with coma for five years following manipulation of the cervical spine.* J. Neurol. 218:97–105, 1978.

39. OKUDERA, T., UEMURA, K., NAKAJAMA, K., ET AL.: *Primary pontine hemorrhage: correlations of pathologic features with postmortem microangiographic and vertebral angiographic studies.* Mt. Sinai J. Med. 45:305–321, 1978.

40. OSBORN, A.G., HEASTON, D.K., AND WING, S.D.: *Diagnosis of ascending transtentorial herniation by cranial computed tomography.* Am. J. Roentgenol. 130:755–760, 1978.

41. OTT, K.H., KASE, C.S., OJEMANN, R.G., ET AL.: *Cerebellar hemorrhage: diagnosis and treatment.* Arch. Neurol. 31:160–167, 1974.

42. PAILLAS, J.E., SEDAN, R., AND BONNEL, J.: *On the changes of consciousness produced by subtentorial lesions.* Acta Neurochir. 12:315–388, 1965.

43. REIGH, E.E., AND O'CONNELL, T.J.: *Extradural hematoma of the posterior fossa with concomitant supratentorial subdural hematoma.* J. Neurosurg. 19:359–364, 1962.

44. ROSENBERG, G.A., AND KAUFMAN, D.M.: *Cerebellar hemorrhage: reliability of clinical evaluation.* Stroke 7:332–336, 1977.

45. SELBY, G., LANCE, J.W.: *Observations of 500 cases of migraine and allied vascular headache.* J. Neurol. Neurosurg. Psychiatry 23:23–32, 1960.

46. STEEGMAN, A.T.: *Primary pontile hemorrhage.* J. Nerv. Ment. Dis. 114:35–65, 1951.

47. STOCKARD, J.J., ROSSITER, V.S., WIEDERHOLT, W.C., ET AL.: *Brainstem auditory evoked responses in suspected central pontine myelinolysis.* Arch. Neurol. 33:726–728, 1976.

48. SWANSON, J.W., AND VICK, N.A.: *Basilar artery migraine. 12 patients, with an attack recorded electroencephalographically.* Neurology 28:782–786, 1978.

49. SYPERT, G.W., AND ALVORD, E.C.: *Cerebellar infarction.* Arch. Neurol. 32:357–363, 1975.

50. TEILMAN, N.K.: *Hemangiomas of the pons.* Arch. Neurol. Psychiatry 69:208–223, 1953.

51. TOMLINSON, B.E., PIERIDES, A.M., AND BRADLEY, W.G.: *Central pontine myelinolysis. Two cases with associated electrolyte disturbance.* Q. J. Med. (new series) 45:373–386, 1976.

52. VASTINE, J.H., AND KINNEY, K.K.: *The pineal shadow as an aid in the localization of brain tumors.* Am. J. Roentgenol. 17:320–324, 1927.

174

53. WACKENHEIM, A., BRAUN, J.P., BABIN, E., ET AL.: *The herniation of the superior cerebellar vermis.* Neuroradiology 7:221–227, 1974.

54. WEICKHARDT, G.D., AND DAVIS, R.L.: *Solitary abscess of the brainstem.* Neurology 14:918–925, 1964.

55. WILKINSON, I.M.S., AND RUSSELL, R.W.R.: *Arteries of the head and neck in giant cell arteritis: a pathological study to show the pattern of arterial involvement.* Arch. Neurol. 27:378–391, 1972.

56. WILSON, C.B., U, H.S.: *Surgical treatment for aneurysms of the upper basilar artery.* J. Neurosurg. 44:537–543, 1976.

57. WOOD, M.W., AND MURPHY, F.: *Obstructive hydrocephalus due to infarction of a cerebellar hemisphere.* J. Neurosurg. 30:260–263, 1969.

58. WRIGHT, D.G., LAURENO, R., AND VICTOR, M.: *Pontine and extrapontine myelinolysis.* Brain 102:361–385, 1979.

59. YOUNG, A.C., SAUNDERS, J., AND PONSFORD, J.R.: *Mental change as an early feature of multiple sclerosis.* J. Neurol. Neurosurg. Psychiatry 39:1008–1013, 1976.

60. HOCKADAY, J.M.: *Basilar migraine in childhood.* Dev. Med. Child Neurol. 21:455–463, 1979.

61. KNUPLING, R., FUCHS, E.C., STOLTENBURG, G., ET AL.: *Chronic and acute transtentorial herniation with tumors of the posterior cranial fossa.* Neurochirurgia 22:9–17, 1979.

62. MATTHEWS, W.B.: *Multiple sclerosis presenting with acute remitting psychiatric symptoms.* J. Neurol. Neurosurg. Psychiatry 42:859–863, 1979.

63. MURPHY, M.J., BENTON, D.W., ASCHENBRENNER, C.A., ET AL.: *Locked-in syndrome caused by a solitary pontine abscess.* J. Neurol. Neurosurg. Psychiatry 42:1062–1065, 1979.

CHAPTER 4

Multifocal, Diffuse, and Metabolic Brain Diseases Causing Stupor or Coma

This chapter describes the biochemical and physiological mechanisms (where known) by which multifocal and diffuse disorders interfere with the metabolism of the brain so as to produce stupor and coma. It also describes the signs and symptoms that characterize these disorders and differentiate them from localized intracranial mass lesions and unifocal destructive lesions.

Three criteria have determined which specific illnesses are discussed in this section. These are that the disorders (1) commonly cause stupor or coma, (2) are reversible if treated promptly, but potentially lethal otherwise, so that sound clinical judgment must govern the brief time available to make a diagnosis and institute treatment, and (3) have certain neurologic signs that are either characteristic or strongly suggest the diagnosis.

Among the specific conditions discussed, acquired and systemic disorders with relatively rapid development and progression have received the greatest attention. The chapter additionally discusses a limited number of established or suggested genetic abnormalities that affect the adult so as to produce stupor and coma. The text largely omits consideration of neoplasms or mass lesions, except when these produce diffuse involvement of the brain. All the disorders discussed in this chapter when they cause stupor or coma do so by interfering with the metabolism of wide areas of the brain, either directly or indirectly. Therefore, we often group them under the rubric "Metabolic Encephalopathy."

A physician confronted by a stuporous or comatose patient must address two major questions: (1) Which of the major etiologic categories of dysfunction (i.e., supratentorial, subtentorial, diffuse, or psychologic) caused the coma? Chapters 2, 3, and 5 discuss the signs that indicate whether a patient is suffering from supratentorial, subtentorial, or psychologic dysfunction, respectively. The next section of this chapter describes the clinical signs of diffuse, multifocal, or metabolic disease of the brain. Once the physician has determined that the patient's signs and symptoms indicate an illness of this last category, he must answer the second question: (2) Which of the large number of diffuse abnormalities of the brain is responsible for this particular patient's stupor or coma? This question often requires a rapid answer since many metabolic disorders that cause coma are fully reversible if treated early and appropriately, but lethal if treatment is delayed.

Table 11 lists some of the diffuse multifocal and metabolic causes of stupor and coma. It attempts to classify these causes of stupor and coma in such a way that the table can be used as a checklist of the major causes to be considered when the physician is presented with an unconscious patient suspected of suffering from an illness in this category. Heading *A* concerns itself with deprivation of oxygen, substrates, or metabolic co-factors. Headings B through E are concerned with systemic diseases that produced abnormalities of cerebral metabolism (metabolic encephalopathy). Headings F and G are concerned with primary disorders of nervous system function, which, because of their diffuse involvement of brain, resemble the metabolic encephalopathies more than they do focal structural disease. Heading H lists a variety of miscellaneous disorders of brain whose cause is unknown. Although they represent a heterogeneous group of disorders, the diseases listed in

Table 11. Some Diffuse, Multifocal or Metabolic Causes of Delirium, Stupor, and Coma

A. Deprivation of oxygen, substrate, or metabolic cofactors
  *1. Hypoxia (interference with oxygen supply to the entire brain—cerebral blood flow [CBF] normal)
    a. Decreased blood PO_2 and O_2 content
      Pulmonary disease
      Alveolar hypoventilation
      Decreased atmospheric oxygen tension
    b. Decreased blood O_2 content, PO_2 normal—"anemic anoxia"
      Anemia
      Carbon monoxide poisoning
      Methemoglobinemia
  *2. Ischemia (diffuse or widespread multifocal interference with blood supply to brain)
    a. Decreased CBF resulting from decreased cardiac output
      Stokes-Adams; cardiac arrest; cardiac arrhythmias
      Myocardial infarction
      Congestive heart failure
      Aortic stenosis
      Pulmonary infarction
    b. Decreased CBF resulting from decreased peripheral resistance in systemic circulation
      Syncope (see Table 15)
      Carotid sinus hypersensitivity
      Low blood volume
    c. Decreased CBF associated with generalized or multifocal increased vascular resistance
      Hyperventilation syndrome
      Hyperviscosity (polycythemia, cryoglobulinemia or macroglobulinemia, sickle cell anemia)
      Subarachnoid hemorrhage
      Bacterial meningitis
      Hypertensive encephalopathy
    d. Decreased CBF owing to widespread small-vessel occlusions
      Disseminated intravascular coagulation
      Systemic lupus erythematosus
      Subacute bacterial endocarditis
      Fat embolism
      Cerebral malaria
      Cardiopulmonary bypass
  *3. Hypoglycemia
    Resulting from exogenous insulin
    Spontaneous (endogenous insulin, liver disease, etc.)
  4. Cofactor deficiency
    Thiamine (Wernicke's encephalopathy)
    Niacin
    Pyridoxine
    Cyanocobalamin
    Folic acid

*Alone or in combination, the most common causes of delirium seen on medical or surgical wards.

178

Table 11. Some Diffuse, Multifocal or Metabolic Causes of Delirium, Stupor, and Coma (*Continued*)

B. Diseases of organs other than brain
    1. Diseases of nonendocrine organs
        Liver (hepatic coma)
        Kidney (uremic coma)
        Lung (CO_2 narcosis)
        Pancreas (exocrine pancreatic encephalopathy)
    2. Hyper- and/or hypofunction of endocrine organs
        Pituitary
        Thyroid (myxedema-thyrotoxicosis)
        Parathyroid (hypo- and hyperpararthyroidism)
        Adrenal (Addison's disease, Cushing's disease, pheochromocytoma)
        Pancreas (diabetes, hypoglycemia)
    3. Other systemic diseases
        Diabetes
        Cancer
        Porphyria
        Sepsis
C. Exogenous Poisons
    *1. Sedative drugs
        Barbiturates and nonbarbiturate hypnotics
        Tranquilizers
        Bromides
        Ethanol
        Opiates
    2. Acid poisons or poisons with acidic breakdown products
        Paraldehyde
        Methyl alcohol
        Ethylene glycol
        Ammonium chloride
    3. Psychotropic drugs
        Tricyclic antidepressants and anticholinergic drugs
        Amphetamines
        Lithium
        Phencyclidine
        Phenothiazines
        LSD, mescaline
        Monoamine oxidase inhibitors
    4. Others
        Penicillin
        Anticonvulsants
        Steroids
        Cardiac glycosides
        Cimetidine
        Heavy metals
        Organic phosphates
        Cyanide
        Salicylate
D. Abnormalities of ionic or acid-base environment of CNS
        Water and sodium (hyper- and hyponatremia)
        Acidosis (metabolic and respiratory)
        Alkalosis (metabolic and respiratory)
        Magnesium (hyper- and hypomagnesemia)
        Calcium (hyper- and hypocalcemia)
        Phosphorus (hypophosphatemia)

*Alone or in combination, the most common causes of delirium seen on medical or surgical wards.

179

Table 11. Some Diffuse, Multifocal or Metabolic Causes of Delirium, Stupor, and Coma (*Continued*)

E. Disordered temperature regulation
    Hypothermia
    Heat stroke, fever
F. Infections or inflammation of CNS
    Leptomeningitis
    Encephalitis
    Acute "toxic" encephalopathy
    Parainfectious encephalomyelitis
    Cerebral vasculitis
    Subarachnoid hemorrhage
G. Primary neuronal or glial disorders
    Creutzfeldt-Jakob disease
    Marchiafava-Bignami disease
    Adrenoleukodystrophy
    Gliomatosis cerebri
    Progressive multifocal leukoencephalopathy
H. Miscellaneous disorders of unknown cause
    Seizures and postictal states
    Concussion
   *Acute delirious states
      sedative drug withdrawal
      "postoperative" delirium
      intensive care unit delirium
      drug intoxications

*Alone or in combination, the most common causes of delirium seen on medical or surgical wards.

Table 11, when they cause stupor and coma, can usually be distinguished by clinical signs alone from supratentorial and infratentorial focal lesions and from psychologic disorders. In addition, many of the specific diseases have manifestations that help to distinguish them from other disorders listed in Table 11. These conditions are addressed in the remainder of the chapter.

CLINICAL SIGNS OF METABOLIC ENCEPHALOPATHY

Each patient with metabolic coma has a distinctive clinical picture, depending on the particular causative illness, the depth of coma, and the complications provided by other illnesses or by treatment. Despite these individualities, however, specific illnesses often produce certain clinical patterns that recur again and again, and once these are recognized, they betray the diagnosis. A careful evaluation of consciousness, respiration, pupillary reactions, ocular movements, motor function, and the EEG may differentiate metabolic encephalopathy from psychiatric dysfunction on the one hand, and from supratentorial or infratentorial structural disease on the other. Since these general characteristics of metabolic coma are so important, they are discussed before the specific disease entities.

180

Consciousness

Clinical Aspects

Changes in mentation and awareness are the earliest and most reliable warnings of the more slowly developing varieties of metabolic encephalopathy and almost invariably precede coma. As noted by Lipowski, psychologic manifestations of cerebral disorders most often first involve information processing, i.e., perception, thinking, and memory.[237] The associated symptoms are usually referred to as *cognitive defects,* which in many metabolic disorders precede stupor or coma. Some workers believe that impairment of attention, with its underlying components of level of consciousness, degree of arousal, motivation, perceptual integration, and motor mechanisms for scanning and exploration, is the underlying abnormality in all acute confusional states.[263] The importance of these early behavioral warnings is so great that we have stepped outside the literal bounds of coma to review briefly some of the mental symptoms that often precede metabolic coma and, by their presence, suggest the diagnosis. The mental changes are best looked for in terms of: attention, alertness, orientation and grasp, memory, affect, and perception.

ATTENTION. An early and consistent mental derangement in patients with metabolic encephalopathy is a failure of selective attention. The patient is unable to concentrate with his accustomed intensity on the matters at hand. On the contrary, his mind appears to wander, with little evidence of sustained interest in the examiner or other important aspects of his environment. In addition to his inability to sustain attention, the patient is unable to channel selectively what attentional abilities he retains. Thus, he may focus inappropriately on an extraneous stimulus (such as a conversation in the hall) or wander back and forth between his conversation with the examiner and his regard for extraneous stimuli. At times, after being distracted to another stimulus, he will forget to return to the activity in which he was engaged before distraction.

ALERTNESS. With metabolic encephalopathy, the level of alertness and awareness of the environment varies from extreme hyper-vigilance and agitation through drowsiness to unresponsiveness. Some patients alternate between hyper-alertness and drowsiness during the same episode of encephalopathy. Altered alertness is an early sign of metabolic brain disease, and at either end of the spectrum it interferes with attention. Drowsy patients are unable to attend appropriately to even important stimuli, and hyper-vigilant patients are so distracted by inappropriate stimuli that their attention suffers as well.

Initially the patient may appear preoccupied or just uninterested. He foregoes reading to lie quietly, or sleeps when left alone. Often he concedes that thinking or reading requires undue effort. As the disease progresses, drowsiness becomes more apparent, and the patient must be prodded or shaken to give answers, many of which emerge with insouciant incorrectness.

Alterations of alertness preceding other changes is more characteristic of acute or subacutely developing metabolic encephalopathy than of more slowly developing dementia; demented patients tend to lose orientation and cognition before displaying an alteration in alertness. Severe metabolic encephalopathy eventually leads to stupor and finally coma, and when this point is reached, mental testing no longer helps to distinguish metabolic from other causes of brain dysfunction.

TESTS OF MENTAL STATUS. It is often difficult to assess cognitive function in patients with impairment of attention and alertness. However, careful quantitative assessment of these functions is exceedingly important, since changes in cognition often indicate whether the physician's therapeutic efforts are improving the patient's general condition. Several bedside tests that can be given in a few minutes, even to confused patients, have been developed. These tests allow one to score cognitive functions and to follow the patient's course in quantitative fashion. [123,194]

ORIENTATION AND GRASP. Although attention and cognition are the first of man's faculties to be impaired with metabolic encephalopathies, they are difficult to test and interpret unless the physician knows his patient's pre-illness personality and intellect. As a result, defects in orientation and immediate grasp of test situations often become the earliest unequivocal symptoms of brain dysfunction. When examining patients suspected of metabolic or cerebral disorders, one must ask specifically the date, the time, the place, and how long it takes to reach home or some other well-defined place. Even patients with limited intellects should know the month and year, and most should know the day and date, particularly if there has been a recent holiday. Patients with early metabolic encephalopathy lose orientation for time and as frequently miss the year as the month or the day. Orientation for distance is usually impaired next, and finally, the identification of persons and places becomes confused. Disorientation for person and place but not time is unusual in structural disease but sometimes is a symptom of hysteria.

COGNITION. The content and progression of thought are always disturbed in delirium and dementia, sometimes as the incipient symptoms. To detect these changes requires asking specific questions employing abstract definitions and problems. Since attention and concentration are nearly always impaired, patients with metabolic brain disease usually make errors in serial subtractions, and rarely can they repeat more than three or four numbers in reverse.

MEMORY. Loss of recent memory is a hallmark of dementia and a frequent accompaniment of delirium. Most patients with metabolic brain disease have a memory loss that is proportional to other losses of highest integrative functions. When the maximal pathologic changes involve the limbic system, however, recent memory loss outstrips other intellectual impairments (p. 183). Thus, memory loss and an inability to form new associations can be a sign of either diffuse or bilateral focal brain disease.

AFFECT. Many patients with metabolic brain disease tend to be apathetic and withdrawn, and since they volunteer little, the examiner must directly test their highest integrative functions. (The apathy of these patients sometimes has pathetically ludicrous consequences. One elderly patient suffering from brain damage caused by a hypotensive episode during a herniorrhaphy responded on each postoperative day to his doctor's question of, "How are you?" by saying, "Fine!" Only when an effort was made to send him home was it discovered that this was nearly his total vocabulary and that he had no idea of where he was, much less of the date or the purpose of his hospitalization.) A smaller proportion of patients, especially those suffering from anoxia, sepsis, acute withdrawal of drugs or alcohol, acute intermittent porphyria, or liver necrosis, are anxious, fearful, agitated, and tremulous. The two affective responses, the one quiet and the other agitated, sometimes alternate in the same patient. More frequently, the two occur in different subjects, with quiet delirium chiefly characterizing slowly developing, recurrent, or chronic processes and agitated delirium characterizing rapidly developing changes of an acute process in a previously healthy or at least metabolically stable subject.

PERCEPTION. Patients with metabolic brain disease frequently make perceptual errors, mistaking the members of the hospital staff for old friends and relatives, and granting vitality to inanimate objects. Illusions are common and invariably involve stimuli from the immediate environment. Quiet and apathetic patients suffer illusory experiences, but these must be asked about since they are rarely volunteered. Anxious and fearful patients, on the other hand, frequently express concern about their illusions and misperceptions to the accompaniment of loud and violent behavior. Visual or combined visual and auditory hallucinations are more common than pure auditory ones.[241]

Pathogenesis of the Mental Changes

Both global and focal cerebral functional abnormalities can cause the mental symptoms of metabolic brain disease. The global symptoms include alterations in the level of alertness, attention, comprehension, and cognitive synthesis. Well-recognized focal cerebral abnormalities include specific abnormalities in language recognition and synthesis, in recent memory storage and recall, in gnosis and praxis, and perhaps in the genesis of hallucinations. Most of the severe metabolic encephalopathies produce combinations of global and focal changes.

Studies of the quantitative or global relationship of forebrain function to mental function received their greatest initial impetus from Lashley's pioneering work in animals. The view received strong support from the work of Chapman and Wolff,[56] who concluded that in diseases of the forebrain, man's highest integrative functions were reduced in proportion to the total quantity of brain destroyed by injury, operation, or degeneration. Except when speech and motor areas were involved, the behavioral impairment was directly related to the total mass of inadequately functioning neurons, regardless of whether the neuronal loss was aggregated in one area or diffusely distributed throughout the cortex.

Our present understandings of the focal mechanism of certain symptoms of cognitive insufficiency had their beginnings in late 19th and early 20th century clinical-pathologic studies and were extended by the results of psychologic testings of patients having neurosurgical removals of certain parts of the cerebrum. Both surgical and disease-related lesions, for example, have demonstrated by their effects that relatively restricted damage to the cingulum,[450] the hippocampal areas, or to the medial-dorsal nucleus of the thalamus can be followed by profound abnormalities in recent and intermediate memory.[431] Geschwind and his colleagues[264] have reported acute confusional states resulting from infarctions in the distribution of the right (nondominant) middle cerebral artery. They have suggested that these abnormalities of attention resulted from damage to cortical regions that represented "nodal convergence sites for afferent fibers from association cortex." The fact that some drugs such as amphetamines or LSD possess exceptional capacities to produce vivid hallucinations must imply that they exert their effects over relatively selective and specific neural pathways, a conclusion that leads one to search for more specific mechanisms in other mental symptoms. Most recently, new techniques for studying regional cerebral blood flow and cerebral metabolism have brought out strong evidence that at least certain types of altered thinking involve regions of brain that differ from the normal pattern.[355]

A combination of diffuse and focal dysfunction probably underlies the cerebral symptoms of most patients with metabolic encephalopathy. The extensive cortical-cortical physiologic connectivity of the human brain discussed in Chapter 1 implies that large focal abnormalities inevitably will produce functional effects that extend well beyond their immediate confines. Furthermore, the more rapidly the lesion develops, the more extensive will be the acute functional loss. Thus, the general loss of highest integrative functions in metabolic diseases is compatible with a diffuse dysfunction of neurons and, as judged by measurements of cerebral metabolism, the severity of the clinical signs is directly related to the mass of neurons affected. However, certain distinctive clinical signs in different patients and in different diseases probably reflect damage to more discrete areas having to do with memory and other selective aspects of integrative behavior. An example is the encephalopathy resulting from thiamine deficiency (Wernicke-Korsakoff syndrome).[431] In this illness patients show acutely the clinical signs of delirium. All neuronal areas lose thiamine at about the same rate, but certain nuclear collections such as the mammillary bodies, the medial-dorsal nucleus of the thalamus, the periaqueductal gray matter, and the oculomotor nuclei are morphologically and probably biochemically more sensitive to the deficiency and show the major pathologic change. A diffuse disease thus has a focal maximum. Clinically, recent memory is impaired more severely than are other mental functions and indeed, memory loss may persist to produce the Korsakoff syndrome after other mental functions and overall cerebral metabolism have improved to a near-normal level.

Respiration

Sooner or later metabolic brain disease nearly always results in an abnormality of either the depth or rhythm of breathing. Most of the time this is a nonspecific alteration and simply a part of a more widespread brainstem depression. Sometimes, however, the respiratory changes stand out separately from the rest of the neurologic defects and are more or less specific to the disease in question. Some of these specific respiratory responses are homeostatic adjustments to the metabolic process causing encephalopathy. The others occur in illnesses that particularly affect the respiratory mechanisms. Either way, proper evaluation and interpretation of the specific respiratory changes facilitate diagnosis and often suggest an urgent need for treatment.

As a first step in appraising the breathing of patients with metabolically caused coma, increased or decreased respiratory efforts must be confirmed as truly reflecting hyperventilation or hypoventilation. Increased chest efforts do not spell hyperventilation if they merely overcome obstruction or pneumonitis, and conversely, seemingly shallow breathing can fulfill the reduced metabolic needs of subjects in deep coma. Although careful clinical evaluation usually avoids those potential deceptions, the bedside observations are most helpful when anchored by direct determinations of the arterial blood pH, PCO_2, PO_2, and bicarbonate concentration.

Neurologic Respiratory Changes Accompanying Metabolic Encephalopathy

Lethargic or lightly obtunded patients have posthyperventilation apnea, and those in stupor or light coma commonly exhibit Cheyne-Stokes respiration. With more profound brainstem depression, transient neurogenic hyperventilation can ensue from suppression of brainstem inhibitory regions. As an illustration, poisoning with short- or intermediate-acting barbiturate preparations often induces brief episodes of hyperventilation and motor hypertonus, either during the stage of deepening coma or as patients reawaken. Hypoglycemia and anoxic damage are even more frequent causes of transient hyperpnea. In these instances, the increased breathing sometimes outlasts the immediate metabolic perturbation, and if the subject also has decerebrate rigidity, the clinical picture may superficially resemble structural disease or severe metabolic acidosis. However, attention to other neurologic details usually leads to the proper diagnosis, as the following case illustrates.

Patient 4–1. A 28-year-old man was brought unconscious to the emergency room. Fifteen minutes earlier, with slurred speech, he had instructed a taxi driver to take him to the hospital, then "passed out." His pulse was 100 per minute, and his blood pressure was 130/90 mm. Hg. His respirations were 40 per minute and deep. The pupils were small (2 mm.), but the light and ciliospinal reflexes were preserved. Oculocephalic reflexes were present. His deep tendon reflexes were hyperactive; there were bilateral extensor plantar responses, and he periodically had bilateral decerebrate spasms. After 25 gm. of glucose were given intravenously, respirations quieted, the decerebrate spasms ceased, and he withdrew appropriately from noxious stimuli. After 75 gm. of glucose, he awoke and disclosed that he was diabetic, taking insulin, and had neglected to eat that day. The preglucose blood sugar level was 20 mg./dl.

Comment: This man's hyperpnea and decerebrate rigidity initially suggested structural brainstem disease to the emergency room physicians. Normal oculovestibular and oculocephalic responses, normal pupillary reactions, and the absence of focal signs made metabolic coma more likely, and the diagnosis was confirmed by the subsequent findings.

The effectiveness of respiration must be evaluated repeatedly when metabolic disease depresses the brain, because the brainstem reticular formation is especially vulnerable to chemical depression. Anoxia, hypoglycemia, and drugs all are capable of relatively selectively inducing hypoventilation or apnea while concurrently sparing other brainstem functions such as pupillary responses and blood pressure control.

Metabolic Respiratory Changes Accompanying Metabolic Encephalopathy

Respiration is the first and most rapid defense against systemic acid-base imbalance, and chemoreceptors located in the carotid body and aortic arterial wall as well as in the low brainstem quickly respond to alterations in the blood of either hydrogen ion concentration or PCO_2.

HYPERVENTILATION. In a stuporous or comatose patient, hyperventilation is a danger sign meaning one of two things: either compensation for metabolic acidosis or a response to primary respiratory stimulation (respiratory alkalosis). Metabolic acidosis and respiratory alkalosis are differentiated by blood biochemical analyses. In the first instance, the arterial blood pH is low (less than 7.30 if hyperpnea is to be attributed to acidosis), and the serum bicarbonate is also low (usually below 10 mEq. per liter). In the second case, the arterial pH is high (over 7.45), and the serum bicarbonate is normal or slightly reduced. In both respiratory alkalosis and metabolic acidosis, the arterial carbon dioxide tension ($PaCO_2$) is reduced, usually below 30 mm. Hg. Mixed metabolic acidosis and respiratory alkalosis may occur in several metabolic abnormalities. It is particularly common in salicylism and in hepatic coma. A diagnosis of mixed metabolic abnormality can be made when the degree of respiratory or metabolic compensation is excessive.[345] Table 12 lists some of the causes of hyperventilation in patients with metabolic encephalopathy.

Metabolic acidosis sufficient to produce coma and hyperpnea has four important causes: uremia, diabetes, lactic acidosis (anoxic or spontaneous), and the ingestion of poisons that are acidic or have acidic break-down products. In any given patient, a quick and accurate selection can and must be made from among these. Diabetes and uremia are diagnosed by appropriate laboratory tests, and diabetic acidosis is confirmed by identifying serum ketonemia. It is important to remember that severe alcoholics without diabetes occasionally can develop ketoacidosis after prolonged

Table 12. Some Causes of Abnormal Ventilation in Unresponsive Patients

I. Hyperventilation
  A. Metabolic acidosis
    1. Anion gap[301]
      *Diabetic ketoacidosis
      *Diabetic hyperosmolar coma
      Lactic acidosis
      *Uremia
      Alcoholic ketoacidosis
      *Acidic poisons
       ethylene glycol
       methyl alcohol
       paraldehyde
      Salicylism (primarily in children)
    2. No anion gap
      Diarrhea
      Pancreatic drainage
      Carbonic anhydrase inhibitors
      NH_4Cl ingestion
      Renal tubular acidosis
      Ureteroenterostomy
  B. Respiratory alkalosis
    *Hepatic failure
    *Sepsis
    Pneumonia
    Anxiety (hyperventilation syndrome)
  C. Mixed acid-based disorders (metabolic acidosis and respiratory alkalosis)
    Salicylism
    *Sepsis
    *Hepatic failure
II. Hypoventilation
  A. Respiratory acidosis
    1. Acute (uncompensated)
      *Sedative drugs
      Brainstem injury
      Neuromuscular disorders
      Chest injury
      Acute pulmonary disease
    *2. Chronic pulmonary disease
  B. Metabolic alkalosis
    Vomiting or gastric drainage
    Diuretic therapy
    Adrenal steroid excess (Cushing's syndrome)
    Primary aldosteronism
    Bartter's syndrome

*Common causes of stupor or coma.

drinking bouts.[197] An important observation is that diabetics, especially those who have been treated with oral hypoglycemic agents, are subject to lactic acidosis as well as to diabetic ketoacidosis, but in the former condition ketonemia is lacking. If diabetes and uremia are eliminated in a patient as causes of acidosis, it can be inferred either that he has spontaneous lactic acidosis or has been poisoned with an exogenous toxin such as ethylene glycol, methyl alcohol, or decomposed paraldehyde. Anoxic lactic acidosis would be suspected only if anoxia or shock was present, and severe anoxic acidosis is relatively uncommon even then. Unfortunately, tests for most ingested agents causing acidosis cannot be made quickly. However, once diabetes, uremia, and acute anoxia have been ruled out, the other causes of metabolic acidosis can be effectively treated by giving intravenous infusions of sodium bicarbonate in quantities sufficient to restore the blood pH to normal (see Patient 4–13). Since action must be prompt to avoid fatality, final diagnosis can await determination of blood lactate and other acids after treatment has been instituted.

Sustained *respiratory alkalosis* has five important causes among disorders producing the picture of metabolic stupor or coma: salicylism, hepatic coma, pulmonary disease, sepsis, and psychogenic hyperventilation. As is true with metabolic acidosis, these usually can be at least partially separated by clinical examination and simple laboratory measures.

Salicylate poisoning causes a combined respiratory alkalosis and metabolic acidosis that lowers the serum bicarbonate disproportionately to the degree of serum pH elevation. Salicylism should be suspected in a stuporous hyperpneic adult if the serum pH is normal or alkaline, and the serum bicarbonate is between 10 and 14 mEq. per L. Salicylism in children lowers serum bicarbonate still more and produces serum acidosis. The diagnosis of severe salicylism is supported by the purple color produced by adding ferric chloride to boiled urine and confirmed by finding a serum salicylate level in excess of 40 mg./dl. Occasionally misleading is the fact that the ingestion of sedative drugs in addition to salicylates may blunt the hyperpnea and lead to metabolic acidosis.[475]

Hepatic coma producing respiratory alkalosis rarely depresses the serum bicarbonate below 16 mEq. per L., and the diagnosis usually is betrayed by other signs of liver dysfunction. The associated clinical abnormalities of liver disease are sometimes minimal, particularly with fulminating acute yellow atrophy or when gastrointestinal hemorrhage precipitates coma in a chronic cirrhotic. Liver function tests must be relied upon in such instances.

Gram-negative sepsis is always associated with hyperventilation, probably a direct central effect of the endotoxin.[394] Early in the course of the illness, the acid-base defect is that of a pure respiratory alkalosis ($HCO_3 > 15$ mEq. per L.), but in critically ill patients lactic acid later accumulates in the blood and the stuporous patient usually presents a combined acid-base defect of respiratory alkalosis and metabolic acidosis ($HCO_3 < 15$ mEq. per L.). Fever and hypotension usually accompany the neurologic signs and suggest the diagnosis.

Respiratory alkalosis caused by pulmonary congestion, fibrosis, or pneumonia rarely depresses the serum bicarbonate significantly. This diagnosis should be considered in hypoxic, hyperpneic subjects in coma who have normal or slightly lowered serum bicarbonate levels and no evidence of liver disease. Psychogenic hyperventilation does not cause coma but may cause delirium and may be present as an additional symptom in a patient with psychogenic "coma."

HYPOVENTILATION. In an unconscious patient, hypoventilation means either respiratory compensation for metabolic alkalosis or respiratory depression with consequent acidosis. The differential diagnosis is outlined in Table 12. In metabolic alkalosis the arterial blood pH is elevated (> 7.45), as is the serum bicarbonate (> 35 mEq. per L.). In untreated respiratory acidosis with coma, the serum pH is low (< 7.35), and the serum bicarbonate is either normal or high, depending on prior treatment and how rapidly the respiratory failure has developed. The $PaCO_2$ is always elevated in respiratory acidosis (usually > 55 mm. Hg) and often elevated because of respiratory compensation in metabolic alkalosis. In respiratory acidosis, the pH of the CSF is always low if artificial respiration has not been used.[48,337] The arterial PCO_2 is elevated in both metabolic alkalosis and respiratory acidosis, but is usually less than 50 mm. Hg in alkalosis and almost invariably rises considerably higher than this when respiratory acidosis causes stupor or coma. In both disorders, the oxygen tension is reduced. A normal serum bicarbonate level is consistent with untreated respiratory acidosis but not with metabolic alkalosis.

Metabolic alkalosis results from either excessive ingestion of alkali or excessive loss of acid via gastrointestinal and renal routes. To find the specific cause often requires exhaustive laboratory analyses, but delirium and obtundation owing to metabolic alkalosis are rarely severe and never life-threatening, so that time exists for careful diagnostic considerations.

Respiratory acidosis is a more pressing problem, caused by either severe pulmonary or neuromuscular disease (peripheral respiratory failure) or by depression of the respiratory center (central respiratory failure). Both causes induce hypoxia as well as CO_2 retention. Chest examinations almost always can differentiate neuromuscular from pulmonary disease and the presence of tachypnea distinguishes pulmonary or peripheral neuromuscular failure from central failure with its irregular or slow respiratory patterns. Severe respiratory acidosis of any origin is best treated by artificial respiration.

Pupils

Among patients in deep coma, the state of the pupils becomes the single most important criterion that clinically distinguishes between metabolic and structural disease. The presence of preserved pupillary light reflexes despite concomitant respiratory depression, caloric unresponsiveness, decerebrate rigidity, or motor flaccidity suggests metabolic coma. Conversely, if asphyxia, anticholinergic or glutethimide ingestion, or preexisting pupillary disease can be ruled out, the absence of pupillary light reflexes strongly implies that the disease is structural rather than metabolic.

Pupils cannot be considered conclusively nonreactive to a light stimulus unless care has been taken to examine them with magnification and a very bright light. Ciliospinal reflexes are less reliable than the light reflexes, but, like them, are usually preserved in metabolic coma even when motor and respiratory signs signify lower brainstem dysfunction.

Ocular Motility

The eyes usually rove randomly with mild metabolic coma and come to rest in the forward position as coma deepens. Although almost any eye position or random movement can be observed transiently when brainstem function is changing rapidly, a maintained conjugate lateral deviation or dysconjugate positioning of the eyes at rest suggests structural disease. Conjugate downward gaze can occur in metabolic as well as in structural disease and by itself is not helpful in differential diagnosis. [395]

Patient 4-2. A 63-year-old woman with severe hepatic cirrhosis and a portacaval shunt was found in coma. She groaned spontaneously but otherwise was unresponsive. Her respirations were 18 per minute and deep. The pupillary diameters were 4 mm. on the right and 3 mm. on the left, and both reacted to light. Her eyes were deviated conjugately downward and slightly to the right. The doll's head maneuver elicited conjugate eye movement in all directions. Her muscles were flaccid, but her stretch reflexes were brisk and more active on the right with bilateral extensor plantar responses. No decorticate or decerebrate responses could be elicited. Her arterial blood pH was 7.58, and her $PaCO_2$, was 21 mm. Hg.

188

Two days later she awoke, at which time her eye movements were normal. Four days later she again drifted into coma, this time with the eyes in the physiologic position and with sluggish but full oculocephalic responses. She died on the sixth hospital day, with severe hepatic cirrhosis. No structural CNS lesion was found at autopsy.

Comment: This patient exhibited conjugate deviation of the eyes downward and slightly to the right that lasted 24 hours and initially suggested a deep, right-sided cerebral hemispheric mass lesion. The return of gaze to normal with awakening and nonrepetition of the downward deviation when coma recurred ruled out a structural lesion. At autopsy, no intrinsic cerebral pathologic lesion was found to explain the abnormal eye movements. We have subsequently observed transient downward deviation of the eyes in several other patients in metabolic coma.

Since reflex eye movements are particularly sensitive to depressant drugs, cold caloric stimulation often provides valuable information about the depth of coma in patients with metabolic disease. The ocular response to passive head movement is less reliable than the caloric test since absence of doll's head eye movements may imply purposeful inhibition of the reflex and does not dependably distinguish psychogenic unresponsiveness from brainstem depression. Cold caloric stimulation produces tonic conjugate deviation toward the irrigated ear in patients in light coma and little or no response in those in deep coma. If caloric stimulation evokes nystagmus, it means that cerebral connections are intact and the impairment of consciousness is either very mild and not metabolic or the "coma" is psychogenic. Finally, if caloric stimulation repeatedly produces dysconjugate eye movements, structural brainstem disease should be suspected (but see Chapter 1).

Patient 4–3. A 20-year-old girl became unresponsive while riding in the back seat of her parents' car. There was no history of previous illness, but her parents stated that she had severe emotional problems. On examination, her vital signs and general physical examination were normal. She appeared to be asleep when left alone, with quiet shallow respiration and no spontaneous movements. Her pupils were 3 mm. and reactive. Oculocephalic responses were absent. She lay motionless to noxious stimuli but appeared to resist passive elevation of her eyelids. Cold caloric testing elicited tonic deviation of the eyes with no nystagmus. She awoke the next morning and admitted ingesting both phenobarbital and meprobamate to frighten her mother.

Comment: The coma in this patient initially appeared light or even simulated. However, tonic deviation of the eyes in response to cold caloric irrigation signified that normal cerebral effects were in abeyance and indicated that her unresponsiveness was the result of organic cerebral dysfunction.

Motor Activity

Patients with metabolic brain disease generally present two types of motor abnormalities: (1) nonspecific disorders of strength, tone, and reflexes, as well as focal or generalized seizures, and (2) certain characteristic adventitious movements that are almost diagnostic of metabolic brain disease.

"Nonspecific" Motor Abnormalities

Diffuse motor abnormalities are frequent in metabolic coma and reflect the degree and distribution of central nervous system depression (Chapter 1). Paratonia, snouting, and prehensile sucking and grasp reflexes frequently go hand in hand with early mental changes, especially with dementia, and may also be elicited in patients in light coma. With increasing brainstem depression, decorticate and decerebrate rigidity and flaccidity appear. The rigid states are sometimes asymmetrical.

Patient 4–4. A 60-year-old man was found in the street, stuporous, with an odor of wine on his breath. No other history was obtainable. His blood pressure was 120/80 mm. Hg, pulse rate 100 per minute, respirations 26 per minute and deep. His neck was supple. There was fetor hepaticus, and the skin was jaundiced. The liver was palpably enlarged. He responded to noxious stimuli only by groaning. There was no response to visual threat. His left pupil was 5 mm. and right pupil 3 mm., and both reacted to light. The eyes diverged at rest, but passive head movement elicited full conjugate ocular movements. The corneal reflexes were decreased but present bilaterally. There was a left facial droop. The gag reflex was present. He did not move spontaneously but grimaced and demonstrated decerebrate responses to noxious stimuli. The limb muscles were symmetrically rigid, and stretch reflexes were hyperactive. The plantar responses were extensor. The lumbar spinal fluid pressure was 120 mm. and the CSF contained 30 mg./dl. protein and one cell. Skull x-ray films were normal. The serum bicarbonate was 16 mEq. per L., chloride 104 mEq. per L., sodium 147 mEq. per L., and potassium 3.9 mEq. per L. Liver function studies were grossly abnormal.

The following morning he responded appropriately to noxious stimulation. Hyperventilation had decreased, and the decerebrate responses had disappeared. Diffuse rigidity, increased deep tendon reflexes, and bilateral extensor plantar responses remained. Improvement was rapid, and by the fourth hospital day he was awake and had normal findings on neurologic examination. However, on the seventh hospital day his blood pressure declined and his jaundice increased. He became hypotensive on the ninth hospital day and died. The general autopsy disclosed severe hepatic cirrhosis. An examination of the brain revealed old infarcts of the posterior second and third frontal convolutions on the left and of the left inferior cerebellum. There were no other lesions.

Comment: In this patient, the signs of liver disease suggested the diagnosis of hepatic coma. At first, however, anisocoria and decerebrate rigidity hinted at a supratentorial mass lesion such as a subdural hematoma. The normal pupillary and doll's eyes reactions favored metabolic disease and the subsequent absence of signs of rostral-caudal deterioration supported that diagnosis.

Focal weakness is surprisingly common with metabolic brain disease. Our series includes five patients in whom hypoglycemia produced transient hemiplegia, four patients with hepatic coma who were transiently hemiplegic, and several patients with uremia or hyponatremia who had focal weakness of supranuclear origin. Others have reported similar findings.[238,273,317]

Patient 4–5. A 37-year-old man had been diabetic for 8 years. He received 35 units of protamine zinc insulin each morning in addition to 5 units of regular insulin when he believed he needed it. One week before admission, he lost consciousness transiently upon arising, and when he awoke, he had a left hemiparesis, which disappeared within seconds. The evening before admission the patient had received 35 units of protamine zinc and 5 units of regular insulin. He awoke at 6 A.M., on the floor, soiled with feces. His entire left side was numb and paralyzed. His pulse was 80 per minute, respirations 12, and blood pressure 130/80 mm. Hg. The general physical examination was unremarkable. He was lethargic but oriented. His speech was slurred. There was supranuclear left facial paralysis and left flaccid hemiplegia with weakness of the tongue, the trapezius, and the sternocleidomastoid muscles. There was a left extensor plantar response but no sensory impairment. The blood sugar was 31 mg./dl. EEG was normal with no slow wave focus. He was given 25 gm. of glucose intravenously and recovered fully in 3 minutes.

Comment: Cerebral infarction initially seemed to be the most likely diagnosis. However, the patient was a little more drowsy than expected with an uncomplicated stroke unless the infarct were massive. The fact that his attack might have begun with unconsciousness made his physicians suspect hypoglycemia. Although the history of a previous similar episode was compatible with the natural history of an attack of carotid artery insufficiency, unconsciousness does not ordinarily occur

190

with hemispheral ischemic attacks and probably that episode also represented hypoglycemia. Of our other four patients with hypoglycemic hemiplegia, three were children and all have been unconscious. The hemiplegia cleared rapidly in all after treatment.

Patients with metabolic brain disease often have both focal and generalized convulsions, particularly the latter, which are indistinguishable from the seizures of structural brain disease. When focal seizures occur, the focus tends to shift from attack to attack. Migratory seizures are especially common and hard to control in uremia.

Motor Abnormalities Characteristic of Metabolic Coma

Tremor, asterixis, and multifocal myoclonus are prominent manifestations of metabolic brain disease and are less commonly seen with focal structural lesions unless these latter have a toxic-infectious component.

TREMOR. The tremor of metabolic encephalopathy is coarse and irregular and has a rate of 8 to 10 per second. Usually these tremors are absent at rest and when present are most evident in the fingers of the outstretched hands. Severe tremors may spread to the face, tongue, and lower extremities, and they frequently interfere with purposive movements in agitated patients such as those with delirium tremens. The physiologic mechanism responsible for this type of tremor is unknown. It is not seen in patients with unilateral hemispheral or focal brainstem lesions.

ASTERIXIS. First described by Adams and Foley[2] in patients with hepatic coma, asterixis is now known to accompany a wide variety of metabolic brain diseases and even some structural lesions. (See Patient 2–8, p. 129, for an example of asterixis accompanying subdural empyema.) Asterixis is a sudden palmar flapping movement of the hands at the wrists.[386] It is most easily elicited in lethargic but awake patients by directing them to hold their arms outstretched with hands dorsiflexed at the wrist and fingers extended and abducted. In its incipiency, asterixis comprises a slight irregular tremor of the fingers beginning after a latent period of 2 to 30 seconds. Leavitt and Tyler[225] have described the two separate components of this tremulousness. One is an irregular oscillation of the fingers, usually in the anterior-posterior direction but with a rotary component at the wrist. The second consists of random movements of the fingers at the metacarpal-phalangeal joints. This second pattern becomes more and more marked as the patient holds his wrist dorsiflexed until finally the fingers lead the hand into a sudden downward jerk followed by a slower return to the original dorsiflexed position. Both hands are affected, but asynchronously, and as the abnormal movement intensifies, it spreads to the feet, tongue, and face. Indeed, with severe metabolic tremors it sometimes becomes difficult to distinguish between intense asterixis and myoclonus.

Asterixis is generally seen in awake but lethargic patients and generally disappears with the advent of stupor or coma, although occasionally one can evoke the arrhythmic contraction in such subjects by passively dorsiflexing the wrist. Unilateral asterixis has been described in several patients with focal brain lesions. Young and his colleagues describe several patients who developed contralateral asterixis after stereotactic thalamotomy for Parkinson's disease.[462] Tarsy and his colleagues[412] describe a patient with unilateral asterixis associated with a mesencephalic infarct, while Massey and associates note that contralateral asterixis occasionally can follow upon discrete lesions involving the thalamus adjacent to the internal capsule.[253] In these instances there was no clear evidence of an underlying metabolic disorder, but superimposed metabolic dysfunction accentuated the asterixis.[108,462] Degos and colleagues have recently reported 20 patients with asterixis contralateral to mesencephalic or parietal lobe lesions.[471]

Electromyograms recorded during asterixis show a brief absence of muscular activity during the downward jerk, followed by a sudden muscular compensatory contraction, much like the sudden bobbing of the head that normally accompanies drowsiness. The sudden electrical silence is unexplained and not accompanied by EEG changes.[2,225]

MULTIFOCAL MYOCLONUS. This consists of sudden, nonrhythmic, nonpatterned gross twitching involving parts of muscles or groups of muscles first in one part of the body, then another, and particularly affecting the facial and proximal musculature. It most commonly accompanies uremic encephalopathy, a large dose of intravenous penicillin, CO_2 narcosis, and hyperosmotic-hyperglycemic encephalopathy. Multifocal myoclonus always signifies severe metabolic disturbances and usually is confined to patients in stupor or coma. Its physiology is unknown; the motor twitchings are not reflected by a specific EEG abnormality and have, in fact, been reported in a patient with electrocerebral silence.[485]

Differential Diagnosis

Distinction between Metabolic and Psychogenic Unresponsiveness

In awake patients, differences in the mental state, the EEG, the motor signs, and, occasionally, the breathing pattern distinguish metabolic from psychiatric disease.

Most conscious patients with metabolic brain disease are confused, and many are disoriented, especially for time. Their abstract thinking is defective; they cannot concentrate well and cannot easily retain new information. Early during the illness, the outstretched dorsiflexed hands show irregular tremulousness and, frequently, asterixis. Snouting, sucking, and grasp reflexes are seen. The EEG is generally slow. Posthyperventilation apnea may be elicited and there may be hypoventilation or hyperventilation, depending on the specific metabolic illness. By contrast, awake patients with psychogenic illness, if they will cooperate, are not disoriented and can retain new information. They lack abnormal reflexes or adventitious movements, although they may have irregular tremor, and they have normal EEG frequencies. Ventilatory patterns, with the exception of psychogenic hyperventilation, are normal.

Unresponsive patients with metabolic disease have even slower activity in their EEGs than responsive patients with metabolic disease, and caloric stimulation elicits either tonic deviation of the eyes or, if the patient is deeply comatose, no response. Psychogenically unresponsive patients have normal EEGs and a normal response to caloric irrigation, with nystagmus having a quick phase away from the side of ice water irrigation; there is little or no tonic deviation of the eyes (see Chapter 5).

Distinction betweeen Coma of Metabolic and Structural Origin

Motor and EEG changes provide the most important distinctions between metabolic brain disease and gross structural disease when patients are merely obtunded or lethargic. Most patients with metabolic brain disease have diffusely abnormal motor signs, including tremor, myoclonus, and, especially, bilateral asterixis. The EEG is diffusely, but not focally, slow. The patient with gross structural disease, on the other hand, generally has abnormal focal motor signs and if asterixis is present, it is unilateral. The EEG may be slow, but in addition, with supratentorial lesions, a focal abnormality will usually be present.

Finally, metabolic and structural brain diseases are distinguished from each other by combinations of signs and their evolution. Comatose patients with metabolic brain disease usually suffer from partial dysfunction affecting many levels of the neuraxis simultaneously, yet concurrently retain the integrity of other functions originating at the same levels. The orderly rostral-caudal deterioration that is characteristic of supratentorial mass lesions does not occur in metabolic brain disease, nor is the anatomic defect regionally restricted as it is with subtentorial damage.

ASPECTS OF CEREBRAL METABOLISM PERTINENT TO COMA

Earlier chapters of this book have described the physiologic relationships among the brainstem, the diencephalon, and the cerebral hemispheres that underlie the wakeful state and normally generate the psychologic activities that constitute full consciousness. The brain's sensorimotor and mental activities are closely coupled to cerebral metabolism so that neurochemical impairment or failure from any cause is likely to produce rapidly evolving neurologic abnormalities.

Neurons and glial cells undergo many chemical processes in fulfilling their specialized functions. The nerve cells must continuously maintain their membrane potentials, synthesize and store transmitters, manufacture axoplasm, and replace their always decaying structural components (Fig. 33). The oligodendroglial cells at the very least generate myelin, and the protoplasmic astrocytes regulate much of the ion homeostasis of the brain's extracellular fluid. Undoubtedly, the astrocytes also serve a variety of other, still incompletely examined functions in maintaining the nutritional and metabolic balance of the neurons. All these complex activities require energy, in fact more of it per kilo weight of cells than in any other organ in the body. Furthermore, many of the enzymatic reactions of both neurons and glial cells, as well as of the specialized cerebral capillary endothelium,[304] must be catalyzed at some point by the energy-yielding hydrolysis of adenosine triphosphate (ATP) to adenosine diphosphate (ADP) and inorganic phosphate. Without a constant and generous supply of ATP, cellular synthesis slows or halts, neuronal functions decline or cease, and cell structures quickly crumble.

The brain depends entirely on the process of glycolysis and respiration within its own cells to synthesize its energy needs. The enzymes that regulate glycolysis are confined to the cellular cytoplasm, while those that generate the much more efficient ATP-producing respiratory citric acid cycle lie within the mitochondria. Normally, glucose provides the entire substrate for energy production by the brain, each mole generating ATP from ADP according to the formula:

$$\text{glucose} + 2\text{ADP} + 2\text{P}_i \rightarrow 2 \text{ lactate} + 2\text{ATP (glycolysis)}$$

$$\text{glucose} + 6\text{O}_2 + 38\text{ADP} + 38\text{P}_i \rightarrow 6\text{CO}_2 + 6\text{H}_2\text{O} + 38\text{ATP (respiration)}$$

The oxygen-requiring process of respiration is far more efficient than glycolysis in generating the brain's energy requirements; the actual ratio is 18:1, as respiration

193

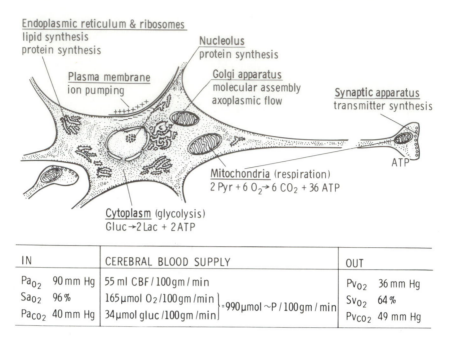

Figure 33. The energy balance of the brain.

adds 36 moles of ATP per mole of glucose to the 2 already produced by glycolysis. Since the enzymes in the glycolytic pathway can increase their rates only about sixfold, glycolysis alone is unable to meet the brain's energy needs in man, even if the circulation and other support systems could sustain an increase in the delivery of the glucose substrate by an improbable 600 percent. This insufficiency in glycolytic enzymatic action explains the constant need for oxygen by the mammalian brain.

Oxygen, glucose, and cerebral blood flow operate interdependently to supply the brain with the substrate and cofactors it requires to carry out the chemical reactions that generate its energy and synthesize its structural components. Awake or asleep, the brain metabolizes at one of the highest rates of any organ in the body. In addition, it suffers a special vulnerability in that it possesses almost no reserves of its critical nutrients so that even a brief interruption of blood flow or oxygen supply threatens the tissue's vitality. These considerations are central to an understanding of many of the metabolic encephalopathies, and the next few paragraphs discuss them in some detail.

Cerebral Blood Flow

Under normal resting conditions, the total cerebral blood flow (CBF) in man is about 55 cc. per 100 gm. per minute, an amount that equals 15 to 20 percent of the resting cardiac output. A number of studies have found that the overall CBF remains relatively constant during the states of wakefulness or slow-wave sleep as well as in the course of various mental and physical activities.[204,221] Recent research,

194

however, reveals that this apparent uniformity masks a regionally varying and dynamically fluctuating CBF, which is closely adjusted to meet the metabolic requirements posed by local physiologic changes in the brain. Overall flow in gray matter, for example, is normally 3 to 4 times higher than in white.[189] Using Lassen and Ingvar's ingenious multidetector techniques for measurement, many investigators have demonstrated in'man that regional cerebral blood flow increases in the appropriate physiologically active cerebral areas during such efforts as hand movement,[305] speech,[220] and the process of stereoperception.[357] Even the mental anticipation of hand movement causes focal increases in frontal lobe blood flow according to Ingvar and Philipson.[190]

Several studies demonstrate that these functionally associated changes in cerebral blood flow are closely coupled to concurrent changes in regional oxygen and glucose metabolism. As an example, Raichle and associates[346] found that flow and oxygen consumption in the cerebral motor area of the brain of normal man rose and fell in parallel during hand movement and its cessation. Investigations in experimental animals have demonstrated repeatedly that the close couple between flow and metabolism during physiologic stimulation holds true for many parts of the cerebral cortex as well as for subcortical structures.[352]

The precise nature of the messenger that normally links blood flow to metabolism in the brain has proved elusive. Although either an excess of CO_2 or a decline in oxygen tension in the blood or brain tissue can induce vasodilatation, neither of these perturbations of the respiratory gases can be identified locally in the brain during physiologic activation.[217] Indeed, during increased brain activity, such as with seizures, the increase in local blood flow often exceeds tissue oxidative demands, so that the oxygen tension rises slightly in venous blood.[325] It appears that the well-known cerebral vascular response to hypercarbia or hypoxia must be regarded as predominantly a fail-safe mechanism for inducing vasodilatation during extreme or pathologic threats. For most physiologic circumstances, increases in lactic acid,[184] potassium, adenosine, or various neurotransmitters have been proposed as the critical signal,[217,342] but none so far has individually satisfied the criteria necessary to assign it a universal role.

Several pathologic states of brain are marked by a disproportionately high rate of local blood flow in relation to metabolism. Examples of such reactive hyperemia or "uncoupling" of flow and metabolism occur in areas of traumatic or post-ischemic tissue injury as well as in regions of inflammation or in the regions surrounding certain brain tumors. So far, the nature of the local stimulus to such pathologic vasodilatation also has eluded investigators. The effects of the process, however, can act to increase the bulk of the involved tissue and thereby to accentuate the pathologic effects of compartmental swelling in the brain, as discussed in Chapter 2.

Reduced cerebral blood flow has several causes. As described in Chapter 2, the cerebral vasculature's capacity for autoregulation protects the CBF against all but the most profound drops in systemic blood pressure. The process of autoregulation also means that conditions causing a lowered cerebral metabolism are usually accompanied by a secondary fall in cerebral blood flow,[221] although in many such cases the initial decline in CBF is less than the metabolic reduction.[168] This delayed response may reflect the relatively slow adaptation of the tonic contractile state of vascular smooth muscle rather than a true uncoupling of flow and metabolism. Intrinsic *arterial spasm* in cerebral vessels, which reduces tissue flow below metabolic needs, is an uncommon phenomenon limited largely to arteries at the base of the brain. Such arterial spasm occurs with local surgical trauma as well as with subarachnoid bleeding, occasional examples of meningitis, and, possibly, the prodromal phases of migraine. Multifocal cerebral arteriolar spasm has been invoked to explain the regional cerebral vascular injury of malignant hypertension; recent work, however, offers a different interpretation of the pathogenesis of that disorder (see p. 214).

Primary reductions in CBF can be regional or general (global). *Regional impairments of CBF* result from intrinsic diseases of the cervical and cerebral arteries (atherosclerosis, thrombosis, and, rarely, inflammation), from arterial embolism, and from the extrinsic pressure on individual cerebral arteries produced by compartmental herniation. *General or global reductions in CBF* result from systemic hypotension, complete or functional cardiac arrest (e.g., ventricular arrhythmias in which output falls below requirements of brain perfusion), and increased intracranial pressure. As noted earlier in this volume, however, unless some primary abnormality of brain acts to increase regional vascular resistance, an increase in the intracranial pressure must approach the systemic systolic pressure before cerebral blood flow declines sufficiently to produce recognizable changes in neurologic functions.

Cessation of blood flow to the brain (*ischemia*), as discussed in subsequent paragraphs, appears to produce a greater risk of irreversible tissue damage than does even a profound reduction in the arterial oxygen tension (*anoxemia*). The precise lower level of arterial perfusion required to maintain the vitality of the tissue is not known in man. Observation in experimental animals places the critical figure at about 15 ml./100 gm. brain min.$^{-1}$ in gray matter. At or below this level the electrical potential fails and potassium leaks rapidly from the cells. Cellular necrosis begins soon afterwards.[43,250] It is of interest that a roughly similar figure may apply in man: reductions in cerebral blood flow below about 20 ml./100 gm. brain min.$^{-1}$ fairly consistently produce ipsilateral EEG slowing in patients undergoing carotid artery ligation in preparation for carotid endarterectomy or aneurysm removal.[488]

Several factors may explain why ischemia so severely threatens tissue structure. A change in pH or in lactic acid concentration is one. Anaerobic metabolism produces large amounts of lactic acid and other reducing equivalents, and changes in the pH can substantially alter chemical reactions. Several pieces of indirect evidence support the inference that lactic acid accumulation endangers brain tissue. Some years ago, Friede and van Houten found that cerebellar slices degenerated much less rapidly in vitro if glycolysis and lactic acid production were inhibited.[131] Ames and Gurian similarly observed a prolonged survival of the anoxic-exposed retina in an in-vitro preparation that minimized lactate accumulation.[7] Myers and Yamaguchi noted that brain damage following cerebral ischemia was greater in hyperglycemic than in fasting animals,[282] an effect possibly attributable to increased lactate accumulation from post-ischemic glycolysis. (A contradictory consideration against lactic acid being the lethal factor in anoxia, however, is that hypoglycemia, which essentially halts lactate production in the brain, causes neuropathologic effects identical to ischemia.) An elevated potassium level is another potentially damaging by-product of ischemia. High extracellular concentrations of potassium are known to depolarize nerve membranes and cause seizures.[318] An additional potential danger is a change in osmolality. Ischemia rapidly leads to a rise in local brain tissue osmolality to levels approaching or exceeding 600 mOsm.[181] Such high values are sufficient to draw a potentially explosive volume of water into the brain cells when blood reperfuses the ischemic area.

196

Glucose Metabolism

Glucose is the overwhelmingly predominant blood-borne substrate for brain metabolism. One might question why this is so since it is known that slices of cerebral cortex in vitro can utilize a variety of substrates, including fatty acids and other compounds, to synthesize acetoacetate for entry into the citric acid cycle. The answer appears to lie in the specialized properties of the blood brain barrier, which, by rigorously limiting or facilitating the entry or egress of substances to and from the brain, guards the narrow homeostasis of that organ.[243,348]

Glucose moves across the blood brain barrier by a non-energy-requiring system called facilitated transport that speeds its entry over other hexoses some 16 times or more at physiologic blood concentrations. Insulin does not appear to affect either cerebral glucose uptake or metabolism in any important way, although insulin does appear to promote glucose uptake into brain.

In net metabolic terms, each 100 gm. of brain in a normal human being utilizes about 0.31 μmol. (5.5 mg.) of glucose per minute, so that in the basal prolonged fasting state the brain's consumption of glucose almost equals the total amount that the liver produces.[309] This net figure, however, hides the fact that glucose consumption in local regions of the brain varies widely according to local functional changes. Because of its rapid transfer into brain, glucose represents essentially the organ's only substrate under physiologic conditions. Ketone bodies, however, can diffuse into brain and also are transported across the blood brain barrier. These substances provide increased fuel to the brain when beta-hydroxy-butyrate, acetoacetate, and other ketones increase in the blood during states such as starvation, the ingestion of high-fat diets, or ketoacidosis. During starvation, in fact, liver gluconeogenesis may fall below the level required to meet cerebral substrate needs; at such times ketone utilization can contribute as much as 30 percent of the brain's fuel for oxidative metabolism.[309] For unknown reasons, however, brain does not appear able to subsist entirely on ketone bodies,[400] and as mentioned below, some investigators believe that ketones contribute to the neurologic toxicity of diabetic ketoacidosis.

Under normal circumstances, all but about 15 percent of glucose uptake in the brain is accounted for by combustion with O_2 to produce H_2O and energy. Whether the remaining glucose is glycolyzed to lactic acid as diagrammed on page 193 is disputed: some studies reveal a consistent but small lactate output by brain and others none. In any event, the fact that glucose fully accounts for the oxidative metabolism of the brain should not be taken to imply that other metabolic pathways are not operative. Only about 35 percent of the glucose that enters the brain is rapidly metabolized to CO_2, the rest being incorporated into cerebral amino acids, proteins, and lipids. It appears, then, that while there is no net use of blood-borne substrate other than glucose under normal circumstances, other internal substrates are nevertheless constantly being catabolized from brain stores, and these must be replenished by synthesis from glucose.

The brain contains about 1 mmol./kg. of free glucose in reserve, and another 3 mmol./kg. of glycogen, about 70 percent of which stands readily available for immediate conversion to glucose. At the brain's normal rate of metabolism (with oxygen present), these tiny stores would maintain the brain's normal function for no more than 2 to 3 minutes if the blood supply was abruptly cut off. If the supply of both oxygen and glucose was interrupted, as occurs in cardiac arrest or strangulation for example, glycolysis would increase to a maximum and available glucose stores would support a normal rate of energy metabolism for no more than about 14 seconds. These considerations emphasize the singular metabolic dependence of the brain on its external nutritional supply.

The energy balance of the brain is influenced both by its supply of energy precursors (i.e., its input) and by the work the organ does (i.e., its output). Just as intrinsic mechanisms appropriately increase or decrease the rate of metabolism in different regions of the brain during periods of locally increased or decreased functional activity, so also intrinsic mechanisms appear able to "turn down" general cerebral metabolic activity and produce stupor or coma when circumstances threaten to deplete blood-borne substrate.

Several metabolic disorders are known to produce a decrease in the brain's rate of metabolism and physiologic function without initially resulting in any encroachment on the energy reserves of the tissue. The reversible hypometabolism of anesthesia is discussed in a following section. Mechanistically less well understood than anesthesia is a reversible hypometabolism that accompanies the early stages of hypoglycemia, severe hypoxemia, reduced states of cerebral blood flow, and hyperammonemia. The response appears to be important in protecting the brain against irreversible damage, however, and is well illustrated by describing the neurochemical changes that accompany hypoglycemia.

Hypoglycemia

METABOLIC EFFECTS. Hypoglycemia deprives the brain of its substrates for respiration and according to the first equation on page 193 can be expected to interfere with cerebral metabolism by reducing the brain's energy supply in a manner similar to that caused by hypoxia. With very severe or prolonged hypoglycemia this turns out to be true, but with less severe or transient reductions of glucose availability one finds that brain function and metabolism decline before one can detect a decline in ATP levels in the tissue.

Soon after the discovery of insulin it was realized that hypoglycemic coma could last for up to an hour or so without necessarily leaving any residual neurologic effects or structural brain damage. (This capacity to induce transient but fully reversible coma was important in developing the use of insulin coma in attempts to treat psychiatric disorders.) Since equally long periods of hypoxemic coma almost always leave neurologic damage in their wake, the difference between the effects of a deficiency of oxygen and a deficiency of substrate engendered considerable interest. Accordingly, the mechanism of hypoglycemic coma has received repeated attention by biochemists with results important to the understanding of many aspects of human cerebral metabolism.

Hypoglycemia affects cerebral blood flow, glucose consumption, and oxygen consumption in different ways. Clinical studies of cerebral blood flow and metabolism during hypoglycemia in man indicate that at all levels of blood sugar thus far studied, CBF either remains the same or may occasionally rise.[79,101,153] With a relatively mild reduction of blood glucose in man down to levels of 1.7 to 2.6 μmol./ml. (31–46 mg./dl.), consciousness is preserved, and cerebral glucose consumption (CMR_{gl}) declines moderately, but cerebral oxygen consumption remains normal. In a few patients with hypoglycemic coma, Kety found that cerebral metabolic rate for oxygen (CMR_{O_2}) declined, but that CMR_{gl} fell disproportionately.

198

Della Porta and associates generally confirmed Kety's results in patients with hypoglycemic coma, but found that CMR_{gl} declined from its control level by more than half while CMR_{O_2} was reduced only to an insignificant degree.[79] These changes imply that during hypoglycemia the brain is utilizing substrates other than glucose for oxidative metabolism, presumably endogenous glycogen and even structural components. Furthermore, despite a normal oxygen consumption the qualitative change in substrate results in profound functional changes in the neural systems that normally subserve consciousness.

Studies in animals extend the above studies in man and indicate that even with degrees of hypoglycemia sufficient to produce convulsions or deep coma, whole brain energy reserves at least briefly can be well maintained. Ferrendelli and Chang,[114] Lewis and associates,[235] and Norberg and Siesjo[297] all reported that during hypoglycemia, levels of phosphocreatine and ATP remained normal in the brains of mice or rats so long as EEG activity remained. Energy reserves began to fail only after prolonged convulsive activity ensued.[235] Ferrendelli and Chang's animals maintained phosphocreatine and ATP levels even after the EEG became isoelectric. Norberg and Siesjo, however, always found a decline in these compounds once the EEG became flat. Despite profound hypoglycemia (blood sugar $< 1/\mu$mol. min.$^{-1}$) and a rate of cerebral glucose consumption that fell to about half of normal, Norberg and Siesjo observed that cerebral oxygen consumption remained approximately normal during deep hypoglycemia.

The above studies imply that, at least in its early stages, metabolic coma from hypoglycemia cannot be attributed simply to a failure of overall cerebral energy supply. A possible contributory mechanism is that hypoglycemia impairs acetylcholine synthesis in the brain, which may lead to a block in cholinergic pathways.[139] Failure of cholinergic transmission seems an unlikely explanation for all the physiologic alterations, however, in view of the continued high rate of oxygen consumption. Other possible toxic mechanisms include the fact that a number of amino acids including several with putative neurotransmitter functions decline significantly in brain during hypoglycemia. These include glutamate, glutamine, GABA, and alanine. Aspartate rises fourfold, and ammonia increases fourteenfold to levels equalling or exceeding those associated with coma in humans or experimental animals.[176,324,391] At the present time it is not known whether these amino acid changes involve the neurotransmitter pool, nor does one have many clues about what, if any, functional effects the transmitters in question may have. Accordingly, the ultimate mechanisms of the remarkably reversible effects of hypoglycemia on the brain remain unexplained.

PHYSIOLOGIC EFFECTS. When alterations in consciousness occur in hypoglycemia, which neural structures are physiologically the most impaired? The discussion on mechanisms of consciousness presented in Chapter 1 provides two choices: either the cortex must be diffusely impaired or the brainstem-activating structures must be functionally affected (or both). Experimental work supports both choices. Himwich took the first view and conceived of hypoglycemia and anoxia as damaging the brain in progressively descending phylogenetic levels; at first dysfunction of cortical neurons occurred, then subcorticodiencephalic, mesencephalic, premyelencephalic, and myelencephalic areas became involved, in that successive order.[175] Neuropathologic changes in man[354] and animals dying from hypoglycemia demonstrate that the earliest and most severe damage strikes neurons of the cerebral cortex; the neurons of the brainstem and basal ganglia are less vulnerable. In physiologic studies, Hoagland and his colleagues found grossly abnormal cortical EEGs in animals with hypoglycemia at a time when direct recordings from anterior and posterior hypothalamic areas remained normal.[178]

Arduini and Arduini took the second view and postulated a subcortical cause for metabolic coma, since their experiments indicate selective reticular depression by hypoglycemia.[12] Using auditory stimuli, the Arduinis recorded responses from both the cerebral cortex and the brainstem reticular formation. When hypoglycemia was induced, the response to sound was diminished or absent in the reticular formation but remained unchanged in the auditory cortex. Anoxia yielded similar results, with responses in the auditory cortex persisting long after the reticular response disappeared. These authors and others made similar observations of the susceptibility of the reticular formation to cyanide,[12] anesthetic drugs,[12,130] and concussion.[124]

In contrast to the orderly conclusions derived from experimental data, clinical evidence suggests that several different levels of the rostral neuraxis can almost randomly suffer the first physiologic dysfunction in hypoglycemia, with the locus sometimes varying capriciously from attack to attack. In some patients hypoglycemia heralds itself with loss of consciousness and bilaterally synchronous slow waves in the EEG, suggesting an initial involvement of arousal mechanisms. Other patients first exhibit restricted signs of cerebral motor or sensory dysfunction unaccompanied by either EEG abnormalities or impaired consciousness. Sometimes each subsequent attack irreversibly damages more cortical neurons; a substantial incidence of permanent dementia occurs in patients who survive repeated hypoglycemia. These inconsistencies among different patients illustrate how in the clinical situation regional cerebral factors such as blood flow and energy requirements must vary from moment to moment to predispose first one part of the brain and then another to metabolic insult.

ACETYLCHOLINE IN HYPOGLYCEMIC AND HYPOXIC ENCEPHALOPATHY. A defect in acetylcholine synthesis has been proposed by Gibson and Blass to explain at least some of the early functional changes in hypoglycemic and hypoxic encephalopathy.[139,140,141] Lying behind the hypothesis is the observation that in both of these conditions changes in brain function occur with deficiencies much less severe than required to reduce the energy reserves of the tissue (Fig. 34).[391] Furthermore, scopolamine, which blocks muscarinic cholinergic transmission in brain, impairs cognitive function in a manner somewhat reminiscent of the hypoxic state.[89]

Acetylcholine (ACh) synthesis depends directly on oxidative metabolism. The acetyl group is generated in mitochondria from the oxidation of pyruvate and transported into cytoplasm for combination with choline to form the transmitter. Although only a tiny fraction of oxidized pyruvate is converted to ACh, synthesis of the transmitter has been demonstrated to decline in proportion to any reduction in glucose availability as well as to even modest degrees of hypoxia.

Direct evidence is lacking that synaptic impairment produced by reduced acetylcholine synthesis causes the early or late cerebral manifestations of hypoxia. Studies by Dolivo in peripheral ganglia, however, demonstrate that, when one removes oxygen or glucose from the bathing medium, synaptic transmission fails many hours before conduction becomes impaired in nerve fibers.[87] An analogous change in brain could at least partially explain early hypoxic symptoms as well as the increased arousal that the cholinergic agonist physostigmine produces in states marked by impaired oxidative metabolism.

Pathogenesis of Reversible and Irreversible
Brain Damage in Metabolic Coma

The above discussion on hypoglycemia postulated that the presence or absence of energy failure in the tissue may be the major factor that determines whether cells die or recover in this condition. The following section extends the point and compares some of the cerebral metabolic effects of reversible anesthesia with those of anoxic-ischemic and other metabolic conditions producing stupor or coma.

Many directly applied physical and chemical agents can injure the brain. Ultimately, most lethal injuries of a nongenetic origin probably exert their effects either by directly producing tissue anoxia, or by indirectly producing its equivalent, thereby blocking cerebral energy production by the mitochondria.[391] (Viral invasion or other injuries, such as radiation, that alter the cellular genome may be exceptions to these rules.) As discussed above, the body normally maintains its nervous tissue in a constant "high energy" state in which the oxidative metabolism of glucose generates a constant supply of ATP and phosphocreatine to maintain membrane potentials, transmit neuronal impulses, and synthesize protoplasm. When the mechanisms that sustain these energy reserves go awry, ATP and phosphocreatine levels decline, membranes lose their pumping mechanisms, the cells swell,[425] and, at some point, the neuron loses its capacity to recover. Histologic evidence, discussed below, indicates that the mitochondria bear the first brunt of irreversible damage, while histochemical evidence suggests that oxidative enzymes themselves are destroyed.[247] Since the precise lethal point of no return is unknown in cellular-molecular terms, one generally must turn to physiologic models when trying to find out just when and why the nervous system dies. Evidence from such models indicates that the brain can harmlessly suspend its activities almost indefinitely when metabolically depressed or cooled, but quickly succumbs when it loses its functional activities in the absence of oxygen or substrate.

Anesthesia

The brain can be depressed to essentially functionless levels by anesthetic depressant drugs, yet lose none of its capacity for total recovery when the anesthetic disappears. Several workers have demonstrated that experimental animals can be fully resuscitated to full functional activity after periods of deep anesthesia producing up to 6 hours of isoelectric EEG flattening. Similar observations have been made in man.[185]

At the present time, no fully satisfactory physiologic or chemical explanations have been found for the action of anesthetic drugs. Pentobarbital has been shown to depress selectively excitatory post-synaptic potentials in invertebrates and in vertebrate sympathetic ganglia,[292] possibly by decreasing the lifetime of open, post-synaptic ionic channels.[420] It is not known whether these findings apply to the mammalian central nervous system. Barbiturates and other anesthetics inhibit mitochondrial respiration in vitro,[284] and at high, nonphysiologic concentrations can uncouple oxidative phosphorylation. However, it seems unlikely that anesthesia results from a generalized depression of cellular respiration.[216] For one thing, not all agents that inhibit cellular respiration cause anesthesia, and some cause convulsions.[283] More importantly, inhibition of mitochondrial oxidation would lead eventually to energy failure in the brain, while measurements of the effects of anesthetics on energy reserves show just the opposite effect.

Chemically, anesthesia depresses the function of the brain but keeps the organ in a high energy state, poised for the resumption of normal function. Nilsson and Siesjo subjected well-ventilated rats to various concentrations of general anesthesia, including halothane, nitrous oxide, and barbiturates.[294,295,296] In all instances, concentrations of ATP and phosphocreatine remained normally high, even during deep anesthesia, and normal lactate-pyruvate ratios were maintained in the brain, indicating that no tissue hypoxia had occurred. By implication, the brain during anesthesia was in a state of primed, energy-rich suspended animation and was neither damaged nor was its potential impaired for future functional activity.

Clinical experience with anesthesia and drug poisoning reviewed in Chapter 7 confirms the implications of the animal studies. Given good medical care, most patients usually survive anesthesia from the self-administration of barbiturates and other sedative drugs, even when coma is so deep that artificial respiration must be provided for several days and the blood pressure supported by vasopressor agents for a week or more. Nor does any apparent or measurable impairment of brain function follow such flirtations with death.

The complete reversibility of anesthetic coma, plus the low metabolic rate that accompanies deep anesthesia has inspired efforts to determine whether barbiturate anesthesia can minimize the expected extent of post-anoxic ischemic brain damage. (Barbiturates also scavenge free radicals from reoxygenated tissue,[80] but it remains to be proved that this represents an important biologic function in resuscitation.[391]) Barbiturate anesthesia already has been applied to patients in coma from head trauma with somewhat encouraging results.[356] In several animal species, investigators have found that the induction of barbiturate anesthesia during or immediately after experimentally occluding a cerebral artery or arresting systole appeared to reduce the expected degree of consequent brain damage.[65,232] Scattered observations on patients suffering from cardiac arrest during surgical operations under deep anesthesia also have suggested that the degree of subsequent injury was less than expected if anesthesia were not present. However, experienced clinicians view these early reports cautiously. Deep barbiturate anesthesia has been applied with only indeterminate results to a few patients immediately following an acute stroke or acute circulatory arrest. The procedure lacks any controlled studies and available reports are insufficient to draw conclusions on the results, particularly because the naturally occurring outcome of such patients is not well known. For example, one preliminary report of post-resuscitation anesthetic treatment for patients in coma from cardiac arrest describes favorable outcomes, but they are essentially identical with those resulting from bystander-initiated resuscitation alone.[366,415] A practical consideration in all this work is that highly complex anesthetic treatment can itself create medical risks that must be weighed against potential benefits. Also, anesthetic treatment will inevitably be expensive. For all these reasons, the approach deserves careful evaluation before being applied widely.

Mechanisms of Irreversible Anoxic-Ischemic Brain Damage

Anoxia, ischemia, and hypoglycemia can combine under several different primary and secondary circumstances to damage the brain. Somewhat similar pathologic changes characterize irreversible brain injury from all three conditions, although

202

systemic and local circulatory differences among them influence the exact geography and type of cellular response. Anoxic-ischemic changes in the brain mark the postmortem findings of several conditions, including patients dying in coma after fatal status epilepticus, carbon monoxide poisoning, or several of the systemic metabolic encephalopathies. Despite these overlapping histologic similarities, investigators hold sharply differing views about the effects of anoxia on the brain. These include disagreement about just how much anoxia is required to damage the organ, the nature of the earliest subcellular injury, whether ischemia damages neurons in a manner identical to anoxia, and even whether nerve cells or blood vessels are the first to undergo fatal injury.

EXPERIMENTAL STUDIES. Complete cerebral ischemia in man causes loss of consciousness in 8 to 10 seconds, and in animals electroencephalographic activity disappears after only a few seconds more. Many clinicians including ourselves believe from experience with patients that even brief anoxic-ischemic periods lasting perhaps two minutes or less are sufficient to produce brain damage in adults, but the observations vary from person to person and clinical conditions make the exact time threshold for producing permanent damage difficult to establish.

Early experimental work in animals indicated that about 4 minutes of severe anoxia was followed by irreversible coma and death. Schneider, however, found that he could prolong this interval by giving meticulous attention to maintaining the animal's systemic circulation.[379] As a result, he postulated that heart failure actually preceded brain failure during anoxia. Subsequently, several investigators claimed that experimental animals could recover from periods of cerebral anoxia-ischemia lasting as long as 20 minutes provided that one prevented severe hypotension or episodes of asystole following the anoxic or ischemic period.[271,367] All these experiments have shortcomings that limit their applicability to man. The brain of subprimate species is generally more resistant to ischemia than is man's. Furthermore, most such experiments have been performed on relatively young animals, whereas most ischemic injury in humans occurs during the later decades. Some of the experiments were performed under anesthesia, a circumstance known to protect the brain against anoxia. Others failed to provide satisfactory evidence that anoxia or ischemia was complete. Several experiments lacked detailed neuropathologic examinations of the brain, leaving moot questions of whether partial damage existed or what was the potential for full neurologic recovery. Nevertheless, the fact that at least some parts of the brain could survive relatively prolonged exposure to anoxia-ischemia gave strong impetus to efforts to find ways of protecting the human cerebrum during comparable assaults. Such efforts received an additional uplift from the findings of K. A. Hossmann and collaborators that at least fragments of neurophysiologic and neurochemical activity could be temporarily restored in the primate brain following periods of apparently total ischemia lasting as long as 60 minutes.[182]

Studies of retinal ganglion cells in vitro also suggested a higher resistance to anoxia by nerve cells than expected from clinical experience. Ames and Gurian dissected out retinas and their attached optic nerves and bathed the tissue in physiological solutions in which oxygen or glucose supplies could either be maintained in the bath or individually removed from it.[7] (The choice of the thin retinal membrane bathed in nutrient fluids sidestepped the need for an intact vascular supply.) It was discovered that reoxygenation restored the optic nerve action potential almost to its control levels after exposures to pure nitrogen lasting as long as 20 minutes. Similarly, van Harreveld and Tachibana demonstrated that the neuron retained the capacity to expel chloride after anoxic exposures lasting as long as 20 to 72 minutes. [425]

The above experimental results led some to postulate that vascular rather than neuronal abnormalities might account for the seemingly brief periods of anoxia that can damage the brain in clinical circumstances. Seemingly in keeping with this idea, Ames and his coworkers reported that if they occluded the great vessels in the neck for a period lasting more than about 7 minutes, immediate recirculation of the brain became increasingly difficult to obtain, in direct proportion to the time of occlusion. The apparent cause was multifocal obstructions in the cerebral capillaries and arterioles. [8,58,214] This condition they termed the *no-reflow phenomenon.*

The hypothesis that a failure of reperfusion (no-reflow) contributes importantly to post-ischemic brain damage has received wide attention, but neither experimental nor clinical evidence gives it a great deal of support. In carefully controlled histologic studies of cerebral ischemia, one always observes dying nerve cells before any detectable change occurs in capillary or other vascular structures. [142,234] In fact, even Fischer and Ames were unable to reproduce their earlier findings of cerebral capillary occlusion by glial compression and intravascular bleb formation when they reinvestigated the ultrastructural effects of cerebral ischemia. [115] Other workers have demonstrated that impaired cerebral vascular perfusion with or without previous ischemia can be readily demonstrated when one injects the vascular marker into the arterial bed, but not after injecting it intravenously. [233] Our inference is that intravascular precipitation of dye marker causes the "phenomenon," and that as originally proposed, an immediate post-ischemic no-reflow is probably an experimental artifact.

If one cannot explain the Ames and Hossman demonstrations of prolonged post-anoxic neuronal survival as owing to the fact that vascular problems were eliminated, how is one to interpret them? The answer is not clear at this time. One must emphasize that both sets of experiments described only a limited amount of functional recovery in a small amount of nervous tissue observed for a brief period of time. Experimental work has demonstrated that following ischemic injury to brain, neuropathologic cellular abnormalities increase in number and intensity for several hours after the injury, [191,340] implying a ripening of the lethal injury. Even so, the Ames and Hossmann experiments have provided a strong stimulus for further work. The demonstration that neural tissue possesses even a small capacity for being resuscitated after anoxic-ischemic injury brings hope of finding ways of ameliorating the enormous amount of neurologic damage produced in patients by cerebral vascular and allied disorders.

In contrast to the apparently minimal importance of immediate reperfusion problems following ischemia, later blood flow difficulties in the brain probably are an important abnormality. After cardiac arrest or cerebral vascular obstruction lasting 15 to 30 minutes or more, several workers have demonstrated that while initial blood flow may be normal or above normal, regions of cerebral nonperfusion subsequently develop, which rapidly increase in their extent as the duration of severe ischemia lengthens. [142,286] We suspect that the circulation fails secondarily in these circumstances, declining only *after* the parenchymatous elements of the brain have already lost their vitality, but this conclusion remains debatable.

Surprisingly enough, neither the precise causes nor the exact sequence of the molecular events that underlie the evolution of anoxic-ischemic injury from first functional change to brain death are fully known. Few intrinsic mechanisms protect

204

the brain during anoxia-ischemia. Duffy and associates obtained evidence that in the face of oxygen lack, oxidative metabolism in the brain immediately declined, providing a kind of hypoxic anesthesia.[95] However useful such a mechanism may be with *partial* anoxia-ischemia, such hypometabolism could only briefly protect the cell against the severe energy depletion that total ischemia produces. Exemplifying this principle is the rate at which the reserves fall: by 1 minute after the onset of total ischemia, ATP concentrations in brain fall by 80 percent, and by the end of 2 minutes residual energy reserves are barely detectable.

Partial or incomplete anoxia-ischemia from stroke is a far more frequent cause of brain damage in man than is complete ischemia, which generally is confined to conditions such as severe systemic hypotension or cardiac arrest. With experimental animals exposed to severely reduced blood flow (oligemia) to the brain or oligemia plus hypoxemia, one can follow a progressive sequence of neuropathologic changes that begins with mitochondrial swelling a vacuolation in neurons of the selectively vulnerable zones of the hippocampus after insults as brief as 10 minutes.[370,371,372] The process gradually enlarges to include an ever wider zone and intensifies to produce typical ischemic cell changes and, finally, necrosis that involves progressively larger areas of the brain. The time sequence of such changes depends on the severity of the injury. In experimental animals, periods of severe hypoxia (PaO_2 20 to 25 mm. Hg), coupled with relative cerebral hypoperfusion such as would result from moderate hypotension or carotid artery occlusion, can produce extensive microvacuolation and ischemic cell change in cerebral hippocampal neurons after exposures of less than 30 minutes duration.[370,371,372] More prolonged periods of hypotension coupled with a somewhat less severe degree of anoxemia produce a pattern of prominent white matter injury in addition to neuronal damage.[144,341] This demyelinating response is the typical change that one observes in the brain of man and animals after periods of coma-producing hypoxemia induced by carbon monoxide.[145,326]

Following cardiac arrest, the presence or absence of systemic circulatory abnormalities as well as the extent of neurologic injury influences the brain's potential for recovery. Several workers have found that lower animals, including the dog and monkey, could be fully revived by meticulous cardiorespiratory care after periods of total or severe global brain ischemia lasting 11 to 15 minutes or more.[282,286,367] In these experiments, attention to maintaining the post-ischemic systemic blood pressure as well as to correcting potential abnormalities in blood electrolytes, blood volume, and respiration appeared important. Increased platelet aggregability, increased intravascular coagulability, and increased serum osmolality all have been observed following periods of global cerebral ischemia and may contribute to impaired cerebral perfusion in such circumstances.

EPITOME. Biochemical evidence obtained during experimental hypoxia, ischemia, hypoglycemia, or hyperammonemia indicates that brain tissue can restore itself fully so long as ATP levels do not fall from normal.[3,176,371,372,391] Histologic evidence indicates that following anoxic-ischemic insults, first the mitochondria and then neuronal cells bodies themselves undergo lethal cell changes.[43] These changes begin in regions of the brain that represent empirically well-defined but mechanistically poorly understood regions of selective vulnerability. They progressively enlarge and, if severe enough, can involve either an entire vascular territory (with regional arterial occlusions) or the entire brain (with global anoxia-ischemia). Compounding the lethal initial injury can be cerebral edema (which with ischemia always appears to follow tissue necrosis in onset[319,323,380]); peripheral circulatory failure from systemic anoxic injury; and impaired cerebral perfusion that owes its pathogenesis to systemic and local circulatory abnormalities as well as abnormal intravascular coagulability. It remains to be seen whether in man these complicating aspects provide a contributory cause or are only a consequence of already severe brain injury, representing a late change occurring after the damage is complete.

Evaluation of Neurotransmitter Changes in Metabolic Coma

The number of known and putative neurotransmitters and transmitter-modulating agents has grown rapidly in recent years. Alterations in the function of these agents have been proposed to explain the pathogenesis of several of the metabolic encephalopathies. Examples of such hypotheses are described in the sections on hypoxia, hepatic failure, and thiamine deficiency. Table 13 lists the experimentally most well established alterations among the known and putative neurotransmitters in the brain during metabolic encephalopathies.

The clinical implications of transmitter changes observed in the experimental setting often become difficult to evaluate. Many of the alterations observed in experimental metabolic perturbations are small, are susceptible to nonspecific trauma, and can occur to an equal degree in conditions that are not accompanied by apparent alterations of consciousness. Furthermore, the interlocking nature of the different neurotransmitter pathways in the brain makes it almost impossible to determine whether transmitter changes caused the observed functional deficits or vice versa. Similarly, when a change does occur, it is equally difficult to place a finger on the first vulnerable pathway. It is a maxim of this field that the mere measurement of static tissue concentrations or excretion levels of a putative transmitter gives no information about the *activity* of a given neurotransmitter pathway. Such dynamic information derives only from measuring the turnover of the transmitter in question. Even that measurement cannot separate primary from secondary changes in activity when trying to judge the biologic significance of a departure from the norm.

Several investigators have proposed the involvement of specific neurotransmitters in certain encephalopathies because drugs that interact with a particular biochemical system improve the animal's behavior or the patient's symptoms, as the case may be. Such conclusions, while interesting, must be regarded with caution. L-dopa, for example, has been reported to improve the neurologic function of certain patients with hepatic encephalopathy.[244,324] But dopamine agonists are inconsistent in eliciting such improvements,[423] and L-dopa also sometimes produces an arousal effect in other types of coma, so the effect may be nonspecific. Similar cautions must be applied to conclusions derived from observing increased attention or alertness in stuporous patients following the use of physostigmine. The drug, through its powerful muscarinic cholinergic action, causes a generalized increase in the arousal state of the organism; it could mediate its effects in stupor by inducing supranormal activity in unaffected pathways rather than reversing or substituting for a transmitter deficiency in a metabolically impaired pathway. To our knowledge, present evidence makes it impossible to incriminate confidently transmitter deficiency or failure as the primary neurologic abnormality in any metabolic encephalopathy, except those produced by poisoning with pharmacologic blocking agents. Thus the sometimes inconsistent findings referred to in Table 13 must be regarded as only the first signposts to a potentially important area of understanding in the metabolic brain diseases.

206

Table 13. Major Reported Neurotransmitter Changes in Metabolic Encephalopathy

I. Hypoxia
 Acetylcholine (ACh) synthesis inhibited[140]
 5-HT (serotonin) synthesis decreased[75,76]
 Dopamine (DA) and norepinephrine synthesis decreased[45]
 GABA levels in brain increased[460]
 Aspartate levels in brain decreased[95]
 Incorporation of glucose into alanine, glutamate, aspartate, GABA, glutamine[461] in brain decreased
 Tyrosine hydroxylase in brain reduced[75,76]
 DA release in brain decreased[45]
II. Ischemia or postischemia
 DA, 5-HIAA, tyrosine, and tryptophan in brain increased; noradrenalin and 5-HT decreased[50,212,446,447]
 Norepinephrine and DA levels in brain decreased[277]
 DA in brain decreased[446,447,463]
 Serotonin synthesis and degradation in brain decreased[278,446,447]
 GABA levels in brain increased[245]
 GABA uptake in brain reduced[38]
 ACh levels decreased in striatum and cortex, increased in hippocampus, cerebellum, midbrain, and hypothalamus[445]
 Glutamate decarboxylase activity in brain reduced[38]
 Mg^{++} requiring ATPase associated with neuronal vesicles reduced[344]
 Adenosine in brain increased[29]
III. Hypoglycemia
 ACh turnover in brain decreased[139]
 Alanine, GABA, and glutamate decreased in brain; aspartate increased[391]
IV. Cofactor deficiency
 A. Thiamine (B_1)
 ACh level and turnover in brain decreased[170,432]
 ACh turnover in superior cervical ganglion decreased[365]
 ACh release impaired[98]
 Catecholamine synthesis in brain decreased[192]
 Serotonin uptake in brain decreased[322]
 GABA glutamate and aspartate levels in brain reduced[134,160]
 Alanine, glutamate, glutamine, aspartate, and GABA synthesis decreased[134]
 B. Pyridoxine (B_6)
 Glutamic decarboxylase (GABA synthesis) and 5-hydroxytryptamine decarboxylase (serotonin synthesis) in brain reduced;[90,91,92] GABA reduced[443]
 C. Cyanocobalamin (B_{12})
 Methylmalonic acid increased in brain, which inhibits ACh synthesis[140]
V. Hepatic encephalopathy
 Octopamine synthesis increased and norepinephrine synthesis decreased in brain[116]
VI. Ammonia intoxication
 ACh in brain decreased[41]
 Glutamate and aspartate decreased in brain[176]
VII. Enzyme inhibitors
 A. Lead
 Norepinephrine in brain increased; dopamine and ACh unchanged[150,393]
 Homovanillic acid and vanillylmandelic acid in brain and urine increased[393]
 B. Mercury
 ACh release in brain increased by low levels and decreased by high levels[30]

SPECIFIC CAUSES OF METABOLIC COMA

General Considerations

The differential diagnosis of metabolic coma is not always easy. The history often is unobtainable and the neurologic examination in many instances suggests only that the cause of coma is metabolic, without identifying the specific etiology. Thus, laboratory examinations and x-ray contrast studies may ultimately be required to make a final diagnosis. But when the patient is acutely and severely ill, and time is short, the major treatable causes of acute metabolic coma (which are comparatively few) must be considered systematically. In obscure cases, it is remarkable how often an accurate clue is derived from careful observation of the respiratory pattern accompanied, when indicated, by analysis of blood pH and serum bicarbonate, determination of blood sugar, and lumbar puncture.

Because hypoglycemic coma is frequent, dangerous, and often clinically obscure, it is well in any instance of undiagnosed stupor or coma to first draw blood for glucose analysis, then give 25 gm. of glucose intravenously (see Chapter 8 for therapeutic approach to the comatose patient). The injection can do no harm and is enough to protect the brain against hypoglycemia until the results of blood sugar examination are available.

Deprivation of Oxygen, Substrate, or Metabolic Cofactors

Ischemia and Anoxia

Hypoxia of the brain almost always arises as part of a larger problem in oxygen supply, either because the ambient pressure of the gas falls or systemic abnormalities in the organism interrupt its delivery to the tissues. Disturbances in oxygen supply in most instances can be divided into *anoxic anoxia*, *anemic anoxia*, and *ischemia*, the last being due to circulatory disturbances. (Histoxic anoxia, a result of the tissue being unable to utilize available oxygen supplies, as in cyanide poisoning, is a rare clinical problem.) Though caused by different conditions and diseases, all three categories share equally the potential for depriving brain tissue of its critical oxygen supply, the main differences between the anoxic, anemic, and ischemic forms lying on the arterial side. All three forms of anoxia share the common effect of producing *cerebral venous hypoxia*, which is the best guide in vivo to estimate the partial pressure of the gas in the tissue.[391]

In *anoxic anoxia*, insufficient oxygen reaches the blood so that both the arterial oxygen content and tension are low. This situation results either from a low oxygen tension in the environment (e.g., high altitude or displacement of oxygen by an inert gas such as nitrogen) or from an inability of oxygen to reach and cross the alveolar capillary membrane (pulmonary disease, hypoventilation). With mild or moderate hypoxia the cerebral blood flow increases to maintain the cerebral oxygen delivery, and no symptoms occur. However, clinical evidence suggests that in chronic conditions the cerebral blood flow can only increase to about twice normal. When the increase is insufficient to compensate for the degree of hypoxia, the $CMRO_2$ begins to fall and symptoms of cerebral hypoxia occur.

In *anemic anoxia*, sufficient oxygen reaches the blood but the amount of hemoglobin available to bind and transport it is decreased. Under such circumstances, the blood oxygen content is decreased even though the physical tension of the gas in the arterial blood is normal. Either low hemoglobin content (anemia) or chemical changes in hemoglobin that interfere with oxygen binding (e.g., carbon monoxyhemoglobin, methemoglobin) can be responsible. Coma occurs if the oxygen content drops so low that the brain's metabolic needs are not met even by an increased cerebral blood flow. The lowered blood viscosity that occurs in anemia makes it somewhat easier for the cerebral blood flow to increase than in carbon monoxide poisoning.

In *ischemic anoxia*, the blood may or may not carry sufficient oxygen, but the cerebral blood flow is insufficient to supply cerebral tissues; the usual causes are diseases that greatly reduce the cardiac output, such as myocardial infarction, arrhythmia, shock, and vasovagal syncope, or diseases that increase the cerebral vascular resistance by arterial occlusion (e.g., stroke) or spasm (e.g., migraine).

The development of neurologic signs in most patients with ischemia or hypoxia depends more on the severity and duration of the process than on its specific cause. Ischemia (vascular failure) is generally more dangerous than hypoxia alone because potentially toxic products of cerebral metabolism such as lactic acid are not removed.

The clinical categories of hypoxic and ischemic brain damage can be subdivided into acute, chronic, and multifocal.

ACUTE DIFFUSE (OR GLOBAL) HYPOXIA OR ISCHEMIA. This circumstance occurs with conditions that rapidly reduce the oxygen content of the blood or cause a sudden reduction in the brain's overall blood flow. The major causes include: obstruction of the airways, such as occurs with drowning, choking, or suffocation; massive obstruction to the cerebral arteries, such as occurs with hanging or strangulation; and conditions causing a sudden decrease in cardiac output, such as asystole, severe arrhythmias, vasodepressor syncope, pulmonary embolism, or massive systemic hemorrhage. Embolic or thrombotic disorders, including thrombotic thrombocytopenic purpura, disseminated intravascular coagulation, acute bacterial endocarditis, falciparum malaria, and fat embolism, all cause such widespread multifocal ischemia that they can give the clinical appearance of acute diffuse cerebral ischemia. If the cerebral circulation stops completely consciousness is lost rapidly, within 6 to 8 seconds.[360] It takes a few seconds longer if blood flow continues but oxygen is no longer supplied. Fleeting lightheadedness and blindness sometimes precede unconsciousness. Generalized convulsions, pupillary dilatation, and bilateral extensor plantar responses quickly follow if anoxia is complete or lasts longer than a few seconds. If tissue oxygenation is restored immediately, consciousness returns in seconds or minutes without sequelae. If, however, the oxygen deprivation lasts longer than 1 or 2 minutes, or if it is superimposed upon preexisting cerebral vascular disease, then stupor, confusion, and signs of motor dysfunction may persist for several hours or permanently. Under clinical circumstances, total ischemic anoxia lasting longer than about 4 minutes starts to kill brain cells, with the neurons of the cerebral cortex (especially the hippocampus) and cerebellum (the Purkinje cells) dying first.[234,440] In man, severe diffuse ischemic anoxia lasting 10 minutes or more begins to destroy the brain.[439] In rare instances, particularly drowning in which cold water rapidly lowers brain temperature, recovery of brain function has been noted despite more prolonged periods of anoxia. Thus, resuscitation efforts after drowning should not be abandoned just because the patient has been immersed for more than 10 minutes.[389]

As noted above, much experimental evidence indicates that the initial mechanism of anoxia's rapidly lethal effect on the brain may to some degree lie in the inability of the heart and the cerebral vascular bed to recover from severe ischemia or oxygen

Table 14. Principal Causes of Brief Episodic Unconsciousness*

1. Syncope
2. Akinetic or absence seizures
3. Drop attacks from cerebral vascular insufficiency
4. Transient global amnesia
5. Hypoglycemia
6. Conversion reactions

*In Conditions 1 and 2, the altered consciousness is apparent to the observer. Condition 3 often is so brief that neither subject nor observer can be sure whether full consciousness was retained. In conditions 4 and 5, the patient may appear awake and "conscious" to observers, but has no exact memory of the episode and often recalls it simply as an unconscious attack.

lack. It has been reported that if one makes meticulous efforts to maintain the circulation, the brains of experimental animals can recover from as long as 30 minutes of very severe hypoxemia with arterial PO_2 tensions of 20 mm. Hg or less.[370] Equally low arterial blood oxygen tensions have been reported in conscious humans who recovered without sequelae.[155] These laboratory findings suggest that guaranteeing the integrity of the systemic circulation offers the strongest chance of effectively treating or preventing hypoxic brain damage.

Acute, short-lived hypoxic-ischemic attacks causing unconsciousness are most often the result of transient global ischemia caused by syncope (Table 14). Much less frequently, transient attacks of vertebrobasilar ischemia can cause unconsciousness. Seizures occasionally can provide problems in differential diagnosis.

Syncope or fainting results when cerebral perfusion falls below the level required to supply sufficient oxygen and substrate to maintain tissue metabolism. The critical blood flow figure in man required to maintain effective cerebral activity is about 20 ml 100 gm. min. $^{-1}$; lower flows rapidly lead to cerebral insufficiency.[40,407] Syncope has many causes, the most frequent being listed in Table 15. Among young persons, most syncope results from psychophysiologic dysfunction of autonomic reflexes pro-

Table 15. Major Causes of Syncope

I. Primarily vascular
  A. Decreased peripheral resistance
    1. Vasodepressor
      a. Psychophysiologic
      c. Reflex from visceral trauma (pain, gastric distention, postmicturition, etc.)
      c. Carotid sinus syncope, type 2 (vasodepressor)
      d. Cough syncope (impaired right heart return)
    2. Blood volume depletion
    3. Neurogenic autonomic insufficiency
II. Primarily cardiac
  A. Vagovagal attacks (transient sinus arrest)
    a. Psychophysiologic
    b. Visceral trauma (tracheal stimulation, glossopharyngeal neuralgia, swallow syncope, etc.)
    c. Carotid sinus syncope, type 1
  B. Cardiac arrhythmia or asystole
  C. Aortic stenosis
  D. Carotid origin emboli in presence of severe vascular disease of other cervical-cranial arteries

210

ducing vasodepressor hypotension. Vasodepressor responses remain the predominant cause of syncope in older persons as well, but with advancing age vasovagal attacks and other forms of heart block occur with increasing frequency. In persons over the age of 40 years, one increasingly finds the cause of syncope to lie in visceral disease stimulating excessive vagal responses, in peripheral or central nervous system disease, or in intrinsic disease of the cardiac conduction system.

Vasodepressor syncope usually but not always heralds itself with brief sensations of giddiness, weakness, and sweating before consciousness is lost. Both it and vasovagal attacks almost always occur when the victim is in the standing position and almost never when he is prone or supine.[427] Asystole, on the other hand, characteristically produces unheralded, abrupt unconsciousness in which the subject suddenly sinks or falls to the ground. The presence of brief unconsciousness and the appearance of pallor differentiates asystolic syncope from transient vertebrobasilar insufficiency.

Vertebrobasilar transient ischemic attacks produce short-lived neurologic episodes characterized by symptoms of neurologic dysfunction arising from subtentorial structures. Brief confusion or amnesic episodes sometimes occur, but stupor and coma are rare. Basilar ischemia involving the descending motor pathways in the basis pontis sometimes results in drop attacks, which may superficially resemble asystolic syncope. The absence of either unconsciousness or the physical appearance of circulatory failure differentiates the condition from true syncope. An unusual kind of sudden falling has been reported in otherwise asymptomatic, relatively young (mean age 44.5 years) women. Labeled *cryptogenic drop attacks* by Stevens and Matthews,[405] the abrupt episodes apparently come without warning, produce no associated neurologic abnormality, and recur as an isolated symptom for years without implying a serious prognosis. We have not encountered such patients.

Epileptic seizures occasionally may be difficult to distinguish from syncope as a cause of unconsciousness, especially in children and young adolescents. Tonic body movements need not necessarily indicate an epileptic disorder because brief but profound cerebral ischemia can lead to a tonic seizure. Generally speaking, fits caused by hypoxia are more brief, less intense, primarily tonic[136] and occur singly, whereas grand mal epileptic attacks usually last 3 to 5 minutes, are tonic and clonic, and tend to recur independently of body position. Fisher believes that some patients suffer from "a type of akinetic seizure" that resembles cardiac syncope.[474]

Laboratory tests sometimes help to implicate hypoxia as the cause of coma and may be necessary for diagnosis in doubtful cases. The principal difficulty in diagnosis is that the neurologic effects of a brief exposure to hypoxia can long outlast abnormalities in the blood gases or detectable residual concentrations of carbon monoxy-hemoglobin. The electrocardiograph may suggest that ischemic hypoxia was the cause of coma if the record discloses cardiac arrhythmia, complete heart block, or configurational changes consistent with acute myocardial infarction. When the cause of the hypoxia is a transient cardiac arrhythmia, the routine electrocardiogram is often normal and more prolonged monitoring of the cardiac rhythm may be required to establish the diagnosis.[424] Any electrocardiographic abnormalities accompanying syncope must be interpreted with caution, however, since subarachnoid hemorrhages, encephalitis, or even cerebral infarction can induce similar electrocardiographic abnormalities (Chapter 1).

The prognosis for cerebral recovery cannot be judged accurately immediately following removal from hypoxia. Brief syncope almost never leaves residual difficulties, although recurrent asystolic syncope in the elderly carries the threat of producing a gradually developing dementia. With longer periods of hypoxia-ischemia, the degree of recovery depends largely on the duration of the insult. Some patients recover fully even though they remain unresponsive for several days after the exposure, while others arouse promptly only to relapse and die a fortnight later (see below). Chapter 7 discusses more fully prognosis in these patients.

Pulmonary embolism is an important and little recognized cause of acute generalized cerebral anoxia. Cerebral ischemia in such instances results from the fall in cardiac output and the consequent fall in cerebral blood flow that accompanies sudden occlusion of the pulmonary arteries. Whether humoral and reflex vascular factors play an additional role is unclear.[186] The incidence of neurologic symptoms resulting from pulmonary embolus varies, but mental changes occur in approximately 60 percent of patients,[215] and in two large series syncope was the initial or a predominant clinical feature in 13 percent of patients.[27, 413] The clinical symptoms are usually those of abrupt, diffuse cerebral ischemia. The patient suddenly loses consciousness, either while exerting himself[313] or while at rest. There may be seizure activity coincident with syncope.[129] If the patient recovers consciousness by the time the physician sees him, he may be confused, tachypneic, and anxious, or the physical and neurologic examinations may be normal. However, if the embolus has been large enough to cause a profound fall in cardiac output and more prolonged unconsciousness, the typical clinical manifestations of systemic hypotension, tachypnea, and hypoxia are usually present in addition to the evidence of diffuse cerebral dysfunction. Focal neurologic signs are sometimes prominent. Fred, Willerson, and Alexander reported four patients in whom the presenting signs of pulmonary embolization were predominantly neurologic.[129] One had syncopal attacks, two developed focal neurologic signs without changes in consciousness, and the fourth was stuporous with focal neurologic signs. At autopsy every patient showed evidence of cerebral neuronal hypoxia, but none had evidence of focal infarction in the brain or of paradoxical cerebral embolization.[381] The diagnosis of pulmonary infarction should be considered in any patient who suddenly suffers a profound faint or who develops acute confusion or loses consciousness without obvious reason. Virtually all such patients complain of chest pain and dyspnea, either at rest or on exercise,[27] and most will be tachypneic when examined. Arterial blood gases are typical of intrapulmonary shunting with a decreased PaO_2 (less than 60 mm. Hg) and a decreased $PaCO_2$.[411] Blood gas determinations and radioactive lung scan are sensitive tests for screening, and if either is normal, massive pulmonary embolism is essentially excluded. Abnormal lung scans, however, accompany a variety of pulmonary diseases and are not diagnostic of pulmonary emboli; arteriography is required to establish the diagnosis. The most frequent incorrect diagnosis is acute myocardial infarction, a disease in which brief syncopal attacks are comparatively rare.

SUBACUTE OR CHRONIC DIFFUSE HYPOXIA. This occurs with severe anemia, myocardial infarction, congestive heart failure, and pulmonary disease. Extreme degrees of any of these conditions can produce stupor or coma, but the clinical picture is nonspecific. Judgment slips away early, and confusion, disorientation, and lethargy follow. More profound ischemia or hypoxia provokes periodic breathing, diffuse changes in deep tendon reflexes, and small but reactive pupils. Ultimately, progressive hypoxia precipitates multifocal myoclonus, paratonic rigidity, and, occasionally, focal neurologic signs in the form of monoplegia, hemiplegia, and tonic postural responses. Such severe neurologic changes usually ensue only after either a prolonged period of cerebral underperfusion, or when the arterial PO_2 values have fallen to the range of 20 to 30 mm. Hg. Anemia per se cannot be incriminated as a cause of delirium or coma unless the blood oxygen-carrying capacity is reduced by more than half.

Patients in stupor or coma from subacute or chronic hypoxia usually come to medical attention with the provoking cause still evident, allowing one to detect physical abnormalities or direct laboratory evidence for the suspected cause. Differential diagnosis requires attention to the following details. The cerebral blood flow never falls as the result of cardiac failure unless the cardiac output drops profoundly,[100] so that one should obtain evidence for severe degrees of congestive heart failure or cardiac arrhythmias in order to assign the cause of stupor or coma to cardiac causes alone. Similarly, in the absence of defects in cerebral blood flow, arterial blood oxygen tensions below 40 mm. Hg are required for hypoxia to produce prominent cerebral symptoms (Fig. 34).

Encephalopathy is seldom caused by a change in either the circulation or the blood oxygen-carrying capacity alone, and most often results from a combination of several causes. This may help to explain why silent myocardial infarcts so often produce metabolic encephalopathy in moderately anemic, elderly subjects with cerebral atherosclerosis, even when the reduction in cardiac output fails to precipate overt heart failure.

Multifocal cerebral ischemia or anoxia occurs in a number of conditions affecting the arterial bed or its contents. Typical of the effects is hypertensive encephalopathy, a disorder wherein malignant hypertension causes multifocal cerebral arterial vasoconstriction and dilatation leading to blood brain-barrier disruption, fibrinoid necrosis of arterioles, and diffuse parenchymal lesions, including micro infarcts and petechial hemorrhages.[57,406,466] Other ischemic insults that can result in similar dif-

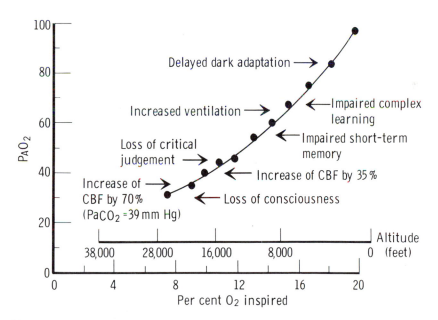

Figure 34. Behavioral responses to hypoxia. Redrawn with permission from Siesjö, B.K., et al.: "Brain dysfunction in cerebral hypoxia and ischemia." In Plum, F. (ed.) *Brain Dysfunction in Metabolic Disorders.* Res. Proc. Assoc. Res. Nerv. Ment. Dis. 53:75–112, 1974.

213

fuse or multifocal end-stage damage to the brain include: (1) increased viscosity of the blood (e.g., in polycythemia, cryoglobulinemia, macroglobulinemia, or sickle cell anemia); (2) multivascular in situ clotting (disseminated intravascular coagulation); (3) multiple small emboli arising in the heart (subacute bacterial endocarditis, non-bacterial thrombotic endocarditis) or the effects of mechanical pump oxygenators substituting for the heart (the cardiopulmonary bypass syndrome); (4) fat embolism; (5) the parasitemia of cerebral malaria; or (6) direct disease of cerebral vessels, as in disseminated lupus erythematosus, periarteritis nodosa, syphilis, or generalized arteriosclerosis. All the above abnormalities, except perhaps arteriosclerosis in which coma is uncommon, are characterized by a similar neurologic picture consisting of delirium, stupor, or coma, frequently combined with generalized or focal seizures. Local or multifocal neurologic signs are common and, often, transient or fleeting, but may last permanently. The combination of diffuse plus focal neurologic signs progressing over time differs from that of most metabolic encephalopathies and even from the other anoxic encephalopathies, which usually present more abruptly with diffuse and symmetrical neurologic pictures. The following paragraphs provide greater details on the multifocal anoxic-ischemic disorders that most frequently cause coma.

The widespread use of antihypertensive drugs has made *hypertensive encephalopathy* relatively rare during recent years.[347] Nevertheless, the importance of treating the condition promptly and correctly makes the diagnosis important.[466] Typically, the involved patients are moderately or severely hypertensive ("malignant hypertension") and have suffered a recent abrupt rise in blood pressure. Most patients with hypertensive encephalopathy have both retinal artery spasm and papilloretinal edema, and the majority have retinal exudates as well. The crises are typically transient and recurrent and can take several forms. One consists of moderate to severe headache and agitation leading into progressive confusion, delirium, stupor, or coma. Another, and perhaps the most common, includes generalized or focal convulsions combined with headache, vomiting, and multifocal neurologic weakness or cortical blindness. Typically, the neurologic signs last minutes, hours, or days, then disappear, leaving little or no residuum. The spinal fluid pressure is usually elevated to over 180 mm. and sometimes rises as high as 300 to 400 mm. of CSF. The CSF protein often ranges between 60 and 200 mg./dl.

The clinical picture of severe hypertensive encephalopathy can resemble that of uremia, brain tumor, or the recurrent transient ischemic attacks of cerebral vascular disease. Clinical judgment is important in diagnosis since laboratory tests sometimes fail to be diagnostic, particularly when uremia and hypertension coexist. Transient and recurrent attacks accompanied by severe headache, an accentuation of hypertension, and visual difficulties are likely to be hypertensive, even in patients with accompanying azotemia; clearing of the signs with reduction of blood pressure favors the diagnosis. A BUN over 100 mg./dl. favors uremia as the diagnosis, as does the presence of multifocal myoclonus and increased neuromuscular irritability. Brain tumor seldom gives the kind of multifocal, bilateral, and transient cerebral attacks that characterize hypertensive disease. The transient ischemic attacks of vascular disease of the large cervical vessels usually differ by producing more stereotyped and short-lived episodes than hypertensive attacks. However, too rapid lowering of blood pressure in patients with malignant hypertension may cause cerebral ischemia.[227] In addition, in ischemic cerebral vascular disease the blood pressure is rarely as high as with hypertensive encephalopathy, and the patients rarely have severe hypertensive eyeground changes.

Disseminated intravascular coagulation is a clinical-pathologic entity that is not bound to a single illness but can be triggered by several; McKay has called it an intermediary mechanism of disease.[255] In the disorder there is free thrombin activity within the circulation that causes platelet aggregation and fibrin formation. The disorder may be associated with bleeding, but more frequently fibrin deposits itself in arterioles, venules, and capillaries to cause widespread ischemia of the organs involved. The pathologic entities that commonly lead to disseminated intravascular coagulation are sepsis with the release of bacterial endotoxin,[28] malignancy,[63] and unknown causes often leading to spontaneous attacks (idiopathic thrombotic thrombocytopenic purpura).[9] Several authors believe that disseminated intravascular coagulation may play a symptom-producing role in entities such as fat embolism, cerebral malaria, and hypertensive encephalopathy.

McKay has described the clinical and pathologic picture.[255] The symptoms of the disorder are primarily cerebral. This is probably because other organs, not having area-specific functions, can tolerate a greater volume of multifocal ischemia without presenting clinical abnormalities. Patients may complain of headache and difficulty in concentrating as well as a variety of fleeting and minor neurologic symptoms, including vertigo, visual blurring, and speech difficulty. The major neurologic signs are those of diffuse cerebral dysfunction beginning with confusion and disorientation and leading in some instances to stupor and coma. Many of the patients who are delirious or stuporous have at the same time fleeting and changing neurologic signs, including visual field defects, generalized or focal seizures, and hemiparesis. Bleeding phenomena are common, including petechiae in the skin or optic fundi, purpura, and, occasionally, subdural or intracerebral hemorrhages. A diagnosis is usually established by examination of coagulation factors in the blood, but neurologic signs may precede identifiable coagulation abnormalities.[63] The platelet count is low and the prothrombin time elevated. Hypofibrinogenemia is usually present, and products split from fibrin can often be identified in the blood.

Cerebral malaria is a well-recognized complication of infection with *Plasmodium falciparum* and is usually the cause of death in that disease. Cerebral malaria was well recognized in World War II and in various reported series had a mortality of 5 to 48 percent, usually depending on how severe the cerebral complications were when treatment was undertaken. The disease became important again in the U.S. during the Vietnam war and still provides an occasional problem among recent foreign travelers. Cerebral malaria usually begins after the systemic disease is well under way, so that almost all involved patients will have had chills and fever for one to several days. The most common neurologic abnormality is a disturbance of consciousness ranging from acute confusion to lethargy, stupor, and, occasionally, frank coma. Focal neurologic signs were encountered in only one of Daroff's 19 cases, and that was a transient, unilateral hyperreflexia and hemisensory disturbance.[73] Other series report a higher incidence of focal neurologic signs.[121] Granted that one thinks of it, the diagnosis is not difficult, since the patients are all systemically ill with high fevers, and thick smears of the blood always contain abundant numbers of *Plasmodium falciparum*. The spinal fluid is usually under increased pressure but is otherwise normal. Occasional patients have been reported who had CSF pleocytosis, a protein increase, or both.

The pathogenesis of the cerebral ischemia is not entirely clear. Plugging of cerebral vessels by parasite-infected erythrocytes combined with endothelial proliferation has been described by several authors. In addition to the occluded vessels, there are frequently perivascular hemorrhages.[487] Maigraith[248] has suggested that anoxia from decreased oxygen-carrying capacity of the infected erythrocytes is the primary process, which then leads to endothelial proliferation and plugging of vessels. Devakul, Harinasuta, and Reid suggested that disseminated intravascular coagulation may be important, as they noted a fall in plasma fibrinogen in two patients with severe cerebral malaria.[83] Schmid believes that inflammation of vessels accompanied by increased permeability plays a major role in producing symptoms.[377] Toro and Román believe that an allergic response of the CNS to the parasite leads to a cerebral vasculopathy.[487]

Fat embolism is a common pathologic entity. Its frequency following trauma, particularly to the extremities, varies from 15 percent in clinical series[230] to 76 percent in some autopsy series.[6] The syndrome is not restricted to patients with musculoskeletal trauma, but occasionally follows burns, pancreatitis, treatment with corticosteriods, hip replacement, and even delirium tremens.[180] Fat embolism has also been described in patients with acute fatty necrosis of the liver, and in sickle cell anemia. Pathologically, small vessels, particularly those in lungs and brain, are occluded by lipid particles and at times by fibrin clots. There is some dispute as to the origin of the fat that plugs small vessels. Some authors believe that the material originates from the traumatized area, particularly bones, and finds its way to the lungs and then the systemic circulation.[369] Others believe that the emboli originate from plasma proteins and that the fibrin that plugs the vessels is probably a manifestation of disseminated intravascular coagulation.[385]

Two clinical syndromes arise from fat embolus. The first, or pulmonary syndrome, is a result of multiple pulmonary microemboli that lead to progressive hypoxia with resulting tachypnea and hypocarbia. The hypoxia can be initially corrected by oxygen, but if the emboli occlude enough alveolar capillaries, the patient eventually develops respiratory failure. The second, or cerebral syndrome, is characterized by confusion, lethargy, stupor, or coma. Characteristically, the symptoms are not present immediately following the traumatic injury. After a period of several hours to as long as 2 or 3 days the patients become lethargic and, in fulminant instances, comatose. The body temperature usually rises to 38 to 39°C, and the heart rate quickens. Most patients are tachypneic from pulmonary emboli, but even when obvious respiratory abnormalities are not present, blood gases reveal a telltale depression of PaO_2 and $PaCO_2$ which reflects pulmonary shunting. Accompanying the diffuse neurologic signs of stupor and coma can be a variety of focal signs, including focal seizures, hemiparesis, or conjugate deviation of the eyes. The diagnosis can be difficult to establish in mild to moderately severe cases. In severe or fulminating instances, a characteristic petechial rash usually develops over the neck, shoulders, and upper part of the anterior thorax on the second or third day after injury. Biopsy of the petechiae reveals lipid emboli in small vessels. Similar petechiae may be seen in the conjunctivae and eyegrounds.[11] The spinal fluid is normal. The prognosis with supportive care is good, and patients who survive an acute episode usually recover without significant neurologic residua.

Patient 4–6. A previously healthy woman, 27 years of age, was examined through the courtesy of Dr. Philip Swanson of the University of Washington, Seattle. While skiing she suffered a noncompound fracture of the left tibia and fibula. Except for pain, her condition was uncomplicated until 36 hours later when nurses recorded that she was making no verbal responses. Shortly thereafter, she received pentothal sodium and nitrous oxide-oxygen anesthesia for closed reduction of the fracture and failed to awaken postoperatively. Examination at the University Hospital recorded intact pupillary responses, and intermittent abnormal extensor posturing of the extremities, more on the left than the right. Blood gases showed a PaO_2 of 60 mm. Hg and $PaCO_2$ of 20 mm. Hg. Fat droplets were found in the urine and the CSF, and successive small numbers of petechial hemorrhages appeared in the optic fundi and the conjunctivae.[11] No episode of hypotension or cardiac arrhythmia was ever recorded.

Seven days after the onset of coma the woman lay in an eyes-open state with roving eye movements and gave no sign of psychologic awareness. Constant posturing of head and extremities was present. She perspired heavily and chewed briskly during times that the eyes were open. There was hypertonus in all four extremities with the postures as noted. The left leg remained in a cast.

The patient remained vegetative for another 48 hours, then began to talk and follow commands. Her somatic neurologic defects gradually subsided. Successive psychologic tests reflected gradual intellectual improvement. Four months following the accident the neurologic examination showed she had returned to normal. She scored 100 on the Wechsler Adult Intelligence Scale and 110 on the Memory Scale. She returned to full employment.

Cardiac surgery with its attendant use of pump-oxygenation produced at one time at least transient neurologic damage in as many as half the patients operated on.[422] Various technical improvements, including the placing of filters in the blood perfusion lines to remove intravascular micro debris, have greatly reduced the neurologic complications of the procedure. Complications still occur, but nowadays can almost always be ascribed to either inadvertent embolism from air or surgical fragments to specific problems with vascular surgery or to difficulty in maintaining intraoperative or postoperative blood pressures. When complications do occur, mortality is often high. The symptoms are similar to those of the other multifocal ischemic entities described above and include delirium, stupor, and coma, with or without focal neurologic dysfunction. In some of the patients, cutaneous petechial hemorrhages reminiscent of those occurring in fat emboli appear on the second or third day after surgery. If patients survive the acute episode without signs of severe focal neurologic damage, they usually make a fairly complete recovery. Nevertheless, Tufo, Ostfeld, and Shekelle identified signs of cerebral damage at discharge from the hospital in 15 percent of postoperative patients,[422] while Heller and associates could detect residual psychologic abnormalities in one third of such patients examined 1 year later.[171]

Delirium also frequently follows coronary artery surgery, the sydrome running the same usually benign course as postoperative delirium after other cardiac surgery. Russell and Bharucha, however, have recently reported four patients who suffered severe parietal-occipital ischemia during coronary bypass surgery,[362] presumably as a result of hypotension. Improvement was slow, but all patients regained good function.

Acute neurologic disorders including seizures and coma sometimes follow liver[403] or heart transplants.[183] The cause appears to be cerebral air embolism occurring during the operative procedure.

Endocarditis produces a high incidence of neurologic damage, whether caused by a chronic infection of the cardiac valves (subacute bacterial endocarditis) or by a noninfected valvular thrombus. The latter occasionally occurs in previously normal individuals, but more often in patients with cancer (nonbacterial or "marantic" thrombotic endocarditis). The ensuing thrombi can trigger widespread embolic ischemia and infarction of the brain. The most common clinical picture with both causes of endocarditis is of an acute focal stroke. In some instances, particularly with fulminating cases, smaller widespread emboli produce a clinical picture of a diffuse encephalopathy with or without focal signs. Jones, Siekert, and Geraci describe the neurologic manifestations of bacterial endocarditis.[200] Twenty-one of their one hundred and ten patients developed severe "toxic encephalopathy," and these symptoms were the initial or presenting manifestations of endocarditis in nine patients. An additional 44 patients had focal neurologic signs, and these were the initial manifestations of endocarditis in 17. Pruitt and associates, in a more recent report, present roughly similar figures; in their series of 218 patients, 84 had neurologic complications.[339] Accurate diagnosis of the endocarditis comes more easily when the valvular lesion is bacterial, for such patients usually have signs of underlying heart disease and are febrile and anemic with changing cardiac murmurs. The CSF may contain white cells and increased protein, fortifying one's suspicion of septic embolization. The diagnosis is more elusive in nonbacterial thrombotic endocarditis, for such patients can have a similar cerebral picture, but cardiac abnormalities are usually minimal or absent.[81] The following patient illustrates the typical combination of diffuse and focal signs that characterize this group of disorders.

Patient 4–7. A 55-year-old man developed a mass in the right buttock diagnosed as metastatic carcinoma 2 weeks prior to his admission to Memorial Hospital. Except for the mass, his physical examination was normal, as was a blood count, urinalysis, liver function tests, and blood electrolyte determinations. An enlargement of the left hilum was apparent on the chest x-ray film. The drainage from the buttock grew enterococci. In the hospital, he was treated with cyclophosphamide and radiation as well as antibiotics. The mass did not respond and produced progressively more pain, which required large doses of narcotics to control. Approximately 40 days after his admission, he became increasingly lethargic, a symptom at first attributed to narcotics. However, on the forty-third day he was noted to be stuporous with a stiff neck. His respirations were 36 per minute; the right pupil was 7 mm. and the left 4 mm., but both were reactive. The optic fundi were normal. He had a full range of roving eye movements. There was a depressed left corneal response accompanied by a left facial paresis, and a left hemiparesis and hemisensory defect. The stretch reflexes were hyperactive on the left and both plantar responses were extensor. A carotid arteriogram demonstrated occlusion of the right middle cerebral artery 2 cm. beyond the bifurcation. The remaining vessels looked normal. A hematologic search for disseminated intravascular coagulation revealed no abnormalities except for a platelet count of 16,000. He remained in coma and gradually became hypotensive and azotemic. He died 5 days after the stupor began.

At autopsy the tumor turned out to be a malignant melanoma apparently arising in the buttocks and involving the regional lymph nodes, subcutaneous tissue, and peritoneal surfaces. The aortic and mitral valves were covered with nonbacterial vegetations, and emboli were identified in intramyocardial vessels, producing myocardial necrosis, as well as in cerebral vessels, producing infarction in the distributions of the right middle cerebral artery, the right posterior cerebral artery, and the left posterior inferior cerebellar artery. There were renal infarcts bilaterally and splenic infarcts as well.

SEQUELAE OF HYPOXIA. Following apparent recovery from an acute hypoxic insult, a small number of patients relapse into a severe *delayed postanoxic encephalopathy*. Our own experience with this disorder now extends to well over 20 cases (e.g., Patient 1–1). The onset in our patients has been as early as 4 days and as late as 14 days after the initial hypoxia; reports from other authors give an even longer interval.[326] The clinical picture includes an initial hypoxic insult that usually is sufficiently severe that patients are in deep coma when first found but awaken within 24 to 48 hours. Occasionally, however, relapse has been reported after a mild hypoxic insult that was sufficient only to daze the patient and not to cause full unconsciousness. In either event, nearly all patients resume full activity within 4 or 5 days after the initial insult and then enjoy a clear and seemingly normal interval of 2 to 10 days or so. Then, abruptly, affected subjects become irritable, apathetic, and confused. Some are agitated or develop mania. Walking changes to a halting shuffle, and diffuse spasticity or rigidity appears. The deterioration may progress to coma or death or may arrest itself at any point. A few patients have a second recovery period that leads to full health.

Delayed coma after hypoxia has been reported most often after carbon monoxide or asphyxial gas poisoning, but cases are known in which hypoglycemia, cardiac arrest, strangling, or a complication of surgical anesthesia has provided the antecedent insult. Often, the neurologic changes are at first mistaken for a psychiatric disorder or even a subdural hematoma because of the lucid interval. Mental status examination

218

clarifies the first of these errors, and the diffuse distribution of the neurologic changes, the lack of headache, and the absence of signs of rostral-caudal deterioration should eliminate the second.

Pathologically, the brains of patients dying of delayed postanoxic deterioration contain diffuse, severe, and bilateral leukoencephalopathy of the cerebral hemispheres with sparing of the immediate subcortical connecting fibers and, usually, of the brainstem (Fig. 4). Demyelination is prominent and axis cylinders appear reduced in number. The basal ganglia are sometimes infarcted, but the nerve cells of the cerebral hemispheres and the brainstem remain mostly intact. The mechanism of the unusual white matter response is unknown. Recent experimental work shows that during hypoxia cerebral white matter is as much or more susceptible to biochemical damage as gray matter.[448] Glucose uptake rises sharply in the white matter[341] and lactic acid production in white matter rises more than in gray.[448] Taken together, the findings imply the presence of an increased glycolysis in the white matter in an effort to meet with local energy needs. So far, however, no good clues exist as to why the white matter degeneration should be delayed rather than immediate.

The diagnosis of coma caused by postanoxic encephalopathy is made from the history of the initial insult and by recognizing the characteristic signs and symptoms of metabolic coma. There is no specific treatment, but bed rest for patients with acute hypoxia may prevent the complication.[326]

Another sequela of severe diffuse hypoxia is the syndrome of *intention or action myoclonus.*[218] Patients suffering from this syndrome generally have had an episode of severe hypoxia caused by cardiac arrest or airway obstruction and have usually had generalized convulsions during the hypoxia episode. Affected patients usually awaken from posthypoxic coma with dysarthria, and attempted voluntary movements are marked by myoclonic jerks of trunk and limb muscles. The pathophysiologic basis of this disorder has not been established, although the salutory effect of treatment with serotonin precursors[78,426] suggests that either the structure or metabolism of some serotinergic system is disordered. Valproate has also been reported to be effective in treating the disorder.[484]

Hypoglycemia

Hypoglycemia is a common and serious cause of metabolic coma and one capable of remarkably varied combinations of signs and symptoms.[456] Among our own series of patients with severe hypoglycemic coma, most have suffered from excessive doses of insulin for the treatment of diabetes. At least two subjects had administered large doses of insulin to themselves in suicide attempts. Less frequent causes of hypoglycemic coma were insulin-secreting pancreatic adenomas, retroperitoneal sarcomas, and alcoholism or hemochromatosis with liver disease. Hypoglycemia in the latter type of patient is recognized to result from a depletion of liver glycogen stores and impaired gluconeogenesis coupled with fasting.[128] A few patients have developed symptoms of hypoglycemia when hyperalimentation therapy, having induced endogenous hyperinsulinism, was suddenly withdrawn.

Patient 4–8. A 72-year-old woman received hyperalimentation via a central venous catheter following gastrostomy to relieve gastric obstruction. Five days later, the venous line slipped out and the patient was found obtunded and confused. Neuroophthalmologic functions were normal. She could barely follow commands, had diffusely increased muscle tone with hyperactive stretch reflexes, and had a mild left hemiparesis with bilateral extensor plantar responses. The blood sugar level was 38 mg./dl. The neurologic abnormalities cleared promptly after a glucose infusion and restoration of feeding.

Pathologically, hypoglycemia directs its main damage at the cerebral hemispheres, producing laminar or pseudolaminar necrosis in fatal cases, but largely sparing the brainstem. The pathogenesis of these changes is discussed on page 198. Clinically, the picture of acute metabolic encephalopathy caused by hypoglycemia usually presents in one of four forms. (1) It may present as a delirium manifested primarily by mental changes with either quiet and sleepy confusion or wild mania. (2) The encephalopathy may present as coma accompanied by signs of multifocal brainstem dysfunction, including neurogenic hyperventilation and decerebrate spasms. In this form, pupillary light reactions, as well as oculocephalic and oculovestibular responses, are usually preserved to suggest that the underlying disorder is metabolic. The patients sometimes have shiver-like diffuse muscle activity and many are hypothermic (33 to 35°C). (3) The encephalopathy may develop as a stroke-like illness characterized by focal neurologic signs with or without accompanying coma. Montgomery and Pinner have stressed this picture of transient focal hypoglycemic encephalopathy,[273] and an example is described in Patient 4-5. The pathologic physiology of such focal signs in hypoglycemia is unknown. Meyer and Portnoy suggested on the basis of laboratory studies that in the conditions of hypoglycemia, hypoxia, and hypotension, focal paralysis results from nutritional deprivation of an area already threatened by a borderline vascular supply.[268] This may or may not be true experimentally, but in man permanent motor paralysis is uncommon and the weakness tends to shift from one side to another during different episodes of metabolic worsening. This kind of shifting deficit as well as the fact that focal neurologic signs also occur in children in coma with severe hypoglycemia stands against explaining the localized neurologic deficits as being caused by cerebral vascular disease. (4) The encephalopathy may present as an epileptic attack with single or multiple generalized convulsions and postictal coma. Many hypoglycemic patients convulse as the blood sugar level drops, and some have seizures as their only manifestation of hypoglycemia, leading to an erroneous diagnosis of epilepsy. The varying clinical picture of hypoglycemia often leads to mistaken clinical diagnoses, particularly when in a given patient the clinical picture varies from episode to episode.[384]

Neither the history nor the physical examination always distinguishes hypoglycemia from other causes of metabolic coma, although (as is true also in hepatic coma) an important clinical point is that the pupillary and oculovestibular reflex pathways are almost always spared. The great danger of delayed diagnosis is that the longer hypoglycemia lasts, the more likely it is to produce irreversible neuronal loss. This may be the reason that more diabetics treated with insulin have EEG abnormalities than those treated with diet alone.[193] Insidious and progressive dementia is by no means rare among zealously controlled diabetics who often suffer recurrent minor hypoglycemia. Prolonged and irreversible coma also can result from severe hypoglycemia, as was illustrated by the following patient.

Patient 4-9. A 58-year-old woman whom we studied several years ago had been admitted to a hospital in an unresponsive state. A history was not obtainable on admission, but the family later related that she had been nervous, depressed, and afraid of being alone. She had had an episode of unresponsiveness for which she was hospitalized several years earlier and from which she had recovered spontaneously after 2 days. The previous episode was believed, but never proved, to have been psychogenic.

Her general physical examination was essentially normal, as were her vital signs. She lay quietly in bed, unresponsive to speech but able to move all extremities when stimulated noxiously. The pupils were equal and reactive. Muscle tone and strength appeared good, and the stretch reflexes were equal and active bilaterally. The plantar responses were flexor. Urinalysis revealed a 4+ sugar reaction and a 1+ test for acetone (she was not previously known to have been diabetic). A diagnosis of diabetic coma was made, and she was given 50 units of regular insulin intravenously and 50 units subcutaneously. Ninety minutes later her urine sugar was still 4+, and 100 additional units of regular insulin were given intravenously. Forty-five minutes later she had a generalized convulsion, and 50 cc. of 50 percent dextrose were given intravenously. The seizure stopped, but she remained in deep coma with decerebrate motor responses. She had constricted but equal and reactive pupils, hyperactive deep tendon reflexes, and bilateral extensor plantar responses.

The following day she became less rigid and opened her eyes spontaneously, but otherwise paid no attention to her environment. An EEG recorded background activity of 4 cps interspersed with frequent bursts of 1 to 3 cps activity. The cerebral oxygen uptake was measured to be 1.1 cc. per 100 gm. brain per minute (normal 3.3 cc. per 100 gm. per minute).[206] Three days later she spoke but she remained confused, disoriented, lethargic, and unable to solve simple problems. Her cerebral metabolic oxygen uptake was 2.2 cc. per 100 gm. brain per minute. Two days later (five days after admission) she was more alert but still confused and disoriented. The cerebral oxygen uptake had increased to 2.6 cc. per 100 gm. brain per minute.

Ten days following admission she was oriented to person and place and could identify the correct year but not the month. She could add small numbers but was often wrong on problems of simple multiplication. She was unable to do serial 7s. She could read some words and a few sentences and was able to write simple sentences. At that time her cerebral metabolic oxygen uptake was 3.0 cc. per 100 gm. brain per minute. Her EEG contained 6 to 7 cps activity with interspersed bursts of 2 to 4 cps. Three months later, her dementia remained unchanged. The cerebral oxygen uptake was again 3.0 cc. per 100 gm. brain per minute. Her mild diabetes did not require insulin or other hypoglycemic medications.

Comment: This woman's tragedy teaches several important lessons. The first is the importance of accurate clinical and laboratory diagnosis. An initial failure to recognize correctly what was almost certainly psychogenic unresponsiveness (oculovestibular tests were not performed) led to mild diabetes being incorrectly diagnosed as acidotic coma and treated with large amounts of insulin. Although never completely proved, all the circumstances indicated that severe hypoglycemia with convulsions ensued, from which her brain never completely recovered. A second important point is that when hypoglycemia is profound or prolonged, glucose injections may not immediately restore brain function even though they raise the blood sugar level. This makes it imperative to obtain blood for glucose analysis before giving glucose to suspected hypoglycemics. Otherwise, all chance of accurate diagnosis may escape. Finally, the cerebral metabolic data from this patient illustrate that profound, chronic changes in mental function can be associated with only minimal reductions in total cerebral metabolism. After her acute illness had passed, she was left with the mentality of a 6-year-old, but her cerebral oxygen consumption returned to the lower limits of normal.

Cofactor Deficiency

Deficiency of one or more of the B vitamins is frequently the cause of delirium, dementia, and possibly stupor, but only thiamine deficiency seriously contends for a place in the differential diagnosis of coma.[431, 435]

Thiamine deficiency produces Wernicke's disease, a symptom complex caused by neuronal and vascular damage of the gray matter and blood vessels surrounding the third ventricle, aqueduct, and fourth ventricle.[431, 477] Why the lesions have such a focal distribution is not altogether understood, since, with deficiency, thiamine disappears from all brain areas at about the same rate.[91] However, a thiamine-dependent enzyme, transketolase, loses its activity in the pontine tegmentum more rapidly than in other areas,[90] and it is presumed that a focal effect such as this is related to the restricted pathologic changes. Thiamine reverses at least some of the neurologic defects in Wernicke's diseases so rapidly that physicians for years have speculated that the action of the vitamins was involved in synaptic transmission. Several years ago, Muralt inferred that the turnover of thiamine increased with nerve stimulation.[279] More recently Berl's laboratory[322] and Chan-Palay[55] have demonstrated that thiamine-deficient animals have a marked impairment of serotonergic neurotransmitter pathways in the cerebellum, diencephalon, and brainstem. The areas of diencephalic and brainstem involvement corresponded closely to the known distribution of pathologic lesions in Wernicke's diseases. Waldenline[490] has reported that thiamine affects active ion transport at nerve terminals and is necessary for regeneration and maintenance of the membrane potential.

The ultimate cause of thiamine deficiency is absence of the vitamin from the diet, and the most frequent reason is that patients have substituted alcohol for vitamin-containing foods. A danger is that the disease can be precipitated by giving vitamin-free glucose infusions to chronically malnourished subjects. As would be expected with lesions involving the diencephalic and periaqueductal structures, the patients are initially obtunded, confused, and often have a striking failure of memory. Deep stupor or coma is unusual, dangerous, and, often, a preterminal development. However, such behavioral symptoms are common to many disorders. They can be attributed to Wernicke's disease only when accompanied by nystagmus, oculomotor paralysis, and impaired oculovestibular responses and when reversed by thiamine treatment. In advanced cases, involvement of oculomotor muscles may be sufficient to produce complete external ophthalmoplegia; fixed, dilated pupils are a rarity.[249] Most patients also suffer from ataxia, dysarthria, and a mild peripheral neuropathy, in addition to eye signs. Many affected patients show a curious universal indifference to noxious stimulation and some are hypothermic.[477] Autonomic insufficiency is so common that orthostatic hypotension and shock are constant threats.[31] The hypotension of Wernicke's disease appears to result from a combination of neural lesions and depleted blood volume and is probably the most common cause of death.

Diseases of Nonendocrine Organs Other than Brain

Liver Disease

Cerebral dysfunction occurs either when liver function fails or when the liver is bypassed so that the portal circulation shunts intestinal venous drainage directly into the systemic circulation.

Morphologic changes are few in the brains of most patients with encephalopathy caused by chronic liver disease except for an increase in large, Alzheimer type II astrocytes.[2,472] A very few patients with chronic liver disease in addition to having episodic hepatic coma also suffer from a progressive mental, cerebellar, and extrapyramidal deterioration; when examined postmortem the brains of such individuals contain zones of pseudolaminar necrosis in the cerebral and cerebellar cortex, small cavitations, nerve cell loss in the basal ganglia and cerebellum, and glycogen-staining inclusions in the enlarged astrocytes.[430]

Several authors describe the gross appearance of swollen brains attributed to "cerebral edema" in patients dying of fulminant hepatic failure either acutely or superimposed on subacute liver disease.[137,436] A small percentage of such brains have shown evidence of transtentorial or cerebellar tonsilar herniation. Most, but not all, of the patients have received artificial respiration for periods lasting for hours or days until death and none of the reports include descriptions of the brain by experienced neuropathologists. Since any number of preterminal events including vascular congestion can cause the dead brain to look swollen, these findings are difficult to evaluate, especially since they correlate poorly with clinical events. Up until the preterminal stage of hepatic encephalopathy when severe brainstem dysfunction occurs, the clinical signs are characteristic of metabolic coma (see below) and not reminiscent of evolving transtentorial herniation or other intracranial pressure shifts. Furthermore, most nonsurgically induced experimental hepatic failure produces only modest changes in the water content of the brain.[158,165] Whether true cerebral edema occurs in hepatic encephalopathy needs to be confirmed; if present, it must be established whether it contributes to the clinical disorder or emerges only as a terminal complication.

Many possible toxic agents or deficiencies have been suggested as potential causes for hepatic coma, but none successfully explains all instances of the condition.[97] An elevated blood and brain ammonia level, which results from the products of intestinal digestion bypassing the urea-synthesizing mechanisms of the liver, has most often been incriminated as the agent at fault.[324] Ammonia, in high concentrations, can be directly toxic to brain, potentially interfering with the chloride pump[266] and possibly replacing intracellular potassium to affect Na-K-ATPase activity.[397] In addition, ammonia in high concentrations interferes with the energy metabolism of brain cells in a manner similar to that of severe hypoxia.[176] Evidence for a direct neurotoxicity in man comes from children with congenital hyperammonemia caused by inherited diseases of the urea cycle. Such youngsters, who lack other metabolic toxins, develop severe cerebral degeneration producing stupor and coma in association with abruptly elevated blood ammonia levels.[46]

Ammonia is constantly produced in brain by deamination, and its concentration in that organ is always higher than in blood. Normally, the brain contains powerful mechanisms for detoxifying ammonia by doubly combining it first with α-keto-glutarate to make glutamate and in turn with glutamate itself to generate the nontoxic substance, glutamine. This last step requires the enzyme glutamine synthetase, which resides in the astrocytes.[298] Ammonia in blood rapidly enters brain in amounts proportional to the arterial blood concentration and the blood flow.[240] Essentially all this ammonia from the blood normally is converted almost instantly into glutamine.[64] Presumably this occurs in the astrocyte, since in experimental animals with portocaval shunts, chronic hyperammonemia induces astrocytosis with a proportional increase in glutamine synthetase.[53,252] Such hyperammonemic animals are neurologically abnormally sensitive to additional ammonia loads, at least partially because modest elevations of blood ammonia produce proportionately greater rises in brain ammonia than in normals, thereby quickly reaching toxic levels.[99]

Several additional neurotoxic mechanisms have been identified in animals with chronic hyperammonemia induced by portacaval shunting. These include an increased permeability of the blood brain barrier to large molecules;[222] an impaired uptake into brain of the short chain monocarboxylic fatty acids, acetate, butyrate, and pyruvate, as well as of glucose;[374] and enhancement of transport from blood to brain of the serotonin-precursor tryptophan, as well as other members of the large neutral amino acid group.[195] This last abnormality bears on the theory that hepatic encephalopathy may be due at least in part to abnormal neurotransmitter mechanisms.

According to Fischer, the neurotransmitter norepinephrine is decreased in the brains of experimental animals with hepatic coma, while serotonin is moderately increased.[116,117] Octopamine, a presumed "false" or competitive transmitter-like amine, is increased. The plasma of patients with hepatic encephalopathy has been found to contain increased concentrations of the amino acids tyrosine, glutamate, aspartate, and methionine. Tyrosine in particular is believed to contribute to an increased synthesis of octopamine in acute hepatic coma. The theory of transmitter abnormality gathers strength from the observation that treatment aimed at normalizing the plasma amino acid pattern appears to result in transient improvement of encephalopathy. Against the theory is the observation that in animals elevated octopamine levels in the brain are not necessarily associated with neurologic abnormalities, nor have injections of octopamine in very high concentrations into the lateral ventricles succeeded in producing any neurologic changes more severe than transient immobility. [116,117]

The immediate pathogenesis of hepatic coma depends on the underlying cause. Many patients with severe liver disease develop encephalopathy as an inexorable step in progressive hepatic failure, and no sudden load or stress need be imposed. Patients with portal-systemic shunts, however, can have almost normal baseline parenchymal liver function as judged by standard laboratory tests, yet develop hepatic encephalopathy when increased loads of nitrogenous substances are suddenly presented to their circulations, such as with gastrointestinal bleeding, infections, or high protein diets. These latter factors also can precipitate hepatic coma in patients with liver disease, as can the ingestion of sedative drugs (mechanism unknown) or acetazolamide, which increases the ammonia concentration in renal effluent blood, increases the brain CO_2 tension,[335] and impedes brain oxygenation by impeding oxyhemoglobin dissociation. [223]

The clinical picture of hepatic encephalopathy is fairly consistent, but its onset often is difficult to define exactly. The incipient mental symptoms usually consist of a quiet, apathetic delirium, which either persists for several days or rapidly evolves into profound coma. Less often, in perhaps 10 to 20 percent of the cases, the earliest symptoms are of a boisterous delirium verging on mania, an onset suggesting rapidly progressive liver disease such as acute yellow atrophy. Neither type of delirium is specific, as was illustrated by one of our patients with chronic cirrhosis who suffered two episodes of hepatic coma spaced 2 weeks apart. The first began with an agitated delirium; the second, with quiet obtundation. It was impossible to distinguish between the two attacks by biochemical changes or rate of evolution. Respiratory changes are a hallmark of severe liver disease. Hyperventilation, as judged by low arterial PCO_2 levels, occurs at all depths of coma and usually becomes clinically obvious as patients become deeply comatose. This almost invariable hyperventilation is well confirmed by our own series of 83 patients: all had serum alkalosis and all but three had low PCO_2 values. These three exceptions had concomitant metabolic alkalosis, correction of which was followed by hyperventilation and respiratory alkalosis. Although some authors have reported instances of metabolic acidosis, particularly in terminal patients, the implication is that encephalopathy unaccompanied by either respiratory or metabolic alkalosis is not hepatic in origin.

Moderately obtunded patients with hepatic encephalopathy sometimes have nystagmus on lateral gaze. Tonic conjugate downward or downward and lateral ocular deviation has marked the onset of coma in several of our patients, and we have once observed reversible, vertical skew deviation during an episode of hepatic coma. Caplan and Scheiner report a single patient with hepatic encephalopathy showing a 2-day period of dysconjugate eye movements. [469] Ocular bobbing also has been described in hepatic coma. [483] Peripheral oculomotor paralyses are rare in hepatic coma unless patients have concomitant Wernicke's disease, and, in fact, easily elicited brisk and conjugate oculocephalic and oculovestibular responses are generally a striking finding in unresponsive patients. The pupils are usually small but react to light. Asterixis is characteristic and frequently involves the muscles of the feet, tongue, and jaw, as well as the hands. Patients with mild to moderate encephalopathy are usually found to have bilateral gegenhalten. Decorticate and decerebrate postural responses, muscle spasticity, and bilateral extensor plantar responses frequently accompany deeper coma. Focal neurologic signs can appear in patients with deep coma and indeed were encountered in five of our unconscious patients. Four of these had hemiparesis, and in two the focal weakness shifted from side to side during the illness. The incidence of convulsions in hepatic coma varies in different series. Only one of our patients convulsed, but Adams and Foley[2] reported seizures in a third of their subjects. The higher incidence in the Boston series may have been related to alcohol withdrawal in those patients. Signs of severe brainstem dysfunction are rare until terminal stages. Loss of pupillary responses, oculovestibular responses, or of spontaneous breathing are late and usually fatal signs.

Hepatic coma is rarely a difficult diagnosis to make in patients who suffer from severe chronic liver disease and who gradually lose consciousness, displaying the obvious stigmata of jaundice, spider angiomata, fetor hepaticus, and enlarged livers and spleens. The diagnosis can be more difficult in patients whose coma is precipitated by an exogenous factor and who have either mild unsuspected liver disease or portal-systemic shunts. In this situation hepatic coma can be suspected by finding clinical evidence of metabolic encephalopathy combined with respiratory alkalosis and brisk oculocephalic reflexes. The diagnosis is strengthened by identifying a portal-systemic shunt, plus an elevated serum ammonia level. The blood sugar should be measured in patients with severe liver disease since diminished liver glycogen stores may induce hypoglycemia and complicate hepatic coma. When diagnosis remains doubtful, analysis of spinal fluid can be helpful. Duffy and Plum found in patients with liver disease that markedly elevated levels of either glutamine or α-ketoglutaramate (αKGM) in the CSF occurred only with encephalopathy.[97] Of the two, αKGM levels gave almost no false positives as well as the strongest discrimination between patients with and without brain involvement (Fig. 35). The spinal fluid in hepatic encephalopathy is usually clear, free of cells, and has a normal protein content. It is rare to detect bilirubin in the CSF unless patients have serum bilirubin levels of at least 4 to 6 mg./dl. and chronic parenchymal liver failure as well. The EEG undergoes progressive slowing in hepatic coma, with slow activity beginning symmetrically in the frontal leads and spreading posteriorly as unconsciousness deepens. The changes are characteristic but not specific; they thus help in identifying a diffuse abnormality but do not necessarily diagnose hepatic failure.

In differential diagnosis, mild hepatic encephalopathy is sometimes confused with psychiatric disturbances or acute alcoholism. Comatose patients in whom hepatic coma has rapidly developed often have motor signs (but not neuroophthalmologic changes) that may suggest structural disease of the brainstem, and they are sometimes mistakenly believed to have subdural hematoma or basilar artery thrombosis. In anything short of preterminal hepatic coma, however, pupillary and caloric responses are normal or inconsistent with a fixed lesion, there is hyperventilation, and signs of rostral-caudal deterioration are absent, all of which rule out subdural hematoma. Subtentorial structural disease is ruled out by the normal pupillary and caloric responses as well as the fluctuating and inconstant quality of motor signs.

Renal Disease

Renal failure leads directly to one metabolic encephalopathy, that of uremia. The treatment of uremia, in turn, potentially causes two additional disorders of cerebral function, the dialysis dysequilibrium syndrome and progressive dialysis en-

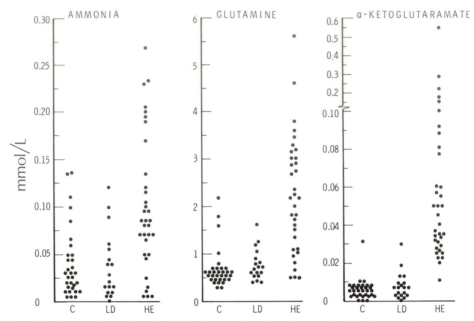

Figure 35. Comparative values in CSF of ammonia, glutamine, and α-ketoglutaramate in controls, patients with neurologically uncomplicated liver disease (LD), and patients with moderate to severe hepatic encephalopathy (HE). Controls included a variety of sick hospital patients, none of whom had detectable liver involvement. Upper limits of normal for this laboratory are ammonia 0.05 mmol./liter, glutamine 0.7 mmol./liter, and αKGM 0.01 mmol./liter.

cephalopathy. Confusion, delirium, stupor, and sometimes coma can occur with each of these conditions.

UREMIC ENCEPHALOPATHY. Before the presently widespread use of hemo- or peritoneal dialysis, the uremic syndrome was common in North America and western Europe. Nowadays, the early correction of biochemical abnormalities in patients with known acute or chronic renal disease often prevents the development of cerebral symptoms. As a result, one more often encounters uremic encephalopathy as a problem of differential diagnosis in patients with a systemic disease such as a collagen vascular disorder, malignant hypertension, the ingestion of a toxin, bacteremia, or disseminated anoxia-ischemia. Most of these primary disorders themselves produce abnormalities of brain function, adding to the complexities of diagnosis.

Despite extensive investigations, the precise cause of the brain dysfunction in uremia eludes identification. However, certain notable associations exist. Once azotemia develops, the uremic syndrome correlates only in a general way with biochemical changes in the blood. As with other metabolic encephalopathies, the more rapid the development of the toxic state, the less perturbed need be the systemic chemical equilibrium. The associated level of the BUN accompanying uremic encephalopathy can vary widely. Urea itself cannot be the toxin, since urea infusions do not reproduce uremic symptoms and hemodialysis reverses the syndrome even when urea is added to the dialyzing bath so as not to lower the blood level.[262] Most other serum biochemical or electrolyte abnormalities correlate no better with the

226

neurologic state. Serum sodium or potassium levels can be abnormally low or high in uremia, depending on its duration and treatment, but symptoms associated with these electrolyte changes are distinct from the typical panorama of uremic encephalopathy. Systemic acidosis is not the cause: the systemic acidosis does not involve the central nervous system,[337] and treatment of the reduced blood pH has no effect on uremic cerebral symptoms.

Morphologically, the brains of patients dying of uremia show no consistent abnormality. Uremia uncomplicated by hypertensive encephalopathy does not produce cerebral edema.[306] The cerebral oxygen consumption declines in uremic stupor, just as it does in most other metabolic encephalopathies, although perhaps not as much as might be expected from the degree of impaired alertness.[376] Levels of cerebral high energy phosphates remain high during experimental uremia, while rates of glycolysis and energy utilization are reduced below normal. Uremic brains show a decrease in sodium and potassium flux along with depressed sodium-stimulated, potassium-dependent ATPase activity.[350] All the above changes appear to be effects rather than causes of the disorder.

Results from several experimental studies suggest potential causes for uremic brain dysfunction, and the evidence for several is strong enough to suggest that more than one factor is involved. Fishman and Raskin several years ago found in uremia a generalized increased permeability of cell membranes, including those of the blood-brain barrier.[118] They suggest that such increased permeability could allow access to the brain of normally excluded, potentially neurotoxic compounds, such as circulating organic acids, which rise in the blood during uremia.[350] Since hemodialysis rapidly clears the uremic syndrome, a neurotoxic dialyzable molecule of small or moderate size is presumably at fault, but the precise offender so far has escaped a good deal of searching.

Several laboratories have found an elevated brain calcium content in uremia, apparently as an effect of increased parathyroid activity.[18,149] Furthermore, artificially raising the calcium content of the brain with parathyroid hormone produces uremic-like EEG abnormalities in animals, while lowering the brain calcium of uremic animals by parathyroidectomy returns the EEG towards normal.[21] The relation of calcium change to the clinical encephalopathy is still unclear, although calcium participates in several major neurochemical steps, including neurotransmitter release. It may be pertinent to the central effects that parathormone-related increases in calcium also occur in the peripheral nerves during experimental uremia. The result is a slowed nerve conduction velocity that can be simulated in control animals by giving parathormone and prevented in uremic animals by prior parathyroidectomy.[149] In human uremics, circulating parathormone levels have been reported to correlate inversely with nerve conduction velocities: the higher the level, the lower the velocity. It is more difficult to obtain comparable correlations with central symptoms of uremia since most such subjects now undergo dialysis before cerebral symptoms develop. However, Avram and associates now report that uremic patients with elevated parathormone levels have slower EEG frequencies and lower congnitive scores than do those with normal parathormone levels.[467]

The clinical picture of uremic encephalopathy is nonspecific in most instances, although the characteristic combination of dulled consciousess, hyperpnea, and motor hyperactivity should immediately give high suspicion to the diagnosis. Like many other metabolic encephalopathies, uremia, particularly when it develops rapidly, can produce a florid delirium marked by noisy agitation, delusions, and hallucinations. More often, however, progressive apathetic, dull, quiet confusion with inappropriate behavior blends slowly into stupor or coma accompanied by characteristic respiratory changes, focal neurologic signs, tremor, asterixis, muscle paratonia, and convulsions. Untreated patients with uremic encephalopathy all have serum acidosis. Pupillary and oculomotor functions are seldom disturbed in uremia, certainly not in any diagnostic way. On the other hand, motor changes are rarely absent. Patients with chronic renal disease are weak and unsteady in their movements. As uremia evolves many of them develop diffuse tremulousness, intense asterixis and, often, so much multifocal myoclonus that the muscles can appear to fasciculate. Action myoclonus (see p. 219) has also been reported.[470] Tetany is frequent. Stretch reflex asymmetries are common, as are focal neurologic weaknesses: 10 of our 45 patients with uremia had a hemiparesis that cleared rapidly after hemodialysis or shifted from side to side during the course of the illness. Convulsions are distressingly common; either focal or generalized, they occurred in 15 of our patients and in 5 of the 13 reported by Locke, Merrill, and Tyler.[238] In our patients at least, little evidence indicated that water intoxication caused the fits, and several examples occurred in patients who were free of serious hypertension.

Laboratory determinations tell one only that patients have uremia, but do not delineate this as the cause of coma. Renal failure is accompanied by complex biochemical, osmotic, and vascular abnormalities, and the degree of azotemia varies widely in patients with equally serious symptoms. One of our patients, a child with nephritis, had severe delirium proceeding to stupor despite a BUN of only 48 mg./dl. Other patients were free of cerebral symptoms with BUN values over 200 mg./dl. Uremia also causes aseptic meningitis, accompanied by stiff neck with as many as 250 lymphocytes and polymorphonuclear leukocytes per cu. mm. in the cerebrospinal fluid. The spinal fluid protein often rises as high as 100 mg./dl. and the CSF pressure can be abnormally elevated to over 160 to 180 mm. in some patients.[350] EEG slowing correlates with increasing degrees of azotemia, but many patients with slow records have little or no accompanying mental changes.[163] The electrophysiologic changes are nonspecific and of no help in diagnosis.

In differential diagnosis, uremia must be distinguished from other causes of acute metabolic acidosis, from acute water intoxication, and from hypertensive encephalopathy. Pencillin intoxication can be a diagnostic problem since it produces delirium, asterixis, and myoclonus and ordinarily requires renal failure for its appearance.[485]

Distinction from other causes of metabolic acidosis is straightforward if a laboratory is available. Among the severe acidoses causing the triad of clouded consciousness, hyperpnea, and a low serum bicarbonate (uremia, diabetes, lactic acidosis, ingestion of exogenous poisons), only uremia is likely to cause multifocal myoclonus, tetany, and generalized convulsions, and the others do not cause azotemia during their early stages.

Water intoxication is common in uremia and can be difficult to diagnose or rule out as a cause of symptoms. Patients with azotemia are nearly always thirsty, and they have multiple electrolyte abnormalities. Excessive water ingestion, inappropriate fluid therapy, and hemodialysis all potentially reduce the serum osmolality in uremia and thereby risk inducing or accentuating delirium and convulsions. The presence of water intoxication is confirmed by measuring a low serum osmolality (less than 260 mOsm. per L.), but the disorder can be suspected when the serum sodium concentration falls below 120 mEq. per L. (p. 251).

The greatest problem in clinical differential diagnosis is to separate the symptoms of uremia from those of hypertensive encephalopathy, since both azotemia and advanced hypertension often plague the same patient. Each condition can cause seizures, focal neurologic signs, increased intracranial pressure, and delirium or stupor. The following points may help to differentiate: Uremia seldom fluctuates so rapidly or causes such fleeting neurologic signs as does hypertensive encephalopathy, and uremia rarely causes papilledema, arterial spasm in the optic fundi, cortical blindness, aphasia, or a substantial increase in the spinal fluid protein content, whereas hypertensive encephalopathy produces all of these. Finally, despite occasional exceptions, uremia *usually* is associated with a very high BUN and hypertensive encephalopathy *usually* is associated with either a sustained very high blood pressure (diastolic pressure of 120 mm. Hg or greater) or a recently elevated blood pressure.

The treatment of uremia by hemodialysis sometimes adds to the neurologic complexity of the syndrome. Neurologic recovery does not always immediately follow effective dialysis, and patients often continue temporarily in coma or stupor. One of our own patients remained comatose for 5 days after his blood nitrogen and electrolytes returned to normal. Such a delayed recovery did not imply permanent brain damage, for this man, like others with similar but less protracted delays, now enjoys normal neurologic function on chronic hemodialysis.

DIALYSIS DYSEQUILIBRIUM SYNDROME. Perhaps as many as half of all patients develop uncomfortable neurologic symptoms during correction of their uremic abnormalities by hemodialysis. A small fraction, perhaps 5 percent, undergo more alarming changes, including asterixis, myoclonus, delirium, convulsions, stupor, or coma.[334] The severe disorder arises more commonly during hemo- than peritoneal dialysis, during rapid changes in blood solutes, and in children more than adults. The associated obtundation and delirium can last several days.

All agree on the general mechanism of the dialysis dysequilibrium syndrome, although not on the details. The blood-brain barrier is only slowly permeable to urea as well as to a number of other biologic molecules, including electrolytes and idiogenic osmols that form in brain during serum hyperosmolality.[239,350] The brain and blood are in osmotic equilibrium in steady states such as uremia; electrolytes and other osmols are adjusted so that brain concentrations of many biologically active substances (e.g., H^+, Na^+, K^+) remain more normal than those in blood. A rapid lowering of the blood urea by hemodialysis is not paralleled by equally rapid reductions in brain osmols. As a result, during dialysis the brain becomes hyperosmolar relative to blood and probably loses sodium, the result being that water shifts from plasma to brain, potentially resulting in water intoxication. Concurrently, rapid correction of blood acidosis can induce brain tissue acidosis because of the slow movement of bicarbonate into the brain.[15,336] Symptoms of water intoxication can be prevented by slower dialysis and by adding agents such as fructose to maintain blood osmolality. Port and Goldsmith believe that cerebral sodium loss is an important factor in pathogenesis, since in their hands a high dialysate sodium concentration prevents the syndrome.[334]

OTHER PROBLEMS FOLLOWING DIALYSIS. Two other considerably less frequent complications can occasionally produce severe brain dysfunction following dialysis. Several cases of acute or chronic subdural hematoma have been observed in dialyzed patients receiving anticoagulants. Wernicke's encephalopathy with its attendant confusional state (p. 221) has developed in patients receiving chronic dialysis who were not being given vitamin supplements.

PROGRESSIVE DIALYSIS ENCEPHALOPATHY (DEMENTIA DIALYTICA). Techniques allowing repeated hemodialysis for patients with renal failure became widely available during the 1960s. First in 1972 and often since, a distinctive progressive encephalopathy has been reported in a fraction of these individuals,[5] most of whom had been chronically dialyzed for periods of 3 to 7 years before neurologic changes began. Starting with a stammering, partially aphasic hesitancy of speech, the progressive dialysis encephalopathy progresses to include delusional thinking, dementia, seizures, myoclonus, asterixis, and, occasionally, focal neurologic abnormalities. Repeated postdialysis somnolence is fairly frequent, stupor or coma, rare. The EEG is abnormal with, initially, characteristic bursts of high voltage slowing in the frontal leads arising from normal background frequencies. Later, with more advanced neurologic deterioration, tracings become diffusely slowed. The clinical disorder at first emerges or is accentuated during or immediately after dialysis; later the changes become unremitting. The brain at autopsy contains no distinctive abnormalities.

Alfrey first suggested that aluminum intoxication causes progressive dialysis dementia.[5] Although some authorities disagree,[465] several observations support Alfrey's suggestion. Patients with renal failure ingest aluminum hydroxide gels to bind intestinal phosphate, and this mechanism was initially incriminated as the source for the high aluminum levels found in blood and brain of affected subjects. Another and perhaps more important source is the municipal water supplies that can contain substantial amounts of aluminum, which enters the patient via the dialysate. Epidemiologic studies have linked the appearance of the syndrome to water heavily contaminated with aluminum.[122] At least one report describes remission of progressive dialysis encephalopathy when aluminum was removed from the diet and the dialysate.[333] Considerations that somewhat weaken the aluminum hypothesis in this disorder are that brain aluminum is elevated to an almost similar degree in many dialyzed patients who never develop dementia. Aluminum intoxication under other circumstances is rare in man. In experimental animals, aluminum produces seizures[213] when injected into cerebral cortex and neurofibrillary degenerations of adjacent nerve cells when injected into the subarachnoid space.[209] Some authors have implicated a neurotoxicity for aluminum in the genesis of neurofibrillary degeneration in the brain with Alzheimer's disease.[69]

Pulmonary Disease

Hypoventilation owing to advanced lung failure or to neurologic causes can lead to a severe encephalopathy or coma. The mechanistic basis for the neurologic changes has not been fully explained and in most instances the encephalopathy probably depends on a variable interaction of hypoxemia, hypercapnia, congestive heart failure, systemic infection, and the fatigue of prolonged, ineffective respiratory efforts. Airway obstruction sometimes awakens these subjects at night (sleep apnea), adding to their daytime lethargy. However, unless some complication such as respiratory arrest occurs, leading to prolonged hypoxia, permanent changes in the brain are lacking and the encephalopathy is fully reversible. Serum acidosis per se is probably not an important factor since alkali infusions unaccompanied by ventilatory therapy fail to improve the neurologic status of these patients. Also, although hypoxia may potentiate the illness, it is unlikely that it is the sole cause of the cerebral symptoms, since patients with congestive heart failure commonly tolerate equal degrees of hypoxemia with no encephalopathy. Sieker and Hickam pointed out that of all the variables, the degree of carbon dioxide retention correlates most closely with the neurologic symptoms.[390] The development of cerebral symptoms also depends in part on the duration of the condition. For example, some subjects with chronic hypercarbia have no cerebral symptoms despite $PaCO_2$ levels of 55 to 60 mm. Hg, whereas

230

others become stuporous in the face of a recent rise in $PaCO_2$ to the same level. A factor explaining these discrepancies may be the existence of better brain buffering in states of chronic CO_2 retention as opposed to acute retention. Posner, Swanson, and Plum found in patients with pulmonary insufficiency a good correlation between the intensity of neurologic symptoms and the severity of carbon dioxide-induced acidosis in the spinal fluid.[337] Their findings suggest that whether or not a neurologic defect accompanies CO_2 retention depends at least partly on the degree of concomitant intracellular acidosis in the brain.

In experimental animals, hypercapnia of mild to moderate degree includes first reduced, then increased excitability of the brain, as judged by the threshold to an electric shock stimulus.[391] Extreme hypercapnia is anesthetic to man or animals. The neurochemical changes accompanying these states are modest and a bit difficult to interpret. Cerebral metabolic rate for oxygen either does not change or increases only moderately during hypercapnia,[62,205,269] but cerebral glucose consumption declines as much as 40 to 50 percent.[82,269] The degradation of endogenous amino acids and other tissue intermediates increases to a degree sufficient to explain the continued high oxygen consumption. Ammonia in the tissue rises, reflecting the increased catabolism of amino acids. These brain tissue changes during hypercapnia resemble those found during hypoglycemia or barbiturate anesthesia. In none of these three conditions, however, do the chemical alterations clarify precisely why the physiologic abnormalities take place.

The clinical picture of pulmonary encephalopathy is similar regardless of the cause of the respiratory decompensation. Among 52 patients with CO_2 narcosis in our own series, 29 had emphysema, 3 had hypoventilation associated with obesity, and 20 had hypoventilation secondary to neuromuscular disease or depression of brainstem respiratory mechanisms. Symptoms include dull, diffuse headache accompanied by slowly developing drowsiness, stupor, or coma. The mental changes usually begin insidiously as pulmonary function fails, but coma can occasionally come on abruptly if infection or sedative drugs precipitate rapid pulmonary decompensation. All patients with respiratory failure hypoventilate as determined by elevated blood PCO_2 levels, and most of them are cyanotic as well. Those with obstructive emphysema usually wheeze, gasp, and puff with obviously increased efforts, but those with hypoventilation owing to obesity or diseases of the nervous system breathe quietly, shallowly, and often irregularly in a pattern that may escape cursory examination. The pupils are small and briskly reactive to light unless hypoxia is profound, in which case fixed dilatation follows. The ocular movements are usually normal. A striking phenomenon found in perhaps 10 percent of patients with severe pulmonary insufficiency is distended ophthalmic veins and papilledema, reflecting increased intracranial pressure associated with the chronic hypercarbia and hypoxia. Signs of motor dysfunction tend to be less prominent in pulmonary encephalopathy than in other metabolic comas. Seizures are comparatively rare. Asterixis and multifocal myoclonus, on the other hand, are almost the rule, and sometimes the myoclonus is so prominent that the subject grossly quivers and shakes. Friedreich described paramyoclonus multiplex in a subject with chronic pulmonary disease, and this may have been the earliest, unknowning description of these metabolic neuromuscular changes.[132] The muscles show moderately increased tone, but the stretch reflexes are more often depressed than hyperactive. The plantar responses are usually extensor.

The diagnosis of hypoxic-hypercarbic encephalopathy is not difficult when patients have obvious pulmonary or cardiopulmonary failure and go on gradually to develop obtundation, tremor, and twitching. A greater diagnostic problem occurs when pa-

231

tients with previously compensated, but marginal, pulmonary function suddenly become hypoxic and hypercapnic because of an infection or excess sedation. Such patients may be erroneously suspected of having sedative poisoning or other causes of coma, but as in the following example, blood gas measurements make the diagnosis.

Patient 4–10. A 60-year-old woman with severe chronic pulmonary disease went to a physician complaining of nervousness and insomnia. An examination disclosed no change in her pulmonary function, and she was given 100 mg. of pentobarbital to help her sleep. Her daughter found her unconscious the following morning and brought her to the hospital. She was comatose but withdrew appropriately from noxious stimuli. She was cyanotic, and her respirations were labored at 40 per minute. Her pupils were 3 mm. in diameter and reacted to light. There was a full range of extraocular movements on passive head turning. No evidence of asterixis or multifocal myoclonus was encountered, and her extremities were flaccid with slightly depressed tendon reflexes and bilateral extensor plantar responses. The arterial blood pH was 7.17; the $PaCO_2$ was 70 mm. Hg; the serum bicarbonate was 25 mEq. per L.; and the PaO_2 was 40 mm. Hg. She was intubated and received artificial ventilation with a respirator for several days before she awakened and was able by her own efforts to maintain her arterial $PaCO_2$ at its normal level of 45 mm. Hg.

Comment: This is not an unusual history. It is likely that the increased nervousness and insomnia were symptoms of increasing respiratory difficulty. The sedative hastened the impending decompensation and induced severe respiratory insufficiency as sleep stilled voluntary respiratory efforts. The rapidity with which she raised her $PaCO_2$ from normal to a level of 70 mm. Hg is indicated by her normal serum bicarbonate, there having been no time for the development of the renal compensation that usually accompanies respiratory acidosis.

Austen, Carmichael, and Adams[20] emphasized that when CO_2 accumulates slowly, the complaints of insidiously appearing headache, somnolence, and confusion may occasionally attract more attention than the more direct signs of respiratory failure. If the patient also has increased intracranial pressure, papilledema, and bilateral extensor plantar responses, it is easy to see how the physician can at first reach the diagnosis of brain tumor or some other equally inappropriate conclusion. The important differential features are that in CO_2 retention focal signs are rare, blood gases are *always* abnormal, and the encephalopathy usually improves promptly if artificial ventilation is effectively administered. (After severe and protracted narcosis, occasional patients can remain stuporous for several days after the blood gases are returned to normal, yet still recover. However, this sequence is rare.)

Two associated conditions are closely related to CO_2 narcosis and often accentuate its neurologic effects. One is hypoxemia and the other is metabolic alkalosis, which often emerges as the result of treatment. Hypoxia accompanying CO_2 retention must be treated, because oxygen lack is immediately dangerous both to heart and brain. But administering inhaled oxygen often depresses the breathing of patients with severe CO_2 retention, making carbon dioxide levels climb even higher. In such patients it can be concluded that the previous hypoxemia stimulated respiration considerably through carotid body and aortic chemoreceptors. Removal of the stimulus by oxygen therapy eliminates these drives, reduces ventilation, and intensifies hypercapnia. This potential sequence has made some physicians reluctant to give oxygen to patients with severe pulmonary disease. An effective solution is to give low concentrations of oxygen (25 percent) in air while observing the patient closely. If respiration declines and CO_2 retention occurs even with this minimal increase in oxygen tensions, oxygen therapy should be combined with artificial ventilation.

Renal bicarbonate excretion is a relatively slow process. As a result, correction of CO_2 narcosis by artificial respiration sometimes induces severe metabolic alkalosis if the carbon dioxide tension is returned quickly to normal in the face of a high serum bicarbonate level. Although metabolic alkalosis is usually asymptomatic, Rotheram, Safar, and Robin[361] reported five patients with pulmonary emphysema treated vigorously by artificial ventilation in whom metabolic alkalosis was associated with serious neurologic symptoms. These patients, after initially recovering from CO_2 narcosis, developed severe alkalosis with arterial blood pH values above 7.55 to 7.60 and again became obtunded. They developed multifocal myoclonus, had severe convulsions, and three died. Two patients regained consciousness after blood CO_2 levels were raised again by deliberately reducing the level of ventilation. We have observed a similar sequence of events in deeply comatose patients treated vigorously with artificial ventilation, but have found it difficult to conclude that alkalosis and not hypoxia was at fault. What seems likely is that too sudden hypocapnia induces cerebral vasoconstriction, which more than counterbalances the beneficial effects to the brain of raising the blood oxygen tension. Rotheram and his colleagues believe that the PCO_2 should be lowered gradually during treatment of respiratory acidosis to allow renal compensation to take place and prevent severe metabolic alkalosis. This is a reasonable approach so long as hypoxemia is prevented.

Pancreatic Encephalopathy

Failure of either the exocrine or endocrine pancreas can cause stupor or coma. Failure of the endocrine pancreas (diabetes) is discussed on page 234. Failure of the exocrine pancreas causes encephalopathy acutely and as a result of pancreatitis. Chronic relapsing pancreatitis may cause episodic stupor or coma.[396] Encephalopathy as a complication of acute pancreatitis is believed to be rare. Scharf and Levy were able to identify only 25 reported cases up to 1976.[388] However, Estrada and associates reported that 6 of 17 nonalcoholic patients with acute pancreatitis, whom they followed prospectively, developed encephalopathy.[109] The pathogenesis of pancreatic encephalopathy is not known. Postmortem evidence of patchy demyelination of white matter in the brain has led to the suggestion that enzymes liberated from the damaged pancreas are responsible for the encephalopathy.[109] Other hypotheses include coexistent viral pancreatitis and encephalitis, disseminated intravascular coagulation complicating pancreatitis, and fat embolism.[198] In one patient with relapsing pancreatitis and episodic coma, there were marked increases in CSF and plasma citrulline and arginine levels, and moderate increases of other amino acids.[396] Pathologically, autopsies have revealed cerebral edema, patchy demyelination, occasional perivascular hemorrhages, and, at times, plugging of small vessels with fat or fibrin thrombi. Biochemical complications of acute pancreatitis also may cause encephalopathy. These include cerebral ischemia secondary to hypotension, hyperosmolality, hypocalcemia,[257] and diabetic acidosis.

Pancreatic encephalopathy usually begins between the second and fifth day after the onset of pancreatitis. The clinical features include an acute agitated delirium with hallucinations, focal or generalized convulsions, and often signs of bilateral corticospinal tract dysfunction. The mental status may wax and wane, and patients often become stuporous or comatose. Akinetic mutism has been reported.[388] The cerebrospinal fluid is usually normal or occasionally has a slightly elevated protein concentration. The CSF lipase level is elevated.[109] The electroencephalogram is always abnormal with diffuse or multifocal slow activity. Radionuclide scans sometimes show evidence of abnormal uptake of isotope, suggesting cerebral infarction.

The diagnosis usually suggests itself when, after several days of abdominal pain, the patient develops acute encephalopathy. The differential diagnosis should include other factors complicating pancreatitis listed above, including, of course, the mumps virus infection that commonly causes both pancreatitis and encephalopathy.[22]

Endocrine Disorders

Diabetes is the most common endocrine disease presenting as undiagnosed stupor or coma. Pituitary, adrenal, or thyroid failure may occasionally present similarly, and these disorders are the subject of this section. Hyper- and hypoparathyroidism are discussed with abnormalities of electrolyte metabolism (p. 255).

Diabetes Mellitus

Diabetes is an endocrine disease with protean systemic manifestations. The clinical effects of diabetes may appear in virtually any organ of the body, either alone or in combination with other organs. The brain is indirectly affected by diabetes, and delirium, stupor, and coma are common symptoms of certain stages of the disease. [4,161] The potential causes of stupor or coma in patients with diabetes are many; some are listed in Table 16. When a diabetic patient develops stupor or coma, more than one of the defects listed in Table 16 may be present, and all must be dealt with if one is to bring about an adequate recovery.

Hyperosmolality is the single most common cause of coma in the diabetic patient. [151] This disorder, which is discussed in detail on page 253, can be an isolated cause of coma or a contributing cause in patients with diabetic ketoacidosis or lactic acidosis.

Diabetic ketoacidosis causes coma in only about 10 percent of affected patients, although less than 20 percent of patients with ketoacidosis remain free of any alteration of consciousness at all. Patients comatose from severe diabetic ketoacidosis almost always have some degree of hyperosmolality as well. In patients with diabetic ketoacidosis, there is no correlation between the state of consciousness and the serum pH. The CSF pH is usually normal prior to the onset of treatment.[302,336] The state of consciousness and serum osmolality provide a better correlation.[133]

Diabetic ketoacidosis usually develops acutely or subacutely in a patient with relatively severe diabetes who neglects to take hypoglycemic agents or in whom an acute infection supervenes. Most affected patients are awake when they come to the

Table 16. Some Causes of Stupor or Coma in Diabetic Patients

Nonketotic hyperglycemic hyperosmolar coma
Ketoacidosis
Lactic acidosis
CNS acidosis complicating treatment
Cerebral edema complicating treatment
Hyponatremia (inappropriate secretion of antidiuretic hormone)
Disseminated intravascular coagulation
Hypophosphatemia
Hypoglycemia
Uremia—hypertensive encephalopathy
Cerebral infarction
Hypotension

---

hospital and have a history of thirst, polyuria, anorexia, and fatigue. They are obviously dehydrated, and deep regular respirations mark the hyperventilation, which partially compensates for the metabolic acidosis. There is often some degree of hypotension and tachycardia, because the hyperglycemic induced osmotic diuresis has reduced the blood volume. Such patients are rarely febrile, and if stuporous or comatose are likely to be mildly hypothermic, even when an acute infection has precipitated the ketoacidosis. The lack of fever, coupled with the fact that ketoacidosis itself can produce a leukocytosis, makes the diagnosis of a concomitant infection difficult. Nausea, vomiting, and acute abdominal pain also complicate the early course of most patients with diabetic ketoacidosis. Although it may be difficult to identify the precipitating factors, the diagnosis of ketoacidosis is rarely difficult; the obvious hyperventilation in all but terminal patients should lead the physician to suspect metabolic acidosis and diabetic ketoacidosis as one of its common causes (Table 12, p. 186).

Diabetic lactic acidosis usually occurs in patients receiving oral hypoglycemic agents, particularly phenformin, but has also been reported in patients not being treated for diabetes. The mechanism of excess lactate production is unknown. Clinical signs and symptoms are the same as those of diabetic ketoacidosis or any other severe metabolic acidosis, except that patients with lactic acidosis are more likely to be hypotensive or in shock. Lactic acidosis in diabetics is distinguished from diabetic ketoacidosis by the absence of high levels of ketone bodies in the serum.

The *treatment* of diabetic ketoacidosis or lactic acidosis although usually lifesaving can itself sometimes have serious or even fatal consequences. The cerebrospinal fluid, which is usually normal in the untreated patient with diabetic acidosis, may become transiently acidotic if the serum acidosis is treated by intravenous bicarbonate infusion, and this may be associated with some short-lived worsening of the patient's state of consciousness.[302] Potentially more dangerous is the sudden lowering of serum osmolality that occurs as insulin lowers the serum glucose and intravenous fluids correct the dehydrated state.[13,14,16,265] This lowering of serum osmolality produces a shift of water into the brain, leading to cerebral edema, which is sometimes fatal.[60,94,242,265] The condition should be suspected clinically when patients recovering from diabetic ketoacidosis or lactic acidosis complain of headache and become lethargic and difficult to arouse. Assuming that no evidence of meningitis is present, patients affected with cerebral edema may then develop hyperpyrexia, hypotension, tachycardia, and signs of transtentorial herniation, which, if not promptly and effectively treated with hyperosmolar agents, can culminate in death. At autopsy, the brains show edema with transtentorial herniation. Also complicating the treatment of diabetic ketoacidosis and lactic acidosis is the fact that some patients who suffer from the syndrome of inappropriate release of antidiuretic hormone may become more easily hypoosmolar during rehydration. Other factors that may complicate the course of diabetic ketoacidosis and add to stupor or coma include disseminated intravascular coagulation[291,418] (see p. 215), hypokalemia, and hypophosphatemia. Profound hypophosphatemia can cause generalized convulsions, stupor, and coma.[120,210]

Hypoglycemia is a common cause of stupor or coma in diabetic patients[19,34] and usually occurs in those taking hypoglycemic agents or during the correction of severe diabetic ketoacidosis. However, spontaneous hypoglycemia can be an early manifestation of diabetes in patients not known to be diabetic or in those known to be diabetic and suffering from renal insufficiency.[34]

Diabetes can lead to severe *renal insufficiency*, producing uremic coma or hypertensive encephalopathy. Severe *cerebral arteriosclerosis* associated with diabetes is a cause of cerebral infarction that, if in the posterior fossa distribution, can produce coma.

Finally, *autonomic neuropathy* caused by diabetes can be a cause of syncope or coma, resulting from either orthostatic hypotension, cardiac arrest, or painless myocardial infarction. Page and Watkins have recently described 12 episodes of cardiorespiratory arrest in eight young diabetic patients, all of whom had severe autonomic neuropathy.[311] None had myocardial infarction, cardiac arrhythmia, or hypoglycemia detected at the time of arrest, and in most of the episodes, there appeared to be some interference with respiration. The authors attribute the episodes to defective respiratory reflex function. Faerman and associates[110] report five cases of painless myocardial infarction in patients with diabetes and autonomic neuropathy. These observations emphasize that all patients with diabetes and episodes of unexplained loss of consciousness should be evaluated carefully for autonomic cardiovascular function.

Adrenal Disorders

Both hyper- and hypoadrenalism are occasional causes of altered consciousness.[52,398,452] Adrenocorticosteroids have profound effects on the brain, but the exact mechanism by which they alter brain function is not understood.[251] Glucocorticoid deficiency prolongs the latency of transmission at central synapses, particularly in multisynaptic systems such as the reticular activating formation. High doses of glucocorticoids decrease the latency of synaptic delay. Corticosteroids easily enter the brain and are bound within cells. They stimulate RNA synthesis in neurons and regulate important enzymes. Glucocorticoid administration increases serotonin biosynthesis and adrenalectomy decreases it. Large doses of glucocorticoids reduce the percentage of time spent in REM sleep, but how all these multiple effects on the physiology and biochemistry of the brain affect behavior is still unclear.

ADDISON'S DISEASE. The pathogenesis of the encephalopathy of Addison's disease probably involves several factors in addition to those caused by the removal of cortisone effect on brain tissue. The untreated disease always produces hyponatremia and hyperkalemia, and often hypoglycemia as well. Hypotension is the rule, and, if severe, this alone can cause cerebral symptoms from ischemia. No matter what treatment is given, encephalopathy does not completely clear in addisonian patients unless cortisone is supplied.

A large percentage of untreated and undertreated patients with Addison's disease are mildly delirious. Stupor and coma usually appear only during addisonian crises. Changes in consciousness, respiration, pupils, and ocular movements are not different from those of several other types of metabolic coma. The presence of certain motor signs, however, may be helpful in suggesting the diagnosis. Patients in addisonian crises have flaccid weakness and either hypoactive or absent deep tendon reflexes, probably resulting from hyperkalemia; many of them suffer from generalized convulsions, which have been attributed to hyponatremia and water intoxication. Papilledema is occasionally present and presumably results from brain swelling caused by glucocorticoid lack. The electroencephalogram is diffusely slow and not different from the pattern in other causes of metabolic encephalopathy.[146]

The neurologic signs of addisonian coma are only rarely sufficiently distinctive to be diagnostic, although the combination of metabolic coma, absence of deep tendon reflexes, and papilledema may suggest adrenal insufficiency. A pigmented skin and hypotension are helpful supplementary signs and, when combined with a low serum sodium and a high serum potassium level, are almost diagnostic. The definitive diagnosis of adrenal insufficiency is made by the direct measurement of low blood or urine cortisol levels.

Surgical procedures and other acute illnesses put severe stress on the adrenal glands. A patient whose adrenal function has been marginal prior to an acute illness or surgical procedure may suddenly develop adrenal failure with its attendant delirium. The symptoms may be attributed inappropriately to the acute illness or to a "postoperative delirium" (see p. 282) unless adrenal function studies are carried out. Some patients without known preexisting adrenal insufficiency develop acute adrenal failure following surgical procedures, particularly cardiac surgery. Alford and associates have recently reported several patients who developed an acute postoperative delirium following coronary bypass surgery.[464] The symptoms included flank or abdominal pain, confusion, fever, and hypotension. A variety of diagnoses were considered before it was discovered that the patients suffered from acute adrenal insufficiency secondary to infarction of the adrenal glands.

The main error in differential diagnosis of Addison's disease is to regard the hyponatremia, hyperkalemia, or hypoglycemia as the primary cause of the metabolic coma, rather than as caused by underlying adrenal insufficiency. This error can be avoided only by considering Addison's disease as a potential cause of metabolic coma and by heeding the other general physical signs and laboratory values. Hypotension and hyperkalemia, for example, rarely combine together in other diseases causing hyponatremia or hypoglycemia.

Patients with Addison's disease are exceedingly sensitive to sedative drugs, including barbiturates and narcotics, and ingestion of standard doses of these drugs may produce coma.

CUSHING'S SYNDROME. Just as glucocorticoid deficiency has profound effects on the brain, so does an excess of the hormone.[398,452] Cushing's syndrome, whether naturally occurring or iatrogenic in origin, frequently leads to an encephalopathy characterized primarily by behavioral changes (either elation or depression) and only rarely by stupor or coma. The changes in behavior associated with glucocorticoid excess are almost always a direct result of that agent on the brain. Depression is a more common complication in Cushing's syndrome (usually caused by pituitary ACTH excess), and elation is more common after ingestion of glucocorticoids. This finding has led some investigators to hypothesize that the depressive effect of Cushing's syndrome, is caused by ACTH rather than cortisone. Occasionally, patients with Cushing's syndrome, particularly with adrenocorticotrophic secreting cancers, develop delirium or stupor that is not a direct result of glucocorticoid excess. Profound hypokalemic metabolic alkalosis may occur after a long period of steroid excess, and the respiratory compensation for the alkalosis may raise $PaCO_2$ and lower PaO_2, resulting in deleterious effects on the state of consciousness. Diabetes and hypertension with their attendant neurologic manifestations often complicate Cushing's syndrome.

The number of patients with iatrogenic steroid excess who suffer from encephalopathy is not known. The Boston Collaborative Drug Surveillance Program, assessing the side effects of prednisone in 676 recipients, determined that 21 patients had acute psychiatric reactions.[36] Eight patients were inappropriately euphoric and 13 suffered from frank psychoses. Psychotic manifestations included hallucinations, delusions, and violent behavior; two of the psychotic patients were profoundly depressed and six were maniacal. The symptoms remitted in all patients when steroids were withdrawn, although some required brief courses of psychotropic drugs in addition. In a pilot study assessing the psychologic effects of high-dose steroids, we gave 100 mg. of dexamethasone daily for 3 days to 10 patients suffering from epidural spinal cord compression and compared psychologic changes in those patients with 10 other patients suffering from vertebral body lesions but not cord compression, who did not receive steroids. Four of the 10 steroid-treated patients developed behavioral changes, which included hallucinations. None displayed abnormalities of alertness or state of consciousness. The control patients did not develop similar symptoms.

Thyroid Disorders

Both hyperthyroidism and hypothyroidism interfere with normal cerebral function,[157,451] but exactly how the symptoms are produced is unclear. The two major hypotheses include the effects of thyroid hormone on oxygen consumption and on nucleoprotein and protein synthesis in neurons and synapses.[251] It is well established that thyroid hormone is necessary for the development of the infant brain and that the profound effects of hypothyroidism on brain development cannot be reversed once they have occurred. In the adult, the effects of thyroid hormone are less clear. Cerebral oxygen consumption is decreased in hypothyroidism, but whether this is a primary or secondary effect of hormone action is not established. Thyroid hormone increases oxygen consumption in most tissues, but no consistent effect on the adult brain has been found. Thyroxine administration increases the metabolic rate of the cerebral cortex of experimental animals from birth to early adulthood, although not at full maturity.[251] Data from intact humans with thyroid disease are inconsistent. Gottstein has reported that patients with hyperthyroidism demonstrate an increased cerebral blood flow and increased oxygen uptake over normal subjects, whereas patients with hypothyroidism undergo decreases in these measurements.[152] The cerebral respiratory quotients in both groups of patients remained normal. Others have found decreases in the cerebral blood flow in myxedema and increases in hyperthyroidism, but no changes in the cerebral oxygen uptake, and have related the changes in cerebral circulation to overall hemodynamic alterations rather than changes in brain metabolism.[300] Sokoloff has suggested that the principal effect of thyroid hormone is on protein metabolism, but that the effects are restricted to the immature brain.[399] Whatever the metabolic cause, symptoms of cerebral dysfunction are prominent in thyroid disease. In the adult with myxedema or hyperthyroidism, thyroid replacement or correction of thyroid excess usually restores all neurologic signs to normal; in infantile hypothyroidism, neurologic normality is rarely achieved unless the defect is almost immediately recognized and corrected.

HYPOTHYROIDISM. Coma is a rare but frequently fatal complication of myxedema.[35,236,289] Many authors have commented on the appearance of "suspended animation" in these profoundly hypometabolic patients. Characteristically, the patients are hypothermic with body temperatures between 87 and 91 °F. They appear to hypoventilate and, indeed, usually have elevated blood PCO_2 values and mild anoxemia. The electroencephalogram is slow and the voltage may be either depressed or increased.[147] The onset of myxedema coma is usually acute. or subacute and precipitated by stresses such as infection, congestive heart failure, trauma, exposure to cold, or sedative or anesthetic drug administration in an untreated hypothyroid patient.

The diagnosis of myxedema in a patient in coma is suggest by cutaneous or subcutaneous stigmata of hypothyroidism, plus a low body temperature and the finding of pseudomyotonic stretch reflexes. The diagnosis is also often suggested by the

238

presence of elevated muscle enzyme levels in the serum[148] but can be confirmed definitely only by thyroid function tests. Since myxedema coma is rapidly fatal, however, treatment with intravenous administration of triiodothyronine or thyroxine[254] should begin once the clinical diagnosis has been made. Laboratory confirmation can come later.

The conditions most often confused with myxedema coma are those that often complicate it. The chief diagnostic error is to regard part of the picture as the whole cause of the encephalopathy. Carbon dioxide narcosis may be suspected if hypoventilation and CO_2 retention are present, but $PaCO_2$ values are rarely above 50 to 55 mm. Hg in hypothroidism, and hypothermia is not part of CO_2 narcosis. Some authors have attributed the cause of coma and profound hypothyroidism to respiratory failure with carbon dioxide retention, but this is unlikely since not all patients with myxedema hypoventilate.[290] Severe hyponatremia is often present in severe myxedema, probably the result of inappropriate ADH secretion, and sometimes causes seizures. Gastrointestinal bleeding and shock also can complicate severe myxedema and divert attention from hypothyroidism as a cause of coma. Hypothermia, which is probably the most dramatic sign, should always suggest hypothyroidism, but may also occur in other metabolic encephalopathies, especially hypoglycemia, depressant drug poisoning, and brainstem infarcts. *Episodic encephalopathy* has been reported as a complication of thyroiditis, and in at least one reported patient responded to the treatment of the associated hypothyroidism.[417]

THYROTOXICOSIS. This disease usually presents with signs of increased central nervous system activity, i.e., anxiety, tremor, or hyperkinetic behavior. Subtle changes in cognitive function accompany the more obvious emotional disturbances.[479] Rarely, in "thyroid storm," these symptoms can progress to confusion, stupor, or coma.[157,260] Thyroid storm usually develops in a patient with preexisting thyrotoxicosis, often partially treated, who encounters precipitating factors such as an infection or a surgical procedure. The early clinical picture is dominated by signs of hypermetabolism. Fever is invariably present, profuse sweating occurs, there is marked tachycardia, and there may be signs of pulmonary edema and congestive heart failure. A more difficult problem is so-called *apathetic thyrotoxicosis*.[414] Such patients are usually elderly and present with neurologic signs of depression and apathy. If untreated, the clinical symptoms progress to delirium and finally to stupor and coma. Nothing distinctive marks the neurologic picture. Hypermetabolism is not clinically prominent nor can one observe the eye signs generally associated with thyrotoxicosis. However, almost all the patients show evidence of severe weight loss and have cardiovascular symptoms, particularly atrial fibrillation and congestive heart failure. Many have signs of a moderately severe proximal myopathy. The diagnosis is established by obtaining tests that reflect thyroid hyperfunction, and the neurologic signs are reversed by antithyroid treatment.

Pituitary Disorders

Pituitary failure is a rare cause of stupor or coma. It can cause stupor or coma in one of two ways: (1) A preexisting tumor, either symptomatic or asymptomatic, may suddenly expand because of hemorrhage or infarction (pituitary apoplexy, p. 144). In this instance, the encephalopathy is caused by the mass lesion or the ejection of noxious substances into the subarachnoid space. The hormonal mechanism of encephalopathy in pituitary failure reflects the combined adrenal and thyroid failure that occurs when these organs are deprived of trophic hormones. The clinical picture may resemble either adrenal or thyroid failure or a combination of both. Great care must be taken in treating patients with severe hypopituitarism, since correction of either the adrenal or thyroid dysfunction alone may precipitate clinical signs of acute failure of the untreated organ. (2) Patients with panhypopituitarism, like patients with primary adrenal or thyroid failure, are exceedingly sensitive to narcotic and sedative drugs.

Pituitary excess causes encephalopathy by hyperfunction of the pituitary-adrenal axis. Controversy over whether ACTH or cortisone leads to the behavioral change in Cushing's disease is discussed on page 237.

Other Systemic Diseases

Cancer

Diffuse encephalopathy leading to delirium, stupor, or coma commonly accompanies disseminated cancer. About 20 percent of the neurologic consultations in a cancer hospital are requested for the evaluation of confused or stuporous patients. The causes of the mental changes are many and sooner or later include all those discussed in this book. A study of 118 consecutive encephalopathic patients in a cancer hospital (Sigsbee, Nealon, and Posner—unpublished) determined that 51 suffered from metabolic brain disease with hepatic encephalopathy (23 patients), hypercalcemia (10 patients), and uremia (7 patients) being the commonest. In 15 other patients, encephalopathy was caused by drugs. In 16, brain tumors and meningeal carcinomatosis led to stupor or coma. Twelve patients suffered from vascular disease, of which disseminated intravascular coagulation was most common. In 10 patients, the encephalopathy was caused by infection: diffuse sepsis in 5, cryptococcal meningitis in 2, and, one each, progressive multifocal leukoencephalopathy, herpes simplex encephalitis, and fungal abscess. Only one patient was deemed to be confused (not stuporous or comatose) because of a remote effect of cancer on the nervous system (see below). In many patients in this series, the encephalopathy appeared to result from mixed causes (see p. 283) rather than from a single one. This latter cause is particularly true in patients with known central nervous system metastases whose otherwise stable course may deteriorate acutely when a mild metabolic defect imposes an additional burden on the damaged brain. Such patients benefit from a physician's knowledge that all stupor or coma in patients with cancer is not due to brain tumors and that even patients with known brain tumors may have other causes of encephalopathy. As with other patients suffering from metabolic encephalopathy, the cancer patient can often be restored to a fully sentient state if the underlying metabolic cause is corrected.

Several causes of encephalopathy in patients with cancer deserve particular attention because they are often neglected in the differential diagnosis.

HYPOGLYCEMIA. Hypoglycemia in patients with cancer occurs in two settings. Large sarcomatous tumors, particularly those in the retroperitoneal space, may compete with the rest of the body for available glucose, leading to hypoglycemic coma. Although an attack of hypoglycemia may be the presenting symptom, the abdominal mass is usually easily palpable. Patients with widely disseminated cancer often eat poorly and may have, in addition, severe liver dysfunction from metastases; the combination can produce spontaneous hypoglycemia.

DRUGS. Patients with severe pain owing to widespread cancer are often particularly susceptible to sedative and narcotic drugs because the cancer has compromised liver or renal function. Patient 4-11 illustrates this problem.

Patient 4–11. A 60-year-old man with multiple myeloma became obtunded while in hospital. Treatment with chemotherapy had produced a severe pancytopenia, which had led to a pneumonia. In addition he suffered from renal failure requiring intermittent hemodialysis. At 6:50 A.M. he was given 4 mg. of levorphanol tartrate (Levo-Dromoran) because of low back pain. Early in the afternoon he began hemodialysis, but he became hypotensive and hemodialysis was stopped. He was noted early in the evening to be markedly obtunded, with the right eye slightly deviated outward and upward. His respirations "appeared agonal." On neurologic examination, the patient was stuporous. With vigorous stimuli, however, he could be aroused to say his name and to identify Memorial Hospital. No other verbal responses could be secured. His pupils were 1.5 mm. and reactive. Ice water calorics yielded a few beats of nystagmus in the appropriate direction. His respirations were 8 per minute, irregular, and shallow. In the resting position, the left eye was straight ahead, the right eye slightly externally and superiorly deviated. Bilateral asterixis and extensor plantar responses were present. Laboratory abnormalities that morning had included a white count of 1100/cu. mm., a hemoglobin of 9.3 gm./dl., platelets of 21,000/cu. mm., 5 μg/liter of fibrin split products, and a positive ethanol gelation test (suggesting mild disseminated intravascular coagulation). The serum sodium was 130 mEq./liter, BUN 82 mg./dl., creatinine 5.7 mg./dl., total protein 8.1 gm./liter with an albumin of 3.0 gm., and alkaline phosphatase of 106.

Because of the small pupils and slow and shallow respiration despite the pneumonia, the patient was given 0.4 mg. of naloxone intraveneously. The pupils dilated to 6 mm., respirations went from 8 to 24/per minute, and he became awake and alert, complaining of the low back pain for which he had been given the drug that morning. The following morning he again became obtunded but less than the evening before. Pupils were 3 mm., and respirations were 20 and relatively deep. Another 0.4 mg. of naloxone was given, the pupils dilated to 7 mm., respirations accelerated to 30 and became deeper, and again he became alert and oriented.

Comment. The clues to narcotic overdosage in this patient were the small pupils and the shallow, irregular respirations despite pneumonia. The patient's other metabolic defects made him particularly sensitive to small doses of narcotic, as did the fact that he had not received the drug in the past for pain and thus had not developed tolerance to it. Furthermore, the long action of levorphanol induced a relapse the next morning, after the effects of the naloxone had worn off.

OAT CELL CARCINOMA OF THE LUNG. This, as well as certain other tumors, secretes an ACTH-like hormone capable of causing Cushing's syndrome with severe metabolic alkalosis, compensatory hypoventilation, and stupor. We have cared for one such patient who was severely obtunded, confused, and hypoventilating, and who had asterixis and bilateral extensor plantar responses.

REMOTE EFFECTS OF CANCER ON THE NERVOUS SYSTEM. These paraneoplastic syndromes may lead to mental changes, including memory loss and dementia, but almost never to stupor or coma.[387] Two syndromes likely to present with mental changes are those of limbic encephalitis and thalamic degeneration.

PROGRESSIVE MULTIFOCAL LEUKOENCEPHALOPATHY. This is a viral infection that sometimes complicates the lymphomas. It is discussed on page 279.

Exogenous Poisons

Sedative and Psychotropic Drugs

Many drugs in common use can produce delirium, stupor, or coma when taken in large amounts (Table 17). The agents that produce delirium seldom provide much of a diagnostic problem and for that reason are not further discussed here.[272] Coma from drug overdose, however, deserves greater attention. Not only is the problem ap-

Table 17. Clues to Specific Drugs Frequently Causing Delirium, Stupor, or Coma

DRUG	CHEMICAL DIAGNOSIS	BEHAVIOR	PHYSICAL SIGNS
1. Amphetamine	Blood or urine	Hypertension; Aggressive, sometimes paranoid, repetitive behavior progressing into agitated paranoid delirium; auditory and visual hallucinations.	Hyperthermia, hypertension, tachycardia, arrhythmia. Pupils dilated. Tremor, dystonia, occasionally convulsions.
2. Cocaine	None available	Similar to above but more euphoric, less paranoid.	
3. Psychedelics (LSD, mescaline, STP, PCP)	Blood or urine	Confused, disoriented, perceptual distortions, distractable, withdrawn or eruptive. Can lead to accidents or violence.	Hypertension and tachycardia. Pupils small, nystagmus. Movements hyperactive; myoclonus or dystonia.
4. Atropine-scopolamine (Sominex)	None available	Delirium; often agitated; responding to visual hallucinations. Drowsiness; delirium, agitation; rarely coma.	Fever, flushed face; dilated pupils; sinus or supraventricular tachycardia; hot dry skin.
5. Tricyclic antidepressants Imipramine (Tofranil) Amitryptilene (Elavil)	Blood or urine	Drowsiness; delirium, agitation; rarely coma.	Fever; Supraventricular tachycardia; conduction defects; ventricular tachycardia or fibrillation. Hypotension. Dystonia.
6. Phenothiazines	Blood	Somnolence; coma rare.	Arrhythmias, hypotension, dystonia.
7. Lithium	Blood	Lethargic confusion, mute state, eventually coma. Multifocal seizures can occur. Onset can be delayed by hours or days after overdose.	Appearance of distraction; roving conjugate eye movement; pupils intact; paratonic resistance; tremors, akathisia.
8. Benzodiazepines (Valium, Librium, Dalmane)	Blood or urine	Stupor, rarely unarousable.	Essentially no cardiovascular or respiratory depression.
9. Methaqualone (Quaalude)	Blood or urine	Hallucinations and agitation blend into depressant drug coma.	Mild: resembles barbiturate intoxication. Severe: increased tendon reflexes, myoclonus, dystonia, convulsions. Tachycardia and heart failure.
10. Glutethimide (Doriden)	Blood	Stupor or coma fluctuating over hours or days.	Resembles barbiturate coma but pupils mid-position, often unequal, and sometimes fixed.
11. Barbiturate	Blood or urine	Stupor or coma.	Hypothermia; skin cool and dry. Pupils reactive; doll's eyes absent; hyporeflexia; flaccid hypotension; apnea.
12. Alcohol	Blood or breath	Dysarthria, ataxia, stupor. Rapidly changing level of alertness with stimulation.	With stupor: hypothermia, skin cold and moist; pupils reactive, mid-position to wide; tachycardia.
13. Opiates	Blood or urine	Stupor or coma.	Needle marks; hypothermia; skin cool and moist; pupils symmetrically pinpoint reactive; bradycardia, hypotension; hypoventilation; pulmonary edema.

pallingly frequent, but accurate histories may be all but impossible to obtain, often because of misguided efforts by friends and families to conceal the facts. For these reasons, an accurate immediate diagnosis leans heavily upon the physical findings and clinical deduction. Chemical laboratory confirmation of the clinical diagnosis is desirable, but the delay in conducting the test often means that the information becomes available too late to be useful in guiding treatment. Furthermore, blood levels of sedatives or alcohol sometimes provide a poor guide to the depth or anticipated duration of coma. Several reasons account for the potential discrepancy. Persons who chronically take these drugs develop a tolerance to their effects and require larger doses with resulting higher blood levels to produce coma. Pharmacologic interaction between drug mixtures and the inability to anticipate the effects of still unabsorbed material in the gut further interfere with making a correlation. Despite these limitations, blood and urine samples should be obtained and analyzed promptly so as to confirm or modify the clinical diagnosis and for possible future medicolegal needs.

Sedatives such as barbiturates, benzodiazepines, glutethimide, meprobamate, phenothiazines, bromides, and alcohol can all produce coma if enough is taken. The mechanism of action of each drug depends partly on its structure and partly on the dose. The barbiturates, for example, appear to act by interrupting synaptic transmission when taken in moderate amounts,[25,219] but larger doses interfere with cerebral oxidative enzymes and directly depress cellular metabolism.[343] As well as can be determined, none of the sedatives taken acutely produces permanent damage to the nervous system, making prompt diagnosis and effective treatment particularly important.

Overdoses with most depressant drugs produce fairly consistent clinical findings, individual drugs usually producing relatively minor clinical differences (Table 17). Almost all these agents depress vestibular and cerebellar function as readily as cerebral cortical function, so that nystagmus, ataxia, and dysarthria accompany or even precede the first signs of impaired consciousness. Larger amounts of drug produce coma, and in this quantity all the agents depress brainstem autonomic responses. With few exceptions, such as the benzodiazepines or phenothiazines, respiration tends to be depressed at least as much as and sometimes more than somatic motor function. Except when glutethimide is the poison, or when huge doses of barbiturates exceeding the potentially fatal threshold have been ingested, the pupils are small and reactive and ciliospinal reflexes are preserved. The oculocephalic responses are depressed or absent, and the oculovestibular responses to cold caloric testing are depressed and may be lost altogether in deep coma. Patients with depressant drug poisoning are usually flaccid with stretch reflexes that are diminished or absent. This typical picture is not always immediately seen, especially if coma develops rapidly after the ingestion of a fast-acting barbiturate, such as secobarbital or pentobarbital. In such cases, respiratory depression may ensue almost as rapidly as does unconsciousness; signs in the motor system may initially evolve as if function was being depressed in a rostral-caudal fashion, with a brief appearance of hyperreflexia and even clonus and extensor plantar responses. Failure to recognize this short-lived (it rarely lasts more than 30 to 45 minutes) phase as being due to depressant drugs can be fatal if one leaves the patient temporarily unattended or delays needed ventilatory assistance. The identifying clue to the toxic-metabolic basis of the changes in such cases is that the pupillary reflexes are preserved and the motor signs are symmetrical.

Chemical analyses are usually required to sort out which drug has been taken in a case of poisoning, but clinical clues sometimes suggest a particular agent (Table 17).

Acne, headache, and severe delirium, but rarely coma, are characteristic of bromidism. *Alcoholic stupor* can be a difficult diagnosis because so many patients who are unconscious for other reasons (from head trauma or drug ingestion, for example) will have the odor of "alcohol" (actually caused by impurities in the liquor) on the breath. The patient in an alcoholic stupor (blood level 250 to 300 mg./dl.) usually has a flushed face, a rapid pulse, a low blood pressure, and mild hypothermia, all resulting from the vasodilatory effect of alcohol.[187] As the coma deepens blood level of 300 to 400 mg./dl.), such patients become pale and quiet, and the pupils may dilate and become sluggishly reactive. With deeper depression, respiration fails. The depth of alcoholic stupor or coma may be deceptive when judged clinically. Repetitive stimulation during medical examinations often arouses such patients to the point where they awaken and require little further stimulation to remain awake, only to lapse into a deep coma with respiratory failure when left alone in bed. Alcohol is frequently taken in conjunction with barbiturates or other psychotropic drugs in suicide attempts. In these instances its action appears to synergize with the other depressant drugs. Under such circumstances of double ingestion, blood levels are no longer reliable in predicting the course, and sudden episodes of respiratory failure or cardiac arrythmias are more frequent than in patients who have taken only a barbiturate.

Heroin-opiate overdosage is an increasingly common problem facing not only hospitals located in ghetto neighborhoods but also those drawing patients from other social classes.[93] The drugs can be taken either by injection or sniffing. Overdosage with narcotics may occur from suicide attempts, or, more commonly, when an addict or neophyte misjudges the amount or the quality of the heroin he is injecting or sniffing. Characteristic signs of opiate coma include pinpoint pupils that generally contract to a bright light and dilate rapidly if a narcotic antagonist is given. Respiratory slowing, irregularity, or cessation are prominent features and result either from direct narcotic depression of the brainstem or from pulmonary edema, which is a frequent complication of heroin overdosage but of uncertain pathogenesis. Of 14 patients comatose from narcotic poisoning reported by Steinberg and Karliner, 4 were apneic and 6 had respiratory depression.[404] One patient had slow, gasping respiration. Four patients were dyspneic and tachypneic and had clinical and x-ray findings suggesting pulmonary edema. Although opiates can produce hypothermia, by the time such patients reach the hospital they frequently have pneumonitis, so that body temperatures may be normal or elevated. The absence of needle marks does not rule out narcotic overdosage; in one series, 4 of 11 patients comatose from heroin became so after their first injection.[404]

Glutethimide (Doriden) and *meprobamate (Equanil) overdoses* sometimes cause an unusual neurologic picture. Patients poisoned with these drugs may be initially comatose with absence of responses to noxious stimuli and to oculocephalic testing. If vigorous repetitive stimuli are delivered, such as repeated head turning or repeated supraorbital compression, the subjects may regain oculocephalic responses or even sleepily arouse, only to relapse into coma when the stimuli are withdrawn. Glutethimide especially predisposes the subject to prolonged coma with fluctuating levels of consciousness. The fluctuations may relate to a toxic metabolite[166] or to recurrent drug absorption owing to fluctuating intestinal motility.

The neurologic examination by itself cannot categorically separate drug poisoning from other causes of metabolic brain disease. The most common diagnostic error is to mistake deep coma from sedative poisoning for the coma of brainstem infarction. The initial distinction between these two conditions may be difficult, but small, reactive

244

pupils, absence of caloric responses, failure to respond to noxious stimuli, absence of stretch reflexes, and muscular flaccidity suggest a profound metabolic disorder. Persisting decerebrate responses, hyperactive stretch reflexes, spasticity, dysconjugate eye movements to caloric tests, and unreactive pupils are more likely with brainstem destruction. If both the pupillary light reflexes and ciliospinal responses are present, deep coma is metabolic in origin. If both the pupillary reactions and the ciliospinal reflexes are lost, deep coma can be due to glutethimide poisoning or, less often, overwhelming severe barbiturate intoxications, but in these instances muscular flaccidity, relatively good blood pressure control, and a lack of grossly irregular breathing are more consistent with metabolic than structural low brainstem disease.

Ineffective care of patients with drug depression becomes itself a cause of coma. In diagnosing coma caused by depressant drug poisoning, one must identify not only the cause but also judge the depth of coma, for the latter influences the choice of treatment. Several years ago, Reed, Driggs, and Foote[351] suggested a grading scheme for patients with depressant drug poisoning approximately as outlined in Table 18. The practical aspect of the classification is that only patients with grade 3 or 4 depression stand at risk of losing their lives. By the same token, comparisons of the potential value of one treatment over another can only be judged by comparing them on patients in grade 3 or 4 coma, where essentially all deaths occur.

Very few patients with sedative drug poisoning should die if they reach the hospital. Fatal arrhythmias owing to the ingestion of tricyclic antidepressants, death owing to preexisting illness, or complications arising from prehospital exposure to the elements occur in a few patients, usually less than 5 percent of those in grade 3 or 4 coma. Barring these exceptions, most serious complications come from breaks in effective resuscitation technique or excessively zealous intensive care. When evaluating new recommendations for therapy, the reader should bear in mind that the treatment of depressant drug overdose by physiologic methods produced results 25 years ago as good or better than any being published today.[61,293,330] In experimental animals the lethal dose of barbiturates is seven times the dose required to depress respiration to apnea and twice the dose required to produce severe hypotension.[224] It follows that if respiration and blood pressure are maintained and pulmonary complications are avoided, coma can persist for remarkably long periods and yet be followed by survival and normal function.

Patient 4–12. A 48-year-old woman ingested 50 gm. of chloral hydrate, 1.5 gm. of chlordiazepoxide (150 tablets Librium), and 2.4 gm. of flurazepam (80 capsules Dalmane) in a suicide attempt. Shortly afterwards, her family found her in a lethargic condition and by the time they brought her to the emergency room she was deeply comatose, hypotensive, and apneic. Examination following endotracheal intubation and the initiation of artificial ventilation showed a blood pressure of 60/40 mm. Hg, pupils that were 2

Table 18. Severity of Depressant Drug Coma*

Grade 0: Asleep but arousable.
    1: Unarousable to talk but withdraws appropriately.
    2: Comatose; most reflexes intact; no cardiorespiratory depression.
    3: Comatose; no tendon reflexes; no cardiorespiratory depression.
    4: Respiratory failure, hypotension, pulmonary edema or arrhythmia present. Comatose for more than 36 hours.

*Adapted from Reed, C. E., Driggs, M. F., and Foote, C. C.: Acute barbiturate intoxication: a study of 300 cases based on a physiologic system of classification of the severity of the intoxication. Ann. Int. Med. 37:290–303, 1952.

245

mm. in diameter and light fixed, absent corneal and oculovestibular responses, and total muscle flaccidity accompanied by areflexia. Arterial and Schwann-Ganz catheters were placed to assist in physiologic monitoring in view of the overwhelming large depressant drug dose. There was already evidence of aspiration pneumonia by the time she reached hospital. A broad spectrum antibiotic was given and a dopamine infusion was started, which initially succeeded in raising the blood pressure to 80/60 mm. Hg. By 12 hours following admission, progressively increasing amounts of dopamine to a level of 40 μg./kg./min. were unable to keep the blood pressure above 60/40 mm. Hg and urine flow ceased. Treatment with L-norepinephrine was initiated at an intravenous dose that reached 12 μg./minute. This induced a prompt rise in blood pressure to 80/40 mm. Hg accompanied by a brisk urine flow. Toxicologic analysis of an admission blood sample showed the qualitative presence of chloral hydrate (quantitative assay was not available). Chlordiazepoxide level was 59.4 μg./ml. and flurazepam was 6.6 μg./ml.

Early management was complicated by the effects of radiographically demonstrated aspiration pneumonia and by pulmonary edema, as well as by atrial, junctional, and ventricular premature cardiac contractions. Hypotension hovering between 80/60 and 60/40 mm. Hg was a serious problem for the first 48 hours and declines in blood pressure were repeatedly accompanied by a marginal urinary flow. The woman remained unresponsive, but by day 4 it was possible to maintain mean blood pressures above 80/60 mm. Hg using dopamine and the L-norepinephrine was discontinued. Isosthenuria and polyuria developed, reflecting the probable complication of renal tubular necrosis, but meticulous attention to electrolyte balance, pulmonary toilet, and the avoidance of overhydration managed to prevent the various complications from worsening. Ice water caloric stimulation first elicited a reaction of ocular movement on day 4 and the pupillary light reflexes reappeared on the same day. On day 8 spontaneous breathing began and one could detect stretch reflexes in the extremities. She first responded to noxious stimuli by opening her eyes and withdrawing her limbs on day 10 and she mumbled words 1 day later. Not until day 13 did she fully awaken to follow commands and answer questions. The quick phase of nystagmus to caloric stimulation did not return until day 15. She has since made a complete physical and intellectual recovery and is receiving psychiatric treatment.

Comment. This woman's course emphasizes the maxim that if patients with depressant drug poisoning survive to reach the hospital they are potentially salvageable almost no matter what the blood levels of the ingested agent. The toxicologic analyses in this instance showed an amount of drug in the body that is generally regarded as a fatal dose. Whether hemodialysis or hemoperfusion would have shortened this patient's course can be questioned, since none of the ingested agents were dialyzable.[458] Generally speaking, among the younger patients that one sees with drug intoxication, only those who have ingested phenobarbital or huge amounts of glutethimide usually have periods of unconsciousness that approach the length of this woman's coma. Her case illustrates that probably any sedative taken in sufficiently large amounts is capable of producing many days of coma that require meticulous systemic care to accomplish survival. Her outcome further emphasizes that even very long periods of unresponsive coma need not produce any measure of brain injury so long as blood gases and arterial perfusion pressures are maintained at levels close to the physiologic norm.

ETHANOL INTOXICATION. One would hardly think that it takes a medical education to diagnose a drunk, but the appraisal of ethanol intoxication sometimes turns out to be deceptively difficult. In Belfast, for example, where events should provide no lack of experience, the diagnosis of alcohol or nonalcohol ingestion in patients with head injury was incorrectly made a full 12 percent of the time. Of even greater potential consequence, 6 of 42 subjects with blood levels over 100 mg./dl. went clinically unrecognized as being intoxicated.[363]

Ethyl alcohol acts on the nervous system in a manner similar to the general anesthetics.[208] Moderately large doses represent a frequent cause of stupor, most examples of which recover spontaneously and neither reach nor, happily, need medical attention. Large doses produce a coma that is potentially fatal and can result from suicide attempts, competitive drinking bouts, hazings, or, less often, accidental overindulgence. A major problem with alcohol ingestion is that the ensuing uninhibited behavior leads to the impulsive ingestion of other sedative, hypnotic, or antidepressant drugs or to careless, headstrong, and uncoordinated activity that invites head trauma. As a result, the major diagnostic problem in altered states of consciousness associated with acute alcoholic intoxication lies in separating the potentially benign and spontaneously reversible signs of alcoholic depression from evidence of more serious injury from other drugs or head trauma.

In pure alcohol intoxication, as noted above, blood levels correlate fairly well with clinical signs of intoxication. Dose levels correlate less well because the rate of absorption from the stomach and intestine depends heavily on the presence or absence of other stomach contents. Chronic ingestion induces moderate tolerance, but in general the associations in Table 19 represent dependable guidelines. When estimating dosage, the physician should recall that in the U.S. the alcoholic content of distilled spirits equals 50 percent of the stated proof on the label.

Clinical signs of acute drunkeness can closely resemble those caused by several other metabolic encephalopathies, including especially depressant drug intoxication, diabetic ketoacidosis, and hypoglycemia. Innate psychologic traits influence the behavior of many drunks, adding to the complexities of diagnosis. As mentioned above, the odor of the breath depends on impurities and is an unreliable sign. Patients with alcohol intoxication are ataxic, clumsy, and dysarthric. They are easily confused, often uninhibited and boisterous (or, more severely, stuporous), and commonly vomit. The conjunctiva are often hyperemic and with severe poisoning the pupils react sluggishly to light. Severe intoxication or stupor produces a remarkable degree of analgesia ("feeling no pain") to noxious stimuli. Blood levels over 300 mg./dl. can depress breathing and lead to fatal coma.

A secure diagnosis of alcoholic intoxication and of its severity requires blood level determinations. When these are unavailable, Champion and associates have recommended determining serum osmolality.[54] Alcohol adds osmols to blood in a degree

Table 19. Clinical Effects and Blood Levels in Acute Alcoholism

Symptoms	Blood Level (mg./dl.)
Euphoria, giddiness, verbosity	25–100
Long reaction time, impaired mental status examination	
Mild incoordination, nystagmus	
Hypalgesia to noxious stimuli	
Boisterousness, withdrawal, easily confused	100–200
Conjunctival hyperemia	
Ataxia, nystagmus, dysarthria	
Pronounced hypalgesia	
Nausea, vomiting, drowsiness	200–300
Diplopia, wide sluggish pupils	
Marked ataxia and clumsiness	
Hypothermia, cold sweat, amnesic stupor	>300
Severe dysarthria or anarthria	
Anesthesia	
Stertor, hypoventilation	
Coma	

proportional to its blood level. Champion found that no patient with a blood level over 150 mg./dl. had a serum osmolality less than 320 mOsm./kg., and patients with blood alcohol levels of 200 mg./dl. had greater than 340 mOsm./kg. Because alcohol is uniformly distributed in body water, the hyperosmolality it produces does not lead to fluid shifts out of the brain (p. 253), and thus the hyperosmolality produced by alcohol is not in itself a cause of symptoms.

Drugs Causing Metabolic Acidosis

The metabolism and mechanisms of neurologic changes in acid-base disorders are discussed on pages 256–258. This section considers specific exogenous poisons causing metabolic acidosis. These include methyl alcohol, ethylene glycol, and paraldehyde. Salicylate poisoning also produces a metabolic acidosis in the tissues, but in adults this aspect of the disorder often is overshadowed in the blood by evidence of respiratory alkalosis.[475]

The metabolic acidosis and neurotoxicity of methyl alcohol, ethylene glycol, and paraldehyde all result from their metabolic breakdown products rather than the original agent. Poisoning from all three drugs is most common in chronic alcoholics who ingest the agents either by mistake or in ignorance of their risks as a substitute for ethanol. All three agents initially produce symptoms of alcohol intoxication progressing to confusion and stupor, by which point symptoms and signs of severe acidosis and systemic organ complications usually emerge as well.

METHANOL. Methanol is degraded into formaldehyde, formic acid, and possibly other acids as well.[106] It is mainly metabolized by alcohol dehydrogenase in the liver and kidney, and the presence of ethanol in the system slows its metabolic breakdown, thereby influencing the clinical course. The earliest and most frequent neurologic damage of methyl alcohol poisoning affects retinal ganglion cells; this injury is attributed by most workers to the effects of formaldehyde. The brains of patients dying of methanol poisoning may be normal or, variably, may show congestion, edema, petechiae, or necrosis of cerebellar cortex or putaminal neuroglial elements.[378] More widespread pathologic abnormalities have in rare instances been noted,[256] along with clinical parkinsonism in the recovery period. It is difficult to appraise the specificity of these neuropathologic changes for methanol (as opposed to systemic circulatory failure) in such severely ill patients. Clinically, methanol poisoning can evolve over several days or appear abruptly. Stupor, coma, or seizures occur only in severely poisoned patients. Clinically, most subjects at first give the appearance of advanced inebriation and develop visual loss ("blind drunk"). Hyperpnea is the rule. The crucial clinical step consists of immediately recognizing the presence of an organic acidosis and treating it vigorously. The following patient illustrates the point.

Patient 4–13. A 39-year-old man had been intermittently drinking denatured alcohol for 10 days. He was admitted complaining that for several hours his vision was blurred and he was short of breath. He was alert, oriented, and coherent, but restless. His blood pressure was 130/100 mm.Hg, his pulse was 130 per minute, and his respirations were 40 per minute, regular, and deep. The only other abnormal physical findings were 20/40 vision, engorged left retinal veins with pink optic discs, and sluggishly reactive pupils, 5 mm. in diameter. His serum bicarbonate level was 5 mEq./liter, and his arterial pH was 7.16. An intravenous infusion was begun immediately; 540 mEq. of sodium bicarbonate were infused during the next 4 hours. By that time his arterial pH had risen to 7.47 and his serum bicarbonate to 13.9 mEq./liter. He was still hyperventilating, but less restless. The infusion was continued at a slower rate for 20 hours to a total of 740 mEq. of bicarbonate. He recovered completely.

Comment: This patient had profound acidosis, as was reflected by the requirement of 540 mEq. of parenteral sodium bicarbonate to raise his serum bicarbonate from 5 to 13 mEq./liter. Even larger amounts have been required by other acidotic patients. The acidosis of methyl alcohol poisoning can be lethal with alarming rapidity: One of our patients walked into the hospital, complaining of blurred vision. He admitted drinking "a lot" of methyl alcohol and was hyperventilating. During the 10 minutes that it took to transfer him to a treatment unit, he lost consciousness. By the time an intravenous infusion could be started, his breathing and heart had stopped. No bicarbonate could be detected in a serum sample drawn simultaneously with death.

PARALDEHYDE ACIDOSIS. This acidosis is uncommon, essentially confined to drug-alcohol abusers, and perhaps related to the ingestion of already decomposed paraldehyde. Paraldehyde is metabolized to acetic acid, but the degree of acidosis in these patients exceeds the amount of detectable acetic acid in the serum, implying the presence of other acid products as well.[106] Distinctive clinical features in addition to the manifestations of metabolic acidosis include the odor of paraldehyde on the breath, abdominal pain, a marked leucocytosis, and obtunded, lethargic behavior. All patients reported to date have recovered.

ETHYLENE GLYCOL (ANTIFREEZE) POISONING. This results from the deleterious effect of the compound's metabolites, including glycoaldehyde, oxalic acid, and hippuric acid.[314] A relatively severe metabolic acidosis occurs during the early hours of toxicity. The inital clinical signs are of alcohol intoxication without ethanol's characteristic odor. Patients with severe poisoning go on to disorientation, stupor, coma, convulsions, and death. Neuroophthalmologic abnormalities including papilledema, nystagmus, and ocular bobbing can be prominent. Metabolic abnormalities, if uncorrected, can lead to cardiopulmonary failure. A late problem of ethylene glycol poisoning is renal damage caused by oxalate and hippurate crystalluria. Diagnosis should be suspected by a history of ingestion of antifreeze in an alcoholic or after a suicide attempt, the identification of an anion-gap metabolic acidosis, and the detection of characteristic oxalic acid crystals in the urine.

LACTIC ACIDOSIS. This has emerged increasingly in recent years as a metabolic disorder sometimes associated with neurologic symptoms and a poor prognosis. Mild and asymptomatic elevations of serum lactate up to 6 mEq./liter or so accompany a number of conditions, including alkalosis, carbohydrate infusions, anxiety or epinephrinemia, diabetic ketoacidosis, and alcohol intoxication. More intense, but still systemically benign lactic acidosis with arterial blood levels of 20 mEq./liter or more and blood pH levels below 7.00 can follow vigorous muscular exercise. We have observed similar degrees of acidosis and acidemia following major motor convulsions, but in neither exercise nor epilepsy was there evidence that the lactacidemia affected brain function. Lactic acid crosses the blood-brain barrier via a carrier mechanism that saturates at about three to four times the normal plasma concentration of 1 mEq./liter. Thus, although high concentrations of lactate in the brain are believed to be neurotoxic,[281] these probably only occur when produced by local brain ischemia or in conditions in which systemic hypoxia, circulatory failure, or drug poisoning also affect directly the oxidative metabolism of the central nervous system.

SALICYLATE INTOXICATION. In adults, salicylate intoxication appears in two principal forms. Relatively younger persons sometimes take aspirin or similar agents in suicide attempts. Although many become severely ill and a few die with terminal coma or convulsions, most of these younger patients lack prominent neurologic complaints except for tinnitus and dyspnea. Older persons, by contrast, often ingest salicylates in excessive amounts more or less accidentally in proprietary analgesics; in them, neurologic symptoms can dominate the early illness, producing an encephalopathy that initially obscures the etiologic diagnosis.[10]

Salicylates act as a "metabolic uncoupler" in oxidative phosphorylation and stimulate net organic acid production. Aspirin (salicylic acid) also contains 1.7 mEq. of acid per 300-mg. tablet.[106] In experimental animals, death from salicylate poisoning comes from convulsions and relates directly to the concentration of the drug in the brain;[174] clinical evidence suggests that similar principles apply in man.

Salicylates in adults stimulate respiration neurogenically to a degree that nearly always produces a respiratory alkalosis in the blood unless simultaneous ingestion of sedative drug suppresses the respiratory response.[475] The metabolic acidosis of the tissues is reflected usually by a disproportionately lowered serum bicarbonate and always by an acid urine. Depending on age, associated illness, and the rapidity of accumulation, first symptoms of salicylate intoxication usually appear at a blood level of about 40 to 50 mg./dl. Blood levels over 60 mg./dl. usually produce symptoms of severe toxicity. Initial complaints are of tinnitus and, less often, deafness. As many as half of older persons with severe salicylate intoxication develop confusion, agitation, slurred speech, hallucinations, stupor, or convulsions and coma.[10] With stupor go hyperpnea, intact pupillary responses, intact oculocephalic responses, diffuse paratonia, and in many instances extensor plantar responses. In a patient with metabolic encephalopathy, a respiratory alkalosis and mildly abnormal anion gap in the blood, combined with aciduria, are almost diagnostic of salicylism and can be quickly confirmed by determination of salicylate blood levels. The following patient illustrates the problem.

Patient 4-14. A 74-year-old woman with osteoarthritis and peptic ulcer disease was noted to be lethargic and confused after she fell out of bed on the surgical service. With a dysarthric, deepened voice, she complained of a recent loss of hearing. The examination showed fluctuating lethargy, asterixis, and bilateral extensor plantar responses, but little else. A CT scan was unremarkable and the changes were at first ascribed to the nonfocal effects of trauma. The next day, however, she was barely arousable, severely dysarthric, and disoriented when she did respond. The pupils were 2 mm. and equal, the oculocephalic responses full and conjugate, and prominent bilateral asterixis involved the upper extremities. Both plantar responses were extensor and the respiratory rate was 32 per minute. Arterial blood gases were pH 7.48, PCO_2 24 mm. Hg, PO_2 81 mm. Hg, and HCO_3^- 19 mEq./liter. Serum sodium was 134, potassium 3.5, and chloride 96 mEq./liter, giving an anion gap of approximately 19. Serum salicylate level was 54 mg./dl. She was treated cautiously with alkaline diuresis and became alert and without abnormal neurologic symptoms or signs within 48 hours.

Abnormalities of Ionic or Acid-Base Environment of the CNS

Abnormalities of Osmolality

The term osmolality refers to the number of solute particles dissolved in a solvent. Osmolality is usually expressed as milliosmoles per kilogram of solvent (mOsm./kg.). It can either be measured directly on the serum by the freezing point depression method or, for clinical purposes, calculated from the concentrations of sodium, glucose, and urea in the serum. The formula below gives a rough but clinically useful approximation of the serum osmolality:

$$mOsm./kg. = 2(Na + K) + \frac{glucose}{18} + \frac{BUN}{2.8}$$

Sodium and potassium are expressed in mEq. per liter, and the divisors convert glucose and BUN, expressed in mg./dl. to mEq./liter. If the glucose and BUN are normal, the serum osmolality can be approximated by doubling the serum Na^+ and adding 10. Normal serum osmolality is 290 ± 5 mOsm./kg. The development of

250

hypoosmolality leads to an increased cellular water content and tissue swelling, and unless the agent altering osmolality is equally distributed throughout the body water (e.g., alcohol), hyperosmolality leads to cerebral shrinkage. Since the brain has protective mechanisms against osmolar shifts,[202,364] which take time to develop, rapid changes in serum osmolality produce more prominent neurologic symptoms than slow changes. Accordingly, it is not possible to give exact values above or below normal at which symptoms will develop. However, serum osmolalities below about 260 mEq./liter or above about 330 mEq./liter are likely to produce cerebral changes. In addition, cerebral symptoms can be produced by sudden restorations of osmolality towards normal when an illness has produced a sustained osmolal shift away from normal. This is particularly true when chronic hyperosmolality is rapidly corrected, which leads to a sudden shift of water into the brain, resulting in cerebral edema and attendant neurologic complications.

HYPOOSMOLAR STATES. Sodium is the most abundant serum cation, and for practical purposes systemic hypoosmolarity reduces itself to hyponatremic states. *Hyponatremia* or *"water intoxication"* is a comparatively frequent cause of delirium, obtundation, and coma, many examples being encountered annually in almost all large hospitals.

Hyponatremia means that body water is increased relative to solute. Symptoms result from water excess in the brain, hence the name water intoxication. The major accumulation of water in hypoosmolar cerebral edema lies within the cells and the pathogenesis of the accompanying symptoms is believed to be related in some way to altered excitability of the neural membrane. The membrane potential is influenced by the ratio of sodium outside to sodium inside the cell, and, more importantly, by the ratio of potassium outside to potassium inside the cell. Dilution of body compartments by water causes a greater absolute decrease in the extracellular sodium than in the less concentrated intracellular sodium and, conversely, a greater absolute decrease in the intracellular potassium than in the extracellular potassium. The sodium change affects the membrane potential relatively little, but the potassium alteration decreases the potential and thereby increases neuronal excitability. It is doubtful, however, that this dilutional change in itself alters the membrane potential sufficiently to cause the observed convulsions. During hyponatremic episodes there may be concomitant shifts of sodium into and potassium out of neurons that accentuate the increased excitability and contribute to the neurologic symptoms.[202]

No satisfactory physiologic evidence completely explains why rapidly developing hyponatremia produces much greater neurologic changes than does slowly developing or chronic hyponatremia. Rymer and Fishman in an experimental study demonstrated three striking features of cerebral edema with hyponatremia.[364] First was that during acute hypoosmolality, brain tissue swells only about half as much as muscle, a difference at least partly explained by an associated loss of potassium from the brain but not muscle. Second was that the potassium loss could not explain the neurologic changes, since no improvement in brain potassium content accompanied the return from coma to alertness in the animals. Finally, the water content of the brain was the most important factor influencing consciousness, since recovery of alertness paralleled a decline of brain water toward normal along with a proportionately smaller increase in brain sodium. These results as well as those of Arieff and associates[17] imply that hypoosmolar encephalopathy is best treated intravenously with hypertonic saline solutions. Although hypertonic saline is effective therapy for the acute life-threatening hypoosmolar encephalopathy, its effects are usually transient and the patient will relapse if the underlying cause remains. In the chronic situation the administration of lithium or demeclocycline[126] promotes renal excretion of water and thereby increases serum sodium concentrations.

Several clinical conditions cause hypoosmolality severe enough to induce confusional states, stupor, or coma. *False hyponatremia* is a rare but misleading depression of the serum sodium measurement resulting from the presence of an excess of lipid or protein; the serum water concentration is decreased and the sodium, which is dissolved only in the aqueous phase of the serum, is low when expressed as mEq./liter of serum. The serum osmolality is normal and the condition has no neurologic consequences. Otherwise, if the urea and glucose concentrations are near normal, the degree of hyponatremia fairly accurately reflects the intensity of hypoosmolality. Hyponatremia can be caused by either a sudden hypotonic water load that exceeds the capacity of the normal kidney to excrete a dilute urine or by a renal water-excreting capacity that is reduced by disease or antidiuretic hormone (ADH) activity in excess of the level required to maintain the normal concentration of serum sodium. Most cases of *acute hyponatremia* probably reflect a combination of these mechanisms, although one occasionally encounters chronic schizophrenic or alcoholic patients who precipitate acute hyponatremic encephalopathy by drinking massive volumes of water or beer. *Chronic hyponatremia* has many causes, principal among which are renal disease, diseases that shrink the blood volume or otherwise reduce renal glomerular filtration, and diseases or conditions than enhance ADH output (inappropriate ADH secretion). Neurologic disorders that actively stimulate ADH include neoplasms or infections in the hypothalamic region, meningitis, head injury, and acute or subacute peripheral neuropathy. A variety of drugs and endocrine disorders (e.g., myxedema and adrenal insufficiency) enhance ADH secretion and predispose to hyponatremia. ADH-secreting bronchogenic carcinomas and chest infections also cause an excess of circulating ADH.

Most patients with slowly developing or only moderately severe hyponatremia are confused or delirious. They have asterixis and, often, multifocal myoclonus. Coma is

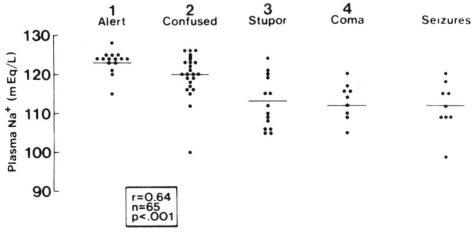

Figure 36. The relationship between plasma Na$^+$ concentration and depression of sensorium in 65 patients with plasma Na$^+$ of 128 mEq./liter or less. It can be seen that although there is a highly significant overall correlation, substantial overlap among groups of patients is present. All patients who had seizures had plasma Na$^+$ of less than 121 mEq./liter. (With permission from Arieff, A.L., Llach, F., and Massry, S.G.: *Neurological manifestations and morbidity of hyponatremia: correlation with brain water and electrolytes.* Medicine 55:121–129, 1976.)

a late and life-threatening phase of water intoxication and both coma and convulsions are more common with acute than chronic hyponatremia. When convulsions or coma do occur, it usually is in the setting of serum sodium values between 95 to 110 mEq./liter. Permanent brain damage often follows upon hyponatremic convulsions. Arieff and associates[17] correlated neurologic symptoms with serum sodium concentrations in 65 patients with acute and chronic hyponatremia (Fig. 36). The 14 patients with acute hyponatremia had a mean plasma sodium concentration of 112 mEq./liter; all were either stuporous or in coma and 4 had convulsions. Five died. Among 51 patients with chronic hyponatremia, 27 with a mean serum Na$^+$ of 122 mEq./liter had no neurologic symptoms. The remaining 24 patients had a mean serum Na$^+$ of 115 mEq./liter; 11 were lethargic, 2 had convulsions, and 3 were in coma. Three died, but not, apparently, because of their hyponatremia. Most patients with acute hyponatremia had abruptly received excessive amounts of hypotonic fluids either intravenously or by bladder irrigation. Among the symptomatic patients with chronic hyponatremia, 12 were chronically receiving diuretics and 9 had the syndrome of inappropriate ADH secretion.

The following report describes a patient with severe hyponatremia who was suspected of having acute, inappropriate ADH secretion.[159] Coma and severe convulsions were followed by permanent brain damage.

Patient 4–15. A 33-year-old schoolteacher was admitted to the hospital in coma. She had been working regularly until 2 days prior to admission, when she stayed home with nausea and vomiting. Two hours before admission she was noted to be dysarthric when speaking on the telephone. Later she was found by friends on the floor, unconscious, and cyanotic. She had three generalized convulsions and was brought to hospital. Her blood pressure was 130/180 mm. Hg, her pulse 140 per minute, her respirations 24 per minute and regular, and her body temperature 38.7° C. She did not respond to noxious stimulation. Her eyes deviated conjugately to the left at rest but turned conjugately to the right with passive head turning. Her pupils were 6 mm. on the right, 5 mm. on the left, and they briskly constricted to light stimulation. Both corneal reflexes were present. Her arms, hands, and fingers were flexed with plastic rigidity and irregular athetoid movements. Her legs and feet were rigidly extended. There were bilateral extensor plantar responses. She had three more convulsions that began in the right hand and then rapidly became generalized.

Despite extensive investigations and tests for metabolic aberrations or poisons, the only abnormalities found in this woman were of acute water intoxication. Her serum values were as follows: sodium 98 mEq. per liter, potassium 3.4 mEq. per liter, osmolality 214 mOsm. per liter (normal = 290 ± 5). The BUN was 10 mg./dl.

Water restriction and infusion of 5 percent NaCl rapidly returned the electrolyte values to normal. After several days she opened her eyes, grimaced when pinched, and moved all extremities. Her muscles remained rigid, however, especially on the right side, and she continued to have bilateral extensor plantar responses. She had no further seizures. Six months later she remained severly demented and unable to care for herself.

Comment: Hyponatremia has no pathognomonic signs or symptoms to suggest it in preference to other metabolic abnormalities, but should be suspected in patients who suddenly develop an unexplained encephalopathy or seizures, particularly if they are receiving diuretics, have carcinoma of the lung, or have neurologic disease. The diagnosis is possible if the serum sodium level falls below 120 mEq./liter and highly likely when the sodium is below 115 mEq./liter.

HYPEROSMOLAR STATES. Physicians often induce transient hyperosmolality therapeutically, using hypertonic solutions containing mannitol, glycerol, or, nowadays less often, urea in an effort to clear cerebral edema or renal insufficiency. Complications of hyperosmolality only occasionally arise during such efforts. Much more frequent are hyperosmolarity problems arising with hypernatremia or with severe hyperglycemia. *Hypernatremia* can be chronic or acute, the latter type being more prone to produce neurologic symptoms. Mild chronic hypernatremia occasionally occurs in chronic untreated diabetes insipidus, caused by uncompensated water loss, but severe chronic hypernatremia with serum sodium levels in excess of 155 to 160 mEq./liter is practically confined to the syndrome of essential hypernatremia. Essential hypernatremia usually is caused by a diencephalic abnormality and is characterized by a lack of thirst and a failure of ADH secretion to respond to osmoreceptor stimulation. In essential hypernatremia[402] serum sodium concentrations sometimes rise in excess of 175 mEq/liter. The patients usually become lethargic when sodium levels exceed 160 mEq./liter; with elevations above 180 mEq./liter, most become confused or stuporous, and some die.[331] A danger is that too rapid rehydration of such chronically hypernatremic subjects can produce symptoms of water intoxication in the presence of serum sodium levels as high as 155 mEq./liter (i.e., about 25–30 mEq. below the level at which hydrating efforts began). The problem is especially frequent in children.

Severe water depletion, producing acute hypernatremia, occurs in children with intense diarrhea and, occasionally, in adults with diabetes insipidus during circumstances that impair their thirst or access to adequate water replacement. Acute hypernatremia also occurs in obtunded patients receiving excessively concentrated solutions by tube feeding. As with other hyperosmolar states, blood volumes tend to be small because of excess free water losses (solute diuresis). Elevated levels of urea nitrogen, and sometimes glucose contribute to the hyperosmolality. Symptoms of encephalopathy usually accompany serum sodium levels in excess of about 160 mEq./liter or total osmolalities of 340 or more mOsm./kg., the earliest symptoms being of delirium or a confusional state. Hypernatremic osmolality also should be considered when patients in coma receiving tube feedings show unexplained signs of worsening, especially if their treatment has included oral or systemic dehydrating agents.

Nonketotic hyperglycemic hyperosmolality is a disorder reported with increasing frequency during recent years as a cause of acute or subacute stupor and coma, especially in elderly subjects. The condition occurs principally in patients with mild or noninsulin requiring diabetes, but has occasionally been encountered in nondiabetics with a hyperglycemic response after severe burns. Most, but not all, of the affected subjects are middle aged or older and a large percentage have an associated acute illness precipitating the hyperglycemic attack. In patients with symptoms, blood sugars usually range from 800 to 1200 mg./dl. or more with total serum mOsm./kg. in excess of 350.[14] An absence of, or very low levels of ketonemia differentiates the condition from diabetic ketoacidosis with coma. In addition, one finds substantially more evidence of dehydration and hemoconcentration than in most examples of early diabetic ketoacidosis. The pathogenesis of nonketotic hyperglycemia is believed to relate to a partial insulin deficiency, severe enough to interfere with glucose entry into cells but not intense enough so that activation of the hepatic ketogenic sequence occurs.[127] Certain drugs, including phenytoin, corticosteroids, and immunosuppressive agents, enhance the tendency to hyperglycemia. Dehydrating agents such as mannitol or glycerol given unthinkingly to such patients can greatly intensify the hyperosmolality.[382] In addition to its spontaneous occurrences, nonketotic hyperglycemia represents a prominent risk in neurologic patients already obtunded from other illnesses who receive steroid drugs and restricted fluids in their treatment.[312] Fulop and associates have argued persuasively that hyperosmolality contributes an important component to the neurologic symptoms of many patients believed to have classic diabetic ketoacidosis.[133]

254

The clinical presentation of hyperglycemic hyperosmolal coma consists of signs of systemic dehydration accompanied by lethargic confusion progressing into deep stupor or coma. Generalized, focal, or partial continuous seizures occur in about one fifth of the cases, and focal, stroke-like motor deficits affect about a quarter. Laboratory studies disclose severe hyperglycemia combined with evidence of severe dehydration of body fluids. Perhaps a quarter of the patients have a mild to moderate lactic acidosis and many have signs of at least mild renal insufficiency. Untreated, all patients die, and even the best efforts at therapy fail in a large percentage, largely because of the seriousness of associated illnesses.

Calcium

Both high and low serum calcium values can be associated with neurologic abnormalities.

HYPERCALCEMIA An elevated serum calcium level may be due to the effects of primary hyperparathyroidism, immobilization, or cancer. Hypercalcemia is a common and important complication of cancer, resulting from either metastatic lesions that demineralize the bones or as a remote effect of parathormone secreting tumors. The systemic clinical symptoms of hypercalcemia include anorexia, nausea, and frequently vomiting, intense thirst, polyuria, and polydipsia. Muscle weakness can be prominent and neurogenic atrophy has been reported.[316] Some patients with hypercalcemia have as their first symtoms a mild diffuse encephalopathy with headache, rather than evidence of systemic disease. Delusions and changes in the affect can be prominent, so that many such patients have been initially treated for a psychiatric disorder until the blood calcium level was measured. With severe hypercalcemia, stupor and finally coma occur. Generalized or focal seizures occur rarely. Hypercalcemia should be suspected in a delirious patient who has a history of renal calculi, recent immobilization, cancer, or evidence of any other systemic disease known to cause the condition.[74] Lacking evidence for these prodromata, it is still sometimes rewarding to obtain a serum calcium determination in patients with unexplained delirium or confusional states.

HYPOCALCEMIA. This is caused by hypoparathyroidism (often occurring late and unsuspected after thyroidectomy) or, rarely, by an idiopathic disorder of calcium metabolism. Hypocalcemia also occurs with uremia, but as discussed on page 226, in this instance parathyroid hormone levels are elevated and brain calcium is high, not low. Presumably, therefore, the central mechanisms of encephalopathy in uremic hypocalcemia differ from those in hypoparathyroid hypocalcemia. The cardinal peripheral manifestations of hypocalcemia are neuromuscular irritability and tetany, but these may be absent when hypocalcemia develops insidiously. Accordingly, patients with hypoparathyroid hypocalcemia can sometimes present with a mild diffuse encephalopathy as their only symptom. Convulsions are common, especially in children. With more severe cases, excitement, delirium, hallucinations, and stupor have been reported.[74] Except postictally, however, coma is rare. Papilledema has been reported, associated with an increased intracranial pressure. This hypocalcemic pseudotumor cerebri apparently is a direct effect of the metabolic abnormality, but the precise mechanism remains unexplained.

Hypocalcemia is commonly misdiagnosed as mental retardation, dementia, or epilepsy, and occasionally as brain tumor. Hypocalcemia should be suspected if the patient has cataracts, and the correct diagnosis sometimes can be inferred from observing calcification in the basal ganglia on skull roentgenography or CT scan. Serum calcium levels below 4.5 mEq./liter are diagnostic of pathologic hypocalcemia.

The level of serum calcium varies with the level of serum albumin such that for each 1.0 gm./L. decrease in the level of serum albumin, there is a 0.8 mg./dl. decrease in the serum calcium level. The ionized calcium, however, remains normal, and thus symptomatic hypocalcemia is not present. When the serum albumin level is normal, a serum calcium below 4.0 mEq./L. is diagnostic of hypoparathyroidism, and whatever the serum albumin, a serum ionized calcium below 4.0 mg./dl. or 2.0 mEq./L. is diagnostic.

Disorders of Systemic Acid-Base Balance

Systemic acidosis and alkalosis accompany several diseases that cause metabolic coma, and the attendant respiratory and acid-base changes can give important clues about the cause of coma (see p. 185 and Table 12). However, of the four disorders of systemic acid-base balance (respiratory and metabolic acidosis, respiratory and metabolic alkalosis), only respiratory acidosis acts as a direct cause of stupor and coma with any regularity. Perhaps even then the associated hypoxia is as important as is the acidosis in producing the neurologic abnormality. Metabolic acidosis, the most immediately medically dangerous of the acid-base disorders, by itself only rarely produces coma. Usually, metabolic acidosis is associated with delirium, or, at most, confused obtundation. Respiratory alkalosis, as such, causes no more than lightheadedness and confusion. Therefore, if patients with acid-base disorders other than respiratory acidosis or severe and protracted metabolic acidosis are in stupor or coma, it is unlikely that the acid-base disturbance by itself is responsible. What is more likely is that the metabolic defect responsible for the acid-base disturbance (e.g., uremia, hepatic encephalopathy, or circulatory depression leading to lactic acidosis) also is directly interfering with brain function.

One reason that disorders of systemic acid-base balance often do not interfere with brain function is that physiologic mechanisms protect the acid-base balance of the brain (as reflected by the pH of its extracellular fluid, the CSF) against even large changes in the serum pH.[329] This protection, involves several physiologic and biochemical defense mechanisms. These include respiratory compensation, a change in the cerebral blood flow, the establishment of ionic gradients between the blood and the brain, and cellular buffering in nervous tissue. These homeostatic defenses work particularly well in metabolic acidosis, largely through effective respiratory compensation. They are less completely effective in protecting the brain against the systemic abnormalities of metabolic alkalosis and respiratory alkalosis and largely ineffective in respiratory acidosis because the causative disease in the respiratory system directly impairs the elimination mechanism for CO_2. Posner and Plum suggested that measurement of CSF pH correlates better with clinical symptoms in patients with acid-base disorders than does measurement of the serum pH.[336] In their studies, it appeared that in many patients with severe metabolic acidosis, coma developed only when compensatory mechanisms failed and the brain became acidotic along with the serum acidosis. Unfortunately, in the physiologic nonsteady states of acute-base disorders, the measurement of pH values in the lumbar CSF has little clinical value. This is because the lumbar fluid exchanges relatively slowly with the extracellular fluid of the brain and therefore often fails to reflect rapid changes in brain pH.[328]

Acidosis exerts profound biochemical[410,437] and physiologic[391,409] effects on nervous tissue. The pH of the tissue affects the ionization of drugs and metabolites as well as their rates of diffusion across membranes, including those that comprise the blood brain barrier. The kinetics of many biologic enzymes change as the pH falls or rises.

The exact mechanisms by which changes in pH interfere with brain metabolism and function are far from clearly defined, although both acidosis and anoxia lower the pH of the cell and thereby interfere with its energy metabolism.

Among clinical conditions causing systemic acidosis *severe respiratory acidosis* produces a depression of alertness and arousal to a degree that parallels fairly well the degree of acidosis. As mentioned above, because of the solubility of carbon dioxide across membranes, in respiratory failure the pH of the brain and CSF falls proportionately to that of the blood.

Pure or mixed *metabolic acidosis* has several causes as listed in Table 12, p. 186.

The presence or severity of neurologic symptoms in metabolic acidosis depends on several factors, including the nature of the systemic metabolic defect, whether or not the fall in systemic pH affects the pH of the brain and CSF, the rate at which the acidosis develops, and the specific anion causing the metabolic disorder. We have observed arterial blood pH values as low as 6.86 in patients with intestinal bicarbonate loss and no neurologic symptoms.[336] Equally low pH values in the blood without neurologic symptoms have been reported in trained athletes because of lactic acid accumulation resulting from vigorous muscular exercise.[307]

Several points can be noted about neurologic dysfunction in acid-base disorders. With diabetic ketoacidosis or uremia, stupor or coma is a late development. With uremia, despite the presence of serum acidosis, CNS acidosis almost never ensues,[337] and neurologic symptoms must be attributed to other mechanisms. In diabetic ketoacidosis, the CSF pH does eventually fall with severe cases.[336] However, present evidence on the subject is insufficient to determine whether diabetic coma results mainly from the neurologic effects of acidosis, from hyperosmolality,[133] or from a direct effect on the brain of the severely disturbed systemic carbohydrate metabolism. The last-mentioned seems most likely.

Except for intestinal bicarbonate losses and muscle activity, almost all the disorders associated with metabolic acidosis listed in Table 12 can cause an encephalopathy severe enough eventually to cause stupor, coma, and, in several instances, convulsions. Although only well established for salicylate intoxication,[174] it seems likely that the specific metabolic agent or disorder rather than the altered pH is the main neurotoxic mechanism in these conditions. This principle especially applies to acidosis caused by exogenous poisons.

All the metabolic acidoses produce hyperpnea as their first neurologic symptom. Subsequent manifestations are nonspecific and include lethargy, drowsiness, and confusion accompanied by mild, diffuse skeletal muscle hypertonus. Extensor plantar responses are found at a late stage. Deep stupor, coma, or convulsions, if they occur, usually develop only preterminally. Diagnosis is helped greatly by obtaining a history of metabolic disease or drug ingestion.

A useful clinical clue to the presence and possible cause of metabolic acidosis or certain other electrolyte disorders comes from estimating the *anion gap* from the measured blood electrolytes.[106] The calculation is based on the known electroneutrality of the serum, which requires the presence of an equal number of anions (negative charges) and cations (positive charges). For practical purposes, sodium and potassium (or sodium alone) represent 95 percent of the cations, whereas the most abundant and conveniently measured anions, chloride and bicarbonate, add up to only 85 percent of the normal total. The result is an anion gap in unmeasured electrolytes that amounts normally to about 12 ± 4 mEq./liter:

$$Na^+ - (Cl^- + HCO_3^-) = 8\text{-}16 \text{ mEq./liter}$$

An increase in the anion gap ordinarily implies the presence of an undetected electrolyte causing a metabolic acidosis and should prompt an immediate search by deduction and specific test for the "missing anion."

Severe metabolic acidosis has a dangerously depressing influence on the cardiovascular system and must be reversed by giving bicarbonate-containing solutions. As the serum bicarbonate is raised, the PCO_2 in the serum also rises. The charged bicarbonate ion does not diffuse readily across the blood-brain barrier into the cerebral extracellular space, but the CO_2 molecule does, thereby increasing the concentration of carbonic acid and at least transiently lowering the pH of the CSF and brain extracellular fluid. Thus, the too rapid correction of metabolic acidosis, although raising the serum pH, can paradoxically and temporarily lower the extracellular pH of the brain. During this period, short-lived neurologic depression may appear, but this is neither profound nor dangerous and does not outweigh the requirement for prompt correction of serum acidosis.

Alkalosis produces only mild encephalopathy. Acute *respiratory alkalosis* constricts the cerebral arterioles and decreases the cerebral blood flow. With the reduction of blood flow, lactic acid production by the brain increases, and whether it is caused by lactic acid or by a reduced blood supply, the patient may develop confusion, accompanied by slow waves in the EEG. However, the decrease in CBF is transient, and it is doubtful that prolonged respiratory alkalosis significantly interferes with cerebral function, except perhaps in rare instances in which too vigorous and prolonged hyperventilation is used to overcorrect preexisting respiratory acidosis (p. 233).[361] It follows that when respiratory alkalosis coexists with stupor or coma, one should search for the underlying cause, such as sepsis, hepatic coma, pulmonary infarction, salicylism, or cardiopulmonary hypoxemia. Profound *metabolic alkalosis* produces a blunted confusional state rather than stupor or coma. The mechanism by which alkalosis interferes with cerebral function is unknown, although such patients undergo a large change in pH of the CSF toward the alkaline side. Respiratory mechanisms via hypoventilation partially compensate for the metabolic alkalosis, but add their own neuropathologic threat since the hypoventilation characteristically lowers the arterial PO_2 to levels of approximately 50 mm. Hg. This degree of hypoxemia probably contributes to the mental symptoms in severe metabolic alkalosis.[329]

Disorders of Temperature Regulation

Both hyperthermia and hypothermia can interfere with cerebral metabolism, producing diffuse neurologic signs, including delirium, stupor, or coma.

Hypothermia

Hypothermia results from a variety of illnesses,[353] including disorders of the hypothalamus, myxedema, hypopituitarism, and bodily exposure. A low body temperature may accompany metabolic coma, particularly hypoglycemia and drug-induced coma, especially that resulting from barbiturate overdose, phenothiazine overdose, or alcoholism. With decreasing body temperature, cerebral metabolic needs decrease and thus cerebral blood flow and oxygen consumption fall. In the absence of any underlying disease that may be producing both coma and hypothermia, there is a rough correlation among the body temperature, and cerebral oxygen uptake, and the state of consciousness. Patients with body temperatures above 32.2°C are usually conscious unless there is some other metabolic reason for stupor or coma, whereas patients whose body temperatures decline below that level usually have at least clouding of consciousness, whatever the primary clinical condition.

Clinically, accidental hypothermia (i.e., hypothermia in the absence of any predisposing causes) is a disease mainly of elderly people exposed to a moderately cold environment. It occurs in the winter months, and most of the reports have come from England. Hypothermic patients are often found unconscious in a cold environment, although fully a third have been in their beds rather than out in the street. The patients who are unconscious are strikingly pale, have a pliable consistency of subcutaneous tissue, and may have the appearance of myxedema, even though that disease is not present. Shivering is absent if the temperature declines below about 30°C, but there may be occasional fascicular twitchings over the shoulders and trunk, and there is usually a diffuse increase in muscle tone leading almost to the appearance of rigor mortis. The body feels cold to the touch even in protected areas such as the perineum. Respirations are slow and shallow and there can be CO_2 retention. The blood pressure may be unmeasurable and the pulse very slow or absent. Some patients are thought to be dead when first encountered. At times the deep tendon reflexes are absent,[353] but usually they are present and may be hyperactive; they may, however, have a delayed relaxation phase resembling that of myxedema. The pupils may be constricted or dilated and reportedly may not respond to light. The electroencephalogram is diffusely slow without reduction in amplitude.[167] One makes the diagnosis by recording the body temperature and ruling out precipitating causes other than exposure. Since most clinical thermometers do not register below 35°C (95°F), simple perusal of the chart of temperatures taken by the nursing staff may not reveal the true severity of the hypothermia, and the perceptive physician must procure a thermometer that records sufficiently low readings to verify his clinical impression. Hypothermia carries a high mortality (40–60 percent). However, those who do recover rarely suffer residual neurologic changes. Pathologic changes in the brains of patients who die include perivascular hemorrhages in the region of the third ventricle with chromatolysis of ganglion cells. Multifocal infarcts have been described in several viscera, including the brain, and probably reflect the cardiovascular collapse that complicates severe hypothermia.

Hyperthermia

Hyperthermia sufficient to produce stupor or coma generally occurs only with *heat stroke*.[66,441,442] There are several metabolic studies on the effects of heat on the nervous system. Nemoto and Frankel reported an increase in the cerebral metabolic rate at temperatures between 38 and 42°C, but at 43°C cerebral metabolic uptake was decreased.[287] However, the cerebral anaerobic index (reflecting an increased lactate production) did not increase with elevated temperature, and the authors concluded that the failure of cerebral metabolism resulted from a limited supply of nucleotides required in cerebral glucose transport rather than from cerebral hypoxia. Meyer and Handa reported decreases in cerebral oxygen metabolism and slowing of the EEG at temperatures above 42°C.[267] These experimental studies correlate well with clinical studies, which consistently find that body temperatures of the order of 42°C or 43°C are required to produce coma, although lower temperatures may be associated with delirium. Heat stroke occurs both in young people who exercise unduly in heat to which they are unacclimatized[476] and in older people (who presumably possess less plastic adaptive mechanisms) during the summer's first hot spell. It is a particular threat in patients taking anticholinergic drugs (e.g., for Parkinson's disease), which interfere with heat dissipation by inhibiting sweating.

Clinically, heat stroke may begin suddenly with stupor or coma or the patient may pass through a period of agitated and violent delirium, sometimes punctuated by generalized convulsions. The patient's skin is usually hot and dry, but sweating occasionally persists during the course of heat stroke. The patient is tachycardic, may be normotensive or hypotensive, and may have a serum pH that is normal or slightly acidotic.[66] The pupils are usually small and reactive, caloric responses are present except terminally, and the skeletal muscles are usually diffusely hypertonic. The diagnosis is made by recording a body temperature in excess of 42°C. Unlike patients with coma caused by hypothermia, who regain neurologic normality if they survive, some patients who survive heat stroke are left with permanent neurologic residua, including cerebellar ataxia, dementia, and hemiparesis. However, if heat stroke is detected early and treatment is vigorous, permanent residua are rare.[66] Polyneuropathy may complicate *iatrogenic* hyperthermia.[49]

Malignant hyperthermia is a rare disorder of muscle metabolism that is characterized by a sudden fulminating and unexpected increase in body metabolism and temperature when susceptible patients or experimental animals[473] are exposed to a variety of anesthetic agents. The clinical symptoms of the disorder include high fever, respiratory and metabolic acidosis, and diffuse rigidity of skeletal muscles. The disorder may be precipitated by a variety of anesthetic agents, including halothane, succinylcholine, or methoxyflurane. Malignant hyperthermia reflects an abnormality of muscle metabolism that is inherited as an autosomal dominant trait. It occurs in 1 out of 20,000 anesthetized patients. If the disorder is recognized immediately, it can be treated by rapid cooling, pH normalization, and sometimes by procainamide or dantrolene. Otherwise it is commonly fatal.

Infectious and Inflammatory Disorders of the Central Nervous System

This section describes a group of disorders in which an accurate diagnosis of stupor or coma carries the highest priority. The conditions are relatively common and many of them perturb or depress the state of consciousness as a first symptom. Symptoms of central nervous system infection can easily mimic those of other illnesses. Yet quick and accurate action is nowhere more necessary, since proper treatment often is brain-saving or even life-saving, while delays or errors often result in irreversible neurologic deficits or death.

Acute Leptomeningitis

Acute leptomeningeal infections[231,358] frequently cause stupor or coma. In one unselected series 49 percent of 104 consecutive patients with acute meningitis had impaired consciousness and an additional 7 percent were comatose.[358] Leptomeningeal infections produce stupor and coma in one of several ways:

Cerebral Herniation. Severe leptomeningeal infection is often accompanied by considerable cerebral edema, especially in young persons. Cerebral edema is an almost invariable finding in fatal leptomeningitis,[358] and the degree may be so great that it produces both transtentorial and cerebellar tonsillar herniation.[85] In addition, leptomeningeal infections occlude cerebrospinal fluid absorptive pathways and, depending on the site of occlusion, cause either communicating or noncommunicating *hydrocephalus* in about 15 percent of patients. As many as 1 to

260

3 percent of patients may require shunting of the ventricles.[231] The enlargement of the ventricles by nonreabsorbed cerebrospinal fluid adds to increased intracranial pressure and increases the risk of cerebral herniation.

Bacterial Encephalitis and Vasculitis. The bacteria that cause acute leptomeningitis often invade the cerebrum, penetrating via the Virchow-Robin perivascular spaces and causing inflammation of both penetrating meningeal vessels and the brain itself.[85,226,438] The effects on the brain are both vascular and metabolic. Vasculitis induces diffuse or focal ischemia of the underlying brain and can lead to focal areas of necrosis. Diffuse necrosis of the subcortical white matter has also been reported as a complication of such bacterial vasculitis.[47] Cerebral veins may be occluded, as well as arteries.

Toxic Encephalopathy. Both the bacterial invaders and the inflammatory response to them can have profound effects on cerebral metabolism, with bacterial or cellular toxins directly competing for nutrients and inhibiting enzyme reactions. Fishman and his colleagues have demonstrated that membrane fractions of white cells incubated with brain slices produce cytotoxic brain edema with increased glucose oxidation, increased lactate production, and evidence of energy depletion.[119]

Inappropriate Therapy. The fluid therapy employed for patients with acute leptomeningitis carries a potential risk of inducing acute water intoxication unless carefully regulated. Many patients with bacterial meningitis suffer from inappropriate ADH secretion, which leads to hyponatremia and cerebral edema when excessive amounts of water are infused. All these mechanisms lead to a form of stupor and coma that closely resembles that produced by other metabolic diseases, leading us to include acute leptomeningitis in this section.

The meningeal infections that produce coma are principally those caused by acute bacterial organisms, particularly *H. influenzae, D. pneumoniae,* and *N. meningitides,* streptococci and *L. monocytogenes.* The three organisms listed first are the major causes of bacterial meningitis in the general population.[203,358] Meningococcal and influenza infections frequently produce meningitis as their only manifestation; pneumococcal and streptococcal meningitis usually arise secondary to infection elsewhere in the body, requiring in these patients a careful search for another source of infection. The search should include careful otolaryngologic examination.[203]

The clinical appearance of acute meningitis is one of an acute metabolic encephalopathy with drowsiness or stupor accompanied by the toxic symptoms of chills, fever, tachycardia, and tachypnea. Most patients have either a headache or a history of it. Distinct meningeal signs are present in over 75 percent of the patients on admission and in about 85 percent at some time during their hospitalization.[358] Polymorphonuclear leukocytes are usually present in the CSF (or at least heavy bacterial counts plus hypoglycorrhachia) by the time the patient reaches the hospital. Patients with meningococcal infection may have the cutaneous stigmata of spotted fever, and those with other bacterial infections often have a suppurative source in the lung, a paranasal sinus, or the middle ear. If meningitis follows its usual evolution, it produces respiratory, ocular, and motor signs that generally resemble those of several other metabolic comas. In addition, however, there is a high incidence of focal neurologic signs, either from localized cerebral ischemia or postictal states. Both focal and generalized convulsions are common, particularly when pneumococci and streptococci are the invading organisms.

In the diagnosis of meningitis, the presence of acute headache, fever, nuchal rigidity, and somnolence combined with a CSF containing polymorphonuclear leukocytes and a low sugar content hardly allows an alternative. However, there are special circumstances in which either life-threatening coma complicates the course of meningitis or the diagnosis is difficult to separate from other causes of insidiously developing coma. Williams, Swanson, and Chapman emphasized a fulminating course in children who, during the first few hours of illness, suddenly developed signs of acute transtentorial rostral-caudal herniation superimposed on the initially characteristic signs of *H. influenzae* meningitis.[455] The complication was attributed to severe edema of the brain. Clinically, such children rapidly lose consciousness and develop hyperpnea disproportionate to the degree of fever. The pupils dilate, at first moderately and then widely, then fix, and the child develops decerebrate motor signs. Urea, mannitol, or other hyperosmotic agents, if used properly, can prevent or reverse the full development of the ominous changes that are otherwise rapidly fatal. Dodge and Schwartz warn that lumbar puncture must be undertaken cautiously in patients with acute meningitis to minimize risks of cerebral herniation.[85] The necessity of an accurate bacteriologic diagnosis in acute meningitis is so overwhelming, however, that lumbar puncture must be carried out, no matter what the risks. If symptoms of cerebral herniation are present before or immediately after lumbar puncture, hyperventilation should be applied immediately and a hyperosmolar agent such as mannitol should be infused rapidly (see Chapter 8).

In elderly patients, bacterial meningitis sometimes presents as insidiously developing stupor or coma in which there may be focal neurologic signs but little evidence of severe systemic illness or stiff neck. In one series, 50 percent of such patients with meningitis were admitted to hospital with another and incorrect diagnosis.[358] Such patients can be regarded incorrectly as having suffered a stroke, but this error is readily avoided by accurate spinal fluid examinations. Accurate spinal fluid examinations also avoid another potential error in the diagnosis of meningitis, namely, that of erroneously making a diagnosis of subarachnoid hemorrhage simply because the blood of a traumatic lumbar puncture obscures the elevated spinal fluid white cell count. With acute, intrinsic bleeding, there is approximately 1 white cell to each 1000 red cells in the CSF. Ratios higher than this should be investigated immediately with supplementary Gram stains and measurement of glucose content.

Patients are occasionally observed who develop the encephalopathy of meningitis before white cells appear in the lumbar spinal fluid. The series of Carpenter and Petersdorf[51] includes several such cases, and the following is an example from our own series.

Patient 4–16. A 28-year-old man complained of mild diurnal temperature elevation for several days with intermittent sore throat, chills, and malaise. He had no muscle or joint complaints or cough, but his chest felt tight. He saw his physician, who found him to be warm and to appear acutely ill, but he lacked significant abnormalities on examination, except that his pharynx and ear canals were reddened. A diagnosis of influenza was made, but the next afternoon he had difficulty thinking clearly and was admitted to the hospital.

His blood pressure was 90/70 mm. Hg, pulse 120 per minute, respirations 20 per minute, and body temperature 38.6 °C. He was acutely ill, restless, and unable to sustain his attention to cooperate fully in the examination. No rash, petechiae, or wheals were seen. There was slight nuchal rigidity and some mild spasm of the back and hamstring muscles. The remainder of the physical and the neurologic examination was normal. The white blood count was 18,000 per cu. mm. with a shift to the left. Urinalysis was normal. A lumbar puncture was performed with the patient in the lateral recumbent position; the opening pressure was 210 mm., the closing pressure was 170 mm., and the clear CSF contained 1 red cell and no white cells. The next morning the protein was reported as 80 mg./dl., the glucose content as 0.

The first evening at 9 o'clock his temperature had declined to 38°C, and he was seemingly improved. Two hours later he had a chill followed by severe headache, and he became slightly irrational. The body temperature was 37.6 °C. There was an increase in the nuchal rigidity and in the hamstring and back-muscle spasm. The white blood count had increased to 23,000 per cu. mm. Shortly before 1:30 A.M. he became delirious and then comatose with irregular respiration. The pupils were equal and reactive; the optic fundi were normal; the deep tendon reflexes were equal and active throughout. The left plantar response was extensor; the right was equivocal. Because of the high white cell count, fever, and coma, administration of large doses of antibiotics was started, but the diagnosis was uncertain.

The next morning the spinal fluid and throat cultures that had been obtained the evening before were found to contain *Neisseria meningitides* and a lumbar puncture now revealed purulent spinal fluid containing 6000 white cells per cu. mm. under a high pressure, with high protein and low glucose contents. His treatment with penicillin and sulfadiazine continued, and he recovered without sequelae.

Comment: The error in diagnosis in this patient was in failing to examine the original spinal fluid sample microscopically or immediately for its glucose concentration. Bacteria can often be seen on Gram stain of centrifuged spinal fluid of a patient with meningitis even when cells have not yet increased and the glucose and protein remain normal. If meningitis or other CNS infection is strongly suspected and no cells are found in the initial examination, the lumbar puncture should be repeated. Patients with overwhelming meningococcal septicemia and few or no polymorphonuclear leukocytes in their spinal fluid represent the worst prognostic group of patients with acute bacterial meningitis. Although a high concentration of polymorphonuclear leukocytes and a decreased spinal fluid glucose strongly suggest the diagnosis of bacterial meningitis, viral infections including mumps and herpes simplex[1,453] can also cause hypoglycorrhachia.

Acute Encephalitis

Viruses, bacteria, rickettsia, protozoa, and nematodes can all invade brain parenchyma. However, only viruses and bacteria invade the brain acutely and diffusely enough to cause altered states of consciousness and to demand immediate attention in the diagnosis of stupor or coma. Bacterial encephalitis has been considered above as a part of meningitis. Viral encephalitis is discussed in this section.

Viral encephalitis can be divided into five pathologic syndromes. These syndromes are sometimes clinically distinct as well, but the clinical signs of the first three are often so similar as to preclude specific diagnosis without biopsy or autopsy. (1) *Acute viral encephalitis* results from invasion of the brain by a virus that produces primarily or exclusively a central nervous system infection.[24,177] (2) *Parainfectious encephalomyelitis* also occurs during or after viral infections, particularly the childhood infections of measles, mumps, and varicella. (3) *Acute toxic encephalopathy* usually occurs during the course of a systemic infection with a common virus. (4) *Progressive viral infections* are encephalitides caused by conventional viral agents but occurring in susceptible patients, usually those who are immunosuppressed or develop the infection before birth or early childhood. Such infections lead to slow or progressive destruction of the nervous system. The disorders include subacute sclerosing panencephalitis, subacute measles encephalitis, progressive rubella panencephalitis, and progressive multifocal leukoencephalopathy. These latter disorders are subacute or gradual in onset, producing stupor or coma in their terminal stages. Most are not dealt with in detail here since they rarely cause problems in the differential diagnosis of stupor or coma. Progressive multifocal leukoencephalopathy is considered along with the primary neuronal and glial disorder of brain (Table 11, heading G). (5) *"Slow virus" infections* are caused by unconventional agents. These include Creutzfeldt-Jakob disease, kuru, and perhaps other progressive dementing illnesses. With the occasional exception of Creutzfeldt-Jakob disease (also under heading G), these disorders likewise are gradual in onset; they do not represent problems in differential diagnosis and are not discussed here.

In each of these pathologically defined illnesses, the viruses produce neurologic signs in one of three ways: (1) They invade, reproduce in, and destroy neurons and glial cells. Cell dysfunction or death may occur even in the absence of any inflammatory or immune response.[338] (2) They evoke an immune response that can cause hemorrhage, inflammation, and necrosis (acute viral encephalitis) or demyelination (postinfectious encephalomyelitis). (3) They provoke cerebral edema and sometimes vascular damage, both of which increase the intracranial pressure and, like a supratentorial mass lesion, lead to transtentorial herniation (usually of the central type; see Patient 4-17 below).

The clinical findings in each of the five pathologically defined viral encephalitides are sometimes sufficiently different to allow clinical diagnosis even when the illness has progressed to the stage of stupor or coma. Furthermore, within each of these categories specific viral illnesses may have individual clinical features that strongly suggest the diagnosis. Unfortunately, all too often the first three categories, which cause acute brain dysfunction, cannot be distinguished on a clinical basis, and the generic term acute encephalitis must be used unless biopsy or autopsy material establishes the exact pathologic change. To compound the complexity, certain viruses can cause different pathologic changes in the brain, depending on the setting. For example, acute toxic encephalopathy, parainfectious encephalomyelitis, subacute sclerosing panencephalitis, and subacute measles encephalitis can all be caused by the measles virus. Despite these difficulties in diagnosis, an attempt should be made to separate the acute encephalitides into pathologic categories and to establish the causal agent, since the treatment and prognosis are different in the different categories. How often brain biopsy is justified in diagnosis remains an unsettled question, discussed in detail on page 270.

ACUTE VIRAL ENCEPHALITIS. Although a number of viruses cause human encephalitis, only two major types are both common and produce coma in the United States: arboviruses (Eastern equine, Western equine, and St. Louis encephalitis) and herpes simplex encephalitis. (The varicella-zoster virus, a rare cause of stupor in the normal population, produces cerebral vasculitis [p. 273], and the enteroviruses Coxsackie, echovirus, and polio cause meningoencephalitis but rarely stupor or coma.) The arboviruses produce their symptoms in epidemics and are thereby easy to diagnose once the epidemic has started. Herpes simplex virus is the most commonly identified sporadic form of acute encephalitis and is discussed here as the model of an acute encephalitic cause of coma. Often, however, the cause of acute viral encephalitis is not established, despite careful serologic and often pathologic evaluation.[177] We recently reviewed our experience at New York Hospital and Memorial Sloan-Kettering Cancer Center with 51 patients whose final diagnosis was acute encephalitis. A viral cause was established in 20; 8 suffered from herpes simplex virus encephalitis, 8 varicella-zoster virus, 2 infectious mononucleosis, 1 Reye's syndrome, and 1 subacute sclerosing panencephalitis. Seven additional patients suffered from a postinfectious encephalomyelitis, with the viral origin of the systemic infection not being identified. After all diagnostic efforts were exhausted, 24 patients, almost half the group, carried a diagnosis of acute viral encephalitis of unknown cause.

Herpes Simplex Encephalitis.[23] This disease is pathologically characterized by

264

extensive neuronal damage in the cerebral hemispheres with a remarkable predilection by the virus for the gray matter of the medial temporal lobe as well as other limbic structures and the insula, cingulate gyrus, and inferior frontal lobe. Neuronal destruction is accompanied by perivascular invasion with inflammatory cells and proliferation of microglia with frequent formation of glial nodules. The vascular endothelium often swells and proliferates. Areas of focal cortical necrosis are common. A diapedesis of red cells into brain tissue is sufficient to produce petechiae or frank hemorrhage in the areas of necrosis. Cowdry type A inclusion bodies in neurons and glial cells are a distinctive feature.

Clinically, herpes simplex encephalitis begins with the acute onset of a confusional state, often accompanied by headache, fever, and seizures. The illness progresses acutely or subacutely to produce stupor or coma. This early stage may be fulminating, and in some instances only a few hours sees a transition from full health to stupor. Often behavior disturbances, selective memory loss, or an agitated delirium, particularly with olfactory or gustatory hallucinations, precedes coma by hours or days—a pattern so characteristic as to suggest the diagnosis. Focal motor signs frequently accompany the onset of coma, and tremors of the extremities, face, and even trunk commonly complement the agitated delirium of herpes encephalitis. Occasionally the somatic signs of herpes simplex encephalitis are limited to the brainstem with cranial nerve palsies predominating.[104,113]

The cerebrospinal fluid pressure is usually increased (180–400 mm. CSF) and the white cell count is usually elevated (10–1000 cells per cu. mm., mostly mononuclear). Both may be normal, particularly early in the course of the illness. Up to 500 red cells per cu. mm. are common and the CSF protein content usually is elevated (values up 870 mg./dl. having been reported). The CSF sugar is usually normal but occasionally depressed.[1] The EEG is always abnormal. Distinctive, periodic, high voltage, 1 Hz. sharp waves from one or both temporal lobes are highly characteristic of herpes simplex encephalitis[59] and suggest a poor prognosis.[102] The radionuclide scan is often abnormal, even early in the illness, revealing an increased uptake of the radionuclide in necrotic areas of the temporal lobe. Such scans may be abnormal even if the CT scan is normal. If the CT scan is abnormal, it usually demonstrates a low density lesion with contrast-enhancement in one or both temporal lobes. The diagnosis can be established early in the illness only by brain biopsy, with culture of the virus from the biopsy specimens or demonstration of viral antigen by immunofluorescence. The former technique is more sensitive. Early diagnosis of herpes simplex encephalitis is vital since effective treatment now available[449] yields the best results when patients are treated before becoming comatose.

Herpes simplex encephalitis is often a difficult diagnosis to make, in part because of its sporadic appearance. Its subacute onset, in which headache and fever can be overshadowed by inappropriate behavior, agitation, tremor, and memory loss, can be misinterpreted as being caused by delirium tremens, drug intoxication, or catatonia[349] unless appropriate laboratory tests are performed. Even with the suggestive clinical picture, the wrong diagnosis may be reached. In the Herpes Simplex Cooperative Study (Whitley, personal communication), cerebral biopsies from patients clinically suspected of harboring herpes simplex encephalitis were positive only 55 percent of the time. Other diagnoses were established 35 percent of the time, and in 15 percent the biopsy was nondiagnostic.

In a large proportion of cases, untreated herpes simplex encephalitis progresses to produce coma, focal motor signs, and seizures. Sometimes, as in the following case, severe hemispheral brain swelling produces transtentorial herniation and death.

Patient 4-17. A 32-year-old children's nurse was admitted to the hospital in coma. She had felt vaguely unwell 5 days before admission and then developed occipital headache and vomiting. Two days before admission, a physician carefully examined her but found only a temperature of 39°C and a normal blood count. She remained alone for the next 48 hours and was found unconscious in her room just before admission.

Examination showed an unresponsive woman with her head and eyes deviated to the right. She had small ecchymoses over the left eye, left hip, and knee. Her neck was moderately stiff. The right pupil was slightly larger than the left, both reacted to light, and the oculocephalic reflex was intact. The corneal reflex was bilaterally sluggish, and the gag reflex was intact. Her extremities were flaccid, the stretch reflexes were 3+, and the plantar responses were flexor. In the emergency room she had a generalized convulsion associated with deviation of the head and the eyes to the left. The lumbar puncture pressure was 130 mm. of CSF. There were 550 mononuclear cells and 643 red blood cells per cu. mm. The CSF sugar was 65 and the protein was 54 mg./dl. Skull x-ray findings were normal. A right carotid arteriogram showed marked elevation of the sylvian vessels with only minimal deviation of the midline structures. Burr holes were placed; no subdural blood was found. A ventriculogram showed the third ventricle curved to the right. The EEG contained 1 to 2 cps. high amplitude slow waves appearing regularly every 3 to 5 seconds from a background of almost complete electrical silence. Low amplitude 10 to 12 cps. sharp wave bursts of gradually increasing voltage began over either frontal area and occurred every 1 to 2 minutes; they lasted 20 to 40 seconds and were associated with seizure activity.

Her seizures were partially controlled with anticonvulsants and she received 20 million units of penicillin and 3 gm. of chloramphenicol per day. Her condition gradually deteriorated, and on the eighth hospital day she developed midposition fixed pupils with absence of oculovestibular responses and diabetes insipidus with a serum osmolality of 313 mOsm. per liter and urine specific gravity of 1.005. Eight days after admission, lumbar puncture yielded a serosanguineous fluid with 26,000 RBC and 2200 mononuclear cells. The protein was 210 mg./dl. Examination of the serum for complement fixing antibodies to herpes simplex virus at the onset of hospitalization disclosed no response at a 1:4 dilution, but a positive response at a 1:32 dilution was obtained just prior to death. She died 10 days after admission, having been maintained with artificial respiration and pressor agents for 48 hours.

At autopsy the herpes simplex virus was cultured from the cerebral cortex. The leptomeninges were congested, and the brain was swollen and soft with bilateral deep tentorial grooving along the hippocampal gyrus. The diencephalon was displaced an estimated 8 to 10 mm. caudally through the tentorial notch. On cut section the medial and anterior temporal lobes as well as the insula were bilaterally necrotic, hemorrhagic, and soft. Linear and oval hemorrhages were found in the thalamus bilaterally and extended down the central portion of the brainstem as far as the pons. Hemorrhages were also found in the cerebellum, and there was a small, intact arteriovenous malformation in the right sylvian fissure. There were meningeal infiltrations of predominantly lymphocytes, some plasma cells, and polymorphonuclear leukocytes. The perivascular spaces were also infiltrated in places extending to the subcortical white matter. In some areas the entire cortex was necrotic with shrunken and eosinophilic nerve cells. Numerous areas of extravasated red blood cells were present in the cortex, basal ganglia, and upper brainstem. Marked microglial proliferation and astrocytic hyperplasia were present. Cowdry type A intranuclear inclusion bodies were present primarily in the oligodendroglia, but were also seen in astroglia, small neurons, and occasional capillary endothelial cells.

Comment: This patient's history, findings, and course were characteristic of herpes simplex encephalitis. In her, as in others with this disease, the tendency for the virus to cause focal and asymmetrical temporal lobe edema and necrosis created focal signs prompting mistaken suspicions of subdural hematoma or brain tumor. The latter error is frequently reinforced in such cases by arteriographic evidence of temporal lobe enlargement secondary to edema and compounded by evidence secured from a radioactive brain scan showing a focal breakdown of the blood-brain barrier, such as also occurs with neoplasms. However, a history of 5 to 7 days or less of headache, fever, confusion, and other signs of bilateral cerebral dysfunction along with pleocytosis is incompatible with either subdural hematoma or operable neoplasm and obviates the need for surgery and emergency contrast studies other than CT scan. More careful attention to the needs for accurate viral diagnosis and treatment as well as to the signs of impending transtentorial herniation followed by early treatment with dehydrating agents might have delayed or prevented this patient's death.

Arbovirus Encephalitis. The clinical diagnosis of epidemic viral encephalitis caused by an arbovirus is rarely a problem once an outbreak has occurred, being easily made in patients who develop headache, fever, nuchal rigidity, and pleocytosis. Indeed, care must be taken during an epidemic not to make a diagnosis of encephalitis when faced with other neurologic illnesses or injuries causing coma. There are slight differences in the clinical pictures of the arbovirus infections. St. Louis encephalitis is usually a milder infection, more often causing lethargy and confusion than stupor or coma. Eastern equine encephalitis, on the other hand, often causes coma, seizures, and paralysis. Western equine encephalitis may be complicated by post-encephalitic parkinsonism.[24]

ACUTE TOXIC ENCEPHALOPATHY. Acute toxic encephalopathy[246] is the term applied to a nervous system disorder usually occurring during or after a systemic viral infection and characterized clinically by the acute onset of increased intracranial pressure with or without focal neurologic signs and without CSF pleocytosis. The disorder is distinguished pathologically from acute viral encephalitis by the absence of inflammatory change or other pathologic abnormalities of acute viral encephalitis, save for cerebral edema and its consequences. Pathophysiologically, acute toxic encephalopathy is distinguished from acute viral encephalitis in that the clinical symptoms produced by acute toxic encephalopathy are due to cerebral edema with its attendant increased intracranial pressure and transtentorial herniation, and not to cellular destruction, inflammation, or necrosis. The cause of acute toxic encephalopathy is unknown and may represent several different illnesses (the most well defined of which is Reye's syndrome, p. 268) rather than a single disorder. It often accompanies viral infection, including the common exanthems such as measles and mumps, but it also appears without evidence of preceding systemic viral infection. In some instances viruses have been identified in the brain at autopsy. There may be accompanying evidence of an acute systemic illness, such as liver and kidney damage in Reye's syndrome, or the patient may be free of symptoms other than those of central nervous system dysfunction. Death is caused by cerebral edema with transtentorial herniation. At autopsy neither inflammation nor demyelination are encountered in the brain, only evidence of severe and widespread cerebral edema. Acute toxic encephalopathy is predominantly a disease of children under the age of 5, but is occasionally encountered in adults as well.[489]

Clinically, the disease is characterized by an acute or subacute febrile onset associated with headache, sometimes nausea and vomiting, and often delirium or drowsiness followed by stupor or coma. Focal neurologic signs usually are absent but may be prominent and include hemiparesis or hemiplegia, aphasia, or visual field defects. In its most fulminant form, the untreated illness progresses rapidly, with signs of transtentorial herniation leading to coma with impaired ocular movements, abnormal pupillary reflexes, abnormal posturing, and, eventually, respiratory failure and death. Status epilepticus marks the early course of a small proportion of the patients. Patient 4–18 illustrates such a case.

Patient 4–18: A 46-year-old man was in hospital 10 days following a negative inguinal node lymph dissection for the treatment of urethral cancer. He was well and was ready for discharge when he complained of a sudden left temporal headache and was noted by his roommate to be confused. Neurologic examination revealed a modest temperature elevation to 38.1 °C and an awake but confused individual who was disoriented to time and had difficulty carrying out three-step commands. The segmental neurologic examination was entirely intact, and laboratory evaluation for infection or metabolic abnormalities was entirely normal. The electroencephalogram was bilaterally slow, more so on the right side than left. The lumbar puncture pressure was 160 mm. CSF. There were two red cells, one white cell, and a protein of 41 mg./dl. The glucose was 75 mg./dl. Within 48 hours he became agitated and mildly aphasic, with a right homonymous visual field defect. He then had a generalized convulsion. The day following the seizure, the lumbar puncture pressure was 230 mm. CSF; there was one white cell, a protein of 90 mg./dl., and glucose of 85 mg./dl. A CT scan was normal, as were bilateral carotid arteriograms. Cultures of blood and CSF for bacteria and viruses and viral titers were all negative, as was a coagulation profile. Within 48 hours after the convulsion, the patient lapsed into coma, with evidence of transtentorial herniation leading to respiratory arrest and death despite treatment with mannitol and steroids. At autopsy, the general examination was normal except for evidence of his previous surgery. There was no evidence of residual cancer. The brain weighed 1500 gm. and was grossly swollen, with evidence of both temporal lobe and tonsillar herniation and a Duret hemorrhage in the pons. Microscopic examination was consistent with severe cerebral edema and herniation, but there was no inflammation nor were there inclusion bodies.

Comment: Except for a somewhat protracted course, this patient is typical of patients with acute toxic encephalopathy. The pathogenesis of this disorder is unknown, but its common occurrence associated with viral infections, makes us include it among the infectious and inflammatory diseases of the nervous system.

A clinical distinction between acute sporadic viral encephalitis and acute toxic encephalopathy often cannot be made. Certain clues, when present, help to differentiate the two entities: acute encephalopathy appears with or shortly after a banal viral infection, usually occurs in children under 5 years of age, may be associated with hypoglycemia and liver function abnormalities, and usually produces only a modest degree of fever. Rapidly developing increased intracranial pressure in the absence of focal signs or neck stiffness also suggests acute toxic encephalopathy. Conversely, prominent focal signs, particularly those of temporal lobe dysfunction and particularly accompanied by an abnormal CT or radionuclide scan, indicate an acute viral encephalitis such as herpes simplex. The presence of pleocytosis (with or without additional red cells) in the CSF suggests acute viral encephalitis, whereas a spinal fluid under very high pressure but with a normal cellular content suggests acute toxic encephalopathy. In many instances, however, neither a clinical nor laboratory diagnosis can be made immediately. If one is uncertain, brain biopsy should be carried out to detect the treatable herpes simplex encephalitis (see p. 270). Even a brain biopsy sometimes does not distinguish between viral and toxic encephalitis, probably because some examples of acute viral encephalitis are multifocal and the abnormal area is missed.

Reye's Syndrome. A variant of acute toxic encephalopathy is Reye's syndrome. This disorder, like other acute toxic encephalopathies, is characterized by progressive encephalopathy with persistent vomiting, often following a viral illness (particularly influenza B and varicella). It differs from other forms of acute toxic encephalopathy in that it occurs in epidemics and there is usually evidence of hepatic dysfunction and often hypoglycemia. The illness is pathologically characterized by fatty degeneration of the viscera, particularly the liver but also the kidney, heart, lungs, pancreas, and skeletal muscle. The cause of death in most cases, as in acute toxic encephalopathy, is cerebral edema with transtentorial and cerebellar herniation. The pathogenesis of Reye's syndrome is unknown. There is substantial chemical[84] and electron microscopic[315] evidence to indicate that the primary pathologic abnormality lies in the mitochondria. The disease was once thought to be uniformly fatal, but with meticulous control of intracranial pressure many patients now survive without sequelae.[421] Some of those who die do so of complications of therapy with hyperosmolar agents, including hypotension and serum hyperosmolality.[105]

PARAINFECTIOUS CNS DISORDERS. Parainfectious disseminated encephalomyelitis and acute hemorrhagic leukoencephalopathy are terms applied to distinct but related clinical and pathologic disorders, both of which probably are caused by an immunologic reaction either to the virus itself or to a virus-triggered autoimmune reaction. The neurologic signs of parainfectious encephalomyelitis appear to result exclusively or predominantly from the effects of the body's immune reactions and do not appear to be a direct result of the viral infection. Similar clinical and pathologic disorders can be produced in experimental animals by the injection of brain extracts of myelin basic protein mixed with appropriate adjuvants. Here, the hemorrhagic changes appear to signify a hyperacute form of allergic encephalomyelitis.[26] In a few instances a causal virus has been isolated from the brain at autopsy.

Encephalomyelitis. In parainfectious disseminated encephalomyelitis, the brain and spinal cord contain multiple perivascular zones of demyelination in which axis cylinders may be either spared or destroyed. There is usually striking perivascular cuffing by inflammatory cells. Clinically, the illness occasionally arises spontaneously, but usually it follows by several days a known or presumed viral infection, frequently an exanthem (e.g., rubella, varicella) but occasionally a banal upper respiratory infection or another common viral infection (e.g., mumps[22] or herpes[211]). The onset is usually rapid, with headache, a return of fever, and delirium, stupor, or coma. Nuchal rigidity may be present. Both focal and generalized convulsions are common, as are focal motor signs such as hemiplegia or paraplegia.

Careful examination often discloses evidence for disseminated focal CNS dysfunction in the form of optic neuritis, conjugate and dysconjugate eye movement abnormalities, and sensory losses distributed differently from motor weaknesses. In 80 percent of cases, the CSF white cell count is elevated, usually to less than 500 lymphocytes per cu. mm. The CSF protein may be slightly increased, but the glucose is normal. In about one out of five patients, the CSF is normal. The diagnosis of acute disseminated encephalomyelitis is suspected when a patient becomes neurologically ill following a systemic viral infection. Evidence of widespread or multifocal nervous system involvement and of mild lymphocytic meningitis supports the diagnosis.

Acute Hemorrhagic Leukoencephalopathy. This disorder is marked pathologically by an inflammation and demyelination similar to disseminated encephalomyelitis, plus widespread hemorrhagic lesions in the cerebral white matter. These latter vary in diameter from microscopic to several centimeters and are accompanied by focal necrosis and edema. The perivascular infiltrations frequently contain many neutrophils, and there is often perivascular fibrinous impregnation. The clinical course is as violent as the pathologic response. The illness may follow a banal viral infection or may complicate septic shock,[154] but often no such history is obtained. The illness begins abruptly with headache, fever, nausea, and vomiting. Affected patients rapidly lapse into coma with high fever but little or no nuchal rigidity. Convulsions and focal neurologic signs, especially hemiparesis, are common. Focal cerebral hemorrhages and edema may produce both the clinical and radiographic signs of a supratentorial mass lesion.[68] The CSF is usually under increased pressure and contains from 10 to 500 mononuclear cells and up to 1000 RBC per cu. mm. The CSF protein may be elevated to 100 to 300 mg./dl. or more.

As a rule, the problem in the differential diagnosis of coma presented by disseminated and hemorrhagic encephalomyelitis is to distinguish it from viral encephalitis and acute toxic encephalopathy. At times a distinction may be impossible, either clinically or virologically. As a general rule, patients with viral encephalitis tend to be more severely ill and to have higher fevers for longer times than patients with disseminated encephalomyelitis, with the exception of the hemorrhagic variety. Acute toxic encephalopathy usually is more acute in onset and is associated with higher intracranial pressure and with fewer focal neurologic signs, either clinically or radiographically. Neither infectious nor parainfectious encephalitis much resembles in its course coma caused by supratentorial mass lesions per se, and neither group produces symptoms and signs simulating subtentorial destructive lesions. Bacterial endocarditis sometimes produces a multifocal encephalopathy accompanied by coma, fever, and pleocytosis; here diagnosis is assisted by the presence of changing cardiac murmurs, by finding emboli in other organs, and by identifying bacterial organisms in blood cultures.

CEREBRAL BIOPSY FOR DIAGNOSIS OF ENCEPHALITIS. When faced with a delirious or stuporous patient suspected of suffering acute encephalitis, the physician is often perplexed about how best to proceed. The clinical pictures of the various forms of encephalitis are often so similar that only cerebral biopsy will distinguish them, but the treatment of the various forms differs. Of the acute viral encephalitides, herpes simplex can be effectively treated by antiviral agents, and it is likely that in some immune-suppressed patients other viral infections such as varicella-zoster and cytomegalovirus also respond to antiviral treatment. Acute toxic encephalitis does not respond to antiviral treatment, but, at least in Reye's syndrome, meticulous monitoring and control of intracranial pressure is effective therapy. Acute parainfectious encephalomyelitis is not reported to respond to either antiviral treatment or control of intracranial pressure; some have recommended the use of steriods or immunosuppressive agents, since it is the immune reaction that is probably responsible for the destructiveness of the illness. However, cerebral biopsy is not a procedure to be undertaken lightly, and one might argue that because herpes simplex encephalitis is the only major viral encephalitis with a specific treatment, one might treat on clinical suspicion without securing a biopsy. On the other hand, the high incidence of incorrect diagnosis in patients biopsied for suspected herpes simplex and the presence of other treatable lesions in that series of patients suggests that biopsies are often important and valuable for the patient: In Whitley's series (personal communication), 35 percent of patients undergoing cerebral biopsy for a presumptive diagnosis of herpes simplex encephalitis had other diseases identified by the biopsy. These included tuberculosis, toxoplasmosis, cryptococcosis, and carcinoma—all illnesses for which some treatment is available.

Weighing the pros and cons, we tentatively conclude the following: (1) Patients suffering from acute nonepidemic encephalitis with focal features, particularly if those focal features suggest temporal lobe dysfunction, should be subjected to cerebral biopsy but treated immediately for herpes simplex, even preceding definitive interpretation of the biopsy results. (2) Patients suffering from encephalitis characterized by increased intracranial pressure without focal features should not be biopsied, but instead treated, when necessary, to reduce intracranial pressure. (3) Patients in whom acute encephalitis follows a known exanthem do not require biopsy. (4) For patients suffering with acute encephalitis in whom an identifying cause is not available, and in whom there are focal features other than the limbic involvement that suggests herpes simplex, cerebral biopsy should *probably* be carried out. The benefits of making a diagnosis of a potentially treatable disease outweigh the short and long-term risks of the biopsy itself.

Procuring the maximum useful information from a cerebral biopsy requires close cooperation between the primary physician, the neurosurgeon, the pathologist, and the microbiologist-immunologist. All should be alerted when a cerebral biopsy is contemplated. The biopsy site should include the area of maximum pathology as defined by clinical signs, electroencephalographic foci, or areas of abnormality on radionuclide or CT scan. Biopsies cannot be taken from motor cortex when focal motor signs are prominent, but they can be taken from premotor cortex on the involved side. If there are no clear focal signs, biopsies should be taken from the nondominant temporal tip if herpes simplex encephalitis is suspected, or the frontal lobe if that is not the major clinical diagnosis. The biopsy should include both gray and white matter and should be large enough to supply tissue for all relevant diagnostic laboratories (3 mm.[3] is probably the smallest feasible size). The pathologist should be immediately available to prepare the fresh tissue for routine histology, electron microscopy, and immunofluorescence or immunoperoxidase assay. A microbiologist should be available to prepare the material for viral, bacteriologic, and fungal culture. Ideally, these investigators should be present in the operating room to direct the handling of the tissue, but, if not, two samples of fresh tissue should be delivered in sterile condition to the pathology and microbiology laboratories for immediate processing.

Cerebral Vasculitis

Certain inflammatory vascular disorders of the brain are either restricted to CNS vessels (e.g., granulomatous angiitis) or produce such prominent CNS symptoms as to appear to be primarily a brain disorder. Recent reviews classify and detail the clinical and arteriographic findings in a large number of illnesses that produce cerebral or systemic vasculitis.[111,401] Only those specific illnesses that may be perplexing causes of stupor or coma are considered here.

GRANULOMATOUS ANGIITIS. In this acute disorder of the nervous system, the pathologic changes in blood vessels may be limited to the brain or involve other systemic organs.[196,486] When the disease is limited to the brain, it tends to affect small leptomeningeal and intracerebral blood vessels. When more widespread it affects larger blood vessels. The cause is unknown. Infection by mycoplasma, rickettsia, or virus has been suggested, as has an autoimmune or immune complex disorder. The inflammatory lesion of the blood vessel causes ischemia of the surrounding brain and may lead to infarction.

Clinically, the onset is usually acute or subacute, with headache, mental changes, impairment of consciousness, focal or generalized seizures, and frequently focal neurologic signs, including hemiparesis, visual loss, and extrapyramidal disorders. Most patients who are alert at onset rapidly progress to stupor or coma, and the disease usually is fatal in days to a few weeks. A more chronic and progressive form exists and can last months or years.

The laboratory examination usually is characterized by an elevated blood erythrocyte sedimentation rate. There is mild CSF pleocytosis (20–40 lymphocytes per cu. mm.) with an elevated total protein and an increased gamma globulin level. If larger blood vessels are involved, the cerebral arteriogram may show the configuration of vasculitis. If only small vessels are involved, the arteriogram may be normal. The specific diagnosis can only be established by cerebral biopsy, and at times even that fails to show the lesion.[299] Jellinger considers granulomatous angiitis restricted to the central nervous system to be a local variety of giant cell angiitis (temporal arteritis), with the same underlying etiology and pathophysiology.[196] If so, steroid therapy might be helpful when an antemortem diagnosis can be established.

SYSTEMIC LUPUS ERYTHEMATOSUS. Acute neurologic dysfunction, including seizures, delirium, and occasionally stupor or coma, frequently complicates the course of systemic lupus erythematosus.[112,321,383,459] The central nervous system disorder may occur early in the course of the systemic disease; in 63 percent of the patients of Feinglass and associates, CNS symptoms either preceded the diagnosis or occurred within the first year of diagnosed disease.[112] In only one instance, however, was the central nervous system disorder the sole initial feature. When Feinglass and associates compared patients with and without brain involvement with respect to the clinical and laboratory findings of SLE, vasculitis and thrombocytopenia were especially present in those with brain involvement. The finding suggests that the central nervous system symptoms of SLE may well be related to a cerebral vasculitis with attendant cerebral ischemia. Others have suggested that the pathogenesis of brain dysfunction in SLE is that of brain injury from immune complexes such as DNA/anti-DNA or from lymphocytotoxic antibodies that cross-react with brain cells. Serologic studies by Winfield and associates fail to support such a postulate.[459]

The clinical onset of CNS lupus is abrupt, often with seizures and/or delirium and sometimes accompanied by focal neurologic signs. Most patients have fever; some have papilledema and elevations of CSF pressure on lumbar puncture. The spinal fluid contents are usually normal, but in about 30 percent of patients the CSF is abnormal with a modest pleocytosis and/or an elevated protein concentration. The electroencephalogram is usually abnormal, with either diffuse or multifocal slow wave activity. The radionuclide brain scan, CT scan, and arteriogram are usually normal. The diagnosis should be considered in any febrile patient, particularly a young woman, with undiagnosed delirium or stupor, especially if complicated by seizures. The diagnosis is supported by systemic findings, particularly a history of arthritis and arthralgia (88 percent), skin rash (79 percent), and renal disease (48 percent),[112] and is established by laboratory evaluation. Ninety percent of patients with nervous system involvement by lupus have antinuclear antibodies in their serum. Lupus erythematosus cells are present in 79 percent, and there is hypo-complementemia in 64 percent. However, many of these findings may be absent if the lupus is *restricted* to the central nervous system.[459] Even when the diagnosis of systemic lupus erythematosus is established, one must be careful not to attribute all neurologic abnormalities that develop directly to the lupus. In patients with lupus, neurologic disability can be caused by uremia, intercurrent central nervous system infection, or the effects of glucocorticoids given for treatment.

SUBACUTE DIENCEPHALIC ANGIOENCEPHALOPATHY. DeGirolami and colleagues described a patient with the subacute onset of a confusional state followed by progressive dementia, obtundation, and diffuse myoclonus.[77] The cerebrospinal fluid showed a progressive rise in the protein concentration. On postmortem examination there were extensive destructive lesions of the thalami bilaterally associated with a focal vasculitis of small arteries and veins (20–80 microns in diameter). The vascular lesions were characterized by thickening of all layers of the vessel wall, with occasional scattered polymorphonuclear leukocytes in the wall and some collections of mononuclear inflammatory cells in the adventitia. Giant cells were absent. The authors were unable to find similar patients reported in the literature. The disease is so rare and its clinical signs so nonspecific as to make it unlikely to be diagnosed in the antemortem state. The presence of diffuse myoclonus in a patient with declining mental status, normal metabolism, and no other clinical or pathologic stigmata of Creutzfeldt-Jakob disease might lead one to suspect the diagnosis, but since the lesions are restricted to the thalamus, premortem laboratory diagnosis seems impossible.

VARICELLA-ZOSTER ENCEPHALITIS. Herpes zoster rarely causes stupor or coma, and even when it does the diagnosis is usually not difficult since the cutaneous dermatomal rash identifies the infection. As many as 40 percent of patients with uncomplicated herpes zoster have meningitis, usually asymptomatic and characterized only by mild CSF pleocytosis, but sometimes accompanied by fever, headache, and stiff neck. Less commonly, particularly in immunosuppressed patients, more profound central nervous system changes may result from herpes zoster infection. These changes take the form of two overlapping clinical syndromes.[86] The first, called "zoster encephalitis," is characterized by headache and confusion progressing to stupor or coma, sometimes with multifocal or generalized convulsions. Focal neurologic signs, including hemiplegia, are sometimes present. The second, called "ophthalmic zoster, hemiplegia," follows herpes zoster involving the trigeminal ganglion and is characterized by sudden headache followed by contralateral hemiplegia.[428] Confusion, stupor, and coma are less common in this disorder than in herpes zoster encephalitis, but sometimes occur.

In both instances, cerebral vasculitis, either involving small vessels (herpes zoster encephalitis) or the carotid artery (ophthalmic zoster, hemiplegia), appears to be the pathophysiologic cause of the symptoms. In herpes zoster encephalitis there is some evidence for invasion of the brain by the virus or for a postinfectious encephalomyelitis as well.

The diagnosis is not difficult. The central nervous system dysfunction almost always occurs after the rash has developed, usually during its healing phase. Arteriography reveals cerebral vasculitis in the hemiplegic syndrome.

Subarachnoid Hemorrhage

The term subarachnoid hemorrhage refers to intracranial bleeding in which the majority of blood is ejected into the subarachnoid space rather than the parenchyma of the brain.[71] Most subarachnoid hemorrhages originate from rupture of a so-called congenital intracranial aneurysm, a berry-shaped out-pouching at the junction of two or more arteries at the base of the brain. In a few cases, subarachnoid hemorrhage is a result of head trauma or of rupture of aneurysms produced by trauma or infection. Sometimes arteriovenous anomalies and hypertensive parenchymal hemorrhages rupture out of the substance of the brain to produce major subarachnoid bleeding.

Several potential mechanisms may interact to produce coma in patients with subarachnoid hemorrhage: (1) Acutely, there is sudden ejection of blood under high pressure into the subarachnoid space. The hemorrhage raises intracranial pressure and distorts intracranial structures in a manner akin to acute concussion. Continuous recording of intracranial pressure in patients with subarachnoid hemorrhage indicates that the initial level of consciousness correlates best with the level of intracranial pressure rather than with the presence of hydrocephalus or vasospasm (see below).[169] (2) Later on (between about 4 days and 2 weeks after the initial hemorrhage), cerebral vasospasm develops in about half the patients, contributing to drowsiness or stupor and going on to produce cerebral ischemia or infarction in a significant percentage.[408] The presence of subarachnoid blood has also been reported to interfere with autoregulation of the cerebral circulation.[468,482] (3) Communicating hydrocephalus may develop rapidly after acute subarachnoid hemorrhage, presumably because blood components deposit themselves along the outflow foramina of the fourth ventricle, in the basal cisterns, and along the large venous sinuses, positions in which they block spinal fluid absorptive pathways. Hydrocephalus may contribute to the acute increase in intracranial pressure seen after subarachnoid hemorrhage or may, at times, be responsible for deterioration in the patient's state of consciousness 2 to 3 weeks after a successfully treated subarachnoid hemorrhage. (4) Sudden masses of blood injected into either the anterior or posterior fossa produce a mass effect that can induce transtentorial herniation. (5) It is possible that subarachnoid blood or its products also directly interfere with cerebral metabolism. The blood products irritate the meninges and produce chemical meningitis. (6) Hypothalamic disturbances appear to be caused by subarachnoid hemorrhage, perhaps because the ejected column of blood is often so close to the hypothalamus. Hypothalamic damage may lead to the syndrome of inappropriate secretion of antidiuretic hormone and to autonomic dysfunction, including unexplained fever and electrocardiographic changes. (see Patient 4–19).[72,164,444] Hormonal abnormalities, including abnormal levels of hydroxycorticosteroids, abnormal dexamethasone suppression tests, and disturbance of normal circadian secretion of adrenal hormones have been reported.[308,454] Finally, hypothalamic damage, by interfering with the function of the reticular activating formation, may itself produce stupor or coma. The clinical picture of subarachnoid hemorrhage is that of widespread cerebral dysfunction resembling metabolic brain disease, and, for this reason, the topic is discussed here.

In the clinical picture of subarachnoid hemorrhage, signs of metabolic coma commonly coexist with focal signs of cerebral dysfunction, making precise localization of the ruptured aneurysm by clinical deduction a notoriously inaccurate exercise. Almost all the patients have headache at onset, but hemogenic chemical meningitis requires several hours to develop and produce its symptoms, so that neck stiffness is often absent during the first hours after bleeding, particularly in unconscious patients. In patients in coma, respiratory, ocular, and motor signs may be those of either metabolic coma or of rostral-caudal deterioration of brain function, depending on the distribution and evolution of the primary hemorrhage and its consequent effect on distorting the brain. Thus, as is true with meningitis, a change in breathing from eupnea to hyperventilation can herald the onset of midbrain compression owing to transtentorial compression. A dilated pupil or total third nerve palsy may be more difficult to interpret, but usually implies that the aneurysm is on the ipsilateral carotid or posterior communicating artery and has either directly compressed the oculomotor nerve or bled into it. Less often, oculomotor paralysis is due to transtentorial herniation. The decision as to which process is responsible must be based on the remainder of the clinical findings. Focal motor signs and focal or generalized seizures are common with acute subarachnoid hemorrhage. Focal motor signs that occur early in the period after bleeding are sometimes caused by hemorrhage into the cerebral substance, but sometimes reflect ischemia, apparently from severe vasospasm. In either case, the resulting hemiparesis is more often contralateral to the aneurysm but can be ipsilateral, depending on where the major vasospasm lies. Focal motor signs occurring later in the illness are usually due to cerebral infarction and are by no means always confined to the distribution of the artery that contained the ruptured aneurysm.[70]

The acute intracranial hypertension that subarachnoid hemorrhage induces may produce papilledema[310] and retinal hemorrhages[478] within minutes or hours. Subacute and chronic intracranial hypertension caused by communicating hydrocephalus can start within hours of the ictus, prolonging coma or even leading to gradually developing dementia and stupor after an initial posthemorrhage improvement.[125] Such a mechanism is the usual explanation for the delirium and obtundation that characteristically start 3 to 4 days after bleeding.

The diagnosis of typical subarachnoid hemorrhage should not be difficult; it is signalled by the sudden onset of piercing, intense headache followed by blunted alertness or stupor, with or without focal signs. If the diagnosis is clinically suspected, a CT scan usually can identify the presence of blood in the subarachnoid spaces and also determine whether there is a hemorrhagic mass lesion or hydrocephalus. If the diagnosis can be made by CT scan, then lumbar puncture should not be performed. Since most patients in whom blood cannot be identified on CT scan are awake and alert, lumbar puncture can generally be performed without difficulty or risk.

A careful history will often help with the clinical diagnosis of subarachnoid hemorrhage. King and Saba reviewed the records of 175 patients with berry aneurysms; 60 percent reported unusual clinical symptoms preceding either the rupture of the aneurysm or its clinical diagnosis.[207] In 95 percent of these patients, an unusual headache preceded other symptoms. It was sudden in onset, severe and disabling, frontal in 26 percent, retroorbital in 14 percent, and bilateral occipital in 39 percent. It usually subsided over several hours to days. Recurrent acute and intense headaches had been present from 1 to 4 weeks before admission in one third of the group, and for more than 6 months in 40 percent. Several other premonitory symptoms included nausea and vomiting, meningismus, brief syncopal attacks, or coma, all usually associated with headache. Since it is likely that these represent small hemorrhages preceding the major bleed, a lumbar puncture performed early might have led to treatment that would have prevented the major rupture. Many of these patients had carried erroneous diagnoses such as viral meningitis, migraine, sinusitis, or tension headaches.

If the physician performs a lumbar puncture and encounters bloody spinal fluid, he may erroneously attribute it to a traumatic tap. This error can be avoided by centrifuging the bloody spinal fluid: intrinsic bleeding discolors the supernatant fluid with oxyhemoglobin within 2 hours, whereas fresh trauma does not. Another source of error is avoided by recognizing the neurologic meaning of certain symptoms and by an awareness that intracranial bleeding affects the cardiovascular system so as to produce potentially misleading EKG changes. The following patient illustrates these principles.

Patient 4–19. A 44-year-old man was admitted to the hospital at 11 A.M. At 10:30 A.M. he had been climbing stairs when he suddenly fell unconscious, not striking his head. He awoke after several minutes, mildly confused and complaining of a generalized headache. By the time he arrived at the hospital, he was clear-headed and felt well. His pulse was 76 per minute; his blood pressure was 108/76 mm. Hg. An electrocardiogram showed a sinus rhythm with a 3:2 sinoauricular block and complete atrioventricular (AV) dissociation with a nodal escape rhythm at 52 per minute. He became lethargic during the examination and gradually lapsed into coma, which was at first attributed to acute myocardial infarction.

Forty minutes later, his blood pressure was 160/90 mm. Hg. He was unconscious and breathed irregularly at about 30 per minute. He moved his left arm spontaneously, but no other movement was seen. His right pupil was larger than the left and reacted sluggishly to light. Corneal reflexes could not be elicited. Bilateral papilledema with some hemorrhages around the disc was noted. His neck was supple. He was thought to have mild cardiac enlargement and gallop rhythm.

Twenty minutes later the patient awoke. Five minutes after that he again lost consciousness, this time permanently. An electrocardiogram showed a normal sinus rhythm with ST elevation and T wave inversion in lead AVL. The changes were believed consistent with an early anterolateral myocardial infarction or ischemia. Ten minutes later his electrocardiogram showed a sinus arrhythmia, changing in 15 minutes to complete AV dissociation with a nodal rhythm of 50 per minute, then to ventricular tachycardia followed by supraventricular tachycardia. The ST and T wave abnormalities persisted.

He was seen by a neurologic consultant shortly after he lapsed into coma for the final time. He had bilateral decerebrate response to noxious stimuli. The pupils were small, briskly reactive, and equal. Bilateral oculovestibular responses were present but depressed. Bilateral diffuse hypertonus was found in the extremities along with extensor plantar responses. A lumbar puncture revealed grossly bloody spinal fluid under a pressure of 400 mm. and with a hematocrit of 23 percent and pink discoloration of the supernatant fluid. An hour later the patient's pupils were found in midposition and were fixed to light with absence of oculovestibular responses. Hypertonus of the extremities gradually changed into flaccidity. Respiration ceased, and, following a brief period of artificial ventilation, he died. The autopsy disclosed a massive subarachnoid hemorrhage from rupture of an aneurysm of the anterior communicating artery.

Comment: Despite the patient's complaint of headache, and unconsciousness, it was several hours before his physicians realized that his coma was not the result of myocardial infarction. The important distinction is that, although mild encephalopathy is fairly common from the decreased cardiac output of myocardial infarction, coma is rare and probably occurs only in patients having a cardiac arrest. Subarachnoid hemorrhage often causes electrocardiographic abnormalities,[164,444,481] some of which mimic closely the abnormalities that accompany a myocardial infarction. The finding emphasizes the importance of considering the diagnosis of subarachnoid hemorrhage in the comatose patient.

Primary Neuronal and Glial Disorders

This category includes several primary central nervous system disorders of diverse or unknown cause that usually culminate in stupor or coma. Most primary neuronal and glial disorders cause coma only after a period of profound dementia has led the physician to the appropriate diagnosis. The disorders included below occasionally produce unconsciousness sufficiently early in their course that they may be confused with other conditions described in this book. As a result, a brief discussion of their clinical picture and differential diagnosis seems warranted. Although some of these diseases are caused by transmissable agents (e.g., Creutzfeldt-Jakob disease, progressive multifocal leukoencephalopathy), they are arbitrarily categorized separately from the encephalitides and acute toxic encephalopathies because their onset is less acute and their course not so explosive.

Creutzfeldt-Jakob Disease

Creutzfeldt-Jakob disease is a subacute disorder producing widespread neuronal degeneration and spongiform pathologic changes in the neocortex and cerebellum.[359] The disease is caused by a transmissable agent and has infected chimpanzees and guinea pigs when tissue from affected persons was injected into those animals. The disease has reportedly been spread from one human to another by corneal transplantation and the implantation of cerebral electrodes.[135]

Clinically, the illness usually affects middle-aged adults, causing dementia, which progresses over a period of weeks to severe obtundation, stupor, and finally unresponsiveness. The motor system suffers disproportionately, and early in the disease there is diffuse paratonic rigidity with decorticate posturing and extensor plantar responses developing later. Early in the course, myoclonus appears in response to startle; later the myoclonus occurs spontaneously. There also may be generalized convulsions. The EEG is characteristic, consisting of a flat, almost isoelectric background with superimposed synchronous periodic sharp waves.[285] The cerebrospinal fluid examination is usually normal. In the final stage of the disease, all spontaneous movements cease, and the patients remain in coma until they die of intercurrent infection.

The appearance of subacute dementia with myoclonic twitches in a middle-aged or elderly patient without systemic disease is diagnostic. Although there is a tendency to mistake the early symptoms for an involutional depression, the organic nature of the disorder rapidly becomes apparent. A similar picture is produced only by severe metabolic diseases (e.g., hepatic encephalopathy) or CNS syphilis (general paresis). However, these latter illnesses have characteristic chemical and laboratory signs and lack the typical EEG of Creutzfeldt-Jakob disease.

Histologic examination in Creutzfeldt-Jakob disease discloses widespread neuronal degeneration in the neocortex and cerebellum as well as marked astrocytic gliosis. Neurons of the basal ganglia, brainstem, and hippocampus are often spared.[201] The disease appears to be caused by a slow virus infection[199] and can be transmitted to chimpanzees by cerebral inoculation of brain tissue from affected patients.[138]

Adrenoleukodystrophy (Schilder's Disease)

Adrenoleukodystrophy (ALD) is a subacute disease of white matter inherited as a sex-linked recessive trait that affects male children or adolescents and occasionally causes coma after an illness that lasts only days or weeks.[375] Most patients with so-called Schilder's disease have in fact suffered from adrenoleukodystrophy. Other such patients have probably suffered from acute multiple sclerosis. Although there are pathologic changes in the adrenal glands, and many patients with ALD have melanoderma and adrenocortical atrophy, most do not have clinical signs of adrenal insufficiency. Cytoplasmic inclusion bodies specific for the condition have been identified in the adrenal gland, the testes, and the Schwann cells of patients. The central nervous system disorder is one of diffuse demyelination with cytoplasmic inclusions in the central nervous system similar to those in other organs. The cause of the disorder is unknown, but Menkes and Corbo state that the basic enzymatic defect may be a disorder of the one-carbon degradation system responsible for the metabolism of long chain fatty acids.[261] Moser and associates report abnormally high concentration of very long chain fatty acids in cultured skin fibroblasts of patients with ALD, thereby providing a diagnostic test.[276]

The central nervous system symptoms can begin either acutely or insidiously, often with behavioral changes, disturbances of gait, or loss of vision. Most patients become cortically blind before they die. Seizures are common.

One should suspect ALD in a male child or adolescent suffering from a subacute and progressive confusional state associated with hyperpigmentation of the skin and the chemical stigma of adrenal failure. The diagnosis can be confirmed by biopsy of one of several organs possessing the characteristic cytoplasmic inclusion bodies. Brain biopsy is the least reliable test since the evidence of inflammation and active demyelination is multifocal and may not be present in the biopsy specimen. Schaumberg and his colleagues found adrenal biopsy to be the most reliable test, whether or not the patient had evidence of adrenocortical failure.[375] Testicular biopsy and sural nerve biopsy are also sometimes positive. The value of fibroblast analysis is mentioned above.

Routine laboratory tests are usually not helpful in diagnosing ALD. Many patients will have biochemical evidence of adrenocortical failure even in the absence of clinically apparent insufficiency. Cerebrospinal fluid protein is usually elevated and the gamma globulin sometimes elevated. The electroencephalogram is usually slow, with focal slow and sharp abnormalities. There are sometimes areas of focal abnormality identified on radionuclide brain scan. When these are coupled with evidence of increased intracranial pressure, resulting from cerebral edema, they can falsely suggest a diagnosis of brain tumor. The CT scan often reveals multiple areas of white matter hypodensity. The pathologic changes are well-described by Schaumberg and colleagues and consist of widespread demyelination of the white matter, with a mononuclear inflammatory response in some areas and marked gliosis in others.[375] Many of the macrophages in the demyelinated areas contain distinctive cytoplasmic inclusions, which mark the disease as adrenoleukodystrophy.

Marchiafava-Bignami Disease

Marchiafava-Bignami disease is a rare disorder of the white matter, which was originally believed to affect predominantly Italian males who were heavy drinkers of red wine.[429] It is now recognized, however, that the disease has no demographic restriction and affects chronic alcoholics no matter what form of alcohol they take; most of the victims are males. The essential lesion is demyelination of the corpus callosum, with extension of the demyelination into the adjacent hemispheres. Axis cylinders may either be preserved or destroyed, and there are an abundance of fatty macrophages without evidence of inflammation in the lesion. Presumably, the ultimate cause is a deficiency of some critical nutrient.

The malady usually begins with delirium, followed by seizures, tremor, and hallucinations. These beginning symptoms may represent alcohol withdrawal. Patients then decline into stupor or coma and usually die within a few weeks of onset. Some patients spontaneously recover from the illness, and the disease is identified at autopsy when they die of other causes later. In another group there is a progressive dementia, which evolves slowly over months to years. The diagnosis can be suspected clinically, but can be confirmed only at autopsy.

The disease is closely related to pontine myelinolysis, which is described in Chapter 3, page 172.

Gliomatosis Cerebri

Infiltrating brain tumors can sometimes invade both supra- and subtentorial structures early in their course so as to resemble a diffuse process. This is particularly true of the neoplasm that Nevin called gliomatosis cerebri.[288] The term gliomatosis cerebri describes a condition of diffuse malignant alteration of the brain's astrocytes. The neoplasm arises multicentrically and usually affects multiple regions of the brain simultaneously to produce a clinical picture of widespread forebrain and, usually, brainstem dysfunction. Microscopically, one finds in the hemisphere and brainstem normal neuronal and glial elements interspersed with multiple foci of individual and clustered collections of large and small abnormal astrocytes, whose appearance of malignancy can vary widely from patient to patient and even from area to area within the same brain. Since gross tumor masses, hydrocephalus, or transtentorial herniation often fail to appear, arteriograms may be uninformative and CT scans can be normal or show no more than a smaller-than-normal ventricular system.

Gliomatosis cerebri produces symptoms that begin insidiously and progress slowly with clinical illnesses lasting from less than a month to as long as a decade or more.[67] Mental and personality symptoms predominate with memory loss, lethargy, slowed thinking, and confusion gradually leading into sleepiness, stupor, and often prolonged coma. Hemiparesis is fairly common, but rapidly evolving focal neurologic defects are rare. Less than half the patients have seizures. About a quarter of the patients show signs of direct brainstem involvement. Indirect evidence of increased intracranial pressure has marked the course of over half the reported cases because of continued tumor growth producing either simple enlargement of the brain or a narrowing of CSF fluid drainage pathways. The following case description typifies the course and findings.

Patient 4–20. A 61-year-old woman insidiously became disinterested in her surroundings and slow in thought during the early spring of 1978. By June, she was lethargic, forgetful, and apathetically incontinent and could no longer walk unassisted. In another hospital a ventricular shunt was placed without changing her symptoms. She gradually became mentally unresponsive and was admitted to New York Hospital in September 1978. On examination she was awake but psychologically unresponsive, reacting only to noxious stimuli with an extensor (decerebrate) response. The pupils were 2 mm. in diameter, equal, and fixed to light. She had roving eye movements with a gaze preference to the right. Oculocephalic responses were full and conjugate but caloric irrigation with cold water in the right ear produced irregular upbeat nystagmus, while irrigation in the left ear evoked irregular nystagmus to the right. She had a spastic left hemiparesis and a flaccid right hemiparesis with bilateral extensor plantar responses.

Numerous laboratory tests, including examination of the CSF, CT scan, and arteriogram were either normal or nonspecifically altered. A brain biopsy taken from the grossly normal-appearing right frontal lobe gave the appearance of a diffuse gemistocytic astrocytoma with considerable variation in the degree of malignant change as well as areas of normal-looking neurons and astrocytes. The patient died in a nursing home soon afterwards.

Comment. The insidious onset of changes in cognition and arousal accompanied by signs of fractional damage to the midbrain (fixed pupils), pontine vestibular complex (abnormal calorics), and corticospinal systems placed the lesion diffusely in the brainstem and perhaps the diencephalon. The CT scan and other tests showed no discrete mass lesions and led to performance of a cerebral biopsy as one of the few possible ways of making a firm diagnosis.

Progressive Multifocal Leukoencephalopathy (PML)

PML is a subacute demyelinating disorder produced when a strain of papovavirus (the JC virus) infects the nervous system.[434] The disorder usually occurs in patients who are immunosuppressed from Hodgkin's disease, lymphomas, or sarcoidosis, but has been reported in individuals whose immune system appears intact. The neurologic symptoms are implied by the name of the disorder: a progressive asymmetric disorder of white matter with hemiparesis, visual impairment, sensory abnormalities, and ataxia. Headaches and seizures are rare. The course is usually progressive over several months, terminating in coma. Rarely, there may be edema associated with the demyelinating plaques, leading to hemispheral swelling and transtentorial herniation. Patients are comatose terminally but rarely have substantial behavioral disorders at onset, and thus the entity does not usually arise in the differential diagnosis of stupor or coma. The cerebrospinal fluid is usually normal; the EEG is usually diffusely or multifocally abnormal. CT scans delineate multifocal radiolucent lesions in the white matter, which sometimes contrast-enhance. The pathology is one of diffuse multifocal demyelination of white matter, with oligodendroglial nuclei containing eosinophilic inclusions and viral particles and bizarre giant astrocytes, suggesting neoplastic transformation. There is little inflammation.

Miscellaneous Disorders

Epilepsy

Seizures are characterized by intense cerebral neuronal activity followed by postictal metabolic cerebral depression of varying degrees and duration. In the experimental animal, one can demonstrate that major seizures produce a 200 to 500 percent increase in cerebral metabolic demand, a substantial degree of systemic hypertension, and an enormously increased cerebral blood flow.[179,258,327] Repetitive convulsions result in a progressive, abnormal increase in the permeability of the blood-brain barrier.[320] If substrate depletion or a relative decline in blood flow occurs during seizures, the brain maintains its metabolism by the consumption of endogenous substrates.[33] With sustained status epilepticus in such animals, progressive hypoxic-ischemic structural neuronal damage results soon after.[259] Similar but necessarily less comprehensive analyses indicate that seizures cause comparable changes in the human brain.[325]

Postictal coma in man ranges in intensity from complete unresponsiveness to stupor; protracted deep unresponsiveness lasting more than 15 to 30 minutes suggests that the onset or extension of an underlying structural lesion caused the seizure. Postictal patients in coma usually are hyperpneic until the lactic acidemia produced by the muscular exercise of the convulsion clears; pupillary light reflexes are intact and oculovestibular responses active. The motor system usually is unremarkable except for extensor plantar responses in about half the patients. Postictal coma rarely produces problems in its differential diagnosis because the patient usually quickly awakens to give his history. The problem the physician most frequently faces is retrospective: Was a past, unobserved episode of unconsciousness caused by epilepsy or syncope? This differential diagnostic problem is considered on page 210. Engle provides a more complete discussion.[107] In three conditions, coma associated with seizures can be sufficiently prolonged to present diagnostic problems.

The first instance is status epilepticus, a series of generalized convulsions occurring at intervals so closely spaced (i.e., every few minutes) that consciousness is not regained between. This state strikes about 10 percent of patients with untreated or inadequately treated epilepsy[229] and often follows the abrupt withdrawal of anticonvulsants. Status epilepticus is a serious medical emergency since the cumulative systemic and cerebral anoxia induced by repeated generalized seizures can produce irreversible brain damage or death[332] (see Patient 4-15); its diagnosis is readily made when repeated convulsions punctuate a state of otherwise nonspecific coma.

A second example of prolonged coma, stupor, or delirium following seizures can occur in elderly patients with an epileptogenic scar or lesion (e.g., from past cerebral infarction) who also suffer from cerebral vascular insufficiency, or mild to moderate senile cerebral degeneration with dementia. In these patients, the enormous cerebral metabolic demand imposed by the seizures, plus systemic hypoxemia during the attack, often is sufficient to compromise an already borderline cerebral function and produce several hours of postictal coma followed by several days of delirium. Most such patients ultimately recover their preseizure cerebral function, but each attack risks damaging more and more brain, making effective prevention and prompt treatment important.

A third condition in which sustained coma may be associated with seizures occurs when the unconsciousness is not simply postictal but is the result of a cerebral disease that also caused the seizures. Many underlying destructive and metabolic cerebral disorders produce both seizures and coma and must be differentiated by other signs, symptoms, and laboratory studies. If one takes previously healthy patients in our own series, a single or brief series of convulsions were followed by sustained unconsciousness only when caused by acute encephalitis or encephalomyelitis or acute hyponatremia. However, one may not always have the history available, and many other structural lesions of brain can cause repetitive convulsions followed by a prolonged postictal stupor. It is an axiom of treatment that convulsions should be stopped as promptly as possible, since both the seizures themselves and the accompanying systemic hypoxemia are sources of potentially serious brain damage.

Confusional states blending into stupor also can be caused by prolonged "minor" seizure discharges. Lennox recognized several years ago that children with closely spaced 3 Hz spike and wave discharges on the EEG could demonstrate dull repetitive behavior reflecting *petit mal status*.[228] Possibly as a variant on this condition, susceptible adults can develop intermittent or prolonged *epileptic confusional attacks* associated with concurrent 3 Hz or slightly slower (2–2.5 Hz) spike and wave discharges on the EEG. The behavior varies from dull, apathetic confusion to states of agitated hallucinatory delirium. A few instances have been marked by a withdrawn stupor.[103] There may be focal signs (e.g., hemiparesis or asphasia) and the EEG may also be focal.[480] Unresponsive coma has not been observed. Among adult patients described with epileptic confusional attacks, many have not had previous seizure disorders. Clinical examinations in affected patients show a high associated incidence of systemic and cerebral vascular disease as well as of systemic salt and water or other metabolic abnormalities. In reported patients or those in our own series, neither CT scans nor other diagnostic procedures have disclosed specific structural neurologic lesions. The anticonvulsants diazepam or phenytoin correct the EEG abnormality and interrupt the abnormal behavior, thereby aiding diagnosis.

Acute Delirious States

Delirium and confusional states usually precede metabolic stupor or coma and can be the presenting problem in many of the diseases described in this chapter or listed in Table 11. There is, in addition, a group of disorders causing a severe and acute delirium that is usually self-limited, which may be fatal if not appropriately treated. Because these states usually do not cause stupor or coma, they have not been discussed elsewhere in this text, but they are responsible for acute changes in the state of consciousness that often challenge and perplex the physician. These conditions are listed under miscellaneous disorders in Table 11 and discussed as a group here. The disorders include withdrawal from sedative drugs or alcohol, acute intoxications by drugs such as propranolol[419] and digitalis[368] that are not generally considered to have psychotropic effects, intoxications with a wide range of psychotropic and hallucinogenic drugs,[37,156] and postoperative states.[275] Intoxication with therapeutic drugs is a problem particularly likely to affect the elderly. The few drugs and pathophysiologic states mentioned above and in Tables 11 and 17 by no means exhaust the list of causes of acute delirium, which are legion, but only identify especially common or perplexing problems.

Although the causal agent in drug ingestion and withdrawal is by definition known, the biochemical abnormality that produces the delirious state is uncertain, and in disorders such as postoperative delirium and intensive care unit delirium, neither the causal agent nor the pathophysiology is well understood.

The clinical picture in most of these states is similar. A patient who was previously alert and oriented (although frequently with some underlying mild dementia) suddenly becomes restless. His affect changes such that while previously calm he becomes agitated, fearful, or depressed, and emotionally labile. He is less able than previously to give attention to his environment; minor defects in cognitive functions can be detected on careful testing, if he will cooperate. Most of the patients become insomniac, many are paranoid and misinterpret sensory stimuli, both auditory and visual.[241] They often hallucinate. Autonomic dysfunction including tachycardia, hypertension, diaphoresis, dilated pupils, and at times fever is common. (Fever should never be dismissed simply as a result of delirium until a careful search has ruled out infection, which may contribute to the genesis of the delirium.) In its florid form, the patient is tremulous, extremely restless, and often fearful; asterixis and multifocal myoclonus may be present. Many patients are totally disoriented but elaborately describe an incorrect environment. When the delirium is severe, such patients are so restless that they cannot lie still, and their thrashing and rolling about in bed may damage a recently operated site and put additional strain on an impaired cardiovascular system. Such patients are so distractible that cognitive testing is impossible. They may engage equally the examiner and imaginary figures in conversation. The speech is so dysarthric that even when the delirious patient does reply correctly to questions he often cannot be understood. If untreated, the agitation of delirium may lead to exhaustion and even death. However, even the most severe of the deliria, delirium tremens, has only a modest mortality if treated with appropriate sedative therapy.

DELIRIUM TREMENS. The most common of the acute and florid delirious states is delirium tremens.[172,373] Although it is caused by withdrawal of alcohol and generally follows complete cessation of drinking, it may occur in a patient still drinking a diminished amount.[429] Similar clinical findings may follow barbiturate or other sedative drug withdrawal, and in the latter case generalized convulsions are prone to occur as well. Particularly perplexing to the physician are those patients not known to be alcoholics who enter hospital for elective surgery and, during the course of work-up or shortly following the operation, become acutely delirious. Various biochemical abnormalities, including hypomagnesemia and hypokalemia, have been implicated in the pathogenesis of delirium tremens, but its exact cause is not established.[280,429,433] The disease generally runs its course in less than a week. If treated with sedative drugs and good supportive therapy, most patients recover fully, although a mortality ranging from 2 to 15 percent has been reported from various sources.[416] Much of this mortality is probably due to other complications of alcoholism, such as liver failure.

POSTOPERATIVE DELIRIUM. Postoperative delirium is one of the most florid and frightening postoperative complications to confront the surgeon. Morse and Litin encountered 60 patients with postoperative delirium at the Mayo Clinic over a 6-month period.[274,275] The disorder occurred in 0.54 percent of operated patients, but only the most florid delirious states were evaluated. In no instance was the precise cause of the disorder established, although several contributing factors were cited. Twenty-two percent of the cases followed open heart surgery, and these illnesses may have resulted from cerebral embolization (see p. 217). Thirty-seven percent followed orthopedic procedures; fat embolism may have played a role in these patients (see p. 216). Precipitating factors included infection, hemorrhage, pain, and psychological stress, but could be identified in only 22 percent of patients.

The clinical picture was as described above. The duration of the illness ranged from 2 to 50 days; but lasted 7 days or less in more than half the patients. The patients were treated by sedative drugs, and most recovered completely; there was one death.

A study of the potentially causative factors in the above 60 patients, when compared with patients undergoing similar operations but who did not become delirious, revealed that more patients with postoperative delirium were over 60 years of age or were anemic, azotemic, infected, or suffered cardiac failure. Some of the delirious patients were undergoing drug withdrawal, particularly alcohol. Long surgical procedures and emergency operations were more likely to result in postoperative delirium, and postoperative complications such as hemorrhage also seemed to play a role. Those patients who developed postoperative delirium were more likely to have a history of alcoholism, depression, or other psychiatric problems.

INTENSIVE CARE UNIT DELIRIUM. Acute delirium frequently occurs in patients hospitalized in intensive care units. Many such patients are postoperative, and all the factors listed under postoperative complications undoubtedly play some causal role. Wilson, however, found that the incidence of postoperative delirium in an intensive care unit without windows was more than double that in patients housed in a unit with windows.[457] He concluded that sensory deprivation was a factor in postoperative delirium. The findings stress the importance of environmental stimulation to help potentially confused patients orient themselves.

DRUG-INDUCED DELIRIUM. A myriad of drugs, both licit and illicit, can cause acute delirium. Some of these are listed in Tables 11 and 17, but these are only partial listings. Any patient, particularly an elderly one, who develops an unexplained acute delirium should be considered as having a drug intoxication until proved otherwise. In addition to the supportive care given for delirium, all drugs not essential for maintenance of life should be withdrawn until it can be determined that they are not contributing to the patient's confusion.

Mixed Metabolic Encephalopathy

All too often, clinical signs and symptoms suggest that a stuporous or comatose patient is suffering from a diffuse metabolic disorder of brain, but laboratory evaluation either reveals a variety of modest abnormalities, none of which appears severe enough to be responsible for the patient's abnormal state of consciousness, or there is no metabolic or toxic abnormality detected. In the first instance, the additive effect of multiple mild metabolic abnormalities may lead to a severe encephalopathy, which can sometimes be remedied by correcting any one of the modest abnormalities.

Patient 4–21. A 74-year-old man with disseminated carcinoma of the prostate was admitted to hospital confused and disoriented. The findings on general physical examination included normal vital signs, cachexia, and an enlarged liver. He was stuporous but rousable by noxious stimuli. When aroused, he was confused and disoriented. His respirations were 16 per minute, his pupils were 2 mm. and reactive, and there was a full range of ocular movement to doll's head maneuver. He withdrew all four extremities appropriately, deep tendon reflexes were hyperactive, and plantar responses were flexor. When he was roused to hold his hands outstretched, there was bilateral asterixis. The remainder of the segmental neurologic examination was within normal limits. Laboratory abnormalities included a hemoglobin of 8 gm./dl., a calcium of 11.5 mg./dl., a grossly elevated alkaline phosphatase, and modestly elevated liver enzymes. Arterial blood gases revealed an oxygen tension of 55 mm. Hg, a pH of 7.49, and a PCO_2 of 30 mm. Hg. A small infiltrate was present in the right middle lobe of the lung on chest x-ray. A diagnosis of mixed metabolic encephalopathy was made, with anemia, hypoxia, liver metastases, and hypercalcemia all playing a role.

Oxygen given by nasal prongs raised the arterial blood PO_2 but failed to change his clinical state. Two units of blood raised his hemoglobin to 10 gm./dl.; when this was combined with the oxygen, he awoke and, although disoriented at the time, was otherwise alert and behaved appropriately. At the time he awakened, no change had developed in his serum calcium or abnormal liver function tests.

A more difficult problem arises when no metabolic or toxic abnormalities are detected. In that circumstance, the first step in diagnosis should be to check all medications the patient has received in the past 48 hours. Barring sedative or narcotic drugs, one should check the platelet count and coagulation profile. Some of these patients have subsequently proved to have disseminated intravascular coagulation with neurological symptoms appearing before coagulation profiles became abnormal. In others, a biochemical defect present prior to the patient's being examined may have left residual brain damage even though the underlying biochemical abnormality has corrected itself. Carbon monoxide poisoning and hypoglycemia are examples of this. In still other patients, drug ingestion with chemical substances not detected by usual laboratory tests may be the cause. In some patients, the diagnosis is never established, and one must presume that some unidentified toxin or not understood metabolic abnormality was present. When faced with such a problem, the physician should apply supportive therapy, as outlined in Chapter 8, while continuing to search diligently to identify metabolic abnormalities as the illness pursues its course.

REFERENCES

1. ABRAMSKY, O., CARMON, A., AND FELDMAN, S.: *Cerebrospinal fluid in acute necrotizing encephalitis. Hypochlorrhachia as a diagnostic aid.* J. Neurol.Sci. 14:183–187, 1971.

2. ADAMS, R.D., AND FOLEY, J.M.: *The neurological disorder associated with liver disease.* Res. Publ. Assoc. Res. Nerv. Ment. Dis. 32:198–237, 1953.

3. AGARDH, C.D., FOLBERGROVA, J., AND SIESJÖ, B.K.: *Cerebral metabolic changes in profound insulin-induced hypoglycemia, and in the recovery period following glucose administration.* J. Neurochem. 31:1135–1142, 1978.

4. ALBERTI, K.G., AND HOCKADAY, T.D.: *Diabetic coma: a reappraisal after five years.* Clin. Endocrinol. Metabol. 6:421–455, 1977.

5. ALFREY, A.C.: *Dialysis encephalopathy syndrome.* Ann. Rev. Med. 29:93–98, 1978.

6. ALHO, A.: *Clinical manifestations of fat embolism syndrome.* Arch. Orthop. Traumat. Surg. 92:153–158, 1978.

7. AMES, A., III, AND GURIAN, B.S.: *Effects of glucose and oxygen deprivation on function of isolated mammalian retina.* J. Neurophysiol. 26:617–634, 1963.

8. AMES, A., III, WRIGHT, R.L., KOWADA M., ET AL.: *Cerebral ischemia. II. The no-reflow phenomenon.* Am. J. Pathol. 52:437–454, 1968.

9. AMOROSI, E.L. AND ULTMANN, J.E.: *Thrombotic thrombocytopenic purpura: report of 16 cases and review of the literature.* Medicine 45:139–159, 1966.

10. ANDERSON, R.J., POTTS, D.E., GABOW, P.A., ET AL.: *Unrecognized adult salicylate intoxication.* Ann. Int. Med. 85:745–748, 1976.

11. ARBUS, L., FABRE, J., BECHAC, G., ET AL.: *Clinical, ophthalmoscopic and biological findings in system fat embolism: pathogenetic theory and treatment in 30 cases.* Acta Neurochirurgica 29:89-104, 1973.

12. ARDUINI, A., AND ARDUINI, M.G.: *Effects of drugs and metabolic alterations on brain stem arousal mechanism.* J. Pharmacol. Exp. Ther. 110:76-85, 1954.

13. ARIEFF, A.I., AND CARROLL, H.J.: *Cerebral edema and depression of sensorium in nonketotic hyperosmolar coma.* Diabetes 23:525-531, 1974.

14. ARIEFF, A.I., AND CARROLL, H.J.: *Non-ketotic hyperosmolar coma with hyperglycemia: clinical features, pathophysiology, renal function, acid-base balance, plasma-cerebrospinal fluid equilibria and the effects of therapy in 37 cases.* Medicine 51:73-94, 1972.

15. ARIEFF, A.I., GUISADO, R., MASSRY, S.G., ET AL.: *Central nervous system pH in uremia and the effects of hemodialysis.* J. Clin. Invest. 58:306-311, 1976.

16. ARIEFF, A.I., KLEEMAN, C.R., ET AL.: *Studies on mechanisms of cerebral edema in diabetic comas; effects of hyperglycemia and rapid lowering of plasma glucose in normal rabbits.* J. Clin. Invest. 52:571-583, 1973.

17. ARIEFF, A.I., LLACH, F., AND MASSRY, S.G.: *Neurological manifestations and morbidity of hyponatremia: correlation with brain water and electrolytes.* Medicine 55:121-129, 1976.

18. ARIEFF, A.I., AND MASSRY, S.G.: *Calcium metabolism of brain in acute renal failure.* J. Clin. Invest. 53:387-392, 1974.

19. ARKY, R.A., AND ARONS, D.L.: *Hypoglycemia in diabetes mellitus.* Med. Clin. N. Am. 55:919-929, 1971.

20. AUSTEN, F.K., CARMICHAEL, M.W., AND ADAMS, R.D.: *Neurologic manifestations of chronic pulmonary insufficiency.* N. Engl. J. Med. 257:579-590, 1957.

21. AVRAM, M.M., FEINFELD, D.A., AND HUATUCO, A.H.: *Decreased motor nerve conduction velocity and elevated parathyroid hormone in uremia.* N. Engl. J. Med. 298:1000-1003, 1978.

22. BALFOUR, H.H., JR., HABLE, K.A., CARLSON, G.S., ET AL.: *Mumps associated with coma or exanthems.* Clin. Pediatr. 11:88-92, 1972.

23. BARINGER, J.R.: "Herpes simplex virus infections of the nervous system." In Vinken, P.J., and Bruyn, G.W. (eds.): *Handbook of Clinical Neurology,* Vol. 34: *Infections of the Nervous System,* Part II. Elsevier North-Holland, New York, 1978, pp. 145-159.

24. BARINGER, J.R.: "Viral diseases of the nervous system." In Tyler, H.R., and Dawson, D.M. (eds.): *Current Neurology,* vol. 2, Houghton Mifflin, Boston, 1979, pp. 441-445.

25. BARKER, J.L.: "Selective depression of postsynaptic excitation by general anesthetics." In Fink, B.R. (ed.): *Molecular Mechanisms of Anesthesia.* Prog. Anesthesiol. Raven, New York 1:135-153, 1975.

26. BEHAN, P.O., KIES, M.W., LISAK, R.P., ET AL.: *Immunological mechanisms in experimental encephalomyelitis in non-human primates.* Arch. Neurol. 29:4-9, 1973.

27. BELL, W.R., SIMON, T.L., AND DEMETS, D.L.: *The clinical features of submassive and massive pulmonary emboli.* Am. J. Med. 62:355-360, 1977.

28. BELLER, F.K.: *The role of endotoxin in disseminated intravascular coagulation.* Trans. 17th Ann. Symp. Blood, 1969, p. 125-149.

29. BERNE, R.M., RUBIO, R., AND CURNISH, R.: *Release of adenosine from ischemic brain: Effect on cerbral vascular resistance and incorporation into cerebral adenine nucleotides.* Circ. Res. 35:262-271, 1974.

30. BINAH, O., MEIRI, U., AND RAHAMINOFF, H.: *The effects of $HgCl_2$ and mersalyl on mechanisms regulating intracellular calcium and transmitter release.* Eur. J. Pharmacol. 51:453-457, 1978.

31. BIRCHFIELD, R.I.: *Postural hypotension in Wernicke's disease.* Am. J. Med. 36:404-414, 1964.

32. BIRD, T.D., AND PLUM, F.: *Recovery from barbiturate overdose coma with a prolonged isoelectric electroencephalogram.* Neurology 18:456-460, 1968.

33. BLENNOW, G., FOLBERGROVA, J., NILSSON, B., ET AL.: *Effects of bicuculline-induced seizures on cerebral metabolism and circulation of rats rendered hypoglycemic by starvation.* Ann. Neurol. 5:139-151, 1979.

34. BLOCK, M.G., AND RUBENSTEIN, A.H.: *Spontaneous hypoglycemia in diabetic patients with renal insufficiency.* J.A.M.A. 213:1863-1866, 1970.

35. BLUM, M.: *Myxedema coma.* Am. J. Med. Sci. 264:432-443, 1972.

36. Boston Collaborative Drug Surveillance Program: *Acute adverse reactions to prednisone in relation to dosage.* Clin. Pharmacol. Ther. 13:694-698, 1972.

285

37. Boston Collaborative Drug Surveillance Program: *Adverse reactions to the tricyclic-antidepressant drugs.* Lancet 1:529–531, 1972.

38. Bowen, D.M., Smith, C.B., White, P., et al.: *Neurotransmitter-related enzymes and indices of hypoxia in senile dementia and other abiotrophies.* Brain 99:459–496, 1976.

39. Bowen, D.M., Goodhardt, M.J., Strong, A.J., et al.: *Biochemical indices of brain structure, function and hypoxia in cortex from baboons with middle cerebral artery occlusion.* Brain Res. 117:503–507, 1976.

40. Boysen, G.: *Cerebral hemodynamics in carotid surgery.* Acta Neurol. Scand. 49:(suppl. 52) 1–84, 1973.

41. Braganca, B.M., Faulkner, P., and Quastel, J.H.: *Effects of inhibitors of glutamine synthesis on the inhibition of acetylcholine synthesis in brain slices by ammonium ions.* Biochem. Biophys. Acta 10:83–88, 1953.

42. Branston, N.M., Symon, L., Crockard, H.A., et al.: *Relationship between the cortical evoked potential and local cortical blood flow following acute middle cerebral artery occlusion in the baboon.* Exp. Neurol. 45:195–208, 1974.

43. Brierley, J.B., Brown, A.W., and Meldrum, B.S.: *The nature and time course of the neuronal alterations resulting from oligaemia and hypoglycemia in the brain of Macaca mulatta.* Brain Res. 25:483–449, 1971.

44. Broderson, P., Paulson, O.B., Bolwig, T.G., et al.: *Cerebral hyperemia in electrically induced epileptic seizures.* Arch. Neurol. 28:334–338, 1973.

45. Brown, R.M., Kehr, W., and Carlsson, A.: *Functional and biochemical aspects of catecholamine metabolism in brain under hypoxia.* Brain Res. 85:491–509, 1975.

46. Bruton, C.J., Corsellis, J.A.N., and Russell, A.: *Hereditary hyperammonemia.* Brain 93:423–434, 1970.

47. Buchan, G.C., and Alvord, E.C., Jr.: *Diffuse necrosis of subcortical white matter associated with bacterial meningitis.* Neurology 19:1–9, 1969.

48. Bulger, R.J., Schrier, R.W., Arend, W.P., et al.: *Spinal-fluid acidosis and the diagnosis of pulmonary encephalopathy.* N. Engl. J. Med. 274:433–437, 1966.

49. Bull, J.M., Lees, D., Schuette, W., et al.: *Whole body hyperthermia: a Phase-I trial of a potential adjuvant to chemotherapy.* Ann. Intern. Med. 90:317–323, 1979.

50. Calderini, G., Carlsson, A., and Nordstrom, C.H.: *Influence of transient ischemia on monoamine metabolism in the rat brain during nitrous oxide and pentobarbitone anesthesia.* Brain Res. 157:303–310, 1978.

51. Carpenter, R.R., and Petersdorf, R.G.: *Clinical spectrum of bacterial meningitis.* Amer. J. Med. 33:262–275, 1962.

52. Carpenter, W.T., Jr., Strauss, J.S., and Bunney, W.E., Jr.: "The psychobiology of cortisol metabolism: clinical and theoretical implications." In Shader, R.I. (ed.): *Psychiatric Complications of Medical Drugs.* Raven Press, New York, 1972, pp. 49–72.

53. Cavanagh, J.B., and Kyu, M.H.: *Type II Alzheimer change experimentally produced in astrocytes in the rat.* J. Neurol. Sci. 12:63–75, 1971.

54. Champion, H.R., Caplan, Y.H., Baker, S.P., et al.: *Alcohol intoxication and serum osmolality.* Lancet 1:1402–1404, 1975.

55. Chan-Palay, V.: *Indoleamine neurons and their processes in the normal rat brain and in chronic diet-induced thiamine deficiency demonstrated by uptake of ^3H-serotonin.* J. Comp. Neurol. 176:467–494, 1977.

56. Chapman, L.F., and Wolff, H.G.: *The cerebral hemispheres and the highest integrative functions of man.* Arch. Neurol. 1:357–424, 1959.

57. Chester, E.M., Agamanolis, D.P., Banker, B.Q., et al.: *Hypertensive encephalopathy: a clinicopathological study of 20 cases.* Neurology 28:928–939, 1978.

58. Chiang, J., Kowada, M., Ames, A., III, et al.: *Cerebral ischemia. III. Vascular changes.* Am. J. Pathol. 52:455–476, 1968.

59. Ch'ien, L.T., Goehm, R.M., Robinson, H., et al.: *Characteristic early electroencephalographic changes in herpes simplex encephalitis; clinical and virologic studies.* Arch. Neurol. 34:361–364, 1977.

60. Clements, R.S., Jr., Blumenthal, S.A., Morrison, A.D., et al.: *Increased cerebrospinal-fluid pressure during treatment of diabetes ketosis.* Lancet 2:671–675, 1971.

61. CLEMMESON, C.: *New line of treatment in barbiturate poisoning.* Acta Med. Scand. 148:83–89, 1954.

62. COHEN, P.J., WOLLMAN, H., ALEXANDER, S.C., ET AL.: *Cerebral carbohydrate metabolism in man during halothane anesthesia.* Anesthesiology 25:185–191, 1964.

63. COLLINS, R.C., AL-MONDHIRY, H., CHERNIK, N.L., ET AL.: *Neurological manifestations of intravascular coagulation in patients with cancer: a clinicopathologic analysis of 12 cases.* Neurology 25:795–806, 1975.

64. COOPER, A.J.L., MCDONALD, J.M., GELBARD, S., ET AL.: *The metabolic fate of ^{13}N-labeled ammonia in rat brain.* J. Biol. Chem. 254:4982–4992, 1979.

65. CORKILL, G., SIVALINGAM, S., REITAN, J., ET AL.: *Dose dependency of post-insult protective effect of pentobarbital in the canine experimental stroke model.* Stroke 9:10–12, 1978.

66. COSTRINI, A.M., PITT, H.A., BUSTAFSON, A.B., ET AL.: *Cardiovascular and metabolic manifestations of heat stroke and severe heat exhaustion.* Am. J. Med. 66:296–302, 1979.

67. COUCH, J.R., AND WEISS, S.A.: *Gliomatosis cerebri.* Neurology 24:504–511, 1974.

68. COXE, W.S., AND LUSE, S.A.: *Acute hemorrhagic leukoencephalitis. A clinical and electron-microscopic report of 2 patients treated with surgical decompression.* J. Neurosurg. 20:584–596, 1963.

69. CRAPPER, D.R., KRISHNAN, S.S., AND DALTON, A.J.: *Brain aluminum distribution in Alzheimer's disease and experimental neurofibrillary degeneration.* Science 180:511–513, 1973.

70. CROMPTON, M.R.: *Cerebral infarction following rupture of cerebral berry aneurysms.* Brain 87:263–280, 1964.

71. CROWELL, R.M., AND ZERVAS, N.T.: *Management of intracranial aneurysm.* Med. Clin. N. Am. 63:695–713, 1979.

72. CRUICKSHANK, J.M., NEIL-DWYER, G., AND STOTT, A.W.: *Possible role of catecholamines, corticosteroids, and potassium in production of electrocardiographic abnormalities associated with subarachnoid haemorrhage.* Br. Heart J. 36:697–706, 1974.

73. DAROFF, R.B., DELLER, J.J., JR., KASTL, A.J., JR., ET AL.: *Cerebral malaria.* J.A.M.A. 202:679–682, 1967.

74. DAVIS, F., AND SCHAUF, C.L.: "Neurologic manifestations of calcium imbalance." In Vinken, P.J., Bruyn, G.W., and Klawans, H.L. (eds.): *Handbook of Clinical Neurology,* Vol. 28. Elsevier North-Holland, New York, 1976, pp. 527–543.

75. DAVIS, J.N., AND CARLSSON, A.: *The effect of hypoxia on monoamine synthesis, levels and metabolism in rat brain.* J. Neurochem. 21:783–790, 1973.

76. DAVIS, J.N., CARLSSON, A., MACMILLAN, V., ET AL.: *Brain tryptophan hydroxylation: dependence on arterial oxygen tension.* Science 182:72–73, 1973.

77. DEGIROLAMI, U., HAAS, M.L., AND RICHARDSON, E.P., JR.: *Subacute diencephalic angio-encephalopathy; a clinicopathological case study.* J. Neurol. Sci. 22:197–210, 1974.

78. DELEAN, J., RICHARDSON, J.C., AND HORNYKIEWICZ, O.: *Beneficial effects of serotonin precursors in postanoxic action myoclonus.* Neurology 26:863–868, 1976.

79. DELLA PORTA, P., MAIOLO, A.T., NEGRI, V.U., ET AL.: *Cerebral blood flow and metabolism in therapeutic insulin coma.* Metabolism 13:131–140, 1964.

80. DEMOPOULOS, H.B., FLAMM, E., AND RANSOHOFF, J.: "Molecular pathology of lipids and CNS membranes." In Jobsis, F.F. (ed.): *Oxygen and Physiological Function.* Professional Information Library, Dallas, 1977.

81. DEPPISCH, L.M., AND FAYEMI, A.O.: *Non-bacterial thrombotic endocarditis: clinicopathologic correlations.* Am. Heart J. 92:723–729, 1976.

82. DESROSIERS, M.H., KENNEDY, C., SHINOHARA, M., ET AL.: *Effects of CO_2 on local cerebral glucose utilization in the conscious rat.* Neurology 26:346, 1976.

83. DEVAKUL, K., HARINASUTA, T., AND REID, H.A.: *^{125}I-labelled fibrinogen in cerebral malaria.* Lancet 2:886–888, 1966.

84. DE VIVO, D.C.: *Reye syndrome: a metabolic response to an acute mitochondrial insult?* Neurology 28:105–107, 1978.

85. DODGE, P.R., AND SWARTZ, M.N.: *Bacterial meningitis: II. Special neurologic problems, postmeningitic complications and clinicopathological correlations.* N. Engl. J. Med. 272:954–960, 1965.

86. DOLIN, R., REICHMAN, R.C., MAZUR, M.H., ET AL.: *Herpes zoster-varicella infections in immunosuppressed patients.* Ann. Intern. Med. 89:375–388, 1978.

87. Dolivo, M.: *Metabolism of mammalian sympathetic ganglia.* Fed. Proc. 33:1043–1048, 1974.

88. Dooling, E.C., and Richardson, E.P.: *Delayed encephalopathy after strangling.* Arch. Neurol. 33:196–199, 1976.

89. Drachman, D.A.: *Memory and cognitive function in man: does the cholinergic system have a specific role?* Neurology, 27:783–790. 1977.

90. Dreyfus, P.M.: *The quantitative histochemical distribution of thiamine in deficient rat brain.* J. Neurochem. 8:139–145, 1961.

91. Dreyfus, P.M.: *The regional distribution of transketolase in the normal and the thiamine deficient nervous system.* J. Neuropath. Exp. Neurol. 24:119–129, 1965.

92. Dreyfus, P.M., and Geel, S.E.: "Vitamin and nutritional deficiencies." In Siegel, G.J., Albers, R.W., Katzman, R., et al. (eds.): *Basic Neurochemistry.* ed. 2. Little, Brown, Boston, 1976, Chapter 29, pp. 605–626.

93. Duberstein, J.L., and Kaufman, D.M.: *A clinical study of an epidemic of heroin intoxication and heroin-induced pulmonary edema.* Am. J. Med. 51:704–514, 1971.

94. Duck, S.C., Weldon, V.V., Pagliara, A.S., et al.: *Cerebral edema complicating therapy for diabetic ketoacidosis.* Diabetes 25:111–115, 1976.

95. Duffy, T.E., Nelson, S.R., and Lowry, O.H.: *Cerebral carbohydrate metabolism during acute hypoxia and recovery.* J. Neurochem. 19:959–977, 1972.

96. Duffy, T.E., and Plum, F.: "Seizures and comatose states." In Siegel, G.J., Albers, R.W., Katzman, R., et al. (eds.): *Basic Neurochemistry.* ed.3. Little, Brown, Boston, in press, 1980.

97. Duffy, T.E., Vergara, F., and Plum, F.: "α-Ketoglutaramate in hepatic encephalopathy." In Plum, F. (ed.): *Brain Dysfunction in Metabolic Disorders.* Res. Publ. Assoc. Nerv. Ment. Dis. 53:39–51, 1974.

98. Eder, L., Hirt, L., and Dunant, Y.: *Possible involvement of thiamine in acetylcholine release.* Nature 264:186–188, 1976.

99. Ehrlich, M., Plum, F., and Duffy, T.E.: *Blood and brain ammonia concentrations after portocaval anastomosis. Effects of ammonia loading.* J. Neurochem. In press, 1980.

100. Eisenberg, S., Madison, L., and Sensenbach, W.: *Cerebral hemodynamic and metabolic studies in patients with congestive heart failure: II. Observations in confused subjects.* Circulation 21:704–709, 1960.

101. Eisenberg, S., and Seltzer, H.S.: *The cerebral metabolic effects of acutely induced hypoglycemia in human subjects.* Metabolism 11:1162–1168, 1962.

102. Elian, M.: *Herpes simplex encephalitis; prognosis and long-term follow-up.* Arch. Neurol. 32:39–43, 1975.

103. Ellis, J.M., and Lee, S.I.: *Acute prolonged confusion in later life as an ictal state.* Epilepsia 19:119–128, 1978.

104. Ellison, P.H., and Hanson, P.A.: *Herpes simplex: a possible cause of brain-stem encephalitis.* Pediatrics 59:240–243, 1977.

105. Ellison, P.H., and Largen, J.A.: *Iatrogenic complications of Reye Syndrome—hypotension, hyperosmolality and renal insult.* Ann. Neurol. 6:179, 1979 (abstract).

106. Emmett, M., and Narins, R.G.: *Clinical use of the anion gap.* Medicine 56:38–54, 1977.

107. Engle, G.L.: *Fainting.* ed. 2. Charles C Thomas, Springfield, Ill., 1962.

108. Ericson, G., Warren, S.E., Gribik, M., et al.: *Unilateral asterixis in a dialysis patient.* J.A.M.A. 240:671, 1978.

109. Estrada, R.V., Moreno, J., Martinez, E., et al.: *Pancreatic encephalopathy.* Acta Neurol. Scand. 59:135–139, 1979.

110. Faerman, I., Faccio, E., Milei, J., et al.: *Autonomic neuropathy and painless myocardial infarction in diabetic patients; histologic evidence of their relationship.* Diabetes 26:1147–1158, 1977.

111. Fauci, A.S., Haynes, B.F., and Katz, P.: *The spectrum of vasculitides; clinical, pathological, immunologic and therapeutic considerations.* Ann. Intern. Med. 89:660–676, 1978.

112. Feinglass, E.J., Arnett, F.C., Dorsch, C.A., et al.: *Neuropsychiatric manifestations of systemic lupus erythematosus: diagnosis, clinical spectrum and relationship to other features of the disease.* Medicine 55:323–339, 1976.

113. Fenton, T.R., Marshall, P.C., and Cavanagh, N.: *Herpes simplex infection presenting as a brainstem infection.* Lancet 2:977–978, 1977.

114. FERRENDELLI, J.A., AND CHANG, M.M.: *Brain metabolism during hypoglycemia. Effect of insulin on regional central nervous system glucose and energy reserves in mice.* Arch. Neurol. 28:173–177, 1973.

115. FISCHER, E.G., AMES, A., III, HEDLEY-WHYTE, E.T., AND O'GORMAN, S.: *Reassessment of cerebral capillary changes in acute global ischemia and their relationship to the "no-reflow phenomenon."* Stroke 8:36–39, 1977.

116. FISCHER, J.E., AND BALDESSARINI, R.J.: "Pathogenesis and therapy of hepatic coma." In Schaeffner, F., and Popper, H., (eds.): *Progress in Liver Disease.* vol. 5. Grune and Smith, New York, 1976.

117. FISCHER, J.E., ROSEN, H.M., EBEID, A.M., ET AL.: *The effect of normalization of plasma amino acids on hepatic encephalopathy in man.* Surgery 80:77–91, 1976.

118. FISHMAN, R.A., AND RASKIN, N.H.: *Experimental uremic encephalopathy. Permeability and electrolyte metabolism of brain and other tissues.* Arch. Neurol. 17:10–21, 1967.

119. FISHMAN, R.A., SLIGAR, K., AND HAKE, R.B.: *Effects of leukocytes on brain metabolism in granulocytic brain edema.* Ann. Neurol. 2:89–94, 1977.

120. FITZGERALD, F.: *Clinical hypophosphatemia.* Ann. Rev. Med. 29:177–189, 1978.

121. FITZ-HUGH, T., JR., PEPPER, D.S., AND HOPKINS, H.U.: *The cerebral form of malaria.* Bull. U.S. Army Medical Dept. 83:39–48, 1944.

122. FLENDRIG, J.A., DRUIS, H., AND DAS, H.A.: *Aluminum intoxication: the cause of dialysis dementia?* Proc. Eur. Dial. Transplant Assoc. 13:355–361, 1976.

123. FOLSTEIN, M.F., FOLSTEIN, S.E., AND McHUGH, P.R.: *"Mini-mental status." A practical method for grading the cognitive state of patients for the clinician.* J. Psychiatr. Res. 12:189–198, 1975.

124. FOLTZ, E.L., AND SCHMIDT, R.P.: *The role of the reticular formation in the coma of head injury.* J. Neurosurg. 13:145–154, 1956.

125. FOLTZ, E.L., AND WARD, A.A., JR.: *Communicating hydrocephalus from subarachnoid bleeding.* J. Neurosurg. 13:546–566, 1956.

126. FORREST, J.N., COX, M., HONG, C., ET AL.: *Superiority of demeclocycline over lithium in the treatment of chronic syndrome of inappropriate secretion of antidiuretic hormone.* N. Engl. J. Med. 298:173–177, 1978.

127. FOSTER, D.W.: *Insulin deficiency and hyperosmolar coma.* Adv. Int. Med. 19:159–173, 1974.

128. FRANKEL, N., COHEN, A.K., ARKY, R.A., ET AL.: *Alcohol hypoglycemia: II. A postulated mechanism of action based on experiments with rat liver slices.* J. Clin. Endocrinol. Metab. 25:76–94, 1965.

129. FRED, H.L., WILLERSON, J.T., AND ALEXANDER, J.K.: *Neurological manifestations of pulmonary thromboembolism.* Arch. Intern. Med. 120:33–37, 1967.

130. FRENCH, J.D., VERZEANO, M., AND MAGOUN, H.W.: *A neural basis of the anesthetic state.* Arch. Neurol. Psychiatr. 69:519–529, 1953.

131. FRIEDE, R.L., AND VAN HOUTEN, W.H.: *Relations between post mortem alterations and glycolytic metabolism in the brain.* Exp. Neurol. 4:197–204, 1961.

132. FRIEDREICH, N.: *Paramyoklonus multiplex.* Virchow Arch. Path. Anat. 86:421–430, 1881.

133. FULOP, M., TANNENBAUM, H., DREYER, N.: *Ketotic hyperosmolar coma.* Lancet 2:635–639, 1973.

134. GAITONDE, M.K., FAYEIN, N.A., AND JOHNSON, A.L.: *Decreased metabolism in vivo of glucose into amino acids of the brain of thiamine-deficient rats after treatment with pyrithiamine.* J. Neurochem. 24:1215–1223, 1975.

135. GAJDUSEK, D.C., GIBBS, C., ASHER, D.M., ET AL.: *Precautions in medical care of, and in handling materials from, patients with transmissible virus dementia (Creutzfeldt-Jakob disease).* N. Engl. J. Med. 297:1253–1258, 1977.

136. GASTAUT, H., AND FISCHER-WILLIAMS, M.: "The physiopathology of epileptic seizures." In Field, J., Magoun, H.W., and Hall, V.E. (eds.): *Handbook of Physiology. Sect. I, Neurophysiology.* American Physiological Society, Washington, D.C., 1959, Volume 1, Chapter 14, p. 329.

137. GAZZARD, B.G., PORTMANN, B., MURRAY-LYON, I.M., ET AL.: *Causes of death in fulminant hepatic failure.* Q.J. Med. 44:615–626, 1975.

138. GIBBS, C.J., JR., GAJDUSEK, D.C., ASHER, D.M., ET AL.: *Creutzfeldt-Jakob disease (spongiform encephalopathy): transmission to the chimpanzee.* Science 161:388–389, 1968.

139. GIBSON, G.E., AND BLASS, J.P.: *Impaired synthesis of acetylcholine in brain accompanying mild hypoxia and hypoglycemia.* J. Neurochem. 27:37–42, 1976.

140. GIBSON, G.E., AND BLASS, J.P.: *Proportional inhibition of acetylcholine synthesis accompanying impairment of 3-hydroxybutyrate oxidation in rat brain slices.* Biochem. Pharmacol. 28:133–139, 1979.

141. GIBSON, G.E., SHIMADA, M., AND BLASS, J.P.: *Alterations in acetylcholine synthesis and in cyclic nucleotides in mild cerebral hypoxia.* J. Neurochem. In press.

142. GINSBERG, M.D., BUDD, W.W., AND WELSH, F.A.: *Diffuse cerebral ischemia in the cat: I. Local blood flow during severe ischemia and recirculation.* Ann. Neurol. 3:482–492, 1978.

143. GINSBERG, M.D., GRAHAM, D.I., WELSH, F.A., ET AL.: *Diffuse cerebral ischemia in the cat. III. Neuropathological sequelae of severe ischemia.* Ann. Neurol. 5:350–358, 1979.

144. GINSBERG, M.D., HEDLEY-WHYTE, E.T., AND RICHARDSON, E.P.: *Hypoxic-ischemic leukoencephalopathy in man.* Arch. Neurol. 33:5–14, 1976.

145. GINSBERG, M.D., MYERS, R.E., AND MCDONAGH, B.F.: *Experimental carbon monoxide encephalopathy in the primate. II. Clinical aspects, neuropathology and physiologic correlations.* Arch. Neurol. 30:209–216, 1974.

146. GLASER, G.H.: "The EEG in certain metabolic disorders." In Remond, A. (ed.): *Handbook of Electroencephalography and Clinical Neurophysiology.* Vol. 15 (Part C). Elsevier North-Holland, New York, 1976, pp. 15C/16-15C/25.

147. GLASER, G.H.: "EEG in thyroid dysfunction." In Remond, A. (ed.): *Handbook of Electroencephalography and Clinical Neurophysiology.* Vol. 15 (Part C). Elsevier North-Holland, New York, 1976, pp. 15C/70–15C/76.

148. GOLDMAN, J., MATZ, R, MORTIMER, R. ET AL.: *High elevations of creatine phosphokinase in hypothyroidism.* J.A.M.A. 238:325–326, 1977.

149. GOLDSTEIN, D.A., CHUI, L.A., AND MASSRY, S.G.: *Effects of parathyroid hormone and uremia on peripheral nerve calcium and motor nerve conduction velocity.* J. Clin. Invest. 62:88–93, 1978.

150. GOLTER, M., AND MICHAELSON, I.A.: *Growth, behavior, and brain catecholamines in lead-exposed neonatal rats: a reappraisal.* Science 187:359–361, 1975.

151. GORDON, E.E., AND KIBADI, U.M.: *The hyperglycaemic, hyperosmolar syndrome.* Am. J. Med. Sci. 271:252–268, 1976.

152. GOTTSTEIN, U.: *Der hirnkreislauf bei hyperthyreose und myxödem.* Verh. dp. Ges inn Med. 70:921–924, 1964.

153. GOTTSTEIN, U., AND HELD, K.: *Insulin wirkung auf den menschlichen.* Hirnmetabolisms von Stoffwechselgesunden und Diabetikern Klin. Wschr. 45:18–23, 1967.

154. GRAHAM, D.I., BEHAN, P.O., AND MORE, I.A.R.: *Brain damage complicating septic shock; acute haemorrhagic leucoencephalitis as a complication of the generalized Schwartzman reaction.* J. Neurol. Neurosurg. Psychiatr. 42:19–28, 1979.

155. GRAY, F.D., JR., AND HORNER, G.J.: *Survival following extreme hypoxemia.* J.A.M.A. 211:1815–1817, 1970.

156. GREENBLATT, D.J., AND SHADER, R.I.: *Anticholinergics.* N. Engl. J. Med. 288:1215–1219, 1973.

157. GREENE, R.: "The thyroid gland: its relationship to neurology." In Vinken, P.J., and Bruyn, G.W. (eds.): *Handbook of Clinical Neurology,* Vol. 27 (Part I). Elsevier North-Holland, New York, 1976, pp. 255–277.

158. GRÖFLIN, U.B., and Thölen, H.: *Cerebral edema in the rat with galactosamine-induced severe hepatitis.* Experientia 34:1501–1503, 1978.

159. GRUMER, H.A., DERRYBERRY, W., DUBIN, A., ET AL.: *Idiopathic, episodic, inappropriate secretion of antidiuretic hormone.* Am. J. Med. 32:954–963, 1962.

160. GUBLER, C.J., ADAMS, B.L., HAMMOND, B., ET AL.: *Effect of thiamine deprivation and thiamine antagonists on the level of γ-aminobutyric acid and on 2-oxoglutarate metabolism in rat brain.* J. Neurochem. 22:831–836, 1974.

161. GUISADO, R., AND ARIEFF, A.I.: *Neurologic manifestations of diabetic comas: correlation with biochemical alterations in the brain.* Metabolism 24:665–679, 1975.

162. GUISADO, R., ARIEFF, A.I., AND MASSRY, S.G.: *Changes in the electroencephalogram in acute uremia.* J. Clin. Invest. 55:738–745, 1975.

163. HAGSTAM, K.E.: *EEG frequency content related to chemical blood parameters in chronic uremia.* Scand. J. Urol. Nephrol. Suppl. 7, 1971.

164. HAMMER W.J., LUESSENHOP, A.J., AND WEINTRAUB, A.M.: *Observations on the electrocar-diographic changes associated with subarachnoid hemorrhage with special reference to their genesis.* Am. J. Med. 59:427–433, 1975.

165. HANID, M.A., MACKENZIE, R.L., JENNER, R.E., ET AL.: *Intracranial pressure in pigs with surgically induced acute liver failure.* Gastroenterology 76:122–131, 1979.

166. HANSEN, A.R., KENNEDY, K.A., AMBRE, J.J., ET AL.: *Glutethimide poisoning. A metabolite con-tributes to morbidity and mortality.* N. Engl. J. Med. 292:250–252, 1975.

167. HARNER, R., AND NAQUET, R.: "Electroencephalography in metabolic coma." In Remond, A. (ed.): *Handbook of Electroencephalography and Clinical Neurophysiology.* Vol. 12. Elsevier North-Holland, New York, 1975, pp. 12/47–12/62.

168. HASS, W.K., HAWKINS, R.A., AND RANSOHOFF, J.: *Reduction of cerebral blood flow, glucose utiliza-tion, and oxidative metabolism after bilateral reticular formation lesions.* Trans. Am. Neurol. Assoc. 102:19–22, 1977.

169. HAYASHI, M., MARUKAWA, S., FUJII, H., ET AL.: *Intracranial hypertension in patients with ruptured intracranial aneurysm.* J. Neurosurg. 46:584–590, 1977.

170. HEINRICH, C.P., STADLER, H., AND WEISER, H.: *The effect of thiamine deficiency on the acetyl-coenzyme and acetylcholine levels in the rat brain.* J. Neurochem. 21:1273–1281, 1973.

171. HELLER, S.S., FRANK, K.A., KORNFIELD, D.S., ET AL.: *Psychological outcome following open-heart surgery.* Arch. Intern. Med. 134:908–914, 1974.

172. HEMMINGSEN, R., KRAMP, P., AND RAFAELSEN, Q.J.: *Delirium tremens and related clinical states.* Acta Psychiatr. Scand. 59:337–369, 1979.

173. HERISHANU, Y., ABRAMSKY, O., AND LAVY, S.: *Focal neurological manifestations in hypercalcemia.* Eur. Neurol. 4:283–288, 1970.

174. HILL, J.B.: *Salicylate intoxication.* N. Engl. J. Med. 288:1110–1113, 1973.

175. HIMWICH, H.E.: *Brain Metabolism and Cerebral Disorders.* Williams and Wilkins Co., Baltimore, 1951.

176. HINDFELT, B., PLUM, F., AND DUFFY, T.E.: *Effect of acute ammonia intoxication on cerebral metabolism in rats with portacaval shunts.* J. Clin. Invest. 59:386–396, 1977.

177. HO, M.: "Acute viral encephalitis." In Vinken, P.J., and Bruyn, G.W. (eds.): *Handbook of Clinical Neurology,* Vol. 34: *Infections of the Nervous System,* Part II. Elsevier North-Holland, New York, 1978, pp. 63–82.

178. HOAGLAND, H., ET AL.: *Effects of hypoglycemia and pentobarbital sodium on electrical activity of cerebral cortex and hypothalamus (dogs).* J. Neurophysiol. 2:276–288, 1939.

179. HOUGAARD, K., OIKAWA, T., SVEINSDOTTIR, E., ET AL.: *Regional cerebral blood flow in focal cortical epilepsy.* Arch. Neurol. 33:527–535, 1976.

180. HOROWITZ, I., KLINGENSTEIN, R.J., LEVY, R., ET AL.: *Fat embolism syndrome in delirium tremens.* Am. J. Gastroenterol. 68:476–480, 1977.

181. HOSSMANN, K.A., AND TAKAGI, S.: *Osmolality of brain in cerebral ischemia.* Exp. Neurol. 51:124–131, 1976.

182. HOSSMANN, K.A. AND ZIMMERMAN, V.: *Resuscitation of the monkey brain after one hour complete ischemia. 1. Physiological and morphological observations.* Brain Res. 81:59–74, 1974.

183. HOTSON, J.R., AND PEDLEY, T.A.: *The neurological complications of cardiac transplantation.* Brain 99:673–694, 1976.

184. HOWSE, D.C., CARONNA, J.J., DUFFY, T.E., ET AL.: *Cerebral energy metabolism, pH and blood flow during seizures in the cat.* Am. J. Physiol. 227:1444–1451, 1974.

185. HUGHES, J.R.: *Limitations of the EEG in coma and brain death.* Ann. N.Y. Acad. Sci. 315:121–136, 1978.

186. HUME, M., SEVITT, S., AND THOMAS, D.P.: *Venous Thrombosis and Pulmonary Embolism.* Harvard University Press, Cambridge, Massachusetts, 1970, pp. 252–278.

187. IMRIE, J.A.: *Acute alcoholic poisoning.* Brit. Med. J. 2:428–430, 1955.

188. INGVAR, D.H., CRONQVIST, S., EKBERG, R., ET AL.: *Normal values of regional cerebral blood flow in man, including flow and weight estimates of gray and white matter. A preliminary summary.* Acta Neurol. Scand. 41: suppl. 14, 72–78, 1965.

189. INGVAR, D.H., AND LASSEN, N.A. (EDS.): *Regional cerebral blood flow.* Acta Neurol. Scand. 41: suppl. 14, 1965.

190. INGVAR, D.H., AND PHILIPSON, L.: *Distribution of cerebral blood flow in the dominant hemisphere during motor ideation and motor performance.* Ann. Neurol. 2:230-237, 1977.

191. ITO, U., SPATZ, M., WALKER, J.T., ET AL.: *Experimental cerebral ischemia in mongolian gerbils. 1. Light microscopic observations.* Acta Neuropath. 32:209-223, 1975.

192. IWATA, H.: *Catecholamine metabolism in thiamine deficient rat.* J. Nutr. Sci. Vitaminol. 22:25-27, 1976.

193. IZZO, J.L., SCHUSTER, D.B., AND ENGEL, G.L.: *The electroencephalogram of patients with diabetes mellitus.* Diabetes 2:93-99, 1953.

194. JACOBS, J.W., BERNHARD, M.R., DELGADO, A., ET AL.: *Screening for organic mental syndromes in the medically ill.* Ann. Int. Med. 86:40-46, 1977.

195. JAMES, J.H., ESCOURROU, J., AND FISCHER, J.E.: *Blood-brain neutral amino acid transport activity is increased after portacaval anastomosis.* Science 200:1395-1397, 1978.

196. JELLINGER, K.: *Giant cell granulomatous angiitis of the central nervous system.* J. Neurol. 215:175-190, 1977.

197. JENKINS, D.W., ECKEL, R.E., AND CRAIG, J.W.: *Alcoholic ketoacidosis.* J.A.M.A. 217:177-183, 1971.

198. JOHNSON, D.A., AND TONG, N.T.: *Pancreatic encephalopathy.* South. Med. J. 70:165-167, 1977.

199. JOHNSON, R.T., AND JOHNSON, K.P.: "Slow and chronic virus infections of the nervous system." In Plum, F. (ed.): *Recent Advances in Neurology.* F.A. Davis Co., Philadelphia, 1969, pp. 33-78.

200. JONES, H.R., JR., SIEKERT, R.G., AND GERACI, J.E.: *Neurologic manifestations of bacterial endocarditis.* Ann. Intern. Med. 71:21-28, 1969.

201. KATZMAN, R., KAGAN, E.H., AND ZIMMERMAN, H.M.: *A Case of Jakob-Creutzfeldt disease. I. Clinicopathological analysis.* J. Neuropath. Exp. Neurol. 20:78-94, 1961.

202. KATZMAN, R., AND PAPPIUS, H.M.: *Brain Electrolytes and Fluid Metabolism.* Williams and Wilkins Co., Baltimore, 1973.

203. KEIM, R.J.: *Meningitis: the influence of routine otolaryngologic consultation on morbidity and mortality in 290 cases.* Laryngoscope, (suppl. 9) 88:1-30, 1978.

204. KETY, S.S., EVARTS, E.V., AND WILLIAMS, H.L. (EDS.): *Sleep and Altered States of Consciousness.* Res. Publ. Assoc. Res. Nerv. Ment. Dis., Proc., Vol. 45, 1967.

205. KETY, S.S., AND SCHMIDT, C.F.: *The effects of altered arterial tensions of carbon dioxide and oxygen on cerebral blood flow and cerebral oxygen consumption of normal young men.* J. Clin. Invest. 27:484-497, 1948.

206. KETY, S.S., AND SCHMIDT, C.F.: *The nitrous oxide method for the quantitative determination of cerebral blood flow in man; theory, procedure and normal values.* J. Clin. Invest. 27:476-483, 1948.

207. KING, R.B., AND SABA, M.I.: *Forewarnings of major subarachnoid hemorrhage due to congenital berry aneurysm.* N.Y. State J. Med. 74:638-639. 1974.

208. KISSIN, B., AND BEGLEITER, H. (EDS.): *The Biology of Alcoholism,* vol. 2, *Physiology and Behavior.* Plenum Press, New York, 1972.

209. KLATZO, I., WISNIEWSKI, H., AND STREICHER, E.: *Experimental production of neurofibrillary degeneration.* J. Neuropath. Exp. Neurol. 24:187-199, 1965.

210. KNOCHEL, J.P.: *The pathophysiology and clinical characteristics of severe hypophosphatemia.* Arch. Intern. Med. 137:203-220, 1977.

211. KOENIG, H., RABINOWITZ, S.G., DAY, E., ET AL.: *Post-infectious encephalomyelitis after successful treatment of herpes simplex encephalitis with adenine arabinoside.* N. Engl. J. Med. 300:1089-1094, 1979.

212. KOGURE, K., SCHEINBERG, P., MATSUMOTO, A., ET AL.: *Catecholamines in experimental brain ischemia.* Arch. Neurol. 32:21-24, 1975.

213. KOPELOFF, L.M., BARRERA, S.E., AND KOPELOFF, N.: *Recurrent convulsive seizures in animals produced by immunologic and chemical means.* Am. J. Psychiatr. 98:881-902, 1942.

214. KOWADA, M., AMES, A., III, MAJNO, G., AND WRIGHT, R.L.: *Cerebral ischemia. I. An improved experimental method for study; cardiovascular effects and demonstration of an early vascular lesion in the rabbit.* J. Neurosurg. 28:150-157, 1968.

215. KRAUSE, S., AND SILVERBLATT, M.: *Pulmonary embolism: a review with emphasis on clinical and electrocardiographic diagnosis.* Arch. Intern. Med. 96:19-25, 1955.

216. KRNJEVIC, K.: "Is general anesthesia induced by neuronal asphyxia?" In Fink, R.B. (ed.): *Molecular Mechanisms of Anesthesia.* Raven, New York, 1975, pp. 93–98.

217. KUSCHINSKY, W., AND WAHL, M.: *Local chemical and neurogenic regulation of cerebral vascular resistance.* Physiol. Rev. 58:656–689, 1978.

218. LANCE, J., AND ADAMS, R.D.: *The syndrome of intention or action myoclonus as a sequel to hypoxic encephalopathy.* Brain 86:111–135, 1963.

219. LARRABEE, M.G., AND POSTERNAK, J.M.: *Selective action of anesthetics on synapses and axons in mammalian sympathetic ganglia.* J. Neurophysiol. 15:91–114, 1952.

220. LARSEN, B., SKINHØJ, E., AND LASSEN, N.A.: *Variations in regional cortical blood flow in the right and left hemispheres during automatic speech.* Brain 101:193–209, 1978.

221. LASSEN, N.A.: *Control of cerebral circulation in health and disease.* Circ. Res. 34:749–760, 1974.

222. LAURSEN, H., AND WESTERGAARD, E.: *Enhanced permeability to horseradish peroxidase across cerebral vessels in the rat after portacaval anastomosis.* Neuropath. Appl. Neurobiol. 3:29–44, 1979.

223. LAUX, B.E., AND RAICHLE, M.E.: *The effect of acetazolamide on cerebral blood flow and oxygen utilization in the rhesus monkey.* J. Clin. Invest. 62:585–592, 1978.

224. LAVENSON, G.S., JR., PLUM, F., AND SWANSON, A.G.: *Physiological management compared with pharmacological and electrical stimulation in barbiturate poisoning.* J. Pharmacol. Exp. Ther. 122:271–280, 1958.

225. LEAVITT, S., AND TYLER, H.R.: *Studies in asterixis.* Arch. Neurol. 10:360–368, 1964.

226. LECHTENBERG, R., SIERRA, M.F., PRINGLE, G.F., ET AL.: Listeria monocytogenes: brain abscess or meningoencephalitis? Neurology 29:86–90, 1979.

227. LEDINGHAM, J.G.G., AND RAJAGOPALAN, B.: *Cerebral complications in the treatment of accelerated hypertension.* Q. J. Med. 48:25–41, 1979.

228. LENNOX, W.G.: *The treatment of epilepsy.* Med. Clin. N. Am. 29:1114–1128, 1945.

229. LENNOX, W.G.: *Epilepsy and Related Disorders.* Little, Brown and Co., Boston, 1960, Chapter 12.

230. LEPISTO, P., AND ALHO, A.: *Diagnostic features of the fat embolism syndrome.* Acta Chir. Scand. 141:245–250, 1975.

231. LEVIN, S., HARRIS, A.A., AND SOKALSKI, S.J.: "Bacterial meningitis." In Vinken, P.J., and Bruyn, G.W. (eds.): *Handbook of Clinical Neurology,* Vol. 33: *Infections of the Nervous System,* Part I. Elsevier North-Holland, New York, 1978, pp. 1–19.

232. LEVY, D.E., AND BRIERLEY, J.B.: *Delayed pentobarbital administration limits ischemic brain damage.* Ann. Neurol. 5:59–64, 1979.

233. LEVY, D.E., BRIERLEY, J.B., AND PLUM, F.: *Ischemic brain damage in the gerbil in the absence of 'no-reflow.'* J. Neurol. Neurosurg. Psychiatr. 38:1197–1205, 1975.

234. LEVY, D.E., BRIERLEY, J.B., SILVERMAN, D.G., ET AL.: *Brief hypoxia-ischemia initially damages cerebral neurons.* Arch. Neurol. 32:450–456, 1975.

235. LEWIS, L.D., LJUNGREN, B., RATCHESON, R.A., ET AL.: *Cerebral energy state in insulin-induced hypoglycemia related to blood glucose and to EEG.* J. Neurochem. 23:673–679, 1974.

236. LINDBERGER, K.: *Myxoedema coma.* Acta. Med. Scand. 198:87–90, 1975.

237. LIPOWSKI, Z.J.: *Organic brain syndromes: a reformulation.* Compr. Psychiatry. 19:309–322, 1978.

238. LOCKE, S., MERRILL, J.P., AND TYLER, H.R.: *Neurologic complications of acute uremia.* Arch. Intern. Med. 108:519–530, 1961.

239. LOCKWOOD, A.H.: *Acute and chronic hyperosmolality. Effects on cerebral amino acids and energy metabolism.* Arch. Neurol. 32:62–64, 1975.

240. LOCKWOOD, A.H., McDONALD, J.M., REIMAN, R.E., ET AL.: *The dynamics of ammonia metabolism in man. Effects of liver disease and hyperammonemia.* J. Clin. Invest. 63:449–460, 1979.

241. LOWE, G.R.: *The phenomenology of hallucinations as an aid to differential diagnosis.* Br. J. Psychiatr. 123:621–633, 1973.

242. LUFKIN, E.J., REAGAN, T.J., DOAN, D.H., ET AL.: *Acute cerebral dysfunction in diabetic ketoacidosis: survival followed by panhypopituitarism.* Metabolism 26:363–369, 1977.

243. LUND-ANDERSEN, H.: *Transport of glucose from blood to brain.* Physiol. Rev. 59:305–349, 1979.

244. LUNZER, M., JAMES, I.M., WEINMAN, J., ET AL.: *Treatment of chronic hepatic encephalopathy with levodopa.* Gut 15:555–561, 1974.

245. Lust, W.D., Mrsulja, B.B., Mrsulja, B.J., et al.: *Putative neurotransmitters and cyclic nucleotides in prolonged ischemia of the cerebral cortex.* Brain Res. 98:394–399, 1975.

246. Lyon, G., Dodge, P.R., and Adams, R.D.: *The acute encephalopathies of obscure origin in infants and children.* Brain 84:680–708, 1961.

247. MacDonald, M., and Spector, R.G.: *The influence of anoxia on respiratory enzymes in rat brain.* Br. J. Exp. Pathol. 44:11–15, 1963.

248. Maigraith, B.G.: *Pathological Processes in Malaria and Blackwater Fever.* Blackwell Scientific Publications, Oxford, 1948.

249. Mancall, E.L., and McEntee, W.J.: *Alterations of the cerebellar cortex in nutritional encephalopathy.* Neurology 15:303–313, 1965.

250. Marcoux, F.W., Morawetz, R.B., Halsey, J.H., et al.: *Infarction threshold in the basal ganglia and adjacent structures determined by cerebral blood flow measurement during middle cerebral artery occlusion in anesthetized monkeys.* Soc. Neuroscience Abstr. 4:1262, 1978.

251. Martin, J.B., Reichlin, S., and Brown, G.M.: *Clinical Neuroendocrinology.* F.A. Davis Co., Philadelphia, 1977.

252. Martinez-Hernandez, A., Bell, K.P., and Norenberg, M.D.: *Glutamine synthetase: glial-localization in brain.* Science 195:1356–1358, 1977.

253. Massey, E.W., Goodman, J.C., Stewart, C., et al.: *Unilateral asterixis: motor integrative dysfunction in focal vascular disease.* Neurology 29:1188–1190, 1979.

254. McConahey, W.M.: *Diagnosing and treating myxedema and myxedema coma.* Geriatrics 33:61–66, 1978.

255. McKay, D.G.: *Disseminated Intravascular Coagulation: An Intermediary Mechanism of Disease.* Harper & Row, New York, 1965.

256. McLean, D.R., Jacobs, H., and Mielke, B.W.: *Methanol poisoning: a clinical and pathological study.* Ann. Neurol., 1980, in press.

257. McMahon, M.J., Woodhead, J.S., and Hayward, R.D.: *The nature of hypocalcaemia in acute pancreatitis.* Br. J. Surg. 65:216–218, 1978.

258. Meldrum, B.S., and Nilsson, B.: *Cerebral blood flow and metabolic rate early and late in prolonged epileptic seizures induced in rats by bicuculline.* Brain 99:523–542, 1976.

259. Meldrum, B.S., Vigououx, R.A., and Brierley, J.B.: Systemic factors in epileptic brain damage. Arch. Neurol. 29:82–87, 1973.

260. Menendez, C.E., and Rivlin, R.S.: *Thyrotoxic crisis and myxedema coma.* Med. Clin. North Am. 57:1463–1470, 1973.

261. Menkes, J.H., and Corbo, L.M.: *Adrenoleukodystrophy; accumulation of cholesterol esters with very long chain fatty acids.* Neurology 27:928–932, 1977.

262. Merrill, J.P., Legrain, M., and Hoigne, R.: *Observations on the role of urea in uremia.* Am. J. Med. 14:519–520, 1953.

263. Mesulam, M.M., and Geschwind, N.: *Disordered mental states in the postoperative period.* Urol. Clin. North Am. 3:99–215, 1976.

264. Mesulam, M.M., Waxman, S.G., Geschwind, N., et al.: *Acute confusional states with right middle cerebral artery infarctions.* J. Neurol. Neurosurg. Psychiatr. 39:84–89, 1976.

265. Metzger, A.L., and Rubenstein, A.H.: *Reversible cerebral oedema complicating diabetic ketoacidosis.* Br. Med. J. 26:746–747, 1970.

266. Meyer, H., and Lux, H.D.: *Action of ammonium on a chloride pump. Removal of hyperpolarizing inhibition in an isolated neuron.* Pfluegers Arch. 350:18, 1974.

267. Meyer, J.S., and Handa, J.: *Cerebral blood flow and metabolism during experimental hyperthermia (fever).* Minn. Med. 50:37–44, 1967.

268. Meyer, J.S., and Portnoy, H.D.: *Localized cerebral hypoglycemia simulating stroke.* Neurology 8:601–614, 1958.

269. Miller, A.L., Hawkins, R.A., and Veech, R.L.: *Decreased rate of glucose utilization by rat brain in vivo after exposure to atmospheres containing high concentrations of CO_2.* J. Neurochem. 25:553–558, 1975.

270. Miller, J.D.: *Barbiturates and raised intracranial pressure.* Ann. Neurol. 6:189–193, 1979.

271. Miller, J.R., and Myers, R.: *Neurologic effect of systemic circulatory arrest in the monkey.* Neurology 20:715–724, 1970.

272. MILLER, R.R.: *Hospital admissions due to adverse drug reactions: a report from the Boston Collaborative Drug Surveillance Program.* Arch. Int. Med. 134:219–223, 1974.

273. MONTGOMERY, B.M., AND PINNER, C.A.: *Transient hypoglycemic hemiplegia.* Arch. Intern. Med. 114:680–684, 1964.

274. MORSE, R.M., AND LITIN, E.M.: *Postoperative delirium: a study of etiologic factors.* Am. J. Psychiatr. 126:388–395, 1969.

275. MORSE, R.M., AND LITIN, E.M.: *The anatomy of a delirium.* Am. J. Psychiatr. 128:111–116, 1971.

276. MOSER, H.W., MOSER, A.B., KAWAMURI, N., ET AL.: *Adrenoleukodystrophy: elevated C_{26} fatty acid in cultured skin fibroblasts.* Ann. Neurol. 7:1980, in press.

277. MRSULJA, B.B., MRSULJA, B.J., SPATZ, M., ET AL.: *Catecholamines in brain ischemia—effects of a-methyl-p-tyrosine and pargyline.* Brain Res. 104:373–378, 1976.

278. MRSULJA, B.B., MRSULJA, B.J., SPATZ, M., ET AL.: *Brain serotonin after experimental vascular occlusion.* Neurology 26:785–787, 1976.

279. MURALT, A. VON: *The role of thiamine in neurophysiology.* Ann. N.Y. Acad. Sci. 98:499–507, 1962.

280. MYERS, R.D.: *Psychopharmacology of alcohol.* Ann. Rev. Pharmacol. Toxicol, 18:125–144, 1978.

281. MYERS, R.E.: "Lactic acid accumulation as cause of brain edema and cerebral necrosis resulting from oxygen deprivation." In Korobkin, R., and Gulleminault, C. (eds.): *Advances in Perinatal Neurology.* SP Medical Books, New York, pp. 85–114, 1979.

282. MYERS, R.E., AND YAMAGUCHI, S.: *Nervous system effects of cardiac arrest in monkeys.* Ann. Neurol. 34:65–74, 1977.

283. NAHRWOLD, M.L., CLARK, P.R., AND COHEN, P.J.: *Is depression of mitochondrial respiration a predicter of* in vivo *anesthetic activity?* Anesthesiology 40:566–570, 1974.

284. NAHRWOLD, M.L., AND COHEN, P.L.: "Anesthetic and mitochondrial function." In Cohen, P.J. (ed.): *Metabolic Aspects of Anesthesia.* Clinical Anesthesia Series, F.A. Davis, Philadelphia, 1:25–44, 1975.

285. NELSON, J.R., AND LEFFMAN, H.: *The human diffusely projecting system.* Arch. Neurol. 8:544–556, 1963.

286. NEMOTO, E.M., BLEYAERT, A.L., STEZOSKI, S.W., ET AL.: *Global brain ischemia: a reproducible monkey model.* Stroke 8:558–564, 1977.

287. NEMOTO, E.M., AND FRANKEL, H.M.: *Cerebral oxygenation and metabolism during progressive hyperthermia.* Am. J. Physiol. 219:1784–1788, 1970.

288. NEVIN, S.: *Gliomatosis cerebri.* Brain 61:170–191, 1938.

289. NEWMARK, S.R., HIMATHONGKAM, T., AND SHANE, J.M.: *Myxedema coma.* J.A.M.A. 230:884–885, 1974.

290. NICHOLS, A.B., AND HUNT, W.B.: *Is myxedema coma respiratory failure?* South Med. J. 69:945–948, 1976.

291. NICHOLSON, G., AND TOMKIN, G.H.: *Successful treatment of disseminated intravascular coagulopathy complicating diabetic coma.* Br. Med. J. 4:450, 1974.

292. NICOLL, R.A.: *Pentobarbital: differential post-synaptic actions on sympathetic ganglion cells.* Science 199:451–452, 1978.

293. NILSSON, E.: *On treatment of barbiturate poisoning. Modified clinical aspect.* Acta. Med. Scand. (suppl. 253) 139:1–127, 1951.

294. NILSSON, L.: *The influence of barbiturate anesthesia upon the energy state and upon acid-base parameters of the brain in arterial hypotension and in asphyxia.* Acta Neurol. Scand. 47:233–253, 1971.

295. NILSSON, L., AND SIESJÖ, B.K.: *The effect of anesthetics upon labile phosphates and upon extra- and intracellular lactate, pyruvate and bicarbonate concentrations in the rat brain.* Acta Physiol. Scand. 80:235–248, 1970.

296. NILSSON, L., AND SIESJÖ, B.K.: *The effect of deep halothane hypotension upon labile phosphates and upon extra- and intracellular lactate and pyruvate concentrations in the rat brain.* Acta Physiol. Scand. 81:508–516, 1971.

297. NORBERG, K., AND SIESJÖ, B.K.: *Oxidative metabolism of the cerebral cortex of the rat in severe insulin-induced hypoglycaemia.* J. Neurochem. 26:345–352, 1976.

298. NORENBERG, M.D., AND MARTINEZ-HERNANDEZ, A.: *Fine structural localization of glutamine synthetase in astrocytes of rat brain.* Brain Res. 161:303–310, 1979.

299. NURICK, S., BLACKWOOD, W., AND MAIR, W.G.P.: *Giant cell granulomatous angiitis of the central nervous system.* Brain 95:133–142, 1972.

300. O'BRIEN, M.D., AND HARRIS, P.W.R.: *Cerebral-cortex perfusion-rates in myxoedema.* Lancet 1:1170–1172, 1968.

301. OH, M.S., AND CARROLL, H.J.: *Current concepts. The anion gap.* N. Engl. J. Med. 297:814–817, 1977.

302. OHMAN, J.L., MARLISS, E.B., AOKI, T.T. ET AL.: *The cerebrospinal fluid in diabetic ketoacidosis.* N. Engl. J. Med. 284:283–290, 1971.

303. OLDENDORF, W.H.: *Carrier mediated blood brain barrier transport of short-chain monocarboxylic organic acids.* Am. J. Physiol. 224:1450–1453, 1973.

304. OLDENDORF, W.H., CORNFORD, M.E., AND BROWN, W.J.: *The large apparent work capability of the blood-brain barrier: a study of the mitochondrial content of capillary endothelial cells in brain and other tissues of the rat.* Ann. Neurol. 1:409–417, 1977.

305. OLESEN, J.: *Contralateral focal increase of cerebral blood flow in man during arm work.* Brain 94:635–646, 1971.

306. OLSEN, S.: *The brain in uremia.* Acta Psychiatr. Scand. (suppl. 156):1–128, 1961.

307. OSNES, J.B., AND HERMANSEN, L.: *Acid-base balance after maximal exercise of short duration.* J. Appl. Physiol. 32:59–63, 1972.

308. OSTERMAN, P.O.: *Hypothalamo-pituitary-adrenal function following subarachnoid hemorrhage.* Acta Neurol. Scand. 52:56–62, 1975.

309. OWEN, O.E., MORGAN, A.P., KEMP, H.G., ET AL.: *Brain metabolism during fasting.* J. Clin. Invest. 46:1589–1595, 1967.

310. PAGANI, L.F.: *The rapid appearance of papilledema.* J. Neurosurg. 30:247–249, 1969.

311. PAGE, M.M., AND WATKINS, P.J.: *Cardiorespiratory arrest and diabetic autonomic neuropathy.* Lancet 1:14–16, 1978.

312. PARK, B.E., MEACHAM, W.F., AND NETSKY, M.G.: *Non-ketotic hyperglycemia hyperosmolar coma. Report of neurosurgical cases with a review of mechanisms and treatment.* J. Neurosurg. 44:409–417, 1976.

313. PARMLEY, L.F., JR., SENIOR, R.M., MCKENNA, D.H., ET AL.: *Clinically deceptive massive pulmonary embolism.* Chest 58:15–23, 1970.

314. PARRY, M.F., AND WALLACH, R.: *Ethylene glycol poisoning.* Am. J. Med. 57:143–150, 1974.

315. PARTIN, J.S., MCADAMS, A.J., PARTIN, J.C., ET AL.: *Brain ultrastructure in Reye's Disease; II, acute injury and recovery processes in three children.* J. Neuropathol. Exp. Neurol. 37:796–819, 1978.

316. PATTEN, B.M., BILEZIKIAN, J.P., MALLETTE, L.E., ET AL.: *Neuromuscular disease in primary hyperparathyroidism.* Ann. Int. Med. 80:182–193, 1974.

317. PEARCE, J.M.S.: *Focal neurological syndromes in hepatic failure.* Postgrad. Med. J. 39:653–657, 1963.

318. PEDLEY, T.A.: *The pathophysiology of focal epilepsy: neurophysiological considerations.* Ann. Neurol. 3(1):2–9, 1978.

319. PETITO, C.K.: *Early and late mechanisms of increased vascular permeability following experimental cerebral infarction.* J. Neuropathol. Exp. Neurol. 38:222–234, 1979.

320. PETITO, C.K., SCHAEFER, J.A., AND PLUM, F.: *Ultrastructural characteristics of the brain and blood brain barrier in experimental seizures.* Brain Res. 127:251–267, 1977.

321. PETZ, L.D.: *Neurological manifestations of systemic lupus erythematosus and thrombotic thrombocytopenic purpura.* Stroke 8:719–722, 1977.

322. PLAITAKIS, A., NICKLAS, W.J., AND BERL, S.: *Thiamine deficiency: selective impairment of the cerebellar serotonergic system.* Neurology 28:691–698, 1978.

323. PLUM, F.: *Brain swelling and edema in cerebral vascular disease.* Res. Publ. Assoc. Res. Nerv. Ment. Dis. 41:318–348, 1966.

324. PLUM, F., AND HINDFELT, B.: "The neurological complications of liver disease," In Vinken, P.J., Bruyn, G.W., and Klawans, H.L. (eds.): *Handbook of Clinical Neurology,* Vol. 27: *In Metabolic and Deficiency Diseases of the Nervous System,* Part I. Elsevier North-Holland, New York, 1976, pp. 349–377.

325. PLUM, F., HOWSE, D.C., AND DUFFY, T.E.: "Metabolic effects of seizures." In PLUM, F. (ed.): *Brain Dysfunction and Metabolic Disorders.* Raven Press, New York, 1974, pp. 141–157.

326. PLUM, F., POSNER, J.B., AND HAIN, R.F.: *Delayed neurological deterioration after anoxia.* Arch. Intern. Med. 110:18-25, 1962.

327. PLUM, F., POSNER, J.B., AND TROY, B.: *Cerebral metabolic and circulatory responses to induced convulsions in animals.* Arch. Neurol. 18:1-13, 1968.

328. PLUM, F., AND PRICE, R.W.: *Acid-base balance of cisternal and lumbar spinal fluid in hospital patients.* N. Engl. J. Med. 289:1346-1351, 1973.

329. PLUM, F., AND SIESJÖ, B.K.: *Recent advances in CSF physiology.* Anesthesiology 42:706-738, 1975.

330. PLUM, F., AND SWANSON, A.G.: *Barbiturate poisoning treated by physiological methods.* J.A.M.A. 163:827-835, 1957.

331. PLUM, F., AND VAN UITERT, R.: "Non-endocrine diseases and disorders of the hypothalamus." In Reichlin, S., Baldessarini, R.J., and Martin, J.B. (eds.): *The Hypothalamus.* Res. Proc. Assoc. Res. Nerv. Ment. Dis. 56:415-473, 1978.

332. PLUM, F., AND WASTERLAIN, C.G.: "Cerebral and systemic anoxia with experimental seizures." In Brierley, J.B., and Meldrum, B.S. (eds.): *Brain Hypoxia.* Heinemann, London, 1971.

333. POISSON, M., MASHALY, R., AND LEBKIRI, B.: *Dialysis encephalopathy, recovery after interruption of aluminum intake.* Br. Med. J. 2:1610-1611, 1976.

334. PORT, I.K., AND GOLDSMITH, R.S.: *Disequilibrium syndrome in hemodialysis.* Ergeb. Inn. Med. Kinderheilkd. 37:1-18, 1975.

335. POSNER, J.B., AND PLUM, F.: *The toxic effects of carbon dioxide and acetazolamide in hepatic encephalopathy.* J. Clin. Invest. 39:1246-1258, 1960.

336. POSNER, J.B., AND PLUM, F.: *Spinal-fluid pH and neurologic symptoms in systemic acidosis.* N. Engl. J. Med. 277:605-613, 1967.

337. POSNER, J.B., SWANSON, A.G., AND PLUM, F.: *Acid-base balance in cerebrospinal fluid.* Arch. Neurol. 12:479-496, 1965.

338. PRICE, R., CHERNIK, N.L., HORTA-BARBOSA, L., ET AL.: *Herpes simplex encephalitis is an anergic patient.* Am. J. Med. 54:222-228, 1973.

339. PRUITT, A.A., RUBIN, R.H., KARCHMER, A.W., ET AL.: *Neurologic complications of bacterial endocarditis.* Medicine 57:329-343, 1978.

340. PULSINELLI, W.A., AND BRIERLEY, J.B.: *Temporal profile of ischemic neuronal damage in the 4-vessel occlusion rat model.* Stroke 10:492, 1979.

341. PULSINELLI, W.A., AND DUFFY, T.E.: *Local cerebral glucose metabolism during controlled hypoxemia in rats.* Science 204:626-629, 1979.

342. PURVES, M.J. (CHAIRMAN): *Cerebral Vascular Smooth Muscle and Its Control.* Ciba Foundation Symposium 56 (new series), Excerpta Medica, New York, 1978.

343. QUASTEL, J.H.: *Effects of anesthetics, depressants, and tranquilizers on brain metabolism.* In Elliot, K.A.C., Page I.H., and Quastel, J.H. (eds.): *Neurochemistry: The Chemistry of Brain and Nerve.* ed. 2. Charles C Thomas, Springfield, Ill. 1962, Chapter 32.

344. QUAYLE, E.S., CHRISTIAN, S.T., AND HALSEY, J.H.: *Effects of ischemia on the Mg^{++} requiring adenosine triphosphatase associated with neuronal synaptic vesicles in gerbil brain.* Stroke 7:36-40, 1976.

345. QUINTANILLA, A.P.: *Acute acid-base disorders. 1. Laboratory characterization.* Postgrad. Med. 60:68-83, 1976.

346. RAICHLE, M.E., GRUBB, R.L., GADO, M.H., ET AL.: *Correlation between regional cerebral blood flow and oxidative metabolism.* Arch. Neurol. 33:523-526, 1976.

347. RAM, C.V.S.: *Hypertensive encephalopathy.* Arch. Intern. Med. 138:1851-1853, 1978.

348. RAPAPORT, S.I.: *Blood Brain Barrier in Physiology and Medicine.* Raven Press, New York, 1976.

349. RASKIN, D.E., AND FRANK, S.W.: *Herpes encephalitis with catatonic stupor.* Arch. Gen. Psychiatry 31:544-546, 1974.

350. RASKIN, N.H., AND FISHMAN, R.A.: *Neurologic disorders in renal failure.* N. Engl. J. Med. 294:143-148, 204-210, 1976.

351. REED, C.E., DRIGGS, M.F., AND FOOTE, C.C.: *Acute barbiturate intoxication: a study of 300 cases based on a physiologic system of classification of the severity of the intoxication.* Ann. Int. Med. 37:290-303, 1952.

352. REIVICH, M.: "Blood flow metabolism couple in brain." In PLUM, F. (ed.): *Brain Dysfunction in Metabolic Disorders.* Raven Press, New York, 1974, pp. 125-140.

297

353. Reuler, J.B.: *Hypothermia: pathophysiology, clinical settings, and management.* Ann. Intern. Med. 89:519–527, 1978.

354. Richardson, J.C., Chambers, R.A., and Heywood, P.M.: *Encephalopathies of anoxia and hypoglycemia.* Arch. Neurol. 1:178–190, 1959.

355. Risberg, J.: *Regional cerebral blood flow measurements by 133 Xe-inhalation: methodology and applications in neuropsychology and psychiatry.* Brain & Language, 9:9–34, 1980.

356. Rockoff, M.A., Marshall, L.F., and Shapiro, H.M.: *High-dose barbiturate therapy in man: a clinical review of 60 patients.* Ann. Neurol. 6:194–199, 1979.

357. Roland, P.E., and Larsen, B.: *Focal increase of cerebral blood flow during stereognostic testing in man.* Arch. Neurol. 33:551–558, 1976.

358. Romer, F.K.: *Bacterial meningitis: a 15-year review of bacterial meningitis from departments of internal medicine.* Dan. Med. Bull. 24:35–40, 1977.

359. Roos, R., Gajdusek, D.C., and Gibbs, C.J.: *The clinical characteristics of transmissible Creutzfeldt-Jakob disease.* Brain 96:1–20, 1973.

360. Rossen, R., Kabat, H., and Anderson, J.P.: *Acute arrest of cerebral circulation in man.* Arch. Neurol. Psychiatr. 50:510–528, 1943.

361. Rotherman, E.B., Jr., Safar, P., and Robin, E.D.: *CNS disorder during mechanical ventilation in chronic pulmonary disease.* J.A.M.A. 189:993–996, 1964.

362. Russell, R.W.R., and Bharucha, N.: *The recognition and prevention of border zone cerebral ischemia during cardiac surgery.* Q. J. Med. 187:303–323, 1978.

363. Rutherford, W.H.: *Diagnosis of alcohol ingestion in mild head injuries.* Lancet 1:1021–1023, 1977.

364. Rymer, M.M., and Fishman, R.A.: *Protective adaptation of brain to water intoxication.* Arch. Neurol. 28:49–54, 1973.

365. Sacchi, O., Ladinsky, H., Prigioni, I., et al.: *Acetylcholine turnover in the thiamine-depleted superior cervical ganglion of the rat.* Brain. Res. 151:609–614, 1978.

366. Safar, P., Mullie, A., Breivik, H., et al.: *Clinical trials of brain resuscitation with barbiturate after cardiac arrest.* Stroke 10:104, 1979.

367. Safar, P., Stezoski, W., and Nemoto, E.M.: *Amelioration of brain damage following cardiac arrest in dogs.* Arch. Neurol. 33:91–95, 1976.

368. Sagel, J., and Matisonn, R.: *Neuropsychiatric disturbance as the initial manifestation of digitalis toxicity.* S. Afr. Med. J. 46:512–514, 1972.

369. Saldeen, T.: *Fat embolism and signs of intravascular coagulation in a posttraumatic autopsy material.* J. Trauma 10:273–286, 1970.

370. Salford, L.G., Brierley, J.B., Plum, F., et al.: *Histology and high energy substrates in rat brain after graded hypoxia.* Panminerva Med. 13:185, 1971.

371. Salford, L.G., Plum, F., and Brierley, J.B.: *Graded hypoxia-oligemia in rat brain. II. Neuropathological alterations and their implications.* Arch. Neurol. 29:234–238, 1973.

372. Salford, L.G., Plum, F., and Siesjö, B.K.: *Graded hypoxia-oligemia in rat brain. I. Biochemical alterations and their implications.* Arch. Neurol. 29:227–233, 1973.

373. Salum, I. (ed.): *Delirium tremens and certain other acute sequels of alcohol abuse; a comparative clinical, social and prognostic study.* Acta Psychiatr. Scand. Suppl. 235, Copenhagen, 1972.

374. Sarna, G.S., Bradbury, M.W.B., Cremer, J.E., et al.: *Brain metabolism and specific transport at the blood brain barrier after portacaval anastomosis in the rat.* Brain Res. 160:69–83, 1979.

375. Schaumburg, H.H., Powers, J.M., Raine, C.S., et al.: *Adrenoleukodystrophy; a clinical and pathological study of 17 cases.* Arch. Neurol. 32:577–591, 1975.

376. Scheinberg, P.: *Effects of uremia on cerebral blood flow and metabolism.* Neurology 4:101–105, 1954.

377. Schmid, A.H.: *Cerebral malaria: on the nature and significance of vascular changes.* Eur. Neurol. 12:197–208, 1974.

378. Schneck, S.A.: "Methyl alcohol." In Vinken, P.J., Bruyn, G.W., and Cohen, M.M. et al. (eds.): *Handbook of Neurology,* Vol. 36: *Intoxication of the Nervous System.* Elsevier North-Holland, New York, 1979, pp. 351–360.

379. Schneider, M.: "Critical blood pressure in the cerebral circulation." In Schade, J.P., and McMenemey, W.H. (eds.): *Selective Vulnerability of the Brain in Hypoxaemia.* F.A. Davis Co. (Blackwell Scientific Publications), Philadelphia, 1963, pp. 7–20.

298

380. SCHNIER, F.J., AND HOSSMANN, K.A.: *Factors contributing to the development of brain edema following middle cerebral artery occlusion in cats.* Reims Satellite Symposium on Cerebrovascular Diseases. Proceedings Seventh International Congress of Pharmacologie 23–26 July, 1978, Reims, France, pp. 41–42.

381. SCOTT, W.W., JR., SIEGELMAN, S.S., HARRINGTON, D.P., ET AL.: *Diagnosis and pathophysiology of paradoxical embolism.* Radiology, 121:59–62, 1976.

382. SEARS, E.S.: *Non-ketotic hyperosmolar hyperglycemia during glycerol therapy for cerebral edema.* Neurology 26:89–94, 1976.

383. SERGENT, J.S., LOCKSHIN, M.D., KLEMPNER, M.S., ET AL.: *Central nervous system disease in systemic lupus erythematosus: therapy and prognosis.* Am. J. Med. 58:664–654, 1975.

384. SERVICE, F.J., DALE, A.J.D., ELVEBACK, L.R., ET AL.: *Insulinoma: clinical and diagnostic features of 60 consecutive cases.* Mayo Clin. Proc. 51:417–429, 1976.

385. SEVITT, S.: *Fat Embolism.* Butterworth, London, 1962.

386. SHAHANI, B.T., AND YOUNG, R.R.: "Asterixis—a disorder of the neural mechanisms underlying sustained muscular contraction." In Shahani, M. (ed.): *The Motor System. Neurophysiology and Muscle Mechanisms.* Elsevier, North-Holland, New York, 1976, pp. 301–306.

387. SHAPIRO, W.R.: *Remote effects of neoplasm on the central nervous system: encephalopathy.* Adv. Neurol. 15:101–117, 1976.

388. SHARF, B., AND LEVY, N.: "Pancreatic encephalopathy." In Vinken, P.J., and Bruyn, G.W.: *Handbook of Clinical Neurology,* Vol. 27, Part 1. Elsevier North-Holland, New York, 1976, pp. 449–458.

389. SIEBKE, H., BREIVIK, H., ROD, T., ET AL.: *Survival after 40 minutes submersion without cerebral sequelae.* Lancet 1:1275–1277, 1975.

390. SIEKER, H.O., AND HICKAM, J.B.: *Carbon dioxide intoxication.* Medicine 35:389–423, 1956.

391. SIESJÖ, B.K.: *Brain Energy Mechanism.* John S. Wiley, New York, 1978.

392. SIESJÖ, B.K., and Plum, F.: "Pathophysiology of anoxic brain damage." In Gaull, G.E. (ed.): *Biology of Brain Dysfunction.* Plenum Publishing Corp., New York, 1972.

393. SILBERGELD, E.K., AND CHISOLM, J.J.: *Lead poisoning: altered urinary catecholamine metabolites as indicators of intoxication in mice and children.* Science 192:153–154, 1976.

394. SIMMONS, R.L., ET AL.: *The role of the central nervous system in septic shock: II. Hemodynamic, respiratory and metabolic effects of intracisternal or intraventricular endotoxin.* Ann. Surg. 167:158–167, 1968.

395. SIMON, R.P.: *Forced downward ocular deviation. Occurrence during oculovestibular testing in sedative drug-induced coma.* Arch. Neurol. 35:456–458, 1978.

396. SJAASTAD, O., GJESSING, L., RITLAND, S., ET AL.: *Chronic relapsing pancreatitis, encephalopathy with disturbance of consciousness, and CSF amino acid aberration.* J. Neurol. 220:83–94, 1979.

397. SKOU, J.C.: *Further investigations on a $Mg^{++} + Na^+$—activated adenosine triphosphatase, possibly related to the active, linked transport of Na^+ and K^+ across the nerve membrane.* Biochem. Biophys. Acta 42:6–23, 1960.

398. SMITH, C.K., ET AL.: *Psychiatric disturbance in endocrinologic disease.* Psychosom. Med. 34:69, 1972.

399. SOKOLOFF, L.: *Action of thyroid hormones and cerebral development.* Am. J. Dis. Child. 114:498–506, 1967.

400. SOKOLOFF, L.: *Metabolism of ketone bodies by the brain.* Ann. Rev. Med. 24:271–279, 1973.

401. SOLE-LLENAS, J., AND PONS-TORTELLA, E.: *Cerebral angiitis.* Neuroradiology 15:1–11, 1978.

402. SRIDHAR, C.B., CALVERT, G.D., AND IBBERTSON, H.K.: *Syndrome of hypernatremia hypodipsia and partial diabetes insipidus. A new interpretation.* J. Clin. Endocrinol. Metab. 38:890–901, 1974.

403. STARZL, T.E., SCHNECK, S.A., MAZZONI, G., ET AL.: *Acute neurological complications after liver transplantation with particular reference to intraoperative cerebral air embolus.* Ann. Surg. 187:236–240, 1978.

404. STEINBERG, A.D., AND KARLINER, J.S.: *The clinical spectrum of heroin pulmonary edema.* Arch. Intern. Med. 122:122–127, 1968.

405. STEVENS, D.L., AND MATTHEWS, W.B.: *Cryptogenic drop attacks: an affliction of women.* Br. Med. J. 1:439–442, 1973.

406. STRANDGAARD, S.: *Autoregulation of cerebral circulation in hypertension.* Acta Neurol. Scand. 57: (suppl. 66) 1–82, 1978.

299

407. Sundt, T.M., Jr., Sharbrough, F.W., and Anderson, R.E.: *Cerebral blood flow measurements and electroencephalograms during carotid endarterectomy.* J. Neurosurg. 41:310–320, 1974.

408. Sundt, T.M., Jr., and Whisnant, J.P.: *Subarachnoid hemorrhage from intracranial aneurysms. Surgical management and natural history of disease.* N. Engl. J. Med. 299:116–122, 1978.

409. Swanson, P.D., Stavney, L.S., and Plum, F.: *Effects of blood pH and carbon dioxide on cerebral electrical activity.* Neurology 8:787–792, 1958.

410. Swanson, P.D.: *Acidosis and some metabolic properties of isolated cerebral tissues.* Arch. Neurol. 20:653–663, 1969.

411. Szucs, M.M., Jr., Brooks, H.L., Grossman, W., et al.: *Diagnostic sensitivity of laboratory findings in acute pulmonary embolism.* Ann. Intern. Med. 74:161–166, 1971.

412. Tarsy, D., Lieberman, B., Chirico-Post, J., et al.: *Unilateral asterixis associated with a mesencephalic syndrome.* Arch. Neurol. 34:446–447, 1977.

413. Thames, M.D., Alpert, J.S., and Dalen, J.E.: *Syncope in patients with pulmonary embolism.* J.A.M.A. 238:2509–2511, 1977.

414. Thomas, F.B., Mazzaferri, E.L., and Skillman, T.G.: *Apathetic thyrotoxicosis: a distinctive clinical and laboratory entity.* Ann. Intern. Med. 72:679–685, 1970.

415. Thompson, R.G., Hallstrom, A., and Cobb, L.A.: *Bystander-initiated cardiopulmonary resuscitation in the management of out-of-hospital ventricular fibrillation.* Ann. Int. Med. 90:737–740, 1979.

416. Thompson, W.L.: *Management of alcohol withdrawal syndromes.* Arch. Intern. Med. 138:278–283, 1978.

417. Thrush, D.C., and Boddie, H.G.: *Episodic encephalopathy associated with thyroid disorders.* J. Neurol. Neurosurg. Psychiatr. 37:696–700, 1974.

418. Timperley, W.R., Preston, F.E., and Ward, J.D.: *Cerebral intravascular coagulation in diabetic ketoacidosis.* Lancet 1:952–956, 1974.

419. Topliss, D., and Bond, R.: *Acute brain syndrome after propranolol treatment.* Lancet 2:1133–1134, 1977.

420. Torda, T.A., and Gage, P.W.: *Postsynaptic effect of I.V. anesthetic agents at the neuromuscular junction.* Br. J. Anaesth. 49:771–776, 1977.

421. Trauner, D.A., Brown, F., Ganz, E., et al.: *Treatment of elevated intracranial pressure in Reye syndrome.* Ann. Neurol. 4:275–278, 1978.

422. Tufo, H.M., Ostfeld, A.M., and Shekelle, R.: *Central nervous system dysfunction following open-heart surgery.* J.A.M.A. 212:1333–1340, 1970.

423. Uribe, M., Farca, A., Marquez, G., et al.: *Treatment of chronic portal systemic encephalopathy with bromocriptine.* Gastroenterology 7:1347–1351, 1979.

424. Van Durme, J.P.: *Tachyarrhythmias and transient cerebral ischemic attacks.* Am. Heart J. 89:538–540, 1975.

425. Van Harreveld, A., and Tachibana, S.: *Recovery of cerebral cortex from asphyxiation.* Am. J. Physiol. 202:59–65, 1962.

426. Van Woert, M.H., Rosenbaum, D., Howieson, J., et al.: *Long-term therapy of myoclonus and other neurological disorders with L-5 hydroxytryptophan and carbidopa.* N. Engl. J. Med. 296:70–75, 1977.

427. Verrill, P.J., and Aellig, W.H.: *Vasovagal faint in the supine position.* Br. Med. J. 4:348, 1970.

428. Victor, D.I., and Green, W.R.: *Temporal artery biopsy in herpes zoster ophthalmicus with delayed arteritis.* Am. J. Ophthalmol. 82:628–630, 1976.

429. Victor, M.: "Neurologic disorders due to alcoholism and malnutrition." In Baker, A.B., and Baker, L.H. (eds.): *Clinical Neurology.* Vol. 2. Harper & Row, New York, 1979, Chapter 22.

430. Victor, M., Adams, R.D., and Cole, M.: *The acquired (non-Wilsonian) type of chronic hepatocerebral degeneration.* Medicine 44:345–396, 1965.

431. Victor, M., Adams, R.D., and Collins, G.H.: *The Wernicke-Korsakoff Syndrome.* F.A. Davis Co., Philadelphia, 1971.

432. Voorhies, C.V., Schmidt, D.E., Barrett, R.J., et al.: *Effects of thiamine deficiency on acetylcholine levels and utilization in vivo in rat brain.* J. Nutr. 107:1902–1908, 1977.

433. Wadstein, J., and Skude, G.: *Does hypokalaemia precede delirium tremens?* Lancet 2:549–550, 1978.

434. WALKER, D.L.: "Progressive multifocal leukoencephalopathy: an opportunistic viral infection of the central nervous system." In Vinken, P.J., and Bruyn, G.W. (eds.): *Handbook of Clinical Neurology,* Vol. 34: *Infections of the Nervous System,* Part II. Elsevier North-Holland, New York, 1978, pp. 307–329.

435. WALLIS, W.E., WILLOUGHBY, E., AND BAKER, P.: *Coma in the Wernicke-Korsakoff syndrome.* Lancet 2:400–403, 1978.

436. WARE, A.J., D'AGOSTINO, A.N., AND COMBES, B.: *Cerebral edema: a major complication of massive hepatic necrosis.* Gastroenterology 61:877–884, 1971.

437. WASTERLAIN, C.G.: *CO_2 anesthesia inhibits RNA synthesis.* Brain Res. 21:452–454, 1970.

438. WATSON, G.W., FULLER, T.J., ELMS, J., ET AL.: *Listeria cerebritis.* Arch. Intern. Med. 138:83–87, 1978.

439. WEINBERGER, L.M., GIBBON, M.H., AND GIBBON, J.H., JR.: *Temporary arrest of the circulation to the central nervous system: I. Physiologic effects.* Arch. Neurol. Psychiatr. 43:615–634, 1940.

440. WEINBERGER, L.M., GIBBON, M.H., AND GIBBON, J.H., JR.: *Temporary arrest of the circulation to the central nervous system: II. Pathologic effects.* Arch. Neurol. Psychiatr. 43:961–986, 1940.

441. WEINER, J.S.: "Heatstroke." In Woodruff, A.W., (ed.): *Medicine in the Tropics.* Churchill Livingston, London, 1974.

442. WEINER, J.S. AND KHOGALI, M.: *Heatstroke.* Lancet 1:1135, 1979 (letter).

443. WEINER, W.J., AND KLAWANS, H.L.: "Vitamin B_6." In Vinken, P.J., and Bruyn, G.W. (eds.): *Handbook of Clinical Neurology.* Vol. 28: *Metabolic and Deficiency Diseases of the Nervous System.* Part 2. Elsevier North-Holland, New York, 1976, Chapter 5, p. 105.

444. WEINTRAUB, B.M., AND McHENRY, L.C., JR.: *Cardiac abnormalities in subarachnoid hemorrhage: a resume.* Stroke 5:384–392, 1974.

445. WEINTRAUB, S.J., MODAK, A.T., AND STAVINOHA, W.B.: *Acetylcholine: postmortem increases in rat brain regions.* Brain Res. 105:179–183, 1976.

446. WELCH, K.M.A., CHABI, E., BUCKINGHAM, J., ET AL.: *Catecholamine and 5-hydroxytryptamine levels in ischemic brain. Influence of p-chlorophenylalanine.* Stroke 8:341–346, 1977.

447. WELCH, K.M.A., WANG, T.B.F., AND CHABI, E.: *Ischemia-induced seizures and cortical monoamine levels.* Ann. Neurol. 3:152–155, 1978.

448. WELSH, F.A., O'CONNOR, M.J., AND MARCY, V.R.: *Effect of oligemia on regional metabolite levels in cat brain.* J. Neurochem. 31:311–319, 1978.

449. WHITLEY, R.J., SOONG, S.J., DOLIN, R., ET AL.: *Adenine arabinoside therapy of biopsy-proved herpes simplex encephalitis.* The Collaborative Study Group. N. Engl. J. Med. 297:289–294, 1977.

450. WHITTY, C.W.M., AND LEWIN, W.: *Vivid day-dreaming: an unusual form of confusion following anterior cingulectomy.* Brain 80:72–76, 1957.

451. WHYBROW, P., AND FERRELL, R.: "Thyroid state and human behavior: contributions from a clinical perspective." In Prange, A.J., Jr. (ed.): *The Thyroid Axis, Drugs and Behavior.* Raven Press, New York, 1974, p. 5.

452. WHYBROW, P.C., AND HURWITZ, T.: "Psychological disturbances associated with endocrine disease and hormone therapy." In Sachar, E.J. (ed.): *Hormones, Behavior and Psychopathology.* Raven Press, New York, 1976, p. 125.

453. WILFERT, C.M.: *Mumps meningoencephalitis with low cerebrospinal-fluid glucose, prolonged pleocytosis and elevation of protein.* N. Engl. J. Med. 280:855–859, 1969.

454. WILKINS, R.H.: *Hypothalamic dysfunction and intracranial arterial spasms.* Surg. Neurol. 4:472–480, 1975.

455. WILLIAMS, C.P.S., SWANSON, A.G., AND CHAPMAN, J.T.: *Brain swelling with acute purulent meningitis.* Pediatrics 34:220–227, 1964.

456. WILLIAMS, R.H.: "Hypoglycemosis." In Williams, R.H. (ed.): *Diabetes.* Paul B. Hoeber, New York, 1960, Chapter 46.

457. WILSON, L.M.: *Intensive care delirium.* Arch. Intern. Med. 130:225–226, 1972.

458. WINCHESTER, J.F., GELFAND, M.C., KNEPSHIELD, J.H., ET AL.: *Dialysis and hemoperfusion of poisons and drug-update.* Trans. Am. Soc. Artif. Intern. Organs 23:762–842, 1977.

459. WINFIELD, J.B., BRUNNER, C.M., AND KOFFLER, D.: *Serologic studies in patients with systemic lupus erythematosus and central nervous system dysfunction.* Arthritis Rheum. 21:289–294, 1978.

460. Wood, J.D., Watson, W.J., and Ducker, A.J.: *The effect of hypoxia on brain γ-aminobutyric acid levels.* J. Neurochem. 15:603–609, 1978.

461. Yoshino, Y., and Elliot, K.A.C.: *Incorporation of carbon atoms from glucose into free amino acids in brain under normal and altered conditions.* Can. J. Biochem. 48:228–235, 1970.

462. Young, R.R., Shahani, B.T., and Kjellberg, R.J.: *Unilateral asterixis produced by a discrete CNS lesion.* Trans. Am. Neurol. Assoc. 101:306–307, 1976.

463. Zervas, N.T., Hori, H., and Negora, M.: *Reduction in brain dopamine following experimental cerebral ischaemia.* Nature 247:283–284, 1974.

464. Alford, W.C. Jr., Meador, C.K., Mihalevich, J., et al.: *Acute adrenal insufficiency following cardiac surgical procedures.* J. Thorac. Cardiovasc. Surg. 78:489–493, 1979.

465. Arieff, A., Cooper, J.D., Armstrong, D., et al.: *Dementia, renal failure and aluminum.* Ann. Int. Med. 9C:741–747, 1979.

466. Auer, L.M.: *The pathogenesis of hypertensive encephalopathy. Experimental data and their clinical relevance with special reference to neurosurgical patients.* Acta Neurochir. (Wien) 27:1–111, 1978.

467. Avram, M.M., Iancu, M., Morrow, P., et al.: *Uremic syndrome in man: new evidence for parathormone as a multisystem neurotoxin.* Clin. Nephrol. 11:59–62, 1979.

468. Boisvert, D.P.J., Pickard, J.D., Graham, D.I., et al.: *Delayed effects of subarachnoid haemorrhage on cerebral metabolism and the cerebrovascular response to hypercapnia in the primate.* J. Neurol. Neurosurg. Psychiatry 42:892–898, 1979.

469. Caplan, L.R., and Scheiner, D.: *Dysconjugate gaze in hepatic coma.* Ann. Neurol. 1980, in press.

470. Chadwick, D., and French, A.T.: *Uraemic myoclonus: an example of reticular reflex myoclonus?* J. Neurol. Neurosurg. Psychiatry 42:52–55, 1979.

471. Degos, J.-D., Verroust, J., Bouchareine, A., et al.: *Asterixis in focal brain lesions.* Arch. Neurol. 36:705–707, 1979.

472. Diemer, N.H.: *Glial and neuronal changes in experimental hepatic encephalopathy. A quantitative morphological investigation.* Acta Neurol. Scand. (suppl. 71) 58:144, 1978.

473. Durbin, C.G., Jr., and Rosenberg, H.: *A laboratory animal model for malignant hyperpyrexia.* J. Pharmacol. Exp. Ther. 210:70–74, 1979.

474. Fisher, C.M.: *Syncope of obscure nature.* Le Journal Canadien des Sciences Neurologiques 6:7–20, 1979.

475. Gabow, P.A., Anderson, R.J., Potts, D.E., et al.: *Acid-base disturbances in the salicylate-intoxicated adult.* Arch. Int. Med. 138:1481–1484, 1978.

476. Hanson, P.G., and Zimmerman, S.W.: *Exertional heatstroke in novice runners.* J.A.M.A. 242:154–147, 1979.

477. Harper, C.: *Wernicke's encephalopathy: a more common disease than realised. A neuropathological study of 51 cases.* J. Neurol. Neurosurg. Psychiatry 42:226–231, 1979.

478. Keane, J.R.: *Retinal hemorrhages. Its significance in 100 patients with acute encephalopathy of unknown cause.* Arch. Neurol. 36:691–694, 1979.

479. MacCrimmon, D.J., Wallace, J.B., Goldberg, W.M., et al.: *Emotional disturbance and cognitive deficits in hyperthyroidism.* Psychosom. Med. 41:331–340, 1979.

480. Niedermeyer, E., Fineyre, F., Riley, T., et al.: *Absence status (petit mal status) with focal characteristics.* Arch. Neurol. 36:417–421, 1979.

481. Parizel, G.: *On the mechanism of sudden death with subarachnoid hemorrhage.* J. Neurol. 220:71–76, 1979.

482. Pickard, J.D., Boisvert, D.P.J., Graham, D.I., et al.: *Late effects of subarachnoid hemorrhage on the response of the primate cerebral circulation to drug-induced changes in arterial blood pressure.* J. Neurol. Neurosurg. Psychiatry 42:899–903, 1979.

483. Rai, G., Buxton-Thomas, M., and Scanlon, M.: *Ocular bobbing in hepatic encephalopathy.* Br. J. Clin. Pract. 30:202–205, 1976.

484. Rollinson, R.D., and Gilligan, B.S.: *Postanoxic action myoclonus (Lance-Adams syndrome) responding to valproate.* Arch. Neurol. 36:44–45, 1979.

485. Sackellares, J.C., and Smith, D.B.: *Myoclonus with electrocerebral silence in a patient receiving penicillin.* Arch. Neurol. 36:857–858, 1979.

486. SANDHU, R., ALEXANDER, S., HORNABROOK, R.W., ET AL.: *Granulomatous angiitis of the CNS.* Arch. Neurol. 36:433–435, 1979.

487. TORO, G., AND ROMÁN, G.: *Cerebral malaria. A disseminated vasculomyelinopathy.* Arch. Neurol. 35:271–275, 1978.

488. TROJABORG, W., AND BOYSEN, G.: *Relation between EEG, regional cerebral blood flow and internal carotid artery pressure during carotid endarterectomy.* Electroenceph. Clin. Neurophysiol. 34:61–69, 1973.

489. VARMA, R.R., RIEDEL, D.R., KOMOROWSKI, R.A., ET AL.: *Reye's syndrome in nonpediatric age groups.* J.A.M.A. 242:1373–1375, 1979.

490. WALDENLIND, L.: *Studies on thiamine and neuromuscular transmission.* Acta Physiol. Scand. [Suppl.](459):1–35, 1978.

CHAPTER 5

Psychogenic Unresponsiveness

Samuel Johnson defined patriotism as the "last resort of a scoundrel."[12] (Ambrose Bierce disagreed, believing it was the first resort.[4]) The medical analogy to these definitions of patriotism is psychogenic illness or hysteria, a diagnostic haven to which uncertain physicians all too often repair when the signs and symptoms seem anatomically or physiologically senseless. Unfortunately, the diagnosis of psychogenic illness or hysteria often tells one more about the physician's lack of knowledge than the patient's disease. In a series by Slater, almost half of a group of 61 patients diagnosed as suffering hysteria were eventually found to have an organic disease that explained their "hysterical" symptoms.[17] Slater concluded that "the diagnosis of hysteria is a disguise for ignorance and a fertile source of clinical error. It is, in fact, not only a delusion but also a snare." For reasons not fully understood, "hysterical" symptoms appear to be especially frequent in patients who turn out to have neurologic disease.

Of all the psychogenic illnesses that mimic structural disease, psychogenic unresponsiveness is among the most difficult to diagnose. With most psychogenic illnesses that mimic structural neurologic disease, the physician pursues a two-pronged diagnostic attack. He must first determine by the neurologic examination that the patient's neurologic signs and symptoms are not in keeping with the anatomy and physiology of the nervous system (i.e., they are anatomically or physiologically impossible), and second he must discern from history and mental status examination that the patient's emotional make-up and current psychologic problems are sufficient to explain the abnormal findings on a psychologic basis. Because the patient with psychogenic unresponsiveness will not communicate, a psychiatric history and mental status examination from the patient is impossible (a history should be obtained from relatives or friends), and the physician is left with only the first portion of his diagnostic armamentarium, i.e., the demonstration that despite apparent unconsciousness, the patient is in fact physiologically awake. Thus, the diagnosis of psychogenic unresponsiveness must be approached with the greatest care. A careful neurologic examination, sometimes supplemented by electroencephalography and an "Amytal interview," as described below, will usually establish the diagnosis and obviate the need for extensive, potentially harmful laboratory investigations. If, however, after such a meticulous examination of a patient with suspected psychogenic unresponsiveness, any question remains about the diagnosis, a careful search for other causes of coma is obligatory.

Psychogenic unresponsiveness is uncommon; it was the final diagnosis in only 4 of our original 386 patients. We have, however, encountered the condition as a challenging diagnostic problem in several further patients at a rate of about one every other year since that time (Table 1). In one study of conversion symptoms in 500 psychiatric outpatients, "unconsciousness" occurred in 17.[8] Two recent series from London each report six patients with psychogenic unresponsiveness who were initially puzzling diagnostically.[10,11] Over how long a period of time these cases were collected or from how wide a patient population is not stated. In our experience, the most frequent suspicion of psychogenic unresponsiveness occurs before the true mechanism is ferreted out of patients with an organic cause for coma.

Several psychiatric disorders can result in psychogenic unresponsiveness. These include (1) conversion reaction, which may in turn be secondary to an hysterical personality, a severe depression, or an acute situational reaction; (2) catatonic stupor, often a manifestation of schizophrenia; (3) a dissociative or "fugue" state; (4) a severe psychotic depression; and (5) malingering.

The two major categories of psychogenic unresponsiveness are that occurring as a conversion symptom (often called conversion hysteria) and that occurring as part of the syndrome of catatonia (often thought to be a manifestation of schizophrenia). The two clinical pictures differ somewhat, but both may closely simulate delirium, stupor, or coma caused by structural or metabolic brain disease. The diagnosis of psychogenic unresponsiveness of either variety is made by demonstrating that both the cerebral hemispheres and the brainstem activating pathways can be made to function in a physiologically normal way, even though the patient will seemingly not respond to his environment.

Conversion Reactions

A conversion reaction is the cause of most psychogenic coma. As used here, the term conversion reaction describes a psychogenic or nonphysiologic loss or disorder of neurologic function involving the special senses or the voluntary nervous system. Many physicians associate conversion reactions with an hysterical personality (conversion hysteria), but in fact conversion reactions may occur as a psychologic defense in a wide range of psychiatric syndromes, including depressive states and neuroses.[8] Furthermore, conversion symptoms, including psychogenic unresponsiveness, may be a reaction to organic disease, and thus occur in a patient already seriously ill.[13] We find it impossible to differentiate conversion reactions, presumably representing involuntary responses by patients to stress, from voluntary malingering except by the direct statement of the subject involved.

Patients suffering from psychogenic unresponsiveness owing to either a conversion reaction or to malingering usually lie with their eyes closed and do not attend to their surroundings. The respiratory rate and depth are usually normal, but in some instances the patient may be overbreathing as another manifestation of his psychologic dysfunction (hyperventilation syndrome).[14] The pupils may be slightly widened, but are equal and reactive except in the instance of the individual who self-instills mydriatic agents. Oculocephalic responses may or may not be present, but caloric testing invariably produces quick-phase nystagmus away from the ice water irrigation, rather than either tonic deviation of the eyes toward the irrigated ear or no response at all. *It is the presence of normal nystagmus in response to caloric testing that firmly indicates that the patient is physiologically awake and that the unresponsive state cannot be caused by structural or metabolic disease of the nervous system.* Henry and Woodruff recently described six patients with psychogenic unresponsiveness in whom the eyes deviated tonically toward the floor when the patient lay on his side.[10] The authors postulate that the deviation of the eyes was psychologically mediated as a way of avoiding eye contact with the examiner. Be that as it may, when one attempts to open the closed lids of a patient suffering from psychogenic unresponsiveness, the lids often resist actively and usually close rapidly when they are released. The slow, steady closure of passively opened eyelids that occurs in many comatose patients cannot be mimicked voluntarily. Similarly, slow roving eye movements are absent in hysteria since they cannot be mimicked voluntarily.[5] Patients suffering from psychogenic unresponsiveness as a conversion symptom usually offer no resistance to passive movements of the extremities, although normal tone is present, and if an extremity is moved suddenly, momentary resistance may be felt. The patient usually does not withdraw from noxious stimuli, but often will avoid self-injury if his raised arm is dropped towards his face by the examiner. The deep tendon reflexes are usually normal, but they can be voluntarily suppressed in some subjects and thus may be absent or, rarely, asymmetrical. The abdominal reflexes are usually present and plantar responses are invariably absent or flexor. The electroencephalogram is that of an awake patient rather than one in coma.

Patient 5-1. A 26-year-old nurse with a history of generalized convulsions was admitted to a hosptial after a night of alcoholic drinking ostensibly followed by generalized convulsions. She had been given 50 percent glucose and 500 mg. sodium amobarbital intravenously. Upon admission she was reportedly unresponsive to verbal command, but when noxious stimuli were administered she withdrew, repetitively thrust her extremities in both flexion and extension, and on one occasion spat at the examiner. Her respirations were normal. The remainder of the general physical examination and the neurologic examination were normal. She was given 10 mg. of diazepam intravenously and 500 mg. of phenytoin intravenously in two doses 3 hours apart. Eight hours later, because she was still unresponsive, a neurologic consultation was requested. She lay quietly in bed, unresponsive to verbal commands and not withdrawing from noxious stimuli. Her respirations were normal; her eyelids resisted opening actively and, when they were opened, closed rapidly. The eyes did not move spontaneously, the doll's eye responses were absent, and the pupils were 3 mm. and reactive. Her extremities were flaccid with normal deep tendon reflexes, normal superficial abdominal reflexes, and flexor plantar responses. When 20 cc. of ice water was irrigated against the left tympanum, nystagmus with a quick component to the right was produced. The examiner indicated to a colleague that the production of nystagmus indicated that she was conscious and that an EEG would establish that fact. She immediately "awoke." Her speech was dysarthric and she was unsteady on her feet when she arose from bed. An EEG was marked by low and medium voltage fast activity in all leads, with some 8 Hz alpha activity and intermittent 6 to 7 Hz activity, a record suggesting sedation owing to drugs. She recovered full alertness later in the day and was discharged a day later with her neurologic examination having been entirely normal. An EEG done at a subsequent time showed background alpha activity 8 to 10 Hz with a moderate amount of fast activity and little or no 5 to 7 Hz slow activity.

This patient illustrates a common problem in differentiating "organic" and psychogenic unresponsiveness. She had been sedated and had a mild metabolic encephalopathy, but the preponderance of her signs was a result of psychogenic unresponsiveness. The presence of nystagmus on oculovestibular stimulation and an EEG that was only mildly slowed without other signs of neurologic abnormality effectively ruled out organic coma.

The converse of Patient 5-1 is illustrated by Patient 4-12. In the latter the initial examination suggested psychogenic unresponsiveness, but vestibular testing elicited tonic deviation of the eyes with no nystagmus. The tonic eye deviation clearly indicated physiologic rather than psychologic unresponsiveness. A rare patient with psychogenic unresponsiveness is able to inhibit nystagmus induced by caloric testing (probably by intense visual fixation[2]), but in this instance there is no tonic deviation of the eyes and the combination of other signs can establish the diagnosis.

When a patient with severe organic illness, whether systemic or neurologic, becomes unresponsive, the physician sometimes fails to entertain the possibility that the unresponsiveness is psychogenic and represents a conversion reaction to a difficult psychologic situation. Patient 5-2 illustrates this.

Patient 5-2. A 69-year-old woman was admitted to the coronary care unit complaining of chest pain. On examination, she was diaphoretic and the EKG showed changes suggestive of an acute anterior wall myocardial infarction. She was awake and alert at the time of admission and had a normal neurologic examination. The following morning she was found to be unresponsive. On examination her respiratory rate was 16 and regular, pulse 92, temperature 37.5, and blood pressure 120/80. The general physical examination was unremarkable, revealing no changes from the day before. On neurologic examination she failed to respond to either verbal or noxious stimuli. She held her eyes in a tightly closed position, actively resisted passive eye opening, and the lids after being passively opened sprung closed when released. Oculocephalic responses were absent. Cold caloric responses yielded normal, brisk nystagmus. Pupils were 4 mm. and reactive. Tone in the extremities was normal. The deep tendon reflexes were equal throughout, and plantar responses were flexor. The neurologist who examined the patient suggested to the cardiologist that the unresponsiveness was psychogenic and that psychiatric consultation be secured. The incredulous cardiologist began at the patient's bedside to discuss how the diagnosis of psychogenic unresponsiveness was arrived at. When the decision was finally made to consult a psychiatrist, the patient, without opening her eyes, responded with the words, "No psychiatrist."

In this instance, the presence of severe heart disease led the patient's physicians to refuse initially to entertain a diagnosis of psychogenic unresponsiveness. In Patient 5–3, the presence of severe, organic neurologic disease masked the diagnosis for a considerable period.

Patient 5–3. A 28-year-old man with liver carcinoma metastatic to the lungs was admitted to hospital complaining of abdominal pain. His behavior was noted to be inappropriate a few days after admission, but this was believed secondary to the narcotic medications he was receiving for pain. The inappropriate behavior progressed to lethargy and then stupor. When first examined by a neurologist, he was unresponsive to verbal stimuli, but grimaced when stimulated noxiously. He held his eyes open and blinked in response to a bright light. Nuchal rigidity and bilateral extensor plantar responses were present, but there were no other positive neurologic signs. A lumbar puncture revealed bloody CSF with xanthochromic supernatant fluid and a CSF glucose concentration of 15 mg./dl. The EEG consisted of a mixture of theta and delta activity, which was bilaterally symmetrical. Carotid arteriography failed to reveal the cause of his symptoms, which were believed to be caused by leptomeningeal metastases. For the next 2 weeks his state of consciousness waxed and waned. When awake, he continued to act oddly. Two weeks after the initial neurologic examination, he was noted to be lying in bed staring at the ceiling, with no responses to verbal stimuli and with 6-mm. pupils, which responded actively to light. Bilateral extensor plantar responses persisted. The EEG now was within normal limits, showing good alpha activity, which blocked with eye opening. Because of the confusion about the exact cause of his diminished state of consciousness, an "Amytal interview" was carried out.[16] After 300 mg. of intravenous Amytal given slowly over several minutes, the patient awoke, was fully oriented, and was able to perform the serial sevens test without error. During the course of the discussion, when the problems of his cancer were broached, he broke into tears. Further history indicated that the patient's brother had a history of hospitalizations for both mania and depression. A diagnosis of psychogenic unresponsiveness superimposed on metastatic disease of the nervous system was made. The patient was started on psychotropic drugs and he remained alert and responsive throughout the remainder of his hospital stay.

The two patients above illustrate the difficulties in making a diagnosis of psychogenic unresponsiveness in patients with organic disease. Merskey and Buhrich have stressed the frequency of conversion hysteria in patients suffering from structural disease.[13] Of 89 patients with hysterical conversion symptoms, 67 percent had some organic diagnosis; 48 percent of the group with organic diagnoses had either an organic cerebral disorder or a systemic illness affecting the brain. The authors believe that organic cerebral disease predisposes patients to the development of conversion reactions.

Catatonia

The second major category of psychogenic unresponsiveness is due to catatonia. Catatonia is a symptom complex usually associated with severe psychiatric disease and characterized by either stupor or excitement accompanied by behavioral disturbances that include among others, mutism, posturing, rigidity, grimacing, and catalepsy.[6] Catatonic stupor is often more difficult to differentiate from "organic" unresponsiveness than is conversion reaction or malingering. There are several reasons for this: The first is that catatonia is a symptom complex that can be caused by a variety of illnesses, both psychologic and "organic." In a recent prospective clinical study of patients admitted to a psychiatric unit with catatonic symptoms, only 4 of 55 were schizophrenic; 39 had affective disorders, 3 reactive psychoses, and 9 suffered from organic brain diseases, which included toxic psychosis, encephalitis, alcoholic degeneration, and drug-induced psychosis.[6] The catatonic syndrome has been reported to result from a wide variety of both structural and metabolic diseases of the nervous system.[1,6] A second reason for the difficulty in distinguishing the catatonia of psychiatric disease from organic nervous system causes of unresponsiveness is that patients with catatonic stupor usually give the appearance of being obtunded or semistuporous rather than comatose. This state is compatible with normal pupillary and oculovestibular function even when the obtundation has a structural origin. In addition, catatonic stupor is accompanied by a variety of autonomic and endocrine abnormalities that give the patient a particularly strong appearance of organic neurologic disease.

Catatonia occurs in two forms: retarded and excited.[15] Of 250 patients diagnosed as catatonic in a psychiatric hospital, 110 were predominantly retarded, 67 were predominantly excited, and 73 were mixed. The patient in catatonic stupor who presents a problem in the differential diagnosis of stupor or coma usually appears unresponsive to his environment, although he retains to a full extent his normal level of consciousness and cognitive functions. This normal level of consciousness is attested to both by a normal neurologic examination at the time he appears stuporous and by the fact that when he recovers he is often (but not always) able to recall all the events that took place during the "stuporous" state.

Severe and prolonged catatonic stupor, as described below, is uncommon, since such patients are usually treated early with psychotropic medications before the full picture develops. The patient in catatonic stupor usually lies with his eyes open, apparently unseeing. His skin is pale and frequently marred by acne and has an oily or greasy appearance.[18] The patient's pulse is rapid, usually between 90 and 120, and he may be hypertensive. Respirations are normal or rapid. The body temperature is often elevated 1.0 to 1.5°C above normal. Such patients usually do not move spontaneously and appear to be unaware of their surroundings. They may not blink to visual threat, although optokinetic responses are usually present. The pupils are dilated and there is frequently alternating anisocoria; they are, however, reactive to light. (Fixed dilated pupils have been occasionally reported, ostensibly as a result of excessive sympathetic stimulation;[18] we have not observed such a phenomenon and wonder whether mydriatics had been self-instilled.) Some patients hold their eyes tightly closed and will not permit passive eye opening. Doll's eye movements are absent and caloric testing produces normal ocular nystagmus rather than tonic deviation. There is sometimes increased salivation, the patient allowing the saliva either to drool from his mouth or to accumulate in the back of the pharynx without being swallowed. Such subjects may be incontinent of urine or feces or, on the contrary, may retain urine, requiring catheterization. Their extremities may be relaxed, but more commonly are held in rigid positions and are resistant to passive motion. Many patients demonstrate waxy flexibility (a mild but steady resistance to passive motion, which gives the examiner the sensation that he is bending a wax rod). Catalepsy (the tonic maintenance for a long period of time of a limb in a potentially uncomfortable posture where it has been placed by an examiner) is present in about 30 percent of retarded catatonics. Choreiform jerks of the extremities and grimaces are common. The deep tendon reflexes are usually present and there are no pathologic reflexes.

While the patient with the retarded form of catatonia may be difficult to distinguish from a patient with stupor caused by structural disease, the patient with the excited type of catatonia may be difficult to distinguish from a patient with an acute delirium. Both may be wildly agitated and combative, and such behavior may make it impossible to test for orientation and alertness. Hallucinatory activity can be caused by either organic or psychologic disease, although pure visual hallucinations are usually due to structural or metabolic disease and pure auditory hallucinations to psychologic disease. The segmental neurologic examination, insofar as it can be tested in a delirious or excited patient, may be normal with either structural or organic disease. Grimacing, stereotypic motor behavior and posturing suggest catatonia rather than metabolic delirium.

Although the passage of time usually resolves the diagnostic problem, the only immediately distinguishing feature between psychogenic and organic delirious reactions is the EEG. In patients with an acute toxic delirium caused by hepatic encephalopathy, encephalitis, alcohol, or other sedative drugs, slow EEG activity predominates. The EEG of the patient with the delirium of withdrawal from alcohol or barbiturates is dominated by low voltage fast activity. The EEG is usually normal in patients with catatonia, but may be abnormal in states of both catatonic stupor and catatonic excitement. Harding and his associates have reviewed the literature concerning the EEG in periodic psychotic states and have reported extensive EEG recordings in three patients with periodic catatonic stupor.[9] In most patients with periodic catatonia, the onset of either catatonic excitement or stupor was accompanied by an *increase* in the frequency of alpha activity, with a decrease in amplitude and total amount of alpha activity present in the record. There was usually an increased amount of theta activity and an increased amount of low to moderate voltage fast activity. A few patients have been reported in whom delta activity in the 2 to 3 Hz range was described. However, catatonia most often presents a low voltage fast normal record rather than the slow record of a comatose patient. At least one reported patient with prominent delta activity during catatonic stupor had become stuporous following a thyroidectomy, and the degree of thyroid dysfunction was never fully evaluated. Thus, an entirely normal EEG with good background alpha activity with response to eye opening and to noise suggests that an either unresponsive or excessively excited patient is suffering from catatonia rather than structural or metabolic disease of the nervous system. If the EEG is dominated by high voltage slow activity in the case of a stuporous patient, or low voltage fast activity in the case of an excited patient, the likelihood is that the disorder is metabolic or structural rather than psychogenic.

AMYTAL INTERVIEW

In many instances, an immediate distinction between organic and psychologic delirium or stupor cannot be made on the basis of the neurologic examination or the EEG, and in these instances an Amytal interview is often helpful. The Amytal interview is conducted by injecting sodium amobarbital intravenously at a slow rate (generally about 25 mg./minute) while talking to the patient and doing repeated neurologic examinations. It is important that the discussion remain fairly neutral and not represent a direct challenge of the patient's veracity. Patients with structural or

310

metabolic disease of the nervous system usually show immediately increasing neurologic dysfunction as the drug is injected. Neurologic signs not present prior to the injection of amobarbital (such as extensor plantar responses or hemiparesis) may appear after only 50 to 150 mg. have been introduced, and behavioral abnormalities, especially confusion and disorientation, grow worse. On the other hand, patients with psychogenic unresponsiveness or psychogenic excitement frequently require large doses of amobarbital before developing any change in their behavior, and the initial change is toward improvement in behavioral function rather than worsening of abnormal findings. Thus, a patient apparently stuporous may fully awaken after several hundred milligrams of the drug and carry out a rational conversation (see Patient 5-3). A stuporous and withdrawn patient who is catatonic may become fully rational. An excited patient may calm down and demonstrate that he is alert, oriented, and has normal cognitive functions.

In a few instances, even the Amytal interview does not make a distinction between organic and psychologic delirium. In such instances, the patient must be hospitalized for observation while a meticulous search for a metabolic cause of the delirium is made. In one of our patients, a diagnosis of catatonic stupor, although strongly suspected, did not make itself certain until the patient fully awoke after a thorough diagnostic evaluation had proved uninformative and electroshock therapy was initiated. Once a psychogenic basis for unresponsiveness is established, a more extensive developmental and psychiatric history must be obtained to determine the type of psychiatric disturbance. The exact psychiatric diagnosis will determine the treatment. While the Amytal interview is a relatively safe procedure for diagnostic purposes, most psychiatrists do not recommend it for treatment if the patient relapses into psychogenic unresponsiveness after the diagnosis has been made. Intravenous barbiturates given with the suggestion that they will remove a symptom could be hazardous, since the patient who has resolved his conflict in developing the conversion symptom may develop more serious psychologic disturbances should that symptom abruptly be removed.

REFERENCES

1. ABRAMS, R., AND TAYLOR, M.A.: *Catatonia. A prospective clinical study.* Arch. Gen. Psychiatry 33:579-581, 1976.

2. BALOH, R.W., SOLINGEN, L., SILLS, A.W., ET AL.: *Effect of different conditions of ocular fixation.* Ann. Otol. Rhinol. Laryngol. 86 (suppl. 43):1-6, 1977.

3. BELFER, M.L., AND D'AUTREMONT, C.C.: *Catatonia-like symptomatology: an interesting case.* Arch. Gen. Psychiatry 24:119-120, 1971.

4. BIERCE, A.: *The Devil's Dictionary.* World Book Co., Yonkers, N.Y., 1948.

5. FISHER, C.M.: *The neurological examination of the comatose patient.* Acta Neurol. Scand. 45 (suppl. 36):1-56, 1969.

6. GELENBERG, A.J.: *The catatonic syndrome.* Lancet 1:1339-1341, 1976.

7. GJESSING, R., AND GJESSING, L.: *Some main trends in the clinical aspects of periodic catatonia.* Acta Psychiatr. Scand. 37:1-13, 1961.

8. GUZE, S.B., WOODRUFF, R.A., AND CLAYTON, P.J.: *A study of conversion symptoms in psychiatric outpatients.* Am. J. Psychiatry 128:135-138, 1971.

9. HARDING, G., JEAVONS, P.M., JENNER, F.A., ET AL.: *The electroencephalogram in three cases of periodic psychosis.* Electroencephalogr. Clin. Neurophysiol. 21:59-66, 1966.

10. HENRY, J.A., AND WOODRUFF, G.H.A.: *A diagnostic sign in states of apparent unconsciousness.* Lancet 2:920-921, 1978.

11. HOPKINS, A.: *Pretending to be unconscious.* Lancet 2:312-314, 1973.

12. JOHNSON, S.: cited in Boswell, J.: *Life of Johnson.*

13. MERSKEY, H., AND BUHRICH, N.A.: *Hysteria and organic brain disease.* Br. J. Med. Psychol. 48:359–366, 1975.

14. MISSRI, J.C., AND ALEXANDER, S.: *Hyperventilation syndrome. A brief review.* J.A.M.A. 240:2093–2096, 1978.

15. MORRISON, J.R.: *Catatonia. Retarded and excited types.* Arc. Gen. Psychiat. 28:39–41, 1973.

16. NAPLES, M., AND HACKETT, T.P.: *The Amytal interview: history and current uses.* Psychosomatics 19:98–105. 1978.

17. SLATER, E.: *Diagnosis of "hysteria."* Br. Med. J. 1:1395–1399, 1965.

18. VON WESTPHAL, A.: *Ueber ein im katatonischen stupor beobachtetes pupillenphanomen sowie bemerkungen uber due pupillenstarre bei hysterie.* Dtsch. Med. Wochenschr. 33:1080–1086, 1907.

312

CHAPTER 6

Brain Death

GENERAL CONSIDERATIONS AND DEFINITIONS

Abundant clinical evidence demonstrates that severe damage to the brain can completely destroy the organ's function and capacity to recover, even when other parts of the body still live. These findings plus advances in resuscitative medicine have made obsolete the traditional clinical definition of death, i.e., cessation of heart beat. Cardiac resuscitation can salvage patients after periods of asystole lasting up to several minutes. Cardiopulmonary by-pass machines permit the patient's heart beat to cease for several hours with full clinical recovery after resuscitation. Other artificial appliances already under development promise in the future to keep patients alive without a normal beating heart for extended periods. The situation is even more striking with respiratory failure. While respiratory depression formerly meant death within minutes, modern mechanical ventilators can maintain pulmonary oxygen exchange indefinitely. Such advances have permitted many patients with formerly lethal cardiac, pulmonary, and neuromuscular diseases to return to relatively full and useful lives, but they have made cessation of heart beat an inadequate definition of death. The result has been to switch the emphasis in defining death to a cessation of brain function. This chapter distinguishes between brain death, on the one hand, and cerebral death or the vegetative state on the other, based on the following definitions.

Brain death occurs when irreversible brain damage is so extensive that the organ enjoys no potential for recovery and can no longer maintain the body's internal homeostasis, i.e., normal respiratory or cardiovascular function, normal temperature control, normal gastrointestinal function, and so on. Although mechanical means may preserve the peripheral organs for a time under such circumstances, a body that is "brain dead" will, despite the most meticulous care, develop failure of the systemic circulation within a few days or, rarely, after several weeks, [17] and the heartbeat will cease. That the brain has been dead for some time prior to the cessation of the heartbeat is attested to by the fact that the organ in such cases is usually autolyzed (respirator brain) when examined postmortem.[28,29]

Irreversible coma, or *cerebral death** (i.e., death of the cerebral hemispheres), or the *vegetative state* occurs when the brain damage is permanent and sufficiently severe that the individual is thereafter unable to maintain external homeostasis

---

*Korein[15] has defined cerebral death as "irreversible destruction of both cerebral hemispheres exclusive of the brainstem and cerebellum" and has differentiated it from brain death, in which there is irreversible destruction of "the neuronal contents of the intracranial cavity," including brainstem and cerebellum. The term "cerebral death" is ambiguous because, as Korein himself points out, it has been used by many neurologists as a synonym for brain death, even appearing as such in the literature.[28] The terms "irreversible coma" and "persistent vegetative state" do not allow for confusion, and thus should be used in preference to the term "cerebral death."

313

(i.e., is unable to respond behaviorally in any major or appropriate way to the environment), even though the brain may continue to maintain internal homeostasis.[21] Actually, very few surviving patients with severe brain damage remain in eyes-closed coma for more than 10 to 14 days. In most, vegetative behavior usually replaces coma by that time. Unlike brain death, in which the cerebral hemispheres and the brainstem both undergo loss of their vitality, the pathology of chronic vegetative states is often limited to the cerebral hemispheres and only occasionally includes focal areas in the brainstem (see Chapter 1).

Three medical considerations make important the application of the concepts of brain death and cerebral death or irreversible coma: (1) Transplant programs require the donation of healthy peripheral organs for success. The early diagnosis of brain death before the systemic circulation fails allows the salvage of such organs. However, ethical and legal considerations demand that if one is to declare the brain dead, the criteria must be clear and unassailable. (2) Even if there were no transplant program, the ability of modern medicine to keep brainless bodies going for extended periods with antibiotics, mechanical respirators, and vasoconstrictor drugs often leads to prolonged, expensive, and futile exercises accompanied by great emotional strains on family and medical staff. Conversely, the recuperative powers of the brain sometimes can seem astounding to the uninitiated, and individual patients whom uninformed physicians might give up for dead sometimes make unexpectedly good recoveries. It is even more important to know when to fight for life than to be willing to diagnose death. (3) Critical care facilities are limited and expensive and inevitably place a drain on other medical resources.[8,10] Their best use demands that one identify and select patients most likely to benefit from intensive techniques, so that these units are not overloaded with individuals who can never recover cerebral function.

Mainly to the neurologist falls the difficult task of trying to decide in patients with badly damaged brains whether further medical effort will fail to produce anything beyond a vegetative existence or, conversely, when even a tiny chance remains that major medical efforts may yield an alive and sentient individual. The following paragraphs review the clinical and laboratory indicants upon which these judgments can be based.

It is important to recognize that these indicants apply only to the present state of our knowledge and medical skills and that future developments in medicine may enhance the salvage rates of patients with badly damaged brains. We must not rest on present efforts to restore brain functions but constantly strive to improve our results. Such efforts to improve the outcome of severe brain damage are probably best left to special intensive care and research centers equipped to deal with these difficult problems.

CRITERIA OF BRAIN DEATH

Since Mollaret and Goulon[20] first examined the question in 1959, many workers have tried to establish criteria that would accurately and unequivocally determine that the brain is dead or about to die no matter what therapeutic measures one might undertake. Several committees and reviewers have sought to establish appropriate clinical and electroencephalographic criteria for brain death based on a retrospective analysis of patients who died.[5,7,13] The most widely known definition is that of the Ad Hoc Committee of the Harvard Medical School to examine the definition of brain death.[3] Those criteria, as well as slightly differing ones emanating from other groups, are outlined in Table 20.

In essence, there is general agreement that brain death has occurred when one can find no discernible evidence of either cerebral hemispheral function or function of the vital centers of the brainstem for an extended period, and when it is unequivocally evident that the abnormality of brain function is the result of structural or known metabolic disease and not the result of either depressant drug (or alcohol) poisoning or hypothermia. Evidence gained from thousands of patients studied in many centers around the world[26] indicates that not a single subject who fulfilled the "Cerebral Survival Criteria" given in Table 20 maintained a heart beat for longer than a few more days, no matter what treatment was delivered. Since these are the only guidelines that possess empirical validation, they have been adopted with minor modifications (Table 21) as the basis for selecting patients for the transplant programs at Memorial Hospital for Cancer and Allied Diseases and The New York Hospital.

The first criterion in Table 21 is crucial to the diagnosis of brain death. The

Table 20. Summary of Sets of Criteria for Brain Death Used by Different Investigators and Clinicians*

Harvard criteria[3]	1. Unresponsive coma
	2. Apnea
	3. Absence of cephalic reflexes
	4. Absence of spinal reflexes
	5. Isoelectric EEG
	6. Persistence of conditions for at least 24 hours
	7. Absence of drug intoxication or hypothermia
Minnesota criteria[18]	1. Basic prerequisite—diagnosis of irreparable cerebral lesion
	2. No spontaneous movements
	3. No spontaneous respiration
	4. Absence of brainstem reflexes
	5. Persistence of condition unchanged for 12 hours
Swedish criteria[12]	1. Unresponsive coma
	2. Apnea
	3. Absent brainstem reflexes
	4. Isoelectric EEG
	5. Nonfilling of cerebral vessels on two aortocranial injections of contrast media 25 minutes apart
Cerebral survival criteria[27]	1. Basic prerequisite—completion of all appropriate and therapeutic procedures
	2. Unresponsive coma
	3. Apnea
	4. Absent cephalic reflexes with dilated, fixed pupils†
	5. Isoelectric EEG
	6. Persistence of the above for 30 minutes to 1 hour, and 6 hours after onset of coma and apnea
	7. Confirmatory test indicating absence of cerebral circulation (optional)

*From Molinari, G.F.: "Review of clinical criteria of brain death." In Korein, J. (ed.): Brain death: interrelated medical and social issues. Ann. N.Y. Acad. Sci. 315:62–69, 1978, with permission.
†See text, p. 317.

physician *must* know the cause of coma and satisfy himself that it is irreversible. Most "coma of unknown origin" that has its onset outside hospital walls is due to depressant drug poisoning. Witnesses cannot be relied upon in this circumstance, for accidental poisoning or efforts at homicide can readily induce false testimony. Even in patients already in hospitals for other illnesses, self-administered drug poisoning can occur and at least temporarily deceive a medical staff. Accordingly, diagnosis of an irreversible lesion by clinical and laboratory means must be fully completed and unequivocally accurate before making a diagnosis of brain death. The ease of being mistaken in such a diagnosis is illustrated by the collaborative study sponsored by the National Institutes of Health, in which results of laboratory tests revealed many more cases in which drugs contributed to the picture of deep coma than had been suspected clinically by experienced physicians. [19]

All observers agree that before a diagnosis of brain death can be made the subject must show total behavioral unawareness to externally applied stimuli and that even the most noxious stimulus must evoke no discernible supraspinal response. The Harvard criteria demand that no reflex activity be present whatsoever. Our own experience and that of others[1,14] suggest that spinal reflex activity, including stretch reflexes and primitive responses to noxious stimuli (e.g., unilateral extension-pronation of the upper extremity and flexion of the lower), can sometimes persist for hours or even days in brain dead patients until the heart finally stops. The absence of cerebral hemisphere function can also be attested to by EEG recordings, the criteria for which are described below. How long cerebral hemisphere function must be absent to diagnose death is somewhat controversial. The Harvard criteria require a 24-hour period under observation, but provide no empirical validation. Unfortunately for transplant purposes, many patients with severe head injuries who meet all other criteria for brain death do not maintain cardiac function for 24 hours despite the use of vasopressor drugs. Thus, when the presence of structural damage is obvious and severe (e.g., head injuries, cerebral hemorrhage, intracranial tumor), we have concluded that a 6-hour period of absent brain function followed by a 30-minute isoelectric EEG is sufficient to determine brain death, particularly when organ transplant is being considered. A recently completed collaborative study on cerebral survival based on 503 unresponsive patients validates these criteria. [27] The study concluded that if reversible conditions have

Table 21. Criteria for Diagnosis of Brain Death, Cornell Affiliated Hospitals, New York

---

1. Nature and duration of coma
   a. Known structural disease or irreversible systemic metabolic cause
   b. No chance of drug intoxication or hypothermia
   c. 6-hour observation
2. Absence of cerebral function
   a. No behavioral or reflex response to noxious stimuli above foramen magnum level
   b. Electroencephalogram isoelectric for 30 minutes at 5–10 μV/mm.
3. Absence of brainstem function
   a. Fixed pupils
   b. No oculovestibular responses to 50 cc. ice water calorics
   c. Apneic during oxygenation for 10 minutes
   d. Systemic circulation may be intact
   e. Purely spinal reflexes may be maintained

---

been thoroughly excluded, brain death could be diagnosed responsibly if appropriate criteria, including EEG silence, were observed for at least 30 minutes, 6 hours or more after the cerebral insult had occurred.

Cerebral Hemispheric Function

Examination of cerebral hemispheric function in the comatose patient is the least useful of all the predictive criteria since many fully reversible structural illnesses can temporarily produce a severe impairment of forebrain activity. The crucial criteria of brain death are those that clinically denote absence of brainstem function and that by laboratory examination denote total absence of cerebral hemispheric and upper brainstem function, i.e., those functions measured by the electroencephalogram.

Brainstem Function

Respiration

Spontaneous respiration must be absent. Most patients when examined will already have been placed on an artificial respirator usually producing a PaO_2 above and a $PaCO_2$ below normal levels. The threshold for respiratory stimulation by the blood gases usually is elevated in patients in deep coma, sometimes to $PaCO_2$ values as high as 50 to 55 mm. Hg. As a result, such patients may be apneic for several minutes when removed from the ventilator, even if they have a structurally normal brainstem. To test brainstem function safely under such circumstances, respiratory activity may be tested by the technique of apneic oxygenation. With this technique, the patient is respired with 100 percent oxygen for a period of 10 to 20 minutes. The respirator is then disconnected and oxygen is delivered through a catheter to a trachea at a rate of about 6 liters per minute. The oxygen tension in the alveoli under such circumstances remains sufficiently high that diffusion across the alveolar membrane will maintain the arterial blood at adequate oxygen tensions, even up to an hour. According to Schafer and Caronna, the $PaCO_2$ rises by about 3 mm. Hg per minute during apneic oxygenation in deeply comatose or clinically brain dead patients.[22] Apneic oxygenation of 10 minutes thus allows the $PaCO_2$ to rise without danger of further hypoxia and assures that one exceeds the respiratory threshold. A $PaCO_2$ that rises above 60 mm. Hg without concomitant breathing efforts provides unequivocal evidence of a nonfunctioning respiratory center.

Pupils

The pupils must be nonreactive. The Harvard criteria require that the pupils be dilated as well as fixed, but midposition fixed pupils are as good or better a sign of failure of brainstem function, as the examination of patients in any morgue will attest. The pupils should be tested with a bright light and the physician should be certain that mydriatric agents (including intravenous atropine) have not been used.

Ocular Movements

Failure of brainstem function should be attested to by the inability to find any ocular responses to head turning and caloric irrigation of the ears with 50 cc. of ice water. Care should be taken to assure that the stimulus reaches the tympanum.

Motor Movements

The Harvard criteria also demand that there be an absence of motor and reflex movements, including absence of corneal responses; no postural activity, including decerebrate rigidity; and no stretch reflexes in the extremities. Physiologic considerations make the last-mentioned an unnecessary criterion if all the other criteria are met, since spinal reflex activity, in response to both noxious stimuli and tendon stretch, often persists in animals whose brains have been destroyed above the spinal or low medullary level. The same reflexes can be found in the isolated spinal cord of man following high cord transection. One should, however, be certain that cranial motor reflexes such as the jaw and snout reflexes are absent before making the diagnosis of brain death. [1]

A variety of unusual, possibly medullospinal motor movements can appear and persist for prolonged periods during artificial animation in patients otherwise brain dead, as the following example illustrates.

Patient 6–1. A 47 year old woman suddenly lost consciousness from cerebral-subarachnoid hemorrhage. Her blood pressure was 180/80 mm. Hg and pulse 64 per minute. Intermittent spontaneous movements involved her right side; the left side did not move and was flaccid. The respirations were 24 per minute, regular, and deep. The pupils were small (3 mm.), equal, and reactive. Full doll's eye responses were obtained both horizontally and vertically. She had intact gag and ciliospinal reflexes. Deep tendon reflexes were brisk bilaterally with absence of ankle and knee jerks and extensor plantar responses. By 5 hours later all responses to stimulation disappeared. Both pupils were midposition and fixed; the doll's eye responses were absent. The plantar responses were also absent, and the systolic blood pressure had fallen below 70 mm. Hg. Shortly thereafter she became apneic, and mechanical ventilation was started.

The next day she remained unresponsive to noxious stimuli, the pupils were fixed at 6 mm. without light response, and no oculovestibular responses were elicited by ice water calorics. She failed to breathe after 10 minutes of apneic oxygenation. The EEG was isoelectric, the blood pressure 160/90 mm. Hg, the pulse 84 per minute, and the body temperature 36.5°C. It was noted for the first time that if her neck was flexed or laterally rotated she developed a sudden jerking flexion of both shoulders and extension of the arms at the elbows. The movement lasted less than 1 second but could be elicited each time the neck was manipulated. Later that day, other neurologic signs being unchanged, one could still produce movement of the arms with neck flexion. There was also occasional movement of the neck toward extension when it was passively flexed, again as a sudden jerk. The movement varied from moment to moment with neck motion, at times one arm taking a decerebrate-like posture and the other a decorticate-like posture, and at times taking the reverse positions. When the neck was laterally rotated, however, the right arm assumed a decerebrate posture with no movement of the legs. Biceps stretch reflexes were now present bilaterally, but no other reflexes could be elicited. The movements and the remainder of the neurologic examination persisted unchanged until the next day, when the blood pressure progressively failed and her heart stopped.

Autopsy revealed a fresh subarachnoid hemorrhage located at the base of the brain on the right side, emanating from a ruptured berry aneurysm just beyond the first bifurcation of the right middle cerebral artery. The brain was severely edematous, and there was transtentorial herniation, more severe on the right, with compression of the brainstem by the herniated uncus. There was also cerebellar tonsillar herniation. Coronal sections revealed rupture of the hemorrhage into the cerebrum on the right side, extending into the white matter adjacent to the basal ganglia. There were no gross lesions in the brainstem other than distortion and pressure by the cone, but, microscopically, severe anoxic changes were present in neurons throughout the brainstem down to the medullary level.

Laboratory Tests

The clinical diagnosis of brain death is generally neither difficult nor likely to be wrong if one follows explicitly the criteria outlined above. The diagnosis carries a heavy ethical and legal responsibility, however, and most medical centers in the U.S. have found it useful to develop objective laboratory tests to supplement the clinical criteria.

Electroencephalogram

The EEG is helpful in the evaluation of absence of cerebral hemispheric function and provides objective, verifiable support to clinical appraisals when organ transplantation is being considered. (In less legally demanding situations, it is doubtful that the experienced physician needs the EEG to tell him when the brain is dead. British criteria for brain death, for example, omit the requirement of obtaining an EEG. [7])

All evidence indicates that an isoelectric EEG for a period of 6 to 12 hours in a patient who is not hypothermic and has not ingested or been given depressant drugs means that no mental recovery is possible and usually means that the brain is already dead. Silverman and associates reported a survey of 2650 isoelectric EEGs that lasted up to 24 hours in duration. [23] Only three patients from this group, each in coma caused by overdose of central nervous system depressant drugs, recovered cerebral function. However, several ostensibly isoelectric tracings were discarded because of faulty technique. A national cooperative group has published the technical requirements necessary to establish electrocerebral silence (Table 22) and has produced an atlas illustrating potential problems of interpretation of the EEG in coma. [4] One should point out that the EEG is not infallible, even with anoxic-ischemic injury. A prolonged vegetative existence is occasionally possible in such cases despite the presence of an initially isoelectric EEG. [6] *Caution: after depressive drug poisoning, total loss of cerebral hemispheric function and isoelectric EEGs have been observed for as long as 50 hours with full clinical recovery.* [11]

Cerebral Circulation

Several laboratories have reported on techniques of examining the cerebral circulation in patients with severe structural brain disease who were thought to be dead. The rationale is that absence of the cerebral circulation would conclusively affirm the presence of a dead brain. Physiologically, two events produce failure of the cerebral circulation. The first is probably rare, but may sometimes acutely follow severe head injuries and includes a massive increase in intracranial pressure that finally equals the arteriolar and capillary perfusion pressure, at which point cerebral

Table 22. Electroencephalographic Recording for Diagnosing Cerebral Death (Am. EEG Soc.)

---

1. A minimum of eight scalp electrodes and ear reference electrodes
2. Interelectrode resistances under 10,000 ohms but over 100 ohms
3. Test of integrity of recording system by deliberate creation of electrode artifact by manipulation
4. Interelectrode distances of at least 10 cm.
5. Gains increased during most of the recording from 7.0 μV to 2.0 μV/mm
6. The use of 0.3 or 0.4 sec. time constants during part of the recording
7. Recording with an EKG and other monitoring devices, such as a pair of electrodes on the dorsum of the right hand, to detect extracerebral responses
8. Tests for reactivity to pain, loud noises, or light
9. A 30-minute total recording time
10. Recording by a qualified technician
11. Repeat record if doubt about electrocerebral silence (ECS)
12. Telephonic transmitted EEGs are not appropriate for determination of ECS

319

circulation ceases and the EEG becomes flat. Such changes are self-evident and have been demonstrated in the experimental animal by many investigators. The second, and probably more common occurrence is a progressive intravascular obstruction that accompanies death of the brain. The pathologic consequence of both events is the so-called respirator brain, a soft and necrotic organ that autolyzes at body temperature when the respiratory and cardiovascular systems are kept functioning for many hours or days after brain circulation has ceased. [29]

The state of the cerebral circulation has been tested in several ways in patients presumed to be dead or overwhelmingly damaged. Several investigators have found no filling of the carotid circulation by cerebral arteriography in such subjects. [30] Goodman, Mishkin, and Dyken studied cerebral perfusion by isotope angiography. [9] They injected 15 mc ^{99m}Te-pertechnetate as a bolus in the antecubital vein and emissions from the head were counted with a gamma camera, with films being taken every 3 seconds for 24 seconds. This technique demonstrates isotope filling of both arteries and veins in the normal state. In three patients believed to be brain dead, no filling of the vessels was found, and all were found to have soft, necrotic brains at autopsy. Korein and associates tested this bolus technique more extensively and found it to be a helpful adjunct in diagnosing brain death. [16] They compared the result with conventional arteriograms in 20 patients and with postmortem examinations in 6 patients. The absence of a bolus tracing from the head in the presence of a control tracing from the femoral artery correlated fully with other signs indicating that brain death had occurred. Other possible laboratory approaches to the diagnosis of brain death include measurement of arm to retina circulation time, isotope angiography, echoencephalography, and measurement of cerebral evoked responses.[26] Although all can undoubtedly add accurate information, none would seem to be necessary when all clinical signs of death are supplemented by an isoelectric EEG and the cause of coma is known.

Brain Biopsy

Brain biopsy or direct surgical inspection has occasionally been suggested to diagnose brain death. The suggestion seems unreasonable. Unless the surgeon drills holes over multiple areas of the cerebrum and brainstem, it is unlikely that either he or the pathologist can examine enough brain tissue antemortem to conclude that the remainder is dead as well.

PITFALLS IN THE DIAGNOSIS OF BRAIN DEATH

Potential pitfalls accompany the diagnosis of brain death, particularly when coma occurs in hospitalized patients or those who have been chronically ill. Almost none of these will lead to serious error in diagnosis if the examining physician is aware of them and attends to them when examining individual patients who are considered brain dead. Some of these pitfalls are outlined in Table 23.

In comatose patients, pupillary fixation does not always mean absence of brainstem function. In rare instances, the pupils may have been fixed by preexisting ocular or neurologic disease. More commonly, particularly in a patient who has suffered cardiac arrest, atropine has been injected during the resuscitation process and widely dilated, fixed pupils may result without indicating the absence of brainstem function. Neuromuscular blocking agents also can produce pupillary fixation, although in these instances the pupils are usually midposition or small rather than widely dilated.

Similarly, the absence of oculovestibular responses does not necessarily indicate absence of brainstem vestibular function. Like pupillary responses, oculovestibular reflexes may be absent if the end organ is either poisoned or damaged. Some otherwise neurologically normal patients suffer labyrinthine dysfunction from peripheral disease that predates the onset of coma. Other patients with chronic illnesses have suffered ototoxicity from a variety of drugs, including antibiotics such as gentamicin. In these patients, oculovestibular responses may be absent even though brainstem processes are still functioning. Finally, a variety of drugs, including sedatives, anticholinergics, anticonvulsants, and tricyclic antidepressants, may suppress vestibular and/or oculomotor function to the point where oculovestibular reflexes disappear.

Pitfalls also exist in the diagnosis of apnea in comatose patients maintained on respirators and have already been discussed above.

The absence of motor activity also does not guarantee loss of brainstem function. Neuromuscular blockers are often used early in the course of artificial respiration when the patient is resisting the respirator; if suspected brain death subsequently occurs, there may still be enough circulating neuromuscular blocking agent to produce absence of motor function when the examination is carried out. A recent report has described the simulation of brain death by excessive sensitivity to succinylcholine.[24] In this case the presence of activity in the EEG established cerebral viability.

Therapeutic overdoses of sedative drugs to treat anoxia or seizures likewise may abolish reflexes and motor responses to noxious stimuli.

There are pitfalls in using the EEG as an ancillary technique in the diagnosis of cerebral death. Isoelectric EEGs with subsequent recovery have been reported with sedative drug overdoses, after anoxia, during hypothermia, following cerebral trauma, and after encephalitis.[27] Bennett and associates have carefully defined the

Table 23. Some Pitfalls in the Diagnosis of Brain Death

Findings	Possible Causes
1. Pupils fixed	Anticholinergic drugs Neuromuscular blockers Preexisting disease
2. No oculovestibular reflexes	Ototoxic agents Vestibular suppressants Preexisting disease
3. No respiration	Posthyperventilation apnea Neuromuscular blockers
4. No motor activity	Neuromuscular blockers "Locked-in" state Sedative drugs
5. Isoelectric EEG	Sedative drugs Anoxia Hypothermia Encephalitis Trauma

artifacts that may appear in an attempt to establish an EEG diagnosis of brain death, and included in their atlas is a protocol for recording variables and the required placement of electrodes to insure that the EEG is isoelectric. [4]

ETHICAL AND LEGAL CONSIDERATIONS

Although not all agree, most religious and ethical authorities have expressed themselves in sympathy with the concept that death of the brain signifies death of the person. Pope Pius XII established the climate for subsequent ethical opinion by his Proclamation in 1958, which declared directly that pronouncement of death was a responsibility of medicine and not the church: "It remains for the doctor . . . to give a clear and precise definition of 'death' and the 'moment of death' of a patient who passes away in a state of unconsciousness." The Pope went on to state that when illnesses reached "hopeless" proportions, death should not be medically opposed by "extraordinary" measures.

Almost all thoughtful observers have recognized that the concept of brain death represents a definition that cessation of life has come to the person and carries no connotation of foreshortening human life merely because matters appear hopeless. Agreement that the brain and the person are one has essentially removed the ethical conflict that otherwise derives from the almost universal respect for the dignity of the individual human being. These and related matters receive detailed discussion in two recent monographs on the subject of brain death.[15,28]

In addition, Veith and associates discuss extensively the acceptance of the concepts of brain death within the contexts of the Orthodox Judiac, Roman Catholic, and Protestant faiths.[25] They quote Paul Ramsay's pithy acceptance of proposals "foretelling when we should stop ventilating and circulating the blood of an unburied corpse because there are no longer any vital functions really alive or recoverable in the patient." Nevertheless opposing views can be found.[31]

From the legal standpoint, death of the brain has been more or less explicitly accepted as indicating death of the person in a series of U.S. court cases. More importantly, 18 states have enacted statutes accepting the diagnosis of brain death as death of the person. Unfortunately, some of these laws retain undesirable imprecisions or ambiguities. In 1975, the American Bar Association approved a model statute that recognizes traditional as well as brain-related criteria for the determination of death and meets many of the medical and legal uncertainties contained in some preexisting statutes. The recommendation already has been incorporated into new laws in California, Georgia, Idaho, and Tennessee. Modified versions underlie new laws in Illinois and Oklahoma. Thirty-two states still lack statutory recognition that death can be determined by brain-related criteria. One hopes that the combined influences of the overwhelming scientific evidence for such a step, its acceptance by major religious leaders and philosophers, and the clear model statute accepted by the Bar Association will soon lead the legislatures of these states to confirm by clear laws what is already the generally accepted pattern of practice.

Given the above principles, how is the doctor to act in the individual case? As the American Neurological Association notes in its guidelines for the determination of brain death,[2] the physician must evaluate all the circumstances surrounding a given case and construct his judgment by the usual and customary methods of medical practice within his community. Life support systems should never be discontinued unless the history of medical findings unequivocally establishes the cause

322

of the brain injury and its irreversibility. Since legislation governing the diagnosis of brain death and the subsequent discontinuation of support remains imprecise in many areas, the diagnosis and planned course of action should be taken only with the informed consent of immediately responsible relatives or guardians. If organ transplantation is contemplated, it seems wise to have the diagnosis of brain death affirmed by two knowledgeable physicians not immediately connected with the transplantation. Although unnecessary in many instances in which the clinical findings are clear and the doctor, patient, and family enjoy a close relationship, EEG confirmation of electrocerebral silence (Table 22) is highly desirable in most circumstances. Such EEG recordings always should be available when one contemplates organ transplant or when legal proceedings are likely, such as occurs in the case of many head injuries.

REFERENCES

1. ALLEN, N.: *Life or death of the brain after cardiac arrest.* Neurology 27:805–806, 1977.

2. AMERICAN NEUROLOGICAL ASSOCIATION: *Revised statement regarding methods for determining that the brain is dead.* Trans. Am. Neurol. Assoc. 102:192–193, 1977.

3. BEECHER, H.K.: *A definition of irreversible coma: report of the Ad Hoc Committee of the Harvard Medical School to examine the definition of brain death.* J.A.M.A. 205:85–88, 1968.

4. BENNETT, D.R., HUGHES, J.R., KOREIN, J. ET AL: *Atlas of Electroencephalography in Coma and Cerebral Death. EEG at the Bedside or in the Intensive Care Unit.* Raven Press, New York, 1976.

5. BLACK, P.M.: *Brain Death.* N. Engl. J. Med. 299:338–344, 393–401, 1978.

6. BRIERLEY, J.B., ADAMS, J.H., GRAHAM, D.I., ET AL.: *Neocortical death after cardiac arrest.* Lancet 2:560–565, 1971.

7. CONFERENCE OF ROYAL COLLEGES AND FACULTIES OF THE UNITED KINGDOM: *Diagnosis of brain death.* Lancet 2:1069–1070, 1976.

8. CULLEN, D.J.: *Results and costs of intensive care.* Anesthesiology 47:203–216, 1977.

9. GOODMAN, J.M., MISHKIN, F.S., AND DYKEN, M.: *Determination of brain death by isotope angiography.* J.A.M.A. 209:1869–1872, 1969.

10. HIATT, H.H.: *Protecting the medical commons: who is responsible?* N. Engl. J. Med. 293:235–241, 1975.

11. HUGHES, J.R.: "Limitations of the EEG in coma and brain death." In Korein, J. (ed.): *Brain death: interrelated medical and social issues.* Ann. N.Y. Acad. Sci. 315:121–136, 1978.

12. INGVAR, D.H., AND WIDEN, L.: *Brain death: summary of a symposium.* Lakartidningen 69:3804–3814, 1972.

13. JENSEN-JUUL, P.: *Criteria of Brain Death. Selection of Donors for Transplantation.* Munksgaard, Copenhagen, 1970.

14. JORGENSEN, E.O.: *Spinal man after brain death.* Acta Neurochir. 28:259–273, 1973.

15. KOREIN, J. (ED.): *Brain death: interrelated medical and social issues.* Ann. N.Y. Acad. Sci. 315:1–454, 1978.

16. KOREIN, J., BRAUNSTEIN, P., GEORGE, A., ET AL.: *Brain death: 1. Angiographic correlation with the radioisotopic bolus technique for evaluation of critical deficit of cerebral flow.* Ann. Neurol. 2:195–205, 1977.

17. KRAMER, W.: *From reanimation to deanimation (intravital death of the brain during artificial respiration).* Acta Neurol. Scand. (suppl. 4) 39:139–153, 1963.

18. MOHANDAS, A., AND CHOU, S.N.: *Brain death. A clinical and pathological study.* J. Neurosurg. 35:211–218, 1971.

19. MOLINARI, G.F.: "Review of clinical criteria of brain death." In Korein, J. (ed.): *Brain death: interrelated medical and social issues,* Ann. N.Y. Acad. Sci. 315:62–69, 1978.

20. MOLLARET, P., AND GOULON, M.: *Le coma depasse.* Rev. Neurol. 101:3–15, 1959.

21. POSNER, J.B.: "Coma and other states of consciousness: the differential diagnosis of brain death."

In Korein, J. (ed.): *Brain death: interrelated medical and social issues.* Ann. N.Y. Acad. Sci. 315:215–227, 1978.

22. Schafer, J.A., and Caronna, J.J.: *Duration of apnea needed to confirm brain death.* Neurology, 28:661–668, 1978.

23. Silverman, D., Masland, R.L., Saunders, M.G., et al.: *Irreversible coma associated with electrocerebral silence.* Neurology 20:525–533, 1970.

24. Tyson, R.N.: *Simulation of cerebral death by succinylcholine sensitivity.* Arch. Neurol. 30:409–411, 1974.

25. Veith, F.J., Fein, J.M., Tendler, M.D., et al.: *Brain death. 1. A status report of medical and ethical considerations. 2. A status report of legal considerations.* J.A.M.A. 238:1651–1655, 1744–1748, 1977.

26. Walker, A.E.: "Cerebral death." In Tower, D.B. (ed.): *The Nervous System.* vol. 2. *The Clinical Neurosciences.* Raven Press, New York, 1975, pp. 75–87.

27. Walker, A.E.: *An appraisal of the criteria of cerebral death. A summary statement. A collaborative study.* J.A.M.A. 237:982–986, 1977.

28. Walker, A.E.: *Cerebral death.* Professional Information Library, 1977.

29. Walker, A.E., Diamond, E.L., Moseley, J.: *The neuropathological findings in irreversible coma: a critique of the "respirator brain."* J. Neuropathol. Exp. Neurol. 34:295–323, 1975.

30. Wertheimer, P., Jouvet, P., and Descotes, J.: *Apropos du diagnostic de la mort du systeme nerveux dans les comas avec arret respiratoire traites par respiration artificielle.* Presse Med. 67:87–88, 1959.

31. Byrne, P.A., O'Reilly, S., and Quay, P.M.: *Brain death—an opposing viewpoint.* J.A.M.A. 242:1985–1990, 1979.

CHAPTER 7

Prognosis in Coma

It is much more difficult to predict the outcome for patients with severe brain damage than to make the usually straightforward diagnosis of brain death. Brain death is a single biologic state with an unequivocal future, while brain damage exists along a continuous scale with the future outcome depending on a number of variables, which include not only the degree of neurologic injury but the severity of the underlying illness and the presence or absence of medical complications. The scientific, philosophic, and emotional uncertainties attending predictions of outcome from human illness can intimidate even experienced physicians. Nevertheless, the problem must be faced: the growth of intensive care facilities for treating the critically ill means that almost every doctor is frequently called upon to treat patients with severe degrees of neurologic insufficiency. To do his or her job responsibly, the physician caring for patients in coma must know whether and when he or she can anticipate accurately if they will either recover or remain permanently, overwhelmingly disabled. All of us know that the financial and emotional costs of caring for those hopelessly damaged or demented by acute illness or trauma can exhaust both family and medical staffs. Part of our medical responsibility is to attempt to reduce those burdens while at the same time retaining our unwavering commitment to do everything possible to deliver humane treatment to those who can benefit from it.

Until recently, there were few attempts to determine in any exact way whether the presence or absence of particular neurologic abnormalities influenced the patient's prognosis. Within the past decade, however, several groups of neurologists and neurosurgeons have instigated efforts to identify and quantify early indicants that might foretell outcome in patients with severe neurologic injury or disease. Although the individual approaches and ways of recording results have differed somewhat from one medical center to the next, many of the findings have been remarkably consistent. They indicate that within a few hours or days after the onset of coma many patients show neurologic signs that differentiate with a high degree of probability the future extremes of no improvement and the capacity for good recovery. As will be seen, for many diseases the presence or absence of certain clinical signs of neurologic damage turns out to be more important in predicting outcome than even the specific illness or injury that damages the brain.

Physicians and patients have traditionally recognized the grave prognosis implied by stupor or coma. Statistics verify the impression: Cullen reported that among 226 patients admitted to an intensive care center, 69 percent of those initially awake and responsive recovered by one year, while 54 percent of those in coma died within 1 month and only 12 percent recovered within 12 months.[12] Several neurosurgical centers report that of patients in coma caused by head injury, about 50 percent will die, even with the best of management.[26,38] Among 310 patients with nontraumatic coma (excluding those with depressant drug poisoning or unconscious from the effects of alcohol), Bates and associates found that 70 percent died or remained vegetative at the end of 1 month, while only 16 percent made a good recovery during that time.[4]

GRADING OUTCOME FROM COMA

Statistics such as the above are too coarse to guide individual patient management. That step requires finely sharpened guidelines that only now are beginning to emerge. This chapter reviews what others have written on the subject of efforts to predict outcome from coma and presents the current results of our own 500 patients in medical coma, studied in collaboration with other medical centers. The reader will find that until recently most studies provided little specific information about the kind of outcome enjoyed or suffered by their patients. As a result, except where specified, descriptions and recovery from coma often connote little more than survival and fail to tell one about the social, vocational, or emotional outcome, i.e., the human qualities of the life that followed.

Our own detailed studies on outcome from medical coma were carried out in close association with those on head injury by Professor Bryan Jennett of Glasgow and his collaborators in the United Kingdom, Holland, and the United States. As part of that effort, we early constructed definitions that would say fairly precisely what was meant by individual outcomes (Table 24).[24,40] Only a small number of outcomes were chosen in the hope that sufficient patients would fall into each class to allow statistical analysis, and yet important differences in medical and social recovery would not be excessively blurred. The classification has worked well, and where such information was supplied by earlier authors, we have applied it in this chapter to our descriptions of results published in the literature. At least for the analysis of outcome from medical coma, however, one shortcoming has emerged: the category of severe disability has turned out to be too broad. Since the class designates all patients who cannot function independently, it includes cripplings that range from demented tetraplegia at one extreme to mentally independent hemiplegia at the other. Future studies of prognosis would do well to subdivide the severe disability group so as to distinguish between those extremes.

PROGNOSIS BY DISEASE STATE

Head Injury

More effort has been directed at trying to predict outcome from head injury than from any other cause of coma. The explanation of this is that the problem is frequent, it predominantly affects young people, and it carries huge financial, social, and emotional stakes. Most available studies have concentrated on signs that predict a poor outcome versus survival, but the results of Jennett and his associates are beginning to identify guidelines that also anticipate which patients have the capacity to make a good functional recovery, as defined in Table 24.

Severe head injury characterized by a stable loss of consciousness lasting 6 hours or more, plus associated signs of brain injury, produces a heavy mortality. About half the patients in coma from head injury will die, and neurosurgeons disagree as to whether treatment influences this outcome and, if so, by how much.[5,26,38,45] Most of the mortality follows within hours or the first few days of the accident. According to Carlsson[9] 96 percent of deaths occur within 48 hours, and Heiskanen[20] gives only a

Table 24. Grades of Outcome from Coma

Good Recovery	Patients who regain the ability to conduct a normal life or, if a pre-existing disability exists, to resume the previous level of activity.
Moderate disability	Patients who achieve independence in daily living but retain either physical or mental limitations that preclude resuming their previous level of function.
Severe disability	Patients who regain at least some cognitive function but depend on others for daily support.
Vegetative state	Patients who awaken but give no sign of cognitive awareness.
No recovery	Patients who remain in coma until death.

moderately lower figure of 54 percent during that time. Even these numbers leave the precise outcome of many patients in doubt: a few surviving subjects will recover no cognitive brain function whatsoever, while others will survive only at the expense of severe neurologic and social disabilities. Still others eventually improve to function at or near the normal level. As will be seen, the age of patients and whether or not they have signs of brainstem dysfunction are the major factors at the outset that influence prognosis.

Age. Advanced age at onset unfavorably influences outcome in traumatic coma. Carlsson calculated that among patients who survived, those under age 20 years all "recovered," almost no matter what their duration of unconsciousness.[9] By contrast, fewer than half the patients older than 50 years returned to work if coma lasted more than 24 hours. Among 206 patients studied by Overgaard, 68 percent less than 10 years of age recovered, while only 30 percent over age 50 enjoyed a good outcome.[34] Jennett and associates give figures that tell an even sadder tale: in 600 patients with severe head injury causing coma, 56 percent of those less than age 20 made a moderate or good recovery.[25] The number fell to 39 percent when age rose to between 20 and 59 years and to a mere 5 percent among those older than 60 years. Becker and colleagues describe a similar experience: mortality among their 160 patients with severe head injury rose from 22 percent in subjects less than 20 years of age to about two thirds of those over age 60.[5] The last-mentioned recovery rate for young persons compares with that found by Pagni and associates: among 178 children less than 14 years old with severe head injury the mortality was 34 percent.[36]

Age-related mortality in head injury takes on more precision when plotted against signs indicating degree of neurologic injury. Table 25 summarizes information from four clinical series totalling 785 severe head injuries. Not all comparisons could be gleaned from each series, but it is evident that even when signs of brainstem dysfunction were absent, patients in older age groups did badly.

Duration of Unconsciousness. Although length of coma provides a good indication of severity of brain damage, it can be determined only retrospectively when the patient awakens and thus cannot be used to prognosticate (the same limitation applies to efforts to correlate outcome with the duration of posttraumatic amnesia). Figure 37 reproduces Carlsson's diagram of the effect of duration of coma on outcomes at different ages. Not surprisingly, the longer the coma the worse the outcome.

Neuroophthalmologic Signs. Absence of pupillary responses, oculocephalic responses, or both at the time of first examination or at any point thereafter indicates a poor outcome in traumatic coma. In Jennett's series, 95 percent of patients died who at 6 hours after onset of coma had either bilaterally nonreacting pupils or absent

DIAGNOSIS OF STUPOR AND COMA

oculocephalic responses.[26] If the pupils were fixed at 24 hours, 91 percent of 1000 patients died and only 4 percent made satisfactory recoveries. Overgaard's figures on the bad prognosis of abnormal neuroophthalmologic signs provide a similar inference.[34] Becker reported that when both pupils were fixed on admission, 85 percent of patients died or remained vegetative.[5] By contrast only 28 percent of patients had such a poor outcome when only one pupil was fixed. In Becker's series 73 percent of subjects with impaired or absent oculocephalic responses did badly, while only 19 percent of those with a normal oculocephalic response had an unfavorable course.

Motor Signs. Neurosurgeons have learned from long experience to make a rough judgment of the seriousness of injury by testing patients' motor responses to noxious stimulation. Statistics quantify the impression. Abnormal flexor (decorticate), abnormal extensor (decerebrate), or predominantly flaccid responses in patients with severe head injury denote a poor prognosis in every reported series. According to Jennett, by 6 hours after onset of coma, motor responses no better than abnormal flexor were associated with a mortality of 63 percent, while abnormal extensor or flaccid responses were linked with an 83 percent mortality.[26] Overgaard states that in patients over age 30 years, abnormal motor responses were 100 percent associated with death or a severe residual deficit.[34] Indeed, when such signs were present only 20 percent of even his younger patients recovered. In Pagni's adult series, 40 percent of patients with abnormal motor responses survived if neuroophthalmologic abnormalities were absent.[36] When abnormal eye signs joined the motor defects, only 7.8 percent lived, no matter what the age.

Table 25. Age, Early Defects, and Outcome from Coma in Severe Head Trauma

Author	Age (yr.) of Patients (and Number)	Mild Motor Defects No eye signs		Severe Motor Deficit No eye signs		Motor Deficit Plus eye signs	
		GR*	D/VS†	GR	D/VS	GR	D/VS
Overgaard[34]	<30 (139)	84%	6%	21%	45%	11%	86%
	>30 (62)	20%	44%	0%	95%		
Pagni[36]	2–14 (73)	83%	17%	50%	50%	40%	60%
Turazzi[56]	0–10 (29)						64%
	11–30 (89)						78%
	31–55 (68)						89%
	>55 (54)						92%
Pazzaglia[38]	<40 (139)	60%	18%			7%	90%
	>40 (132)	24%	56%				96%
TOTAL	785						

*GR = Good Recovery
†D/VS = Disability/Vegetative State

Combined Indicants. As noted, the presence after head injury of either abnormal motor signs (implying, at best, severe diencephalic dysfunction) or abnormal neuro-ophthalmologic signs (implying brainstem dysfunction) indicates that the subject has only a small chance of a good outcome. Furthermore, it matters little for prognosis whether such signs reflect brainstem damage that is directly due to the immediate trauma or is secondary to the effects of transtentorial herniation.[56] But in different reported series, the percentage of those who failed to recover at all, those who died, or those who were left permanently vegetative varies considerably when plotted against single indicants. Furthermore, except for Jennett and his collaborators,[26] no authors have attempted to identify early signs that predict good outcome, i.e., complete recovery or only moderate disability. Jennett and associates first pointed out that by using a simple Bayesian statistical method for combining indicants, one could predict with an accuracy of better than 95 percent between the extremes of death versus survival in many patients within the first 24 hours after injury. By combining indicants in patients who survived until 3 days, they could make confident (97 percent correct) predictions in about half the total, including a substantial number of those destined to make a moderate or good recovery.

Jennett and his coworkers have not yet published sufficient data to allow others to reconstruct their own conclusions, but one suspects that when age and duration of unresponsiveness are included with an appraisal of eye signs and motor function, the

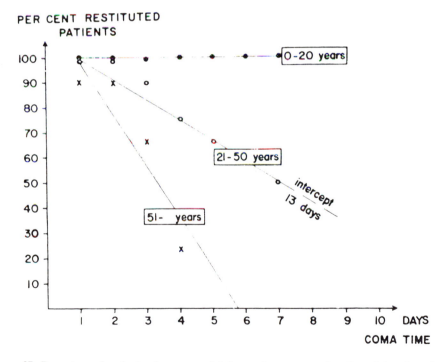

Figure 37. Percentage of patients who recovered full consciousness as a function of duration of coma. (From Carlsson, C.A., von Essen, C., and Löfgren, J.: *Factors affecting the clinical course of patients with severe head injuries.* J. Neurosurg. 29:242–251, 1968. Reprinted by permission of the Journal of Neurosurgery.)

combined data will accurately predict within a day or so of onset between recovery and no recovery for the majority of patients in coma from head injury. Perhaps it also will be possible to predict for most patients the specific degree of recovery within a few days after injury.

Laboratory Indicants. Most efforts to find single laboratory measures to predict the eventual degree of neurologic damage or outcome in traumatic coma have been useless. Appraisals of EEG patterns, of intracranial pressure, or of radiographic changes all have their advantages in diagnosing tissue injuries, guiding management, or diagnosing brain death, but they seldom contribute to one's capacity to predict outcome before clinical signs make conditions obvious. (A partial exception to this rule is CT scanning in the instance in which it detects intracerebral hematoma, a finding that adversely affects prognosis.[26]) Results of measurements of cerebral blood flow and metabolism, of acid-base changes in the CSF, or of other metabolites in the CSF have been too variable or reported in too small numbers of patients to provide helpful guidelines.

Recently, investigators have utilized cerebral evoked responses in an effort to predict eventual outcome and degree of neurologic damage in patients with head injury. Early results indicate that in at least some cases electrophysiologic changes may correlate with eventual outcome, and that changes in the wave forms can assist in the localization of hemispheric versus brainstem injury.[19] It requires more information to determine whether this complex and time-consuming approach will add a substantial or practical dimension to clinical appraisals based on the patient's signs, symptoms, and course of illness.

Coma Owing to Nontraumatic Causes

Depressant Drug Poisoning

Most fatal suicide attempts from depressant drug poisoning occur outside the hospital. Once such patients reach treatment, experienced centers all over the world generally report an overall mortality among patients with altered consciousness of about 1 percent. The death rate climbs to approximately 5 percent in those with grade 3 to 4 coma (p. 245). The mortality can be substantially higher when institutions treat only small numbers of cases and lack experience and proper facilities.[18] Adverse prognostic factors in depressant drug coma include an advanced age of the patient, the presence of complicating medical illnesses (especially systemic infections, hepatic insufficiency, and heart failure), and a lengthy coma. Alkaline diuresis (for phenobarbital), hemodialysis, and charcoal hemoperfusion all have been reported to shorten coma and improve prognosis for patients with severe poisoning, especially from phenobarbital and glutethimide.[60] No controlled figures support these claims, however, and some institutions report equally good results with conventional intensive care as described in Chapter 8.

Barring unexpected complications, patients recovering from depressant drug poisoning suffer no residual brain damage even after prolonged coma lasting 5 days or more. Rare exceptions to this rule occur in poisoned patients who suffer cardiac arrest, e.g., during tracheal or gastric intubation. A small number of poisoned subjects develop cutaneous pressure sores or pressure neuropathies from prolonged periods of immobility. Such compressions often occur during the period of immobile coma before the victim is found and brought to hospital.

Cardiac Arrest

Coma is relatively uncommon when hospitalized patients develop cardiac arrest in intensive care units and are resuscitated.[6] The incidence of at least temporary brain dysfunction rises among patients in whom prolonged asystole occurs on the general units of hospitals, and coma is frequent after out-of-hospital cardiac resuscitations by passersby or ambulance personnel.[52] Available information indicates that fewer than 40 percent of patients who are in coma for as long as 12 hours following cardiac arrest make a functional recovery.[6,15,16,52,59] Furthermore, neurologic recovery is particularly in doubt during the early postarrest period when important management decisions must be made.

Neurologists have correlated outcome following cardiac arrest with the following indicants: duration of anoxia,[6,50] duration of postanoxic coma,[4,16,52,61] changes in the EEG,[6,41] the pattern of motor response to stimulation,[3,16,59] the presence or absence of brainstem reflexes,[1,4,15,16,52] levels of cerebral blood flow and oxygen metabolism,[57] and CSF acid-base and electrolyte changes.[28]

The circumstances of resuscitation are such that one rarely knows accurately the duration of anoxia-ischemia or circulatory arrest after cardiac arrest. Furthermore, even the meanings of the terms "cardiac" and "circulatory arrest" are confused. Circulatory arrest is defined as that interval between the onset of cardiac arrest and the initiation of cardiac massage, but does not allow for individual variations in the effectiveness of resuscitative efforts.

The duration of postresuscitation coma is a more certain and useful prognostic indicant. Bokonjic and Buchthal reported that 90 percent of patients in coma less than 48 hours made a complete recovery.[8] Other medical programs have had less cheering experiences. Snyder and associates found that 78 percent of patients who improved awakened within 10 hours and 90 percent by 24 hours.[52] Several observers have noted that persistence of unresponsive coma for 48 hours after cardiac arrest uncomplicated by recurrences or deep sedative therapy has been associated with almost certain death or vegetative survival.[61]

Willoughby and Leach evaluated the motor response to a noxious stimulus at 1 hour after cardiac arrest as a predictor of outcome in 48 cases.[59] They reported that no response or merely stereotyped reflex responses indicated a generally poor prognosis. Withdrawal from the stimulus or a localizing motor response correlated well with neurologic recovery. Subsequent observations, however, reveal these conclusions to be too pessimistic. Bates and coworkers noted that when motor response poorer than withdrawal persisted for as long as 6 hours following resuscitation, 4 percent of patients still made a good recovery.[4] Similarly, Finklestein and Caronna reported that even after 12 hours, abnormal flexor or extensor responses did not reliably predict outcome, although their presence at 24 hours indicated an outcome no better than death or the vegetative state.[16]

Several studies report that impaired brainstem or spinal reflexes overwhelmingly point to a poor prognosis following cardiorespiratory arrest. Absence of the pupillary reflexes, the corneal reflexes, the oculovestibular reflexes or the deep tendon reflexes at 12 hours has correlated with a high probability of an outcome of death or vegetative survival in every study reporting on the state of these variables. Even at 6 hours or less after cardiac arrest, Bates and colleagues found that the combination of nonreactive pupils or absent corneal responses with absent oculovestibular reflexes predicted death or overwhelming disability.[4] Earnest and associates reached similar conclusions based on examination at the time of admission to an intensive care unit.[15] By contrast, when patients had intact pupils, preserved oculocephalic responses, and preserved motor responses on admission, 87 percent recovered a high quality of brain function.

Cerebral Vascular Disease

The presence of any degree of altered consciousness substantially reduces the chance of a good outcome of patients with acute stroke. Among Marquardsen's 769 patients, less than 1 percent of those admitted in unresponsive coma survived beyond 5 days, and even among those who were merely drowsy, 71 percent died within 3 weeks.[31] These poor results reflect a high proportion of acute cerebral hemorrhage. Among the 153 patients who came to autopsy examination, 75 percent of those in coma had intracranial bleeding, while among the somnolent group 40 percent had primary brain hemorrhages. Absent pupillary light reflexes invariably predicted a fatal issue. Paralysis of conjugate ocular gaze reduced chances of survival. Bilateral extensor plantar responses, severe motor paralysis, or periodic breathing all unfavorably influenced prognosis, even among awake subjects.

Obtundation, stupor, or coma with ischemic stroke predicts an outcome almost equally as poor as the above. Carter reported that among 95 patients with cerebral infarction in coma for less than 24 hours, 44 percent died within 4 weeks.[10] More longlasting unresponsiveness continuing up to 48 hours led to a mortality of 86 percent, and when over 48 hours led to a mortality of 95 percent. Cooper and associates[11] gave similar figures, while Jones and Millikan[27] noted that in carotid stroke the addition of altered consciousness to hemiplegia increased mortality from 2 to 41 percent. Oxbury, Greenhall, and Grainger found that any alteration in consciousness with ischemic stroke predicted at least a 30 percent mortality and the death rate climbed as coma deepened.[35]

The neurologic causes of death in those who die acutely from ischemic stroke consist of either acute primary damage to the brainstem as a consequence of basilar artery occlusion or of brain shift and transtentorial herniation secondary to necrotic swelling and edema of the affected cerebral hemisphere.[51] Clinically, impaired consciousness, dense hemiplegia, and conjugate gaze paralysis toward the side of the paralyzed limb each and all correlate with extensive hemispheric infarction and the likelihood of fatal brain edema.

Several years ago we noted in a large study of patients with acute, massive infarcts of the cerebral hemispheres that more than one fifth developed altered consciousness and the characteristic clinical picture of progressive rostral-caudal diencephalic and brainstem dysfunction.[39] Patients who subsequently recovered stopped their neurologic progression at the diencephalic level and then improved. Those who died developed characteristic signs of progressively impaired midbrain and lower brainstem functions. No patients with hemispheric stroke recovered who developed fixed, irregular pupils or other signs of midbrain damage.

Prognosis in cerebral hemorrhage is generally worse than with cerebral infarction. The advent of CT scanning, however, has demonstrated that many patients with small cerebral hemorrhages never develop an alteration of consciousness and most such patients enjoy good neurologic outcomes. With larger intraparenchymal hemorrhages, the prognosis is directly related to the initial impairment of consciousness and to the size of the hematoma as evaluated by CT scanning. Hier and colleagues reported that all their patients in coma at the time of admission had large hemorrhages and died within the first week.[21] Awake patients showing at least some form of voluntary motor function on the affected side lived and experienced a fairly satisfactory outcome. Bates and associates found a somewhat better outcome among 47 patients in coma from cerebral hemorrhage; 6 recovered consciousness, of whom 3 attained an independent existence.[4]

Extensive studies have been made on changes in acid-base determinants and various other metabolites in blood and CSF in patients with acute cerebrovascular diseases, including spontaneous or traumatic subarachnoid hemorrhage. Red cell glycolysis following brain trauma or hemorrhage produces a lactic acidosis in the CSF that may correlate with the degree of respiratory alkalosis in the blood, but the results have been too selective and inconsistent to be helpful in indicating prognosis. Rout and coworkers reported that patients with stroke showing a $PaCO_2$ of less than 35 mm. Hg had a 70 percent mortality.[47] Fujishima and associates found that among CSF changes in patients with intracranial hemorrhage, a lactate concentration greater than 2.5 mM. per liter, a lactate/pyruvate ratio of greater than 20, a bicarbonate level of less than 21 mEq. per liter, a pH below 7.28, or a PCO_2 less than 32 mm. Hg, each indicated a poor prognosis.[17] However, the specificity of these acid-base findings is doubtful. Mazzara and colleagues reported that in hospital patients suffering from a variety of serious illnesses the degree of hyperventilation and hypocapnia directly correlated with a poor outcome, but noted that respiratory alkalosis affects many critically ill patients with or without neurologic disease.[32] Such overbreathing reflects mainly the severity of the underlying systemic disease and its pulmonary complications rather than any specific neurologic deficit.

Subarachnoid Hemorrhage

Spontaneous subarachnoid hemorrhage, (SAH) carries a high risk: reported overall mortality from an initial subarachnoid hemorrhage ranges from 14 to 43 percent.[37,55] According to Locksley 40 percent of deaths from subarachnoid hemorrhage occur in the first 7 days; 67 percent by 21 days.[30] The chance for 1-year survival of a patient who is alert at the time when angiography is performed is 60 percent, and the chance of this patient making a reasonable recovery is 45 percent. Level of consciousness is of major importance in anticipating outcome from subarachnoid hemorrhage. According to Richardson the mortality in the first 6 months is 29 percent for alert patients, 55 percent for drowsy patients, 71 percent for stuporous patients, and 90 percent for patients in coma.[43] Age is important: young and alert patients have a mortality one third that of elderly, drowsy patients.[33] Vascular spasm (by arteriographic criteria), hypertension, and an aneurysm greater than 9 mm. in diameter all increase the mortality risk.[43] The site of aneurysm appears not to be a major factor unless it either arises on the basilar or vertebral system or multiple aneurysms are present, both of which factors worsen the outcome. Patients who are obtunded and have lateralizing neurologic deficits but no intracerebral mass lesions have a high mortality that is apparently unaffected by surgical therapy.[2]

Intraocular, subhyaloid hemorrhages occur in approximately 20 percent of patients with subarachnoid hemorrhage and worsen the prognosis. Mortality in patients with SAH and subhyaloid hemorrhages is 50 to 60 percent and even higher when the hemorrhages are bilateral. The evidence suggests that the presence of subhyaloid hemorrhages relates directly to the severity of the intracranial bleeding and the concomitant elevation of the intracranial pressure.[58]

Central Nervous System Infection

Altered states of consciousness consisting of drowsiness, confusion, or delirious reactions are so common in bacterial meningitis that they usually attract little detailed discussion in summaries of large series of patients. Deep stupor or coma is cited as carrying mortalities of 50 percent or higher,[3,14] but writers on the subject usually give more attention to the attendant virulence of the infecting organism or to delays in beginning effective treatment than to neurologic details. The slant is understandable, but makes it impossible to offer precise information about prognosis based on neurologic signs. Increasing age of the patient, the presence of debilitating associated disease, a low spinal fluid sugar, and the development of seizures all worsen the outcome in meningitis, but accurate statistics are lacking. Correlations between altered states of consciousness, the presence of other neurologic abnormalities, and outcome are equally difficult to deduce from published reports on fungal and viral infections of the nervous system.

Hepatic Coma

Hepatic coma develops either as an inexorable stage in progressive hepatic failure, or as a more reversible process in patients with portal systemic shunts when increased loads of nitrogenous substances are suddenly presented to their circulations (see Schenker and associates[49] for a review). Prognosis in hepatic coma depends on the cause, the acuteness and severity of the liver failure, and the presence or absence of dysfunction of other organs.[42,44,54]

The cause of hepatic coma importantly influences the outcome, prognosis being far worse in fulminant hepatic failure than in coma associated with chronic cirrhosis or portacaval shunting. Survival also correlates with age in infectious and serum hepatitis. With the latter illness, Trey reported a 22 percent survival in patients under 45 years of age, but only a 5 percent survival in those over 45 years of age.[44] Only 18 percent of patients in deep coma survived. As might be expected, recovery from coma also depends on the extent of liver damage. Biopsy specimens from 30 patients in coma with acute hepatic failure caused by viral hepatitis revealed massive liver-cell necrosis in 19 fatal cases, and only moderate changes in survivors.[13]

The prognosis is less discouraging in coma with chronic liver disease. Prytz and Sloth reported that in 100 cases of hepatic coma among 61 patients with cirrhosis, survival after the first episode of coma was 55 percent at 1 month, 20 percent at 1 year, and 10 percent at 4 years.[42] A fatal outcome was associated with a higher frequency of ascites, edema, prolonged prothrombin time, depressed renal function, abnormal electrolytes, and age over 60 years. Quality of survival was not discussed.

Few studies of patients with severe hepatic encephalopathy provide sufficient neurologic details to allow a correlation between early neurologic signs and outcome. Dilated reactive pupils, brisk deep tendon reflexes, ankle clonus, and extensor plantar responses occur frequently in patients in coma from hepatic insufficiency; in our experience none of these changes are incompatible with survival. The presence of decerebrate posturing similarly does not rule out potential recovery.

Bates and associates found sharp differences between the outcome of patients in coma associated with chronic portacaval encephalopathy and those with acute hepatic failure caused by virus or acetaminophen intoxication. None of the comatose patients with acute hepatitis survived, while 22 of 48 patients in coma secondary to subacute or chronic hepatic disease made a moderate or good recovery. Neither abnormal motor responses to stimulation nor coma lasting over 3 days ruled out a good recovery in this latter group. Absent pupillary responses or, especially, disappearance of oculovestibular responses, however, nearly always was associated with subsequent death.

PROSPECTIVE ANALYSIS OF OUTCOME FROM NONTRAUMATIC COMA

With the exception of Jennett's figures in traumatic coma and Bates' initial report on 310 patients with medical coma, the prognostic correlations given in the preceding sections of this chapter all suffer limitations that hinder their practical use. Most were gleaned retrospectively from patients' charts, exposing them to the potential flaws of omission of observations and the inconsistencies of inexperienced examiners. Many of the reports describe too few patients to allow one comfortably to conclude that the findings are applicable to a larger severely ill universe. Most of the studies correlate outcome with either a single set of observations made acutely or, at best, a few examinations conducted over a very few days. Furthermore, only a few studies attempt to quantify outcome as to degree of residual physical, psychologic, or occupational disability. None of the analyses compare outcomes among different diseases causing coma or determine whether signs anticipating a good or bad result take their predictive strength from the nature of the illness they accompany or from the extent of the acute neurologic dysfunction that reflect.

To remedy the above limitations we initiated at The New York Hospital in the late 1960s prospective studies of the outcome from coma as caused by medical disorders. Fortunately other neurologists shared our interests, so that we collaborated with colleagues at the Royal Victoria Hospital, Newcastle-upon-Tyne, United Kingdom, and, subsequently, at the San Francisco General Hospital in order to evaluate a full 500 patients in acute coma from medical illnesses. Data from all the patients were entered initially on the University of Glasgow computer, and the early statistical analyses were conducted largely by Dr. Robin Knill-Jones at Glasgow using approaches developed in association with Professor Bryan Jennett for the head injury studies. Patients with head trauma or any form of exogenous intoxication were excluded from the medical coma study, but otherwise persons at the several hospitals over age 12 years and in acute coma were identified and repeatedly examined at frequent intervals. Meticulous efforts were made to see every patient in coma at the several institutions over a several-year period and to adopt examining techniques that guaranteed consistency in the observations. To avoid any bias in the way that patients in the study were treated, the examiners refrained from either making recommendations for therapy or disclosing preliminary results to the various treatment staffs. All the patients were followed for a minimum of 12 months (unless death came first) and many for much longer. (Only 2 of the 500 patients were lost to follow-up.) The large population provided data on substantial numbers of individuals in all the major disease categories, permitting one to make correlations between outcome and both the severity of early signs of neurologic dysfunction as well as the nature of the illness.

A neurologic profile similar to that described in Chapter 8 was employed to evaluate these patients. Coma was defined as continuous, unarousable, eyes-closed unconsciousness with the patient giving no response to verbal stimulation and no localizing or appropriately resisting motor responses. In order to eliminate transient

335

and benign unconsciousness from self-limited disorders, patients were admitted to the study only if their state of unresponsiveness lasted at least 6 hours. Their outcomes were defined as indicated in Table 24.

Since the main purpose of the study was to determine how neurologic factors affected outcome (as opposed to the influence of the underlying systemic illness or of systemic complications), the results were described by the patient's *best neurologic outcome* as the end-point after coma, a grading that most accurately reflected the neurologic capacity for recovery. As one might expect, *actual outcome* from the illness in many instances was worse than this best neurologic state, since some patients who temporarily recovered neurologically died from complicating conditions, such as recurrent cardiac arrhythmias, infections, and pulmonary infarction.

The results of the medical coma study reaffirm that loss of consciousness lasting 6 hours or more bestows a bad prognosis. Of the 500 patients, 379 (76 percent) were dead within the first month and 88 percent by the end of a year. Three quarters of those dying by 1 month never regained consciousness, and within that month, only 15 percent of the entire 500 made a neurologically satisfactory recovery (i.e., achieved the level of moderate disability or good recovery).

Table 26 charts the *best* 1-month recovery of these patients by disease state. Some of the patients died during that first month of nonneurologic causes, but the table is constructed so as to indicate the highest possible chance of recovery by the brain.

The presence of coma, while always a serious sign, implies in some diseases a less grave outcome than in others. About 30 percent of the patients with hepatic and miscellaneous causes of coma did well, three times the recovery rate of patients with vascular-ischemic neurologic injuries (subarachnoid hemorrhage, cerebral vascular diseases, and hypoxia-ischemia). The best explanation for this difference is that most of the hepatic-miscellaneous patients had reversible biochemical, infectious, or extracerebral intracranial (e.g., subdural hematoma) lesions that may have transiently depressed the brain centers regulating consciousness and cognition, but nevertheless left the structure of those centers intact. By contrast, many of the patients with stroke and ischemia suffered direct destruction to these crucial regions. Reflecting this difference, a detailed analysis disclosed that the metabolic-miscellaneous group of pa-

Table 26. Best One-Month Outcome Related to Cause of Coma

Cause of Coma (n)*	Best One-Month Outcome (%)				
	No Recov.	Veg. State	Sev. Disab.	Mod. Disab.	Good Recov.
All Patients (500)	61	12	12	5	10
Subarachnoid Hemorrhage (38)	74	5	13	5	3
Other Cerebrovascular Disease (143)	74	7	11	4	4
Hypoxia-Ischemia (210)	58	20	11	3	8
Hepatic Encephalopathy (51)	49	2	16	10	23
Miscellaneous (58)	45	10	14	5	26

*Hypoxia-ischemia includes 150 patients with cardiac arrest, 38 with profound hypotension, and 22 with respiratory arrest. Other cerebrovascular diseases include 76 with brain infarcts and 67 with brain hemorrhage. Miscellaneous includes 19 patients with mixed metabolic disturbances, 16 with infection, 11 with reversible coma owing to mass lesions, and 12 with isolated disorders such as hypoglycemia.

tients throughout their illness showed significantly fewer signs of severe brainstem dysfunction than did those with vascular-ischemic disorders (Table 27). As an example, corneal responses were absent in less than 20 percent of the metabolic group, but in more than 30 percent of the remaining patients. Furthermore, when patients with hepatic-miscellaneous causes of coma *did* show abnormal neuroophthalmologic signs (see below), their prognosis was equally as poor as that of patients in the other disease groups with similar signs.

Patients who survived medical coma by and large made most of their improvement by the end of the first month. Among the 121 patients still living at that time, 61 died within the next year, usually from a progression or complication of the illness that caused coma in the first place. There were 7 moderately disabled patients who improved to a good recovery. Of 39 patients severely disabled at 1 month, 9 later improved to a good recovery or moderate disability rating. At the end of the year, three patients remained vegetative and four severely disabled.

Since the composition of age, sex, and disease states causing coma was similar in the patients treated in the United States and the United Kingdom, the study provided some interesting contrasts of medical practice and its effect on outcome between the two countries. A detailed analysis of the first 310 patients revealed that three times as many laboratory tests (e.g., EEGs, angiograms, CT scans) were performed on the patients in the U.S. as in the U.K., and procedures such as artificial ventilation, the use of corticosteroid hormones, and the application of neurosurgical treatment (e.g., to evacuate cerebral hemorrhage) were far more frequently applied in the U.S. than in the U.K.[4] The most visible effect of these increased diagnostic and therapeutic efforts was that of the timing of the total deaths at 1 month: 71 percent occurred within the first 3 days in the U.K., but only 46 percent within this time in the U.S. By the end of the month, however, the proportional number of deaths was similar in the two countries, being 77 percent of 152 patients in New York and 80 percent of 156 patients in Newcastle-upon-Tyne.

A bad outcome in medical coma correlated most strongly with the duration of the unconscious state and the presence of abnormal neuroophthalmologic abnormalities

Table 27. Independent One-Month Outcome Related to Neurologic Responses at Admission and Cause of Coma

Absent Neurologic Response	Percentage (Actual Number) of Patients Achieving Moderate Disability or Good Recovery with Coma Caused by:				
	HI*	SAH*	CVD*	HEP*	OTHER
Verbal	11 (82)	7 (30)	6 (103)	23 (30)	28 (25)
Eye Opening	10 (185)	3 (33)	7 (111)	36 (31)	24 (37)
Pupillary Reaction	0 (52)	0 (17)	4 (55)	0 (2)	0 (8)
Spontaneous Eye Movements	6 (140)	4 (24)	5 (55)	45 (11)	17 (23)
Oculocephalic	7 (83)	0 (18)	2 (51)	50 (2)	0 (12)
Oculovestibular	5 (56)	0 (17)	2 (41)	0 (2)	0 (6)
Corneal	4 (71)	0 (12)	4 (48)	0 (5)	12 (8)
Motor	4 (102)	0 (9)	6 (32)	20 (5)	21 (14)
Deep Tendon Reflexes	3 (63)	0 (10)	10 (21)	14 (7)	33 (15)
Skeletal Muscle Tone	9 (124)	6 (16)	5 (39)	20 (10)	14 (21)

*HI = Hypoxia-Ischemia; SAH = Subarachnoid Hemorrhage; CVD = Cerebral Vascular Disease; HEP = Hepatic Coma.

at the outset. Thus, only one patient who remained in coma for a week made a good recovery within a month. Conversely, the earlier consciousness returned the better was the outcome. Among patients who awakened and regained their mental faculties within 1 day, nearly half did well (i.e., achieved a moderate disability or good recovery), compared with only 14 percent among those who at 1 day remained vegetative or in coma. Among patients who survived 3 days, 60 percent who were awake and talked made a satisfactory recovery within the first month, compared with only 5 percent of those still vegetative or in coma. Furthermore, patients who improved from day to day, even if they started at a low level, did better than patients whose condition remained stable during the first few days. Contrary to initial expectations, no consistent relationship emerged between age and prognosis either for the study as a whole or for individual illnesses. The sex of the patient had no apparent influence on outcome.

Coma of 6 hours or more turned out to be such an innately serious state that in most cases it became difficult to predict accurately who would do well (i.e., make a moderate or good recovery) much before the third day of illness. By contrast about one third of patients destined to do badly showed overwhelmingly strong indications of that outcome on admission and for the next several days.

As Table 28 indicates, abnormal neuroophthalmologic signs, at first in combination and after 3 days singly, indicated a poor or hopeless prognosis. The presence of normal eye signs on the other hand already indicated by the end of the first day a 38 percent chance of satisfactory recovery, and the association became stronger and was joined by other even more favorable indicants thereafter.

Given the above associations, how is one to act on them? This is for the physician, his patient, and the patient's family to decide. Knowledge that a patient who has been in coma for 6 hours from a known nonpharmacologic cause and with abnormal neuroophthalmologic signs has essentially no chance of making a satisfactory recovery will deter many physicians from applying heroic and extraordinary measures of care. (Nevertheless such patients may be candidates for well-controlled new or unconventional treatments, since conventional therapy offers such a dismal outcome.) Conversely, the recognition that a seriously ill and still unresponsive patient who shows normal eye or motor signs at 1 to 3 days has about a 50 percent chance of making a good neurologic recovery should provide strong encouragement to intensive care staffs. The latter individuals often feel they are working blindly and with little chance of success when caring for the severely brain damaged, and knowledge of a potentially favorable outcome greatly improves morale and the associated level of care.

PROGNOSIS IN THE VEGETATIVE STATE

Long-term survival in the vegetative condition is uncommon and affects only 1 to 2 percent of all patients in coma from either head injury or severe medical illness.[26,29] Nevertheless, this still can represent a substantial problem in individual chronic patient care. Sato and associates estimated in a recent epidemiologic study that Japan, with a population of 100 million, had 2000 to 3000 permanently vegetative patients requiring care.[48] A major question posed by physicians is just when such a hopeless condition can be predicted confidently and whether one can identify neurologic signs that point to such an outcome early enough and accurately enough to avoid prolonging inappropriately intensive treatment.

Some details about these patients may describe more clearly the pattern of their course of illness and the factors that influence their prognosis.

Our own studies indicate that signs predicting a future vegetative state with high probability are difficult or impossible to identify during the very first days after onset of coma. The explanation of this limitation lies in the pathologic basis of the vegetative state, which usually consists of badly damaged cerebral hemispheres combined with a relatively intact brainstem. Such a combination during the early days of illness yields impaired consciousness, often accompanied by signs of relatively good brainstem function; a similar initial picture occurs in patients with only functional and reversible cerebral injury. A permanently damaged cortex shows its irreversible losses only as the convalescent days blend into weeks. Under the circumstances, the

Table 28. Best One-Month Outcome in Medical Coma vs. Early Neurologic Signs

Time (and Number) of Subjects in Categories	Number (and Percentage) of Patients Making Poor Outcome, i.e., No Recovery or Vegetative State	Number (and Percentage) of Patients Making Good Outcome, i.e., Moderate Disability or Good Recovery
Admission		
a. All patients (500)	365 (73)	75 (15)
b. Any two absent: corneals, pupils, OC-OV (119)	117 (98)	1 (0.8)*
c. Remaining patients (381)	250 (66)	71 (19)
One day		
a. Surviving patients (387)	256 (66)	74 (19)
b. Any two absent: corneals, pupils, OV-OC, motor (86)	85 (99)	1 (1)*
c. OC or OV normal, or roving eye movements, or orienting eye movements (159)	64 (40)	58 (36)
d. Comprehensible words (25)		15 (60)
e. Voluntary motor responses (40)		20 (50)
Three days		
a. Surviving patients (261)	135 (52)	71 (27)
b. Absence of any: corneals, pupils, OV-OC, spontaneous eye movements (63)	61 (97)	0 (0)
c. Presence of any of the following: (106)		
Comprehensible words (68)	1 (2)	47 (69)
Obeys commands (55)	0	36 (65)
Orienting eye movements (69)	3 (4)	48 (70)
Normal OC or OV (64)	5 (8)	43 (67)
Localizing motor response (93)	3 (3)	56 (60)
Seven days		
a. Surviving patients (179)	62 (35)	63 (35)
b. Absence of any: corneals, pupils, OC-OV, spontaneous eye movements, motor response (24)	20 (83)	0 (0)
c. Presence of any of the following: (111)		
Comprehensible words (86)	0	62 (72)
Obeys commands (74)	0	49 (66)
Orienting eye movements (84)	3 (4)	59 (70)
Normal OC or OV (70)	4 (5.7)	60 (86)
Localizing Motor Response (100)	3 (3)	66 (66)

*This patient died within a month.

evolution of clinical changes after the first week has more prognostic value than specific neurologic signs observed during the first few days.

One cannot construct highly accurate prognoses on vegetative patients with intact brainstem function much before the end of the second week after onset of coma. This is illustrated by our experience. Among 45 patients who were vegetative at the end of 1 week, 13 later awakened and 5 had satisfactory outcomes. Even after being vegetative for close to 2 weeks, eight patients awakened and one recovered to the level of a moderate disability, his chief difficulty being intellectual losses that precluded his return to work. For patients who remained vegetative after 2 weeks, however, the prognosis became uniformly poor. Twenty-four such individuals survived to 1 month and of them only five were alive at the end of a year. Three remained permanently vegetative; the other two had overwhelming neurologic limitations as well as incapacitating mental impairments.

Reports from other authors generally indicate a similarly poor outlook for patients still vegetative at 1 month. Higashi and colleagues report following 110 chronically vegetative subjects. Only 3 percent of the patients recovered and survived for 3 years, and none were able "to resume activity as a social human being." Most other reports describe only small numbers of patients. Jacobson reported on five patients with protracted "unconsciousness" after head injury.[23] Though reconstruction of the details is incomplete, three seem to have been in the vegetative state after 1 month and two later recovered speech. One had a vocabulary of 10 words, the other was able to verbalize requests, but was wheelchair bound, aggressive, and dependent upon others for support.

Word-of-mouth stories or news reports crop up from time to time claiming dramatic recovery from prolonged coma or a vegetative state. Seldom do these reports provide enough detail to evaluate the biologic accuracy of the event, and we have seen little to confirm any such remarkable recoveries from coma caused by organic brain disease. Only one reasonably well-documented report of such a recovery has appeared in medical sources.[46] The patient was a 43-year-old man who remained vegetative after an anoxic-ischemic injury for approximately 1 to 1½ years. He neither opened his eyes nor had motor responses to noxious stimuli for 6 months. He then awakened and remained vegetative for another year, after which time he began to speak and follow commands. After 2 years he scored 100 on the verbal section of the Weschsler Adult Intelligence Scale (the precoma IQ was not given), but even then the man was paralyzed in three extremities and totally dependent.

REFERENCES

1. ALLEN, N.: *Life or death of the brain after cardiac arrest.* Neurology 27:805–806, 1977.

2. BAILEY, W.L., AND LOESER, J.D.: *Intracranial aneurysms.* J.A.M.A. 216:1993–1996, 1971.

3. BAIRD, D.R., GREENWOOD, B.M., AND WHITTLE, H.C.: *Mortality from pneumococcal meningitis.* Lancet 2:1344–1346, 1976.

4. BATES, D., CARONNA, J.J., CARTLIDGE, N.E.F., ET AL.: *A prospective study of non-traumatic coma: methods and results in 310 patients.* Ann. Neurol. 2:211–220, 1977.

5. BECKER, D.P., MILLER, J.D., WARD, J.D., ET AL.: *The outcome from severe head injury with early diagnosis and intensive management.* J. Neurosurg. 47:491–502, 1977.

6. BELL, J.A., AND HODGSON, H.J.F.: *Coma after cardiac arrest.* Brain 97:361–372, 1974.

7. BINNIE, C.D., PRIOR, P.F., LLOYD, D.S.L., ET AL.: *Electroencephalographic prediction of fatal anoxic brain damage after resuscitation cardiac arrest.* Br. Med. J. 4:265–268, 1970.

8. BOKONJIC, N., AND BUCHTAL, F.: "Post anoxic unconsciousness as related to clinical and EEG recovery in stagnant anoxia and carbon monoxide poisoning." In Meyer, J.S., and Gastaut, H. (eds.):

Cerebral Anoxia and the Electroencephalogram. Charles C Thomas, Springfield, Ill., 1961, pp. 118-127.

9. CARLSSON, C.A., VON ESSEN, C., AND LOFGREN, J.: *Factors affecting the clinical course of patients with severe head injuries. Part 1. Influence of biological factors. Part 2. Significance of posttraumatic coma.* J. Neurosurg. 29:242-251, 1968.

10. CARTER, A.B.: *Cerebral infarction.* New York, MacMillan Company, 1964.

11. COOPER, E.S., IPSEN, J., AND BROWN, H.D.: *Determining factors in the prognosis of stroke.* Geriatrics 18:3-9, 1963.

12. CULLEN, D.J.: *Results and costs of intensive care.* Anesthesiology 17:203-216, 1977.

13. DEMEDTS, M., DEGROOTE, J., VANDAMME, B., ET AL.: *Discriminative and prognostic signs in acute hepatic coma, treated by exchange transfusions.* Digestion 11:105-114, 1974.

14. DODGE, P.R., AND SWARTZ, M.N.: *Bacterial meningitis—a review of selected aspects. II. Special neurologic problems, postmeningitis complications and clinicopathological correlations.* N. Eng. J. Med. 272:954-960, 1003-1010, 1965.

15. EARNEST, M.P., BRECKINRIDGE, J.C., YARNELL, P.R., ET AL.: *Quality of survival after out-of-hospital cardiac arrest: predictive value of early neurologic evaluation.* Neurology 29:56-60, 1979.

16. FINKELSTEIN, S., AND CARONNA, J.J.: *Outcome of coma following cardiac arrest.* Neurology 27:367-368, 1977.

17. FUJISHIMA, M., SUGI, T., CHOKI, J., ET AL.: *Cerebrospinal fluid and arterial lactate, pyruvate and acid-base balance in patients with intracranial hemorrhages.* Stroke 6:707-714, 1975.

18. GHODSE, A.H.: *Deliberate self poisoning: a study in London casualty departments.* Br. Med. J. 1:805-808, 1977.

19. GREENBERG, R.P., BECKER, D.P., MILLER, J.D., ET AL.: *Evaluation of brain function in severe human head trauma with multimodality evoked potentials. Part 2. Localization of brain dysfunction and correlation with post-traumatic neurological conditions.* J. Neurosurg. 47:163-177, 1977.

20. HEISKANEN, Q.: *Cerebral circulatory arrest caused by acute increase of intracranial pressure.* Acta Neurol. Scand. (suppl. 7) 40:1964.

21. HIER, D.B., DAVIS, K.R., RICHARDSON, E.P., ET AL.: *Hypertensive putaminal hemorrhage.* Ann. Neurol. 1:152-159, 1977.

22. HIGASHI, K., SAKATA, Y., HATANO, M., ET AL.: *Epidemiological studies on patients with a persistent vegetative state.* J. Neurol. Neurosurg. Psychiatry 40:876-885, 1977.

23. JACOBSON, S.A.: *Protracted unconsciousness due to closed head injury.* Neurology 6:281-287, 1956.

24. JENNETT, B., AND BOND, M.: *Assessment of outcome after severe brain damage. A practical scale.* Lancet 1:480-484, 1975.

25. JENNETT, B., TEASDALE, G., BRAAKMAN, R., ET AL.: *Predicting outcome in individual patients after severe head injury.* Lancet 1:1031-1034, 1976.

26. JENNETT, B., TEASDALE, G., BRAAKMAN, R., ET AL.: *Prognosis of patients with severe head injury.* Neurosurgery, 4:283-288, 1979.

27. JONES, H.R., AND MILLIKAN, C.H.: *Temporal profile (clinical course) of acute carotid system cerebral infarction.* Stroke 7:64-71, 1976.

28. KALIN, E.M., TWEED, W.A., LEE, J., ET AL.: *Cerebrospinal fluid acid-base and electrolyte changes resulting from cerebral anoxia in man.* N. Eng. J. Med. 20:1013-1016, 1975.

29. LEVY, D.E., KNILL-JONES, R.P., AND PLUM, F.: *The vegetative state and its prognosis following non-traumatic coma.* Ann. N.Y. Acad. Sci. 315:293-306, 1978.

30. LOCKSLEY, H.B.: *Natural history of subarachnoid hemorrhage, intracranial aneurysms and arteriovenous malformations. Based on 6,368 in the cooperative study.* J. Neurosurg. 25:219-239, 321-368, 1966.

31. MARQUARDSEN, J.: *The natural history of acute cerebrovascular disease.* Acta Neurol. Scand. 45:(suppl. 38) 1-192, 1969.

32. MAZZARA, J.T., AYRES, S.M., AND GRACE, W.J.: *Extreme hypocapnia in the critically ill patient.* Am. J. Med. 56:450-456, 1974.

33. McKISSOCK, W., RICHARDSON, A., AND WALSH, L.: *Posterior communicating aneurysms: a controlled trial of the conservative and surgical treatment of ruptured aneurysms of the internal carotid artery at or near the point of origin of the posterior communicating artery.* Lancet 1:1203-1206, 1960.

341

34. OVERGAARD, J., CHRISTENSEN, S., HVID-HANSEN, O., ET AL.: *Prognosis after head injury based on early clinical examination.* Lancet 2:631–635, 1973.

35. OXBURY, J.M., GREENHALL, R.C.D., AND GRAINGER, K.M.R.: *Predicting the outcome of stroke: acute stage after cerebral infarction.* Br. Med. J. 3:125–127, 1975.

36. PAGNI, C.A., SIGNORONI, G., CROTTI, F., ET AL.: "Longterm results after resuscitation in post-traumatic coma of infancy and childhood." In Bushe, K.A., Spoerri, O., and Shaw, J. (eds.) *Progress in Pediatric Neurosurgery.* Hippokrates-Verlag, Stuttgart, 1974, pp. 196–201.

37. PAKARINEN, S.: *Incidence, etiology and prognosis of primary subarachnoid hemorrhage.* Acta Neurol. Scand. 43: (suppl. 29) 1–27, 1967.

38. PAZZAGLIA, P., FRANK, G., FRANK, F., ET AL.: *Clinical course and prognosis of acute post-traumatic coma.* J. Neurol. Neurosurg. Psychiatry 38:149–154, 1975.

39. PLUM, F.: "Brain swelling and edema in cerebral vascular disease." In *Cerebrovascular Disease.* Vol. 41. Res. Publ. Assoc. Res. Nerv. Ment. Dis., Williams and Wilkins, Baltimore, 1966, Chapter 12, pp. 318–348.

40. PLUM, F., AND CARONNA, J.J.: "Can one predict outcome of medical coma?" In *Outcome of Severe Damage to the Central Nervous System.* CIBA Foundation Symposium #34, Elsevier-North Holland, Amsterdam, 1975, pp. 121–139.

41. PRIOR, P.F.: *The EEG in acute cerebral anoxia: assessment of cerebral function and prognosis in patients resuscitated after cardiorespiratory arrest.* Amsterdam, Excerpta Medica, 1973.

42. PRYTZ, H., AND SLOTH, K.: *Hepatic coma in cirrhosis of the liver.* Scand. J. Gastroenterol. 8:229–233, 1973.

43. RICHARDSON, A.E.: *The natural history of patients with intracranial aneurysm after rupture.* Prog. Brain Res. 30:269–273, 1968.

44. RITT, D.J., WHELAN, G., WERNER, D.J., ET AL.: *Acute hepatic necrosis with stupor or coma. An analysis of 31 patients.* Medicine 48:151–172, 1969.

45. ROCKOFF, M., MARSHALL, L., AND SHAPIRO, H.: *High dose barbiturate therapy in man. A clinical review of sixty patients.* Ann. Neurol. 6:194–199, 1979.

46. ROSENBERG, G.A., JOHNSON, S.F., BRENNER, R.P.: *Recovery of cognition after prolonged vegetative state.* Ann. Neurol. 2:167–168, 1977.

47. ROUT, M.W., LANE, D.J., AND WOLLNER, L.: *Prognosis in acute cerebrovascular accidents in relation to respiratory pattern and blood gas tensions.* Br. Med. J. 3:7–9, 1971.

48. SATO, S., UEKI, K., ARAI, H., ET AL.: *Epidemiological survey of vegetative state patients in Tokohu District in Japan.* Neurol. Med. Chir. (Tokyo) 8:141–145, 1978.

49. SCHENKER, S., BREEN, K.J., AND HOYUMPA, A.M.: *Hepatic encephalopathy: current status.* Gastroenterology 66:121–151, 1974.

50. SCHNEIDER, M.: "Critical blood pressure in the cerebral circulation." In Schade, J.P., and McMenemey, W.H. (eds.): *Selective Vulnerability of the Brain in Hypoxaemia.* F.A. Davis Co. (Blackwell Scientific Publications), Philadelphia, 1963, pp. 7–20.

51. SHAW, C.M., ALVORD, E.C., JR., AND BERRY, R.G.: *Swelling of the brain following ischemic infarction with arterial occlusion.* Arch. Neurol. 1:161–177, 1959.

52. SNYDER, B.D., RAMIREZ-LASSEPAS, M., AND LIPPERT, D.M.: *Neurologic status and prognosis after cardiopulmonary arrest: 1. A retrospective study.* Neurology 27:807–811, 1977.

53. THOMPSON, R.G., HALLSTROM, A.P., AND COBB, L.A.: *Bystander-initiated cardiopulmonary resuscitation in the management of out-of-hospital ventricular fibrillation.* Ann. Int. Med. 90:737–740, 1979.

54. TREY, C., LIPWORTH, L., AND DAVIDSON, C.S.: *Parameters influencing survival in the first 318 patients reported to the fulminant hepatic failure surveillance study.* Gastroenterology 58:306, 1970.

55. TRUMPY, J.H.: *Subarachnoid hemorrhage. Time sequence of recurrences and their prognosis.* Acta Neurol. Scand. 43:48–60, 1967.

56. TURAZZI, S., ALEXANDRE, A., AND BRICOLO, A.: *Incidence and significance of clinical signs of brainstem traumatic lesions.* J. Neurosurg. Sci. 19:215–222, 1975.

57. TWEED, W.A., AND BECKSTEAD, J.E.: *Cerebral blood flow and metabolism in patients following anoxia.* Clin. Res. 23:642A, 1975.

58. VANDERLINDEN, R.G., AND CHISHOLM, L.D.: *Vitreous hemorrhages and sudden increased intracranial pressure.* J. Neurosurg. 41:167–176, 1974.

342

59. WILLOUGHBY, J.O., AND LEACH, B.G.: *Relation of neurological findings after cardiac arrest to outcome.* Br. Med. J. 3:437–439, 1974.

60. WINCHESTER, J.F., GELFAND, M.C., KNEPSHIELD, J.H., ET AL.: *Dialysis and hemoperfusion of poisons and drugs—update.* Trans. Am. Soc. Artif. Intern. Organs 23:762–842, 1977.

61. YARNELL, P.R.: *Neurological outcome of prolonged coma survivors of out-of-hospital cardiac arrest.* Stroke 7:279–282, 1976.

CHAPTER 8

Approach to the Unconscious Patient

A CLINICAL REGIMEN FOR DIAGNOSIS AND MANAGEMENT

Of the acute problems in clinical medicine, none is more difficult than the prompt diagnosis and effective management of the patient in coma. The difficulty exists partly because the causes of coma are so many and partly because the physician possesses only a limited time in which to make the appropriate diagnostic and therapeutic judgment. The coma caused by a subdural or epidural hematoma may be fully reversible when the patient is first seen, but if treatment is not promptly undertaken, the brain injury may become either irreparable or fatal within a very short period of time. A comatose patient suffering from diabetic ketoacidosis or hypoglycemia may rapidly return to normal if appropriate treatment is begun immediately, but may die or be rendered permanently brain-damaged if treatment is deferred. In extradural hematoma, meticulous evaluation of acid-base balance and substrate availability is not only useless, it is dangerous, since time may be too short. In untreated diabetic coma, time spent performing cerebral arteriography or CT scanning is not only meddlesome and fruitless, but potentially dangerous.

The physician evaluating comatose patients requires a systematic approach that will allow him to direct his diagnostic and therapeutic endeavors along appropriate pathways and not waste time on irrelevant considerations. The preceding chapters of this text presented what may appear to be a bewildering variety of disease states that cause stupor or coma. However, these chapters have also indicated that for any disease or functional abnormality of the brain to cause unconsciousness, it must either (1) produce bilateral dysfunction of the cerebral hemispheres; (2) damage or depress the physiologic activating mechanisms that lie along the central core of the upper brainstem and diencephalon; or (3) metabolically damage or depress both mechanisms. Conditions that can produce these effects can be divided into (1) supratentorial mass lesions that compress or displace the diencephalon and brainstem; (2) subtentorial destructive or expanding lesions that damage or compress the reticular formation; and (3) metabolic encephalopathies that diffusely affect the brain. Another condition, (4) psychiatric unresponsiveness, must be included in the differential diagnosis. Using these physiologic principles, one may considerably narrow the diagnostic possibilities and start specific treatment rapidly enough to make a difference in outcome. This chapter outlines a clinical approach that in most instances allows the physician to assign the cause of unresponsiveness promptly into one of the above four main categories while he acts to prevent irreversible damage to the patient's brain.

The key to making a categorical clinical diagnosis in coma consists of two steps: first, the accurate interpretation of a limited number of physical signs that reflect the integrity or impairment of various levels of the brain, and second, the determination of whether the pathologic physiology of supratentorial masses, subtentorial destructions, or metabolic encephalopathies best explains the pattern and evolution of these signs. As Table 29 indicates, each of these pathophysiologic categories produces a characteristic group of symptoms and signs, which usually evolve in a predictable manner. Once the patient's disease can be assigned to one of the three main categories, specific radiographic, electrophysiologic, or chemical laboratory studies can be employed to make disease-specific diagnoses or to detect conditions that potentially complicate the patient's management. Once diagnosis is made and treatment started, changes in these same clinical signs and laboratory tests then can be used serially to extend or supplement treatment (medical or surgical), to judge its effect, and, as indicated in Chapter 7, to arrive at estimates of recovery and prognosis.

Many efforts have been made to find an ideal clinical approach to the unconscious patient. Most such approaches more-or-less repeat or even enlarge upon the complete neurologic examination, which makes them too time-consuming for practical daily use. A few are admirably brief and to the point,[42] but have been designed for limited purposes, such as the following of patients with head injury; generally they provide too little information to allow diagnosis or the monitoring of metabolic problems. The clinical profile described in a later section no doubt falls short of perfection, but it has been employed extensively by ourselves and others,[3] and found to have advantages. The examination judges the normal and abnormal physiology of the functions described earlier in Chapter 1: arousal, pupillary responses, eye movements, corneal responses, the breathing pattern, skeletal muscle motor function, and deep tendon reflexes. Most of these functions undergo predictable changes in association with localizable brain abnormalities and help to tell where the lesion or lesions lie. How the signs of abnormal function then group themselves together and evolve points to whether the cause of altered con-

Table 29. Differential Characteristics of States Causing Sustained Unresponsiveness

---

I. *Supratentorial Mass Lesions Compressing or Displacing the Diencephalon or Brainstem*
   Initiating signs usually of focal cerebral dysfunction
   Signs of dysfunction progress rostral to caudal
   Neurologic signs at any given time point to one anatomic area (e.g., diencephalon, midbrain-pons, medulla)
   Motor signs often asymmetrical
II. *Subtentorial Masses or Destruction Causing Coma*
   History of preceding brainstem dysfunction or sudden onset of coma
   Localizing brainstem signs precede or accompany onset of coma and always include oculovestibular abnormality
   Cranial nerve palsies usually present
   "Bizarre" respiratory patterns common and usually appear at onset
III. *Metabolic Coma*
   Confusion and stupor commonly precede motor signs
   Motor signs are usually symmetrical
   Pupillary reactions are usually preserved
   Asterixis, myoclonus, tremor, and seizures are common
   Acid-base imbalance with hyper- or hypoventilation is frequent
IV. *Psychiatric Unresponsiveness*
   Lids close actively
   Pupils reactive or dilated (cycloplegics)
   Oculocephalics are unpredictable; oculovestibulars physiologic (nystagmus is present)
   Motor tone is inconsistent or normal
   Eupnea or hyperventilation is usual
   No pathologic reflexes are present
   EEG is normal

---

sciousness is supratentorial (starts rostrally and evolves caudally), subtentorial (starts focally in the brainstem), metabolic (produces from the onset signs of diffuse or multifocal dysfunction), or psychiatric (lacks signs of physiologic brain dysfunction).

PRINCIPLES OF EMERGENCY MANAGEMENT

Even before the diagnostic process begins, the patient's unclothed body should be inspected (especially for signs of trauma) and his *vital signs* measured. No matter what the diagnosis or the cause of coma, certain general principles of management apply to all patients[37] and should be addressed as one pursues the examination and undertakes definitive therapy (Table 30).

1. ASSURE OXYGENATION. The brain must have a continuous supply of oxygen, and adequate blood oxygenation depends on sufficient respiration. Scrupulous attention must be given to the airway and the lungs themselves. *Check the airway.* If the airway is obstructed, attempt to clear it by suctioning and then arrange for a cuffed endotracheal tube to be placed by the most skilled practitioner available. Prior to placing the tube, extend the head gently, elevate the jaw, and ventilate the patient with oxygen using a mask and bag to assure maximal possible blood oxygenation during the procedure. Tracheal irritation usually produces a sympathetic discharge with hypertension, tachycardia and occasional premature ventricular contractions. Rarely, particularly in hypoxemic patients, a vagal discharge leading to bradycardia or cardiac arrest occurs. Maximal oxygenation plus 1 mg. atropine given intravenously before intubation helps prevent cardiac arrhythmias that otherwise may result from the vagal stimulation. Remember that to place an endotracheal tube usually requires that one extend the neck; if there is a potential cervical spine injury, the head should not be moved before radiologic assessment has been made. (The same principle applies to testing oculocephalic reflexes.) When cervical spine injury exists, intubation should be performed either without extension of the neck or by tracheostomy. If upper airway obstruction is severe and immediate intubation is not possible or is inadvisable, a #14 needle inserted through the membranous anterior junction of the thyroid and cricoid cartilage will bypass the obstruction while the physician prepares for a tracheostomy.

Evaluate Respiratory Excursions. Arterial blood gas measurement is the only certain method of determining adequate ventilation, but, as a rule of thumb, if breath sounds can be heard at both lung bases and if the respiratory rate is greater than 8 per minute, ventilation is probably adequate. If a respirometer is available, measure tidal volume, but remember that patients comatose from drug overdose or

Table 30. Principles of Management of Comatose Patients

1. Assure oxygenation
2. Maintain circulation
3. Give glucose
4. Lower intracranial pressure
5. Stop seizures
6. Treat infection
7. Restore acid-base balance and electrolyte balance
8. Adjust body temperature
9. Administer thiamine
10. Consider specific antidotes
11. Control agitation

who are hypothermic have depressed metabolism and require less ventilation than awake normals. If respirations are insufficient, support them by artificial means (mouth-to-mouth, mask and bag, mechanical ventilation) before completing the examination. The comatose patient ideally should maintain a PaO_2 greater than 100 mm. Hg. and a $PaCO_2$ between 30–35 mm. Hg.

After initial management, patients with metabolic coma should be kept in a semiprone Trendelenburg position and turned from side to side each hour. Frequently perform chest physical therapy and suction the airway using sterile technique. Attach a freely vented hose to the endotracheal tube and deliver humidified air (or oxygen, if necessary) at body temperature to minimize the inspissation of dried mucus in the tube. Deflate the endotracheal cuff intermittently unless the patient is on artificial ventilation or a soft cuff tube is used. With due care, a soft cuff endotracheal tube can be maintained up to a week without the necessity of a tracheostomy. However, if prolonged coma seems likely, a tracheostomy usually should be performed after about 48 hours.

2. MAINTAIN THE CIRCULATION. The circulation must be maintained if the brain is to receive adequate oxygen. *Check the blood pressure and pulse.* Insert an intravenous line, replace blood volume loss, and infuse vasoactive agents as needed. Remember that in badly brain-injured subjects, dopamine produces less damage to the kidneys than levarterenol bitartrate (Levophed). *Monitor the cardiac rate and rhythm and treat unstable vital signs and cardiac arrythmias.* If the patient is in shock, seek an extracerebral source. Damage to the brain at levels rostral to the low brainstem is rarely responsible for systemic hypotension (see Chapter 1).

Try to maintain the mean arterial pressure at about 100 mm. Hg using hypertensive and/or hypotensive agents as necessary. In an older patient with known chronic hypertension, take care not to let the blood pressure fall much below previously accustomed levels, because the relative hypotension may cause cerebral hypoxia. In young, previously healthy patients, particularly those with depressant drug poisoning, a blood pressure of 80 mm. Hg is probably adequate.

3. GIVE GLUCOSE. The brain depends not only on oxygen and blood flow, but also on an obligate use of glucose for its homeostasis (see Chapter 4). Hypoglycemia can be diagnosed only by laboratory test, but in the time required for the laboratory to carry out and report such results, the brain may be irreversibly damaged. Therefore, after the blood is drawn for laboratory evaluation, 25 gm. glucose (50 ml. of 50% solution) should be given intravenously to any comatose patient in whom the diagnosis is not entirely clear. The glucose will prevent hypoglycemic brain damage while results of laboratory tests are awaited and will not damage the brain of patients who are not hypoglycemic. One might argue that hyperosmolar glucose given to a patient in diabetic or hyperosmolar coma would further shrink the brain, thus worsening the clinical situation. However, we believe that the risk of permanent brain damage in the hypoglycemic patient outweighs the probably temporary worsening of encephalopathy in the hyperosmolar patient when glucose is given. Even after a hypoglycemic patient has been treated with glucose, care must be taken to prevent recurrent hypoglycemia. Therefore, infuse glucose and water intravenously until the situation has stabilized.

4. LOWER INTRACRANIAL PRESSURE. The methods are described below under Supratentorial Mass Lesions.

5. STOP SEIZURES. Repeated seizures of whatever cause, in and of themselves, produce brain damage and must be stopped. Treat generalized convulsions with intravenous diazepam in doses large enough to stop the seizure (somewhere between 3–10 mg.). Have a ventilator available, since large doses of the drug depress

breathing. Once the seizures have stopped, give intravenous phenytoin (between 500 mg. and 1 gm. at a rate of <50 mg./min.) to maintain seizure control. If seizures recur, give more diazepam. At times, generalized seizures cannot be stopped with intravenous drugs, and barbiturate anesthesia is necessary. Focal continuous epilepsy, which frequently occurs with metabolic brain disease, is less damaging to the brain and does not require the use of anesthetic doses of anticonvulsant drugs.

6. TREAT INFECTION. Several kinds of infection cause delirium and coma, and infection may exacerbate coma from other causes. Draw blood cultures on all febrile patients and perform lumbar puncture if indicated. Begin antibiotic treatment immediately after procuring the appropriate cultures and smears.

7. RESTORE ACID-BASE BALANCE. With severe metabolic acidosis or alkalosis, the pH should be returned toward a normal level since metabolic acidosis can lead to cardiovascular abnormalities and metabolic alkalosis can depress respiration. Respiratory acidosis presages respiratory failure and warns the physician that ventilatory assistance may soon be needed. Respiratory alkalosis can cause cardiac arrhythmias and hinders easy weaning from respiratory care.

8. ADJUST BODY TEMPERATURE. Several metabolic and structural abnormalities lead to either hyperthermia or hypothermia, and these states may exacerbate abnormalities of cerebral metabolism. Hyperthermia is dangerous because it increases cerebral metabolic demands and at extreme levels can denature brain cellular proteins. The body temperature of hyperthermic patients should be reduced on a cooling blanket to near normothermic levels. Hypothermic patients with temperatures below 34°C should be gradually warmed to maintain a body temperature above 35°C.

9. ADMINISTER THIAMINE. Wernicke's encephalopathy is a rare cause of coma.[45] However, many patients admitted as emergencies in stupor or coma are chronic alcoholics or otherwise malnourished. In such a patient, a glucose load may precipitate acute Wernicke's encephalopathy. Therefore, inject 50 to 100 mg. thiamine at the time glucose is given or shortly thereafter.

10. CONSIDER SPECIFIC ANTIDOTES. Most patients entering an emergency room in coma are suffering from drug overdose. Any of the gamut of sedative drugs, alcohol, narcotics, tranquilizers, and hallucinogens may have been ingested singly or in combination. Most drug overdose is best treated by the supportive measures considered in a subsequent section. However, certain antagonists specifically reverse the effects of several coma-producing drugs. For narcotic overdose give 0.4 mg. intravenous naloxone hydrochloride every 5 minutes until consciousness is restored. This drug must be used with great care since in a patient addicted to narcotics it may produce acute withdrawal symptoms requiring narcotic therapy. (If the patient is a known or suspected narcotic addict, 0.4 mg. naloxone should be diluted in 10 cc. saline and given slowly. One should use the minimum amount necessary to establish the diagnosis by pupillary dilatation and reverse the comatose state.) Naloxone has a duration of action of 2 to 3 hours, much shorter than the action of several narcotic drugs, especially methadone. Thus, patients who have taken an overdose of narcotic and whose toxic reactions are reversed by naloxone may relapse after a period of 4 to 5 hours and need retreatment. Naloxone has been reported to be effective in reversing the effects of excessive alcohol and other sedative drugs as well as narcotics.[19]

Certain of the effects of sedative drugs with anticholinergic properties, particularly the tricyclic antidepressants, can be reversed by the intravenous injection of 1 mg. physostigmine intravenously. Physostigmine has arousal properties because of its cholinergic action on the nervous system. Therefore, if the patient rouses it does not necessarily indicate that the cause of coma was an anticholinergic drug.[27,28] However, full awakening suggests that such a drug was ingested. Physostigmine thus possesses both diagnostic and therapeutic uses. The drug has a short duration of action and its use may have to be repeated. The specific antidotes for several other drugs are considered elsewhere.[2,38]

11. CONTROL AGITATION. Many patients who are delirious or stuporous are grossly agitated. The hyperactivity is distressing to patients and family and may lead to self-injury. Sedative drugs should not be used until the diagnosis is relatively clear and one is certain that the problem is metabolic rather than structural. Sometimes agitation can be controlled by keeping the patient in a lighted room and asking a relative or staff member to sit at the bedside and talk reassuringly to the patient. If this proves insufficient, use minor or major tranquilizers. Small doses of diazepam (5-10 mg. every 3-4 hours) may be sufficient to control agitation. In patients who have habitually ingested alcohol or sedative drugs, larger doses may be necessary because of cross-tolerance. Sometimes major tranquilizers, such as haloperidol beginning at a low dose of 1 mg. twice a day and raising as necessary, may achieve quietude without causing excessive sedation. For very short-term sedation, as might be necessary to perform a CT scan, one should consider intravenous fentanyl or morphine because they are short-acting and can be reversed at the end of the procedure. Slower-acting narcotics often produce sedation too late to be useful for an emergency scan and cause respiratory depression after the naloxone has worn off.

12. PROTECT THE EYES. Corneal erosions can occur within 4 to 6 hours if the eyes of comatose patients remain partially or fully opened.[39] Exposure keratitis may lead to secondary bacterial corneal ulcerations. To prevent such changes, lubricate the eyes with an ophthalmic ointment and passively close them with tape or a corneal bandage. The tape and ointment should be reapplied about every 12 hours as long as unconsciousness lasts.[4]

EXAMINATION OF THE PATIENT

Once the vital functions have been protected, proceed with the history and examination.

The examination of the unconscious patient should include, to whatever extent possible, a complete history and physical examination (Table 31). The history must be obtained from relatives, friends, or sometimes even the police. The history of onset is important. Coma of unknown cause in a previously healthy patient, especially with sudden onset, most often turns out to be due to self-induced drug poisoning, subarachnoid hemorrhage, head trauma, or, in older persons, brainstem hemorrhage or infarction. Most examples of supratentorial mass lesions produce a more gradual impairment of consciousness, as do the metabolic encephalopathies.

In the general physical examination, after assessing and dealing with abnormalities of vital signs, look for evidence of trauma or signs that might suggest an acute or chronic systemic medical illness or the ingestion or self-administration of drugs. Evaluate nuchal rigidity, but take care lest the cervical spine has been fractured.

It is the neurologic examination that is most helpful in assessing the nature of the patient's unconsciousness. Table 31 outlines the clinical neurologic functions that provide the most useful information in making a categorical diagnosis. These clinical indices have been extensively tested and applied to patients and have proved themselves to be easily and quickly obtained and to have a high degree of consistency from examiner to examiner.[43] Furthermore, they give valuable informa-

Table 31. Examination of the Comatose Patient

HISTORY (from relatives or friends)
    Onset of coma (abrupt, gradual)
    Recent complaints (headache, depression, focal weakness, vertigo)
    Recent injury
    Previous medical illnesses (diabetes, uremia, heart disease)
    Previous psychiatric history
    Access to drugs (sedatives, psychotropic drugs)
GENERAL PHYSICAL EXAMINATION
    Vital signs
    Evidence of trauma
    Evidence of acute or chronic systemic illness
    Evidence of drug ingestion (needle marks, alcohol on breath)
    Nuchal rigidity (examine with care)
NEUROLOGIC PROFILE
    Verbal responses
      Oriented speech
      Confused conversation
      Inappropriate speech
      Incomprehensible speech
      No speech
    Eye Opening
      Spontaneous
      Response to verbal stimuli
      Response to noxious stimuli
      None
    Pupillary Reactions
      Present
      Absent
    Spontaneous Eye Movements
      Orienting
      Roving conjugate
      Roving dysconjugate
      Miscellaneous abnormal movements
      None
    Oculocephalic Responses
      Normal
      Full
      Minimal
      None
    Oculovestibular Responses
      Normal
      Tonic conjugate
      Minimal or dysconjugate
      None
    Corneal Responses
      Present
      Absent
    Respiratory Pattern
      Regular
      Periodic
      Ataxic
    Motor Responses
      Obeying commands
      Localizing
      Withdrawal
      Abnormal flexion
      Abnormal extension
      None
    Deep Tendon Reflexes
      Normal
      Increased
      Absent
    Skeletal Muscle Tone
      Normal
      Paratonic
      Flexor
      Extensor
      Flaccid

tion upon which to base both diagnosis and prognosis. When serially recorded on a day sheet as best-worst changes during each 24 hours, the result reflects accurately the patient's clinical course. The following paragraphs give the detailed description of each clinical sign.

VERBAL RESPONSES. The best response, oriented speech, implies awareness of self and the environment. The patient knows who he is, where he is, why he is there, and the year, season, and month. Confused conversation indicates conversational speech with syntactically correct phrases but with disorientation and confusion in the content. Inappropriate speech means intelligible but isolated words. The content can include profanity but no sustained conversation. Incomprehensible speech refers to the production of word-like mutterings or groans. The worst verbal response, no speech, applies to total mutism.

EYE OPENING. Patients with spontaneous eye opening have some tone in the eyelids and generally demonstrate spontaneous blinking, which differentiates them from completely unresponsive patients whose eyes sometimes remain passively open. Though spontaneous eye opening rules out coma by our definition, it does not guarantee awareness. (Some vegetative patients with eye opening have been shown postmortem to have total loss of the cerebral cortex [see Chapter 1].) Eye opening in response to verbal stimuli means that any verbal stimulus, whether an appropriate command or not, produces eye opening. More severely damaged patients demonstrate eye opening only in response to a noxious stimulus applied to the trunk or an extremity. (A noxious stimulus to the head commonly evokes eye closing.) The worst response, no eye opening, applies to all remaining patients except when local changes such as periorbital edema preclude examination.

PUPILLARY REACTIONS. Pupillary reactions to an intense flashlight beam are evaluated for both eyes, and the better response is recorded; use a hand lens to evaluate questionable responses. Record pupillary diameters and note the presence of any somatic third-nerve paresis.

SPONTANEOUS EYE MOVEMENT. The best response is spontaneous orienting eye movements, in which the patient looks toward environmental stimuli. Record roving conjugate and roving dysconjugate eye movements when present and reserve a miscellaneous movement category for patients without orienting eye movements who have spontaneous nystagmus, opsoclonus, ocular bobbing, or other, unclassified eye movement. Absent spontaneous eye movements should be noted, as should the presence of lateral deviation to either side or dysconjugate gaze at rest (e.g., skew).

OCULOCEPHALIC RESPONSES. These are evaluated in conjunction with passive, brisk, horizontal head turning. When appropriate, the response to vertical head movement should also be recorded. Patients with normal responses retain orienting eye movements. Full oculocephalic responses are brisk and tonic and generally include conjugate eye movements opposite to the direction of turning. Minimal responses are defined as conjugate movements of less than 30 degrees or bilateral inability to adduct the eyes. Absence of response is the poorest level of function. *Remember, do not test oculocephalic reflexes in patients suspected of having sustained a severe neck injury.*

OCULOVESTIBULAR RESPONSES. These are tested by irrigating each external auditory canal with up to 50 ml. ice water with the head 30 degrees above the horizontal plane. A normal (awake) response includes rapid nystagmus toward the nonirrigated ear and minimal, if any, tonic deviation. Patients with tonic responses exhibit conjugate deviation toward the irrigated ear. Minimal and no response are coded as with oculocephalic testing.

CORNEAL RESPONSES. Responses to a cotton wisp drawn fully across the cornea are recorded as present or absent for the eye with the better response.

RESPIRATORY PATTERN. The pattern is recorded as regular, periodic, ataxic, or combinations of these. Respiratory rate should be determined in patients not being mechanically ventilated.

MOTOR RESPONSES. These should be tested and recorded in all extremities and strength noted as normal or weak. The best score is given to patients who obey commands; care should be taken to avoid interpreting reflex grasping as obedience. If a command evokes no responses, apply a noxious stimulus gently but firmly to each extremity (compression of finger or toenail beds or of Achilles tendon) and to the supraorbital notches. Localizing responses designate the use of an extremity to locate or resist a remote noxious stimulus (e.g., the arm crossing the midline toward a cranial stimulus or reaching above shoulder level toward a cranial stimulus). A more primitive response consists of a nonstereotyped, rapid withdrawal from a noxious stimulus; this response often incorporates hip or shoulder adduction. An abnormal flexion response in the upper extremities is stereotyped, slow, and dystonic and the thumb is often held between the second and third fingers. Abnormal flexion in the lower extremities (the reflex triple flexion response) sometimes can be difficult to distinguish from withdrawal. An abnormal extension response in the upper extremity consists of adduction and internal rotation of the shoulder and pronation of the forearm. No response is coded only when strong stimuli are applied to more than one site and when muscle relaxants have not recently been administered.

DEEP TENDON REFLEXES. These reflexes are recorded for the best limb as normal, increased, or absent; minimal responses are best regarded as normal.

SKELETAL MUSCLE TONE. This should be recorded for the best limb as normal, paratonic (diffuse resistance throughout the range of passive motion), flexor (spasticity), extensor (rigidity), or flaccid.

GUIDES TO SPECIFIC MANAGEMENT

Supratentorial Mass Lesions

The differential characteristics that suggest a supratentorial mass lesion producing stupor or coma are outlined in Table 29. The procedures and laboratory tests useful for the differential diagnosis of stupor and coma are listed in Tables 32 and 33. If the physician elicits a history of headache (other than that limited to the suboccipital region) or of prior head trauma, no matter how trivial, he should suspect a supratentorial mass lesion. At times the historian will be able to describe symptoms or signs (facial asymmetry, weakness of one arm, dragging of the leg, or complaints of unilateral sensory loss) that existed prior to coma and suggest the presence of a supratentorial lesion. The presence at the initial examination of strikingly asymmetrical motor signs or of dysfunction progressing in a rostral-caudal fashion provides strong presumptive evidence of a supratentorial mass. The combination of neurologic signs should point to a single plane of diencephalic or brainstem dysfunction, as illustrated in Chapter 2. Both third-nerve motor dysfunction and poor pupillary responses evolving as coma deepens suggest a supratentorial mass. The major problem in differential diagnosis arises when supratentorial mass lesions, either extracerebral or in "silent" areas of the brain, cause stupor or coma at the diencephalic stage without producing preceding or accompanying focal motor signs. Because such patients often have reactive pupils, intact oculocephalic and oculovestibular responses, and abnormal motor signs that are symmetrical or only mildly asymmetrical, the physician may suspect metabolic encephalopathy rather than a supratentorial mass. Unless there is a clear history to help one differentiate, the physician should consider both diagnostic categories and direct the evaluation accordingly.

If you suspect that the patient is suffering from a supratentorial mass, determine how severe are the symptoms and estimate how rapidly they are worsening. If the patient is stuporous or comatose but relatively stable, procure an emergency CT scan, if available. If a CT scan is not available, carotid arteriography or radionuclide brain scan are second and third choices. (Skull films waste time and give considerably less information than any of the above tests. It is not of immediate consequence whether or not the patient has suffered a fractured skull, since fractures per se do not produce stupor or coma. What is of consequence is the presence of an epidural or subdural hematoma, with or without a skull fracture.)

If the patient is deeply comatose or if transtentorial herniation is evolving rapidly in a stuporous patient, *treat intracranial hypertension first.*[35] The most rapid technique for lowering intracranial pressure is hyperventilation.[16] The resulting decrease in $PaCO_2$ causes cerebral vasoconstriction, thus decreasing cerebral blood volume. With the airway secured, hyperventilate the patient to a $PaCO_2$ between 20 to 25 mm. Hg. This technique lowers intracranial pressure rapidly, but its effect is transient. Administer hyperosmolar agents at the same time; they decrease the water content of the brain by creating an osmolar gradient between the blood and that portion of the brain with an intact blood-brain barrier. Because most brain lesions cause local breakdown of the blood-brain barrier, hyperosmolar agents pull water from normal brain (not from the lesion) to lower intracranial pressure. The agent of choice is mannitol given in a 20 percent solution at a dose of 1.5 to 2 gm./kg. by bolus injection. Its effects are rapid and last several hours.[26] Glycerol has a similar effect but is less widely available.[34]

For appropriate lesions, give adrenocorticosteroids (steroids). Steroids decrease cerebral edema around brain tumors and certain other mass lesions and thus lower

Table 32. Procedures Useful in Evaluating the Comatose Patient

Cause	Tests of Diagnostic Value	Tests of Prognostic Value
Supratentorial lesions	CT scan Carotid arteriography (EEG)	Caloric tests Evoked potentials (?) EEG (if isoelectric) Arteriography (if no filling)
Infratentorial lesions	Vertebral arteriography CT scan (EEG) Rarely air or contrast ventriculogram Caloric tests	

intracranial pressure.[23] They also improve compliance of brain tissue[46] and diminish plateau waves (sudden transient increases in intracranial pressure that may increase transtentorial herniation).[1] The first dose should be given intravenously immediately, although its full effects will not be felt for several hours. Steroids are most effective in treating the cerebral edema of brain tumors and that produced by extracerebral masses such as sub- and epidural hematomas; they are least effective (some believe ineffective) in treating edema associated with cerebral contusion, laceration, infarction, hemorrhage, or anoxia. [10,13] (However, see Gobeit[11] and Hooshmand and associates. [15]) The appropriate dose of steroids is not established. Some studies claim that patients whose increased intracranial pressure fails to respond to standard doses (e.g., 16 mg. dexamethasone daily) will respond to higher doses (e.g., 32–100 mg. daily). [11,31] Whatever their effects on pressure, these high doses given for a few days appear to cause no more deleterious side effects than do standard doses. [11,20] We have given single doses of dexamethasone as large as 100 mg. by intravenous injection without untoward effect. After the first intravenous injection, administer steroids at 6-hour intervals until the acute problem has resolved. Some physicians add furosemide (40–120 mg.i.v.) or acetazolamide to the giving of steroids and believe the combination is better than steroids alone. [18,24]

The above steps should require no more than a few minutes to bring the intracranial pressure under control. Once it is controlled, procure a CT scan. Almost always the scan will demonstrate the nature of the supratentorial mass lesion and it often determines the degree of transtentorial herniation as well. [29,40] If a subdural or epidural hematoma is identified, evacuate it immediately. If you suspect an epidural or subdural hematoma clinically and the patient is deteriorating rapidly, it may be wise for a neurosurgeon to place burr holes, which are both diagnostic and therapeutic, without waiting for a CT scan. Emergency surgery to treat other supratentorial mass lesions is less effective, and opinions vary as to whether it is ever helpful. Our view is that acute intraparenchymal masses (hemorrhages, primary or metastatic tumors, cerebral abscess, or infarction) that produce deep stupor or coma are best managed nonsurgically, at least initially.

Monitor the patient's vital signs and the neurologic examination constantly during therapy. If an endotracheal tube has not been placed before, do it now. Measure the blood gases and ventilate the patient to maintain the PaO_2 at greater than 100 mm. Hg. Keep the $PaCO_2$ between 25 to 35 mm. Hg. Mannitol may be repeated as often as every 4 to 6 hours, depending on the patient's clinical state. In patients suffering from cerebral tumors or abscess, continue dexamethasone (about 25 mg. every 6 hours) or an equivalent steroid. Keep the head slightly elevated and move the patient from side to side each hour. Insert a Foley catheter and record urine output each hour. Measure electrolytes frequently if mannitol or diuretics are being given, because the use of these drugs can result in severe electrolyte imbalance.

Many neurosurgeons believe that monitoring the intracranial pressure aids in the management of intracranial hypertension. The pressure is measured via either a screw placed in the subdural or epidural space or a catheter inserted into the lateral ventricle. The effect of treatment can then be quantified and often aimed at reducing increasing intracranial pressure before its clinical signs become apparent.[12,21] This technique has already proved useful in the treatment of Reye's syndrome;[44] whether it will increase the salvage rate in other supratentorial mass lesions is not presently clear. [21]

Some investigators have advocated barbiturate anesthesia to treat severe intracranial hypertension from head injury.[22] The drugs used are thiopental or pentobarbital given intravenously: for pentobarbital, 3 to 5 mg./kg. initially followed by an intravenous infusion sufficient to keep a blood barbiturate level of 2.5 to 3.5 mg./dl.;[22] for thiopental, up to 30 mg./kg. by titrated intravenous infusion.[6] Other workers use a constant infusion of thiopental of 150 mg./hour after a preliminary 100 to 150 mg. dose.[8] With such therapy, the intracranial pressure decreases rapidly and usually remains low as long as the patient is anesthetized. This technique requires extremely careful monitoring of vital signs and, if performed at all, should be carried out only in the best equipped intensive care units. There are reports of decreases in mortality with the use of barbiturate anesthesia in head injuries, drownings, cerebral infarction, and other supratentorial mass lesions.[6,22,36] These reports, however, are based on retrospective analyses, are not based on controlled data, and are at least partially contradicted by other studies.[25,32] How barbiturates act to reduce the intracranial pressure is unknown. It is not simply through anesthesia, since in experimental animals gas anesthesia appears to have no such salutary effect. The clinical usefulness of barbiturate therapy for coma must be regarded as still in the stage of experimental evaluation.

If the patient with a supratentorial mass lesion responds to emergency treatment, undertake definitive treatment when his condition stabilizes. Definitive treatment includes surgical extirpation of primary brain tumors, radiation therapy for primary and secondary brain tumors, and surgical clipping of cerebral aneurysms that have produced subarachnoid and/or intracerebral hemorrhages. Remember, however, that emergency intracranial surgery performed on patients in coma seldom produces a favorable outcome. The treatment of brain abscess is controversial; there is increasing evidence that if monitoring by CT scan is available, brain abscesses can be effectively treated by antibiotics rather than by surgical extirpation.[5,33]

Subtentorial Lesions

Subtentorial lesions fall into two groups: those that are intrinsic to the brainstem and those that compress it. In patients with subtentorial mass or destructive lesions causing coma, one may elicit a history of occipital headache or of complaints of vertigo, diplopia, or other symptoms and signs suggesting brainstem dysfunction. Frequently, however, the onset of the coma is sudden and the headache occurs only moments before the patient loses consciousness. If the onset of the headache is accompanied by vomiting, one should suspect a subtentorial lesion, since acute vomiting is less common with supratentorial masses. Characteristic oculovestibular abnormalities including skew deviation, dysconjugate gaze, fixed gaze palsies, or dysconjugate responses to oculocephalic and oculovestibular testing are strong presumptive evidence of a subtentorial lesion. Cranial nerve palsies are often present and unusual respiratory patterns usually are present from onset. The major problem in differential diagnosis arises when a patient with a supratentorial mass lesion has progressed far enough to arrive at the pontine or medullary level of coma. In this instance it is virtually impossible to distinguish by physical examination between the effects of supratentorial and subtentorial masses. Metabolic coma can usually be distinguished from the above two because the pupils remain reactive. A CT scan usually distinguishes between supra- and subtentorial masses and often establishes the diagnosis definitively. However, if you suspect the patient of harboring a subtentorial lesion and he is deteriorating rapidly, treat him as if he had brainstem compression as from a cerebellar or extraaxial lesion, even before the CT scan is performed. Treatment should be initiated to lower intracranial pressure by the methods described above. Secure the airway early because with subtentorial lesions respiratory failure often occurs abruptly.

At times it is impossible to distinguish on clinical grounds an intrinsic brainstem lesion (such as infarction from basilar artery occlusion) from an extrinsic compressive lesion (such as cerebellar hematoma), but the latter is potentially reversible and the former is not. If the distinction cannot be clearly made, treat with hyperventilation, hyperosmolar agents, and probably steroids. After treatment for edema is underway, procure a CT scan. Surgically evacuate large hematomas of the cerebellum or the subdural space if the patient is stuporous or comatose, if his state of consciousness is decreasing, or if signs indicate progressive brainstem compression.[7,30] A cerebellar infarct causing stupor or coma from brainstem compression appears on CT scan as a hypodense area and likewise responds to surgical decompression and removal of infarcted tissue.[17] Despite a few reports of successful surgical evacuation of brainstem hematomas,[41] intrinsic lesions of the brainstem usually do not respond to surgery, and most such patients do better if managed conservatively. If the intrinsic lesion is a tumor, management with steroids and mannitol may stabilize matters and allow for radiation therapy. Infarction of the brainstem should be treated conservatively. If the patient is not comatose and appears to be worsening, anticoagulant therapy with heparin may help.

Metabolic Encephalopathy

Metabolic coma (Table 29) is characterized by a history of confusion and disorientation having preceded the onset of stupor or coma, usually in the absence of any motor signs. When motor signs (decorticate or decerebrate rigidity) appear, they are usually symmetrical. If the patient is stuporous rather than comatose, asterixis, myoclonus, and tremor are common, and in comatose patients the presence of repetitive seizures, either focal or generalized, provide presumptive evidence of metabolic dysfunction. Many patients with metabolic coma are either hyper- or hypoventilating, but it is rare to see the unusual and irregular respiratory patterns that characterize subtentorial mass or destructive lesions. There are two major errors in the diagnosis of metabolic coma. The first is in differentiating patients with the diencephalic stage of supratentorial masses from those with metabolic coma. In the absence of focal motor signs, one initially tends to suspect metabolic coma even in patients who turn out to have a supratentorial mass lesion. The second error occurs in those occasional patients with metabolic coma (e.g., hepatic coma or hypoglycemia) who have strikingly asymmetrical motor signs with hyperventilation and deep coma. Here the preservation of intact and symmetrical pupillary and oculovestibular responses provides strong presumptive evidence for metabolic rather than structural disease.

It is stupor and coma caused by metabolic brain disease that most challenges the internist, neurologist, or general physician likely to be reading this monograph. If patients suffer from major damage caused by supratentorial mass lesions or by subtentorial mass or destructive lesions, specific treatment is most often surgical. If psychogenic unresponsiveness is the problem, the ultimate management of the patient rests with a psychiatrist. In metabolic brain disease, however, the physician of first contact is on his own, and the task of preserving the brain from permanent damage rests with him. The physician should first evaluate the vital signs, provide adequate ventilation and arterial pressure, and then draw blood for metabolic studies. Metabolic studies that should be secured from the first blood drawing are indicated in Table 33. Because drug ingestion is the most common cause of coma, procure blood and urine for toxicologic study on all patients. Those metabolic encephalopathies that are most likely to produce either irreversible brain damage or a quick demise and that are potentially treatable include drug overdose, hypoglycemia, metabolic acidosis (from several causes), hyperosmolar states, hypoxia, bacterial meningitis or endocarditis, and severe electrolyte imbalance. Accordingly, immediately *after*

Table 33. Emergency Laboratory Evaluation of Metabolic Coma

I. Immediate Tests
  A. Venous Blood
    1. glucose
    2. electrolytes (Na, K, Cl, CO_2, Ca, PO_4)
    3. urea or creatinine
    4. osmolality
  B. Arterial Blood
    1. check color
    2. pH
    3. PO_2
    4. PCO_2
    5. HCO_3
    6. HbCO (if available)
  C. Cerebrospinal Fluid
    1. cells
    2. Gram stain
    3. glucose
  D. Electrocardiogram
II. Deferred Tests*
  A. Venous Blood
    1. sedative and toxic drugs
    2. liver function tests
    3. coagulation studies
    4. thyroid and adrenal function
    5. blood cultures
    6. viral titers
  B. Urine
    1. sedative and toxic drugs
    2. culture
  C. Cerebrospinal Fluid
    1. protein
    2. culture
    3. viral and fungal titers

*Samples to be procured before treatment is begun, to be processed later.

358

drawing blood for laboratory studies, if the diagnosis is uncertain give 25 gm. glucose (50 ml. of a 50 percent solution) intravenously to treat possible *hypoglycemia.* Be cautioned that if the patient awakens, he may not have been hypoglycemic, since the hyperosmolar load might have rapidly but transiently lowered elevated intracranial pressure. On the other hand, if the patient fails to awaken, it does not rule out hypoglycemia, because if enough cerebral depression has already occurred, prolonged coma may follow even effective immediate treatment of hypoglycemia. The diagnosis awaits the already drawn blood glucose. Infusion of hyperosmolar glucose may somewhat worsen hyperglycemic hyperosmolar coma, but the benefits to be gained by treating hypoglycemia (thus preventing permanent brain damage) outweigh the relatively minor risk of making hyperosmolality slightly worse.

Comprehensive treatment of *acid-base imbalance* should await securing arterial samples for blood gas analysis to establish an accurate diagnosis but emergency management may have to begin even before laboratory results are returned. Both acidosis and alkalosis can cause cardiac arrhythmias, but acute metabolic acidosis is more likely to be rapidly lethal. Therefore, treat such a patient with metabolic brain disease who is hyperventilating and in whom the cardiovascular system appears to be failing by injecting sodium bicarbonate intravenously, 1 mEq./kg body weight, while awaiting the results of the blood gas determinations. The procedure may be lifesaving.

Relieve hypoxia immediately by assuring an adequate airway and delivering sufficient oxygen to keep the blood fully oxygenated. Even in the presence of a normal PaO_2, blood oxygen content may be insufficient to supply the brain's needs for several reasons. (1) The hemoglobin may be abnormal (carbon monoxyhemoglobinemia, methemoglobinemia, or sulfhemoglobinemia). Methemoglobin or sulfhemoglobin are diagnosed by the typical "terra cotta" appearance of oxygenated blood, and patients are treated with methylene blue.[2] Carbon monoxide binds hemoglobin with 200 times the affinity of oxygen and thus displaces oxygen and yields carbon monoxyhemoglobin. The PaO_2 is normal and the patient's color is pink or "cherry red," but he is hypoxic because insufficient hemoglobin is available to deliver oxygen to the tissue. Such patients should be given 100 percent oxygen and hyperventilated to increase excretion of the carbon monoxide. (2) Severe anemia by itself will not cause coma but lowers the blood O_2 content even when the PaO_2 is normal, and thus decreases the oxygen supply to the brain. In patients with other forms of hypoxia, anemia may exacerbate the symptoms. Treat severe anemia (hematocrit <25) with transfusion of whole blood or packed red cells. (3) Tissues can be hypoxic even when the PaO_2 and O_2 content is normal if they cannot metabolize the oxygen (e.g., cyanide poisoning). The state is called histotoxic hypoxia and there is no specific antidote. Maintaining the blood pressure, however, may prevent brain damage even in histotoxic anoxia.

In any comatose or stuporous patient who is febrile, whether or not nuchal rigidity and/or other signs of meningeal irritation (e.g., positive Kernig's or Brudzinski's signs) are present, consider *acute bacterial meningitis.* Perform a lumbar puncture immediately (before antibiotics are administered). Perform a cell count; do a Gram stain of the centrifuged sediment and culture the fluid. Remember that the absence of cells in the spinal fluid does not rule out acute bacterial meningitis; the centrifuged sediment must be examined by Gram stain. Even a normal Gram stain does not always rule out bacterial meningitis and, if the diagnosis is suspected, the lumbar puncture should be repeated in a few hours. Remember, however, that lumbar punctures are dangerous in the presence of increased intracranial pressure (see

359

Chapter 2). Unless you suspect acute bacterial meningitis, do not perform a lumbar puncture in stuporous or comatose patients until after a CT scan has been done.

Severe *electrolyte imbalance* usually affects the heart more than the brain. Accordingly, an electrocardiogram often suggests the diagnosis before serum electrolytes are returned from the laboratory.[9] It usually is advisable to adjust both electrolyte and acid-base imbalances slowly, since too rapid correction often leads to overshoot or intracellular-extracellular imbalances and worsens the clinical situation.[14]

The most common cause of stupor and coma in emergency room patients is *sedative drug or alcohol overdose.* Most of these drugs are not rapidly lethal but, because they are respiratory depressants, they risk producing respiratory arrest or circulatory depression at any time. Therefore, no stuporous or comatose patient suspected of having ingested sedative drugs should ever be left alone. This is particularly true in the minutes immediately following the initial examination; the stimulation delivered by the examining physician may arouse the patient to a state in which he appears relatively alert or his respiratory function appears normal only to have him lapse into coma with depressed breathing when external stimulation ceases. The management of specific drug poisonings is beyond the scope of this chapter (see Schwartz[38]), but certain general principles apply to all patients suspected of having ingested sedative drugs. The type of medication influences the treatment and its duration. Accordingly, search the patient and ask relatives or the police to search the patient's living quarters for potentially toxic agents or empty medication vials that might have contained sedative drugs. Both respiratory and cardiovascular failure occur with massive sedative drug overdose. Anticipation and early treatment of these complications often smooths the clinical course. Insert an endotracheal tube in any stuporous or comatose patient suspected of drug overdose and be certain that respiratory-supporting apparatus is available in case of acute respiratory failure. The placement of a central venous line allows one to maintain an adequate blood volume without overloading the patient. Give generous amounts of fluid to maintain blood volume and blood pressure but avoid overhydrating oliguric patients.

Once the vital signs have been stabilized, one should attempt to remove, neutralize, or reverse the effects of the drug. In an awake patient, the most effective means of removal is by the induction of emesis. Emesis should not be attempted if the ingested substance was a caustic alkali or acid, and some investigators question whether it should be attempted if the patient has ingested a petroleum distillate, since there is danger of aspiration during the course of emesis. Emesis can be produced with either syrup of ipecac or with apomorphine. Syrup of ipecac is given to an adult in a dose of 20 to 30 cc. orally, followed with glasses of water. The dose may be repeated after 20 minutes. If emesis does not occur, the substance must be lavaged, since ipecac is a cardiac irritant. For the awake adult, some physicians use apomorphine 6 mg. intravenously to induce vomiting. Following the use of apomorphine, patients should be given water to drink so that the stomach is filled and watched carefully for respiratory depression. If respiratory depression occurs, naloxone will reverse it.

If the patient is in coma, gastric lavage is indicated. It is doubtful if gastric lavage removes large quantities of drug from most patients with sedative drug overdose, but because sedative drugs may slow gastric motility and emptying, considerable poison may remain in the stomach of some patients. Do not perform gastric lavage until you have placed a cuffed endotracheal tube to prevent aspiration of the lavaged fluid. A large, preferably double-lumened, gastric tube should be placed by the oral route after removing foreign bodies, including false teeth, from the mouth. The lavage is performed in the head-down position, on the left side, to allow for pooling of the gastric contents and to prevent the passage of fluid into the duodenum. Either tap water or half-normal saline can be used in increments of 200 to 300 cc. in adults. Lavage is continued until the return is clear.

After emesis or gastric lavage has been concluded, the patient should be given activated charcoal, which is effective in binding a large variety of toxic substances. Either give the patient 1 or 2 tablespoons of activated charcoal to drink in each glass of water or instill the material down the lavage tube at the termination of gastric lavage.

If the patient's respiratory function is good after the endotracheal tube is placed, position him in a semiprone Trendelenburg position to allow for secretions to drain. Gently suction the lungs at frequent intervals to maintain good pulmonary function. With meticulous, physiologically based intensive therapy, all patients who ingest sedative drugs should sooner or later awaken without complication. Table 34 indicates common pitfalls that result in less successful outcomes.

Although necessary in only a few instances, if massive doses of phenobarbital or glutethimide have been ingested, one can consider speeding elimination by hemodialysis. If the patient has ingested a drug with anticholinergic properties, intravenous physostigmine may be useful. As noted earlier, some evidence indicates that the nonspecific activating effect of physostigmine may awaken patients who have ingested sedative drugs without anticholinergic properties.[27,28,38]

Psychogenic Unresponsiveness

Psychogenic unresponsiveness is characterized by a normal neurologic examination, including normal oculovestibular responses. Once one has considered the possibility of psychogenic unresponsiveness and done the appropriate neurologic examination, little difficulty arises in making the definitive diagnosis. If the patient meets the clinical criteria for psychogenic unresponsiveness, no further laboratory tests are required. If, however, there is still some question after the examination, an electroencephalogram (EEG) is the most helpful diagnostic test. An EEG that shows normal alpha activity inhibited by eye opening and other

Table 34. Errors and Pitfalls in Overdose Management

Error	Result
1. Under-recognition of danger	Patient descends to coma unattended
2. No atropine prior to intubation	Cardiac arrhythmia or arrest
3. Attempt gastric lavage before endotracheal intubation	Aspiration pneumonia
4. Unskillful intubation attempts	Edema of the airway
5. Unskillful central venous insertions	Pneumothorax; femoral hematomas
6. Excessive hydration without diuresis	Congestive heart failure; shock lung
7. Drug screens not taken	Opportunity lost to establish accurate diagnosis
8. Ignorance of delayed (lithium) or fluctuating (glutethimide) course	Intensive treatment undesirably delayed or foreshortened
9. Omission of antibiotics plus failure to culture sputum or secretions.	Overwhelming pneumonitis develops in hypothermic subjects
10. Omission of proper postures for drainage of lungs and to relieve pressure points during prolonged coma	Pressure necroses and palsies

stimuli strongly supports the diagnosis of psychogenic unresponsiveness. The Amytal interview (see Chapter 5) may be both diagnostic and therapeutic. In emergency evaluation of the unresponsive patient, use the Amytal interview to establish the diagnosis and to "wake the patient up," so that one may begin more definitive treatment. Admit patients with psychogenic unresponsiveness to hospital (even if the Amytal has awakened them) and secure emergency psychiatric consultation. The physician must evaluate thoroughly the patient's physical state to rule out coexisting organic disease; psychogenic unresponsiveness often occurs in a setting of serious medical illness.

A FINAL WORD

This book has presented a physiologic approach to the differential diagnosis and the emergency management of the stuporous and comatose patient. The approach is based on the belief that after a history and a general physical and neurologic examination, the informed physician can, with reasonable confidence, place the patient into one of four major groups of illnesses that cause coma. The specific group into which the patient is placed directs the rest of the diagnostic evaluation and treatment. At times, however, the diagnosis is uncertain even after the examination is completed and it is necessary to defer even the preliminary categorization of patients until the CT scan or metabolic tests are carried out and the most serious infections or metabolic abnormalities have been considered. No patient should be denied a CT scan if there is any suspicion of a mass lesion, despite the absence of focal signs. No patient should be denied glucose if there is any suspicion of hypoglycemia, despite the presence of hemiplegia or other focal signs. At all times during the diagnostic evaluation and the treatment of a patient who is stuporous or comatose, the physician must ask himself whether his diagnosis could possibly be wrong and whether he needs to seek consultation or undertake other diagnostic or therapeutic measures. Fortunately, with constant attention to the changing state of consciousness and a willingness to reconsider the situation minute by minute, few mistakes should be made. Good luck!

REFERENCES

1. ALBERTI, E., HARTMANN, A., SCHUTZ, H.J., ET AL.: *The effect of large doses of dexamethasone on the cerebrospinal fluid pressure in patients with supratentorial tumors.* J. Neurol. 217:173–181, 1978.
2. ARENA, J.M.: *Poisoning,* ed. 4. Charles C Thomas, Springfield, Ill., 1978.
3. BATES, D., CARONNA, J.J., CARTLIDGE, N.E.F. ET AL.: *A prospective study of non-traumatic coma: methods and results in 310 patients.* Ann. Neurol. 2:211–220, 1977.
4. BATRA, Y.K., AND BALI, I.M.: *Corneal abrasions during general anesthesia.* Anesth. Analg. (Cleve.) 56:363–365, 1977.
5. BERG, B., FRANKLIN, G., CUNEO, R., ET AL.: *Nonsurgical cure of brain abscess: early diagnosis and follow-up with computerized tomography.* Ann. Neurol. 3:474–478, 1978.
6. BREIVIK, H., SAFAR, P., SANDS, P., ET AL.: *Clinical feasibility trials of barbiturate therapy after cardiac arrest.* Crit. Care Med. 6:228–244, 1978.
7. BRENNAN, R.W., AND BERGLAND, R.M.: *Acute cerebellar hemorrhage: analysis of clinical findings and outcome in 12 cases.* Neurology 27:527–532, 1977.
8. CARLON, G.C., KAHN, R.C., GOLDINER, P.L., ET AL.: *Long-term infusion of sodium thiopental: hemodynamic and respiratory effects.* Crit. Care Med. 6:311–316, 1978.
9. CLEMENTS, S.D., JR.: "Effect of electrolyte abnormalities on the electrocardiogram." In Schwartz, G.R., Safar, P., Stone, J.H., et al. (eds.): *Principles and Practice of Emergency Medicine,* vol. II. W.B. Saunders Company, Philadelphia, 1978, pp. 959–962.

10. COOPER, P.R., MOODY, S., CLARK, W.K., ET AL.: *Dexamethasone and severe head injury; a prospective double-blind study.* J. Neurosurg. 51:307–316, 1979.

11. GOBIET, W.: "The influence of various doses of dexamethasone on intracranial pressure in patients with severe head injury." In Pappius, H.M., and Feindel, W. (eds.): *Dynamics of Brain Edema.* Springer-Verlag, Berlin, 1976, pp. 351–355.

12. GOBIET, W.: *Monitoring of intracranial pressure in patients with severe head injury.* Neurochirurgia (Stuttg.) 20:35–47, 1977.

13. GUDEMAN, S.K., MILLER, J.D., AND BECKER, D.P.: *Failure of high-dose steroid therapy to influence intracranial pressure in patients with severe head injury.* J. Neurosurg. 51:301–306, 1979.

14. HOGAN, G.R., DODGE, P.R., GILL, S.R., ET AL.: *Pathogenesis of seizures occurring during restoration of plasma tonicity to normal in animals previously chronically hypernatremic.* Pediatrics 43:54–64, 1969.

15. HOOSHMAND, H., DOVE, J., HOUFF, S., ET AL.: *Effects of diuretics and steroids on CSF pressure.* Arch. Neurol. 21:499–509, 1969.

16. JAMES, H.E., LANGFITT, T.W., KUMAR, V.S., ET AL. *Treatment of intracranial hypertension.* Acta Neurochir. 36:189–200, 1977.

17. LEHRICH, J.R., WINKLER, G.F., AND OJEMANN, R.G.: *Cerebellar infarction with brain stem compression.* Arch. Neurol. 22:490–498, 1970.

18. LONG, D.M., MAXWELL, R., AND CHOI, K.S.: "A new therapy regimen for brain edema." In Pappius, H.M., and Feindel, W. (eds.): *Dynamics of Brain Edema.* Springer-Verlag, Berlin, 1976, pp. 293–300.

19. MACKENZIE, A.I.: *Naloxone in alcohol intoxication.* Lancet 2:733–734, 1979.

20. MARSHALL, L.F., KING, J., AND LANGFITT, T.W.: *The complications of high-dose corticosteroid therapy in neurosurgical patients: a prospective study.* Ann. Neurol. 1:201–203, 1977.

21. MARSHALL, L.F., SMITH, R.W., AND SHAPIRO, H.M.: *The outcome with aggressive treatment in severe head injuries. Part I: The significance of intracranial pressure monitoring.* J. Neurosurg. 50:20–25, 1979.

22. MARSHALL, L.F., SMITH, R.W., AND SHAPIRO, H.M.: *The outcome with aggressive treatment in severe head injuries. Part II: Acute and chronic barbiturate administration in the management of head injury.* J. Neurosurg. 50:26–30, 1979.

23. MAXWELL, R.E., LONG, D.M., AND FRENCH, L.A.: "The clinical effects of a synthetic gluco-corticoid used for brain edema in the practice of neurosurgery." In Reulen, H.J. and Schurmann, K. (eds.): *Steroids and Brain Edema.* Springer-Verlag, New York, 1972, pp. 219–232.

24. MEINIG, G., AULICH, A., WENDE, S., ET AL.: "The effect of dexamethasone and diuretics on peritumor brain edema: comparative study of tissue water content and CT." In Pappius, H.M., and Feindel, W. (eds.): *Dynamics of Brain Edema.* Springer-Verlag, Berlin, 1976, pp. 301–305.

25. MILLER, J.D.: *Barbiturates and raised intracranial pressure.* Ann. Neurol. 6:189–193, 1979.

26. MILLER, J.D., AND LEECH, P.: *Effects of mannitol and steroid therapy on intracranial volume-pressure relationships in patients.* J. Neurosurg. 42:274–281, 1975.

27. MOGELNICKI, S.R., WALLER, J.L., AND FINLAYSON, D.C.: *Physostigmine reversal of cimetidine-induced mental confusion.* J.A.M.A. 241:826–827, 1979.

28. NATTEL, S., BAYNE, L., AND RUEDY, J.: *Physostigmine in coma due to drug overdose.* Clin. Pharmacol. Ther. 25:96–102, 1979.

29. OSBORN, A.C.: *Diagnosis of descending transtentorial herniation by cranial computed tomography.* Radiology 123:93–96, 1977.

30. OTT, K.H., KASE, C.S., OJEMANN, R.G., ET AL.: *Cerebellar hemorrhage: diagnosis and treatment.* Arch. Neurol. 31:160–167, 1974.

31. RENAUDIN, J., FEWER, D., WILSON, C.B., ET AL.: *Dose dependency of Decadron in patients with partially excised brain tumors.* J. Neurosurg. 39:302–305, 1973.

32. ROCKOFF, M.A., MARSHALL, L.F., AND SHAPIRO, H.M.: *High-dose barbiturate therapy in man: a clinical review of sixty patients.* Ann. Neurol. 6:194–199, 1979.

33. ROSENBLUM, M.L., HOFF, J.T., NORMAN, D., ET AL.: *Decreased mortality from brain abscesses since advent of computerized tomography.* J. Neurosurg. 49:658–668, 1978.

34. ROTTENBERG, D.A., HURWITZ, B.J., AND POSNER, J.B.: *The effect of oral glycerol on intraventricular pressure in man.* Neurology 27:600–608, 1977.

35. ROTTENBERG, D.A., AND POSNER, J.B.: "Intracranial pressure control." In Cottrell, J.E., and Turndorf, H. (eds.): *Anesthesia and Neurosurgery*. C.V. Mosby Co. St. Louis, 1980.

36. SAFAR, P., BLEYAERT, A., NEMOTO, E.M., ET AL.: *Resuscitation after global brain ischemia-anoxia*. Crit. Care Med. 6:215–227, 1978.

37. SAFAR, P.: "Central nervous system failure" (Ch. 5) and "Cardiopulmonary–cerebral resuscitation" (Ch. 9). In Schwartz, G.R., Safar, P., Stone, L.H., et al. (eds.): *Principles and Practice of Emergency Medicine*. W. B. Saunders Co., Philadelphia, 1978.

38. SCHWARTZ, G.R.: "Poisonings. A. Emergency toxicology and general principles of medical management of the poisoned patient." In Schwartz, G.R., Safar, P., Stone, J.H., et al (eds.): *Principles and Practice of Emergency Medicine*. W.B. Saunders Co., 1978, Chapter 58, pp. 1316–1332.

39. SNOW, J. C. KRIPKE, B. J.. NORTON, M. L., ET AL.: *Corneal injuries during general anesthesia*. Anesth. Analg. (Cleve.) 54:465–467, 1975.

40. STROVRING, J.: *Descending tentorial herniation: findings on computed tomography*. Neuroradiology 14:101–105, 1977.

41. SUNDARESAN, N., GALICICH, J., KROL, G., ET AL.: *Successful surgical treatment of pontine vascular malformation in a 3-year old*. Child's Brain 5:131–136, 1979.

42. TEASDALE, G., AND JENNETT, B.: *Assessment of impaired consciousness and coma: a practical scale*. Lancet 2:81–84, 1974.

43. TEASDALE, G., KNILL-JONES, R., VANDER AND SANDE, J.: *Observer variability in assessing impaired consciousness and coma*. J. Neurol. Neurosurg. Psychiatry 41:603–610, 1978.

44. TRAUNER, D.A., BROWN, F., GANZ, E., ET AL.: *Treatment of elevated intracranial pressure in Reye syndrome*. Ann. Neurol. 4:275–278, 1978.

45. WALLIS, W.E., WILLOUGHBY, E., AND BAKER, P.: *Coma in the Wernicke-Korsakoff syndrome*. Lancet 2:400–401, 1978.

46. WILKINSON, H.A.: *Intracranial pressure reserve testing: initial clinical observations*. Arch. Neurol. 35:661–667, 1978.

Index